THE SECOND WORLD WAR

THE SECOND WORLD WAR

A Military History

GORDON CORRIGAN

Atlantic Books
LONDON

First published in Great Britain in 2010 by Atlantic Books Ltd.

This paperback edition published in 2012 by Atlantic Books,
an imprint of Atlantic Books Ltd.

1 2 3 4 5 6 7 8 9

A CIP catalogue record for this book is available
from the British Library.

ISBN: 978-1-84354-895-9
E-Book ISBN: 978-0-85789-135-8

Printed in Italy by ⟨logo⟩ Grafica Veneta S.p.A.

Atlantic Books
Ormond House
26–27 Boswell Street
London
WC1N 3JZ

www.atlantic-books.co.uk

CONTENTS

LIST OF ILLUSTRATIONS

LIST OF MAPS

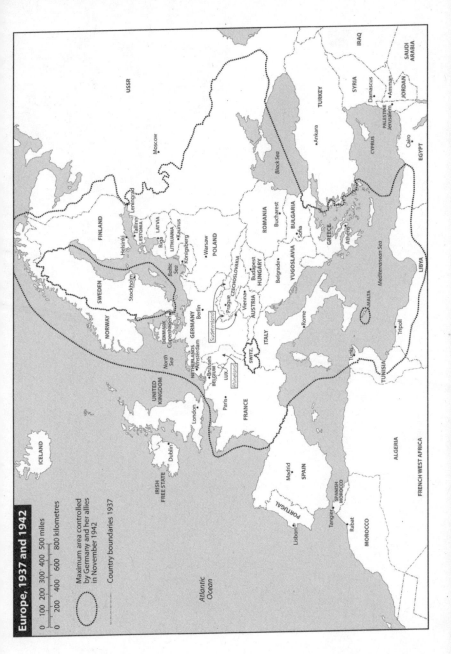

Europe, 1937 and 1942

0 100 200 300 400 500 miles
0 200 400 600 800 kilometres

Maximum area controlled by Germany and her allies in November 1942

Country boundaries 1937

ICELAND

IRISH FREE STATE
Dublin

UNITED KINGDOM
London

Atlantic Ocean

NORWAY
SWEDEN
Stockholm

FINLAND
Helsinki

North Sea
Baltic Sea

DENMARK
Copenhagen

NETHERLANDS
Amsterdam
Brussels
BELGIUM
LUX.
Rhineland

GERMANY
Berlin

ESTONIA
Tallinn
LATVIA
Riga
LITHUANIA
Kaunus
Königsberg

USSR
Moscow
Leningrad

Paris

FRANCE

SWITZ.

Sudetenland
Prague
CZECHOSLOVAKIA
Vienna
AUSTRIA

Warsaw
POLAND

Budapest
HUNGARY

ROMANIA
Bucharest

Black Sea

ITALY
Rome

YUGOSLAVIA
Belgrade

BULGARIA
Sofia

TURKEY
Ankara

PORTUGAL
Lisbon

SPAIN
Madrid

GREECE
Athens

Mediterranean Sea

CYPRUS

SYRIA
Damascus

IRAQ

SAUDI ARABIA

JORDAN
Amman

PALESTINE
Jerusalem

EGYPT
Cairo

MALTA

Tripoli
LIBYA

TUNISIA

ALGERIA

FRENCH WEST AFRICA

MOROCCO
Rabat
Tangier
SPANISH MOROCCO

XI

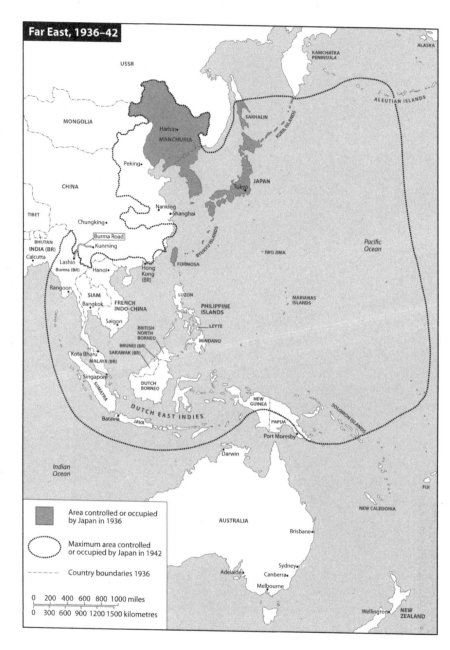

Far East, 1936–42

USSR

MONGOLIA

ALASKA

KAMCHATKA
PENINSULA

ALEUTIAN ISLANDS

SAKHALIN

Harbin
MANCHURIA

KURIL ISLANDS

Peking

CHINA

Tokyo   JAPAN

TIBET

Nanking
Shanghai

Chungking

Burma Road

BHUTAN

Kunming

INDIA (BR)

Pacific
Ocean

RYUKYU ISLANDS

Calcutta

Lashio

FORMOSA

IWO JIMA

Burma (BR)

Hanoi

Rangoon

Hong
Kong
(BR)

SIAM

LUZON

Bangkok   FRENCH
INDO-CHINA

PHILIPPINE
ISLANDS

MARIANAS
ISLANDS

Saigon

LEYTE

BRITISH
NORTH
BORNEO

MINDANO

BRUNEI (BR)

Kota Bharu   SARAWAK (BR)

MALAYA (BR)

Singapore

DUTCH
BORNEO

DUTCH EAST INDIES

NEW
GUINEA

SOLOMON ISLANDS

Batavia   JAVA

PAPUA

Port Moresby

Darwin

Indian
Ocean

FIJI

NEW CALEDONIA

AUSTRALIA

Brisbane

Area controlled or occupied
by Japan in 1936

Sydney

Maximum area controlled
or occupied by Japan in 1942

Adelaide

Canberra

Country boundaries 1936

Melbourne

Wellington   NEW
ZEALAND

| 0 | 200 | 400 | 600 | 800 | 1000 miles |

| 0 | 300 | 600 | 900 | 1200 | 1500 kilometres |

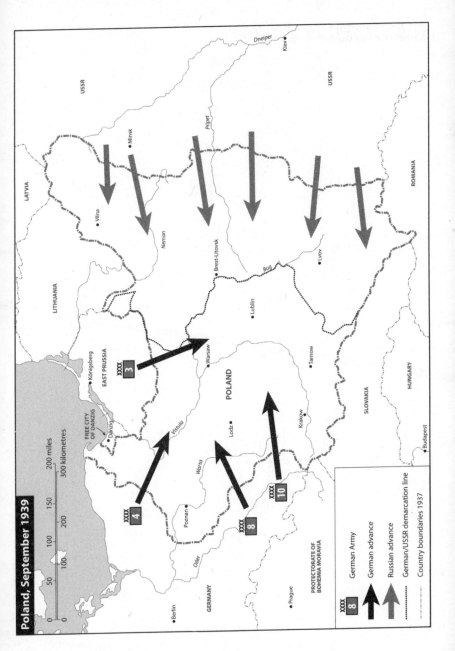

Poland, September 1939

Battle of France, 10 May – 30 May 1940

0 10 20 30 40 50 miles
0 20 40 60 80 kilometres

— · — · — Country boundaries 1936

NETHERLANDS

Ems

•Amsterdam

The Hague• •Utrecht

•Arnhem

Münster•

GERMANY

Waal

Maas

Dortmund•

•Breda

Duisburg• Rhur

Ostend•

•Düsseldorf

•Antwerp

Dunkirk•

Ghent•

Cologne•

Scheldt

Brussels• •Leuven Maastricht•

BELGIUM •Wavre Eben Emael• •Aachen

Liège•

Rhine

•Mons Namur• Meuse

Arras•

•Dinant

Koblenz•

Somme
Amiens•

Givet•

Monthermé•

Mézières•
Sedan•

LUXEMBOURG

•Luxembourg

Oise

FRANCE Reims•

Marne

Meuse

•Paris

•Nancy

Strasbourg•

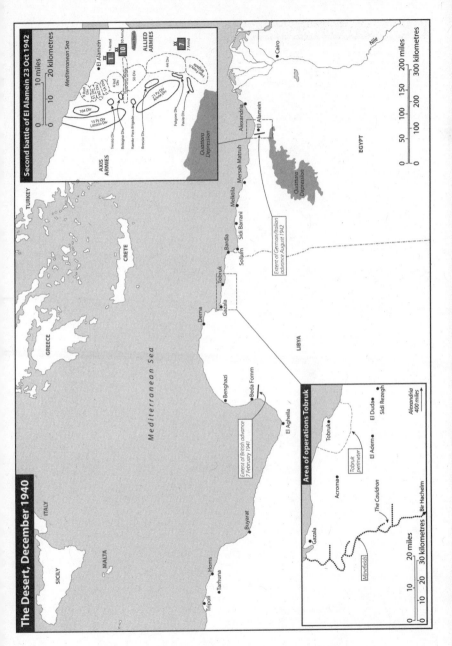

The Desert, December 1940

ITALY

SICILY

MALTA

GREECE

TURKEY

CRETE

Mediterranean Sea

Tripoli
Tarhuna
Homs
Buvarat

Benghazi
Beda Fomm
El Agheila

*Extent of British advance
7 February 1941*

Derna
Gazala
Tobruk
Bardia
Sollum
Sidi Barrani
Mekktila
Mersah Matruh

*Extent of German/Italian
advance August 1942*

El Alamein
Alexandria

Cairo

Nile

EGYPT

LIBYA

Quattara
Depression

Second battle of El Alamein 23 Oct 1942

0   10   20 miles
0   10   20 kilometres

Mediterranean Sea

AXIS
ARMIES

El Alamein

164 Div

Trento Div
Bologna Div

Ital
Div

90 Div

15 Pz Div
Littorio Div

Ramke Para Brigade

Brescia Div

21 Pz Div
Ariete Armd Div

Folgore Div

Pavia Div

Quattara Depression

ALLIED
ARMIES

1 Armd

10 Armd

7 Armd

44 Div

X
1

XX
10

XX
7

0   50   100   150   200 miles
0   100   200   300 kilometres

Area of operations Tobruk

Gazala
Acroma
Tobruk
El Duda
Sidi Rezegh
El Adem
The Cauldron
Bir Hacheim

*Tobruk
perimeter*

Minefields

Alexandria
400 miles

0   10   20 miles
0   10   20   30 kilometres

XV

Russia, June 1941 – November 1942

| 0 | 50 | 100 | 150 | 200 miles |
| 0 | 100 | 200 | 300 kilometres |

·············· Country boundaries 1936

FINLAND

SWEDEN

• Stockholm

Helsinki •

Tallinn •

Leningrad •

VOLKHOV FRONT

USSR

Baltic Sea

• Riga

NORTH WEST FRONT

KALININ FRONT

Kalinin •

Volga

Kaunas

Moscow •

Vyazma •

WEST FRONT

Danzig

Königsberg

• Vilnius

Orsha •

Smolensk •

Tula •

GERMANY

Minsk •

Neman

Bobruisk •

Bryansk •

• Orel

Warsaw •

Western Bug

• Brest Litovsk

Pripet

Lodz •

Vistula

• Lvov

Kiev •

Kursk •

• Voronezh

SOUTH WEST FRONT

Volga

XXXXX

German front line
Dec 1941

German front line
July 1941

Kharkov •

XXXX
2
HUNGARIAN 2ND ARMY

German start line
22 June 1941

SLOVAKIA

Dniester

Uman •

Dnieper

Southern Bug

XXXX
8
ITALIAN 8TH ARMY

XXXX
3
ROMANIAN 3RD ARMY

XXXX
6
GERMAN 6TH ARMY

Stalingrad
• Leninsk

• Budapest

HUNGARY

Odessa •

Rostov •

Don

XXXX
4
4TH PANZER ARMY

XXXX
4
ROMANIAN 4TH ARMY

SOUTH FRONT

ROMANIA

German farthest
advance Nov 1942

Belgrade •

• Bucharest

Danube

Sevastopol •

Krasnodar •

Novorossisk •

• Malkop

XXXX
17
GERMAN 17TH ARMY

XXXX
1
1ST PANZER ARMY

YUGOSLAVIA

• Sofia

BULGARIA

Black Sea

▲ Mt Elbrus

USSR

Istanbul •

Batumi •

GREECE

Ankara •

IRAQ

• Athens

TURKEY

SYRIA

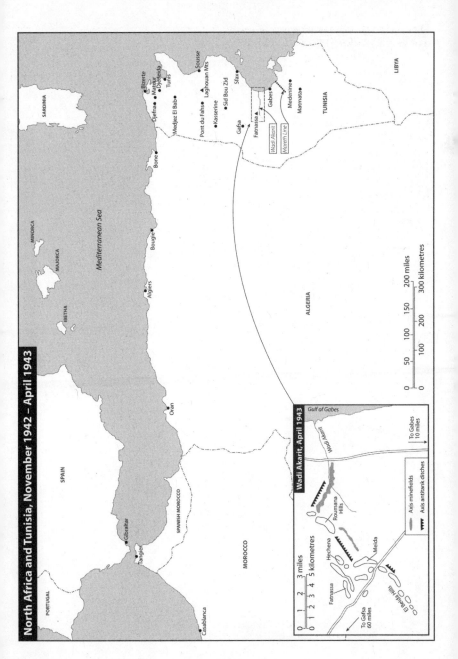

North Africa and Tunisia, November 1942 – April 1943

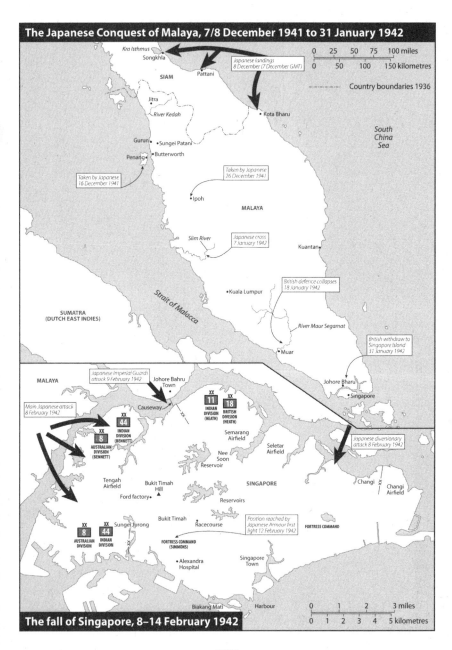

The Japanese Conquest of Malaya, 7/8 December 1941 to 31 January 1942

| 0 | 25 | 50 | 75 | 100 miles |

| 0 | 50 | 100 | 150 kilometres |

Country boundaries 1936

Kra Isthmus

Songkhla

Japanese landings 8 December (7 December GMT)

Pattani

SIAM

Jitra

River Kedah

Kota Bharu

South China Sea

Gurun • Sungei Patani

Penang • Butterworth

Taken by Japanese 16 December 1941

Taken by Japanese 26 December 1941

•Ipoh

MALAYA

Slim River

Japanese cross 7 January 1942

Kuantan•

SUMATRA
(DUTCH EAST INDIES)

Strait of Malacca

•Kuala Lumpur

British defence collapses 18 January 1942

River Maur Segamat

British withdraw to Singapore Island 31 January 1942

•Muar

MALAYA

Japanese Imperial Guards attack 9 February 1942

Johore Bahru Town

XX
11
INDIAN DIVISION (HEATH)

XX
18
BRITISH DIVISION (HEATH)

Johore Bahru

•Singapore

Main Japanese attack 8 February 1942

Causeway

XX
44
INDIAN DIVISION (BENNETT)

XX
8
AUSTRALIAN DIVISION (BENNETT)

Semarang Airfield

Seletar Airfield

Japanese diversionary attack 8 February 1942

Tengah Airfield

Bukit Timah Hill

Nee Soon Reservoir

SINGAPORE

Changi

Changi Airfield

Ford factory•

Bukit Timah

Racecourse

Position reached by Japanese Armour first light 12 February 1942

FORTRESS COMMAND

Sungei Jurong

XX
8
AUSTRALIAN DIVISION

XX
44
INDIAN DIVISION

FORTRESS COMMAND (SIMMONS)

•Alexandra Hospital

Singapore Town

Biakang Mati

Harbour

| 0 | 1 | 2 | 3 miles |

| 0 | 1 | 2 | 3 | 4 | 5 kilometres |

The fall of Singapore, 8–14 February 1942

The battle for Hong Kong, 8 – 25 December 1941

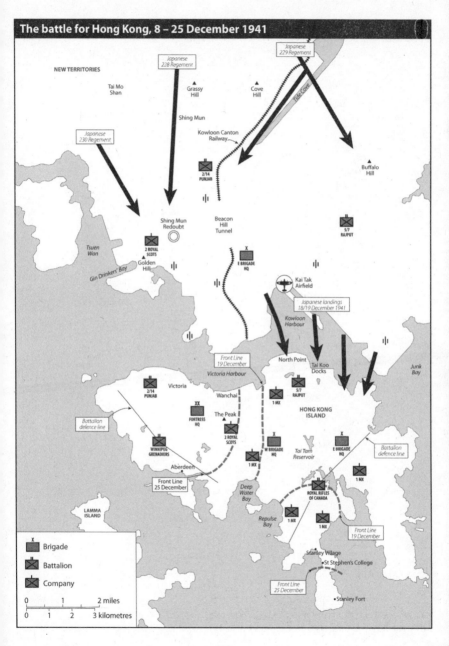

NEW TERRITORIES

Tai Mo Shan

Japanese 228 Regiment

▲ Grassy Hill

Cove Hill

Tide Cove

Shing Mun

Kowloon Canton Railway

Japanese 229 Regiment

Japanese 230 Regiment

2/14 PUNJAB

▲ Buffalo Hill

Shing Mun Redoubt

Beacon Hill Tunnel

5/7 RAJPUT

Tsuen Wan

2 ROYAL SCOTS

Golden Hill

Gin Drinkers' Bay

E BRIGADE HQ

Kai Tak Airfield

Japanese landings 18/19 December 1941

Kowloon Harbour

Front Line 19 December

North Point

Tai Koo Docks

Junk Bay

2/14 PUNJAB

Victoria

Victoria Harbour

Wanchai

5/7 RAJPUT

1 MX

XX FORTRESS HQ

The Peak

HONG KONG ISLAND

Battalion defence line

2 ROYAL SCOTS

WINNIPEG GRENADIERS

1 MX

W BRIGADE HQ

Tai Tam Reservoir

E BRIGADE HQ

Battalion defence line

1 MX

Aberdeen

Front Line 25 December

LAMMA ISLAND

Deep Water Bay

ROYAL RIFLES OF CANADA

1 MX

Repulse Bay

1 MX

1 MX

Front Line 19 December

Stanley Village

• St Stephen's College

Front Line 25 December

• Stanley Fort

Legend

- ▪ Brigade
- ▪ Battalion
- ▪ Company

0   1   2 miles

0   1   2   3 kilometres

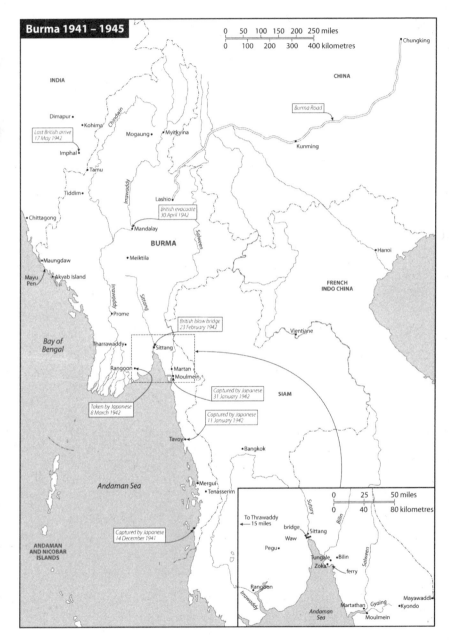

Burma 1941 – 1945

| 0 | 50 | 100 | 150 | 200 | 250 miles |
| 0 | | 100 | 200 | 300 | 400 kilometres |

INDIA

CHINA

Dimapur•
•Kohima

Last British arrive 17 May 1942

Imphal•

•Tamu

Tiddim•

•Chittagong

•Maungdaw

•Akyab Island

Mayu Pen

Bay of Bengal

Tharrawaddy•

Rangoon•

Mogaung •

Myitkyina•

Meiktila•

Mandalay•

BURMA

Lashio•

British evacuate 30 April 1942

Burma Road

Kunming

•Hanoi

FRENCH INDO CHINA

Prome•

British blow bridge 23 February 1942

•Sittang

Martan•
•Moulmein

Captured by Japanese 31 January 1942

Vientiane•

SIAM

Taken by Japanese 8 March 1942

Captured by Japanese 11 January 1942

Tavoy•

•Bangkok

Andaman Sea

•Mergui
•Tenasserim

ANDAMAN AND NICOBAR ISLANDS

Captured by Japanese 14 December 1941

Chungking•

Chindwin

Irrawaddy

Salween

Irrawaddy

Sittang

Inset map

| 0 | 25 | 50 miles |
| 0 | 40 | 80 kilometres |

To Thrawaddy
← 15 miles

bridge•Sittang

Waw

Pegu•

Tungale• •Bilin

Zoka• —ferry

Rangoon•

Irrawaddy

Andaman Sea

Martathan• Gyaing
Moulmein•

Mayawaddi•
•Kyondo

Sittang

Bilin

Salween

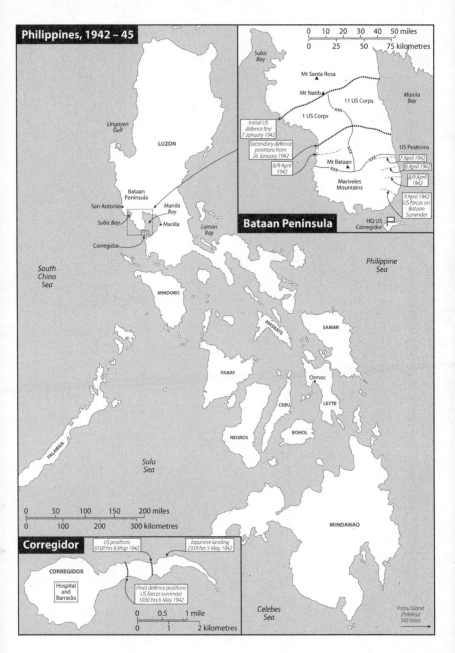

Philippines, 1942 – 45

0 10 20 30 40 50 miles
0 25 50 75 kilometres

Subic Bay

Mt Santa Rosa

Mt Natib

11 US Corps

1 US Corps

Manila Bay

Initial US defence line 7 January 1942

Secondary defence positions from 26 January 1942

8/9 April 1942

Mt Bataan

Mariveles Mountains

US Positions

7 April 1942

8 April 1942

8/9 April 1942

9 April 1942 US forces on Bataan Surrender

Bataan Peninsula

HQ US Corregidor

LUZON

Lingayen Gulf

Bataan Peninsula

San Antonio

Subic Bay

Manila Bay

Manila

Lamon Bay

Corregidor

South China Sea

MINDORO

MASBATE

SAMAR

Philippine Sea

PANAY

Ormoc

CEBU

LEYTE

NEGROS

BOHOL

Sulu Sea

0 50 100 150 200 miles
0 100 200 300 kilometres

MINDANAO

Corregidor

US positions 0100 hrs 6 May 1942

Japanese landing 2359 hrs 5 May 1942

CORREGIDOR

Hospital and Barracks

Final defence positions US forces surrender 1030 hrs 6 May 1942

0 0.5 1 mile
0 1 2 kilometres

Celebes Sea

Palau Island (Pelelieu) 560 miles

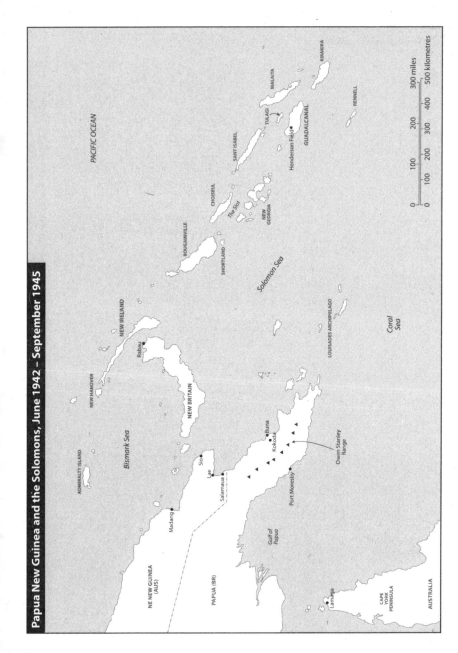

Papua New Guinea and the Solomons, June 1942 – September 1945

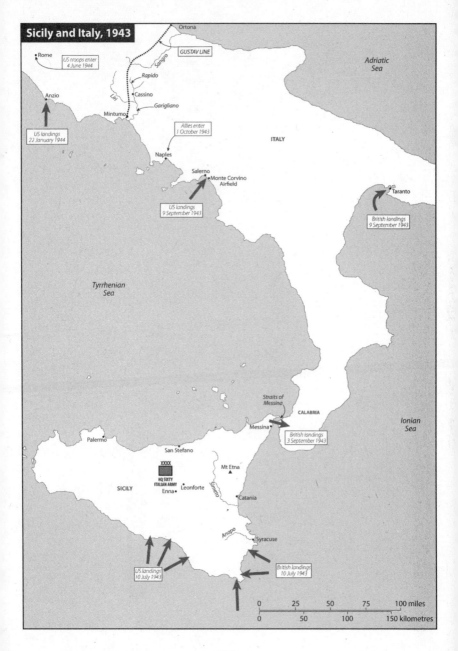

Sicily and Italy, 1943

Rome

US troops enter 4 June 1944

Ortona

Sangro

GUSTAV LINE

Rapido

Liri

Cassino

Garigliano

Mintumo

ITALY

Anzio

US landings 22 January 1944

Allies enter 1 October 1943

Naples

Adriatic Sea

Salerno

Monte Corvino Airfield

US landings 9 September 1943

Taranto

British landings 9 September 1943

Tyrrhenian Sea

Straits of Messina

CALABRIA

Messina

British landings 3 September 1943

Ionian Sea

Palermo

San Stefano

HQ SIXTY ITALIAN ARMY

SICILY

Leonforte

Enna

Mt Etna

Simeto

Catania

Anapo

Syracuse

US landings 10 July 1943

British landings 10 July 1943

| 0 | 25 | 50 | 75 | 100 miles |

| 0 | 50 | 100 | 150 kilometres |

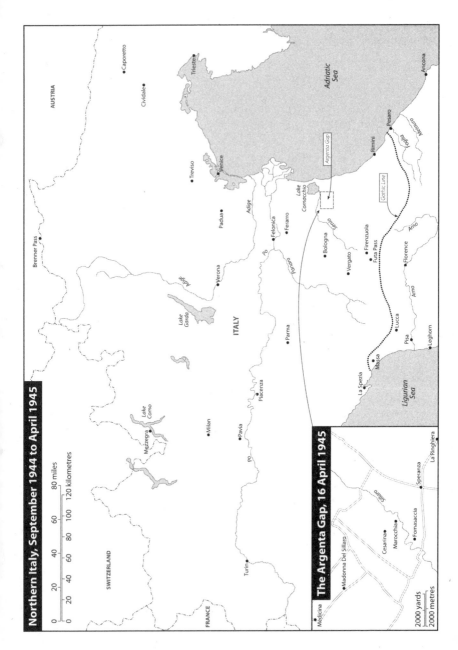

Northern Italy, September 1944 to April 1945

AUSTRIA

Caporetto

Cividale

Trieste

Brenner Pass

Treviso

Venice

Adriatic Sea

Padua

Adige

Felonica

Verona

Ferraro

Lake Cornacchio

Argenta Gap

Reno

Bologna

Po

Lake Garda

Panaro

Vergato

Firenzuola

Futa Pass

Florence

Arno

ITALY

Parma

Lucca

Pisa

Gothic Line

Arno

Leghorn

Massa

La Spezia

Ligurian Sea

Pesaro

Marecchia

Rimini

Conca

SWITZERLAND

Lake Como

Mezzegra

Milan

Pavia

Po

Piacenza

Turin

FRANCE

| 0 | 20 | 40 | 60 | 80 miles |
| 0 | 20 | 40 | 60 | 80 | 100 | 120 kilometres |

The Argenta Gap, 16 April 1945

Medicina

Madonna Del Sillaro

Sillaro

Cesarina

Marocchia

Fornasaccia

Speranza

La Ringhiera

2000 yards
2000 metres

XXIV

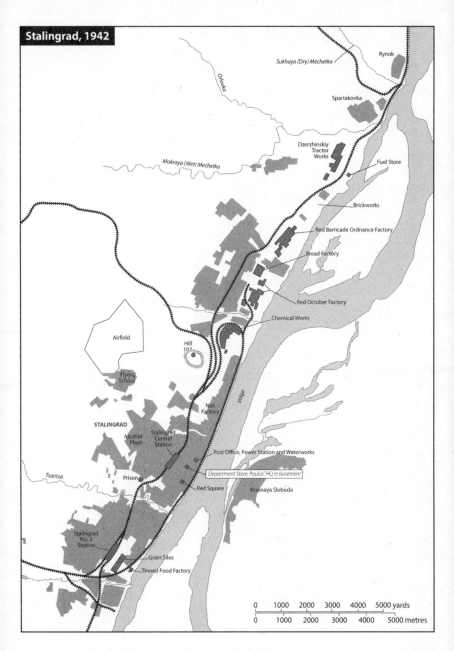

Stalingrad, 1942

Orlovka

Sukhaya (Dry) Mechetka

Rynok

Spartakovka

Mokraya (Wet) Mechetka

Dzerzhinskiy Tractor Works

Fuel Store

Brickworks

Red Barricade Ordnance Factory

Bread Factory

Red October Factory

Chemical Works

Airfield

Hill 102ₘ

Flying School

Volga

Nail Factory

STALINGRAD

Alcohol Plant

Stalingrad Central Station

Post Office, Power Station and Waterworks

Department Store, Paulus' HQ in basement

Tsaritsa

Prison

Red Square

Krasnaya Sloboda

Stalingrad No. 2 Station

Grain Silos

Tinned Food Factory

| 0 | 1000 | 2000 | 3000 | 4000 | 5000 yards |
| 0 | 1000 | 2000 | 3000 | 4000 | 5000 metres |

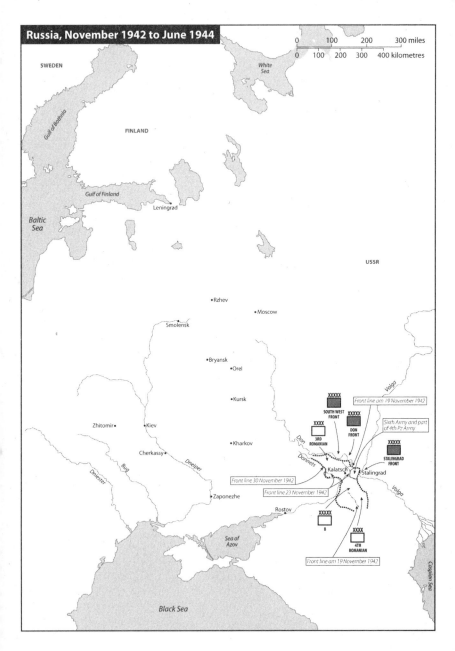

Russia, November 1942 to June 1944

SWEDEN

White Sea

Gulf of Bothnia

FINLAND

Gulf of Finland

Leningrad

Baltic Sea

USSR

•Rzhev

•Moscow

Smolensk•

•Bryansk

•Orel

Zhitomir•

•Kiev

•Kursk

•Kharkov

Cherkassy•

Dnieper

Bug

Dniester

Donets

Don

XXXXX
SOUTH WEST FRONT

XXXX
3RD ROMANIAN

XXXXX
DON FRONT

Front line am 19 November 1942

Sixth Army and part of 4th Pz Army

XXXXX
STALINGRAD FRONT

Kalatsch

Stalingrad

Volga

Volga

•Zaponezhe

Front line 30 November 1942

Front line 23 November 1942

Rostov•

XXXXX
8

XXXX
4TH ROMANIAN

Front line am 19 November 1942

Sea of Azov

Caspian Sea

Black Sea

Don

Donets

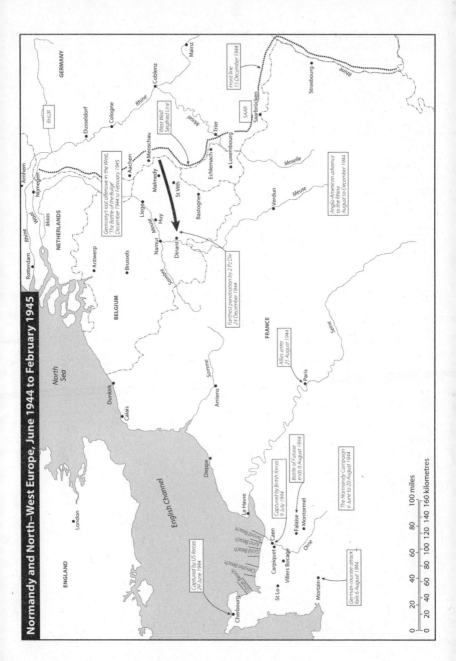

Normandy and North–West Europe, June 1944 to February 1945

ENGLAND

London

North Sea

English Channel

Dunkirk
Calais
Dieppe
Le Havre
Cherbourg
St Lô
Carpiquet
Villers Bocage
Mortain
Caen
Falaise
Montormel
Amiens
Somme
Paris
Seine
Orne

Utah Beach
Omaha Beach
Gold Beach
Juno Beach
Sword Beach

FRANCE

NETHERLANDS
Rotterdam
Antwerp
Brussels
BELGIUM
Namur
Huy
Liège
Dinant
Bastogne
St Vith
Malmedy
Echternach
Luxembourg
Verdun
Meuse
Sambre
Maas
Waal
Rhine
Nijmegen
Arnhem
Aachen
Menschau
Trier
Saarbrücken
SAAR
Strasbourg
Mainz
Coblenz
Cologne
Dusseldorf
RUHR
GERMANY
Rhine
Moselle
Meuse
Moel

West Wall
Siegfried Line

Front line
15 December 1944

Germany's last offensive in the West.
'The Battle of the Bulge'
December 1944 to February 1945

Farthest penetration by 2 Pz. Div
24 December 1944

Anglo-American advance
to the Rhine
August to December 1944

Allies enter
25 August 1944

Battle of Falaise
ends 6 August 1944

The Normandy Campaign
6 June to 20 August 1944

Captured by British forces
9 July 1944

German counter attack
folds 6 August 1944

Captured by US forces
29 June 1944

| 0 | 20 | 40 | 60 | 80 | 100 miles |
| 0 | 20 40 60 | 100 120 140 160 kilometres |

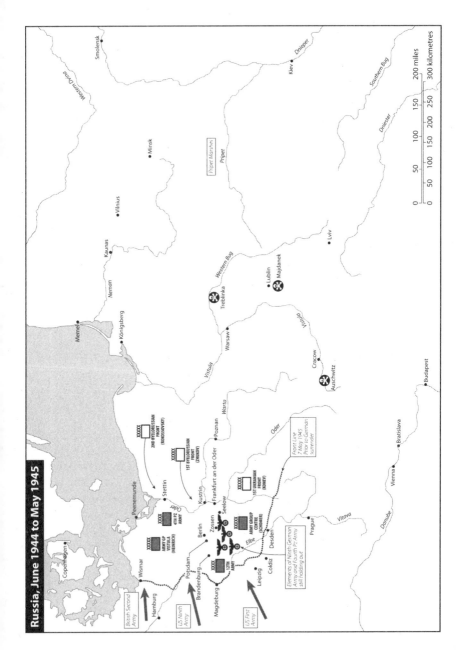

Russia, June 1944 to May 1945

INTRODUCTION

On the first day of September 1939, German forces struck at Poland, and what was to become known as the Second World War officially began. To begin with, despite the involvement of Germany, France and Britain, what fighting that did take place was confined to Europe. Even twelve months later, the only fighting on land was relatively small-scale scuffling in the Horn of Africa and along the Libyan coast, for France had surrendered and the tiny British Expeditionary Force had been driven from Europe. The following year, however, Germany invaded Russia and a whole new dimension opened up. Later in the same year, the involvement of the United States and Japan made the war truly global.

In 1939 the powers of the first rank – or those that considered themselves to be in the first rank, the Great Powers – were Britain, France, Germany, the USA, the USSR and Japan. Of these, all at some stage entered the war, and all but France were still engaged at the end. Of the second- and third-rank powers, Italy, China, Yugoslavia, Hungary, Romania, Bulgaria, Greece, Spain, Holland, Belgium, Norway and Denmark were all involved, although Spain did not declare war, despite providing a contingent of troops and an air squadron under German command on the Eastern Front. When all those who declared war – whether or not they actually provided combat units – and all those who provided troops – whether or not they actually declared war – and all those who were occupied or attacked with or without a declaration of war are totted up, then we find that the perhaps astonishing total of fifty-five nations can be said to have been officially involved in the war.*

---

*If the countries of the British Empire are counted separately, then the total is even greater.

Many – nay, most – of these fifty-five made no military contribution or, if they did, were of little use. Germany's official allies – Italy, Romania, Hungary, Finland and Bulgaria – were more of a hindrance than a help and needed constant bolstering up or bailing out by German resources. On the other hand, it is often forgotten (because it is inconvenient to remember it) that there were many Poles and Russians in German service who fought well until the end, and that the Waffen SS happily recruited Belgians, Dutchmen, Scandinavians, Balts and even Frenchmen, all of whom did well by their masters. Indeed, it is difficult not to have some sympathy with those who afterwards were considered traitors. The USSR had not ratified the Geneva Convention, and was thus not entitled to its protection. When the choice was between languishing (or, more likely, being worked to death) in a German prison camp, and taking part in the international crusade against Bolshevism, with three square meals a day, a salary and a uniform to boot, the argument for collaboration was persuasive. Poles might not have liked the Germans, but they didn't like the Russians either. Similarly, there were many Western Europeans who had no particular love for Britain, and genuinely saw Russia as a threat, as of course she was.

Of those nations which rowed in on the Allied side, many, having been invaded and occupied by Axis forces, had little option, although a finalist for the prize for bare-faced cheek must be the London-based government-in-exile of Luxembourg (population 300,000), which in December 1942 declared war on Germany, Italy and Japan. But Luxembourg was at least occupied by Germany (and indeed annexed by her as Gau Moselland), so the trophy must be awarded to the government of Liberia, most of whose citizens were unlikely to have ever seen a German, or to have known where Germany was, but which nevertheless declared war on Germany and Japan on 27 January 1944. It is not at all clear what contribution Haiti, having declared war on Bulgaria, Hungary and Romania on Christmas Eve 1941, thought she could make to the cause of democracy and the freedom of small nations, but the award for blatant opportunism is shared between Argentina, who declared war on Germany and Japan on 27 March 1945, six weeks before Germany's surrender, and the Soviet Union, who declared war on Japan on 8 August 1945, six days before Japan's unconditional surrender. There is no prize for a complete and total inability to feel national embarrassment, but if there were it would have to go to Italy, who declared war on Britain and France on 10 June 1940, four days before German troops marched into Paris, invaded Greece on 28 October 1940 without telling her German allies and got a very bloody nose, surrendered to the British and Americans on 8 September 1943 and then declared war on Germany five weeks later, thus adhering to Napoleon's dictum that no Italian state had ever finished a war on the same side as that on which it had started, except when it had changed sides twice.

At the height of the Second World War, the battle raged – or, in some cases, stagnated – in three of the world's seven continents. There had, of course, been world wars before, although the term was but recently coined. The 1914–18 war was not referred to as the First World War until the Second started – before that, it was simply the Great War. In that conflagration there had been serious fighting in only two of the seven continents, but, with all the then Great Powers – the USA and the empires of Britain, France, Russia, Austria-Hungary and Germany – involved, and a total of twenty-eight participants, a world war it undoubtedly was. During the nineteenth century's major disagreement between countries that mattered – the French Revolutionary and Napoleonic Wars, which lasted from 1791 to 1814, with a final spasm in 1815* – fighting took place in four continents: Europe, Asia, Africa and America. The Powers – England, France, Austria, Russia and Prussia – and nearly every other European state were all involved, and so that must also qualify as a world war. Prior to that, the Seven Years War, from 1756 to 1763, saw serious combat in three continents – four, if one includes naval engagements – and the involvement of the Powers, leading one inescapably to the conclusion that it too must be classified as a world war.

While it would be perfectly sound, therefore, to nominate the Seven Years War as the First World War, the French Revolutionary and Napoleonic Wars as the Second, and the Kaiser's War the Third, with 1939–45 being the Fourth World War, it is not my intention to tilt at windmills by trying to change the universally accepted nomenclature; it is merely to make the point that global war has not been confined to the disputes of the twentieth century. Some historians, of course, are of the view that the two world wars of the twentieth century were in fact one war, with an armistice between 1918 and 1939, and, in that the settlement at Versailles in 1919 did result in a whole plethora of provocations which Germany was bound to try to resolve once she was strong enough, there is much merit in that argument. Versailles was not, however, the sole forcing house for the rise of extreme German

---

*Starting in 1793, as far as the British are concerned, when France declared war on England.

nationalism; there were economic, cultural and racial factors too, along with an unwillingness, or an inability, on the part of France and Britain to deter Germany and Italy until it was far too late.

Although war on a global scale was nothing new, there are certain aspects of what we shall continue to call the Second World War that were. In previous conflicts civilians had rarely been targeted. True, besieged populations tended to starve, but that was incidental, and marauding armies tended to spread disease, and not only of the venereal variety. More recently, Boer women and children had died in British camps but this was due to a failure to understand health and hygiene rather than, as some South African historians still allege, a deliberate policy of genocide. In the first war, German shelling of English coastal towns along with attacks on London and elsewhere by Zeppelins and Gotha bombers had killed a few British civilians, but the intention here had been clear – to entice units of the Royal Navy into battle or to hit military targets. In the second war, however, both sides deliberately sought to kill each other's civilians, mainly from the air. That the Blitz by the Luftwaffe and the de-housing of the German population by the Royal and United States Army Air Forces failed to bring an end to the war by themselves, or even to dent morale, and that it took a very long time to seriously affect industrial production, is irrelevant. While air forces attacking England or Germany or occupied Europe occasionally remembered to claim that they were aiming for military targets and that civilian deaths were collateral, there was no pretence that the fire-bombing of Tokyo and the dropping of atomic weapons on Japan were anything but the deliberate wiping out of large chunks of the population. There was, too, a racial dimension: large amounts of high explosive dropped on Germans were one thing, but nobody ever suggested dropping an atomic bomb on them. Germans may have been the enemy but they were still, after all, white, civilized and Christian, whereas the Japanese were the Yellow Peril and Japan was a very long way away. However targeted, civilians were nevertheless in the front line and this, along with the mobilization of the whole energies and resources of the combatant nations towards one end, makes the Second World War history's first total war.*

We tend to think of the Second World War as one war, with nations joining – or leaving – at intervals. In many ways, however, there were a number of wars

---

*Even if the Germans, unlike the British, stubbornly refused to conscript women until the final stages.

all going on at the same time. Germany's war with Russia, from 1941 until 1945, is almost a separate conflict: Russia accepted all manner of materiel from the West, particularly wheeled transport (she didn't think much of British or American tanks), but she told her supposed allies very little of her war aims or her operational plans, nor would she have subordinated them to any overall direction that did not coincide with her own agenda. As far as Germany was concerned, it was in the East that the real war was being fought: North Africa and Italy were subsidiary theatres and, even at the height of the Normandy campaign, never less than 75 per cent of the Wehrmacht was deployed on the Eastern Front.

When the United States of America joined the war in 1941, it was one of Churchill's few real contributions to eventual victory (or, perhaps more accurately in the British case, 'eventual not losing') that he persuaded President Roosevelt to adopt the Germany First policy, even though many Americans saw Japan as being a greater and more immediate threat to them. That said, the USA's direct military (as opposed to industrial) contribution to the war in the West was modest until June 1944, and the big American battles were in the Pacific. In contrast, as far as Britain was concerned, the war in the Far East was almost peripheral, and for the most part manpower and materiel were only committed to it if they were surplus to requirements in the West: what happened in the East could not directly affect the existence of the United Kingdom as an independent nation. As for Japan, she did not even inform Germany of her intention to initiate war with the United States and Britain, and, while Germany did immediately declare war on America, there was no coordination of Japanese and German strategy. In many ways, therefore, the Far East theatre was also a separate war.

Countries may operate as part of a coalition – indeed, on land Britain has only very rarely fought alone – but that does not mean that the war aims of that coalition's members necessarily coincide. The preservation of the British Empire was, for example, of no concern to the United States – indeed, some Americans welcomed the thought of its disintegration. Britain seriously considered whether she was obliged to declare war on the USSR when that country gobbled up its agreed share of Poland in September 1939, and she sent RAF fighters to support the Finns in their Winter War.* British and

---

*The British would have sent troops too, if the Norwegians and Swedes had agreed to allow them passage. By 1941 perceptions had changed and Britain declared war on Finland.

American politicians and chiefs of staff disagreed profoundly as to the need for and the merits of the Italian campaign, and there were severe differences of opinion as to the best time to launch Operation Overlord, the invasion of North-West Europe.

As for technology, war has always inspired its development, but this conflict gave birth to little that was actually novel – most was merely a refinement of what was there before. Radar, the delivery of troops by parachute, battlefield radio, ballistic missiles and atomic weapons were certainly new. Aircraft and tanks, however, along with aircraft carriers and submarines, had all been used in the first war, as had plastic surgery, even if their development before and during the second produced machines and weapons systems that would have been almost unrecognizable when set beside those of 1914–18. The frail, single-seater flying machine of 1914 which relied on wing warp to control its progress through the air had metamorphosed into long-range bombers and jet fighters, the Mark I tank of 1916 had become the Panzer Mark VI Tiger, and the 1914 carrier HMS *Ark Royal*, a 7,500-ton converted merchant ship carrying seven sea and land planes, was by 1945 the 60,000-ton USS *Midway* with her complement of 137 of the most modern aircraft.

* * *

Authors of accounts of wars, revolutions, economic collapse and divers catastrophes like to talk about gathering storm clouds, and from the early 1930s onwards there was indeed a plethora of indicators that war was coming. The trouble was that nobody, or almost nobody, paid very much attention. Britain was ostensibly still a superpower; the Royal Navy patrolled the sea lanes, although Britain had surrendered absolute command of the oceans in the Washington Naval Treaty of 1922, unable to fund the naval construction programme necessary to retain it. It was literally true that the sun never set on the British Empire, but despite all the flags and parades there were huge weaknesses. Having been severely mauled by the Geddes Axe of 1921, the British armed forces totalled only half a million men, and the British Army was still armed with much the same equipment that it had fielded in 1918, but with rather less of it. With no money for interwar experimentation, the army that had invented *Blitzkrieg* in 1918 now had few tanks and little experience of air-to-ground cooperation. The only aspect of defence to have received any serious attention at all had been air defence, but with the Royal Air Force funded on the understanding that, in the event of another European war, there would be no land component sent across the Channel, there was a serious shortage of air support for the British Expeditionary Force when political priorities changed and it was, after all, sent to France in 1939.

France possessed a huge army, but its generals were fixated on a rerun of 1914–18 and its soldiers were mostly underpaid and poorly fed conscripts. The French did have some military thinkers of vision and originality and did possess a large number of very good tanks, but the military establishment had not agreed on how they should be used and in the event most were spread far too thinly or employed merely as semi-mobile gun platforms. As a result, they were easily outmanoeuvred by German armour that was of lesser mechanical quality but directed by men who had given a great deal of thought to its employment. Furthermore, the Third Republic was riven by political and social strife and, as the subsequent adherence to Pétain and Vichy showed, there were many French men and women who thought that the whole edifice was so rotten that only by knocking it all down and starting again could France be restored to her proper place in the world.

At around 6 million men, the Soviet army was enormous, but its organization and structure were unwieldy and ramshackle and it was led by an ill-educated and barely competent officer class whose operational decisions were subject to review by a parallel command structure of political commissars at all levels. The ravages of forced industrialization, collectivization of agriculture and Stalin's purges of 1937–38, which despatched to execution, imprisonment or exile around 100,000 army officers, including nearly all the high command, left Russia in no state to resist when invasion came in 1941.

The United States of America was even less prepared for war than Britain. Many Americans thought that it had been a mistake to become involved in the first war. Congress had declined to ratify the Versailles Treaty in 1919 and the nation had withdrawn into isolation, with no intention or expectation of again participating in a European war that could not possibly affect American interests. In the year that Hitler came to power in Germany, America had an army of 132,000 men, which meant it was even smaller than Czechoslovakia's. That army had one acting full general (the Chief of Staff, Douglas MacArthur), no lieutenant-generals and a promotion system by strict seniority. Its tanks were obsolete and its aircraft rapidly becoming so. The army was mainly deployed along the Mexican border or in the Philippines, and, while the USA did have a sizeable navy, the Depression had ensured that the 1916 Fleet, the threat of which had frightened the British into signing the Washington treaty, was never built.

Even Germany, where more thought, energy and money had gone into the armed forces than anywhere else, was unprepared for a long war. Ever since the days of little Brandenburg, German soldiers and statesmen had striven to avoid a war on two fronts. Prussia, and later Germany, had to win a war quickly, or she could not win it at all – a reality determined by geography, economics and the relative size of her population. In 1870 she had defeated France in six weeks – all else was mere mopping up. In 1914 she had tried, via the Schlieffen Plan, to win by Christmas and she had failed. Having taken on the empires of France, Britain and Russia, and then the United States, and having given time for the traditional British weapon of blockade to bite, she had eventually discovered that the odds were simply far too great. In the 1920s and 1930s the only state with which Germany could cooperate in attempting to build up a military machine that might break the shackles of Versailles was the world's other pariah – Soviet Russia – and both Weimar and National Socialist regimes carried out tank and aircraft development deep inside Russia, the quid pro quo being that Russian officers attended German military courses. Despite National Socialist antipathy towards Bolshevism, there was a strong historical justification for alignment with Russia: from 1815 onwards Prussia had usually had what Bismarck called an insurance treaty with Russia to avoid war on two fronts, a treaty which was only discarded on the insistence of Kaiser Wilhelm II, who thought it unnecessary.

In 1939, therefore, the Wehrmacht was a tactical, rather than strategic, organization, and the German armed forces that entered the war were structured for short, sharp campaigns based on mobility and shock action. The Luftwaffe's main role was to provide ground support while the German navy, the Kriegsmarine, was configured for commerce raiding, mine-laying and submarine warfare. Germany did not believe that France and Britain would actually keep their promises to Poland, but thought that, even if they did, they could be swiftly disposed of.

Perhaps the most extraordinary aspect of Germany's conduct of the war is not that she tried to take on the world – fair enough, if you think you can do it – but her treatment of her own and Europe's Jews. There is scant – if any – evidence that German Jews were other than loyal citizens; indeed, during the first war a German government survey was carried out to determine whether Jewish soldiers were being killed at the same rate as other Germans and found that they were.* There is no logic in the German extermination policy of 1942–45, which used up transportation and manpower assets that would have been far better employed in trying to win the war. Behind the rhetoric of racial contamination – which thinking Germans must have known was nonsense – it is impossible to find any good reasons for the judicial killing of millions of people. There was, of course, a long history of anti-Semitism in Europe, but, whereas in America and Britain anti-Semitism was characterized by the blackballing of Jewish applicants for membership of golf clubs, in Europe Jews were subject to pogroms and all manner of discrimination. Nevertheless, if National Socialist Germany really believed that she had to eliminate her Jews entirely, why not win the war first and then slaughter at leisure?

What is even more extraordinary is that, while all this was going on, there were still Jews serving in the German armed forces. Horst Rippert, a former sergeant pilot of the Luftwaffe now aged eighty-eight, has recently come to public attention because he may, or may not, have been the Bf 109 pilot who on 31 July 1944 shot down the French author and Free French pilot Antoine de Saint-Exupéry as he flew a reconnaissance mission from Corsica over south-western France. Rippert, who went on to become a sports journalist after the war, said in passing that he was at one stage taken off flying duties 'because I was Jewish', but was later reinstated and subsequently decorated by the Luftwaffe's Commander-in-Chief, Hermann Göring.[1] Meanwhile, this author was recently introduced to a Jewish student whose German Jewish grandfather, who was blond and blue-eyed, had served happily in the Waffen SS. It was not all as simple as it might now seem.

We tend, of course, to excuse or gloss over Japanese atrocities during the war as being symptomatic of an apparently barbarous people who knew no better, but the Germans were educated, civilized and cultured and most assuredly did know better. I have asked a number of German historians why, morality aside, they did not postpone killing their Jews until after the war. The only reply that seems to make some sort of sense is that to National Socialism the ridding Europe of Jews for all time was more important than

---

*Quoted in Wolfram Wette, *Die Wehrmacht – Feindbilder, Vernichtungskrieg, Legenden*, S. Fischer Verlag GmbH, Frankfurt am Main, 2002.

winning the war. Wars can be re-fought; a race, once extinct, is gone for ever. That said, even if Germany had won the war, it is difficult to see how she could have justified the extermination camps to the world or to her own population, and what happened and the opprobrium that it attached to the very name of Germany has echoes to this day.*

Hitler and the NSDAP did their best to equate, in the public mind, Jewishness and communism. Some Jews were, of course, communist, as were some Roman Catholics, Lutherans and atheists, but the vast majority were not. Europeans were frightened of communism: it had a self-avowed international aspect, whatever Stalin might say about socialism in one country, and it could be a lot nastier than anything the NSDAP came up with. Hitler made officials and generals he lost faith in retire to the country; Stalin had them shot. If you can convince people that communism threatens everything you believe in – which up to a point it did – and you then manage to convince people that Judaism goes hand in hand with communism, then it makes it a lot easier to ship your Jews off to remote areas out of sight and presumably out of mind. No doubt some of the Allgemeine (or general, not to be confused with the Waffen, or armed) SS who ran the death camps were psychopaths but they cannot all have been so – most must have believed that what they were doing was in the national interest.

As to exactly which institutions and individuals were culpable in the policy towards the Jews is still the subject of debate. After the war, it was in the interests of democratic politicians trying to establish the new Germany and of Western governments that needed Germany as an ally in the Cold War against the new threat from the USSR to believe that most Germans knew nothing of the extermination camps and that the German armed forces had fought an honourable war. As most of the camps were either in remote rural areas or in what had been Poland, the majority of the German civilian population were probably ignorant as to what actually went on,† and may

---

*A British private soldier stationed in Moenchengladbach was recently reprimanded by a German *Hausfrau* for smacking his child, who was misbehaving in the street. At the soldier's subsequent interview with his company commander (a close relative of this author), it transpired that the lady had said, 'In Germany we do not strike children', to which the soldier replied, 'And in England we don't gas Jews.' Mud sticks for a very long time.

†But see Goldhagen, *Hitler's Willing Executioners*, where it is stated that 'hundreds of thousands' of Germans were directly involved and 'millions' knew about it.

well have convinced themselves, or at least tried to convince themselves, that, when their Jewish neighbours were rounded up and put on railway wagons, they really were just going to be resettled in the East. Most American and British veterans of the war would agree that by and large the German armed forces, the Wehrmacht, fought decently: the Geneva Convention was adhered to and prisoners were properly treated. Misbehaviour was rare and such deviations that did occur were by individuals or small groups acting without the sanction of higher authority. The position is less clear in the East. That atrocities were committed against civilians is unquestionable; the debate is to what extent the Wehrmacht, primarily the army, was involved.

As the German army was initially welcomed as liberators by many Soviet citizens who had no love for Stalin or communism, it made no military sense to antagonize them. The treating of Russians as sub-humans and the shooting out of hand of political commissars and anyone suspected of political affiliations or, later, partisan activity turned those who might have been sympathetic to Germany, or at least quiescent, into terrorists and tied down large numbers of German troops protecting their lines of communication – troops that would have been far more usefully employed in fighting the Red Army. In the early days of Barbarossa, the German invasion of the USSR, the army was careful to adhere to the norms of civilized behaviour. Very soon, however, responsibility for the administration of occupied territory was taken away from the military and handed over to civilian or SS authorities. Some army commanders refused to promulgate or enforce the so-called Commissar Order, which instructed that political commissars in the Red Army were to be executed; others considered that it was none of their business, but, while they may have provided fatigue parties or guards to assist, they made sure that the actual shootings were carried out by the Allgemeine SS. Legal pedants might argue that, as the USSR had not recognized the Geneva Convention, her citizens and soldiers were not entitled to its protection, but this cannot wash. What appears to have happened is that the soldiers tried to avoid becoming involved in atrocities, found that they could not prevent them and, as time went on and partisan activity became more savage, were inevitably drawn into carrying out reprisals. The war in the East was a brutal one, and men on both sides became brutalized by it.

As for Japan, once she had elected to join the world, rather than remain cut off from it, war was inevitable. Japan wanted to be a great power, at least in the region, but she had no, or almost no, raw materials to sustain the industrial base that great powers need if they are to pursue an independent foreign policy. Oil, iron ore, rubber and the like can, of course, be bought from those countries that do have them, but supply can be suspended at the whim of the seller and the only way to obtain those materials without dependence on the policies of others is to take them. In Japan's instance, this meant seizing the rubber plantations of Malaya and the oil fields of Burma and the Dutch East Indies. Once that was done, however, a defensive ring had to be created to hold the newly acquired territories. That, added to a deepening involvement in China and an opportunist grab for India, stretched Japan way beyond her capabilities. As long as the Western powers held their collective nerve, Japan could not win. She could invade British, Dutch and American possessions, she could sink Allied ships, but she could never pose a realistic threat to the American homeland, nor, unless the Germans did it for her, to mainland Britain either. Japan had a large and well-motivated army and an impressive navy, but the army's logistic machinery was never going to be able to sustain simultaneous campaigns in China, the Pacific and Burma; nor could she hope to maintain air superiority at sea once the American shipyards and aircraft factories got into their stride. Japan was always going to lose.

* * *

After sixty years, it might be felt that, with most of those who fought in the Second World War dead or in their eighties, emotions have had time to cool, and a reasonably detached view might be taken, but, as the crowds passing daily through war museums and the seemingly insatiable appetite for films and television programmes about this war – the last European war – show, the events of 1939–45 still have the capacity to provoke interest, anger, outrage and pride. With nearly all the information about this war now in the public domain, it is perhaps timely to re-examine the aims of the warring nations, analyse why they went to war and why and how they prosecuted the war in the way that they did. Any such study must consider the influence of technology, of economics and of individual personalities, and, while it must inevitably look at the influence of Stalin and Hitler, Roosevelt and Churchill, Mussolini and Tojo, it should include the common soldier too, for how men fight and why they fight is as much part of a nation's character as whether they eat bacon and eggs or beetroot soup for breakfast. While political, economic, social and military history all impinge upon and are affected by each other, this book is primarily a work of operational military history, mainly concerned with why and how the war was fought as it was, and written because it seems, to this author at least, that, at a time when in the Western democracies there is uncertainty and much debate as to how national defence postures should develop, such a study is timely and may even prove helpful.

It is a hackneyed old joke that history does not repeat itself, while historians repeat themselves. Certainly, the wars of the twentieth century have been subjected to a great deal of 'revisionism', where somebody takes what has become the accepted view and turns it on its head. Much revisionism is actually re-revisionism. Immediately upon its close, the first war was widely regarded as having been necessary and well conducted until those with an axe to grind got started. Sir Basil Liddell Hart's influence on military history, for example, and particularly the history of the first war, has been nothing short of pernicious. The long shadow he cast over a later generation of politicians and scholars, whose views inevitably influenced those of the wider reading public, led to a popular view of the generals of the 1914–18 period as being uncaring butchers and unthinking bunglers. That in its time was revisionist history. Later John Terraine led a re-revision, and he and historians including Correlli Barnett, Brian Bond, Peter Simpkins, Gary Sheffield, John Bourne, Mark Connelly and others showed that the conclusions of Liddell Hart, John Laffin, Denis Winter and their ilk were not just mistaken, but in some cases deliberate distortion, and that the British had, within the constraints of the assets and the technology available at the time, fought the war competently until by 1918 they could launch massive all-arms offensives using all available assets which forced the Germans to sue for peace. Most modern military historians would lean more towards the Terraine interpretation than to that of Laffin, although the majority of the public are probably still of the opposite view. What was revisionist history of the first war has now almost become orthodoxy.

The interpretation of the Second World War, too, has been subject to revision. With almost unlimited funding, an army of researchers and, unusually, permission from the prime minister, Clement Attlee, to trawl government papers without restriction, Winston Churchill produced the first British version of the war to appear on the shelves. His was a magisterial view from the mountain top, embracing grand strategy and high politics, in which all that was bad could be blamed on the appeasers, and in which plucky Britain, standing alone until the New World came to the assistance of the Old, played the major role in defeating the aggressors. As more accounts began to be published, on both sides of the Atlantic, and as scholars began to analyse the performance of the British armed forces, and as German generals released from imprisonment began to publish their (admittedly largely self-justificatory) memoirs, the competence of the British armed forces in the war began to be questioned. An accepted version arose, one which viewed the German army as being far superior in fighting quality to that of the British, and which acknowledged that the Germans had lost because once again they had taken on the British Empire, the USSR and the USA at the same time. More recently, revisionist (or perhaps re-revisionist) study is suggesting that the British Army's performance during the war was actually quite good (although in this author's opinion the emphasis must be on the 'quite'), and that its conduct in the North African and North-West European campaigns in particular is deserving of praise. The truth, I fear, is that Britain was very rarely a match for the Germans.

Elsewhere, in the United States there has never been any doubt that the American performance was anything short of superb – which, once the nation was aroused, it by and large was – and some American accounts are severely critical of the British effort, in the main because of the complete inability of Montgomery and his satraps to work harmoniously in a coalition. In the USSR the view has always been that the destruction of fascism was achieved with only a marginal contribution from the other Allies, a position that remains largely unchanged in post-communist Russia today. In Germany historians have painted the Germans themselves as being victims of Nazism and the Hitler era is still surrounded by much sensitivity and self-flagellation. In 2007 a German teacher who suggested that certain aspects of National Socialism might be praiseworthy was dismissed from her post. The aspects she cited were transport (and Germans are still using Hitler's autobahns) and support for the family. In some countries, it is a crime to deny what has become known as the Holocaust.* Making it a crime to express unacceptable opinions is the thin edge of a very thick wedge (equally reprehensible, for

---

*The word means 'compete destruction by fire' and so could equally well refer to the Allied bombing of Dresden, or the fire-bombing of Tokyo, but instead has come to mean, with doubtful etymological accuracy, the elimination of large numbers of the Jewish population of Europe by the Germans from 1942 to 1945.

example, is the refusal of some British academics to have any dealings with Israel because of her perceived attitude to the Palestinians). The way to deal with views with which one disagrees, or which are palpable nonsense, is surely to subject them to rigorous scholarly examination in the full light of day. When opinions are made illegal, it only encourages people to wonder whether there might not be something in them.

My own position is that I am firmly in the Terraine–Sheffield camp as regards the first war. As I have explained both above and elsewhere, I consider that war to have been necessary and to have been well conducted, at least by the British.* As regards the Second World War, I regret that I simply cannot agree with some current work which suggests that the British Army, as opposed to the Royal Navy or Air Force, fought rather well. You simply cannot compare Montgomery's ten divisions and one brigade at Alamein (of which four divisions and the brigade were not actually British)† taking on eleven under-strength German and Italian divisions that were starved of materiel, with, say, the German Sixth Army battling six Russian armies at Stalingrad, nor the shameful incompetence of the British surrender of Singapore with the tenacious and fanatical German defence of Berlin to (almost) the last man and the last bullet.

Between 1914 and 1918, almost the entire British Army was fighting the main enemy (Germany) in the main theatre (the Western Front) for the whole of the war. In 1940, however, the BEF was bustled unceremoniously out of Europe and the British Army subsequently did very little until returning to France in 1944. All else – North Africa, Italy, even the Far East (where only one third of the British Army was actually British) – was peripheral to the defeat of the main enemy. Britain's major contribution to the war was in not losing it in 1940, and thus making herself available as a staging area for British and American forces to launch Operation Overlord, the Normandy landings in June 1944.

The more recent the event, of course, the more difficult it is to form an opinion of it, if only because one tries to avoid giving too much offence to those who were there and are still around to heckle. Evidence from the

---

Mud, Blood and Poppycock (Cassell, London, 2003) won me two death threats, both written in green ink with lots of block capitals and bits underlined. Fortunately, the would-be assassins' map-reading was as bad as their spelling and I am still here.

† 1 South African, 2 New Zealand, 4 Indian, 9 Australian and a French brigade.

veterans of any conflict is sometimes useful, but it becomes less so with the passing of time. Former combatants may come to believe what others think they ought to believe and views formed over the years may be very different from those held at the time. As a result, confusion, however honest, can set in. On a recent visit to one of the three Normandy beaches on which British troops landed in 1944, I was approached by a lovely old boy wearing his medals and his regimental beret complete with cap badge, who told me that he had landed there with his battalion on D-Day. It seemed churlish to tell him that he had landed on the next beach down on D + 1, so I kept quiet.

And finally, a brief point about the structure of the book. As I have alluded to above, the causes of the various wars in Europe, Africa and the Far East were not identical, and in some cases were not even associated. That all these wars happened in the same time frame is, of course, not entirely coincidental, but for ease of understanding I have considered them as separate, albeit related and interlinked, conflicts. I trust that this approach will enlighten rather than confuse.

Gordon Corrigan

Kent 2010

PRELUDE

FEBRUARY 1942

The Russian village of Nikolskoje, a motley collection of log cabins thatched with turf, lay 180 miles south-west of Moscow and was of no importance whatsoever except that in February 1942 it was held by units of the Red Army's 32 Cavalry Division, a mix of horse- and tank-mounted troops, and, like a host of similar villages all along the 1,200 miles of the Eastern Front, it would have to be dealt with to give the Germans a jump-off line for the resumption of the drive east once the snow cleared and the ground hardened.

Nikolskoje had been taken by the Germans in 1941, and for a brief time Field Marshal Fedor von Bock had his headquarters there, but then it had been abandoned as the Germans went into defence for the winter of 1941/42. On 10 February 1942, Major Günter Pape was ordered to take Nikolskoje, along with its outlying hamlet of Solojewka. Pape commanded the Third Motorcycle reconnaissance battalion of 3 Panzer Division, part of Colonel-General Rudolf Schmidt's Second Panzer Army of Army Group Centre commanded by Field Marshal Günter von Kluge, and in addition to his own battalion he was allocated a motorized infantry battalion of the Waffen SS, three tanks and an anti-tank platoon commanded by Oberfeldwebel (Staff-Sergeant) Albert Ernst, a thirty-year-old regular soldier who had joined the Reichswehr in 1930.

Pape's battle group moved off at 0700 hours, an hour before first light, and, as the likely threat was from Russian tanks, the anti-tank platoon led. With its Krupp six-wheeler vehicles to tow the guns, the platoon had a reasonable cross-country capability, but in any case there was little shelter on the snow-covered ground. Soon two Russian machine-gun posts began to chatter: Ernst ordered one of his 50mm guns to unhitch and return fire, and very soon the machine-guns ceased. A little farther on and a Russian mortar opened up, but the effects of its bombs were muffled by the snow

17

and Ernst simply ordered his lead vehicle to drive over it: those of its crew who were not crushed beneath the wheels fled back to Solojewka in their rear. Now the German infantry came up and stormed into the buildings while the Mk III tanks and Ernst's guns provided fire support. As they hurled themselves from hut to hut through the now fiercely burning village, the infantry found that they had stumbled upon the Red Army divisional headquarters – far further forward than it should have been – and accepted the surrender of a bemused divisional commander.

Russian soldiers were now fleeing as fast as they could in the snow to reach the safety – as they thought – of Nikolskoje, but Ernst's anti-tank platoon and the Mk III panzers were in hot pursuit and Ernst reached the outskirts and set up his guns just as his vehicles were consuming their last drops of fuel. Giving the Russians no time to organize a coherent defence, Major Pape ordered the tanks to shoot the infantry in and by eleven o'clock in the morning the German battle group had taken Nikolskoje and had pressed on with the infantry and the tanks, driving the Soviets from the next three villages, or more properly the straggling collections of mud-floored hovels of Nowo-Dankilowo, Moskwinka and Stakanowo.

Pape* was awarded the Knight's Cross of the Iron Cross for the action, and Ernst the Iron Cross First Class, but in the greater scheme of things the four-hour battle was but a minor skirmish: it is covered only in personal memoirs and was mentioned just briefly in Pape's hometown newspaper. It was, nevertheless, one of the first successful attacks of the German army's 1942 campaign, and soon, after many little actions like it, all would be ready for the next phase, when the German army would surge forward to the Volga and then turn south into the Caucasus and the glittering prize of the oil fields that would feed German industry and the Wehrmacht, regardless of Allied blockade or bombing.

* * *

---

*By the end of the war, Pape was a major-general in command of a panzer grenadier division. After the war, he became a major-general in the Bundeswehr but resigned in 1966 during the 'Crisis of the Generals', when the head of the Luftwaffe, Lieutenant-General Werner Panitzki, and the head of the army, General Heinz Trettner, resigned over differences in the method of civilian control of the armed forces. Pape resigned in loyalty to his commander. Ernst finished the war as a captain, when he surrendered the city of Iserlohn to the Americans on 16 April 1945.

As Major Pape's men regrouped and congratulated themselves on the successful first moves to continue the eastwards march of German conquest, 5,000 miles to the south-east it was night and the men of the Japanese 18 Division were filing down to the bank of the estuary of the River Skudai, at the tip of the Malayan peninsula and directly across the strait from the north shore of Singapore Island. In a hastily assembled collection of sampans, army landing craft and rubber assault boats, they would form the first wave of the landings on Britain's impregnable Far East bastion. The soldiers' morale was high but most were resigned to the fact that there was a very good chance of dying for the emperor before the night was over: so far the Japanese advance down Malaya had been unstoppable, but now the British and the Indians and the Australians would surely fight like cornered rats, even if the invading force managed actually to get across the water and land in the teeth of the artillery fire that would swamp the boats and rend the bodies of their occupants.

All day, the positions of the Australians defending the opposite shore had been subjected to bombardment, but, as the little armada moved out into the water, the Japanese had to cease shelling, for fear of hitting their own men. Now, surely, would come the retaliation, but as the boats moved closer and closer to the shore, there was no reply from the defenders, until at last, only fifty yards from landing, a desultory rattle of rifle and Bren gun fire began. It was far too late. The Japanese lieutenants and sergeants and corporals who led that first wave could hardly believe their good fortune as they stormed ashore and through the hastily dug defences. There should indeed have been a devastating artillery barrage to fall upon them, and Vickers machine-guns and anti-tank guns should have ripped through the plywood and rubber of their boats, but the searchlights that the British had sited to illuminate them had never come on (nobody ever knew quite why); the frantic telephone messages from the artillery forward observation officers had not got through as the cables had been severed by the Japanese shelling; there were too few radios and communication by this means was anyway patchy; and the last resort of flares fired in a certain sequence to bring down fire were not seen by the men on the guns in their camouflaged positions two miles behind.

Within hours, the invaders had reached Tengah airfield, abandoned days before by the RAF as the station commander shot himself in shame and desperation, the shore defence had collapsed and more and more Japanese troops were streaming off the landing craft. In a matter of days, it would all be over. Singapore would be in Japanese hands and the myth of British invincibility shattered. Next would come Burma, and then India, the jewel in the crown of the British Empire that, were it not taken by the Japanese themselves, would fall into their hands by internal revolt. The Japanese dream of the Greater East Asian Co-Prosperity Sphere was only a grasp away from becoming reality.

* * *

For any German – or Italian or Japanese – the world view must indeed have seemed a rosy one in mid-February 1942. In 1939, the Wehrmacht had swept into Poland, and then in 1940 had conquered the whole of Western Europe in a mere six weeks, with the opposition either running up the white flag or, in the case of the British, scrambling humiliatingly back across the Channel. The invasion of Russia in June 1941 had been a run of almost unbroken success, with the Luftwaffe ruling the skies and hundreds of thousands of Red Army soldiers encircled, defeated, killed or taken prisoner. True, the German army had been unable to take Moscow in 1940, but, as Hitler had said, Moscow was only a name on a map, and now they had survived the coldest Russian winter for fifty years. Meanwhile, in North Africa Rommel's German and Italian forces were preparing an offensive that would drive the British Eighth Army all the way back from Gazala to the Egyptian border and in the Far East Germany's ally, Japan, had driven the British from Malaya, captured Hong Kong and Singapore, destroyed the Dutch empire in the East Indies and would soon take the surrender of the American and Filipino forces on Corregidor.

It would be both a cliché and simply untrue to remark that, despite all the euphoria in Berlin, Rome and Tokyo, there were dark clouds on the horizon, for dark clouds can be seen, and it would have been a brave man indeed in those heady days of mid-February 1942 who would have been prepared to lay any sort of odds against the Axis winning the Second World War. But wars are not predictable, and, however much we soldiers might wish it to be otherwise, they are not necessarily decided by the courage, leadership, training and loyalty of the troops involved, nor by the quality of the equipment they deploy – these are, of course, important, but money, population and industrial capacity are often the final deciders.

In very short order, the global situation would change utterly. In less than four months, the Japanese Combined Fleet, far from luring the Americans to disaster, would itself suffer a devastating defeat; a month after that, American forces would land on the Japanese-occupied island of Guadalcanal; in October, the British Eighth Army, hitherto beaten and out-generalled, would strike the first blow at Alamein that would drive Panzer Army Africa all the way back to Tunisia, and then the British and Americans would invade Vichy French Algeria and Morocco, spelling the death of the German and Italian campaign in North Africa. Worst of all for the Axis, by the end of 1942 the German drive to the Volga would be halted by the disaster of Stalingrad and most of the Caucasus oil would prove unreachable. The Russian campaign, until now a more or less unbroken string of great German victories, would instead become a grim and bloody defence – an unremitting succession of desperate counter-attacks and heartbreaking retreats back to the gates of Berlin and the heart of the Reich itself. The fortunes of war are indeed fickle.

1

ON YOUR MARKS...

It would be quite unfair to blame the United States of America for starting the Second World War. Hitler did not come to power because of the Wall Street Crash, but, as the Great Depression sparked off by the crash affected the economies of the whole developed world and encouraged the rise of extreme politics, it certainly helped. Indeed, before the crash led indirectly to the collapse of a major Austrian bank in May 1931 – a collapse which brought down the entire German banking system with it – German liberal democracy might, just, have survived; after it, the rise of extreme German nationalism could not be contained.

Stock markets depend on confidence – confidence in the soundness of the market, confidence in the individual companies and utilities quoted on it, and confidence in its regulation. When any of these factors is absent, then it is only a question of time before financial chaos and collapse ensue. The Wall Street Crash was not the first such implosion, nor by any means the last. Economists still argue about the causes of the 1929 crash, but what actually happened is clear enough, even if the reasons for it are not. Democracies and controlled economies are mutually incompatible and in a free market occasional adjustment – recession even – is probably inevitable. The United States had been heading for recession in 1914 and the First World War had got her out of it. The slack in American industry was taken up by British and French contracts for war-making materiel, and indeed there were cynics who claimed (unfairly, in this author's view) that America only entered the war to make sure that the Allies won and she got paid. As the only participant that actually emerged from the war richer than she entered it, America was poised for a period of sustained economic growth after it, and, under the administrations of Presidents Calvin Coolidge from 1921 and Herbert Hoover from 1928, she got it. Among the results of this boom were very large amounts of cash looking for a home, and some of this surplus cash was absorbed by lending to overseas governments and financial institutions: by 1929, American banks had outstanding foreign loans of $8.5bn, about half of this total being to Germany.* A proportion of these loans were undoubtedly dubious, but, as long as the lenders were happy to lend and the borrowers could service the loans at interest rates that were not onerous, nobody minded very much.

It was not just corporations and the US government that used overseas loans as a seemingly safe resting place for spare capital, but individuals too, and many not only bought into loans but piled into the stock market, which seemed as if it would go on rising for ever. By 1929 it was estimated that 9 million individuals were engaged in owning, buying and selling shares, which, if dependants are included, means that around 20 per cent of the entire US population (120 million in 1929) was involved with the stock market and directly affected by it. Many knew perfectly well that shares can go down as well as up, but there was an almost universal suspension of belief that for many years appeared to be justified as the market marched ever upwards.

America had never believed in the regulation of making money, and there was the usual crop of out-and-out swindlers who encouraged investment in companies that either did not exist or were set up purely to fleece the gullible. Most brokers – those who arranged for the purchase and sale of shares – were not dishonest, but too many of them were either incompetent or incurable optimists who encouraged the naive and the greedy to buy and to go on buying. By 1929 shares were changing hands at prices that could not possibly be justified by the underlying assets backing them, and between 1925 and 1929 the total of share prices on the New York exchange had trebled. The trouble about booms, though, is that they nearly always over-extend themselves and are followed by some sort of bust.

Matters were hardly improved by the fact that, alongside the straightforward investment in the Wall Street market, there was a great deal of buying on margin, which was effectively a way of buying shares with borrowed money, the collateral for the loan being the shares themselves. If the market went up, the

---

*There are many ways to calculate inflation but using the conservative Consumer Price Index measure, this is equivalent to over $100bn today, or about one and a half times the UK's annual defence budget.

profits could be enormous,* but, if it went down, then the investor had to keep pumping more and more money in to back the loan, which now became increasingly greater than the value of the shares. As it was, by October 1929 a staggering total of $6.8bn was outstanding in loans to buy shares, most of it backed by the shares themselves. In short, Wall Street had become as much a medium for gambling, with many small investors sucked in by the lure of easy money, as it was a mechanism for economic growth. It had taken twenty years, from 1907 until 1927, for the Dow Jones industrial average – the measure of the total value of a representative basket of shares on the New York market – to double. It took only another two years – from 1927 to 1929 – for it to double again. The bubble could not go on expanding for ever, and eventually it burst.

The twenties had stopped roaring well before October 1929, although very few seemed to notice. On the 17th of that month, the committee of the Investment Bankers Association of New York warned that speculation in utilities (gas, electricity, water) had 'reached danger point and many stocks are selling far above their intrinsic value'.[2] No one seemed to listen. On Wednesday, 23 October, New York prices started to drop and the second-highest number of shares in the history of the exchange was traded. The telegrams demanding increases in margin payments started to go out. The next day's opening saw more selling but there was a modest upturn in late trading when the banks and investment houses pumped money in to steady the market, and the morning's losses were halved. On Friday, 25 October, the Dow Jones closed marginally up, and on Saturday marginally down but in steady trading. Both the optimists and those who were in too deeply to get out without huge losses breathed again.

Their relief was short-lived. On Monday morning, a rumour-fuelled wave of selling saw Wall Street's biggest drop in share prices to date, with $14bn lopped off the value of shares. Worse was to come. On Tuesday, 29 October, massive selling, which was now panic selling, continued. By the close of trading that day, 16.4 million shares had been traded. The Dow, which on 1 October stood at 343, was at 230 and it would be another twenty-five

---

* An investor buys a thousand shares each priced at $10. He puts up 10 per cent ($1,000) and borrows the rest ($9,000) from the broker. A month later the shares have doubled in value to $20 and the investor sells. He gets $20,000 for the sale, pays the broker back the $9,000 plus interest (say, an annual interest rate of 6 per cent, as it was in mid-October 1929, or roughly $45 for the month) and now has $10,955 for an initial investment of $1,000.

years before it would reach its pre-crash levels again. In all, $10bn had been wiped off the market value. To put this sum into perspective, it was equal to the total cost to America of the first war, ten times the Union budget for the Civil War and twice all the money in circulation throughout the entire nation.[3] It was now breathtakingly clear that this really was a crash: there would be no correction, no rally, no pumping in of money by the banks. By the time loans had not been repaid and banks and businesses had failed, the total cost has been estimated at $50bn or $559bn in today's money.

Manufacturing industries, which were slowing down anyway before the crash, now found themselves with warehouses full of goods that nobody could afford to buy, and employers began to lay off workers. Before the crash, there were 1.5 million Americans unemployed, or 3.3 per cent of a workforce of 45 million. By 1932, that had risen to 15 million, or a third of the workforce. Inevitably, recession in the wake of the crash and the collapse of the American domestic economy quickly began to affect the rest of the world. Overseas companies that sold to America found orders were cancelled or not renewed. If Detroit was not making cars, then it did not need rubber to make tyres, and so there was a slump in the rubber plantations of Malaya, then a British colony. Much the same applied to those exporters of tin, oil and European luxury items. One of the first things that people or companies do when faced with a liquidity crisis is to call in outstanding debts, and this is what American banks began to do.

In these days, when goods cross borders with ease, it is sometimes forgotten that free trade, now accepted by most advanced nations, was still hotly argued about in the interwar years. The USA was protectionist – that is, she imposed tariffs on goods imported from abroad, in order to protect domestic producers. Had tariffs not been imposed, then foreign goods might undercut those produced at home and would drive the price of the latter down, and the wages of those who made them down too. Up to the time of the crash, these tariffs were not a serious obstacle to international trade and even those imposed on goods in direct competition with those made at home were not onerous. All that was to change in 1930 with the imposition of the Smoot–Hawley Act, which imposed swingeing import duties on a wider range of foreign goods, raising some of them by an unprecedented 50 per cent.

Now foreign countries could no longer export with ease to the United States, and some began to impose retaliatory tariffs on US goods. If commodity producers could not export to the United States, then neither would they import American wheat and meat. Grain, unsold and so unharvested, rotted in the fields of the Midwest and cattle were slaughtered because it was not worth bringing them to market. Rightly or wrongly, America was widely blamed for exporting recession: foreign governments argued – with some reason – that, if they could only be allowed to export to America, they could earn dollars and thus repay loans owing to the USA, while American exporters argued that, even though US exports were but a very small part of GDP, foreigners were deliberately driving them out of business. Either way, a crisis of global proportions was in the making.

At home, while America was protectionist, she was also non-interventionist. It was unthinkable then for the federal government to finance a public works programme (which might have solved, or at least massively reduced, unemployment) and impossible for it to direct the banking system. There was a Federal Reserve, but it had little real influence and the plethora of banks, many of them badly managed and mainly confined to one state, were generally uncooperative with it. There was no strong central bank with the power to intervene and offer a lifeline to financial institutions in trouble. It was up to the private sector to get itself out of its own mess, and that the private sector was unable to do. Domestically, President Hoover got little thanks from his countrymen for his handling of the recession. Hard though he tried to stimulate recovery – against all his own principles and those of his party, which saw rescue as being the prerogative of the individual and not the state – he could not succeed, largely because the recession was worldwide and deepening, but also because the machinery whereby he could intervene decisively simply did not exist. Then, in the summer of 1931, Hoover announced a moratorium on foreign debts owed to the government, but it was beyond his – or anyone's – power to stay debts owed to private investors and private banks, and it was those non-public debts that would prove critical.

* * *

The first spark that would ultimately ignite the Second World War was struck when Kredit Anstalt collapsed in May 1931. The largest bank in Austria and probably the most important bank in Europe, or at least in Central and Eastern Europe,* it had been in trouble in 1929, but such an institution could

---

*Readers should note that the United Kingdom, despite its geographical location, is not considered part of Europe, at least in regard to matters of finance.

not then have been allowed to fail and it had been bailed out by a consortium of banks that included JP Morgan (America), Schroeder (UK) and Rothschild (Austria). Then, in March 1931, Austria turned to her natural ally, Germany, and formed a customs union or free trade area. To France, this was completely unacceptable – the enemies of 1914–18 were getting together again – and French loans to Germany and Austria were immediately called in. Two months later, in May, a run on the bank again brought support, this time from the Bank of England, the Austrian government and the Federal Reserve, but it was not enough. The bank collapsed and Austrian governmental credit had run out. Shortly afterwards came the collapse of virtually the entire German banking system – and this too had been underwritten by the Bank of England. Then, in September 1931, Britain went off the gold standard. Most of Europe went off it too, but for the Bank of England no longer to back sterling with a guarantee to change it into gold on demand inflicted far-reaching and chaotic effects on the global economy. The Bank of England had been effectively the world's banker, with sterling in wider use as an international currency than even the dollar. Many countries, including France along with most of Europe, kept their national reserves in sterling, which was regarded as totally safe and realizable against gold. Now there was no certainty that these reserves would keep their value.

In America, there was little interest in what was going on in Europe, at least from the general public. The country's own problems – economic, industrial, social – were quite sufficient without having to worry about what effects the slump might be having elsewhere. Besides, despite the fact that they showed a net profit from their involvement in the first war, many Americans had a sneaking suspicion that the wily British and the mercurial French had somehow conned them into entering it, and given that the United States had refused to ratify the Treaty of Versailles, which brought the war to an end, there was little incentive to become embroiled again in the doings of Europeans.

Across the Atlantic, however, the view was very different, and that France called in her loans to Germany and Austria in 1931 so peremptorily should have come as no surprise. Of all Germany's erstwhile opponents, France had more reason to fear and hate her than most. Prussia had played a major part in the downfall of Napoleon and she had defeated and humiliated the second Napoleon's* empire in 1870: as a crowning insult, William of Prussia was declared emperor of a united Germany in the Hall of Mirrors in Versailles. This, combined with the fact that France had to pay a very large indemnity and lost Alsace (which was largely German-speaking) and one third of Lorraine (with rather less justification), left no great love for the Germans in French hearts – indeed, they were probably disliked almost as much as the British, who at least were no threat to metropolitan France on land.

Almost half a century after the indignities of the Franco-Prussian War, France was to emerge on the winning side in 1918, but at fearful cost. With a population 7 million less than that of the United Kingdom, she had suffered twice as many military deaths, and as she already had a declining and ageing population, one in which men of military age comprised a much smaller percentage than they did in Britain, the effects were even worse than the bald statistic might indicate.[4] It was France that was the moving spirit behind the harsh terms of the Versailles Treaty, and she was determined to brook no deviation from them. Suggestions by the British and Americans that payment of reparations might be modified cut no ice with successive French governments and, while Britain had some – even considerable – sympathy with the fledgling Weimar Republic, she was not prepared to break with France.

While Britain, and to a lesser extent the United States, had spent large sums in prosecuting the war, America herself suffered no damage to the homeland and, apart from the occasional air raid or shelling of a coastal town, neither did Britain. In France, however, at least 300,000 dwelling places were destroyed or damaged so badly that they had to be completely rebuilt and 20,000 factories or manufacturing establishments were rendered unusable. The country was faced with the huge problem of reconstruction while at the same time she could make few savings from disarmament as, unlike Britain, which rushed to get rid of her soldiers, sailors and airmen as quickly as possible, France, even with a

---

*Louis Napoleon, the son of Louis, the one-time king of Holland and brother of Napoleon I. He reigned as Napoleon III to sustain the fiction that the first Napoleon's infant son was the rightful ruler of France after his father's exile to St Helena. Like so many deposed emperors, kings and dictators, Napoleon III went into exile in Hampshire and his son (the Prince Imperial) was killed in a particularly foolish escapade while an observer with the British Army in the Zulu War in 1879. Louis Napoleon, his Spanish ex-empress Eugenie and the Prince Imperial are all buried at Farnborough Abbey. Despite the Bonaparte lineage, most of the French considered them to be upstarts and have never asked for the bodies to be repatriated.

defeated and disarmed Germany as a neighbour, felt unable to drop her guard completely. Furthermore, France, like Germany, had opted to finance the war from domestic and international loans rather than from increased taxation and these now had to be paid back. The cost of rebuilding and the repayment of international loans would, the French government hoped, be met from German reparations and any suggestion by the British or the Americans that Germany might not be able to pay were brusquely dismissed. To begin with, even with reparation money coming in, outgoings were only partly covered, and, when reparations lessened and then stopped altogether, serious currency inflation was inevitable. By 1925, the franc was worth only one tenth of its 1914 value, which meant that domestic investors found their wartime loans to the government repaid with a greatly reduced purchasing power. While French inflation was not nearly as bad as Germany's, it caused serious economic, social and political dislocation nevertheless.

Initially, the weak franc helped exports, but this was short-lived. The Wall Street Crash and the Great Depression hit France, with her less advanced industrial and financial base, later than the rest of the developed world, but much French overseas trade depended on the export of relatively expensive items – wines, cognacs, leather goods, textiles – and luxury goods were amongst the first savings to be made by foreign importers. From 1929 French exports fell dramatically, and from a situation of full employment, and in some sectors a shortage of labour, in 1920, unemployment soared to nearly half a million by 1933.[5]

During the first war, the normal political processes of competing parties trying to persuade the electorate to favour them over others had been in abeyance, and the *Union Sacrée* ('Sacred Union') had maintained a more or less stable support for the war. Once peace came, however, the in-fighting began again and many of the strains inherent in the Third Republic* reappeared. In very broad terms, French politics between the wars saw a somewhat incongruous alliance of the rich, the aristocracy, conservative peasant smallholders, small businessmen and investors, and much of the lower middle class – this latter previously a staunch supporter of the republican

---

*The First Republic was that established by the Revolution and lasted until Napoleon I crowned himself emperor in 1804; the second ran from the 1848 revolution which ditched King Louis Philippe until the coup by Napoleon III in 1852, and the Third from the defeat of the Second Empire in 1870 until defeat yet again in 1940.

state – set against the proponents of a welfare state, socialists, communists, radical workers, civil servants and intellectuals.* These groupings were not absolute – there was considerable overlap and the influence of the left was reduced by splits in the socialist and communist ranks between those who wanted to follow Moscow's line (most, but not all, communists) and those who saw themselves as republican patriots (most, but not all, socialists). While supposedly part of the left but in practice in the centre was the Radical Socialist Party, which drew its support from white-collar workers, the lower end of the professions and some of the peasantry. On the right were a number of fairly unpleasant organizations that were opposed to the whole concept of the Republic. These included *L'Action Française*, which had grown out of the debacle of 1870 and was monarchist, Catholic and anti-Semitic, taking the Church's side in the old struggle between secular and clerical influence in government and sending its strong-arm squads out to beat up communists. Allied with them, although not quite so extreme, was the *Croix de Feu* (literally, 'Cross of Fire'), an ex-servicemen's organization, and other bodies whose beliefs varied from a vague feeling that the Third Republic was not working to outright fascism. The actual membership of these organizations was not large, but they wielded considerable influence, particularly amongst those French men and women who looked for stability in an increasingly chaotic world.

The French Army had borne the brunt of the fighting in the war of 1914–18 and had been more involved than any of the Allies in trying to prop up the White Russians after it. Hundreds – perhaps thousands – of individuals had served with military missions, in training teams, as advisers or providing logistical support to the anti-Bolshevik forces, and it was the French navy that provided naval support in the Black Sea and eventually evacuated the last of the White Russian armies along with large numbers of civilians fleeing the new Soviet regime. In the minds of many – perhaps most – professional officers of the French Army, opposition to the Bolsheviks in Russia was, after 1920, translated into fear and hatred of communism in France. To them, it was an alien philosophy imported from abroad and owing allegiance not to France but to its puppet masters in Moscow. It had been the communists and the communist-controlled

---

*The term 'intellectual' is one frequently found in descriptions of political groupings and presumably refers to writers, artists, poets, philosophers and other idlers whose influence is considerably greater than their numbers or contribution would warrant.

press that had fanned the flames of the army mutinies of 1917, and, when the French Army marched into the Ruhr in January 1923 in order to enforce reparations, the high command saw the voluble opposition of a section of French public opinion as being symptomatic of defeatism and treason encouraged by the communists. Professional armies tend to be uninterested in politics except where it affects them directly, but in a conscript army, which the French Army was, it was inevitable that political opinions held in civilian life were carried on into the military. Tracts condemning the Ruhr occupation began to circulate amongst the soldiers and stern action was taken against such inflammatory activity. The leftist newspaper *L'Humanité* was banned and men spreading propaganda critical of the army or of the occupation were arrested and subject to courts martial. Meanwhile, operations in North Africa in the 1920s – against the Moroccan rebel Abd-el-Krim and in putting down incipient nationalist agitation in Algeria and Syria – cost the army 12,000 dead with little thanks from those at home.[6]

As the twenties wore on, many French officers, and a sizeable section of the French right, became increasingly distrustful of the institutions of the Republic, but, just as France was beginning to see some signs of peace and prosperity, the Wall Street Crash and the Depression seemed about to plunge her into chaos. It appeared to many Frenchmen that in America unregulated capitalism and democracy were failing, while at home ministerial crises, financial scandals and unemployment were all symptomatic of the failure of the state. Much military and some civilian opinion lurched to the right, and the evident failure of the attempt to institutionalize the universal brotherhood of man in the shape of the League of Nations intensified the view that only by doing away with the Third Republic and rebuilding the nation anew could a prosperous, stable and powerful France re-emerge.

* * *

Once the British had decided in 1914, somewhat late in the day, that they would, after all, make a major contribution to the war on land, they had to expand their own tiny (by European standards) army and, in most cases, turn token Dominion and colonial armies into contingents large enough to be effective.* It was the

---

*The full-time armies of Canada, Australia, New Zealand and South Africa were tiny at the beginning of the war; only India had a professional regular army almost as large (or as small) as Britain's.

most intensive war in which the British had ever been engaged, and casualties in the inexperienced and under-trained Territorial Force and New Army units created from volunteers in the first two years of the war were inevitably far heavier than anyone imagined they might be. Despite this, the British learned, and they ended the war with the most technologically advanced and best-equipped army in the world, the most powerful navy bar none and the world's first independent air force. On the face of it, Britain emerged victorious with her Empire and her economy intact. But Britain's national debt had increased tenfold since 1914, much of her overseas investments had been liquidated to pay for the war, and the pre-war international trade network that was the basis of British prosperity had been ruptured and could not easily be reassembled. American industry, and to a lesser extent Dominion and Indian industry too, had been stimulated by the war and would now be competitors in the servicing of world markets.

Immediately after the war, there was a short-lived boom as goods not available during the war reappeared on the shelves, but this quickly collapsed. The war had meant full employment; now wartime industries were closing down and demobilized soldiers were swelling the labour pool. In 1918 Lloyd George's Liberal–Conservative coalition government had granted universal suffrage to males from the age of twenty-one and to females from the age of thirty* and this increased the power and influence of the trades unions through the fledgling Labour Party. Britain was the first nation to industrialize and now she would be the first to feel the pains of post-industrialization. As the economy slowed and went into recession followed by depression, a population accustomed to a steady improvement in living standards was not prepared to accept reductions in wages – after all, said many, we won the war, didn't we? Britain received virtually no reparations from Germany and watched anxiously as the German economy began to improve, financed by American loans. Lloyd George's coalition hung on until 1922, by which time one fifth of the workforce was unemployed, and it was the last time the once great Liberal Party held office until the coalition of 2010. The party had never recovered from the Asquith–Lloyd George wartime split and would now be eclipsed by the Labour Party. There were two weak Labour governments, in 1924 and from 1929 to 1931; otherwise, for the rest of

---

*This was to ensure that there would be more male voters than female. When it became apparent that female voting patterns broke down in exactly the same way as men's, the females' age was also set at twenty-one in 1928.

the interwar period Britain would be managed, or mismanaged, by Conservative or Conservative-led governments.

Britain lurched from economic crisis to economic crisis. A plan to create a tariff-protected market within the Empire foundered on the Dominions' reluctance to be mere suppliers of raw materials to and importers of finished goods from Britain. Taxes rose and wages were cut. There were strikes by workers and a mutiny in the navy; the Geddes Axe scythed great swathes through public sector employment (including the armed forces) and cut state subsidies. In 1926 a dispute between the coal miners (and Britain was still hugely reliant on coal, which was privately owned) and the mine owners led to a general strike when workers in other industries came out in sympathy with the miners.* The strike was broken: the army, police and volunteers manned essential communications and supply services, but, while the miners took a cut in pay, the strike did force the government to ameliorate some of its recessional recovery policies.

In a democracy, there are no votes in defence. The aim of every politician is to get into office and, once in power, to stay there. With a restricted franchise, there will be some hope of voters occasionally putting the national interest first, but with universal suffrage, as Britain had from 1918, a greedy and ignorant electorate, which seeks instant gratification and views each issue in the light of how it affects them personally, is one which has to be pandered to. Governments do this by bribery: providing or improving things that directly impinge upon the majority of voters, and this has to be financed. In a time of economic downturn, the money can come from seizing or selling off national assets (Henry VIII and the dissolution of the monasteries), squeezing the rich (Charles II and distraint of knighthood), taxation (William Pitt inventing income tax to pay for the French Revolutionary Wars) or taking money from something else and hoping that no one will notice, or, if they do notice, will not care. After the war Lloyd George said that, while the government could afford to take chances with defence, it could not afford to take chances with social welfare. Navy, army and air force estimates were regularly cut and the nation's defence posture was based on the Ten-Year Rule, which said that there would be no major war for ten years, there was no need for an expeditionary force and all defence planning was to be based upon those assumptions. The rule was particularly pernicious by its being made a rolling assumption, so that the risk of war was always ten years in the

---

* The *Daily Mail* refused to print a government-dictated leader – some things don't change.

future. The British Admiralty (albeit opposed by military dinosaurs like Churchill) had concluded that the all-big-gun battleship should be superseded by the aircraft carrier as the capital ship, but, instead of the planned seven carriers to be built, there was money for only two, and in any case, as has been noted, Britain had surrendered her naval supremacy at the Washington Naval Conference in 1922.*

The Wall Street Crash happened just as the British economy was beginning to recover, and it hit the United Kingdom earlier and more severely than the rest of the developed world outside America. Unemployment doubled, social services were reduced, taxes were raised and a National Government took Britain off the gold standard, thus devaluing the currency.†️ Britain was still a world power with an empire, but underneath – and sometimes on the surface too – all was not well.

* * *

There would have been a Russian Revolution without the first war. The Tsar was not likely to moderate his autocratic style and the nods that had been made in the direction of liberalization prior to 1914 were bound to stimulate demand for more. As it was, the perceived failure of the Protector of the Slavs to intervene during the two Balkan Wars of 1912 and 1913 had not gone unnoticed, while in the wider war a variety of factors – the breakdown of the transport network, the social and economic dislocation inevitable upon rapid industrialization and the provision of food and essential supplies as a matter of priority to the armed forces while civilians, or at least poor civilians, queued for bread – left the Tsar with little room for manoeuvre.

Russia mobilized 12 million men between 1914 and 1917, more than France, or the UK or Germany. While estimates of Russian casualties vary

---

*The USA threatened to build a navy to rival the Royal Navy. To maintain superiority, Britain would have had to build too, and her government was terrified by the cost. At the Washington Conference Britain agreed a ratio of tonnage that made the US Navy equal in size to the Royal Navy. To get to that tonnage, the USA could build, while the British had to decommission and scrap. The result was a Royal Navy unprepared for war when it came. In fact, if the British had shown a bit more gumption, the US would not have built – the Crash and the Depression would in due course have seen to that.

†Britain went formally on to the gold standard in 1844 when the pound sterling was fixed at 113 grains of gold to one pound. She came off it in 1914, went on again in 1925 at the same rate and came off it in 1931. On 1 July 2008 (before recession began temporarily to inflate its price) the same amount of gold cost £109.

greatly, there may have been as many as 2 million military deaths, which as a proportion of the population was a lot less than the equivalent French figure, but the civilian death toll due entirely or partially to the war may have been as much as another 2 million, a far greater figure than those suffered by any ally or enemy. With mounting casualties, no victory in sight and increasing agitation against the Tsar, the army high command made it clear that they would neither accept a transfer of power to the sickly Tsarevitch nor intervene to preserve the monarchy. The Tsar found he had no alternative but to abdicate, which he did on 2 March 1917. The Provisional Government that assumed power was a reasonable coalition, and seemed to be well able to restrain its extremists. What scuppered it was its declared intention of remaining in the war, coupled with the arrival of the exiled Lenin, inserted into Russia by the Germans and unprepared to compromise his communist principles in any way. The publication of the supposedly secret treaties with Britain and France that granted the Dardanelles – hitherto international waters – to Russia brought massive disillusionment as the liberals, socialists and intellectuals realized that they were fighting not for Mother Russia but for the government's expansionist ambitions. After a failed summer campaign – the Brusilov Offensive – desertion and mutiny began to shake the army apart. The October* Revolution followed, the communists seized power and Russia sued for peace.

Russia's chief negotiator, Leon Trotsky, attempted to buy time in the hope that Lenin's prediction of socialist revolutions in Western Europe, including Germany, would come true, and, when he refused German demands for autonomy for Poland, Finland, Estonia, Lithuania and the Ukraine (in all of which territories there were already anti-communist uprisings or resistance), the German army called his bluff and carried on advancing eastwards against no opposition. Persuaded largely by Lenin, Russia returned to the negotiations and the Treaty of Brest-Litovsk was signed on 3 March 1918. Half of the main grain-, iron- and coal-producing areas and almost half the population of the former Russian Empire were lost and German troops occupied the Ukraine with the intention of using its grain supplies to feed a German population reduced to near starvation by the Royal Navy's blockade. It was Foch, the French coordinator of Allied military effort, and Haig, Commander-in-Chief of the British Expeditionary Force, who

---

* Actually the November Revolution – Russia was still on the old calendar.

saved Lenin – had Germany won the war, the communist regime could not have survived. As it was, the communists were not convinced that even the humiliating peace they had signed would hold, and in March 1918 they shifted the capital from St Petersburg–Petrograd to Moscow. Moscow had been a Russian capital in the past – but that was two centuries ago. Versailles cancelled Brest-Litovsk, but the Bolsheviks were by no means in control of the whole country.

The Don Cossacks rebelled against confiscation of their land in 1917; in 1918 Georgia, Armenia and Azerbaijan declared independence and from December 1918 until April 1919 the French occupied the port of Odessa, intending it to be used as a base for supplying the anti-communist forces. In May 1919 an allied force of British, French and American troops, under British command, landed in Murmansk and Archangel and attempted to support the White Russians,* before withdrawing in the autumn, and from December 1917 until 1922 the Japanese occupied Vladivostok. In June 1918, 100,000 Czechs, a mixture of deserters and prisoners of war, made common cause with the Czech Legion, a band of turncoats who were originally to be employed against the Germans alongside the Russians, and finding the situation changed considerably as a result of Brest-Litovsk, they seized control of the Trans-Siberian railway. Providing themselves with weapons by disarming ramshackle communist militias, they marched on Ekaterinburg, getting there just too late to prevent the execution of the Tsar and his family.† They announced that they wished to be transferred to the Western Front, received the backing of the French, and entered into negotiations with the Soviets, before being eventually rescued by the Americans, who intervened to guard the railway and organized the evacuation of the Czechs from Vladivostok. The Soviets were prevented from establishing control of the Caspian Sea by the Royal Navy, which also evacuated cornered White Russian troops. As well as the Russian Civil War, the fledgling Soviet state fought wars against Estonia in 1918, Finland from 1918 to 1920, and Poland from 1920 to 1921 (when the Polish Army was supported and advised by French officers including Marshal Franchet d'Espèrey and General Weygand), all of which she lost.

---

*Strictly speaking, White Russia is Belorussia, that area bounded in the west by Latvia, Lithuania and Poland, and to the south by the Ukraine, but the term quickly became applied to all those in arms against the communists.

†Although it is doubtful if they knew that the Tsar was there, and questionable whether they could have cared less what the communists might do to him.

Within the USSR, the anti-communist forces were eventually defeated: incompetent leadership, over-ambitious plans, an inability to coordinate the activities of the various armies, logistic difficulties, the reluctance of the Allies to become embroiled in a full-scale military campaign and a failure to realize that, apart from some of those who were not ethnic Russians, most people in what had been the Russian Empire wanted peace at almost any price. The Civil War and the wars on the boundaries of the USSR allowed Trotsky, the People's Commissar for Defence, to weld a disparate collection of workers' and peasants' militias, bits of the old Imperial Army and politically motivated bearers of whatever arms they could find into what would become the Red Army. It also convinced most of Lenin's colleagues that rather than a workers' militia, which had been seriously suggested as the future armed force of the state, there was a need for a professional, conventionally organized army.

Not only had the major grain-producing regions been lost to Russia until Versailles restored them in 1919, but the harvest in 1917–18 was bad and there was a serious shortage of food, compounded by peasant growers refusing to sell to the state grain monopoly. Furthermore, it was all very well for Lenin to speak grandly of workers and peasants' control, but the factories had been run by either the derided bourgeoisie or – heaven forfend – bloodsucking capitalists and Tsarist sympathizers. Their removal meant that there was no one capable of running the plants, and medium- and small-sized enterprises collapsed. Factory output in the early years of the USSR fell to a third of what it had been before the war. Wages fell, not returning to their pre-war level until the late 1920s, and strikes by disgruntled workers were rife. The only apparent solution was a state takeover of factories – the banks had already been taken over in December 1918 – which accorded with the communist principle of common ownership of the means of production. Lenin, the instigator and the inspiration of the communist revolution, died in January 1924. As the effective head of state, he was succeeded by Joseph Stalin.

Joseph Stalin, born Dzhughashvili, was born around 1878 in Georgia, one of the most backward parts of a backward empire, where serfdom had only finally been abolished in 1871, ten years after emancipation in the rest of Russia. Joseph came from humble origins, spoke Russian as a second language, had an interrupted education and became an incipient revolutionary at a very early age. 'Stalin' or 'man of steel' was only one of many cover names that he used during his early life, which was marked by regular detention, imprisonment, escapes and exile since he was constantly on the run and agitating against the monarchy and the capitalist system. He was a Bolshevik almost from the start and, while he revered Lenin, he did not agree with all his idol's policies. In essence, Stalin may have been an uneducated terrorist, but, while he organized bank robberies and assassinations, he was none the less a highly intelligent and politically aware terrorist, and he was completely amoral. As editor of the underground party newspaper *Pravda*, he initially supported the 1917 Provisional Government's policy of refusing to negotiate with the Germans. Lenin, the pragmatist, said that anyone who took this line was betraying socialism. Stalin, after gauging grass roots opinion, decided that, while the wind might not be blowing in Lenin's direction just yet, it would do so eventually, and changed his stance.

With the overthrow of the Provisional Government, Lenin appointed Stalin as Commissar (minister) for Nationalities. As he was himself a member of a minority ethnic group, this was an obvious post for him to hold. The trouble was that many of the nationalities had no wish to be communist, and even those who were prepared to tolerate communism had no wish to be organized in the way that Stalin wished. The Bolsheviks' original policy was to grant each nationality self-determination, assuming, somewhat naively, that the new states would be communist and would cleave to Mother Russia. This did not happen and Lenin and Stalin were forced to change the policy from devolution of power to centralization. Much the same happened with the economy, but in reverse: an entirely controlled economy did not work, partly because the people who might have been able to run the factories and the utilities had at worst been shot or exiled and at best were under suspicion of just waiting for the revolution to fail. Lenin, supported by Stalin, forced through the New Economic Policy, which allowed a certain amount of leeway to local entrepreneurs and producers, despite the opposition of diehards who wanted no going back to old ways. In December 1921 the Terror, during which recalcitrant officials or political opponents were subjected to show trials and then executed, imprisoned or exiled, was relaxed somewhat, and the number of secret policemen reduced from 143,000 in December 1921 to 105,000 in May 1922.*

---

*As the population was around 240 million, the one copper's nark per 2.29 thousand people must have been a very busy spy.

Stalin's support for Lenin got him 'elected' – appointed – to the two controlling bodies of the party, and hence government, the Politburo and the Orgburo. The Politburo was the inner circle of the Central Committee of the Communist Party and made policy for, initially, the Russian Federal Republic and, later, for the whole of the USSR. The Orgburo was responsible for the civil service and government organizations and also for personnel matters. A Secretariat maintained liaison between the two bodies. In April 1922, in an attempt to lighten the workload on Lenin, whose health had been failing since an assassination attempt in August 1918,* Stalin was appointed to the newly created post of general secretary to the Secretariat. Most thought that the new general secretary would be a mere dogsbody and Lenin's poodle. How wrong they were would soon be apparent; the general secretary was responsible for appointments, and was able to pack the organs of state with his own supporters, while still professing total loyalty to Lenin – and, to be fair, almost certainly being totally loyal. But Stalin's support for Lenin did not extend to blind, unthinking concurrence in everything. Lenin, despite his pragmatism in ending the war and relaxing the economy, firmly believed that socialist revolutions would follow in Western Europe, and that the USSR would become a loose federation including Hungary, Germany and, perhaps, even France. Stalin, ever the realist, knew that no such revolutions were remotely likely and thought that the Party should concentrate on establishing the communist system in the USSR without wasting time in wishful thinking about what went on abroad. It was Stalin, too, who realized that Lenin's idea of linking the Russian Republic (which included a number of so-called 'autonomous' republics within it) to Belorussia, the Ukraine and the Transcaucasian Federation (Armenia, Azerbaijan and Georgia) with nothing more than bilateral treaties was not going to promote communism in those areas, and that they must be brought under the direct control of Moscow.

With his health deteriorating in the last year of his life, Lenin took no part in the governing of the country and, by the time he died on 21 January 1924, the USSR was governed by a collective which was drawn from the Central Committee and included Stalin. During his time as general secretary, Stalin had been able to advance the careers of his supporters and slow down or halt

---

*By Dora Kaplan, a socialist revolutionary who had done time in Siberia and whose parents had emigrated to the USA. She thought Lenin was betraying the revolution, and put two bullets into him. She was caught and executed shortly afterwards.

altogether those of his opponents. Once Lenin was safely embalmed, his mausoleum built by the Kremlin wall and Petrograd given yet another name change, to Leningrad, the triumvirate of Stalin, Gregory Zinoviev and Lev Kamenev* emerged as his inheritors. The other leading candidate for Lenin's mantle, Trotsky (née Bronstein), was not only associated with the Mensheviks, the relatively liberal revolutionary wing which had split from the communists in 1914, but, like Zinoviev and Kamenev, was Jewish, and anti-Semitism had not disappeared with the revolution, whatever the Bolsheviks might claim. Despite Trotsky's great service in creating the Red Army (and, in the opinion of many, saving the revolution thereby), he was dismissed from his offices, sent into exile and eventually assassinated in Mexico in 1940. It took Stalin a little longer to neutralize Zinoviev and Kamenev,† but by 1927 they were out of favour and out of the Central Committee and Stalin was the undisputed leader of the Soviet Union.

The modest success of the New Economic Policy, the end of starvation and Stalin's caution in regard to world revolution made him genuinely popular with party members, quite apart from the fact that as head of personnel he had been able to pack party and government offices with his own men. Once firmly in the saddle, however, Stalin replaced the New Economic Policy with centralization. This involved the forced collectivization of agriculture, with cereal growers forced to sell to the state and Kulaks (yeoman farmers who owned their land) persecuted, and a Five-Year Plan which took all factories into state ownership and gave them production quotas and targets.

From outside, this forced and central direction of the national economy gained some respectability after the Wall Street Crash. All over the developed world, unfettered capitalism seemed to be failing while in Russia the proletariat appeared to be protected from its effects. Stalin knew that, if the USSR were to be dragged kicking and squealing into the modern industrialized world, then he would need finance, machinery and expertise from the West to do it, and the Western powers would only cooperate if they were sure that the USSR was not about to instigate world revolution by force of

---

*In December 1918 Lenin sent Kamenev to London to explain to the British government what the new communist state was all about. He lasted a week before the British deported him, irritated by his clumsy attempts to spread Bolshevism amongst British workers. Distrustful of foreigners as British workers are, those few who understood what Kamenev was trying to say thought him a joke.

†They were both arraigned on trumped-up charges in 1936 and executed.

arms – hence Stalin's insistence on the slogan 'Socialism in One Country'. The USSR may in fact be the only nation of note that actually profited from the crash and the Depression that followed. With the slowdown in industrial output, unemployment and lack of investment everywhere else, banks and industrialists saw Stalin's Five-Year Plan as an opportunity not to be missed. Loans and credit agreements were arranged, tenders submitted and contracts signed as the great leap forward out of backwardness and into modernization began. Even the Ford Motor Company, that epitome of rampant capitalism, signed an agreement to build a car-manufacturing plant.* There were limits, though, to this commercial largesse. The Red Army much admired the American Christie tank suspension, even if it had been rejected by the US Army, but selling Ford cars was one thing, bits of tanks quite another. The Russians smuggled it out nevertheless and it became the basis for the BT series of Russian tanks that duly led to the highly successful T-34.†

The rush to modernize came with a very great price in human lives. The Kulaks were, understandably, opposed to agrarian collectivization, and there were estimated to be between 5 million and 7 million of them. As officers of the Red Army who came from peasant stock might not be prepared to enforce collectivization with sufficient rigour, the secret police (the OGPU) were reinforced by party militias and bully boys from the cities and the factories. Those who persisted in opposing government policy were either shot, exiled to the Russian Far East or forced to labour in physically demanding and unpleasant industries, such as mining, where the concept of workers' health and safety did not exist. It is thought that up to 5 million people perished from a combination of compulsory grain seizures, punishment for being anti-Stalin or worked to death in labour camps in the winter of 1932–33 alone.[7] But Stalin's paranoid suspicion and distrust of anyone or any institution that might oppose him would soon be extended from recalcitrant farmers to the organs of the Soviet state. The armed forces would not escape, and thousands of officers of the Red Army would be removed.

---

*At Nizhni Novgorod (later renamed Gorky and unrenamed after the collapse of the USSR), the third-largest city in Russia and later the central manufacturing base for MiG aircraft and submarines for the Russian navy – not necessarily all to be blamed on Ford.

†The US would not sell it to the British either, so the British military attaché had one shipped to London in crates marked 'pineapples'.

* * *

According to national legend, the first emperor of Japan was the great-great-great-grandson of the Sun Goddess. The Sun Goddess created Japan – and, presumably, the rest of the world too, although this is not mentioned by the chroniclers. The Japanese imperial family traces its line back to 11 February 660 BC, which puts the creation of the world at around 810 BC, so the planet is even younger than Bishop Ussher's calculations made it.* While the Japanese claim that their emperor is the only reigning monarch whose descent is unbroken from the Sun Goddess, and that his subjects are descendants of the goddess's brother, may not be entirely accurate, Japanese emperors, unlike their Chinese counterparts, were not overthrown or deposed, largely because they had no power other than that exercised by advisers in the imperial name. That is not to say that emperors did not die mysteriously, nor abdicate early, but the emperor himself was seen as being 'above the clouds' or remote from the day-to-day governance of what was actually a loose collection of quasi-independent baronial estates, and, being above mere politics, he was a focus for loyalty and respect (but not yet actual worship) by all classes.

By around 1600 the constant feuding between rival magnates had made the country even more difficult to govern than it already had been, and Tokugawa Ieyasu, a member of a hereditary military clan, achieved supreme temporal power by a mixture of alliances and slaughter, frequently of his own allies. That Ieyasu at one stage during his early career killed his first wife and ordered his son to commit suicide in order to prove his loyalty to a superior is a fair indication of the sort of society Japan had become, and taking the traditional military title of *shogun*, Ieyasu established a form of government which, against all the odds, lasted for 250 years. The emperor was still the emperor, of course, but, instead of decisions being taken by the emperor's advisers, they were now taken by the shogun and, latterly, by the shogun's advisers.

---

*Archbishop James Ussher (1581–1656) was a strange mixture of intellectual, political conciliator, theological liberal, educational reformer and complete nut. He calculated that the creation of the world dated from 22 October 4004 BC, that the British Christian Church dated from AD 36 and that the world would end on 25 October 1996. As the Duke of Wellington said in a different context, 'If you believe that, you will believe anything.' Charles II bought his library of 10,000 books for £2,000 and gave them to Trinity College Dublin.

Japanese society was rigidly hierarchical, bolstered by the Shinto religion, which was part ancestor worship and part a reinforcement of a caste system decreeing that one was born into a station in life out of which one could not escape. As Hinduism, which shares Shinto's belief in caste, has also demonstrated, such a system is a most effective tool for social control, and during the period of the shogunate the stratified layers of precedence – and bloody repression where that failed – enabled the shogun and his successors to hold together the often mutually antipathetic principalities. Loyalty and obedience were everything: to one's elder siblings and parents, to the village, to the local lord, to the ruler of the province, to the shogunate and ultimately to the emperor. The national religion had no moral code, other than loyalty and obedience, and there was no concept of looking after those less fortunate than oneself. Lords might take action to improve the lot of their workers, but only did so because, if they did not, the work would not get done; the idea that one should look after one's subordinates because that is the decent thing to do was quite alien. Confucian and Buddhist influences did moderate behaviour somewhat, but the shoguns were so concerned about Christianity that they banned it and banished its missionaries.

Japan had always been suspicious of outsiders, and under the shoguns she became more so. Japanese merchants did trade with China but the only Europeans allowed to maintain a permanent trading post were the Dutch, and they were confined to an island off Nagasaki. In the first half of the nineteenth century Japan was still feudal when the rest of the world had moved on, but even in its rigidly stratified society things were changing. The relative influence of the four classes into which Japanese were divided – warriors, peasants, artisans and merchants – was not as it was. The shogunate had brought relative peace, and the hereditary warriors – the *samurai*, who made up 10 per cent of the population and insisted on maintaining their traditional dress, carrying two swords and demanding obeisance from all those below them in the pecking order – were becoming redundant. All samurai were supposed to follow a lord, to whom they owed total and unthinking loyalty, but the shoguns had kept the lords in check by taxing them and too many of them were in hock to the merchants and money lenders and could not afford to keep great bands of retainers with nothing to do. Rather like the *Junker* of Prussia or the Anglo-Irish Ascendancy, the magnates and the samurai had aristocratic tastes and pretensions, but increasingly lacked the wherewithal to indulge them. Not only did the samurai consider that working for a living was beneath them, but they were also barred by law and custom from all trades and professions, other than their own, save that of intellectual or bureaucrat. As the number of samurai who could become, say, poets or civil servants was limited, by 1850 it was estimated that there were 400,000 *ronin*, or samurai without a liege lord, who wandered the country at best hoping to find a lord, and at worst indulging in brigandage.[8]

It is generally assumed that it was Commodore Perry and his Black Ships that forced Japan out of the medieval and into the modern. Perry, under orders from the American president, Millard Fillmore, sailed into Edo Bay (now Tokyo Bay) on 8 July 1853 and demanded that Japan open its ports to American trade. Two of Perry's ships were powered by steam and all of them mounted modern cannon; they were met by dummy shore batteries and warriors armed with smoothbore muskets and swords. The Japanese did not have a navy and, after procrastinating and delaying as long as they could, were forced to recognize Perry's presence. Perry delivered his president's demands, and, after announcing that he would return in a year with a fleet, sailed away. While Perry himself made much of the claim that it was he who forced Japan to open itself to the outside world, in fact the system was rotten and falling apart before Perry came on the scene. The merchant class had the money, they wanted trade with the West, and the British and the Russians were pressing for Japanese ports to be opened to them. Japanese of the governing and merchant classes knew very well that the British had trounced China militarily in the 1840s, and drew the obvious conclusion that the Japanese system of government, imported from China, might not last for ever. Japanese suspicion of the outside world had always been mixed with curiosity. There was much about Western technology that was attractive to the Japanese, and it had not escaped their notice that a small island nation such as Britain, which depended on trade, could manage very well if it had colonies and a powerful navy – a point which was reinforced in 1862 when the Royal Navy flattened the capital of a particular clan of samurai as punishment for an attack on a lone Englishman travelling across Japan overland.

While Perry may not have precipitated the period of anarchy, civil war, assassination and chaos that lasted until the Meiji Restoration in 1868, he was certainly one of its catalysts. It was a restoration because the constitution drawn up by those who emerged victorious from the bloody struggles of the previous decade supposedly 'restored' power to the emperor, but in no sense was this a liberal or enlightened revolution in the manner of those that had broken out all over Europe (and in the main failed) in 1848. Rather, it was, as one historian has put it, as if the fox-hunting squirearchy of England had risen up and seized power as the champions of liberalism.* The architects of the restoration concluded that Japan was powerless to resist the unequal treaties that she had signed to permit contact with the West, and that the only way to stand up to the Europeans was to learn their ways and be better at them than they were. Hence a written constitution, top hats and morning dress, political parties, elected assemblies and a monarch who supposedly acted in accordance with the advice of his ministers – but was now officially divine. With all this went massive and rapid modernization, industrialization and expansion; the British built railways and spinning mills and trained a Japanese navy, the Dutch built arsenals, the French built ironworks, Germans drafted the laws, trained the army and introduced the polka; the Italians, the Swiss and the Americans all were involved in one of the most rapid industrializations of a backward agricultural economy; and all the while, looking over their shoulders, were bright young Japanese learning how it was all being done. Long before Stalin, the Japanese squeezed the peasantry to provide capital for industrialization, a side effect being a population drift to the towns and cities that duly provided the workforce for the factories.

While the restoration's slogan of 'Respect the emperor, expel the barbarians' might not have been applicable just yet, that of 'Rich country, strong army' certainly was, and by 1895 the Japanese had an army of 240,000 men armed with modern weapons, mainly peasant conscripts led by Samurai officers and NCOs, and a small but efficient navy of twenty-eight steam-powered warships.†9 That same year Japan, in her first foreign war of modern times, took Korea and Formosa from a decaying Chinese empire, and in 1904–5 defeated the Russians. Even though the latter were already tottering and their armies and navy were operating a long way from home, it was none the less a decisive victory.

But underneath the top hats and Western façade, Japan had not changed all that much. Class divisions may have been legally abolished but power still rested with the aristocracy, the samurai and the merchants; the emperor may have been transformed into a constitutional monarch but he was now to be

---

* If only they would…

† Thirty years later it numbered 250 ships, including two aircraft carriers and forty-nine submarines.

worshipped as divine; political parties may have been tolerated for a time but they had no power, and all the time were stressed the 'virtues' of obedience, loyalty, respect for the emperor, while any show of individualism was discouraged. Huge commercial enterprises grew up, with the power and influence that money brought, but they were expected to work in the interests of the state rather than in those of shareholders, and it was an unwritten alliance between the industrialists and the military, motivated not only by a need to safeguard their own narrow interests but also by a conviction that Japan should be – must be – a powerful and respected country with an empire like the British, the French, the Russians and the Americans that was to send Japan along the road of expansion, conquest and repression. Much the same motivation inspired the newly unified Germany, and it is no surprise that it was to the German, rather than to the British or American, model of government that the shapers of Japanese institutions looked.

The Japanese admiration for all things German was not reciprocated, however, and so the Japanese, in 1902, allied themselves with the British, and English newspapers lauded 'the plucky little Japs' when they went on to smash the Russian colossus. The First World War came as a welcome opportunity. Japan joined the Allies and her economy boomed. Factories proliferated and heavy industry grew, particularly steel mills, which in turn boosted ship-building. Japan supplied the Western powers with textiles and was able to penetrate markets that the British and French could no longer service. While she did no fighting, the presence of her navy in the Far East allowed the British to transfer ships to home waters and in 1915 she took possession of the German concession of Shantung in China. Japanese participation in the war persuaded the British to ignore her penetration of Manchuria, but her seizure of the German Pacific island territories of the Marianas, Palau, the Marshalls and the Carolines increased existing American suspicions of Japanese long-term aims.

Japan ended the war as an industrialized nation with the wherewithal to manufacture but without the necessary raw materials – coal, rubber, iron, oil – which had to be imported, and with a society deeply divided socially and economically, but united by emperor worship and dislike of foreigners. At the top were the army, the navy and the powerful industrialists, and at the bottom were the increasingly exploited toilers – factory workers and peasants. There was virtually no middle class, and, as the administration clamped down mightily on any mutterings from the left, politics revolved around conflicting interpretations of nationalism and loyalty to the emperor. Japan had sent 70,000 troops to Russia, supposedly to assist the anti-Bolshevik forces but in reality to protect her own interests – unsure though she was what those interests were – and she did not withdraw them until 1925, thus earning the permanent hostility of the new Soviet state. Japan increasingly saw herself as becoming isolated internationally – mainly, she thought, owing to the machinations of the British and the Americans, who were both anxious to protect their own interest in Asia – and so the feelings of insecurity and aggressiveness grew. The articles of the Washington Naval Treaty, which gave Japan a ratio in naval tonnage of only three to Britain's and America's five each, and the British refusal to renew the Anglo-Japanese alliance, which ended in 1923, seemed only to confirm the developed world's hostility towards Japan. All the country's most powerful interests now accepted that expansion was needed; the only argument was whether that expansion should be by peaceful persuasion or by military might, and whether it should be north into Soviet-controlled territory or south-west into China.

Japan suffered an economic wobble in 1927, when there were a series of bank failures that also brought down a number of small businesses – many of which were then gobbled up by the *zaibatsu* or big industrialists. This experience did make Japan better prepared for the Wall Street Crash than some other economies but, when the silk trade in the United States collapsed, Japanese exports plummeted. The solution, it seemed to many Japanese, was to expel the colonialists and create an Asian economic trading area in which Japan would provide the manufactured goods from raw materials supplied from within the bloc. The last vestige of influence held by the lobby in favour of peaceful penetration evaporated and increasingly the military, and their allies the *zaibatsu*, would shape Japanese foreign and defence policy.

* * *

It was not long after the first war that the cry 'We wuz robbed', or its Italian equivalent, was raised. Italy had been a unified country only since 1861, and, despite attempts by her founding fathers to link her with the glories of the Roman Empire, the truth was that 1,500 years of invasion, fragmentation and immigration had left precious few of the once rulers of the known world and had replaced them with a distillation of a variety of Balkan tribes. In modern parlance, Italy was desperate to punch above her weight, but, by the time that her king and government realized that a good way to divert attention from domestic problems was to embark on adventures abroad, there was precious little left to colonize. Italy joined the Triple Alliance with Germany and Austria in 1882, but always made it clear that she regarded it as a defensive pact and in any event would not go to war against Britain. As the Mediterranean was a British lake, this was a very sensible reservation.

Italy had interests in Eritrea and attempts to expand there led to war with Abyssinia and a disastrous defeat at Adowa in 1896. She sent a 2,000-strong contingent as part of the relief force to China during the Boxer Rebellion, and in 1911 she embarked on a campaign to seize Libya from a tottering Ottoman Empire. In a conflict marked more by Italian ingenuity in committing atrocities than by any great military skill,* Libya was eventually brought under nominal Italian control in 1912, when Turkey was distracted by the First Balkan War.

The Triple Alliance was unpopular with many Italians, who saw it as an obstacle to the incorporation of areas on her borders belonging to Austria but containing large numbers of ethnic Italians, or at least Italian-speakers. Austrian residents of Trieste were bemused by the apparent attachment of so many of their fellow citizens to opera, to the extent that the most common graffiti on the city walls was 'Viva Verdi', but they were not to know that this was shorthand for *Viva Vittorio Emmanuele Re d'Italia*. When war broke out in 1914, Italy declined to join Germany and Austria, pointing out that, as the alliance was a defensive pact and Austria-Hungary had declared war on Serbia, Italy was not obliged to join in. Both sides courted the Italians. To the Germans, Italian entry on the side of the Central Powers, or at least a guarantee of neutrality, would release Austrian troops for the Western Front, open another front against France and make life difficult for the British navy in the Mediterranean. From the Allied point of view, Italian belligerence would tie down large numbers of Austrians and keep them away from Russia. There was little that Germany could or Austria would offer Italy, but the Allies could hold out the promise of satisfying Italian irredentism at Austria's expense. The Pact of London, signed in April 1915, duly granted Austrian territory to Italy in return for her entering the war on the Allied side no later than 26 May 1915.

---

* Although it was probably the first time that aircraft were used (by the Italians) to bomb ground targets.

Bismarck said that Italy had a large appetite for territorial gains but very poor teeth.[10] Anyone who has served with NATO regards the modern Italian Army as something of a joke, one that lends weight to the old adage, 'If you can't fight, wear a big hat', and assumes that this has always been so, but this is not entirely fair. Italy's performance in the first war was noted for the dogged stoicism of her soldiers, who were let down by her leaders and the lack of a military-industrial base. Estimates of Italian military deaths vary between 460,000 and 650,000 – losses comparable to those of Britain (700,000) and suffered by a smaller population in a shorter war. Italy made few advances and was only saved from complete collapse by the despatch of French and British divisions in late 1917. Even what is celebrated as the glorious victory of Vittorio Veneto was spearheaded by British troops, a fact that is notably absent from Italian history books.*

The Italian economy, kept running at full speed during the war, went into recession after it as contracts for war materials stopped. Soon 10 per cent of the workforce was unemployed and this was made worse by the arrival of 4 million demobilized soldiers on to the labour market. Prices rose, wages could not keep up and the government, saddled with massive war debts, faced long delays before it could begin to pay war pensions to the disabled and the families of the dead. There were strikes, riots, army mutinies and general disorder. Using the old ploy of blaming someone else, the Italian government soon began to blame the Allies. Italy had gone to war to expand her territory at the expense of the Central Powers. She got Trieste, part of the Tyrol, part of modern Slovenia and Istria at the head of the Adriatic (including large numbers of Germans and Slavs who lived there too), but what about German colonies in Africa, and what about the Italian position in the Middle East? Those German colonies and the Italian position in Eritrea had not been specifically promised in the negotiations that brought Italy into the war, but the French and the British had agreed Italy's claim to part of Dalmatia. This arrangement was not, however, agreed by the Americans, who in 1915 had been neutral and therefore not involved in the discussions. At Versailles, President Woodrow Wilson refused to recognize the London pact and took the side of Slav self-determination, thus vetoing any suggestion

---

* In today's Italy something that is a totally incompetent, complete and utter shambles is referred to as *Caporetto totale* after the Battle of Caporetto in September–October 1917.

of an Italian Dalmatia. The erstwhile allies had therefore cheated Italy of her due rewards for all her dead, and all her problems could be blamed on them.

In the uncertainty of post-war Italy, communism began to take hold amongst the have-nots, and the inevitable counter was the rise of the extreme right. Fascism, its principles originally enunciated by Gabriele D'Annunzio, an extreme nationalist writer and son of a hero of the struggle for Italian independence, but taken up by Benito Mussolini, was the counter to communism. Both sides drew their foot soldiers from much the same pool but, while communism focused on the working classes and had an international dimension, fascism focused on the state. Mussolini, a journalist and political activist before the war (and, like many eventual fascists, originally a socialist), was conscripted into the Italian Army, became a sergeant and was invalided out with injuries sustained in training. His charismatic rhetoric, espousing patriotism and pride in race, authoritarian order, anti-corruption, elitism and economic self-sufficiency, all wrapped up in the symbolism of the Roman Empire, was a heady mix for Italians disillusioned by the failure of the war to resolve all social ills, and attracted the landowners, industrialists and Catholics terrified by the prospect of communism. In the summer of 1922 a strike called by the Socialist Party was a failure, and those services that were affected were kept running by fascist volunteers. In October 1922 Mussolini ordered a 'March on Rome', supposedly a demonstration of the Fascist Party's loyalty to the king, but in reality intended to intimidate the government into accepting the fascists into a coalition, and, when the Liberal President of the Council (prime minister) asked the king, Victor Emmanuel III, for special powers to deal with the march, the king refused, the prime minister resigned and the king appointed Mussolini as prime minister.

In the April 1924 general election Mussolini's fascists received 65 per cent of the votes cast, and even without the undoubted intimidation and vote-rigging they would have got a large majority. Mussolini managed to escape, albeit narrowly, the political backlash after the murder of a socialist leader, Giacomo Matteotti, widely believed to have been at the instigation of Mussolini (although this was never proved), and by 1926 he was able to give up all pretence of democracy and rule by decree. Once all political parties except the fascists were abolished, Mussolini was able to bring all the organs of state under fascist control and introduce a planned economy, encourage a rise in the birth rate and undertake a (half-hearted) pruning of a swollen civil service. The Italian currency, the lira, was revalued (in fact, grossly over-valued) from one seventh of its pre-1914 value to one third, and food production was increased.[11] Mussolini really did drain the Pontine Marshes, something that no Roman emperor had been able to manage, and he did make the trains run on time. In 1925–26 Italy managed to secure a promise of loans from the United States, which, it was hoped, would stabilize the economy and allow staged repayments of war loans to Britain. Mussolini also solved the Roman Question – the relationship between the state and the Vatican – which had eluded Italian politicians (and the anti-clerical king) so far.* That this meant withdrawing all copies of Mussolini's pre-war pamphlet *God Does Not Exist*, the banning of freemasonry,† laws banning contraceptives and 'lewd behaviour' during Lent, and considerable financial concessions made to the Church mattered not a jot. Pope Pius XI – a man just as autocratic as Mussolini – declared that the Church now recognized the fascist state and this brought huge domestic and international prestige.

All this had its positive aspects, but it also meant a savage deflation, higher taxes and, once the lira had been revalued and Italy returned to the gold standard in 1927, a drop in exports. The Wall Street Crash and the Great Depression hit Italy as it did the rest of the world, but Italy's financial markets were far less sophisticated than those of America or Britain, and, even though the effects were exacerbated by the withdrawal of loans and the overpriced lira, Mussolini managed to avoid social unrest, although living standards fell and unemployment rose. Far from weakening the fascist position, the Depression – which could be blamed on the Anglo-Saxons and linked to the refusal to award Italy her rightful spoils from the Great War – only strengthened the appeal of order and strong government. Nevertheless, the inescapable fact remained that Italy was a poor – and, in many respects, backward – country and lacked the resources to posture as a great power. In due course she would pay the price of the overweening ambition of her leaders.

---

*Since 1870 and the incorporation of Rome as the nation's capital, the Roman Catholic Church had refused to recognize the legitimacy of the Italian state.

†In the UK freemasons are a harmless collection of middle-aged men who hop backwards with one leg of their trousers rolled up while giving each other funny handshakes. In Europe they are – or are believed to be – a sinister secret society that influences politicians and the judiciary to advance the cause of its members.

2

GET SET...

If Britain and the countries of Europe were still in the recovery room following the Great War, then in the 1920s Germany was still on life support. The Versailles Treaty had apportioned the entire blame for the war, and all the damage and destruction thereof, to Germany and she was forced to accept that responsibility and agree to pay for it. This was only one of the shackles of Versailles but it was the one that was most obvious to the German man in the turnip patch. Germany in the 1920s and early 1930s had a flourishing chemical industry and many of her technical industries were world leaders, but she was far from being a fully industrialized and urban society in the way that Britain was. After unification in 1870, the German population grew from 24 million to 67 million by 1914, but by 1930, after war deaths and the loss of territory resulting from Versailles, it was 65 million, of which 15 million relied on subsistence agriculture. Germany had financed the Great War by raising loans rather than taxes, and as the country embarked painfully on the democratic experiment, with six coalition governments between 1919 and 1923, the wherewithal to repay the loans was not there. The *Reichsmark* declined from 20 to the pound sterling in 1914 to 250 in 1919, 500 in early 1921 and 1,000 at the end of that year, until it stood at 35,000 to the pound in 1922.[12] The Weimar Republic was blamed for failing to live within its means, but the only way it could stave off collapse was by printing more and more money, leading to an even faster decline in the value of the currency. When Germany simply could not pay the reparations demanded and defaulted in 1923, the French, dragging the Belgians behind them, sent 60,000 troops into the Ruhr, Germany's industrial heartland. Britain and America disapproved, but Raymond Poincaré had been president of France throughout the war and was still president, with no love for Germany or sympathy for her problems. This was the final blow to the German economy. Unemployment in Germany rose; hyperinflation set in; Berlin suspended all reparations payments and the value of the mark sank to 16 trillion (16,000,000,000,000) to the pound. Germans embarked on a policy of passive resistance and the only country with money to spare – the United States – was asked to help. The result was the Dawes Plan.

Charles W. Dawes was an American banker who had masterminded inter-Allied procurement during the First World War. Asked to produce a plan to stabilize the German currency and to rationalize reparations payments, Dawes, assisted by Owen Young, the chairman of General Electric, came up with a plan that seemed to satisfy everyone. Reparations payments would be consolidated and would gradually rise until the full instalments became due from 1928. The *Reichsmark* was restored to its pre-war level and inflation was checked by pegging it to the US dollar. A Reparations Office would supervise the German economy and take control of the German central bank with the authority to stop or reduce reparations if such payments would substantially damage the German economy. The Dawes Plan came into effect in 1924 and to everyone but the extreme nationalists (who objected to foreign control and the fact that reparations payments had not been reduced, only delayed) it seemed to meet all requirements: the wartime Allies would get their reparations in due course, the German economy would not be destroyed by inflation and the German currency was worth something once more. Germany could import and it seemed that the Weimar Republic would survive and could concentrate on economic growth rather than military adventures. Unemployment fell dramatically, to less than 1 million in January 1925, and fluctuated between 1 million and 3 million from then until autumn 1929, when it was only just under 1 million prior to the Wall Street Crash.[13]

Of course, somebody had to pay for all this. The German currency's peg to the dollar had to be backed by monetary reserves in Germany, and this was provided by loans. The largest was $100m raised on Wall Street, where it was hugely over-subscribed. In a genuine act of philanthropy, the US government had put its own credibility behind the loan, and, as interest rates in Germany were higher than those in the United States, there was no shortage of banks and private investors to participate. Other loans followed. Germany was now able to begin to pay her reparations to Britain and France with money borrowed from America, and Britain and France could use that to repay their American wartime loans. This led to a mounting burden of international debt for Germany, but, as long as America seemed happy to lend, then the merry-go-round could continue – and it did lead to pressure from America to reduce reparations in order to ensure that Germany could repay her loans, hence the Young Plan of spring 1929.

Owen Young, who had been very much part of the Dawes Plan, now produced a restructuring that reduced the total amount of reparations by about 75 per cent, and extended the repayments until 1988. All the involved governments signed up to it, partly because something was better than nothing, and partly because they realized that, unless they did, the Weimar Republic could not survive. For the democratic parties in Germany, the Young Plan meant stability and peace, while the nationalists once again criticized it and the president of the Reichsbank, Hjalmar Schacht, resigned in protest, throwing his influence behind Hitler, who had asked, not unreasonably, why generations as yet unborn should be saddled with the debts of their parents. The plan's details had been widely leaked and known, but in the May 1928 elections Germans had gone for economic stability first and Hitler's NSDAP* obtained but 2.5 per cent of the vote and twelve seats. The largest party was the Social Democrats, the SPD (liberals, in British terms), with 153 seats, and the communists came fourth with 54.

Then came the Wall Street Crash, and America had no more money to lend, or, if she had, she would not do so in the face of a collapse of international trade, and loans began to be called in. In Germany, the only way to maintain the stability of the currency when unemployment was rising again was to deflate with compulsory cuts in wages and increased taxes (including a poll tax), many of these measures being forced through by emergency decree. In fact, unemployment increased from under 1 million just before the crash to over 3 million in January 1930, and in the general election of September 1930 the NSDAP obtained 18.5 per cent of the popular vote and became the second-largest party in the *Reichstag* with 107 seats; the SPD had 143 and the communists 77. President Hoover's moratorium on foreign debts in the summer of 1931 – by which time Germany owed 8.5bn *Reichsmark*s to the USA and 13bn to European and British lenders – came too late and, in any case, if this was to apply to Britain and France too, as indeed it was, then it was to proceed in tandem with Hoover's other plank of policy, that of

---

* Nationalsozialistische Deutsche Arbeiterpartei, 'National Socialist German Workers' Party' – Nazis.

disarmament. (As it turned out, American efforts to establish a global framework of arms limitation were a failure, the World Disarmament Conference of 1932–34 ending without agreement.)

It is hardly surprising that at times of political, financial and social uncertainty people will turn to those who can, or claim they can, impose stability and order. If this involves giving up a certain amount of personal liberty, then so be it, and anyway the inhabitants of much of Europe had never enjoyed a great deal of personal liberty. In Germany, National Socialism was attractive because it seemed to provide an answer to all the nation's problems: it was against the Young Plan, it would bring down unemployment, boost trade, look after the farmers and repudiate Versailles. Above all, it seemed the only safeguard against communism. The 1930s was a time of instability all over Europe: parliamentary democracy had failed, economies were collapsing, unemployment was rising, wages were going down in real terms and it was not only in Germany that authoritarian regimes obtained power – mostly by consent. Indeed, Yugoslavia, Estonia, Hungary, Bulgaria, Poland, Greece and Spain all rejected democratic parties in favour of fascist or semi-fascist governments, and Italy had been fascist since 1922.

National Socialism was a rather woolly mixture of racial theory, misunderstood genetics, Nietzschean philosophy and unashamed nationalism. While today one would get into all sorts of trouble for implying that any race was in any way superior to any other, it must be remembered that Social Darwinism – a belief that if individual species were as they were as the result of natural selection, a process whereby only those features that helped the organism to survive were passed on and those that were inhibitive were discarded, then the same could be applied to races, only the 'fittest' of which would survive – was considered to be a perfectly tenable, if somewhat eccentric, theory between the wars. It was a widely held view in the most respectable of circles that the European races were of higher intelligence and operated on a higher moral plane than, say, the savages of Africa or the Australian aborigines. In Britain the Eugenics Society believed in positive measures to improve the race by selective breeding, and suggested ways of ensuring that defective genes were not transmitted to future generations. The aims of the Eugenics Society stopped well short of genocide, but its members did lobby for compulsory sterilization of those considered unfit to breed. Many countries and legislatures passed laws to permit compulsory sterilization (including Sweden and some states of the USA), although in the UK the move was defeated by an alliance of the Roman Catholic Church, liberals and the Labour Party. Believers in and supporters of Social Darwinism and eugenics in Britain included the writers and intellectuals Thomas Huxley, J. B. Priestley, George Bernard Shaw, D. H. Lawrence, W. B. Yeats and H. G. Wells, the politicians Arthur Balfour and William Beveridge (the author of the report that led to the creation of the National Health Service), the birth-control advocate Marie Stopes, Bishop Barnes of Birmingham and numerous medical authorities.

Much of what the believers in Social Darwinism and eugenics said in the 1920s and 1930s may now have been scientifically discredited, but it seemed perfectly logical at the time. What the NSDAP did was take it to extremes, with the claim that the Aryan race was superior to all others and destined to rule the world – and indeed, if it did not seize the advantage in the immediate future, then it was fated to be subsumed by the mongrel races of the East, which of course included Soviet communists. That there was (and is) considerable doubt as to exactly what the Aryan race (as opposed to the Aryan language group) is was irrelevant: as far as the NSDAP was concerned, the true Aryan was tall, blonde and blue-eyed, Teutonic and Scandinavian, a definition which included not only the Germans but also the British, the Dutch, some of the French and the Flemish Belgians. The fact that Hitler and most of his senior henchmen did not come anywhere near that description, and that Germany had its share of the short, fat and dark, mattered not. To underwrite the theory of the new creed, the National Socialists hijacked the ideas of Friedrich Nietzsche (1844–1900), a vastly overrated German philosopher who was barking mad for most of his life. Nietzsche's ideas revolved around the concept of the *Übermensch*, the superman or superior man, who would by right dominate the inferior races. That Nietzsche in his rare moments of lucidity had opposed militarism and despised anti-Semitism was conveniently forgotten.

Where the leaders of the NSDAP were clever was in their ability to appeal to all classes, or at least to obtain their tacit approval. The industrialists were promised a massive programme of public works on the table and rearmament under it, the workers full employment (not yet, of course, but in time) and the farmers an increase in domestic food production. The middle classes were promised stabilization of the currency and the traditional elites – the aristocracy, the great landowners, the army – the negation of Versailles and the restoration of Germany to her rightful place among the Great Powers. In particular, the intention to rebut the 'War Guilt Lie' was attractive to all. Of course, many Germans found Hitler and his acolytes vulgar and hysterical but presumed that the realities of power would temper their more extreme policies. Abroad there were those, including many in Britain and America, who thought that only firm government could sort out the German economy and, most important of all, act as a bulwark against communism, which was a threat to everything the West held dear. Very few people in 1930, in Germany or elsewhere, thought that National Socialism was evil. It might have been coarse, noisy, rabble-rousing, silly even, but it was not evil.

By March 1932 there were 6 million Germans unemployed and the chancellor, Heinrich Brüning, was increasingly having to ask President Paul von Hindenburg to force through by decree unpopular measures intended to restore economic stability. Already the democratic credentials of the Weimar Republic were looking distinctly weak and, as civil service and public sector salaries were reduced and even war pensions cut, foreign debt climbed and the street fighting between communist and NSDAP gangs increased in intensity. Brüning managed to ban the SA and the SS, the uniformed militias of the NSDAP, but in the presidential election of March 1932 Hindenburg, the hero of the Great War, only won in a run-off, with Hitler coming second with 37 per cent of the votes cast. In May, Brüning resigned, to be replaced by Franz von Papen, a former junior officer in the army who had been expelled from the United States in 1916 while military attaché at the German embassy in Washington, suspected of planning sabotage of factories producing war material for the British. Von Papen was an old-fashioned nationalist who was happy to work with the NSDAP, and lifted the ban on the latter's uniforms, but his government was too narrowly based – it was very much a collection of well-bred old pals – to command a majority in the *Reichstag*, while his monarchist and Christian beliefs made him suspect to the NSDAP. To try to achieve a majority, he persuaded Hindenburg to dissolve parliament, and in the general election of July 1932 the NSDAP got 37 per cent of the votes cast – 14 million – and 230 seats, while the SPD came second with 133 and the communists third, increasing their 78 seats to 89. Von Papen offered Hitler, now head of the largest party in the *Reichstag* albeit without an overall majority, the post of vice-chancellor, but Hitler held out for chancellor or nothing. On this occasion, it was nothing, as Hindenburg distrusted Hitler, disliked his politics and refused to appoint him.

Von Papen now introduced some measures to ameliorate the plight of the workers and in another election in November 1932 there was some falling off in support for the NSDAP, who nevertheless remained the largest party with 33 per cent of the votes and 196 seats, while the communists gained 11 seats, bringing their total to 100. Von Papen resigned, to be replaced by Kurt von Schleicher. General von Schleicher had been closely involved with the secret rearmament that had started under Weimar, and with the arrangement with the Red Army that allowed German soldiers to train in armoured warfare and develop military aviation well inside Russia and away from the prying eyes of the British and the French. He was an extreme nationalist, prepared to use the NSDAP but not to put them into power, and an arch intriguer and political fixer. He tried to form an alliance between the trade unions and the army aimed at keeping the NSDAP out, but only succeeded in alienating big business and the landowners. Unable to carry the *Reichstag*, and finding Hindenburg unwilling to let him impose a military dictatorship, he resigned in January 1933. Hindenburg now had no options left, and he sent for Hitler.

Von Schleicher is generally regarded as the man who buried the Weimar Republic and made it possible for Hitler to come to power, but it is difficult to see how Hitler could have been prevented from coming to power by legitimate means. Only an unlikely coalition of the SDP and the communists could have outvoted the NSDAP in the *Reichstag*, but even then, if the NSDAP could have obtained the votes of the fifty-two nationalist Deutschnationale Volkspartei (DNVP) members (probable) and the Catholic Centre Party's seventy (possible, if only to block the communists), Hitler could have formed a coalition with an absolute majority. The fact is that most Germans wanted Hitler, if nothing else as a last-ditch antidote to economic chaos, social collapse and unemployment.[14]

Adolf Hitler, appointed chancellor of Germany on 30 January 1933, has possibly had more written about him than anyone else in modern history, and it is still almost impossible to glimpse the real man through the smoke of propaganda (his own and his enemies'), revulsion at what eventually happened in the concentration camps set up by his regime, and the results of the denazification of Germany at the end of the Second World War and since. Today, no German will stand up in public and defend any aspect of the Third Reich* and trying to get officers of the modern

---

*Historians differ over the definition of the First Reich. Most agree that it starts with the Carolingian empire around AD 800. It ends either with the first Crusade, AD 1125, or when Napoleon abolished the Holy Roman Empire in 1806, depending upon whom you listen to. The Second Reich ran from 1871, with German unification and the crowning of William of Prussia as Kaiser, until the end of the Hohenzollern dynasty in 1918. The Third Reich was Hitler's and ran from 1933 until 1945.

German army, the Bundeswehr, to discuss any aspect of the 1939–45 war is like drawing teeth. Certain facts are, however, indisputable. Firstly, Hitler and his party came to power as a result of the normal, albeit in some respects flawed, democratic political process. Secondly, not all of what the NSDAP did when it achieved power was bad – it made provision for old-age pensions, adult education and public health services far better than anything that existed in Britain at the time, and it built the autobahns. Thirdly, Hitler was a charismatic leader and brilliant orator. While he was quite ready to use terror, mere fear could not have kept virtually the whole nation fighting right to the bitter end. Hitler may have been bad, but he certainly was not mad. Indeed, had he stopped after the absorption of the Sudeten Germans in 1938, he might well now be regarded as the greatest German since Charlemagne.*

It is always dangerous (albeit fun) to speculate on what might have happened had not the Wall Street Crash forced the Weimar government into an inescapable round of deflation, higher taxes and unemployment, thus making the promises of Hitler and others to stabilize the currency and restore full employment (and, incidentally, to break free from the shackles of Versailles) so attractive. The Weimar Republic had been rearming in secret; any German government, whatever its political colour, would have wanted to renegotiate the borders fixed by Versailles; the Polish Corridor could not realistically be expected to remain Polish nor Danzig a 'Free City' for ever; even a liberal and democratic Germany would have wanted to station its troops in the Rhineland, extend customs union with Austria into full-blown amalgamation and incorporate the Sudeten Germans. But a democratic Germany might have achieved all of that by negotiation, and she might have stopped short of gobbling up the whole of Czechoslovakia in March 1939. It is also reasonable to suppose that a democratic Germany would have resisted the temptation to have another crack at the old enemy, France, but it is very possible that she would have gone to war with Russia eventually, and quite possibly in alliance with the British and the French. The Second World War might well have happened anyway, although the sides might have lined up differently.

As it was, Hitler's aims were straightforward: all power in Germany was to be in the hands of the NSDAP, the economy was to be restored,

---

*Whom the French claim as one of theirs but who to the Germans is Karl der Grosse. He was a Frank, so both could claim him.

and the Versailles Treaty to be annulled or ignored and the German territories lost after 1918 were to be recovered. Longer-term goals included the establishment of *Lebensraum*, 'living space', or territorial expansion. As this could not be to the west or the south, it would be at the expense of Russia and Poland in the east. With himself as chancellor but with only two others (Frick and Göring) of his own party in the cabinet of what was supposedly a coalition government, Hitler now had to establish NSDAP control of the country and then to consolidate it. The *Reichstag* was dissolved on 1 February and in the March elections the NSDAP got 43.9 per cent of the vote and 288 seats, which in coalition with the nationalist DNVP with its fifty-two seats gave Hitler a small overall majority. The election was marred by intimidation, bullying of opponents and vote-packing by the SA (*Sturmabteilung* or 'Storm Detachment'), the rough trade of the NSDAP, but even so the election was reasonably fair and Hitler would have had a thumping majority without the assistance of the SA gangs.

Hitler now moved remarkably quickly, helped by an arson attack on the *Reichstag* building in February 1933 that could conveniently be blamed on the communists. Despite conspiracy theories then and since, there is no reason to believe that the Berlin police did not get their man – a simple-minded Dutchman, Marinus van der Lubbe, who may or may not have acted on the instigation of a communist, but almost certainly not on the orders of the Communist Party, which had nothing to gain and much to lose from his action. In the event, the communists lost anyway as in March 1933 the newly elected *Reichstag* passed an enabling act, which by law had to have a two-thirds majority, granting emergency powers to the chancellor, Hitler, to rule by decree. As the eighty-one communist members of the *Reichstag* were in jail and not able to vote, the result was a foregone conclusion, but, if they had been there, Hitler would almost certainly still have got his majority. Progress now was rapid. That same month, communist and socialist trades unions and newspapers were taken over and either abolished or transformed into supporters of the regime, the first concentration camp was opened at Dachau (not yet an extermination centre) and the German state legislatures were taken over by NSDAP appointees. In April foreigners and Jews (except those who had served in the 1914–18 war) were dismissed from the public service, and the Secret State Police, the *Geheime Staatspolizei* or Gestapo, was formed. In May all trades unions were subsumed into the NSDAP German Labour Front and in June the Social Democrats, the SPD, were banned and the other political parties, seeing the graffiti on the wall, disbanded 'voluntarily'. By July 1933 Germany was a one-party state and in a referendum in November 1933 92 per cent of the voters approved.

The NSDAP had seized power, or rather had it handed to it, and despite his revolutionary rhetoric Hitler now needed stability in order to consolidate that power. Stability was threatened by the activities of the SA, which had its origins in the working class and the unemployed. Its members wore party uniform (the 'brownshirts') and as stewards and general bully boys had been the standard-bearers of the party in its long upward struggle. Now, however, the SA was an embarrassment with its members taking the law into their own hands, beating up those whom it thought were its enemies (including anyone talking with an odd accent, or of swarthy appearance) and generally behaving as if they were a state within a state. Statements by its commander, Ernst Röhm, a former captain in the army, that the NSDAP revolution was unfinished alarmed industrialists and landowners, while his claim that the 4-million-strong organization should form the army of the new state angered the generals. As all the institutions that Röhm threatened were needed by Hitler for his long-term plans for Germany, the National bit of National Socialism had to stamp on the Socialism bit and Röhm had to go, although this was undoubtedly made easier by his being a drunkard and a homosexual, about which orientation the NSDAP leadership held Presbyterian views. In July 1934 the Night of the Long Knives removed any threat the SA might pose, and settled numerous old scores the while. At least seventy-seven NSDAP members, including the entire SA leadership, were shot or arrested and then shot, along with some 100 others, including the former chancellor, General von Schleicher, and his wife.

In August 1934 Field Marshal Paul von Hindenburg died, aged eighty-seven. He had fought in the Austro-Prussian and Franco-Prussian wars of German unification and from 1916 was Chief of the General Staff, professional head of the German army. He was revered throughout Germany and many saw him as the last link to an honourable past. The NSDAP portrayed him as having handed over all that was best in the old Germany to the vigorous and dynamic new Germany, in the shape of Hitler. Hitler now combined the offices of president and chancellor into one and became Führer (leader) and *Reichskanzler* as well as Commander-in-Chief of the Wehrmacht or 'Armed

Forces'. All members of the Wehrmacht were required to swear an oath to Hitler personally,* and, in a referendum held in August when the voters were invited to approve Hitler's becoming Führer, 89.93 per cent voted 'yes'. That the published result showed that around 4.5 million had voted 'no' would indicate that the referendum was properly conducted and that approval of Hitler was genuine.

By the end of 1934 Hitler and the NSDAP were the unchallenged rulers of Germany, with legal permission to do almost whatever they liked. Now for Versailles and the lost territories.

* * *

At the height of the war to come, the United States would dispose of 100 divisions and 8 million men† in the most technologically advanced army the world had yet seen, but in 1932, when Hitler was preparing his party for power in Germany, America was one of the least militarized societies in the developed world and her army's most visible military operation was against her own people in her own capital.

This was the third year of the Great Depression and there were few signs of it ever ending. For most of the inhabitants of Washington, however, the great unfolding drama was that of the Bonus Expeditionary Force, as the 25,000 veterans of the Great War called themselves. They had come to the capital, unemployed, hungry and broke, many with their wives and children, to seek early redemption of a promise made to them in 1924. Then, in a rare fit of generosity, Congress had passed an act granting a cash bonus of $1,000 to all who had served in the Great War, to be paid in 1945, the idea being that by then the veterans would be entering middle age and could do with a handout, and by then the money to pay it would be easily available from public funds. The veterans had calculated that if the bonus were to be paid now, rather than their having to wait another thirteen years, they would each get $500 – $7,600 or £3,800 at today's values – a sizeable sum. In order to make their point, the veterans marched up and down Pennsylvania Avenue

---

*This is generally considered to have been frightfully bad form on Hitler's part, but in the British Army we are bound by an oath that says that we shall '… bear true and faithful allegiance to Her Majesty Queen Elizabeth II …' so the Germans were only copying us.

†Not counting the air force, which at this time was not a separate service but part of the army.

and held meetings, when they would harangue each other and anyone else who would listen. Squatting in derelict buildings and makeshift camps in parks and fields, they kept themselves alive by begging, generally non-aggressively, or with donations from sympathizers. While the House of Representatives passed a bill to pay the bonus, it was defeated in the Senate. Congress had no intention of redeeming its promise early – it did not have the money, or, if it did, there were more important things to spend it on. President Hoover found the whole thing an unwelcome distraction and refused to see the representatives of the marchers.

To begin with, many of the Washington police, including the commissioner, had some sympathy with the marchers and were reluctant to use force to move them on, but, as the long hot summer wore on, presidential and governmental irritation increased. The marchers would not go home (many had no homes to go to or, if they had, there was nothing to go there for), hygiene in their camps deteriorated and the whole thing was becoming a national embarrassment. The press, initially supportive, began to turn against the marchers and it was claimed that the whole thing was being stirred up by communist agitators. In Michigan a demonstration by unemployed workers outside the Henry Ford factory got out of hand and police fired on the crowd, killing four and wounding a number. While what happened in Michigan was nothing to do with the Bonus Marchers, it fed the paranoia of the conspiracy theorists, who began to see any gathering of the unwashed, veterans or not, as composed of red rabble rousers. On 28 July Congress ordered the Washington police to remove the Bonus Marchers from public buildings and parks. Stones were thrown, the police over-reacted and drew their pistols and two marchers were killed. The president now ordered the army to put an end to what he described as 'rioting and defiance of civil authority' and what General Douglas MacArthur, the army's Chief of Staff, called 'incipient revolution'.[15]

At around 5 p.m. the army moved in, led personally by MacArthur in full uniform. It was unfortunate that office work had just ended for the day, and the streets were packed with office workers leaving for home. The vanguard of the military might about to be unleashed was the 3rd Cavalry commanded by Major George S. Patton. It was doubly unfortunate that instead of charging the Bonus Marchers, which is what they were presumably supposed to do, Patton's warriors laid into the office workers and uninvolved spectators, riding them down and whacking them with the flats of their drawn sabres, before then turning their attention to the marchers. After the cavalry came the infantry, backed up by six tanks (which did more damage to the road surface with their steel tracks than they did to the marchers). An infantry charge preceded by a bombardment of tear gas drove the marchers back and by 10 p.m. two adults and a baby had been killed and the troops were pouring petrol over the marchers' makeshift huts and setting them on fire. It was the end of the Bonus March, and, while the Secretary for Defense lauded MacArthur as the hero of the hour for saving the capital from the ravages of 'communists and persons with criminal records... few if any of whom had ever worn an American uniform', the truth was that this down-at-heel, helpless and hopeless body was made up of men of whom, according to the veterans' administration, 94 per cent had served in the armed forces, 67 per cent had served overseas and 20 per cent had been disabled by war service.

It was not a glorious chapter in the history of the United States Army and a public relations disaster at a time when its very existence and purpose were in question, but this was an army that was under-funded, ill-equipped and with little training, and certainly none in crowd control. The Bonus Expeditionary Force melted away, and the men the army had dispersed drifted back into the population of the nomadic unemployed. Eight years later, when the children of the Depression's 15 million unemployed were conscripted, 40 per cent of them failed the medical examination: the chief reasons were rotting teeth, defective eyesight, heart problems, deformed limbs and mental instability.

In the presidential election of November 1932 the Democrat Franklin Delano Roosevelt defeated the Republican Hoover and became president in February 1933. His priorities were to stabilize the economy and prevent what many people thought was incipient revolution by the lower classes – by which was meant the manual workers and agricultural labourers. Roosevelt withdrew US participation in the International Monetary Conference – an attempt to fix exchange rates – and devalued the dollar. What became known as the New Deal brought the National Recovery Act, the Agricultural Adjustment Administration, the Tennessee Valley Authority (state involvement in the production and distribution of electric power), the Wagner–Connery Act (to regulate labour disputes), the National Labour Relations Board and a flurry of legislation delving into matters that had hitherto been regarded as the responsibility of the private sector, business or the individual. It also took the United States off the gold standard and brought the repeal of the unpopular and increasingly unworkable Eighteenth Amendment to the

Constitution which banned the manufacture, import, export and sale (but not the possession or drinking) of alcohol. Some of Roosevelt's measures were overturned by the Supreme Court as being unconstitutional – leading to a long-running battle between president and court – and those that were not would take time to work through. Strikes by those who were in work became commonplace and increasingly threatening, with police or National Guard regularly opening fire, and self-help organizations sprang up, whereby barter, either of goods or of services, replaced money as the means of exchange.

Despite 420,000 workers being on strike in September 1934, halfway through Roosevelt's term of office, by 1936 his measures were beginning to have an effect. For all the strikes nationwide and black riots in Harlem in 1935, unemployment was halved and industrial production had increased by 20 per cent, company profits were up by 50 per cent and the Dow Jones had risen by 80 per cent. Hindsight says that Roosevelt was a shoo-in for a second term, but all the polls and most of the press said otherwise. For the 1936 presidential election, the smart money was on Roosevelt losing by a landslide, hated as he was by right-wingers, the rich and big business, but also by the extreme left, which reminded anyone who would listen that he had vetoed the spring 1936 passing of an Act to pay the erstwhile marchers their bonus – a veto which was duly overturned by a two-thirds vote of each house. In the event, he won by the largest majority achieved up to that time, carrying every state except Maine and Vermont and gaining 523 Electoral College votes to the Republican Landon's eight. As the Democrats also now controlled 75 per cent of both houses of Congress, Roosevelt could do pretty much as he liked.

The New Deal passed the Minimum Wages Act, which also stipulated a forty-hour week. It was thrown out by the Supreme Court but the Social Security Act, which introduced pensions and unemployment insurance, survived, probably because it specifically did not apply to the bottom of the social scale: migrant and domestic workers and agricultural labourers. All this demanded a huge injection of public funds, and something had to go. As usual in democracies, it was defence that took much of the hit, and, apart from some increases in the naval estimates, the military establishment, already tiny, shrank and then shrank again. Much was made in the press of a forty-two-year-old lieutenant and a sixty-year-old sergeant being on the army's active list, with the average age of captains being forty-three.* Half a million

---

*In today's British Army the average age of captains is twenty-six and a bright officer would expect to be a brigadier at forty-three. Details for the American Army of today are similar.

undergraduates had signed a petition saying that, if Congress declared war, they would refuse to serve. Douglas MacArthur was sent off to the Philippines in 1936 to get him out of the way – probably rightly, Roosevelt regarded him as one of the two most dangerous men in America* – and with him went his staff officer, Major Dwight D. Eisenhower. Pacifism and isolationism were in the air and as ever there were no votes in defence.

Roosevelt's enemies said he had no foreign policy. This was not entirely fair. The president did have views on foreign affairs but he kept them to himself at a time when his, and the nation's, priorities were domestic. Americans took a passing interest in Edward VIII's affair with Mrs Simpson and his subsequent abdication, and they knew Winston Churchill as a writer of anti-communist tracts, but otherwise they had little knowledge of what went on abroad. The United States recognized the USSR in November 1933 but was certainly not interested in foreign entanglements. The Neutrality Acts, passed by Congress in 1935 and reluctantly approved by Roosevelt, were a sop to those in America who insisted that she had achieved none of her goals in the first war, and had merely acted as a provider of loans that were not being repaid. These were the same people who regarded the League of Nations (of which the United States was not a member) as an imperialist plot to lure America into foreign wars that were none of her business, and, while they probably did not represent majority opinion, which was broadly uninterested, they were a vocal and influential lobby.[†] The Acts banned the export or sale of arms and the granting of loans to any belligerent in a war in which the US was not herself engaged. The Democratic Party's election manifesto in 1936 proclaimed, inter alia: 'We shall… guard against being drawn, by political commitments, international banking or private trading, into any war which may develop anywhere.'[16] America refused to join Britain in a condemnation of Japan's actions in Manchuria; declined to apply an oil embargo against Italy when that country invaded Abyssinia; avoided taking any stance in the Spanish Civil War; declined to protest against the ill-treatment of Jews in Germany; and when the Japanese attacked and sank an

---

*The other was the extreme right-wing demagogue Huey Long, Governor of Arkansas, who despite being a Democrat was violently anti-Roosevelt and the New Deal, and had a mass following. He was assassinated in September 1935 and the conspiracy theorists blamed Roosevelt (some still do – and it is almost certainly nonsense).

†Roosevelt, in his unsuccessful campaign for the vice-presidency in 1920, had campaigned on a platform supporting the League.

American gunboat, the USS *Panay*, off Shanghai in 1937, and then claimed it had all been a frightful mistake, American reaction was decidedly muted, a fact that was carefully noted by the Japanese. (They had also noted the result of the American naval exercise of 1932 when an aircraft carrier had evaded the guard ships and notionally sank the warships anchored in Pearl Harbor.) It was not that Roosevelt could not see the threat posed by fascism, particularly by Germany and Japan: he most certainly could see it, but he knew that, at least while America was still in the throes of Depression, he could not carry the country with him in any attempt to intervene.

In 1937 there was more serious labour unrest followed by a mini stock market crash and by the spring of 1938 5 million workers who had found jobs since Roosevelt came into office in 1933 had lost them, and 14 per cent of the workforce was on relief. While things were still better than they had been, the weaknesses in the economy were proving to be deeper and longer-lasting than anyone could have foretold. Fortunately for American business, however, affairs in Europe would soon point a way out of the Depression.

* * *

In Germany the NSDAP government proceeded to do exactly what Hitler had said it would. In October 1933 Germany abruptly left both the League of Nations and the World Disarmament Conference. There was some huffing and puffing from the powers, but nobody did anything. In July 1934 an attempted coup by Austrian National Socialists failed, largely through the Italian dictator Mussolini making it clear by sending troops to the Brenner Pass that he was not ready to see a Greater Germany on his borders. In January 1935 German morale received a boost when voters in a League of Nations plebiscite in the Saarland, administered by the League as part of the Versailles settlement, were offered the choice of becoming French, returning to Germany or continuing with the status quo. Nine out of ten plumped for Germany. In June of the same year, to the fury of the French, the Anglo-German naval agreement allowed Germany to expand her surface fleet to 35 per cent of the size of the Royal Navy, and in the same month Germany re-introduced conscription and not so secretly re-formed the air force, the Luftwaffe – all clear violations of the Versailles Treaty. In March of the following year, 1936, there was even more blatant defiance when German troops marched into the

Rhineland, that portion of Germany bordering on France which Versailles had ordered to be demilitarized to meet French security fears. The German generals crossed their fingers and even Hitler held his breath, but the Allies did nothing except harrumph ineffectually.

In July 1936 the Spanish army garrison in Morocco rebelled against the Popular Front Spanish government, a loose alliance of liberals, communists and socialists whose reforms had angered the landowners and the Catholic Church. German aircraft ferried the troops under General Francisco Franco from Spanish Morocco to Spain and continued to support him with aircraft and weapons, although not with troops on the ground. (Franco's troops could not come by sea because the Spanish navy supported the Republicans.) In August, in Berlin, Germany hosted the Olympic Games, which were a triumph of propaganda and a message to all that Germany was back on the world stage, and in November Germany and Japan signed the Anti-Comintern Pact, which was designed to counter the influence of the USSR.

In 1937 German Jews, having been dismissed from the professions and the civil service, were required to wear a yellow Star of David armband. Having been frustrated in 1934, *Anschluss* was finally achieved in March 1938 when German troops marched into Austria without a shot being fired. A subsequent referendum in Austria gave 99 per cent approval of the merger, and, even with the packing, threatening and blatant fiddling of the results that undoubtedly went on, there can be no doubt that the vast majority of Austrians really did want to be united with their German cousins. In the Munich agreement of September 1938 the British and French agreed to German demands that the Sudetenland, that portion of Czechoslovakia bordering on Germany and containing many ethnic Germans, be ceded to Germany, and pressured the Czech government into agreeing. While that government would have been delighted to get rid of its troublesome German minority, it was not at all happy to lose Czechoslovakia's natural defences of the hills and rivers that made up the Sudeten strip.

It was now clear to Germany that the erstwhile Allies could be safely ignored – they were paper tigers, could do nothing and would do nothing. In November 1938 a German diplomat was assassinated in Paris by a German-Polish Jew, which precipitated *Kristallnacht*, an orgy of looting and destruction aimed at Jewish businesses and individuals. While the civilized world might have accepted polite discrimination against Jews, this sort of behaviour aroused widespread revulsion – which worried the Nazis not a jot. In March

1939 Germany encouraged the Slovaks to agitate for independence and the German army marched into Czechoslovakia. That state ceased to exist, being replaced by the German-administered Protectorate of Bohemia and Moravia and the German client state of Slovakia. For the first time, any pretence that Hitler only wanted to reunite German people and erstwhile German territory was laid bare. The only possible reason for dissolving Czechoslovakia was to give Germany a jumping-off point for adventures in the East, as well, of course, as the opportunity to lay her hands on one of Europe's most sophisticated arms industries. Then, in August 1939, to the amazement and consternation of the rest of Europe, Germany signed a mutual assistance treaty with the USSR. The public provisions not only contained a non-aggression clause but provided for the supply of raw materials and foodstuffs from the Soviet Union in return for manufactured goods and machine tools from Germany. The secret provisions divided Poland between Germany and the USSR at a time in the future. Now the centuries-old fear of German soldiers and statesmen of a war on two fronts was eliminated. Germany's back door was secure.

* * *

That the Germans were allowed to get away with blatant defiance of the Versailles Treaty, and that they were not stopped well short of war in 1939, is generally laid at the door of the pusillanimous British and the almost as pusillanimous French. But there is a very wide gulf between what one should do and what one can do. Popular misconception says that, if the Allies had acted militarily when Germany reoccupied the Rhineland, then Hitler's war of conquest could never have happened. It is true that many German officers were against the reoccupation, and there was some idle talk in officers' messes as to what might happen if it failed. The reality is that neither the French nor the British were in any state to intervene, militarily or otherwise. General Ironside, the Chief of the British General Staff, was quite clear that his men would be no match qualitatively or quantitatively for the Germans, and the French would not act unless the British did. In any case, the Rhineland was German; in January 1935 the British government had accepted that the continuation of a demilitarized Rhineland was not a vital British interest; it had been created to serve French and Belgian interests and was no concern of Britain's. It would be reoccupied legitimately in a few years anyway and no one, bar the outcast Churchill and his eccentric clique, was prepared to go to war to prevent it happening now. Contrary to opinion then and since, it is most unlikely that the German troops in the Rhineland would have scuttled tamely home in the face of French or British intervention. On the contrary, even those few German battalions that had occupied the left (French) side of the Rhine had been instructed to fight.[17] The whole force would have fought a determined and skilful defence, and, given the speedy build-up of the initial twelve battalions and supporting artillery into four divisions, would probably have been at least a match for whatever the Allies might have fielded.

The word 'appeasement' has become something of an insult, with connotations of craven cowardice and toadying to unpleasant bullies, but the word simply means the pacification of the potentially hostile and was a perfectly respectable political tool before it was made into a form of denigration by its failure in the 1930s. The British had generally recognized that much of the Versailles Treaty was unfair, and that the potentially largest and richest nation in continental Europe could not be ground down for ever. They wanted Germany to resume her place in the family of nations, and strove to help her to do so in a way that would suppress any latent revanchist tendencies. Here British policy diverged from that of the French, who were unrepentant, saw no reason why Germany should be forgiven or released from the strictures of Versailles and were convinced (rightly, as it turned out) that, given half a chance, Germany would be at their throats again. The first, half-baked, attempt to restrain German ambitions was the so-called Stresa Front, signed by Britain, France and Italy in April 1935, but it had no teeth and soon fell apart. In June of that same year Baldwin's Conservatives won the British general election and Ramsay MacDonald's coalition government was no more, the Labour opposition now being led by Clement Attlee.* Baldwin was a realist and a world-weary sceptic who had already been prime minister twice. Austen Chamberlain, who had good reason to dislike him, thought him 'self-centred, selfish and

---

*About as far from a red in tooth and claw socialist as it is possible to be, Attlee was a public school- and Oxford-educated barrister, had a pre-Great War commission in the Territorial Force and ended that war as an infantry major. He was one of only two prime ministers since the first Duke of Wellington to have been wounded in action (the other was Harold Macmillan). There would not be another leader of the Labour Party with a background like his until Tony Blair in the 1990s. Blair did not have the opportunity to fight in a war, but his thoroughly robust views on defence made him popular with the Services.

idle, yet one of the shrewdest politicians, but without a constructive idea in his head and with an amazing ignorance of Indian and foreign affairs'.[18] Austen's half-brother, Neville, thought he had 'a singular and instinctive knowledge of how the plain man's mind works'.[19] Within days of becoming leader of the government Baldwin acceded to the Anglo-German Naval Agreement. Despite French anger, there was little else that the British could do. Germany was going to expand her navy regardless, and neither Britain nor anyone else was prepared to go to war to stop her. Better to agree some limitations than to stand back and do nothing at all. The Germans might, of course, sign the agreement and then ignore it, but that was a chance that was seen to be worth taking – after all, there were enough honourable old school diplomats in the German Foreign Office to make sure the agreement held.

Baldwin's first real crisis in foreign affairs was the infamous Hoare–Laval Pact. Sir Samuel Hoare, the man who had saved the RAF when Secretary for Air, was now Foreign Secretary and, as he travelled to Switzerland for a holiday, called on the French foreign minister and acting premier, Pierre Laval. Between them, they hatched a plot to give a large part of Abyssinia to Italy, in the hope of thereby keeping Mussolini on their side as a counterweight to Hitler. The proposal was written down, both men initialled it and Hoare went on his way. It was unfortunate that the plan was almost immediately leaked, probably from the French side, and there was the most almighty kerfuffle in the British and French press and in both parliaments. There was much cant about poor little Abyssinia, the emphasis being on the fact that she was a Christian country, and great sympathy for the Emperor Haile Selassie. That Abyssinia was a backward, corrupt and oppressive autocracy that still tolerated slavery and that most emperors were either hopelessly inbred or mad (or both) was conveniently forgotten, and both Hoare and Laval had to resign. Mussolini was discommoded, continued his Abyssinian war anyway and moved closer to Hitler.*

---

*In 1962 this author, as an officer cadet at the Royal Military Academy Sandhurst, had the misfortune to be briefly in charge of one of Haile Selassie's many grandsons. That he was unable to tie his own shoelaces or knot a tie (tasks that had always been done by a servant), and that he found using a Western lavatory a trial, was not the problem – we could cope with that – but that he dribbled, never understood that you were supposed to get out of bed in the morning and tended to get lost on his way from his room to the showers did rather militate against modern military training. In the event, even Sandhurst gave up on him and he went back to Abyssinia to become a general and commander of the Imperial Guard. It is hardly surprising that the whole ludicrous edifice was overthrown by a Marxist revolution in 1974.

For much of 1936 the attention of the British government was taken up with the problem of the new king, Edward VIII, who succeeded his father when George V died in January. Edward was idle, a playboy and probably not very bright. He was more interested in cheap popularity and the company of louche sycophants than in the traditional roles of a British monarch. King George had doubts about him, and the awful Mrs Simpson did the nation a great service by agreeing to marry him, and thus provoking his abdication in favour of his brother, George VI, a thoroughly good king who produced an excellent successor in Elizabeth II. Even when not engaged in trying to resolve the succession crisis, Baldwin tended to leave foreign affairs to his Foreign Secretary, Eden, who had replaced Hoare. Thus, as a result of the Abyssinian crisis, Italy drew closer to Germany, the Germans began to build the Siegfried Line to defend the Rhineland, the League of Nations was increasingly shown to have no clothes and still there was no serious attempt by the British or the French to bring the two European autocrats to heel. If France would not fight for the Rhineland – the last guarantee of her security – then, thought many, she would not fight at all. Belgium now abandoned her mutual assistance treaty with France and declared 'independence' – in effect, neutrality.

In May 1937 Baldwin resigned and was replaced by Chamberlain, who had hitherto been Chancellor of the Exchequer. It is at Chamberlain's door that most of the blame for 'appeasement' – by which was and is meant the failure to stop Hitler before it was too late – was and is laid, particularly by those who profited by Chamberlain's later fall, namely Churchill and his supporters. In fact, Chamberlain was the first government minister to advocate rearmament, and he wanted to fight the 1935 election on that basis, but was dissuaded by Baldwin, who thought the voters would never stand for it. When one examines the newspapers of the time, particularly the letters columns, and the correspondence between the British and Dominion governments, it is abundantly clear that no British politician could have carried the country to war, or even to full-scale rearmament, at that time, and it is pointless, and unfair, to claim that the Second World War was all Chamberlain's fault. If the Rhineland was not a *casus belli* for the British, then the union of the two German states, Germany and Austria, was certainly not one either, and as for the Sudeten question, resolved, so the British and French thought, by the Munich agreement of September 1938, then it was surely not unreasonable that the Sudeten Germans should be repatriated. The general view in Britain, and in the Empire, was that, while Hitler was clearly a vulgar populist, and his party was very tacky indeed, what he had done so far – the incorporation of Germans living on the borders of Germany into his Reich – was not unacceptable. It was a great pity that he had got what he demanded by threats, when he might well have got them by negotiation, but now that he had no further demands in Europe, things would quieten down and the Germans would revert to the normal diplomatic processes inherent in international relations.

While full-scale rearmament had not been implemented before Munich, what spare British cash that was available for defence had been spent on the Royal Air Force. It was an article of faith, held not just by the British but by the Germans, Italians and Americans too, that aerial bombardment of civilian populations, which all sides publicly eschewed but privately feared and prepared for, would so cripple industry and destroy the population's will that the nation subjected to it would have to give up the fight. In hindsight, of course, bombing from the air had almost the opposite effect on morale, both in Europe and in the United Kingdom, and industry simply moved under-ground or surrounded itself with anti-aircraft defences, but at the time the slogan 'The bomber will always get through' was widely believed.* In the event, more or less the only field in which Britain was militarily reasonably well prepared when war did come was in the nation's air defence. Despite Chamberlain's 'peace in our time' rhetoric, intended for public consumption both in the UK and abroad, it was becoming increasingly apparent that another European war was brewing up nicely. With the German occupation of the rump of Czechoslovakia, it was no longer a question of if, but of when. Britain and France issued a guarantee to Poland – neither country was in any state to actually do anything, but it was hoped that the very existence of the threat of military action might make the Germans stop and think.

In 1939 the Royal Navy was the largest in the world, but many of its ships were old, the planned number of new aircraft carriers had not been built, and the Washington Naval Conference of 1922–23 had forced Britain to lay up or destroy ships to reduce her fleet to the agreed tonnage. The army – volunteer and professional, unlike European conscript armies – was tiny, and spread over the Empire. Not only is a professional army expensive, and therefore small, but it does not have the turnover in manpower that a system of

---

*It was also attractive to those who did not want to spend money on battleships and tanks or to have to maintain manpower-intensive armies.

conscription does, and hence there is the difficulty of producing a first-line reserve available to expand the army in time of major war. This had been recognized in the early years of the century and led to the setting up of the Territorial Force by Lord Haldane and Major-General Sir Douglas (later Field Marshal Earl) Haig. This organization, which changed its name to the Territorial Army in 1920, consisted of civilians, or those who had served in the regular army but had no reserve liability, who trained in the evenings and at weekends and was supposed to mirror the regular army in organization and equipment, but in fact was poorly trained and scantily equipped. This was not the fault of its members who, discounting the drinking-club element, were by and large well-motivated patriots who wanted to 'do their bit', albeit not as a full-time career, but an inevitable consequence of the shortage of funding for and interest in defence between the wars. What few assets were made available naturally went to the regular army, with precious little left over for the part-timers. Thus, the British government's announcement in spring 1939 that the TA was to be doubled in size was an empty gesture militarily, but one which might show the world that the British meant business. In February 1939 the government at last accepted a continental commitment and staff talks with the French, an admission that the British would have to provide land forces in Europe in the event of a war, an eventuality for which the armed services had been training for some years but which had been steadfastly denied by politicians who rather hoped that the British contribution would be a naval blockade and bombers over Berlin. In May of the same year the British government introduced conscription.

* * *

In Spain an attempted coup by the army supported by monarchists, industrialists, conservative landowners, the Church and the Falange fascist party against the Popular Front republic, which began in 1936 when the German and Italian air forces helped to ferry the Army of Africa to mainland Spain, had become a civil war. Both sides were incompetent and corrupt and perpetrated atrocities but the wider world saw it in simplistic terms: republic good, nationalists bad. The Republican side attracted support from the USSR in the shape of 1,000 aircraft, 900 tanks, 1,500 artillery pieces and large quantities of small arms ammunition, but no other formal governmental assistance. The British government preferred the Nationalist cause (as it was less likely to interfere with British trade and investment) while the French were broadly sympathetic to the Republicans, but both governments pursued a policy of non-intervention. The Civil War did, however, become a magnet for communists, anarchists, liberals and naive do-gooders from all over Europe and America. Republican forces included the so-called International Brigades (in practice, rather smaller than brigades) mostly raised under the aegis of Soviet or communist surrogates, unbeknownst to many of those joining them. The French government allowed a training camp to be established at Perpignan and permitted movement to Spain via Marseilles, and, while the brigades caught the imagination of the less sceptical, they were often untrained and poorly equipped.

While the Nationalists too had some volunteers from overseas, notably an Irish contingent led by 'General' Eoin O'Duffy, an old IRA warrior who attempted to form an Irish equivalent of the NSDAP – its members made the raised arm salute and uttered the cry of 'Hail O'Duffy' – and took around 700 Irish Catholics to Spain in the belief that they were fighting to preserve the mother church from the godless Republicans, they had considerable material support from Italy and Germany. In the three years of the war nearly 78,000 Italian troops served in Spain and Italy provided 759 aircraft, 157 tanks, 1,800 artillery pieces of various calibres and 320 million rounds of small arms ammunition. The Germans sent the Condor Legion, mainly an air force but also with a tank unit and some support services. Altogether, Germany provided 600 aircraft and 200 light tanks.[20] While there was no direct German or Italian interest in Spain, a victory for the Nationalist cause would act as a counterweight to France and, in the event of war, might, by closing the Strait of Gibraltar, make things difficult for the British in the Mediterranean. Of more immediate use, perhaps, was the opportunity to practise tactics and operational procedures, particularly the use of dive-bombers, which would reap dividends in any coming war. The Spanish Civil War ended with a Nationalist victory in March 1939 and the new *Caudillo* ('leader'), General Francisco Franco, joined Germany, Japan and Italy in the Anti-Comintern Pact.

* * *

Thus far, the German armed forces' only experience of actual combat since 1918 had been that of the Condor Legion. Italy, on the other hand, had been fighting in Libya until 1932, had committed eighteen divisions to Abyssinia in 1935 and suffered 10,600 casualties. Leaving two divisions and 200,000 colonial troops to maintain order, she had then supported the Republicans in the Spanish Civil

War – thereby incurring another 14,000 casualties – and finally in April 1939 had invaded and annexed Albania, which Italians believed should have been theirs after 1918. The Italian Army and air force had either lost* or given to the Spanish Nationalists huge amounts of military hardware and ammunition and had consequently run out of both. Originally inclined to be suspicious of Germany, Mussolini's regime had been angered by the British sponsoring of (ineffectual) sanctions by the League of Nations against its Abyssinian adventure and the failure of the Hoare–Laval Pact. Italy had signed the Anti-Comintern Pact in 1937 yet in 1939 made it clear that she could not possibly go to war at Germany's side without massive re-equipment of her armed forces – list supplied. It was a list that Germany could not possibly meet.

* * *

In Soviet Russia of the mid-1930s Stalin's position, seemingly impregnable after the death of Lenin, seemed, at least to him, to be under threat. The rapid pace of forced industrialization and the collectivization of farms with the movement of labour from the countryside into the towns produced great hardship at the lower levels of a society where there were supposed to be no levels, and there were outbreaks of unrest and criticism of Stalin's policies, which even extended to delegates to the Seventeenth Party Congress in 1934 and members of the Central Committee. For Stalin the solution was straightforward: anti-Soviet elements, foreign spies, counter-revolutionaries, Trotskyites, saboteurs and anyone who might even think of opposing Stalin must be eliminated, and the Great Terror began. It started in 1937 with the Red Army, then a force of nearly 1 million men in ninety infantry and sixteen horsed cavalry divisions, with around 5,000 ageing aircraft and 3,000 obsolete tanks.† Of the Supreme Military Soviet's eighty members, just five survived; of the nineteen army commanders, thirteen went; and of 135 divisional commanders, 110 were purged. No one knows the exact figures for more junior officers but it has been estimated that up to 30 per cent were imprisoned or executed. What was left lacked staff experience and was of low morale. No officer had any confidence that he would still be in post the following week. Prior to the purge, there had been disagreement between

---

*In the sense of destroyed by enemy action, rather than mislaid.

†The highly successful T-34 did not come into service until 1940 and even then there were very few of them.

the generals, who wanted to concentrate on technology, upgrading weapon systems and modernizing training, and the Central Committee, which insisted that all future wars would be class wars and that it was political ideology which mattered: the Red Army should go on the offensive because there would be pro-Soviet risings by the workers and peasants in the attacked countries. Of course, this was nonsense, but after the purge it was ideology that won and it would take a series of defeats at the hands of the Germans before military common sense was allowed to return, at least in part.

Stalin subsequently turned his attention to the civil service and local party officials, then to the management of industry and the higher levels of the party. Suspects were rounded up by the secret police, the NKVD (the OGPU with a new name), hastily tried and, after a grovelling confession had been extracted, either executed or sentenced to long, or even indefinite, terms in concentration camps. Of the 1,966 delegates to the Seventeenth Congress, which had changed the title of Stalin's post from general secretary to secretary, ninety-eight were executed or imprisoned, and, of the seventy-one members of the Central Committee, fifty-five disappeared. By 1939 the terror had accounted for perhaps 20 million killed and 8 million jailed.[21]

Despite the havoc wreaked upon it by Stalin, the Red Army performed creditably against Japanese border incursions in 1937 and again in a nasty little campaign around Lake Khasan, south-west of Vladivostok, in July and August of 1938. From May to September 1939 there was a major operation involving 40,000 men, tanks and aircraft on the border of Inner Mongolia (Russian) and Manchuria (Japanese) that brought the Japanese to a halt. But this was a campaign of relatively low technology, when the Red Army was defending its own land. The USSR was in no state to engage in military adventures outside the USSR, nor to defend its territory against a first-class enemy – like the Germans. Given the problems with the Japanese in the East and the general condition of the Red Army, the August 1939 pact signed by Joachim von Ribbentrop for Germany and Vyacheslav Molotov for the USSR made enormous sense, whatever Hitler might have said about the Bolshevik menace in the past.

* * *

The French general election of 1936 was won by the Popular Front, a loose coalition of left-wing parties including the communists and backed by the trade unions, headed by Léon Blum, who became prime minister. Blum announced an ambitious programme of nationalization and the extension of workers' rights. A forty-hour week, increased pay scales, holidays with pay and compulsory arbitration of labour disputes were to be implemented, and the Bank of France and some major industries were taken into full or partial public ownership. All this cost money, which alienated the middle classes and business, whose taxes would have to be raised to pay for it, and also investors, who increasingly began to move capital out of the country. When the communists, under orders from Moscow, refused to cooperate with Blum, his programme became unsustainable, the Popular Front collapsed and Blum was replaced by the radical socialist Édouard Daladier. Increasingly, many Frenchmen thought that only some form of totalitarianism could restore France to her former glory, and by 1939 French society was fatally riven between those who clung to the old republican values, and those who thought it was time for a new beginning.

Much of the prestige of the French Army did not long survive the victory parades of 1919. The generals were thought by many to have fought the war in the wrong way and with little regard for the lives of their men. The inter-war military establishment was in no doubt that it would have to fight another war against Germany eventually and home defence was the overriding priority of all military planning, with the defence of the empire and the sea lanes coming a poor second. The French Army, the largest of the three services, relied on a regular cadre of officers and NCOs of around 106,000, and an annual conscription of private soldiers, some of whom might become junior NCOs. In 1918 conscription had been for a period of three years (or until the end of hostilities, whichever came later), reduced to two years in 1921, to eighteen months in 1923 and to one year in 1928. At this stage, the annual intake of conscripts was 240,000, which produced a standing army of almost 350,000 and a reserve which was topped up by the annual discharge of the previous year's 240,000. As long as Germany was held to the 100,000-man army laid down by Versailles, this was more than enough to defend the homeland and police the empire. When, however, it became obvious that Germany had embarked on rearmament, and this realization was coupled with a calculation which showed that because of the huge losses of men of breeding age in the first war, whose sons would have been eligible for military service, the annual intake of conscripts from 1936 onwards would drop to 120,000, the term of conscription was raised to two years in 1935, which maintained the army at its 350,000 strength.

Although it was large in numbers of men, much of the French Army's equipment was outdated and in need of modernization. Despite its pacifist tendencies, the Popular Front government accepted that rearmament was essential and voted the funds for a massive increase in the production of tanks and anti-tank guns. As it happened, industry could not cope and by the time war came nothing like the planned quantities were available. The French defence lobby envisaged the next war as being long and defensive: France would hold her frontiers until blockade, allies and industrial production could combine to weaken Germany to such an extent that one final offensive would end the war. A huge proportion of the defence budget went into the Maginot Line, a series of fortified zones along the Rhine and running from the Belgian frontier in the north to the Swiss border and into southern France. The Line was highly sophisticated with underground barracks, hospitals, gun emplacements, and stores and ammunition depots. It was an attempt to substitute steel and concrete for men's lives and is often derided as a white elephant. In fact it did exactly what it was supposed to do: the Italians in 1940 failed to break through it and the Germans only mastered it by outflanking it. Had it extended around the Belgian frontier – impossible politically – then the story of the Battle of France might well have been different.

While the military establishment thought in terms of a lengthy defensive war, the foreign policy of successive French governments was to counter the threat of German aggression by a network of alliances, with Poland, Yugoslavia, Romania and Czechoslovakia. A military agreement with Italy in 1935 was regarded as a great coup by the French – now they could divert divisions from the Italian to the German border. This understanding was short-lived, however, and fell apart because of British insistence on sanctions being applied to Italy in the latter's Abyssinian campaign. The difficulty with building alliances and mutual assistance pacts was that, should Poland, Yugoslavia *et al* be attacked by Germany, the only assistance France could give would be by an invasion of Germany from the west, and the French Army was organized, trained and equipped for a defensive war. Thus, French foreign and defence policies were at loggerheads, a dichotomy that was never resolved until war and defeat resolved it for them.

And that war came soon enough, for in the early hours of 1 September 1939 1.5 million German soldiers in sixty-seven divisions, supported by air and naval forces, invaded Poland.

3

GO!

The army permitted to Germany by the Versailles settlement was limited to 100,000 men, all to be professionals so that no sizeable reserve could be built up. The limit for the navy was 15,000. There were strict limitations on the numbers and types of weapons, and the amount of ammunition that could be held for them; there were to be no tanks, no aircraft and no gas, nor the means of delivering it, and there was to be no general staff. That in a mere twenty years this tiny military rump, barely sufficient to keep order internally, was transformed into a force of 4.5 million, which could send 1.5 million men, including six armoured divisions fielding 3,600 of the forbidden armoured vehicles, into Poland had a certain amount to do with Hitler and the NSDAP but a great deal more to do with the German army itself. The army of the Weimar Republic, the Reichswehr, was a very carefully selected body. Only the best of the officers and NCOs of the old Hohenzollern military machine were retained, and all ranks were trained to think two ranks up; thus sergeants were expected to be able to command companies, company commanders brigades (regiments in German parlance) and battalion commanders divisions. Versailles had built in safeguards to prevent the Germans from creating a cadre for future expansion (by, for example, having more officers and senior NCOs than needed, who would manage expansion when it came), but Generaloberst* Hans von Seekt, Commander-in-Chief from 1920 to 1926, found numerous loopholes and ensured that the army slipped through them. A Prussian of the old school and still a monarchist at heart, he had no

---

*Translated as 'colonel-general', it is the equivalent of general in the British and US Armies. The German army had no rank of brigadier (British) or brigadier-general (US) so a German *Generalmajor* (major-general) equated roughly to a brigadier, a *Generalleutnant* (lieutenant-general) to a major-general and a *General der...* (insert arm of service) to a lieutenant-general. A *Generalfeldmarschall* was a field marshal (British) or general of the army (US).

sympathy with Weimar democracy and was determined to keep the army out of politics, regain respect for it within society and prepare it for the war that would surely come to restore Germany to her rightful place in the world. It was von Seekt who arranged for the German army to experiment with tanks and aircraft deep inside Russia, who re-created the Great General Staff under inoffensive titles (the 'Head of the Troops Office' was actually the Chief of the General Staff) and who encouraged preparations for mechanization.

Officers of the Reichswehr had noted the lessons of the First World War. They concluded – correctly – that they had been defeated strategically by the Royal Navy's blockade, having to fight a war on two fronts and the industrial muscle of the United States and Britain. Tactically they had been beaten by the adoption by the British of all-arms manoeuvre warfare in 1918, where tanks, infantry, artillery, engineers and aircraft combined to produce shock on the battlefield, probe for weaknesses and bypass strongpoints that could be mopped up later: this was something to which the usual stout German defence had no answer. The German officers of the 1920s concluded that a war on two fronts must be avoided; that a long war would allow blockade and industrial might to slowly strangle Germany, and that the German army must adopt and refine the tactics used against them in 1918 – tactics which came to be known as *Blitzkrieg*. The possibility of a war on two fronts was a long-term German concern, and it was largely for politicians to avoid it, but the German army should prepare for short, sharp wars, using mechanized units to effect rapid and deep strikes into the flanks and rear of enemy formations. The old insistence on the need to hold ground come what may must be forgotten, and tactical withdrawals in order to concentrate and counter-attack should become normal practice.

In 1932, the year before Hitler gained power, the United States military attaché, Lieutenant-Colonel Jacob Wuest, observed the Reichswehr's autumn manoeuvres – based on a supposed invasion of eastern Germany by Poland – and thought it an army of 'thinking individuals with a sense of freedom of action arising from good team training'. The officers, he thought, were 'serious-minded and keen… quiet with a natural sense of dignity'.[22] In a document entitled 'Points for Training 1932–33', the Commander-in-Chief of the army, Colonel-General Kurt Freiherr* von Hammerstein-Equord, summed up the lessons of the training exercises and looked forward to the

---

Freiherr is the German equivalent of a baronetcy, i.e. an hereditary knighthood.

following year. He emphasized the importance of concurrent activity, with warning orders sufficient to get troops on the move issued well in advance. He thought there was too much detail in many operational orders, which as far as possible should be verbal, not written. Rather than telling a subordinate exactly how to carry out his task, commanders should lay down a clear mission, and then allow subordinates to get on with it – in other words, tell them what to do, not how to do it. The speedy passing of information up and down was stressed, but also the need for commanders at all levels to be able to cope with the 'fog of war'. Proper appreciation of the terrain was vital, particularly when faced with enemy armour, and tanks were not to be parcelled out but concentrated to make maximum use of their mobility and shock action. Surprise was the key and tanks were never to be used in less than battalion strength.* Much the same points can be heard after today's military exercises, showing that, while the assets change, the basic principles do not.

Umpiring† methods came in for some criticism, particularly for not insisting that units move at realistic speeds. It was accepted that umpiring dummy tanks (plywood bolted on to wheeled vehicles or motor cycles) was not easy but umpires were not to allow them to exceed 20 kph (12.5 mph).‡ Within the German army all were agreed as to the importance of anti-tank defence, but there was much discussion as to the best method of achieving it. Hammerstein thought that enemy tanks should be engaged well before they reached the defence line, but he accepted that there was merit in the contrary view, which held that, when faced with tanks, the infantry should

---

*With their ability to make a virtue out of necessity, the British, with very few tanks, allowed squadron-sized (or company-sized) and even troop-sized (or platoon-sized) attacks. Today we would say that in most circumstances tanks should not be employed in less than squadron size.

†In training one is not allowed to fire live ammunition – the only certain way of finding out which side wins – so all military exercises are observed by umpires whose duty it is to ensure that timings are realistic and that what units and individuals do conforms as closely as possible to real combat. Everyone has driven through minefields when the umpires were not looking.

‡As the Germans were not ready to admit that they were developing real tanks, they could only exercise with dummies. Lest the reader should snigger, it should be pointed out that in the 1970s, when the defence budget was under even more strain than usual, we in the British infantry were issued with football rattles for exercises to compensate for there being no blank ammunition for machine-guns.

go to ground, allow the enemy armour to pass through to be dealt with by friendly tanks and anti-tank guns in the rear, and then deal with the enemy's infantry following their tanks. What no one doubted was the importance of having lots of anti-tank guns, and when war came it was German anti-tank guns, rather than tanks, which were the main killers of Allied tanks.

What had not yet been resolved was the role of horsed cavalry, of which the Germans still had eighteen regiments, albeit partially motorized. Should cavalry be used in the reconnaissance role or could they be used in combat? Some cavalry officers believed in what the French called the 'oats and oil' solution, where horsed cavalry and light motorized units could work together, while a few still considered that what they called heavy cavalry could be used in attack. A larger number, not all cavalry officers, thought that armoured vehicles would be unsuitable for war in the mud of Poland and Russia, should it come, and that only horsed cavalry could cope with the terrain. By 1939 the Germans had reduced their horsed cavalry to one brigade, although later on horsed cavalry units were raised for service in Russia, where they did prove effective. Huge numbers of horses were still used, and would be used, by the Germans in logistics units and to pull the artillery of non-armoured or non-motorized units, and in 1939 the German army had 400,000 horses on the establishment.

Looking ahead to 1933, the army commander announced test exercises for every combat unit of the Reichswehr, including one of seven days for each infantry battalion. Thus, by the year Hitler came to power, and by 1935, when he was ready to announce publicly that Germany would no longer be bound by Versailles and would rearm, the groundwork had already been done. Armoured tactics had been thrashed out in Russia; the army knew exactly what sort of armoured vehicle it needed; every serving soldier and officer was a highly trained professional well capable of instant promotion; there was a general staff in disguise and senior commanders were highly experienced veterans of the first war. Military aviation too was well advanced thanks to experimentation in Russia and the proliferation of 'gliding clubs', while the navy was a thoroughly proficient service, albeit one not capable of much more than coastal defence and commerce raiding.

The NSDAP government's first ordered increase in the size of the army was from the Reichsheer's seven divisions to twenty-one with a wartime reinforcement of a further fifteen divisions. This was a huge step, to be completed within two years, and was carried out, in the main, by dividing existing single units to form two and then splitting them again. There were enough officers and senior NCOs who could be promoted to provide the command structure, but the rank and file could only come from conscription, which was initially to be for one year, quickly changed to two years (in August 1936) when it was realized that one year was far too short. In 1936 the expansion was increased to forty-two divisions in the standing army with eight in reserve to be reached by 1938. In 1938 this was increased yet again, and by the summer of 1939 the German army could field 103 divisions, a fifteen-fold increase in four years.

Such a huge expansion could not be achieved simply by splitting and more splitting – the inherent military experience and training of the longer-serving soldiers would become far too diluted to produce effective units. The reoccupation of the Rhineland in 1936 meant that the Rhineland Armed Police could now be admitted as being paramilitary and absorbed into the army as twenty-eight battalions of infantry; the absorption of Austria in 1938 added five divisions, and the re-designation of border guards and police formations and the inclusion of recalled veterans of the first war all helped. What is perhaps extraordinary is that, despite this unprecedented peacetime expansion, professional standards were barely compromised. Right to the end of the war, even junior German officers, few of them by then products of the pre-Hitlerian army, were highly skilled, well motivated and formidable opponents. Meanwhile, in 1935 the first three armoured (panzer) divisions were formed, based very much on the British experimental armoured division which German army observers had seen on Salisbury Plain in 1927. The difference was that, while the British put much thought into armoured organization and tactics, they were given very little money to put it into practice.

Of course, there were difficulties: there was a shortage of staff-trained officers and the War Academy struggled to match its output to the expansion; vehicles broke down on exercises and on the drive into Austria; there were shortages of some items of equipment; organizations were not yet finalized and there was suspicion of the efforts of the SS to expand its own armed wing, the Waffen SS, but in general problems were quickly solved, doctrine was developed, tried, tested, amended, refined and promulgated, and by 1939 the German army was well trained, well led, reasonably well equipped and large enough to engage in serious war. Versailles had certainly reduced the size of Germany's war-making capacity, but it had totally failed to eradicate the Prussian military tradition and German flexibility and ability to improvise.

* * *

It is one of life's great mysteries that the Poles have been able to keep their language, culture and religion alive despite inhabiting an area which has usually belonged to either Germany, Russia or Austria, or sometimes to all three. Napoleon Bonaparte gave them the client state of the Grand Duchy of Warsaw, for which they remained forever grateful, and in the attempt to please everyone (except the defeated Germans) the Allies created the Republic of Poland in 1918. The Poles are a hardy race, but if you sit beside the school bully it is as well not to tease him, and this is doubly the case if you sit between two school bullies. Poland had taken advantage of Germany when she was weak in the aftermath of the first war, she had fought a war of aggression with the Soviet Union in the 1920s and had grabbed the Teschen area and some frontier districts in the Carpathians from Czechoslovakia when Germany claimed the Sudetenland. Long before Germany was in any position to threaten her, Poland had discriminated against and oppressed ethnic Germans living in Poland (there were around 70,000 of them). She was bound to be stamped on by somebody sooner or later. Nor do we need to feel too sorry for the Poles, or at least for their government, when their nation was invaded in 1939. The Poles were just as anti-Semitic as the Germans, the only difference being that the Germans were better at it, and the Polish government was only marginally less fascist than that of Germany. The French and British governments had no illusions about Poland, and right up to the last in their dealings with the Poles they urged conciliation. But the Poles do not do conciliation.

It is apparent that the German government, or at least Hitler, did not believe that the French or the British would go to war over Poland, despite their guarantees. They had reluctantly acquiesced in everything else that Germany had done to nullify Versailles, so why should they bother with Poland, where neither country had a vital interest? Whatever the British might say in public, Hitler had no designs on the British Empire, Britain was a maritime power not a European one, and there was no reason why the interests of the two nations could not coexist. The big difference, of course, was that the British, and to a lesser extent the French, could justify appeasement by telling themselves that Germany was only enlarging her borders to incorporate Germans, and that Versailles was unrealistic anyway. Once Germany gobbled up the rump of Czechoslovakia, there was no longer an excuse. The British probably had no great concerns about what the Germans might do to the USSR, but they realized that France could not defend herself against a Germany that had defeated Russia, and in that case a German Europe would very quickly become a threat to Britain. It was very much in the British interest to maintain a reasonable balance of forces in Europe, and the whole aim of British foreign policy in the 1930s, including appeasement, was to maintain that equilibrium without going to war. When it became apparent that Germany could not be dissuaded from further expansion at the expense of her neighbours, war was inevitable.

The German reason for attacking Poland was partly to reduce the Polish Corridor and regain Danzig, but also to clear the way for an eventual expansion to the East, the search for *Lebensraum*. Germany's demands on Poland were not unreasonable – indeed, by Hitlerian standards they were mild: the return of the (unquestionably German) free city of Danzig and a rail link across the Polish Corridor over which Germany would have extra-territorial rights. Poland refused (the British urged acceptance), presumably because she feared being seen as acceding to German demands but not to Russian, or perhaps just through bloody-mindedness. To Germany, the obvious riposte was to take by force what could not be achieved by threats. The German plans for Poland, *Fall Weiss*,* dated January 1939, laid down purely defensive deployments, but in revised orders issued by the *Ober-kommando der Wehrmacht* (OKW, 'Supreme Headquarters Armed Forces') in March and April the operation became an offensive. The invasion would be carried out by two army groups, Army Group North with the Third and Fourth Armies and Army Group South with the Eighth, Tenth and Fourteenth.

Those who are familiar with military organizations need not read this paragraph. But for those who do not have a copy of the *Staff Officer's Handbook* instantly available, the creation of military organizations is affected by two main factors: how many men one commander can reasonably command (and what one headquarters can realistically deal with), and the need for the unit or formation to be structured and equipped to carry out whatever task may be assigned to it. Clearly one general directly commanding 200,000 individual soldiers would not work, nor would a unit equipped solely with snowshoes be of much use in the desert. An organizational pyramid is therefore developed in order that the highest level of command passes on its wishes to the next level down and so on, with each grouping having the assets it needs to fulfil its role. In the German army of 1939 the

---

*'Case White'. The British title their plans 'Operation…', the Germans use 'Case…'.

basic brick of the infantry was the ten-man section, of eight riflemen and two machine-gunners manning one machine-gun, the whole commanded by a non-commissioned officer (NCO) of corporal-equivalent rank. Three sections plus a 50mm mortar made up a platoon, which was commanded (usually) by a senior NCO. A company, commanded by an officer of lieutenant's or captain's rank, had three platoons and a support platoon of three machine-guns and three anti-tank rifles. The next level up was the battalion with three companies and a support company of eight machine-guns and six 81mm mortars. Three battalions plus an anti-tank artillery company, a field artillery company, a motorized reconnaissance company, an engineer platoon and a signals platoon formed a regiment, usually commanded by a colonel. A division had three infantry regiments, an artillery regiment, a reconnaissance battalion, an engineer battalion, a motorized anti-tank battalion and a transport battalion, and was commanded by a major-general or lieutenant-general. A corps had two or more divisions, plus its own supporting and logistic units, and was commanded by a lieutenant-general or general, while an army had two or more corps, plus its own support and logistic units, and was commanded by a general or colonel-general. Two or more armies formed an army group, commanded by a colonel-general or field marshal. In the infantry division outlined above, the field artillery and most of the logistic transport was horse-drawn and would remain so for the duration of the war. There were also motorized divisions, armoured divisions, light divisions and alpine or mountain divisions, but the basic structure was the same.

All armies were, in principle, structured along similar lines, but, while the British regarded their machine-guns as being there to support the riflemen, German riflemen were there to support the machine-gun, and the Germans had much more anti-tank artillery than anyone else. Something that the Germans, unlike their opponents, were very good at was rapid reorganization when confronted by a task which the basic division or regiment was not ideally structured to carry out. A battle group (*Kampf-gruppe*) could rapidly be thrown together from assets needed for the particular task and be sent into action instantly, despite the component parts never having worked together previously. The Germans could do this, not only because their officers and NCOs were well trained, but also because there was a common doctrine throughout the army in which everyone was trained. Thus, an infantry battalion sent off to work with a tank battalion they had never met before knew how to communicate with the tanks, how to move with them and what to do when tanks or infantry came under fire. The US Army paid lip service to flexibility and rapid reorganization but rarely managed it, while the British had little or no common doctrine and relied on battalion, regimental or brigade standard operating procedures, which could vary greatly depending upon the battalion, regiment or brigade.

The German plan for Case White envisaged the Third Army attacking south from East Prussia towards Warsaw and linking up with the Fourth Army, which would attack eastwards from northern Germany, cutting off the Polish Corridor. From Army Group South, Eighth Army would attack north-east towards Warsaw, while Tenth would drive due east and cut Poland in half. Fourteenth Army, attacking from Slovakia, would push north to capture the fortified area of Lvov, and also prevent the Polish forces from retreating into Hungary. To provide an excuse for German aggression, the SS would arrange for 150 concentration camp prisoners to be dressed in Polish uniforms and forced to stage an attack on German frontier positions. They would be repelled, as would a similar faked attack on a German radio station at Gleiwitz.

Poland had originally ordered partial mobilization in March, shortly after the German occupation of Prague, the Czech capital. This had adversely affected already near-to-breaking-point relations with Germany, and sparked off a number of incidents which were coyly referred to as 'collective indiscipline' – mutinies – in the Polish Army, mainly involving conscripts of German origin. On 19 May 1939 the French agreed that, in the event of a German attack on Poland, France would attack Germany on the fifteenth day after mobilization.

By August the Poles were well aware that they were under threat; the only question was when the invasion would come. The Polish thinking saw Germany as the potential aggressor and the intention was to deploy the bulk of the Polish Army against her, leaving very little on the eastern border with the USSR. Instead of trading ground and using the natural defence lines of rivers and mountains, the Poles planned to fight on the frontier. On 28 August full mobilization, including the calling up of the militia (the equivalent of the TA or National Guard), was ordered for 30 August, but on the 29th this was cancelled after British and French protests that mobilization would be seen by Germany as provocation. On 30 August the Poles listened to their own, wiser, counsels and cancelled their cancellation, ordering mobilization for the 31st. The result of all this packs on, packs off nonsense was that, when the attack did come, only about one third of the Polish Army was in its battle positions – which, incredibly, were left to individual army commanders to decide upon.

The Germans too had undergone several false starts. On 23 August Hitler had ordered A-Day* for 26 August, and on the morning of 25 August this had been confirmed, with a jump-off time of 0430 hours, only for the order to be countermanded late that evening, although mobilization and the preparatory build-up were to continue. General Wagner, the German Quartermaster General, said that there was 'total irresolution and chaos in the chain of command',23 as well there might be when an operation of this size and complexity is suddenly halted. It seems that Hitler's irresolution was caused by Italy declining to play and by last-minute British attempts to get both parties to the conference table. On 31 August OKW ordered subordinate army groups that zero hour would now be first light on 1 September.

On paper the relative strengths of the two protagonists' infantry show little disparity: forty German infantry divisions† to thirty-seven Polish, but seven of the German infantry divisions were motorized or partly motorized, and they deployed five armoured divisions against the Poles' one brigade, or 3,600 armoured fighting vehicles against 750, 6,000 artillery pieces against 4,000 and, crucially, nearly 2,000 modern aircraft against 900 mostly obsolete ones. True, the Poles could field eleven horsed cavalry brigades against the Germans' one, but the role of cavalry in this campaign did not go far beyond escort and outpost duties and route reconnaissance. But it was not just numbers and technology that counted. The Germans had far better communications; they also had units organized for the tasks they were given and a tactical doctrine that worked and that all understood. The Poles were brave and patriotic, slow and inflexible. By the end of the first week, only one Polish army had not been broken into separate units, and most of those had been surrounded. A counter-attack on 10 September by the one Polish army still intact only led to its own encirclement and by the end of the second

---

*Angrifftag or 'Attack Day', the equivalent of the British D-Day or the French J-Jour, the day on which a particular operation is to start and from which all timings start (i.e. D – 1 the day before the operation begins, D + 1 the day after and so on).

†Including three Slovak divisions. The Germans also fielded a number of Frontier regiments and two Waffen SS Standarten (brigades).

week the Polish defence had collapsed with only detached pockets holding out. When the Soviet Union invaded eastern Poland on 17 September, in accordance with the secret clauses of the Russo-German pact, there was no hope left. Warsaw surrendered on 27 September and, although sporadic fighting went on until 6 October, that was the end of Polish resistance. Around 120,000 Poles had been killed, 70,000 fighting Germans and 50,000 the Russians, and probably another 300,000–400,000 wounded. Around a million had been taken prisoner, while perhaps 150,000 had escaped abroad. Britain had declared war at 1100 hours on 3 September, with France following at 1700 the same day, but actually did nothing – indeed, there was nothing that either country could do.

The French and British strategic viewpoints differed: as the French saw it, Russia's strict neutrality would have forced the Germans to keep a sizeable proportion of the Wehrmacht in the East to guard against a Russian attack. It was now apparent that Russia and Germany intended to divide Poland between them and that Russia was securing Germany's back door. The best German units would now be available to attack France and the traditional British weapon of blockade would be nullified by supplies of food and raw materials supplied to Germany by Russia. The British build-up in France was moving far too slowly and the concern was that Germany might attack before the Allies were ready. The French produced all sorts of hare-brained schemes to counter Russian influence, including invading southern Europe via Salonika (neutral territory, but never mind) and bombing Russian oil fields. Quite how this would have reduced Russian support for Germany is unclear; indeed, it would have been much more likely to increase it, and in any event the British, with far more confidence in the capabilities of the French Army than the French had themselves, would have none of it.

For their part, the British had briefly considered whether their guarantee to Poland created a legal requirement to declare war on the Soviet Union after the latter's invasion of eastern Poland, but the Attorney General, the senior British law officer, gave it as his considered opinion that it did not. No doubt another attorney general would have been found had the existing one come to a different opinion. Contrary to the French view, the British did not believe that Russo-German amity would survive and urged the need to delay as long as possible in order to give time for the build-up of land forces and for the blockade to work. Eventually, thought the British, German industry would be unable to sustain a war economy for long and, provided enough time was bought, the regime would become enfeebled and either collapse from within or be toppled by a modest Allied invasion.

The Germans, or at least Hitler, rather agreed with the French. He was concerned that British industry could out-build Germany* and wanted a quick resolution of the war in the West prior to embarking on what he had clearly set out in his political manifesto, *Mein Kampf* – the establishment of living space for Germany in the East. Hitler originally asked for an attack on the West for early November 1939, but the general staff persuaded him that the Wehrmacht, particularly the army, could not finish one war and go straight into another. For an army that for a generation had not fired a shot in anger, other than when putting down civil unrest, the success of the Polish campaign was little short of superb, but, hardly surprisingly, not everything had gone according to plan. There were faults in some weapon systems, and much equipment had been lost or damaged and was only partly replaced by captured Polish equipment of inferior quality. Three hundred tanks, 370 artillery pieces and 560 aircraft had been destroyed and, perhaps most seriously of all, 11,000 German soldiers had been killed, with another 30,000 wounded, casualties being disproportionately heavy amongst NCOs and junior officers. While German staff work and reaction to changing situations had been superb, the organization of the armoured divisions was unwieldy – there were too many units within the division to be coordinated and controlled by one headquarters. Equipment had to be replaced, organizations adapted and numbers made up before the army could turn its attention westwards. Hitler's half-hearted peace offering to the Allies received scant attention and the winter of 1939 and the spring of 1940 became known as the Phoney War, when the Allies concentrated on building up their strength while the Germans restructured the Wehrmacht for the next phase of the war.

In the part of Poland conquered by Germany, the areas inhabited by ethnic Germans or considered to be vital to German security were annexed to Germany. The rest was established as the General Government. Military control swiftly gave way to a civil administration with various occupation elements pursuing different agenda. On the one hand, the NSDAP party officials and members of the General SS followed racial theories while attempting to ensure that no Polish individuals or organizations could mount

---

*In that he was right: French and British production of aircraft and tanks in late 1939 and early 1940 far outstripped that of Germany.

any effective resistance to German occupation. Hence Jews were deported from the portion of Poland now incorporated into Germany to the General Government, and Polish army officers, members of the nobility, intellectuals, teachers and writers found themselves imprisoned, while the Roman Catholic Church found its monasteries closed and its influence severely curtailed. Atrocities followed, particularly where disaffected Poles attempted to sabotage German infrastructure or assassinate German officials. On the other hand, there was the German Foreign Office, which saw the damage that such behaviour was doing to Germany's standing in the world and attempted to curb it. Senior Nazis who had actually to govern on the ground also saw the folly of antagonizing the population and urged restraint. The army confined itself to protesting against misbehaviour, recording and reporting it. Little was ever done, although sufficient mitigation was imposed to make the area governable, at least until the Warsaw Rising much later in the war.

Elsewhere, the Russo-German pact had accepted that the Baltic States – Estonia, Latvia, Lithuania and Finland – lay within the Soviet sphere of influence, despite their Germanic racial origins, and in the case of the first three Russia had no great difficulty in establishing hegemony over them. Finland was a different matter, and, when a Russian demand for extra-territorial concessions in the Karelian isthmus and ice-free ports was refused, the Russians attacked. The Winter War, which lasted from 30 October 1939 until 13 March 1940, saw the Red Army (3 million strong) in their initial foray receive a very bloody nose from the Finnish Army (126,000 strong including the NAAFI manager and the guardroom cat) under the splendid seventy-two-year-old Marshal Carl Mannerheim. The British and the French saw an opportunity to help the plucky little underdog Finns and, using this as a cover, do something to prevent the Germans from importing iron ore from Sweden, which was neutral, albeit in Germany's favour. The problem lay in the fact that the only safe route for Allied troops going to Finland was via Norway and Sweden. While the Norwegians might be sympathetic to British wishes, they understandably turned down a request for transit rights on the very sensible grounds that to grant them would only provoke the Germans. The only practical help given to the Finns came in the form of fifty-three aircraft of the RAF, which were swiftly removed when it became apparent that Russia was about to win.

If the Allies could not use troop movements to Finland to interfere with German imports from Scandinavia, then other methods had to be found. Iron ore was exported via the Swedish port of Luleå in the Baltic, which the Allied navies could not get at, and by rail to the Norwegian port of Narvik, which they could. Luleå froze in the winter whereas Narvik was ice-free all the year round. There was a snag. Norway was neutral and German cargo ships could sail from Narvik all the way down to German ports without ever entering international waters and thus making themselves a legitimate target. However, as Machiavelli so wisely said, necessity makes virtue and the British were quite happy to breach international law if there was a reasonable chance of getting away with it. Plans were drawn up to occupy Norway if there was any sign of a German invasion of that country and or Denmark. As it happened, the Germans were already convinced that the Allies harboured ill-intent towards Norway, and had indeed an invasion plan of their own, Case North, which, entirely coincidentally, they activated on 6 April 1940, the very day that the British government informed the governments of Norway and Sweden that the Royal Navy would lay mines in Norwegian waters.

If the history faculties at universities were to run a module on how not to conduct a military campaign, then they should forget Darius' crossing of the Hellespont, McClellan in the Peninsula, the First Afghan War and General Galtieri's invasion of the Falkland Islands. They need look no farther than the Norwegian campaign of 1940, for as complete and utter cock-ups go it would be difficult to better. There was a perfectly good Allied plan to invade Norway, either to forestall a German occupation or to snaffle the raw materials coming from Sweden, which involved four battalions of infantry with all their equipment on board troopships with an escort of the First Cruiser Squadron at Rosyth ready to sail. The French would also provide a contingent composed mainly of the French Foreign Legion and Polish troops who had escaped from Poland and were now under French command. The problem was that this perfectly good plan was not followed.

On 8 April the Royal Navy began to lay mines in Norwegian waters off Narvik and the German navy put to sea towards Norway. On 9 April German paratroopers dropped on Denmark and the German navy landed troops in Copenhagen. The Danes very quickly accepted their lot. But the British wrongly interpreted the German naval activity as indicating that the Kriegsmarine was trying to break out into the North Sea, and the Royal Navy reverted to headless-chicken mode. The troops embarked for Norway were hastily disembarked, leaving their equipment on board, while various ships went rushing off hither and thither chasing a breakout that was not happening. By the time it was accepted that the German naval activity was directed at Norway and the ships chasing a non-existent breakout had returned to port, it was too late to pre-empt the German landings, which had got three divisions ashore in the first wave with another three following up. The admiral commanding the Royal Navy's Home Fleet decided to attack Bergen, a plan vetoed by the Admiralty in London, but then un-vetoed again. An aircraft carrier was sent off with no fighter aircraft for self-protection, and all sorts of naval vessels continued to rush about to no apparent purpose. Eventually, it was decided to send troops to Norway, although neither the army and navy nor the politicians were at one as to what this might achieve.

After much debate and interminable conferences, made worse by the refusal of the War Cabinet to meet before 0830 hours in the morning, it was agreed that two brigades, one regular and one Territorial, would be sent to Narvik, and eventually, on 11 April, the convoy sailed. Now there was order, counter-order and disorder. While still at sea, the convoy was ordered to split, with one brigade diverted to Namsos, 200 miles to the south of Narvik. This meant that the Territorials landing at Namsos would be without their anti-aircraft artillery and without their brigade commander, who was with the force commander in the leading ship heading for Narvik. Meanwhile, the naval commander was changed halfway through the approach, adding to the already strained relations between army and navy, each of whose commanders had been given different instructions. More and more senior officers got involved and at one stage there were four generals commanding what was barely enough for one.

When the landings did eventually take place at Namsos, the Territorials were no match for the Germans, who simply rounded them up, and the landing at Narvik would not take place until 28 May, by which time it had been decided to call the operation off, and even then Narvik was captured not by the British but by a combined force of Norwegians, French and Poles. Between 4 and 8 June the Royal Navy carried out one of its more traditional roles – evacuating a beaten army to be used somewhere else – and took off 29,000 Allied troops. Such was the confusion, chaos and incompetence of the Norwegian campaign that even the politicians noticed and there was a most almighty row in Parliament, leading to the resignation of the prime minister, Neville Chamberlain, and the propelling to supreme office of

Winston Churchill as head of a coalition government,* which, given that Churchill was largely responsible for the shambles of Norway, was, to say the least, somewhat ironic.

Winston Churchill has cult status in the United Kingdom. He was the man who won the war, the man who stood up against the appeasers, the only man who saw that Hitler was a threat, the only politician who as an ex-soldier himself understood the military imperatives. It is almost impossible, even now, to criticize Churchill without attracting vituperation and abuse – as he himself said, 'History will be kind to me, for I shall write it.' And so he did and so it is.

There can be little doubt that Churchill's rhetoric was inspirational, that his speeches in the dark days of 1940 and 1941 contributed hugely to the British people's determination to stick it out, that it was Churchill's resolution that brought it home to the government of the United States that Britain was worth supporting, that he kept alive hope in the peoples of occupied countries. Churchill had entered the Royal Military College Sandhurst in 1893 and was commissioned into fourth Hussars two years later. In his four years as a regular officer before leaving the army to go into politics, he never commanded a soldier in the field but rather used his mother's connections to get himself attached to interesting campaigns where he could earn money as a war correspondent and write books. He was an observer with the Spanish Army in Cuba for six months, reporting for the *Daily Graphic*, accompanied General Sir Bindon Blood's Malakand Field Force on a punitive foray on the North-West Frontier of India in 1897 for the *Daily Telegraph* (and an excellent book), wangled a place in Kitchener's army in 1898 in the Sudan, where, now representing the *Morning Post*, he took part in the unnecessary and incompetently executed charge of the 21st Lancers at Omdurman (another excellent book), left the army in 1899 and failed to get elected to Parliament. He then went off to the South African War for the *Morning Post* again (two quite good books), got captured and escaped in somewhat dubious circumstances and did eventually get elected to Parliament. He was a Conservative Member of Parliament in 1900, defected to the Liberals in 1904 and turned his coat yet again when he reverted to being a Conservative in 1924. As First Lord of the Admiralty

---

*For a full account of the sorry debacle of the Norwegian caper, see my *Blood, Sweat and Arrogance*.

(navy minister), he took much of the blame for the failure of the Gallipoli campaign in 1915–16, and, when his position as a government minister became untenable, he took himself off to France and, improbably, was given command of a New Army battalion, Sixth Royal Scots Fusiliers.* That not a single man in that battalion was killed in the three and a half months at the front had nothing to do with Churchill's skill and a great deal to do with the battalion's location – south of the Ypres Salient, while the real action was well to the south, astride the Somme and at Verdun. Unable to keep away from politics for long, Churchill soon tired of soldiering and resigned. As a government minister again, in 1919 he was in the Cabinet that propounded the Ten-Year Rule (see Chapter 1); in 1921 he argued vehemently in favour of battleships and against aircraft carriers; in 1925 he opposed the construction of defences at the Singapore naval base; in 1927 he demanded cuts in the naval estimates; in 1928 he proposed that the Ten-Year Rule become a rolling assumption rather than being reviewed each year (carried); in 1929 he forced cuts in the army estimates and in 1930 stopped the army obtaining more tanks, before resigning in 1931 in protest over plans to prepare India for Dominion status.

Without office, but as a Privy Councillor and a member of various committees not without influence, he became the leading, or at least the noisiest, opponent of appeasement and when war was declared in 1939 he was recalled to the Cabinet as, again, First Lord of the Admiralty. According to Churchill, a signal was sent from the Admiralty to all ships: 'Winston is back'. No trace of this signal has ever been found and nobody but Churchill has ever admitted to seeing it. One cynic has suggested that, if it was ever sent, it was in exasperation rather than jubilation. An armed forces minister is supposed to oversee the broad direction of the service of which he is the political head. He is not there to usurp the functions of the admirals, generals or air marshals, who have spent a lifetime preparing to wage war. Churchill, who always fancied himself a great strategist and tactician, took to ordering individual ships about and behaving as if he was the admiral commanding the Home Fleet – and indeed every fleet. The results were near

*Field Marshal Sir John French, the Commander-in-Chief of the British Expeditionary Force, had promised Churchill the command of a brigade, but by 1916 French had been superseded by the much harder-headed General Sir Douglas Haig, and in any case, while the government was prepared, just, to stomach an acting Lieutenant-Colonel Churchill, it drew the line at his being a brigadier-general.

disastrous. Aircraft carriers were sent off to hunt for submarines without escort vessels; destroyers and battleships were sent hither and thither with Churchill personally deciding where each ship should go. The impression was one of great and purposeful activity: the reality was chaos and muddle. It was Churchill who interpreted the German naval activity preparatory to invading Norway as an attempt to break out, and Churchill who insisted that the British convoy en route to Narvik should be split. When it was eventually clear even to him that the Norwegian expedition had failed, he argued (fortunately unsuccessfully) that the remnants of the Territorial brigade should remain in Norway with instructions to wage guerrilla warfare.

As prime minister, Churchill sacked generals and admirals who would not tell him what he wanted to hear and insisted on involving British forces in adventures that should never have been contemplated. After a meeting on 8 May 1943, General Sir Alan Brooke, who had become Chief of the Imperial General Staff (professional head of the British Army) after Churchill had sacked his predecessor, General Sir John Dill, for refusing to pander to the prime minister's whims, recorded in his diary: 'A thoroughly unsatisfactory meeting at which he [Churchill] again showed that he cannot grasp the relationship of various theatres of war to each other. He always gets carried away by the one he is examining and in prosecuting it is prepared to sacrifice most of the others. I have never, in the one and a half years that I have worked with him, succeeded in making him review the war as a whole and to relate the importance of the various fronts to each other.'[24] Meanwhile, Beatrice Webb, in her diary, thought him 'egotistical, bumptious, shallow-minded and reactionary, but with a certain personal magnetism, great pluck and some originality, not of intellect but of character. More of the American speculator than the English aristocrat.'

Churchill may have been the 'man who won the war', as was claimed in the 1945 election campaign, but he was also the man who nearly lost it by refusing to listen to sound advice and by allowing his emotions to rule his head. Had Churchill confined his activities to inspiring the people of Britain and of Britain's allies, and not tried to run the war single-handedly, then his iconic status might be justified, but his entry in the *Oxford Dictionary of National Biography* by Paul Addison probably has him absolutely right:

> Among his contemporaries, only the most narrow-minded denied
> him great qualities: volcanic energy, physical and mental courage,

eloquence and vision, humanity and wit. Almost all conceded that he possessed elements of genius. But he was, they concluded, a genius *manqué* whose more brilliant qualities were offset by serious flaws: supreme egotism, an adventurer's love of daring but perilous courses of action, poor judgement of men, erratic changes of course, susceptibility to rhetoric and flights of the imagination.

As it was, on 10 May 1940, a month after their initial landings in Norway and Denmark, the Germans launched *Fall Gelb*, Case Yellow, the attack on Holland, Belgium, Luxembourg and France. In 1936 Belgium had withdrawn from her treaty relationship with France, whereby the latter guaranteed Belgium's territorial integrity, in the naive belief that a declaration of neutrality in any future European war would be enough to ensure that belligerents left her alone. Unfortunately, if you are a Belgian, anyone wanting to invade Western Europe will inevitably choose to trample through your front garden – it is an inescapable fact of geography – and, while any threat from the East might well have dissuaded Germany from adventures in the West, in 1940 there was, thanks to the Russo-German pact, no threat from the East. It was never supposed that the Maginot Line would be impossible to breach, but it was hoped that it would hold up an attacker (and presumably a German attacker) long enough for French mobilization to take place and for a counter-stroke to be mounted. The French were not incapable of working out that the Germans would be unlikely to attack the Line directly; they would instead come through Holland, Belgium and Luxembourg, where, in order not to compromise Belgian neutrality, the Line did not run. There would, in other words, be a rerun of 1914. Then the Schlieffen Plan had failed – there were not enough troops, the Kaiser's army could not march fast enough and the logistic chain could not keep up – but now the German army could move on wheels and tracks and it was supported by the Luftwaffe.

After some very secret discussions with the Dutch and the Belgians, neither of whom wished to provoke German aggression, it was agreed that a German invasion of those countries would trigger the French Plan D with Breda Variant. This would see the French advance along the Channel coast as far as Breda to link up with the Dutch and secure the estuary of the River Scheldt; the Belgians would hold along the Albert Canal and then withdraw to the River Dyle from Antwerp and Louvain; the British would hold the Dyle from Louvain down to Wavre, where 125 years previously they had held off Napoleon Bonaparte during a campaign in which the Prussians had been their allies; and the French would again defend as far as the northern end of the Maginot Line. For their part, the Germans postponed the start date for Case Yellow twenty-nine times, and, had it not been for Hitler and some imaginative German staff officers, the Allied assessment of German intentions would have been about right, for the original Case Yellow was indeed not very different from a motorized Schlieffen.

The military intention was to seize enough of Holland, Belgium and northern France to provide air bases for an eventual attack on England and to protect the economically vital Ruhr, considered (rightly) to be a priority target for RAF bombers; political ends would include the return of Alsace and part of Lorraine to Germany and frontier adjustments. To Hitler this was not sufficiently decisive: he wanted more, including an all-out defeat and occupation of Holland, Belgium and France. At the same time, Lieutenant-General Erich von Manstein, Chief of Staff of Colonel-General Gerd von Rundstedt's Army Group A, who thought the whole plan was pedestrian and unimaginative, was seeking a way to achieve rapid results by capitalizing on what the German army was good at – all-arms cooperation, rapid redeployment, flexibility and communications – while compensating for its weaknesses in numbers and quality of armoured vehicles. Manstein was convinced that the answer was to send one army group (B, commanded by Colonel-General Foder von Bock) into Holland and Belgium, which would attract the weight of the Allies north, and then to send a second army group (Rundstedt's A) in a narrow armoured thrust through the Ardennes forest in southern Belgium, with the aim of cutting the Allied forces in two, while a third army group (C, commanded by Colonel-General Ritter von Leeb) would take on the Maginot Line to fix its defenders (around 400,000 men) in position and prevent them from being used elsewhere. Once the French, British and Belgian armies in the north were destroyed, the Germans would regroup and send Army Groups A and B south to deal with the French armies in central and southern France, thus also outflanking the Maginot Line. Initially, Manstein's ideas got nowhere: the generals were trying to persuade their political masters that a negotiated settlement was preferable to all-out war, but one of Hitler's army liaison officers visiting Army Group A was lobbied by Manstein and took the plan back to OKW and showed it to Hitler, who, having now told his generals that the shilly-shallying was to cease, ordered that the Manstein plan be adopted.

The stalemate of the so-called Phoney War had allowed both sides to build up their strengths. The German army pushed ahead with mechanization while the French completed their mobilization and the British moved more troops to France and to the British Expeditionary Force (BEF). Once the French had completed mobilization, they had available in Europe fifty-one regular and thirty-seven reserve divisions. Of these, ten divisions were on the Italian border and twelve were in fortresses on the Maginot Line, leaving sixty-five divisions for operations. The French Commander-in-Chief, the sixty-eight-year-old General Maurice-Gustave Gamelin, was convinced that the French Army was not yet ready for offensive operations, particularly if the Rhine and the German defensive West Wall were to be negotiated, and to the great disappointment of the Poles authorized only very minor, and ineffective, incursions across Germany's western frontier. Gamelin had cultivated Daladier, the leftist French prime minister who with Chamberlain had signed the Munich agreement in September 1938, but Daladier resigned in March 1940 because of his government's refusal to back him in supporting the Finns against the Soviet Union in the Winter War of 1939–40, and Paul Reynaud, his successor, had little confidence in Gamelin. The two men's relationship went from suspicion and distrust to outright hostility.

On 10 May 1940, *A-Tag* for *Fall Gelb*, the Germans had available 131 infantry divisions and ten armoured divisions, while their opponents had 138 (ninety-seven French, twenty Belgian, thirteen British and eight Dutch) infantry, three armoured and seven cavalry divisions. Even if we discount one of the British divisions locked up with the French in the Maginot Line, and the Dutch and the Belgians on the grounds that they were supposedly neutral and there had been no, or very little, joint planning, the infantry numbers were still reasonably even. The Germans fielded 2,445 tanks, of which only 627 were Panzer Mks III and IV while the rest were either Mk I (armed only with machine-guns), Mk II (with an ineffective 20mm cannon) or inferior captured Czech models. The French had 3,063 tanks and the British 310, not only a numerical advantage but a qualitative superiority too, as 625 of the French tanks were the Somua and Char B, both proper tanks packing a good punch and as well armoured as the German Mks III and IV. All things being equal, the Allies should have had no problem in holding off a German offensive.

All things, however, were not equal. It was the French and British press that first described the German tactics as *Blitzkrieg*, lightning war, and that is certainly what it looked like to those on the receiving end. But there was nothing magic about *Blitzkrieg* and the Germans did not invent it. *Blitzkrieg* was simply a refined version of all-arms cooperation where the infantry, armour, artillery, engineers and aircraft all worked together to produce shock on the battlefield. It was not designed just to kill, although of course it did, but to get inside its opponent's decision-making cycle, to unbalance him, to get him on the back foot and keep him there. It depended on all the various components trusting each other, the use of initiative by junior commanders, a sound understanding of battle drills by all involved and good communications. It was invented, if such a thing can be invented, by the British in the first war, when their last great offensive, one that forced a German surrender, jumped off with the Battle of Amiens on 8 August 1918. Then the infantry, working closely with tanks and with artillery close up, stormed through the German defences. The engineers were following, ready to bridge rivers and destroy obstacles, while aircraft flew overhead in support of the ground troops or ranged further afield, attacking enemy stores dumps, railheads, forming-up places and communications. Strongpoints were bypassed – they could be dealt with later – and the infantry poured through weak points identified by themselves, the tanks or airborne observers. Yet, and the point bears repetition, it was the defeated Germans who had analysed the lessons of Amiens, honed them and incorporated them into their own tactical doctrine. It was not that the British and the French did not understand the principles of *Blitzkrieg*, simply that the Germans had prepared more thoroughly for it and proved much better at it. By the time the French were able to react to what the Germans were doing in May and June 1940, it was too late – the battle had moved on and the situation had changed irrevocably.

The Allies enjoyed superiority in both quantity and, for the last time in the war, quality of tanks. But the Germans concentrated theirs and made full use of armour's ability to move fast and deliver a decisive blow, whereas French doctrine was to use far too many tanks to support the infantry, with the result that they became little more than gun platforms on tracks. There were also far too few genuinely mobile armoured divisions in the French Army, although that commanded by the then Colonel de Gaulle, later to become a major irritant to both Churchill and Roosevelt, did as well as it could; it was, however, short of infantry and, when it went on the offensive, could not be reinforced. As for the British, while it was true that theirs was the only army that had (almost) evicted the equine from the battlefield,* most of the infantry still had to march – years of neglect and underfunding could not be overcome in the mere twelve months since rearmament had begun. And anyway, British doctrine was largely irrelevant since the BEF had only a few real tanks† with a two-pounder gun rather than a machine-gun and a reasonable thickness of armour.

In both numbers and performance of aircraft, the Germans were also well ahead. The Luftwaffe was a modern, tactical air force, structured for just this sort of short, sharp campaign, while most of the French aircraft were obsolescent and the British – wisely, as it turned out – were not prepared to commit their bomber force at this stage and held back most of their fighters for the air defence of the UK.

* * *

Contrary to what is invariably stated in saloon-bar discussions, nobody had ever said that tanks could not come through the Ardennes, a range of.hills and forests lying between Luxembourg, southern Belgium and the River Meuse around the French city of Sedan. Moving tanks and wheeled vehicles through the Ardennes was not easy then and it would not be easy now but it was and is perfectly possible. What people did think and did say was that it would not be possible to get all the various components of a striking force through the Ardennes rapidly enough to be effective before the defenders tumbled to what was going on and reacted to it. They were very wrong. The Germans had carried out a thorough reconnaissance of possible routes through the woods, sometimes with staff officers in civilian clothes cycling along them, and in a marvel of traffic control they sent Panzer Group von Kleist, with 134,000 men and 42,000 vehicles, wheeled and tracked, sixty miles from the German

---

*As the foul winter of 1939–40 had made some of the French roads impassable to motor vehicles, some Indian Army pack transport companies, with mules, had been brought in.

†The British had a handful of A9 and A10 cruiser tanks with a two-pounder gun, and 7 Royal Tank Regiment (7 RTR) were armed with the A12 (Matilda Mk II), which had a two-pounder gun, 3.7 inches of frontal armour and a top speed of 15 mph. Because of its thickness of armour, the Matilda was very difficult to knock out and, had there been several hundred of them and had they been handled properly, the outcome of the Battle of France might have been different. But then, if there had been several hundred of them, the Germans might well not have attacked in the first place.

border to the Meuse in three days.[25] Ten days later, on 20 May, Major-General Erwin Rommel's 7 Panzer Division reached the Channel coast at Abbeville.

Meanwhile, in the north the German attack on Holland and Belgium precipitated the Allied advance into Belgium, although the Breda Variant never came off. The British and French took up a defensive position along the River Dyle, and the Belgians, their frontier fortresses taken out by German glider and parachute troops, were driven back from the Albert Canal. On 13 May the Dutch royal family and government were removed to England, and the Dutch Army surrendered on 15 May. As German attacks intensified, the Allies were pushed back from the Dyle to the River Scheldt and then to the River Lys. On 17 May, after a visit by Churchill intended, rather unfairly, to put a chilli up the collective bottom of the French, the prime minister, Reynaud, appointed the eighty-four-year-old Marshal Philippe Pétain, the hero of Verdun in 1916 and hitherto ambassador to Spain, as deputy prime minister, and on 19 May, when it was increasingly apparent to everyone* that the German thrust through the Ardennes was getting very near the coast and appeared unstoppable, Reynaud sacked Gamelin and replaced him with the seventy-three-year-old General Maxime Weygand. It is never a good idea to change commanders in mid-battle,† and there was now even more military constipation than before. The German gamble – if gamble it was – had come off: responding too late to the Ardennes spearhead, which had now become a spear, the Allies were incapable of cutting the German corridor and were now themselves cut in two, with the forces in the north unable to cooperate with those in the south. All that remained now was for the Germans to deal with the British, the Belgians and the northern French, and then to turn south into Central France.

One of the disadvantages of having a small professional army is that it will nearly always fight as part of a coalition, and the numerically smaller partner in that coalition will perforce have to follow the lead of the larger. The BEF could not operate independently, but only as part of an Allied army and a rather small part at that. (In fact, only five of the British divisions were

---

*Or, at least, nearly everyone. Churchill continued to send increasingly hysterical and completely unrealistic instructions on how to fight the battle. Fortunately for the BEF, its commander ignored them.

†I have avoided making reference to 'changing horses in mid-stream', one of the more ridiculous metaphors in our vocabulary. Why on earth would anyone want to get off one horse and on to another in the middle of a river?

regular, and four of the Territorial divisions were completely unfit for frontline service.) It rapidly became obvious to the British, or at least to the British on the spot – those in London, particularly those who did not wear uniform, took a little longer – that they had placed far too much faith in the supposed strengths of the French Army. Some French units were ill-disciplined and their morale was poor, only two French armoured divisions were up to strength and planning was pedestrian. Some French units were well led, their morale was excellent and they were highly effective: the trouble was that they were nearly always in the wrong place, and, when they were moved to where they could make a difference, once again it was too late.

As early as 15 May, Reynaud had told the British that the road to Paris was open and the battle was lost. Nevertheless, an Anglo-French counter-attack to the south against the German corridor was planned for 26 May, but on 25 May the Belgians had been forced to retreat, leaving a huge gap in the Allied line which, if not closed, would allow the Germans to get in behind the British and cut them off from the Channel ports. Throughout history any British army operating on the Continent, whether that of King Henry V, Marlborough, Wellington or John French, has had to consider the Channel ports and keep open the routes to and from them. It is through those ports that British armies are reinforced and resupplied, and through them that a beaten army can be removed by the Royal Navy to fight somewhere else another day. The British only had one army in 1940 and, if they broke it, they did not have another. The two divisions that would have taken part in the (almost certainly abortive) counter-attack were switched to close the gap. The commander of the BEF, General Viscount Gort VC, DSO, MC, did this entirely on his own initiative and contrary to orders from London, and on 26 May ordered a withdrawal towards Dunkirk, the only port from which an evacuation could take place and to which the roads were still open. By doing so, he saved the BEF as a cadre around which future armies could be built, and he got precious little thanks for it. Gort and his staff had been planning for a possible withdrawal since 19 May, and after it had begun the British government, now at last aware of the impending debacle, ordered Operation Dynamo, the evacuation of the BEF from Europe. At midnight on that same day Belgium surrendered – and, despite the opprobrium directed at the King of the Belgians by both the French and British, there was nothing else he could have done.

The naval staff had anticipated the requirement and, while on 27 May they lifted but 7,669 men from Dunkirk and the adjacent beaches, the daily total thereafter was 17,804, 47,310, 58,823 and, on 31 May, 68,014. On that day, Churchill was in Paris and announced that the evacuation was going satisfactorily. When questioned by the French as to how many of their men had been taken off, Churchill had to admit that it was only 15,000,* and thereafter the Royal Navy was told to take equal numbers of French and British troops. On 1 June, 64,429 were landed in England, on 2 June 26,256, on 3 June 26,746 and in the last lift, on 4 June, 26,175 French troops were taken off.[26] Managing two maritime operations at once – Dunkirk and Norway – the Royal Navy performed its traditional role impeccably, although at great cost. A total of 693 ships took part in the Dunkirk evacuation. Of them six destroyers, eight troop transporters, one sloop, five minesweepers, seventeen trawlers, one hospital ship and 188 smaller vessels were sunk, and about the same number damaged in some way. A total of 338,226 men were safely brought to England, 110,000 of them French. Only a nation with a powerful navy could have done it, and only an air force on which some interwar money had been spent could have kept the Luftwaffe away from the beaches for long enough to allow the navy to do it.

The British Army was helped in getting back to the beaches and defending the bridgehead by an order halting the advance of the German armour on 24 May. This had nothing to do with Hitler's not wanting the British to be humiliated, which might make them less willing to negotiate, but a perfectly sensible military requirement to replenish and repair armoured vehicles that had clocked up a huge amount of track mileage since the Battle of France began, and to prepare them for Phase Two, the advance south. The British were also helped by the willingness of the French to take on more and more of the defence of the embarkation areas, but, despite the ability of the British collective memory to turn failure into heroic myth, the much vaunted 'Miracle of Dunkirk' was a disaster for the British Army. Nearly all its heavy equipment – tanks, artillery pieces, vehicles – had to be left behind, the men had been on half-rations since 23 May, and discipline in some units broke down completely.

On 5 June, *Fall Rot*, 'Case Red', began and 119 German divisions began the conquest of France. On 11 June, after making quite sure that she would be on the winning side and be quite safe from retaliation, Italy declared war

---

* But the French high command had only given permission to their men to embark on 30 May.

on France and Britain. It turned out to be the wrong assessment on both counts, but was probably not unreasonable at the time. As it was, the Italians suffered a seriously bloody nose when they tried, and failed, to break through the Maginot Line in the south. An attempt by Churchill to send a second BEF in through the Normandy port of Cherbourg in a half-baked scheme to hold Brittany against the Germans was called off after wiser military counsel prevailed. On 14 June, German troops entered Paris, and the Royal Navy launched Operation Ariel, the evacuation of Allied troops from ports in Brittany and Normandy and on the Bay of Biscay. On 14 May the French premier, Reynaud, resigned in favour of Marshal Pétain. The 400,000 troops in the Maginot Line were never conquered, but once the Line was outflanked there was no point in fighting on and, on 18 June, France surrendered.

Now Britain stood alone. But in reality, of course, she was not alone: the forces of the Empire – India, Canada, Australia, New Zealand, South Africa and large parts of black Africa – were in the war, and, while their ability to contribute might now be small, it would grow, and grow very quickly.

4

INTERLUDE

BRITAIN AT WAR: MAY 1940–JUNE 1941

It was hardly a joyous homecoming. Most of the troops brought away from the beaches and the port of Dunkirk were landed at night, and in any case the arrival ports were closed to curious spectators. Met by ladies of the Women's Voluntary Service (WVS) and other support organizations and given tea and sandwiches, the men were whisked away in convoys of vehicles or specially chartered trains to whatever barracks were available, often many miles away from their home bases. Many of the men evacuated – perhaps most – thought of themselves as having been defeated, as indeed they had been, and the removal of personal weapons from some units arriving in England compounded the feelings of disgrace and humiliation. None of this could be allowed to leak to the civilian population, and the men were told in no uncertain terms that they were heroes, members of an undefeated army brought home to fight another day, while the newspapers made much of the 'Miracle of Dunkirk' and the supposedly heroic role of the 'little ships' – the privately owned yachts, motor launches and dinghies that were claimed to have brought back huge numbers of troops from the beaches. While the use of the 'little ships' to ferry troops from the beaches to the transport ships was useful, it was only a tiny effort compared with that of the Royal and Merchant Navies and they brought back to England only a tiny proportion of the total troops shifted, but the legend was what mattered – here was the ordinary Englishman mucking in, without being told, to play his part in fighting the beastly Hun.

On 4 June, Churchill made his now famous 'We shall fight on the beaches' speech in the House of Commons, making it clear that whatever happened (and this was two weeks before the French surrender) Britain would carry on the war, if necessary alone. It was stirring stuff but the reality was somewhat different. While nearly 340,000 soldiers had been brought safely back from

France, most of the 110,000 French soldiers had no desire whatsover to join de Gaulle's embryo Free French army and after the surrender availed themselves of the right to be repatriated, and in any case an army without weapons is of little use. Of the 2,794 artillery pieces sent to France with the BEF, only 322 had come back, of 68,678 vehicles, only 4,739 and, perhaps worst of all, of the 445 tanks of various sorts only nine real tanks (those with a gun as opposed to a machine-gun) had returned. The only troops fully equipped and up to strength in the United Kingdom were three infantry divisions and parts of a fourth, and two armoured brigades. The question was not whether Britain would continue the war but whether she could.

As early as 25 May the British Chiefs of Staff, the professional heads of the three services, had drawn up a paper examining the options for continuing the war should the BEF have to be withdrawn from Europe. Churchill had hoped to persuade the French to continue the war from their colonies, but it was becoming increasingly apparent that this was unlikely, and, once British troops began to be evacuated from Europe, inter-Allied rancour increased. The Chiefs of Staff thought that, if the German army could effect a landing in England, and could follow it up, then all would be lost: despite the propaganda about the gallant Local Defence Volunteers, renamed the Home Guard in August, and the more recent claims about the damage that the 'auxiliaries' could have caused an invader, there were not the assets to mount a credible defence. On the other hand, the Royal Navy and the Royal Air Force between them were probably strong enough to prevent a landing, so the main threat, thought the Chiefs, would be from air attacks on British ports, airfields, aircraft factories and radar installations. The effects of submarine warfare (which in the event was far more of a threat than anything from the air) was hardly mentioned. Britain could, therefore, hold out, provided that the RAF could maintain air superiority above the Channel. Within a year or so the Royal Navy's blockade would leave Germany short of food, while a shortage of raw materials would affect her weapons production. In an outburst of very wishful thinking, the paper opined that hunger, the collapse of the industrial base, revolt in the occupied countries and bombing by the RAF would force Germany's defeat in due course. One injection of sound realism was the caveat that all depended upon the full economic and financial support of the United States.

It is part of the received version of Britain's war that the possibility of peace negotiations with Germany was never even considered. Certainly there is no, or almost no, documentary evidence that the peace proposals in Hitler's speech of 21 July were examined seriously and Churchill's private secretary, John Colville, a civil servant on secondment from the Foreign Office, is admant that Churchill refused any reply, even a 'no', on the grounds that 'I am not on speaking terms with that man [Hitler].'[27] Not all agreed. There were those in government, including Lord Halifax, the Foreign Secretary, who thought that there would be no harm in at least finding out what the terms might be. At the risk of appearing to peddle conspiracy theories, it is inconceivable that some consideration was not given to what the German proposals were. You lose nothing by finding out what price you might have to pay for something. It may well be a price that you are not prepared to pay, in which case that is the end of the matter. If the British government did enter into any negotiations, any documents relating to them would, of course, have been destroyed, and, for reasons of public morale and British credibility abroad then, and Britain's perception of herself now, no mention of them could ever be allowed to leak out. Hitler's speech was deliberately vague as to what the settlement might be, but it would surely have demanded that the UK allow Germany a free hand in Europe and have required some British disarmament, particularly reductions in the Royal Navy. The carrot would presumably have been a promise not to interfere with the British Empire and perhaps a parcelling out between Britain and Germany of the French colonies. Those proposed terms, or anything similar, would have been as unacceptable then as they are in hindsight, and, if any negotiations did take place, they came to nothing. As Churchill observed at the time, by fighting on and being defeated the British would have got no worse terms than those that might then have been on the table.

German proposals and planning for an invasion of England were half-hearted. The planning staffs went through the motions, but not even the Luftwaffe's senior commanders, perhaps more politically indoctrinated than their counterparts in the army and navy, really thought it was a starter, barring some extraordinary stroke of luck. The German planners, military and political, had not given much thought to the inconvenience of Britain going to war over Poland and, having gone to war, holding out after defeat on the Continent. There had been virtually no strategic thought given to the possibility of British intransigence: German victory in the Battle of France was supposed to end any threat from the West and allow Germany to embark on her long-term aims, the subjugation of Russia and the acquisition of living room in the East. Hitler was well aware of the practical difficulties of achieving a landing in England and ordered that it should be a last resort. Ideally England should be defeated, or forced to agree to a compromise peace, by indirect methods. Major-General Alfred Jodl,* Chief of Operations in OKW, produced such a plan, which envisaged air attacks to destroy Britain's war economy, a submarine campign to cut off her imports, encouraging and assisting Spain to seize Gibraltar and Italy the Suez Canal, terror raids on the civilian population and then, as a final push, a landing. Hitler vetoed terror raids, at least for now, as he still thought Britain could be brought to the negotiating table and he hoped to drive a wedge between the British population and its leaders. As much for propaganda purposes within the armed services as for any practical reason, he did, however, order planning for an invasion of England – Case Sea Lion. If such an action was to have any chance of success, there were a number of conditions that had to be met. Firstly, there had to be sufficient shipping to transport a force large enough to not only effect a landing but hold it, expand it and then push on to London – initially estimated by the army to be 100,000 men with tanks, guns and vehicles in the first wave; secondly, the weather had to be favourable, which meant that the invasion would have to take place well before the autumn, after which Channel storms, often difficult to predict, were notorious; and finally, and most important of all, there must be German air superiority over the Channel and Southern England.

. All sorts of problems arose, partly because none of the planning staffs really believed in Sea Lion, and partly because of the inherent difficulties of a non-maritime power trying to mount a seaborne invasion. There were insufficient landing craft – indeed, none worthy of the name – and, while Rhine barges were collected and concentrated in ports along the Channel coast, there were not nearly enough (even if they had been suitable for crossing anything other than a mill pond, which they were not) and attempts to procure suitable vessels took up manufacturing capacity needed for other things. The navy could not meet the Luftwaffe's requirements for shipping to move the number of anti-aircraft guns they needed; nor could they sweep channels

---

*Fifty years old in 1940 and a major-general since 1939, Jodl came from a distinguished military family and headed the operations planning staff in OKW until the end of the war. More intelligent than his immediate superior, Field Marshal Keitel, he was well able to spot the flaws in some of Hitler's strategic and tactical ideas and, while not challenging the Führer openly, he often did persuade him to change his mind. In what this author considers a disgraceful travesty of justice, Jodl was tried as a war criminal by the Allies after the war and executed.

free of mines without the Royal Navy relaying them, and concealment of the men, vehicles and shipping from the RAF was well nigh impossible. A plan for an initial landing of thirteen divisions along 180 miles between Weymouth and Margate eventually became ten divisions along eighty miles between Worthing and Folkestone before being abandoned altogether.* Sea Lion was never, of course, officially cancelled, only postponed until further notice. Internal reasons of morale and infallibility demanded that the invasion plans stayed on the drawing board, but by September troops were beginning to be withdrawn from the proposed launch areas as German eyes turned east and south.

The one phase of Sea Lion that did happen was the attempt to gain air superiority, combined with attacks on Britain's industrial capacity and on civilian morale. What to the British are two separate battles – the Battle of Britain and the Blitz – was to the Germans one battle, with a change in emphasis along the way. The Battle of Britain began with a fighter vs fighter struggle when the RAF's Spitfires and Hurricanes took on the Luftwaffe's Bf 109s and 110s. To begin with, the Germans had 964 fighters available against the RAF's 507, but the statistics are deceptive. The twin-engined Bf 110, of which the Germans had 261, was not as manoeuvrable as either British aircraft and, even when flown by a very competent pilot (which it invariably was), would come off worse in a dogfight. The Bf 109 was a match for both the Spitfire and the Hurricane, but it had a limited range and could only spend a relatively short time in British airspace before having to return to base. Furthermore, British aircraft that crash-landed might be repairable, and if their pilots had survived intact they could rejoin the fray; German aircraft that went down were irrecoverable and their pilots either drowned or were captured.

Luftwaffe intelligence during the battle was often over-optimistic about British losses. It also took the Germans some time to realize that the British were using radar both to give early warning of the enemy's approach and to vector fighters into the attack, which meant that these aircraft only had to take off at the last minute and could maximize their time in combat. When the aim of luring the RAF into battle and defeating it failed, the Germans then concentrated on bombing airfields and aircraft factories. If they had

---

*In contrast, Operation Overlord, the Allied invasion of Normandy in June 1944, had an initial landing of five divisions along fifty miles.

succeeded in this phase, particularly if they had rendered airfields unusable, then air superiority would have been gained, but, while it was a close-run thing, they did not succeed. Targeting was too dispersed and, rather than going for the same objectives day after day or night after night, thus making it impossible for the British to repair their airfields, assembly lines or whatever, the Luftwaffe went for far too many targets, and, while damage was considerable, it was always repairable.

There were all sorts of reasons why the Battle of Britain, the attempt to destroy the RAF, turned into the Blitz, the attempt to destroy British morale. It may have happened partly by accident when an RAF raid that had gone off course bombed the suburbs of Stuttgart on 24 August 1940 (result: four German civilians dead), leading to a German attack with 100 bombers on London the following morning. It may have been the result of Hitler's relenting on his banning of terror raids, as the British claimed, or it may have been an attempt to destroy British industrial production, as the Germans claimed. The real reason for the bombing of civilian homes by the Luftwaffe, and for the subsequent campaign by Bomber Command of the RAF, contrary to the spirit, if not the letter, of the Geneva Convention, was that it was simply not possible with the technology of the time to hit precision targets at night, and increasingly as anti-aircraft defences grew and improved both the Luftwaffe and then the RAF had to do most of their bombing under cover of darkness. If it was not possible to hit with precision, and by inference military, targets, then to attack the enemy homeland from the air meant going for the cities, where at least you would hit something. At first the Germans claimed that they were aiming at docks, or railway marshalling yards, or factories, as did the RAF when their own campaign began, but this pretence was soon abandoned and London, Liverpool, Manchester, Sheffield, Newcastle, Bristol, Birmingham and even Belfast soon became regular recipients of German bombs. The destruction of the medieval cathedral by German bombs during a raid on Coventry on 14 November 1940 caused a great hoo-hah at the time and is still quoted as an example of barbarity today. Conspiracy theorists allege that Churchill knew about the raid but let it happen in order to show how beastly the Germans were. The truth is that, if you accept a city as a legitimate target, you cannot exempt listed buildings from your wrath. The Brtish did accept cities as legitimate targets because they did the same to the Germans and it was just good luck that Cologne Cathedral withstood everything that the RAF could throw at that city (and it was raided around 150 times).

In all, around 43,000 British civilians were killed in the Blitz and about three times that number injured, but by the time the campaign tapered off in the spring of 1941, when German eyes and assets were increasingly being directed eastwards, it had failed. It did not break civilian morale, it did not destroy, or even seriously reduce, industrial output, and nor did it provoke the population into demanding an end to the war, as the pre-war theories of Douhet* and his adherents predicted. A great deal of housing was destroyed, but much of this was in slum areas that would have had to be replaced anyway, and reconstruction provided employment. Frightful though living through constant air raids must have been, particularly for the inhabitants of London, which not unnaturally was the target of more German raids than any other city, the Luftwaffe was simply not equipped to do the job properly. Its principal bombers, the Heinkel 111 and Dornier 17, were medium bombers, and even the Junkers Ju 88, by far the most effective German bomber, could not match the load-carrying capabilities of the RAF's heavy bombers such as the Short Stirling, the Handley-Page Halifax and, later, the Avro Lancaster. The He 177, the one German bomber that, depending on variant, could carry a decent load of up to 12,000 pounds, entered service far too late to be effective, was plagued by structural and engine problems, and was regarded as positively dangerous in a dive. Excellent though the Luftwaffe was as a ground-support arm, it had been configured (and equipped) as a tactical rather than a strategic air force, and to expect it to reduce major cities to rubble was just asking too much.

If the Germans could neither invade England nor force a peace from the air, then there might be merit in going for weak points somewhere else. The Mediterranean had long been regarded as a British lake, at least by the British, and their bases in Malta and Gibraltar did allow the Royal Navy to dominate the sea lanes there. The possession of Gibraltar allowed the British to close the straits and prevent shipping from passing into or out of the Mediterranean. Force H, the Royal Navy task force based on Gibraltar, supported the search of all neutral shipping passing through the straits, and the prevention of 'contraband' (what the British considered to be war materials) passing to Italy or to Germany via Vichy French ports. If the

*The Italian General Giulio Douhet pioneered the bombing of ground targets during Italy's conquests of Libya and was an air ace in the First World War. His 1921 book *Command of the Air*, which argued that sufficient aircraft would always get through and that wars could be won from the air, was enormously influential between the wars.

Germans could take Gibraltar, or deny its use to the British, then that would have considerable strategic and propaganda value. Gibraltar had been held by the British since 1704. It was ceded to Britain in perpetuity by Spain on 13 July 1713 as part of the Treaty of Utrecht, which brought to a close the War of the Spanish Succession, in which the British, with their allies the Dutch and the Savoyards, were successful in preventing the French from bagging the Spanish throne and thus becoming a superpower. In the years since, the Spanish, rapidly forgetting that it was England that had twice saved them from becoming a lackey of France, rather regretted giving Gibraltar away and wanted it back.*

Franco and the Falange party were in power because Germany and Italy had put them there. They might, just, have won their civil war without Hitler and Mussolini, depending upon what the USSR and Britain and France might or might not have done, but it would have taken them a lot longer and Spain would have been reduced to even more of a basket case than it already was. Franco had signed the Anti-Comintern Pact and was a fellow fascist. It was not unreasonable, therefore, for the Germans to assume that some gratitude might be forthcoming now that payback time had arrived. Accordingly, OKW was instructed to plan for the capture of Gibraltar, something that Grand Admiral Raeder, commander of the German navy, had been constantly urging.

German reconnaissance parties were duly despatched in civilian clothes and with false passports to Spain, where they received full cooperation from the authorities. Wearing Spanish uniforms, the officers, at various times consisting of mountain infantry, artillery, engineer, secret intelligence service and parachute representatives, were able to get close to the border, observe the Brtish colony from Spanish houses and obtain an aerial view by travelling in Spanish civilian aircraft whose flight plans strayed slightly into British airspace. It soon became clear that what had appeared from Berlin to be a relatively simple operation

---

*Apart from the War of the Spanish Succession, it was a cause of some resentment in Spain that, in what the British call the Peninsular War (1808–14) and the Spanish the War of Independence (1807–14), Spain could only expel the French by accepting British money, equipment and troops. As Spain was old, Catholic, agrarian, on the way down and broke, and England was brash, Protestant, industrialized, on the way up and the richest country in the world, and had long been either an enemy or a competitor of Spain, one can understand the Spanish attitude. Today's Spain would still like it back, although anyone who travels in Spain can see exactly why Britain has no intention of giving it back and why over 90 per cent of Gibraltarians regularly vote to remain British.

would actually pose all sorts of problems. To begin with, the Royal Navy's presence in and around the Rock precluded any form of seaborne landing. From the land the only line of approach was the 1,500 metres of open ground along the narrow isthmus linking Gibraltar with the mainland, and this had been mined by the British and was covered by a large number of artillery pieces. The British had evacuated most of the civilian population, and the garrison, estimated by Admiral Canaris's intelligence service at around 10,000, including five infantry battalions making use of the forty or so miles of tunnels carved into the limestone rock, had supplies for eighteen months, making a siege impractical. Secondly, there was the problem of transporting the assault troops from Germany to Spain. The French and Spanish rail gauges were different, so troops and stores would have to be cross-loaded at the border; all rail lines went through Madrid, the capital, making it impossible to disguise troop movement on such a scale, and there was only one, rather bad, road from the mainland to Gibraltar. Finally, the lack of landing sites on the precipitous slopes and unpredictable winds around the rock ruled out the use of parachute troops or an Eban Emael-style glider assault.*

OKW's first stab at a plan for the capture of Gibraltar -- Case Felix – predicated a force of one infantry regiment, one mountain regiment, two combat engineer battalions, one engineer construction battalion, the perhaps astonishing total of twelve artillery regiments of various types and large numbers of 88mm anti-aircraft guns capable of engaging point targets to take out the British guns emplaced in embrasures cut in the rock. As time went on more and more assets were considered necessary, until the final bill for Felix amounted to 65,400 men and 11,000 horses, the original assault force having been augmented by three observation battalions, a third combat engineer battalion, another fourteen medium and heavy artillery regiments and two smoke battalions. In addition there would be two motorized divisions and nine regiments of medium artillery in support, with a Waffen SS division as flank protection and communication and logistic units as required. Once the troops were assembled in their concentration area near La Linea, there would be a massive artillery bombardment of the rock and the harbour, followed by an attack by Luftwaffe bombers and dive-bombers on whatever British shipping was still afloat. Once that was over, the artillery would start again, aiming to keep the

---

* In 1940 the Germans had taken out the seemingly impregnable Belgian frontier fortress of Eban Emael by landing glider-borne troops on top of it.

defenders in their tunnels, while the 88mm guns would neutralize the British coastal artillery, allowing the infantry and engineers to advance through the minefields under the cover of smoke.

The units nominated for Felix were assembled for training in the French Jura region, where the limestone rock was similar to that of Gibraltar and where there were mountains that resembled it. To command the operation, General of Mountain Troops Ludwig Kuebler with Headquarters XLIX Corps was selected. A superb soldier, albeit a hard taskmaster, Kuebler had been severely disfigured by wounds sustained in the First World War, and was known to his men as the 'Limping Nurmi'.* If anyone could take Gibraltar, Kuebler was that man and by late September 1940 training in rope work, fighting in built-up areas and tunnels, mine clearance and general physical fitness began in earnest. The logistic problems inherent in Felix would be horrific. The Spanish rail system was primitive and could only move one division every twelve days, so most of the troops would have to march, and it is between 1,000 and 1,400 miles from France to Gibraltar, depending upon where one crosses the Pyrenees. Virtually nothing could be obtained in country and the force would need over 13,000 tons of ammunition, 140 tons of food per day and 9,000 tons of petrol, oil and lubricants. Depots would have to be set up in advance and vehicle-repair workshops pre-positioned. Six to eight weeks' notice would be needed to mount the operation and it would be almost impossible to hide what was going on from the British.

All this, of course, assumed full Spanish agreement, and at first it looked as if this would be forthcoming. General Juan Vigón, the Spanish Minister of War, and his staff agreed to improve airfields in southern Spain for use by the Luftwaffe, to improve the roads around Gibraltar and to cooperate fully in intelligence-gathering. While all assured the Germans that Spain would enter the war on the German side, no one was prepared to say when that might be. It was pointed out that Spain was impoverished from the Civil War and would need large quantities of arms, fuel and foodstuffs from Germany before she could commit herself to what might be a long war. A

---

*Paavo Nurmi (1897–1973), the 'Flying Finn', was probably the greatest track athlete of all time. Between 1921 and 1931 he set twenty-nine world records for distances between 1,500 and 20,000 metres and won nine Olympic gold medals. In one of many post-war examples of pots hanging kettles, Kuebler was tried by the Yugoslavs in 1947 and executed.

request by the Germans for Spain to cede one of the Canary Islands to them for use as an airbase was batted into the long grass, and, when the Spanish pointed out that they had territorial claims in North Africa and would like not only Gibraltar but French Morocco as well, discussions stalled.

On 23 October 1940 Hitler and his entourage travelled by train through France to Hendaye, on the Spanish border, for discussions with General Franco. The *Caudillo* expressed his warm friendship for Germany and complete support for her war aims. He would certainly join the war but there were problems. Spain depended on imports for all her oil and also for much of her food, the latter coming mainly from Canada. A blockade by the Royal Navy would easily cut this lifeline and put Franco's regime in serious danger. Certainly Spain regarded Gibraltar as hers, and she had other territorial claims too, but while she very much wished to enter the war she simply could not do so until Britian was defeated – which Franco assured Hitler could only be a matter of weeks, or months at most. Hitler was displeased at such ingratitude, but Felix without Franco could not be mounted. Things might change, however, and the plan, and training for it, continued. Franco's only child, his daughter Carmen Franco Polo, in a book published in Spain in 2008 claims that her father feared that he might be kidnapped by the Germans at the Hendaye conference in order to force him to take Spain into the war, in a rerun of Napoleon's snaffling of the Spanish royal family at the Bayonne conference in 1808. As Carmen was only fourteen at the time of Hendaye, it seems improbable that her father would have confided such matters to her, so this is more likely a reverie in hindsight. In any case, it seems very unlikely that the Germans, unscrupulous though they could be in matters of diplomacy, would risk imprisoning the head of state of a neutral power.

By early 1941 the Germans had virtually given up hope of persuading Franco to join the war – the wily *Caudillo* kept professing his intention to do so but the intransigence of the British allowed him to fall back on the vulnerability of Spain to counter-actions on their part and to insist on the defeat of Britain as a precondition to a Spanish declaration.* In German eyes,

---

*Some years ago this author hired a Spanish postgraduate student as an interpreter. The student professed total antagonism to Franco. When it was suggested that Franco had at least kept Spain out of the Second World War, the student expostulated: 'But that's the whole point – if we had gone in we would have been beaten and we would have got loads of money in Marshall Aid!'

there remained the possibility that the British might launch a pre-emptive invasion of Spain, and thus a further operational plan – Case Isabella – envisaged ten German divisions moving into Spain to counter a British landing. As the focus of German planning turned increasingly towards the East, so interest in Felix and Isabella waned. No doubt German staff officers were well aware of the quarter of a million French troops tied down in Spain in 1812 while Napoleon marched on Moscow, and, although Felix stayed on the books, the troops training for it were withdrawn for other duties, and eventually Isabella was watered down to a paper-only contingency plan to hold a defensive line along the Pyrenees with one armoured and two infantry divisions.[28]

If the capture of Gibraltar would seriously discommode the British, then the capture of the Suez Canal as well would make the Mediterranean an Axis preserve. There would no longer be any risk of British intervention in the Balkans; the shortest British route to India would be severed; Italian troops would be available for operations outside their own immediate area; there would be no risk of the French colonies and the French fleet declaring for de Gaulle; and the Axis could obtain the raw materials of North Africa and be within striking distance of the Middle East oil fields. Some of the OKW planners considered that one German armoured division to support the Italians would be enough for Mussolini's troops in Italian Libya to take the canal; others were sceptical as to the value of armour in the desert, but in any event Mussolini, against the advice of his generals based in Africa, was convinced that Italy could take Egypt without assistance, and hence all the glory would be his.

In the meantime, the British, despite having no army left at home, did manage to show Hitler that they had no intention of giving in by themselves hitting at soft targets. In July 1940 they sequestered French warships in British ports in the United Kingdom and Egypt with little resistance, but when the fleet based in French North Africa declined either to join the Free French Navy, sail for neutral ports or render their ships incapable of action, the Royal Navy opened fire at Mers el Kebir, sinking one battleship, severely damaging two and killing a large number of French sailors. What the British did was entirely illegal, but needs must and, had Vichy France handed her fleet over to the Germans, re-entered the war on the German side, or had her fleet seized by the Germans, the balance of naval power would have shifted dramatically. The British action was entirely understandable in the circumstances, even if the French navy have still not forgiven Britain for it* and de Gaulle accused the British of glorying in it (which, apart from most British admirals, who thought the action unnecessary, they probably did). In September 1940 an attempt to take the port of Dakar, in Vichy French Senegal, by an amphibious operation in conjunction with the Free French was an inglorious failure (see below), largely because of over-optimism by de Gaulle, bad Allied security and the determination of the Vichy garrison, but in November carrier-borne aircraft of the Royal Navy sank three Italian battleships and damaged a large number of other ships at virtually no loss to themsleves in a raid on Taranto naval base, and, when the remnants of the fleet attempted to sail for safer ports, British ships inflicted yet more damage. Increasingly Hitler was forced to recognize that the British were not going to do the sensible thing and agree a peace: all that Germany could do for the moment was to nibble at the vulnerable points, although on several occasions Hitler stated that Britain's only hope lay with Russia, and, once that problem was dealt with, Britain would have no further reason for fighting on.

* * *

In fact, Britain's hope lay not with Russia but with the United States, as had been made clear by the Chiefs of Staff in their assessment of May 1940. Franklin Delano Roosevelt may well go down in history as the cleverest politician of his age. He did not want Britain to be defeated, not because he necessarily had any particular love for the British, although he preferred their system of government to that of Germany, but simply because he realized that it was not in the American interest for Europe and the British Isles to become a National Socialist fiefdom. As long as Britain could be kept in the war, then, however ineffectively the British might wage that war, Germany could never turn her attention exclusively elsewhere. Once convinced that Britain not only would but could continue the war alone, Roosevelt set about creating the conditions for American support. He had been in regular communication with Churchill since September 1939, when the president

---

*The French and the British are, of course, traditional enemies, having fought together for around six years and against each other for more than 200. Every year on the anniversary of Trafalgar, 21 October, the French marines drink a toast to the man who shot and killed Nelson from the rigging of the *Redoubtable*. Cheeky buggers.

sent a letter of congratulation on Churchill's appointment, or reappointment, as First Lord of the Admiralty, telling the recipient to 'keep in touch personally, with anything you want to know about'. For the head of state of one nation to communicate directly with a minister in the government of another was an extraordinary breach of protocol, but it was well for the future of both countries that it continued. While Churchill's influence on American foreign and military policy was less than Churchill thought it was, and while it lessened as the war went on and the United States moved from being a junior member of the alliance to its undisputed leader, there can be no doubt that the personal relationship between the two men was vital to British survival. Whatever Churchill's faults as a war leader – and they were many – his achievement in obtaining American support, which from the earliest days he knew would be essential, cannot be gainsaid.

Although no one in the United States of America would have openly cheered the coming of the Second World War, it was what got America out of the Depression. To begin with, however, the vast majority of the American people wanted nothing to do with the war and the president had to move cautiously. In 1938, in the aftermath of Munich, he rather hoped and expected that the Senate Foreign Relations Committee would vote to repeal the Neutrality Acts, banning American war-making material from being supplied to any belligerent in a war in which the US was not engaged: they declined by twelve votes to eleven. A poll by Gallup in early 1939 showed that in the event of a European war 65 per cent of Americans thought Germany should be boycotted and 57 per cent were in favour of repeal of the Neutrality Acts, but, while 58 per cent of respondents thought that the United States would be drawn in, and 90 per cent would fight if America was invaded, only 10 ten cent would fight if America was not invaded. It appeared that, while public opinion was, just, sympathetic to Britain and France (or at least not well disposed to Germany), there was no mandate for American participation. FDR did his best to modernize the navy, and in 1936 he had forced through an increased naval budget against strong pacifist and non-interventionist opposition, but he had neglected the army, which in 1939 was 227,000 strong but with equipment for only 75,000. Rifles and machine-guns were first-war vintage, none of America's aircraft was a match for those of the British and the French, never mind the Germans, and the field artillery was armed mostly with French 75mm guns brought home in 1918. However, the president selected the fifty-nine-year-old Brigadier-General George C. Marshall as

Chief of Staff of the army, promoting him over the head of a number of his seniors, and this was an inspired appointment. Marshall was a master of logistics and organization, and in a war that would depend upon industrial output and would ultimately be won by materiel, his input as professional head of the US Army and later as a member of the Anglo-American Combined Chiefs of Staff Committee was crucial.

In one of his fireside chats, regular radio broadcasts to the nation, on 3 September 1939, the day Britain and France declared war on Germany, Roosevelt said, 'This nation will remain a neutral nation. But I cannot ask that every American remain neutral in thought as well', and, when asked at a press conference whether the United States could stay out of the war, he replied, 'I not only sincerely hope so but I believe we can, and every effort will be made by this administration to do so.'[29] The president closed American territorial waters to belligerent submarines – which meant German submarines – and declared a 'limited National Emergency'. The legal world was unsure as to exactly what a limited national emergency was, but it did allow the president to persuade both Houses of Congress to amend the Neutrality Acts to allow the provision of armaments to belligerents who could collect and pay for them – the so-called 'cash and carry' provision of the Neutrality Act of 1939. In November British ships began docking in American ports and taking delivery of such weapons as American industry could supply – not a lot at that time, but it would soon get bigger and better. As only the British, who had a blue water navy, could collect and carry, this was a blatant act in support of the Allies and as such became the first political issue of the war for the United States. The cash-and-carry amendment was furiously opposed by the America First Committee, a curious amalgam of pro-Nazis, socialists, communists and those who honestly believed that America should have no part in adventures abroad, but it became an issue of patriotism, and cinemas began to play the American national anthem after all performances, and the well-known firm Dictator Carpets changed its name to Liberty Carpets.*

After the Battle of France in 1940 and the British retreat from the Continent, there were those in power in the United States who thought that

*When the French, forgetting that it is solely due to the USA and the UK that they are not now Germans, refused to support the Coalition in its invasion of Iraq in 2003, there was a move in the USA to rename French fries 'Freedom fries'. Students of linguistics should note that what to the British are chips are fries to the Americans, and what are chips to the Americans are potato crisps to the British.

Britain could not survive. These included Joseph Kennedy,* the American ambassador in London, and Cordell Hull, the Secretary of State, who called for the Royal Navy to be sent to North American ports to prevent it being used as a bargaining chip in the inevitable peace negotiations with Germany. Once it became apparent that Britain would not negotiate, Roosevelt became more vociferous in support of the Allied cause (and after June 1940 the 'Allies' consisted only of the British Empire), although he still had to tread warily and during the 1940 election campaign, when justifying his increased defence expenditure, he said unequivocally, 'Your boys are not going to be sent to any foreign wars.' His victory in that election was not the landslide of 1936, but it was solid enough. He obtained 55 per cent of the popular vote but he carried thirty-eight states and he had bypassed Congress by agreeing to give the British fifty American destroyers in exchange for the use of British bases in the Caribbean. The destroyers were obsolete by modern standards but they were desperately needed by the Royal Navy as escort vessels.

By the summer of 1940 Britain was running out of money with which to pay the necessary cash on the nail demanded for American weaponry, and in March 1941 Roosevelt pushed through the Lend-Lease Act, which not only allowed him to supply equipment to the British on the provisio that after the war it would be returned in kind or paid for, but also gave him very wide powers to grant military aid to whomsoever he pleased. America was to be 'the arsenal of democracy' and the gearing up of the assembly lines to produce ships, vehicles and guns accelerated the dragging of America out of the Depression – now there were jobs for all. Roosevelt likened the act to lending one's neighbour a hose when his house was on fire. The Selective Service Act, which the president signed in September 1940 and which for the first time in peacetime instituted compulsory military service, brought accusations of dictatorship, but the Act was extended by Congress in August 1941, albeit by only one vote. Roosevelt was gradually nursing American public opinion towards involvement in the war on the side of the British (or on the side of the four basic freedoms, as the president put it), but as late as the spring of 1941 a Gallup poll showed that a substantial majority of Americans, while willing the British to win, or rather willing Germany to lose, were opposed to American entry. Roosevelt might want to go farther than his stated 'all help

*An American isolationist who did not like the British very much anyway, Kennedy became increasingly disenchanted with Roosevelt and 'resigned' as ambassador in 1940.

short of war' but public and Congressional opinion would not support him firing the first shot. Fortunately for the British, someone else would soon fire that shot.

* * *

Apart from a brief interlude between 1933 and 1935, the Italian armed forces had been at war since 1923, in either Somaliland, Abyssinia or Spain. Italy's problem was that, while her armed forces had coped adequately against tribesmen armed with spears, or civilian idealists in the International Brigades, they were not ready for a war against a Western enemy. At the outbreak of war Italian equipment was of roughly the same standard as that of the British or the French, but the problem was not quality, but quantity. The Italian industrial base was not sufficiently developed to support a long or intensive war. The League of Nations sanctions in 1936 had helped a little, by forcing Italians to make items that they would otherwise have imported, but it was far from enough. In the whole of the Second World War, Italy manufactured 13,523 aircraft. In 1942 alone Germany produced 15,596.[30] There was little thought given to what Italy's long-term military policy might be, apart from supporting the creation of a new Roman Empire. Italy had failed to obtain the eastern side of the Aegean Sea in 1918, and with the Treaty of Tirana in 1926 Albania became in effect an Italian protectorate. Mussolini decided to go one better and on 7 April 1939 launched Operation Overseas Tirana. An expeditionary force of 22,000 men with eighty-one tanks and sixty-four artillery pieces invaded Albania and in three days it was all over. Italian casualties were twelve dead and eighty-one wounded, and King Victor Emmanuel III added the crown of Albania, which he had described as 'a land containing four stones', to the Emperorship of Abyssinia which he had held since May 1936. Despite telling Hitler that he would not be ready to enter the war on Germany's side until 1942, Mussolini declared war on France and Britain on 10 June 1940, by which time the British had scuttled from Europe and France was on her knees. It was the most blatant piece of opportunism seen in Europe since Henry of Navarre embraced Catholicism, and it infuriated the French, who considered that surrendering to the Germans was fair enough – they had been beaten by them – but they were damned if they would surrender to Italy, whose sole move against the southern portion of the Maginot Line had been firmly repulsed. The Germans too thought it was bad form and General Franz Halder, the German Chief of the General Staff, thought it thoroughly dishonourable,[31] as indeed it was.

As an ex-journalist, Mussolini knew a great deal about propaganda, but a lot less about waging war. He planned to take Egypt from a reeling Britain by launching a simultaneous two-pronged attack eastwards from Libya and northwards from Italian Somaliland. The Italian Commander-in-Chief in Libya, the fifty-eight-year-old Marshal Rudolfo Graziani, who had been in post since his predecessor, Marshal Balbo, had been shot down and killed (presumably accidentally) by his own anti-aircraft guns in June 1940, knew better. He was well aware that butchering Senussi tribesmen was not the same thing as taking on the British, under-equipped and numerically inferior though the Egyptian garrison might be, and much procrastination and prevarication winged its way from Tripoli to Rome. In the view of the Italian staffs in Abyssinia and Italian Somaliland, however, the southern prong might well be a runner, but only if the inconvenient British garrison of British Somaliland, bounded by the Gulf of Aden to the north, Abyssinia to the south and west and Italian Somaliland to the east, was dealt with first. Elimination of this British enclave would ensure that an advance towards Egypt would not be threatened from the rear, and the capture of British Somaliland might allow the Italian navy to close the exit from and approach to the Suez Canal (although how Italian ships could possibly get there was never satisfactorily answered).

In Italian Somaliland and Abyssinia the Duke of Aosta had two Italian colonial infantry divisions, a total of 280,000 mostly locally enlisted natives with Italian officers, and this was increased to 324,000 by conscripting Italian residents. The British had the Somaliland Camel Corps, three Indian and one King's African Rifles infantry battalions, with a fifth battalion, the Second Battalion The Black Watch, sent as a reinforcement just before the Italian attack, or about 4,000 men altogether. When twenty-six Italian battalions supported by light tanks, aircraft and horsed cavalry invaded on 3 August 1940, the camels and the five British battalions dealt them a very bloody nose indeed, and after holding the Italians up for four days their commander, fifty-one-year-old Major-General Alfred Godwin-Austen, withdrew in good order to the coast, embarked his troops and sailed away. The British had around fifty killed (including four soldiers of the Black Watch), the Italians around ten times that. It was thought that the death toll included Captain Eric Wilson, commanding the Somaliland Camel Corps machine-gun section. Hugely outnumbered, Wilson and his tiny detachment held off the Italians until all his men were wounded or killed. Severely wounded himself, he fought on alone, before being eventually overrun. Listed as killed in action, Wilson was awarded a posthumous Victoria Cross 'for most conspicuous gallantry'. It was not until the following year that Wilson turned up at an Italian prisoner-of-war camp and his family could be told that, like those of Mark Twain's, the reports of his death had been much exaggerated. Eric Wilson VC survived being accused of being an imposter, lived to the respectable age of ninety-six and died in December 2008.

There was no point in the British trying to hold on to the colony when they could not be reinforced or resupplied, and Godwin-Austen showed considerable skill in extricating his little command at considerable cost to his enemy. Churchill, who assumed that lack of casualties indicated lack of fighting spirit, did not see it that way and his suspicions of General Sir Archibald Wavell, Commander-in-Chief Middle East Command, were intensified when he refused to sack Godwin-Austen.* The capture of British Somaliland was trumpeted as a great victory for the new Romans, but in truth it was nothing of the sort. The Duke of Aosta was well aware of the difficulties in advancing north into Egypt and in any case he was not left to enjoy the fruits of victory, such as they were, for long.

On 19 January 1941 Lieutenant-General William Platt with two Indian divisions supported by a squadron of 4 Royal Tank Regiment with Matilda infantry tanks invaded Eritrea from the Sudan, followed on 29 January by Lieutenant-General Alan Cunningham (younger brother of Admiral Sir Andrew Cunningham, Commander Mediterranean Fleet) with 1 South African Division, a Rhodesian brigade, a Kenyan brigade and a brigade from the Gold Coast (now Ghana) attacking north-east into Italian Somaliland from Kenya, the whole supported by a diversionary operation against western Abyssinia by local guerrillas led by British officers including Gideon Force commanded by the very dubious Major Orde Wingate.† Every two hours, on the even hour, Royal Signals operators were instructed to radio the Italian high command and ask, 'Do you wish to surrender?' For the first few months the answer was always

---

*Essentially, Wavell was a thinking soldier and a gentleman, whereas Churchill was neither. As Wavell rightly commented, Churchill's tactical understanding stopped somewhere around the middle of the Boer War.

†Another example of the British ability to make a hero out of a wrong 'un, Wingate was probably mad and certainly unbalanced. Lucky to not be court-martialled for getting too close to Jewish terrorists in Palestine, and doubly lucky to not be booted out as a failed suicide in May 1941, he will reappear in Burma.

the same: 'Not yet.'[32] By May the Italians had lost 230,000 men killed, wounded or taken prisoner; the British had lost a few hundred, and on 19 May the Duke of Aosta and his remaining 7,000 troops surrendered.

Meanwhile, to the north, Mussolini had told his army commander in Libya to stop making excuses and get on with the invasion of Egypt, and on 13 September 1940 five divisions crossed the Libyan–Egyptian border, moved down the Halfaya Pass and approached Sollum, the first town in British Egypt.* The garrison, a platoon of the Coldstream Guards, thought it wise to withdraw. The Italians had little intelligence about British deployments west of the Suez Canal and much artillery ammunition was expended bombarding tracts of empty desert. Harassed by the Royal Air Force and inconvenienced by British minefields, the Italians moved at a rate of twelve miles a day and got as far as Sidi Barrani, where they stopped. Sidi Barrani is 50 miles inside Egypt and 400 miles from Cairo. It cannot be described as a one-horse town for there are no horses. It was, and is, a fly-blown collection of ramshackle buildings on either side of the main coastal road, and of no tactical significance whatsoever. Graziani had, however, obeyed his master's orders and invaded Egypt. Now he had his men dig in and build wired and entrenched forts while he set his engineers to improving the road behind him and deliberated what to do next.

The combat element of the British garrison in Egypt was the Western Desert Force, commanded since June by Lieutenant-General Richard O'Connor, fifty-one in 1940 and a thoroughgoing professional who had commanded an infantry battalion in action in 1918 at the age of twenty-nine. O'Connor reported to the General Officer Commanding in Chief (GOC in C) Egypt, another lieutenant-general, Henry Maitland Wilson, who was eight years older than O'Connor. A large (the unkind might say fat) officer who enjoyed riding but who needed a horse well up to weight, 'Jumbo' Wilson was a supportive administrator rather than a field commander, and reported in turn to Wavell, C-in-C Middle East. The Western Desert Force consisted of the British 7 Armoured Division, the Indian 4 Infantry Division and an ad hoc brigade-sized all-arms grouping known as Selby Force, after its

---

*Strictly speaking, Egypt was not British but an independent country. Britain did, however, retain certain rights, including the defence of the Suez Canal and, under a treaty of 1936, the use of all Egyptian facilities, ports and airfields and means of communication in time of war. This meant that the British in effect occupied Egypt with the king and government doing pretty well what they were told.

commander Brigadier 'Uncle Arthur' Selby, hitherto Commander Mersa Matruh Garrison. In support there was 7 Royal Tank Regiment with Matilda infantry tanks.

On the face of it, the Italians had little to worry about. They outnumbered the British by more than two to one in manpower, and by two to one in artillery, generally the most competent component of the Italian Army, and the Italian medium tanks at least should have been able to give a good account of themselves against those of the British. There were problems, however. The Italian 75mm field guns, while generally well handled, were not a match for the British 25-pounders;* there was an acute shortage of vehicles and consequently problems in the resupply of ammunition and fuel; the standards of training of native levy units was not good; technical understanding amongst mainland Italian soldiers was low; and for once the British had more tanks than their enemy. Instead of remaining mobile, or as mobile as they could be given the shortage of transport, the Italians had locked themselves up in their so-called forts and had dispersed their tanks until they were little more than pill boxes – a mistake they might have rectified had they studied French tactics in the Battle of France.

On 7 December 1940 the British struck back. Operation Compass began and the RAF destroyed thirty-nine Italian aircraft on the ground. By 6 February 1941, when the Italian Tenth Army surrendered, in what had been originally intended as a five-day raid, the Western Desert Force (renamed XIII Corps on 1 January 1941 and augmented by an Australian division) had captured Tobruk, Benghazi and Beda Fomm, had covered 700 miles, taken 110,000 prisoners, including twenty-two generals and an admiral, and captured 845 artillery pieces, 380 tanks and huge numbers of soft-skinned vehicles. It was also reported that the British had captured the Italian Army's mobile brothel.† The total butcher's bill for the British was 500 killed (of whom only twenty-four were British Army) and around 1,400 wounded and missing. The RAF shot down in combat or destroyed on the ground 1,249

---

*Probably the only British item of army equipment that was superior to anything deployed by German or Italian, the 25-pounder fired a high-explosive (HE) shell weighing 25lb out to a range of 13,400 yards, whereas the Italian 75mm fired a 14lb shell to 11,000 yards.

†This author has been unable to find any firm evidence for this, and regretfully concludes that, like the report that each Italian platoon was issued with a machine for making cappuccino coffee, it is an old soldiers' tale (the equivalent of an old wives' tale but with rather more alcohol involved).

Italian aircraft at a cost to itself of eleven fighters and four bombers shot down or crashed. O'Connor's famous signal 'fox killed in the open' was sent in clear so that it would be picked up by any Italian listening.* It was a spectacular victory, albeit against a second-class enemy, and if the momentum had been maintained the Italians could have been chased out of North Africa completely, and the Germans never allowed to get there. That, however, was not to be.

Operation Compass was not the only British military operation beginning in 1940, but others had less success. Persuaded that the Vichy French government of Senegal on the western bulge of Africa was only waiting for a suitable moment to declare for the Free French, the British launched Operation Menace. The driving force behind this caper and the man who managed to convince Churchill that it would work was Charles André Joseph Marie de Gaulle, fifty years old and promoted to brigadier-general in May 1940. He was regarded as a maverick in the French Army, largely through his vocal opposition to static fortress defence (the Maginot Line) and his advocacy (rightly) of all-arms mechanized formations. His 4 Armoured Division gave a good account of itself in the battle for France, and appointed under-secretary of state for war and national defence by the prime minister, Reynaud, in June he escaped to England after the surrender. Tried *in absentia* and sentenced to death for desertion by a French military court, he was recognized as head of the Free French by the British on 22 June 1940, largely because there was nobody else. While he had been a competent formation commander, he very quickly developed delusions of grandeur and was perfectly prepared to let the Allies win the war while he plotted how to rule France after it. General Sir Alan Brooke, Chief of the Imperial General Staff from December 1941, would describe his 'overbearing manner, his megalomania and his lack of co-operative spirit', but in his early days in England de Gaulle appealed to Churchill, who shared his apparent wish to be up and at them.[33] A naval task force including two battleships and an aircraft carrier with de Gaulle himself and landing parties of Free French and British troops duly set sail, and on arrival off Dakar, the port and capital of Senegal, on

---

*For any reader who does not hunt – and there may be some – killing the fox in the open, as opposed to sending him to ground and having to drive him out with terriers, is a great compliment to one's pack of hounds. American readers should note that in England hunting means fox hunting; what Americans call hunting is shooting or stalking in England.

23 September they called upon the authorities to forsake Vichy and join the Free French. The Senegal French were perfectly happy as they were, however, and had recently had a stiffening of morale in the shape of two cruisers and three destroyers of the French navy.* In the ensuing naval bombardment and French reply, ships of the Royal Navy were damaged, a French submarine was sunk and a landing party was repulsed. On 26 September the operation was called off. It had been a total failure, largely through faulty intelligence, misplaced faith in de Gaulle and a lack of security in London. The French air force mounted air raids on Gibraltar in retaliation – they had little effect – but Vichy France stopped short of declaring war.

* * *

Having invaded British Somaliland in August and Egypt in September 1940, Mussolini, already vastly overreached if only he had realized it, invaded Greece on 28 October. The original excuse was that Greece had allowed ships of the Royal Navy to refuel in her territorial waters, which the Italians claimed was a breach of her neutrality,† but the real reason was Italian imperialism, rivalry with Germany for control of the Balkans and a wish to control the exit from the Dardanelles, which could easily be done from Greece. The relationship between Germany and Italy was always ambiguous. On the one hand, Italy had been fascist and Mussolini in power long before Hitler; the NSDAP had copied much of the Italian fascists' ideology and methods, including the raised arm salute, and Hitler showed remarkable personal loyalty towards Mussolini long after there was any profit for Germany in so doing. On the other hand, Italy was in no position to fight a modern war, had traditionally favoured the British (a policy that made eminent sense given that the Mediterranean was a British lake), had entered the first war on the Allied side, had opposed *Anschluss* to the extent of sending troops to the Brenner Pass between Austria and Italy, and disapproved of Germany's handling of Czechoslovakia. What tipped Italy into the German camp was British opposition to her Abyssinian adventures, her virulent anti-communism,

---

*It should have been three cruisers but the Royal Navy had managed to persuade one of them to turn back to Toulon.

†It may have been, depending on how long the ships stayed in Greek waters.

a wish to create a second Roman Empire, and resentment over the failure to obtain what she saw as her just rewards in 1918. All these aims were more likely to be achieved by rowing in with Germany – assuming, of course, that Germany won the war, which in the spring of 1940 looked very likely. Despite the alliance, there was resentment of Italy's younger and stronger partner, and the Italians very much wanted to achieve something by themselves, a strong motivating factor for the invasions of British Somaliland, Egypt and Greece.

The British were under no obligation to get involved in Greece. After the dismemberment of Czechoslovakia in 1939, they had tossed out guarantees to all who would listen, including the Greeks. The Greek government was well aware that these commitments could not possibly be honoured and turned the offer down, knowing full well that what forces the British could send in time of war would not be enough to ensure the integrity of Greece but might well provoke the very thing they would be sent to prevent – a German invasion. That Britain did get involved stemmed from one of Churchill's flamboyant rhetorical gestures when a new Greek government, faced with an Italian invasion from Albania, changed its mind and asked for British troops after all. Churchill should have said no – the troops would have been far better employed in Africa – but 'Britain supports her friends' was the cry and troops went to Crete and aircraft to Greece, and the Royal Navy intensified its efforts to get the Italian navy to come out and fight. Had the British contribution stopped at that, then no great damage to her efforts in North Africa would have ensued. As it was, despite sending eight divisons into Greece, the Italian Army soon found itself in trouble. What was hoped to be a lightning campaign degenerated into a bloody struggle in the mountains in which the Italians came off very much the worse: the Albanian roads and ports could not support the logistical effort required, the Greeks did not welcome the Italians as liberators and the Greek Army was able to mobilize a lot more troops than the Italians expected. By the end of 1940 the Greeks had pushed the Italians back into Albania and it began to look as if, rather than Italy conquering Greece, Greece might conquer Albania. The Greeks too, however, were having problems in the mountains. There was a shortage of medical supplies and warm clothing, and they were very nearly out of ammunition. The British were asked for help.

The Italians had not told the Germans of their intention to invade

Greece (nor about the invasions of British Somaliland and Egypt) since they hoped to score a success of their own which, while it could not rival Germany's conquest of Western Europe, might at least make up for Italy's shameful showing against France in June 1940. The Germans were displeased, particularly as it now looked as if they would have to bail their ally out. They already had troops in Romania, sent there in September 1940 ostensibly to train the Romanian Army but in reality to secure the oil fields for Germany and prevent the USSR from gobbling up the whole country (Russia had already annexed two Romanian provinces in accordance with the Molotov–Ribbentrop pact), and planning for Case Marita envisaged German forces in Romania invading Greece from Bulgaria, which was being wooed by Germany and would join the Tripartite Pact in 1941, and from Yugoslavia, across which country Germany had secured transit rights. In February 1941 the British decided to halt operations in Libya, to the considerable chagrin of General O'Connor, who was convinced (probably rightly) that he could be in Tripoli in weeks and have the Italians out of North Africa completely in a month. From London's perspective, what now mattered was Greece, for, if a Greek collapse could be averted, it was here that one enemy was on the run, and in any case Churchill had seen great merit in a Balkan front in the first war and, egged on by the Foreign Secretary, Anthony Eden, saw no reason to change his views in the second.

From March 1941 a British armoured brigade, the Australian 6 Division and the New Zealand Division were removed from Egypt and Libya and sent to Greece under the command of General 'Jumbo' Wilson. German plans were then slightly upset by a British-inspired military coup in Yugoslavia which meant that Germany had to squash that country before attacking Greece. On 6 April 1941 German troops invaded Yugoslavia from Germany to the north and from Romania and Bulgaria to the east. The capital, Belgrade, was bombed that same day – casualties were significant, even if the claimed death toll of 17,000 was almost certainly greatly exaggerated – and German efforts were helped by the mutiny of two mainly Croatian Yugoslav armies.* By 14 April it was all over and the Yugoslav government asked for an armistice. Now for Greece, and when the Germans crossed the

---

*The Croats had no particular love for Germany but objected to being dragged into war. The other group in the country were the Serbs, who disliked just about everybody but remembered that they had been in the Allied camp in the first war.

border from Yugoslavia into Macedonia in the west and into Thrace to the east, both the Greek main force and the British were in the wrong place, having been committed to defending the Metaxas Line north of Salonika facing Bulgaria. It was another humiliating disaster for the British along the lines of Norway, and, when the Germans captured Athens on 27 April, the British began to evacuate their troops to Crete. Once again the Royal Navy saved a British army and by 30 April such men as could be got away had been taken off and Crete was preparing itself against the inevitable German assault.

The defence of Crete, with the depressingly familiar instruction 'to be held at all costs', was entrusted to Major-General Bernard Freyberg, an Englishman who had spent much of his youth in New Zealand. He had won the Victoria Cross commanding a battalion of the Royal Naval Divison during the Somme offensive in 1916, then becoming the youngest brigadier-general in the British Army at the age of twenty-eight. Reverting to his substantive rank of captain after the war, he transferred to the Grenadier Guards, was a major-general when war broke out and was lent to the government of New Zealand to command their expeditionary force (a division plus supporting and logistic units). On Crete he had no chance. Although there were 43,000 men on the island, many were not from the combat arms and the 10,000 Greeks were mostly without weapons. While one British infantry brigade had been there since the previous November (and had done precious little to create defence works), and two squadrons of fighter aircraft had arrived from Egypt, there were only a handful of tanks, only sixty-eight anti-aircraft guns and very few vehicles. The roads that did exist were narrow and could easily be rendered unusable by bombing, while the ports were too small to be used by naval vessels, with the exception of one anchorage on the south of the island. German plans for the airborne assault on Crete were known from intercepts but there is little advantage in knowing that you are about to be attacked by ten very large men with machetes if you are armed only with a cricket bat.

On 14 May the Luftwaffe began to bomb Crete and the air raids went on for six days. There were no hardened shelters for the RAF aircraft and after three days the last six of them were withdrawn back to Egypt before they too were shot down or destroyed on the ground. At 0800 hours on 20 May, Case Merkur began when eight battalions of airborne infantry parachuted in or landed in gliders. Their casualties were severe, but, once the main airport at Maleme was taken the next day, the result was not in doubt. More and more German transport aircraft landed, disgorging mountain troops, and with the Luftwaffe having complete air superiority there was little the Royal Navy could do by day. On 22 May the Royal Navy removed the King of Greece and on 27 May the inevitable evacuation began from the south of the island. The losses to the navy were great, but, when Admiral Sir Andrew Cunningham, Commander-in-Chief of the Mediterranean Fleet, was asked whether the removal to Egypt of so few fighting troops was worth the cost in ships, he replied, 'It takes three years to build a ship, and three hundred to build a reputation.' The evacuation went on until 1 June and 18,000 men were taken off at a cost of three cruisers and six destroyers sunk. If it had been an expensive defeat for the British, it was an expensive victory for the Germans. Of the 11,000 elite airborne soldiers, almost 4,000 were killed and never again would the Germans mount an airborne operation of this magnitude.

It was not only in Greece that the Germans felt obliged to rescue their Italian allies, but in North Africa too. Hitherto, they had taken little interest in what went on in the Mediterranean and in North Africa: Germany's ambitions lay in mainland Europe and not abroad, but the possibility of the whole of the Libyan coast being in British hands, which might encourage the French North African territories to declare for de Gaulle, and the possibility that Italy might have to leave the war, thus allowing the British use of Italian airfields from where they could bomb Germany's main source of oil in Romania, concentrated minds somewhat. After the initial refusal to send anything to Libya, it was now agreed to despatch the *Deutsche Afrika-Korps* (DAK) of one panzer division, one light division* and supporting arms, with forty aircraft and an anti-aircraft battalion of the Luftwaffe, the whole to be commanded by the newly promoted Lieutenant-General Erwin Rommel. Rommel was fifty years old and had come to prominence as a dashing and succesful divisional commander in the Battle of France, when his division had been first to reach the Channel coast and had captured the entire British 51 Highland Division at St Valery.

The DAK began to land in Tripoli harbour on 14 February 1941. The British knew they were arriving but assumed that it would be at least three

---

*An ad hoc formation of two infantry battalions, a reconnaissance battalion, two anti-tank battalions, two machine-gun battalions, one field artillery battalion, one anti-aircraft battalion and an armoured regiment of two battalions of Mk III and Mk IV tanks.

months before they could do anything – they would need to acclimatize, train, reconnoitre and plan. The German army did not operate that way, however, and, when Rommel launched an attack on 24 March 1941, the British were forced to retreat. By 4 April the combined German–Italian offensive had taken Benghazi, and the next day Derna, capturing Generals O'Connor and Neame* on the way. On 10 April, Rommel began the first siege of Tobruk, and on 17 June the British counter-stroke, Operation Battleaxe, aimed at relieving Tobruk, was called off after the loss of ninety of the 190 British tanks to no avail. The year 1941 was not looking good for the British, the only bright flashes in strategic darkness being the putting down of a pro-German revolt in Iraq in May and the taking of Syria after hard fighting against Vichy French forces in June.

In Berlin all this was mere froth. Far greater things were being planned and all attention was focused on the East.

---

*In March 1941 O'Connor was appointed Commander British Troops Egypt and replaced as Commander XIII Corps by Lieutenant-General Phillip Neame VC, who thanks to the Greek nonsense had precious little with which to defend. When Rommel's attack began, O'Connor went forward to advise Neame, but their staff car got lost and both were captured.

5

THE RUSSIAN WAR

JUNE–OCTOBER 1941

While to Germany the defeat of France – 'the perpetual disturber of world peace' as Hitler put it – wiped out the disgrace of 1918 and the stain of Versailles, the opposition of Britain was unfortunate and irrelevant to Germany's war aims. The war against Russia was Hitler's and Germany's real war. It would not only fulfil National Socialist aims of ridding the world of the Jewish-Bolshevik* menace and provide land for expansion of the German population – *Lebensraum* – but would also provide a huge economic area to be exploited for the benefit of the Reich, thus freeing Germany from the effects of blockade, a major factor in her defeat in 1918. Control of the Baltic and of the industrial area of the Ukraine would mean the German economy was no longer dependent on imported raw materials, while the oil fields of the Caucasus could supply the Wehrmacht and German industry. Furthermore, the elimination of Russia would put paid to Britain's last hope in Europe, for Hitler was well aware of Churchill's attempts to draw Stalin into a grand anti-German alliance both before the invasion of Poland in 1939 and in conversations with the newly appointed British ambassador to Moscow, the Labour Party nominee Sir Stafford Cripps, in July 1940.

Of course, many of Germany's economic aims could be achieved by maintaining the status quo as agreed in the pact of 1939, and Russia was scrupulous in adhering to her side of that agreement, with deliveries of foodstuffs, iron ore and oil being made to Germany daily. There were difficulties in adhering to the pact, however. Hitler did not trust Stalin to keep his word, and, as the balance of trade was heavily in favour of the USSR,

---

*Somewhat of a misnomer – while many of the original Bolsheviks had been Jewish (Trotsky being the best known), by the 1930s the USSR was almost as anti-Semitic as Germany, reverting to a long Russian tradition of persecution of her Jews.

deliveries could cease at any time. Soldiers in the German units stationed in Poland were highly suspicious of Russian intentions and the Commander-in-Chief of the army, Colonel-General Walther von Brauchitsch, instructed that all officers and men were to be briefed that there was no breakdown of German–Soviet relations and that the recent move of the German Eighteenth Army into Poland was not to be taken as indicating any aggressive intent. The department of the SS's intelligence apparatus responsible for gauging public opinion reported that the German civilian population was unhappy with this perceived closeness to Russia, long seen as a potential enemy. If the British really were hanging on in the hope that the two dictators would fall out, then the sooner Russia was dealt with, the better.

Hitler had always said, both in his written works and in private conversation, that Russia, communism and the Jews were his and Germany's real enemies; anything else was peripheral. Politically he was at the height of his popularity in the summer of 1940: in a mere nine months Poland, Norway, Denmark, Holland, Belgium and France had been conquered and the British sent unceremoniously back to their island, from where they bayed toothlessly across the Channel. The reservations of the general staff – in any nation far more aware of the effects of war than their political masters and hence more cautious – had been shown to be groundless, and opposition to the NSDAP was at its lowest level since 1933. Hitler could do whatever he wanted and there was no one to argue against him. The war in the East was the one that mattered to Germany: it was there that the overwhelming majority of her soldiers and airmen would fight, it was there where more than three quarters of her dead would lie and it would be there that the Second World War would be decided. It would be this war that would ultimately bring Germany down to defeat, occupation, ignominy and partition for fifty years.

After the Battle of France, General of Artillery Franz Halder, Chief of the General Staff of the German army, said that it would win no more battles for a long time. What he meant was that, even though his staff were pondering their part in Sea Lion, the elimination of England would be a matter for the air force and the navy. Indeed, plans were drawn up to reduce the size of the army to 120 divisions by disbanding thirty-five divisions and their ancillary units, releasing half a million men back into the civilian economy. Then, on 21 July 1940, Hitler addressed the senior officers of the three armed services. He told them that they must consider 'the American and Russian question', again alluding to British hopes of Russian and eventually American support. He was well aware that in the long term Britain and America could build more ships and aircraft and muster more men and equipment than could Germany. America was not a threat yet but could become so. He was determined to deal with Russia in the near future and he regarded the Molotov–Ribbentrop Pact as no more than a temporary tactical manoeuvre. The army general staff were instructed to plan for military intervention to demonstrate to Russia Germany's hegemony in Europe, while at the same time pursuing the half-hearted scheme for a landing in England, while the other two services were told to submit their views on the Russian question.

The Kriegsmarine's assessment, submitted by Rear Admiral Kurt Fricke, chief of operations staff, to Grand Admiral Raeder, Commander-in-Chief of the navy, emphasized the threat from a powerful Russian fleet in the Baltic and the need for Germany to have sufficient terrain in the East to allow her to be economically self-sufficient and for a German Europe to be secure against military action. All this could be achieved by a successful war against the USSR, but should only be embarked upon when Britain had been defeated. Raeder underlined the sentence about British defeat being a prerequisite for action and passed the paper to Field Marshal Wilhelm Keitel, chief of OKW, who presumably showed it to Hitler. The Luftwaffe's view was, perhaps understandably, more tactical than strategic. The Battle of Britain was in the process of being lost and the air force chiefs saw a war with Russia as allowing them to return to what they were good at – the tactical ground support of a swift-moving army.

On 31 July, ten days after Hitler's indication that war with Russia was a serious consideration, the heads of the three services and their senior staff officers were again summoned, this time to the Berghof, Hitler's mountain home in Obersalzburg. After some discussion about Sea Lion, when Hitler ordered a date of 15 September 1940, or, depending upon the results of the air campaign, a postponement until May 1941, discussion moved on to Russia. Hitler explained that Britain's only hope lay in the Soviet Union and, eventually, America. If Russia could be taken out of the picture, then America would never intervene in Europe because she would be too concerned with the threat from Japan, which would be far greater once Russia was eliminated. Russia must therefore be attacked as soon as possible, in the spring of 1941. The offensive, said Hitler, could only be successful if Russia were destroyed in one blow: merely capturing part of it would not do and holding still for the following winter would be perilous. Hitler defined his war aim as 'the liquidation of Russia's manpower and the capture of the Ukraine, the Baltic states and Belorussia'.[34]

War in the East would be very largely the province of the army, with the other two services in a supporting role, and, although the high command of the army, the *Oberkommando des Heeres* (OKH), had recommended earlier that friendly relations with Russia should be maintained to avoid a war on two fronts, its representatives raised no objection to Hitler's stated aims at the Berghof. Army intelligence was of the view that, while there was no direct threat to Germany now (although there might be to Romania and Finland, which fell within the Soviet sphere of influence according to the 1939 pact but were regarded by Germany as her client states), there were signs that the Red Army was embarking on a programme of modernization which would in time enable it to engage in large-scale mobile offensive operations. Meanwhile, America was increasingly moving towards overt support for Britain, and, although Roosevelt would probably bring the USA into the war against Germany, this could not be before 1941 at the earliest. All this indicated that operations against Russia should begin as soon as possible while the Wehrmacht still had a qualitative advantage, and, although the generals took party functionaries' ramblings about the racial inferiority of Slavs and Jewish plots with a pinch of salt, the military requirement to deal with Russia now, before it was too late, coincided completely with the political imperative for living space and the eradication of communism, and with Hitler's wish, also expressed in *Mein Kampf*, to continue what the Teutonic Knights had begun in the fourteenth century. From the Berghof conference of July 1940 onwards, the focus of Wehrmacht thinking was towards a pre-emptive war in the East; all else was secondary. It was a colossal gamble in the Napoleonic style – all or nothing – and, while in the end it failed, in 1940 success seemed assured.

General Halder now issued instructions to the planning staffs. The previous contingency plan to take but a part of western Russia as a source of supply of raw materials and food was scrapped, and a war of annihilation (as it was termed in March 1941) was to be prepared. The rundown of the army to 120 divisions was cancelled: instead it would increase to 180 divisions and the armaments industry was to step up several gears to provide the necessary weapons, vehicles and equipment. To German economists and diplomats, this represented a major about-turn. The economists had planned for a continuation of the arrangement with the USSR and a diversion of manpower from the armed forces to industry; now they had to produce the materiel that the eastern adventure, codenamed Case Barbarossa, would require. The army agreed to release 300,000 skilled workers to be employed in the armaments industry,[35] but even so it would be a mammoth task to fully equip the existing divisions, many of which were armed with captured vehicles and artillery pieces, never mind the projected new ones.

For his part, the foreign minister, Ribbentrop, who averred that foreign policy should be conducted free of ideological considerations, had since 1939 proposed the creation of an anti-British bloc which would bring Britain down, or at least neutralize her, and discourage American involvement without going to war with Russia. The German ambassador in Moscow, Friedrich von der Schulenburg, thought a war with Russia would be a disaster. The Tripartite Pact, signed between Germany, Italy and Japan in September 1940, was designed to warn off the United States,* and Ribbentrop hoped to enlarge this into a Quadripartite Pact to include the USSR. He saw much merit in drawing Franco's Spain and Vichy France closer to Germany in a Continental coalition against Britain. But both these plans crumbled, the first because Hitler and the army saw war with Russia as inevitable, and the second because not only were Spanish and Italian territorial claims on France irreconcilable, but also Franco and Pétain were far too clever to become any more aligned with Germany than perforce they already were.

After reluctantly accepting the need for a Russian war, the German Foreign Office now had to make certain adjustments in preparation for it. A boundary dispute between Hungary and Romania, which could lead to war between the two, was subjected to swift German arbitration, with Germany and Italy guaranteeing Romania's frontiers, and Finland, to which country Germany had refused any assistance in the Winter War with Russia of 1939/40 in accordance with the German–Soviet Pact, was now courted with the offer of assistance in rearming. Neither action was taken to kindly by Stalin, who considered them to be interference in matters properly the concern of the USSR. Meanwhile, as plans were drawn up and forces deployed, a German corps in Austria was instructed to ready itself to thrust through Hungary to occupy the Romanian oil fields should there be any indications of a Russian *coup de main* and German forces in Norway were

---

*In fact, it did exactly the opposite, reinforcing Roosevelt's view that the USA should support Britain.

required to develop a plan to seize the nickel-producing region of Finland should Russia make any moves to do so.

While Hitler was of the view that the Red Army was a paper tiger, the army staff were more realistic. Their assessment of the Red Army, distributed to units in January 1941 as *The Wartime Armed Forces of the Union of Soviet Socialist Republics*, drew its information from a variety of sources, covert and overt, including the reports of Major-General Ernst August Köstring, who had been the German military attaché in Moscow since 1935, spoke fluent Russian and had a wide variety of contacts. On mobilization it was thought that the Red Army could muster between 11 million and 12 million men in twenty armies with twenty rifle (infantry), nine cavalry, and six motorized or mechanized corps, comprising 150 rifle divisions, between thirty-two and thirty-six horsed cavalry divisions and thirty-six motorized or mechanized brigades. The number of armoured fighting vehicles (tanks, armoured cars and self-propelled guns) and heavy artillery units as army and corps troops (that is, those not in divisions but available to the army or corps commander) was not known. When divisions facing Finland and in Leningrad, in the Caucasus, Central Asia and the Far East were deducted, then 120 rifle divisions and most of the armour would face a German invasion. Much Soviet equipment was considered inferior, but was being rapidly replaced. This replacement programme could run into bottlenecks, however, owing to the shortage of skilled industrial workers. There was a shortage of transport and Russian tanks were generally seen as being of poor quality, mainly copies of foreign models, and their crews lacking in training and in the initiative necessary for a war of manoeuvre. The Russian soldier was seen as being frugal, brave, loyal and tough with the ability to hold out 'even in defeat and under heavy pressure'. Unlike his performance in the Winter War, where the average Russian was unenthusiastic about the cause, he was expected to fight to the finish for his motherland. After the Winter War, however, the Russian state and army had taken note of the lessons from its less than distinguished performance and the command structure had been reorganized to reduce the influence of the political commissar and return it to where it should be – with the military commander. A new military code emphasized the importance of discipline and gave commanders authority to use any methods necessary (including shooting their own men) to enforce an order. The biggest weaknesses, thought the German army, were in the middle and senior officer ranks, where the effects of the Great Terror of 1937 and 1938 had not yet been made good, and in the reliance by the Red Army on numbers rather than movement.

* * *

In 1939 the Soviet president, Mikhail Kalinin, described Stalin as 'Father, teacher, great leader of the Soviet people, heir to the cause of Lenin, creator of the Soviet constitution, transformer of nature, great helmsman, great strategist of the revolution, genius of mankind, the greatest genius of all times and peoples.'[36] Despite the hyperbole, by 1940 Stalin had consolidated his rule. Rationing had ended, there was food in the shops, the Moscow underground railway had been completed, new factories provided jobs, new schools were being built, and culture and the arts were being supported. The hated collective farms were still there, of course, but, while life in the people's paradise was still extremely grim by Western standards, things were better than they had been at any time since the revolution. The Great Terror had removed any threat to the regime from within and while people were still arrested for the most trifling offences – or for none at all – the Commissar for Internal Affairs, and head of the secret police, the NKVD, had been removed from office (and shot) in 1939 and replaced by Laventi Beria. Seen in hindsight as a monster, by contemporary standards Beria was a bleeding heart liberal and his brief was to moderate the activities of the NKVD and concentrate on solving murders, fraud and sabotage by agents inserted from without rather than in seeking out traitors and counter-revolutionaries. The course of the war in the West was well covered by the newspapers (all government-run) with a very fair balance between British and German reports. The overwhelming view amongst Russians who knew or cared about such things was that they had no wish to be involved in the war, but if it did come there was great confidence in the mighty Red Army with its superlative air arm and swarms of tanks.

Stalin knew perfectly well that the reality was very different. He was well aware of Hitler's oft-stated intent towards the East and his views on Bolshevism, and, at the time of Munich and after, he calculated that neither Britain nor France was in any position to offer meaningful military support to Russia. Russia should therefore buy time to build up her armed forces by placating Germany. The capitalist powers would fight each other to exhaustion, and Russia could then act as she pleased. The German–Soviet Pact of August 1939 was the obvious result of Soviet thinking and gave the USSR a buffer in the form of eastern Poland and the Baltic States. Yet the sudden and spectacular German victories in the Battle of France threw all Stalin's calculations into disarray. Far from being fought to exhaustion, Germany was stronger than ever, with France defeated and the British forced to abandon the Continent. The Russian military build-up would now have to be accelerated and in the interim all possible means to appease the Germans would have to be implemented.

The lessons of the Winter War with Finland, where the Red Army had not done well, and the Russo-Japanese clashes of 1939, where it had (eventually), were pored over. The Red Army was to be doubled, design of the new tanks was to be accelerated, new aircraft would replace the ageing veterans of the Spanish Civil War, and nine mechanized corps were to be formed immediately and another twenty as soon as possible thereafter. From May 1940 general ranks were reintroduced* and to partially address the shortage of senior officers, many of whom had been imprisoned as a result of the purge but against whom nothing substantive could be proved, were released and reinstated. These included the future Marshals of the Soviet Union Konstantin Rokossovsky, Georgi Zhukov, Semyon Timoshenko, Semyon Budenny and Ivan Koniev, all of whom had been NCOs in the Tsarist army and sided with the Bolsheviks in the revolution. The one general who might have been able to put the Red Army on a war footing rather more swiftly had been Marshal Mikhail Tukachevsky, who, although born of a noble family and an officer in the Tsarist army, had also sided with the Bolsheviks in the revolution. He was a reformer and an advocate of armoured warfare, but as People's Commissar for Defence in 1937 he fell victim to Stalin's purge and was shot. His replacement was a party hack, Marshal Klim Voroshilov, who understood little of modern warfare and achieved less, although he did introduce compulsory folk-dancing lessons for officers.† By 1941 the only officer with any real comprehension of the higher

---

*During the formation of the Red Army, officer ranks were abolished, being replaced by functional titles (company commander, battalion commander etc), then in the 1930s junior and field ranks (second lieutenant to colonel) were reintroduced, but functional titles were still used for what had been generals' ranks. Hence, Army Commander First Rate was a Front (Army Group in British, American and German terms) commander, or five-star general, Army Commander Second Rate was an army commander, or four-star general, and so on down.

†There was a period in the 1960s and 1970s when fervour for Scottish country dancing swept through the British Army like dysentery at the siege of Harfleur. Some commanding officers in perfectly respectable regiments with no Scottish connections made these evenings mandatory. This author found that the only way to survive was either to employ ridicule and sabotage (the eightsome reel is particularly susceptible) or to consume very large quantities of alcohol.

management of war was Marshal Shaposnikov, an ex-colonel of the Tsar and suspect because of it.

From the spring of 1940 the Red Army was supposed to be preparing for a defensive war against Germany. Not only did Stalin and his generals realize that the pact could not last for ever but there was plenty of intelligence indicating that Germany was preparing to attack. The Russians had highly placed agents in Tokyo, London and Berlin, and the movement of German troops eastwards could not be concealed entirely. It is, however, one thing to collect raw intelligence and quite another to assess and interpret it. History abounds with examples of the discarding of useful information in favour of something more convenient, and of officers who only believe that which fits in with their own preconceived ideas, or conforms to what they wish to be true.*

By early 1941 the intelligence being collated and assessed by the Red Army could be interpreted in two ways: either it indicated an attack on Russia in the near future or it could simply be a German attempt to put pressure on the USSR in order to extract more concessions. It was for the GRU, the intelligence arm of the Red Army, and its director to draw conclusions from the intelligence gathered and to brief Stalin and the Politburo accordingly. The director prior to and during the Winter War, General Ivan Proskurov, had been sacked for standing up to Stalin and rebutting the dictator's criticisms of the GRU's performance during that war. The new director, General Filipp Golikov, was by no means a fool but equally was going to look after his own career and had no intention of saying anything that did not support what Stalin already believed, or wanted to believe. Golikov duly described the German build-up as an attempt to blackmail the USSR while the Germans dealt with the British and avoided a war on two fronts – an interpretation that matched the misinformation being put about by German intelligence.

The frontier between German-controlled territory and that of the USSR was approximately 800 miles north to south, with the 100 or so miles of the Pripet Marshes roughly in the middle. The Russian general staff considered that the Germans, when and if they did invade, would most likely attack

---

*For a proof of this, and lots of other explanations as to why the senior officer you thought behaved oddly did so, see Norman F. Dixon, *On the Psychology of Military Incompetence*, Jonathan Cape, London, 1976.

either north or south of the marshes. In January a series of war games indicated that, wherever the Germans came, the defenders would be beaten. Stalin sacked the Chief of the General Staff, General Kirill Meretskov, and replaced him with General Georgi Zhukov. A man of tremendous willpower and fighting spirit, who browbeat any contrary argument into submission, Zhukov followed the old Tsarist tradition of slapping any officer or soldier who displeased him. He was not, however, a man of great acumen, nor greatly suited to administration, nor prepared to oppose anything Stalin wanted.

As late as March 1941 Stalin was convinced, Golikov concurring, that the main sources of reports predicting an imminent attack were British and American and were designed to provoke a breakdown in German–Soviet relations. Stalin knew very well that it was in the British interest that Germany and Russia should fall out, and his suspicions of the British were fuelled when Rudolf Hess, hitherto the German deputy Führer, parachuted into Scotland on the night of 10/11 May 1941 in an attempt, so he claimed, to negotiate a peace between Britain and Germany.* Even at the last minute, Stalin still refused to accept that an attack was likely, although it would have made no difference if he had believed it was. Either way, there was never going to be enough time to put right the lack of professional knowledge in the officer corps and to replace obsolete weapons and equipment. Furthermore, any defensive plans drawn up before 1939 were useless as Russia now had to cover the new territories of Poland, the Baltic States and the annexed Romanian provinces, and Stalin had therefore ordered the demolition of the old frontier defences and the preparation of new ones to the west. The Red Army would fight forward, a policy that played into German hands, and when the time came it found itself with two incomplete lines of defences, neither of which was of much help. The Red Army owned

---

*Hess was an old friend of Hitler's, serving in the same regiment in the first war (albeit commissioned whereas Hitler was a JNCO) before becoming a fighter pilot. He shared a cell with Hitler after the failed Munich *putsch* and became deputy leader of the NSDAP (not, as is so often claimed, deputy leader of the state). Quite what was behind his flight to Britain is still not clear: not all the files have been released by TNA, but most of the conspiracy theories have been disproved. The British government refused to negotiate (or said they did) and Hess ended up in Spandau jail as the last prisoner of the Nuremberg trials, and he died there in 1987, probably by his own hand. This author once commanded the guard on Hess, and discovered that a source of amusement for the old boy was to beg cigarettes from the soldiers and then, having smoked them, report the donors for breaking the rule of no contact with the prisoner.

more tanks than the rest of the world put together but the tank units had few radios and so could not be used for deep penetration or wide flanking manoeuvres. The level of technical understanding was still far too low, all-arms training was deficient and logistics systems were primitive. Some modern historians[37] have suggested that Stalin was very well aware of Hitler's real intentions and was in fact preparing for a pre-emptive strike by the Red Army into Poland and then Germany (as Zhukov urged him to), and it is true that the dispositions of the Russian forces in 1941 look more like preparations for an offensive than for defence. There is very little evidence for this, however, and what there is appears suspect: Russian doctrine in any case emphasized immediate counter-attacks, and so the location of the Russian fronts cannot of themselves be taken as evidence of aggressive intentions. But even if Stalin had pre-empted the Germans and launched an attack, the Red Army would have come off worse.

* * *

In Hitler's Directive Number 21, issued in December 1940 and amended by subsequent OKW and OKH orders, Case Barbarossa,* the invasion of the USSR, was set for 15 May 1941. Then came the inconvenient necessity to rescue Mussolini from his ill-judged invasions of Greece and Egypt, which forced a delay until 22 June 1941. As the spring thaw in Russia was late that year, this delay probably made little difference, and the effects of sending two panzer divisions to Libya were minimal, but the need to garrison the Balkans reduced the number of troops available for Russia, while the Luftwaffe's losses in aircraft and in elite airborne troops in the Crete operation could not be made good in time. The armour had suffered from the bad roads and excessive track mileage in the Balkans and a large number of Germany's total tank strength was in workshops being repaired when Barbarossa was launched. In June 1941 the German army deployed thirty-eight infantry divisions in garrison duties in the Low Countries, France and Germany, eight divisions in Norway† and seven in the

---

*Frederick I (1122–90) was king of Germany and Holy Roman Emperor from 1152. Called Barbarossa because of his red beard, he did much to unify Germany and was drowned while on crusade. German legend says that he sleeps in a mountain cave ready to return and restore Germany to her ancient greatness. This is probably untrue.

†Far more than was needed to keep order, but the Germans were convinced that the British intended to invade Norway, an impression that the British, with constant pinprick commando raids, did their best to reinforce.

Balkans, which left 120 available for Barbarossa plus nineteen panzer and sixteen motorized infantry divisions. Additionally, there would be thirty-six divisions provided by Germany's allies, ranging from fourteen each from Finland and Romania to one division of Spanish volunteers.

Armoured divisions had been reorganized as a result of the Battle of France, although not all had yet implemented the new establishment. They now had either two or three battalions of tanks, between four and six battalions of lorry-borne infantry, a reconnaissance battalion on motorcycles, an artillery regiment of thirty-six 105mm towed field guns, three anti-tank companies each of twelve 37mm or 50mm guns mounted on tank chassis, an armoured reconnaissance company in armoured cars, an engineer company and an anti-aircraft company. The tank battalions were supposed to have two companies each of Mk III tanks with either a 37mm or a 50mm gun, and one company of Mk IVs with a short-barrelled 75mm gun. In practice, of the 3,648 tanks that the German army deployed for Barbarossa, only 1,000 were Mk IIIs and but 450 Mk IVs. The remainder were either Mk IIs with a 20mm gun effective against only the thinnest of armour or captured Czech Panzer 35s and 38s. The infantry divisions which made up the bulk of the German forces had nine battalions of infantry, each of around 600 men, an artillery regiment of forty-eight field (105mm) and medium (150mm) guns and three anti-tank companies each with twelve 37mm anti-tank guns. Motorized divisions had six battalions instead of nine, but all were lorry-borne with their artillery towed by lorries or half-tracks.

As for the Luftwaffe, it fielded 1,945 aircraft in support of Barbarossa, 200 less than it had provided for the Battle of France as losses over Britain and in the Balkans and Crete had not yet been made good. Of these, 150 were transport aircraft and eighty the versatile Fieseler 156 Storch STOL (short take-off and landing) liaison machines. The remainder included 510 twin-engined bombers (Do 17s, Ju 88s, He 111s), 290 dive bombers (Ju 87 Stukas*), 440 Bf 109 single- and forty Me 110 twin-engined fighters and 120 recon-naissance aircraft (Ju 86s and Fw 189s).

---

*Effective in the Battle of France as airborne artillery, the Stuka with its terrifying siren relied on its psychological effect as much as on its ability to deliver a 200lb bomb with pinpoint accuracy. By the time of the Battle of Britain, it was obsolete against RAF fighters and was withdrawn from use in the West.

The army was well trained in what it had to do. Morale was high after the sweeping victories in Poland and France, and the Luftwaffe was the finest air force in the world at providing close support for ground forces. One good kick at the Soviet door and the whole edifice would come tumbling down. There were, however, weaknesses. The Russian rail gauge was not the same as that in use in Germany, so, even if the Russians did not destroy their railway lines, these could only be used by the Germans after cross-loading. The German army used a wide variety of vehicles, many of them captured, all requiring different spare parts and servicing schedules. The failure to have all the armoured divisions on the same establishment meant that the contents of resupply packets had to vary depending on the division to be supported. And in the infantry divisions, the bulk of the forces to be deployed, the soldiers marched while artillery pieces and all administrative transport at battalion level were horse-drawn, adding a huge burden in forage and in the manpower needed to look after the animals. Apart from the armoured and motorized divisions, the army could move no faster than Napoleon's *Grande Armée* in 1812. While the allied contingents were valuable politically, and their manpower could be used to garrison rear areas, the requirement to administer them added to the Germans' logistic difficulties and there were tensions between them. The Slovaks (two divisions) had to be kept away from the Romanians (four divisions), who in turn could not be placed anywhere near the Hungarians (one division and 160 light tanks), while Austrian members of the Wehrmacht were not entirely convinced that Italy (four divisions) did not still have ambitions in the Austrian Tyrol.

Furthermore, the Luftwaffe possessed no heavy bombers comparable with those coming into service with the RAF: it could not therefore mount effective raids on rail communications and industrial plants deep within Russia, and it had too few transport aircraft should resupply by road and rail be insufficient. Neither the army nor the air force was ready for a long war, but it was not intended that it should be a long war: armoured and motorized formations would strike deep into Soviet territory, cutting off whole armies and destroying them before they could mount a defence farther back. The campaign would be over in weeks, and there was no need to order winter clothing – indeed, only the Luftwaffe's Field Marshal Erhard Milch, in charge of procurement, ignored instructions and ordered 800,000 sets of cold-weather clothing to equip the air force officers and men, who he suspected would still be in Russia when the snows came.

The attack on Russia would be mounted by over 3 million men, 625,000 horses, 600,000 motor vehicles of various types and 3,600 armoured fighting vehicles.[38] The army staff calculated that they would take 475,000 casualties (killed, wounded, missing) in the first three months of the war, but the replacement army in Germany was only 385,000 strong and the next call-up, of those born in 1922, was not due until November 1941. This meant that not only could losses not be replaced, but also the units attacking on 22 June could not be relieved and the normal military practice of rotating units in and out of the theatre could not be followed. All this reinforced the need for a short war. If the USSR could be destroyed in six to eight weeks, then large parts of the army could be demobilized and the men released to industry.

The German forces would be in three army groups. Field Marshal Wilhelm Ritter von Leeb's Army Group North would strike from East Prussia through the Baltic States towards Leningrad with three panzer, three motorized and twenty infantry divisions; Field Marshal Fedor von Bock's Army Group Centre would attack north of the Pripet Marshes, mask Brest-Litovsk and take Minsk, Smolensk and, ultimately, Moscow with ten panzer, five motorized and thirty-one infantry divisions; Field Marshal Gerd von Rundstedt's Army Group South would push its seven panzer (including one SS panzer), two motorized and thirty-four (including four light, one air-landing, one mountain and four Romanian) divisions from southern Poland, Hungary and Romania through southern Russia and into the Ukraine.* The intention was for the armoured and motorized divisions to cut through the Russian front in great wide pincer movements, joining behind the enemy, holding that ring and preventing the Russian armies from retreating until they were dealt with by the German infantry divisions following up. It was a perfectly sensible and realistic plan.

Facing the assembling might of the Wehrmacht were four fronts. General Markian Popov's Northern Front faced Finland and the German army in Norway, and had eighteen rifle and one and a half motorized divisions; Colonel-General Fyodor Kutznetsov's North-West Front defended the Baltic States and had twenty-eight rifle, three motorized and two horsed

---

*The army group commanders were aged sixty-five, sixty-one and sixty-six respectively, rather contradicting the widely held (by the young) view that only the young are sufficiently robust to cope with modern war.

cavalry divisions; General Dmitri Pavlov's Western Front faced the German Army Group Centre and had thirty rifle, twelve tank, two horsed cavalry and one and a half airborne divisions; and Colonel-General Mikhail Kirponos's South-West Front had forty-five rifle, five motorized and ten horsed cavalry divisions. There were therefore 121 Russian infantry divisions compared to eighty-five German, twelve Russian to twenty German tank divisions and 9.5 Russian to ten German motorized divisions. Behind the Russian front lines were more infantry and armoured reserves and on numbers alone these should have been more than sufficient to hold off an invasion. Quite apart from the difference in technology and training, however, the figures are deceptive. While a Russian division had the same number of battalions as a German – nine – there were 17,000 all ranks in a German infantry division and only 9,600 in a Russian one. A German tank division had 118 tanks, a Russian one 195, but the Russians communicated by flags whereas the Germans were controlled by radio. A German armoured division had 15,500 all ranks compared to 11,000 for the Russian equivalent. The Russian air force, part of the Red Army in 1941 rather than an independent service like the RAF or the Luftwaffe, had around 10,000 aircraft in 1941 with about half serviceable. Many were obsolete, most had no radios and Russia had no radar network. Many of the aircraft had been moved to recently constructed airfields near the new western border, but hard shelters had not yet been constructed and the aircraft sat parked on the strips.

For the Germans, the logistic support required for the mobile war that they intended to wage was an immense task, the responsibility of the army's Quartermaster General, General Eugen Müller, and his deputy and eventual successor, Lieutenant-General Edouard Wagner. In broad terms, army groups were to jump off with fourteen days' supply of ammunition, fuel and rations, which would translate to the infantry soldier carrying four days' rations on his back and vehicles carrying five days' fuel in jerricans,* followed up by fuel bowsers. During this time, the quartermaster service would set up and stock depots, with major depots to be no more than 100–200 kilometres behind the front. From these, armies would draw what they needed and the depots

---

*This was an excellent steel container holding either fuel or water, two of which could be carried by one man, allowing refuelling of a vehicle to be done by its crew rather than having bowsers come to it. The British first saw them in North Africa (and called them Jerry cans for obvious reasons) and copied them. Today the four-and-a-half-gallon jerrican is still an essential piece of British military equipment.

would move forward as the army did. As it was known that the Russian railway gauge was not compatible with the German, and as Russian rolling stock would not be captured, or, if it was, it would have been rendered useless, it was decided to convert the Russian lines to German gauge. This would take two weeks and thereafter the engineers would aim to develop the lines to keep up with the advance. In the meantime, 15,000 farm carts complete with horses and drivers were hired in German-controlled Poland.

Although the army had some reservations about embarking on the Russian war before the one in the West was finally over, and while there was some tinkering by Hitler with the operational plan, the generals and the politicians were generally agreed as to the military objectives. It was when the post-conflict governance of captured areas came to be considered that divergence of opinion arose. The army's view was that responsibility for keeping order in territories that it overran lay with it until such time as peacetime conditions had been restored, when it would hand over to civil government agencies. During the period of military control, German military and international law would apply. The German government's view was that the army was there to destroy the Russian armies and control of captured territory was a matter for the civil power. A directive issued in Hitler's name on 5 March 1941 and entitled *Practice of Jurisdiction in the Barbarossa Zone of Operations and on Special Measures by Army Personnel* instructed the army to cooperate with SS agencies, allowed collective punishments to be authorized by a battalion commander or above and, astonishingly, stated that there was no obligation to prosecute Germans for offences against the civilian population except for certain acts of violence, and even then only verdicts which were 'in line with Leadership's political intentions' were to be confirmed.[39] Captured political commissars were to be separated from other prisoners and handed over for 'special treatment'. The Commander-in-Chief of the army did his best to water this down, insisting that military discipline was to be maintained, that action was to be taken against a commissar only if he 'places himself or intends to place himself against the German Wehrmacht by a specific identifiable action or attitude', and that officers were to ensure there were to be no arbitrary acts of violence by individuals.

On 15 March 1941 the army's Quartermaster General, now Wagner, had discussions with SS Gruppenführer (lieutenant-general) Reinhard Heydrich, head of the SS State Security Service, the Sicherheitsdienst or SD, to establish the demarcation of roles between the army and the SS security police

Einsatzgruppen or 'action groups' that would move in once the army had pacified the area. Heydrich made no secret of his intention that, as in Poland, his action groups would deal with 'anti-Reich and anti-German elements in the enemy country behind the fighting troops'.[40] These included 'émigrés, freemasons, Jews, intelligentsia, saboteurs, terrorists, clergy and nobility', although in Russia the last two groups would not detain the SS long as most had been eliminated by the communists or had fled abroad. The SS were authorized to take 'executive measures' against the civilian population. The army had not been happy with the behaviour of the SS in Poland, and Wagner insisted on having it laid down on paper that the SS would discharge their duties outside the army's zone of control and on their own responsibility. How much Wagner and his staff knew of the intentions of the SS, concealed as they were behind bureaucratic phraseology, is debatable, but he clearly suspected something and tried to ensure that, whatever the SS got up to, the army would not be tainted by it.

As it was, on 6 June 1941 the 'Commissar Order' was issued by NSDAP decree, stating that political commissars were not of combatant status and not entitled to protection under international law. Commissars were to be shot on capture, either by the army if captured in the operational zone or by the SS elsewhere. Both OKW and OKH struggled long and hard to dress up what was unquestionably illegal and immoral as a military necessity by painting commissars and political functionaries as threats to security. The preamble to the order stressed that the enemy could not be expected to behave in accordance with the principles of humanity or international law, and that political commissars could be expected to 'indulge in hate-filled, cruel and inhuman treatment of those of our men they have taken prisoner'. They were 'the originators of barbaric Asiatic fighting methods' and any consideration by the troops for such people on the grounds of international law would be a mistake. When it was promulgated to the army, various commanders took differing views of the order. Some passed it on and supported it, others put it in the pending tray and left it there, others ordered that only commissars actively resisting should be shot and yet others said that such prisoners should be handed over to the SS out of the combat zone.

In the introduction to his operation order for Panzer Group 4, part of Army Group North, Colonel-General Erich Hoepner wrote:

> The war against Russia is an essential phase in the German nation's struggle for existence. It is the ancient struggle for the Germanic peoples against Slavdom. The defence of European culture against the Muscovite-Asiatic tide, the repulse of Jewish-Bolshevism. That struggle must have as its aim the shattering of present-day Russia and must therefore be waged with unprecedented hardness. Every combat action must be inspired, in concept and execution, by an iron determination to ensure the merciless, total annihilation of the enemy. In particular there must be no sparing the exponents of the present Russian Bolshevik system.[41]

This was strong stuff, although no worse than some of the things Churchill said about the Nazis. Many officers, on the other hand, shared the pragmatic view of Lieutenant-Colonel Henning von Tresckow, on the headquarters staff of Army Group Centre, who wrote: 'If international law is to be infringed, it should be done by the Russians and not by us.'

Such, however, were the seeds of a situation that would cause all sorts of legal and administrative problems later on, not least in post-war trials: who was in charge once the fighting had moved on, and what exactly was the legal position? Both Germany and Russia had signed the Hague Convention of 1907 but the USSR had declined to recognize the Tsarist signature of the accord and therefore it could be argued that she was not entitled to the convention's protection. Furthermore, the USSR had not signed the Geneva Convention of 1929 dealing with the treatment of prisoners of war, although both the USSR and Germany had signed the 1921 and 1925 protocols that dealt with the treatment of wounded and sick in time of war and banned the use of chemical and biological weapons. The 1921 document specifically banned collective punishments and reprisals. It would appear therefore that, while neither country was obliged to follow the strict conditions and small print of Hague or Geneva, they were obliged to behave in what most people would consider a reasonable way. Ultimately neither did, the only difference being that the Germans tried to dress up what they did in a cloak of legality, whereas the Russians did not bother.

Already the SS (*Schutzstaffel*, literally 'guard detachment') was a state within a state. Originally formed in 1923 as small groups of bodyguards, meeting stewards and propagandists for the NSDAP, by 1933 the SS had 200,000 members under the leadership of the Reichsführer SS Heinrich Himmler. It rapidly grew and by

1941 had assumed more and more functions of state, including the Race and Settlement Office, dealing with matters of Aryan descent and decisions as to who was a German and who was not; the secret police;* the Criminal Police; and the management of concentration camps. It had its own intelligence arm, which absorbed the state security organs, and it had expanded into industry, particularly the armaments industry. It had its own armed branch, the Waffen SS, which had been formed in 1939 from various quasi-legal armed groupings. The generals, however, were not prepared to tolerate two armies in the state and so the Waffen SS came under the army for operations, and was integrated into army formations, but retained its own rank structure and training organization. Its units were made up entirely of volunteers and, as the SS grip on industry tightened, it tended to get the most modern weapons. Well trained and highly motivated, the Waffen SS would expand to thirty-eight divisions by 1945. SS divisions were amongst the most effective in the German order of battle, they fought ferociously until the very end and 25 per cent of all the men who served in the Waffen SS were killed. As a very young organization, it lacked staff experience and a number of senior commanders and staff officers were loaned by the army. After the war, the whole of the SS was tarred with the same brush, and, because the concentration camps had been run by the General SS (whose camp guards were mostly men medically unfit or too old for military service), the men of the Waffen SS, who by and large had behaved themselves, at least in the West, and the widows of their dead were denied the pensions to which they were entitled, a wrong not righted until most of them were themselves dead.

* * *

Between 0300 and 0330 on Sunday, 22 June 1941, depending on the time of first light at different parts of the front, the greatest war ever seen anywhere began. As with the attack on Poland and the Battle of France, it was the Luftwaffe that opened the batting. Sixty-six Soviet air bases were attacked. Most had no hard shelters, aircraft were parked wing-tip to wing-tip on the tarmac or earthen strips and 800 were destroyed on the ground, while another 400 or so were shot down. It was, in modern parlance, a target-rich environment and the Luftwaffe very quickly established air superiority. Then, over a frontage of 1,000 miles, the German army began to move.

---

*Geheime Staatspolizei or Gestapo, responsible for combating subversion and espionage within Germany. The nearest equivalent in the UK is the Police Special Branch, although neither might have liked the comparison.

What the Germans were attempting was on a truly massive scale. The USSR covered an area of over 8.5 million square miles: a million square miles more than China and the United States put together and five times the area of the present-day European Union. It was 6,000 miles from its European western border to its Asiatic eastern edge, more than twice as far as the distance from San Francisco to New York. The accounts of German soldiers who served in the Russian war all talk of the vast expanses of un- or under-populated wastes, mile after mile after mile of steppe, forest or, in the winter, snow, often with not a building or an inhabitant to be seen for hours on end. It would soon begin to seem that, however far they drove into Russia, there was still a huge way to go, and that, however many Russians they killed or captured, there were still many more to be dealt with, yet in June 1941 the mood was very different and everything that the German army planned seemed achievable.

Army Group North was the smallest of the three army groups, but the road network in the Baltic States was much better than that in the USSR proper, and in the first phase the tasks of Army Group North were to establish a crossing over the River Dvina, in the process cutting off and destroying Russian forces west of that river, to take the city of Riga and then to swing north and north-east to link up with the Finns advancing south from Finland to surround the city of Leningrad. To do this Field Marshal von Leeb had Panzer Group 4 (Colonel-General Hoepner), Sixteenth Army (Colonel-General Ernst Busch) and Eighteenth Army (Colonel-General Georg von Kuchler). Altogether, the army group fielded three panzer, twenty-two infantry and two motorized infantry divisions, with one motorized division (3 SS *Totenkopf*)* in reserve. The armour would advance as fast as possible in two spearheads. On the left General of Panzer Troops Hans-Georg Reinhardt with XXXXI Corp's two armoured, one motorized and one infantry division would push towards Jacobstadt on the Dvina, while on the right General of Infantry Erich von Manstein's† LVI Corps would head for

---

*The SS *Totenkopfverbände* were originally armed units with some military training who guarded concentration camps when those camps had not yet become extermination centres. They were embodied into the Waffen SS as the nucleus of the *Totenkopf* Division in 1939 and replaced by members of the General SS.

†Born the tenth child of General of Artillery von Lewinski, he was adopted at birth by his mother's childless sister and her husband, Lieutenant-General von Manstein, thus his full name was Fritz Erich von Lewinski gennant von Manstein, and in this author's opinion he was the best general of the war on any side. Prior to Barbarossa, he had instructed his corps that the Commissar Order was not to be implemented.

Dunaburg, also on the Dvina, with one armoured, one motorized and one infantry division. The two armies, Eighteenth on the left and Sixteenth on the right, would deal with Russian units bypassed by the panzer group, establish a bridgehead over the Dvina once crossing points had been seized by the armour, and protect the panzer group's flanks as far as they could. Once all that had been achieved, the army group would take Riga and then link up with the Finns.

Army Group North knew it outnumbered the Russian forces opposing it – one armoured division, four armoured brigades and eighteen infantry divisions of the Baltic Military District – but it had only vague intelligence as to how they might fight. It could be that the Baltic States would not be defended at all, and despite reconnaissance flights by the Luftwaffe it was unclear whether the bridges over the lesser rivers between the jump-off line and the Dvina had been prepared for demolition. The probability was that the population would welcome the Wehrmacht as liberators, so, while civilian resistance need not be feared, there would inevitably be Russian troops cut off by the rapid advance who would have to be dealt with. It was a huge task – both Jacobstadt and Dunaburg were 200 miles from the start line and were fifty miles apart. To get to their assembly areas for the attack, the German troops had to cross the River Nemen where it flowed through East Prussia and this could not be concealed from the Russians; nor the quantities of bridging equipment being stockpiled behind the frontier. Resupply of the armoured columns would be impossible because of the speed at which it was intended they would move, and the presence of enemy units bypassed but still on the supply routes, so they would carry all the fuel and rations they needed with them. Although the mud of the spring thaw had dried up, the threat now was dust, which got into vehicle engines, clogged up air filters and radiators and for the marching infantry made it difficult to see beyond a hundred yards. In four months the snows would come, but by then the war would be won.

The Russians were caught completely unprepared. Although Timoshenko had become increasingly convinced that the intelligence suggesting a German attack was genuine, he could not convince Stalin, who insisted on doing everything possible to avoid a war. Thus, when the attack came, the Russian army was deployed neither for an offensive into German-occupied Poland nor for defence, but for something in between and that not very well. Most units were in barracks when the blow fell and even then Stalin took some while to accept that Hitler really had broken his word and that all Soviet Russia's cooperation since the pact of 1939 had only bought him a little time. There was less excuse for General Kuznetsov as, even under the contingency plan for an offensive, his troops were supposed to remain on the defensive, but in his North-Western Front headquarters in Mitau in Latvia, 200 miles from the front line, there was first confusion and then panic. Information was slow coming in and, when it did arrive, it was incomplete. What was happening? What were the enemy trying to do? Where were they heading for? How many were there? Crossing the Nemen south of Memel, Manstein's armour pushed bewildered frontier guards out of the way, burst through the right flank of the Russian Eighth Army and drove deep into Lithuania through negligible opposition. By early afternoon Manstein had crossed the River Dubissa and was advancing through wooded country in the direction of the rail junction at Schaulen. That the terrain was unsuitable for armour mattered not – the few Russians that he met were quickly dealt with. Reinhardt's corps attacking from Tilsit met stiffer opposition as he hit the one division in the centre of the Eighth Army that was able to put up some resistance but that was quickly dealt with and, after a series of skirmishes, he was through Tauragé and well beyond the frontier. Now the two infantry armies began to move, the Eighteenth along the coast towards Libau to force the Russian Eighth Army back from the sea, and the Sixteenth at the junction between the Russian Eighth and Eleventh Armies. Both armies met scattered groups of Russians, some of which put up a fight before being destroyed or driven back into the woods. Kuznetsov was still trying desperately to work out what was happening, but an attempt to counter-attack the Germans at Tauragé with his armour failed when units were unable to communicate with each other, and Reinhardt's tanks stopped another attempt to move armour south to stem the advance of Army Group Centre.

It was Army Group Centre, which it was intended would eventually capture Moscow, that would deliver the main thrust of Barbarossa and so it had as much armour as the other two army groups combined. The Chief of the General Staff of the army, General Franz Halder, already concerned that Hitler would start to interfere with the drive on Moscow, had posted his own chief of operations branch, Major-General Hans von Greiffenberg, as Chief of Staff to Field Marshal von Bock in order, as Halder put it, to 'avoid cross-fire from the upper atmosphere'. The plan was to strike north and south of Minsk to the area north of Smolensk to destroy the Russian forces in Belorussia with two pincer arms provided by Panzer Group 2 (Colonel-General Heinz Guderian with six panzer and six infantry divisions and the German army's one horsed cavalry division) on the right and Panzer Group 3 (Colonel-General Herman Hoth and four panzer, three motorized and four infantry divisions) on the left. The armour would push on, bypassing any major enemy formations, the cavalry would look after the northern edge of the Pripet Marshes and the two armies, Fourth commanded by Field Marshal Gunther von Kluge and Ninth commanded by Colonel-General Adolf Strauss, would deal with the city of Brest-Litovsk, strongly garrisoned by NKVD troops,* and follow up the armour to deal with Russian forces caught in their encirclement. Opposing them would be the southern army (11th) of the North-Western Front and the thirty rifle, twelve tank, two horsed cavalry and two airborne divisions of General Dimitri Pavlov's Western Front. Pavlov was one of the Red Army's better generals. Aged forty-four in 1941, he had fought as a young soldier in the Russian Civil War, earning rapid promotion after it. He had commanded the Russian troops sent to Spain, survived Stalin's purges, commanded one of the few successful Russian attacks of the Winter War, and both understood and was an advocate of armoured warfare. It would be of little avail.

As the German armour crossed into Russia, Field Marshal Albert Kesselring's Second Air Fleet hit Kutznetsov's southern army and Pavlov's supporting air fleet, which was virtually wiped out. Unwilling to report the disaster to Moscow, the air commander, the forty-nine-year-old Major-General Ivan Koppets,† shot himself, probably only anticipating his fate once Stalin had learned what had happened. On the right of Army Group Centre's advance, Guderian's Panzer Group 2 bypassed Brest-Litovsk, dropping off its 45 Infantry Division to take the town, crossed

---

*Originally lightly armed border troops under the Interior Ministry, there were about 100,000 of them along the western frontier of the USSR in June 1941, including the Brest-Litovsk garrison. Later they were formed into fifteen infantry divisions and as the most politically indoctrinated units of the Red Army were used for a variety of tasks, including rear area security, apprehending deserters and partisan activity, as well as being deployed in major battles as combat divisions.

†Koppets had done rather well, rising from captain to major-general in three years as those above him were progressively purged.

the River Bug and headed for Minsk, while from south-west of Vilnius Hoth's armour drove through the southern flank of the Russian Eleventh Army, already under attack from Reinhardt to the north, captured three bridges over the River Nemen and struck the junction of the North-Western and Western Fronts. General Kutznetsov eventually learned of this rupture and tried to send his armour south to deal with it. Harried by the Luftwaffe from the air, those Russian tanks that were not knocked out on the way were stopped by Reinhardt's XXXXI Corps. It would have made little difference to the result had the commander of the Western Front not been on his way back from a concert party when the blow fell.*
There was no one at his Western Front headquarters capable of making a decision, and, when Pavlov did get there at around 0400 hours, he found his staff and much of his command in panic mode. The Luftwaffe had hit headquarters, radio relay stations, supply routes and ammunition dumps, and communications, never particularly good at the best of times, were in disarray. Pavlov tried to find out what was going on but was not in contact with most of his subordinates. Unable to get through to HQ Tenth Army by telephone or radio, he sent two of his staff officers to find out what was happening. As nobody at Tenth Army knew either of them, they were both assumed to be German spies and shot. Pavlov did manage to move some of his tanks, which held up one of Guderian's armoured divisions for a while, but by last light the Germans were investing Brest-Litovsk and the Russian armies were withdrawing behind the Nemen.

Army Group South covered a frontage equal to the other two army groups put together and its combat formations were split by 250 miles of the Hungarian frontier, which was to be defended by the Hungarians themselves. Commanded by Field Marshal Gerd von Rundstedt, the doyen of the German officer corps, the army group's Sixth Army (Field Marshal Walter von Reichenau) and Seventeenth Army (Colonel-General Karl-Heinrich von Stülpnagel), mustering between them twelve infantry, one mountain and three light divisions, began the war from Poland. There too was the Group's armour, Panzer Group 1 with seven panzer, two motorized and six infantry divisions commanded by Colonel-General Ewald von Kleist, who had commanded the armoured thrust through the Ardennes to the Channel coast in the Battle of France. Also under the command of von

---

*At three in the morning? Quite a concert party!

Rundstedt was Eleventh Army in Romania, commanded by Colonel-General Ritter von Schobert with six German and four Romanian infantry divisions, one German air-landing division, three Romanian mountain brigades and three Romanian cavalry brigades. All told, Rundstedt faced the Russian Southern and South-Western Fronts with fifty-six infantry, around thirty armoured and eleven horsed cavalry divisions. In sheer numbers the Germans did not stand a chance but what looked like an overwhelming Soviet superiority in armour was negated by the inability of the Russian armoured formations to manoeuvre independently, their lack of radios and the Luftwaffe's ability to pounce on any vehicle column. The tasks given to the army group were to destroy Soviet forces in Galicia and western Ukraine and to capture crossings over the River Dnieper at and south of Kiev, in the words of the OKH operation order 'at an early stage'. Kiev was 300 miles from the jump-off line.

The plan was for the Sixth Army with the panzer group under command to create a breach in the Soviet defences to allow the armour to break through and strike at the junction of the Russian Fifth and Sixth Armies, while farther south the Seventeenth Army would strike at Lvov, which was a mere 100 miles from the start point. In the south, there had been some discussions regarding the command of Romanian units. They were resolved with the appointment of the Romanian dictator, Marshal Ion Antonescu, as overall commander; HQ German Eleventh Army would, however, exercise operational command over Romanian units attached to it, although those of the latter nominated to defend their frontier to the south and not taking part in the attack would remain under Romanian command. The initial assault was entirely successful; the Luftwaffe knocked out 300 Soviet aircraft and the Sixth Army forced a way through the forward frontier defences. Even the Romanian units whose only remit was to hold the frontier managed to capture crossings over the River Prut to their front. Then, as the Russians realized what was happening, resistance stiffened. All three elements of the army group found that they were faced with a determined defence and Panzer Group 1's advantage in communications and training was largely negated by the heavily wooded country, which made it difficult for the armour to manoeuvre.

At the end of the first day of Barbarossa, despite the slower than expected progress of Army Group South, the German high command had every reason to be pleased. The Germans had broken through at numerous locations, the armour was racing ahead to complete a series of encirclements and Russian armies, broken and disorganized, were retreating in disorder. In Moscow, Stalin had eventually accepted that this was no private venture by a disaffected German general but the real thing, a fact confirmed when a somewhat embarrassed German ambassador delivered a formal declaration of war some hours after hostilities had opened. His reaction was to send Zhukov off to find out what was happening – thus depriving himself of a chief of staff in Moscow just when one was needed – and to order all fronts to mount immediate counter-attacks but, perhaps still hoping that it was all a terrible mistake, to pursue the Germans only as far as the border.

On 24 June the wings of the Fourth and Ninth Armies met east of Bialystok, and Panzer Groups 2 and 3 drove on to complete the encirclement. When Hoth and Guderian met east of Minsk on 28 June, 170 miles from their start line, the best part of four Russian armies were still within the pocket. Stalin had ordered that on no account was Minsk to fall to the Germans: it was of no strategic consequence whatsoever – neither a communications hub nor an industrial centre – but it was the capital of Belorussia, White Russia, a constituent republic of the USSR and so to Stalin a symbol that must not be lost, and, when it was, the game was up for Pavlov. He and his staff were summoned to Moscow, interviewed by the NKVD, forced to confess to all sorts of sins, including being in the pocket of foreign enemies of the state, and he, his chief of staff, artillery commander and chief intelligence officer were shot. Such a reversion to the tactics of the Great Terror was not likely to boost morale in a paranoid army of a paranoid country.

The creating of the Minsk pocket was a great success for the Germans, but the elimination of the Russian troops trapped within it would take time and tie down the mobile units, particularly as the infantry, despite prodigious feats of marching, could not keep up with the tanks. The Chief of the General Staff of the army, Halder, knew perfectly well that the two panzer group commanders were trying to get as free a hand and as much independence as they could, but at the same time he recognized that to use armoured units merely to hold a ring was not to make the most of their capabilities, and so he reorganized Army Group Centre. Field Marshal Kluge, Fourth Army commander, would take under command the two panzer groups and two of his own infantry corps, the whole to be renamed Fourth Armoured Army (*Panzerarmee*), to continue the drive on Moscow. Second Army, commanded by Colonel-General Maximilian Freiherr von Weichs, hitherto in OKH reserve, would now take under command the rest of Fourth Army and Sixth Army and reduce the pocket.

On 29 June, the day after the closing of the Minsk pocket, Brest-Litovsk, stoutly defended by the NKVD, fell to 45 Infantry Division of Guderian's Panzer Group 2, although by then 'Fast Heinz' was on the road to Moscow. The Soviet defences, such as they were, were fast falling apart and Kuznetsov attempted to pull what troops he could still control to the east of the Dvina. In the north, as the Russian Eighth Army retreated north into Estonia and the Eleventh east towards home, a gap opened up that Kuznetsov could not close and into which General Busch's German Sixteenth Army marched. On 26 June, Manstein's armour captured intact a bridge across the River Dvina at Dunaburg – he had fought his way 150 miles in four days – and on the 30th Reinhardt did the same at Jacobstadt. The Dvina line was now breached and the wretched Kuznetsov was sacked, narrowly escaping being shot. In the far north, Finland too was now at war. The Finns had always intended to enter the war on the German side but were biding their time and declared neutrality on 22 June when Barbarossa began. However, when the Russians opened fire on Finnish shipping and bombed the mainland (quite possibly accidentally), the Finns declared war on 26 June, coordinating their movements with two German mountain divisions which were crossing the Norwegian–Russian border and moving to threaten the Russian port of Murmansk. Meanwhile, in the south, despite stubborn resistance the Germans captured Lvov on 26 June. A counter-attack by Russian tanks was broken up by the Luftwaffe, and as they retreated through the city, NKVD troops settled old scores with the population (Poles and Ukrainians), shooting several thousand political prisoners out of hand.* On 27 June, Hungary declared war on the Soviet Union.

Three hundred miles east of the German jump-off line, the River Dvina, which has hitherto run from east to west, changes its course and turns north-west for the Gulf of Riga in the Baltic. Fifty miles south, the River Dnieper, which has also run from east to west, turns south into the Ukraine. Between those two rivers is an eighty-mile-wide corridor. It is the traditional invasion

---

*Quite apart from the legality, shooting large numbers of prisoners is not an efficient method of disposal. One shot may not kill and each victim must be examined and if necessary finished off. The whole process takes time, manpower and ammunition better used elsewhere. A more effective method, as the Russians followed by the Germans discovered, is the gas chamber.

route to Moscow and it was a major objective of Army Group Centre in the first phase of Barbarossa. It was here that Napoleon took the *Grande Armée* in 1812 and back again, now distinctly less grand, in 1813, and here that Barclay de Tolly marched a Russian army westwards in 1815. At the eastern end of the corridor on the Dnieper is the city of Smolensk. The plan now was for Hoth's Panzer Group 3 to cross the River Berezina in the area of Lepel and attack along the northern side of the corridor, while Guderian's Panzer Group 2 would cross the Dnieper where it bent to the south and push along the southern side. The two armoured groups would meet at Smolensk and seal the eastern end of the corridor, while the infantry armies would block the western end. To give the infantry sufficient troops to surround and subdue the huge 4,000-square-mile pocket, XXXV Corps, a large corps of five divisions, and XXXXII Corps, comprising two divisions, were brought out of reserve and placed under the command of Army Group Centre. On 3 July the armour began its 150-mile advance. Progress was not as fast as had been hoped: despite covering thirty miles a day, the infantry could not keep up; the weather turned wet and thundery; the roads were bad and this particularly affected Panzer Group 3, which was largely equipped with captured French vehicles, and there were disagreements between von Kluge and Guderian over routes and speed of advance. Guderian was never an easy subordinate and had had similar arguments with his superior, von Kleist, in the advance through the Ardennes in 1940. Most of all, however, Russian resistance was stiffer than expected. Marshal Timoshenko had brought up five so far uncommitted armies with the aim of stopping the Germans from getting to Smolensk. The requirement to defeat Soviet units in the corridor and disarm roving bands of enemy stragglers conflicted with the need to press on to close the pocket at Smolensk. Despite the problems, and increasing interference from Hitler that at this stage of the war could be largely deflected by Halder in Berlin, the two armoured groups met at Smolensk on 24 July. Timoshenko was unable, or not permitted by Stalin, to extricate his armies and, although large numbers of Russians did escape to the east and resistance inside the pocket did not end until 5 August, the result was another resounding success for German encirclement tactics. The number of Russian dead is unknown but Army Group Centre took 330,000 prisoners of war and captured 3,300 tanks at Minsk, and now another 348,000 prisoners and huge numbers of tanks and artillery pieces at Smolensk. Army Group Centre had advanced nearly 400 miles in just over a month and, in the view of those at OKH at least, was now well poised to press on and take Moscow, only 200 miles away.

In the north, von Leeb's army group had taken Riga, crossed the old Russian–Latvian border and was preparing to advance on Leningrad. Militarily, Leningrad was a naval base for the Red Banner Baltic Fleet, which, if left alone, could close the Gulf of Finland to shipments of Swedish iron ore to Germany, and an important centre of the Soviet armaments industry. Politically it was important to Stalin because of its name, and, if the main railway line from Leningrad to Moscow could be cut, then troops in and around Leningrad could not be removed by the Russians for use elsewhere. Panzer Group 4 cut off Leningrad from the outside world by land on 8 July, although a tenuous sea link across Lake Lagoda remained. Field Marshal von Leeb thought he could hook round and join up with the Finns, advancing from the north, and then take Leningrad in four days, but problems arose. So far the Finns had been able to deal with such Russian counter-attacks that had been launched. The north of their country was safe from the large Russian garrison in Murmansk as its attention was fully focused on the two mountain divisions under the German Lieutenant-General Eduard Dietl, who had crossed the Norwegian–Russian border and was attacking in the direction of Murmansk. Despite this, the Finns were not prepared to advance beyond their 1939 frontier – their main objective in joining the war was to regain the territory lost in the Winter War, and they had now done that. Besides the problem of the uncooperative Finns, the ground was increasingly difficult for vehicles, particularly for tanks, and, with Hitler demanding that the city be razed to the ground, the attack on Leningrad settled down into a rather untidy blockade.

In Army Group South the results were less spectacular than in the centre, but impressive none the less. On 11 July von Kleist's armour reached the outer defensive positions of Kiev on the Dnieper. He had advanced 250 miles in nineteen days but was rightly reluctant to get involved in fighting in built-up areas so turned south along the Dnieper, intending to cross and get east of the city while he waited for the infantry of Sixth and Seventeenth Armies to come up. In fact, General Kirponos's South-West Front had performed better than any of the other Russian fronts and was expected by Stalin (and by Kirponos himself) to be able to hold Kiev. Field Marshal von Rundstedt now had a problem. He wanted to encircle Kiev and trap Kirponos's troops in the pocket thus created, but with only one panzer group he could not be

A Panzer Mark IV leads
German forces into
Graudenz (now Grudziadz)
in Poland 100 miles south
of Danzig, to cheering
crowds of the mainly ethnic
German inhabitants on
3 September 1939.

The view from the nose of a
German Heinkel He 111
twin-engined bomber over
Poland in September 1939.

The Commander-in-Chief of the German Army, Colonel-General (later Field-Marshal) Walther von Brauchitsch, with Hitler on the Polish Front, 5 October 1939.

A patrol of the British Army's Somaliland Camel Corps, summer 1940.

Operation Ariel: the Royal Navy organises the evacuation of British and allied soldiers from Brest, Britanny, just ahead of the German columns, June 1940.

RAF air crew and their land transport, sometime during the Battle of Britain, summer 1940.

German horse-drawn artillery in Russia, August 1941.

Russian partisans captured and executed by the Germans on the Eastern Front, December 1941. The notice says 'Takov Konchitsa Partizan' – 'So perish partisans'.

The Russian commander of a T-26B infantry tank surrenders to German troops in late summer 1941. The T-26 was a virtual copy of the British Vickers light tank and had a 37mm gun.

Australian troops take shelter during the first siege of Tobruk in June 1941.

A signaller on the bridge of HMS *Sheffield* on Arctic convoy, winter 1941/42.

Reichsführer SS Heinrich Himmler inspects men of the Waffen SS on the Eastern Front, summer 1942.

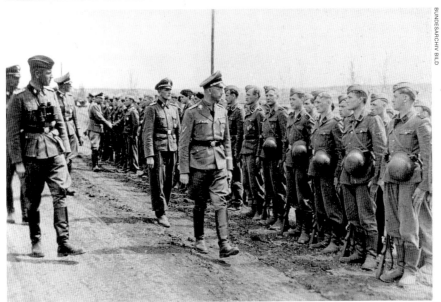

Russian prisoners of war being marched away to German captivity through Kharkov in May 1942. Many would die on the way.

A German flamethrower team at Stalingrad sometime in the autumn of 1942.

German mountain troops in the Caucusus in September 1942.

A German 105mm light howitzer battery in action in the Western Desert, summer 1942.

The deck of the aircraft carrier USS *Yorktown* after she was hit by three Japanese bombs, Battle of Midway, 4 June 1942.

Disgrace and humiliation: British officers surrendering Singapore to the Japanese, 14 February 1942.

German prisoners of war, mostly from the Sixth Army at Stalingrad, being paraded through Moscow (contrary to the laws of war) in summer 1943.

sure that the ring would be strong enough to prevent the Russians from breaking out before the German infantry armies could get up.

Now occurred the first serious example of Hitler overruling his generals on an operational matter. He had overruled them before – on *Anschluss* and on the invasion of Czechoslovakia – but these had been cases where Hitler considered that the political imperative outweighed the military risks. He had also tinkered with operational plans, but so far he had generally decided the strategic objectives and then allowed the generals to get on with waging the war. Once the Smolensk battle was over, the army wanted to press on to capture Moscow. Field Marshal von Brauchitsch, Commander-in-Chief of the army, and Colonel-General Halder, the Chief of the General Staff, urged the Führer to ignore Leningrad and Kiev and allow the army to go for the big prize, Moscow. Hitler, on the other hand, wanted the Russian armies west of Kiev to be enveloped and destroyed. There were insufficient reserves to do both simultaneously without an unacceptable risk to Army Group South and Hitler decided on the Kiev option. He ordered that, once the Smolensk battle was over, the advance on Moscow was to halt and Guderian's Panzer Group 2 from Army Group Centre was to turn south and form the northern arm of the encirclement of Kiev, with Army Group South turning north and forming the southern arm. Guderian's tanks and lorries left the Smolensk pocket on 6 August and began to attack south. On 12 August Field Marshal Keitel's OKW, on Hitler's orders, directed that Army Group Centre, which had already lost Panzer Group 2, was to go over to the defensive and send Hoth and his Panzer Group 3 north to assist Army Group North in the attack on Leningrad.

In the south, Kiev still held out but Army Group South had achieved a limited encirclement at Uman, 120 miles south of Kiev, which shattered twenty Russian divisions and yielded 103,000 prisoners. By the end of August the army group was closing up to the Dnieper, against far harder resistance than anywhere else, and on 31 August its armour had forced a crossing ninety miles south-east of Kiev and established a bridgehead. Now von Kleist's Panzer Group 1 could begin to move round east of Kiev to link up with Guderian coming down from the north. Soon all the assets would be in place for the biggest envelopment battle so far of the campaign.

The two armoured arms of the pincers met on 13 September at Lubny, 125 miles east-south-east of Kiev, and by the 16th the outer ring was secure as infantry divisions hurried up to seal the exits from the pocket. Inside the city of Kiev and the pocket were four Soviet armies. Stalin gave permission for Kiev to be given up, and while there were still gaps in the ring he sent a senior staff officer to General Kirponos to tell him to withdraw from the pocket – but in Stalin's Russia nobody did anything on verbal orders. Kirponos insisted on written permission to withdraw, and by the time it arrived it was too late. Kiev was abandoned on 19 September, and fighting in the pocket was virtually over by 25 September. General Kirponos was himself killed trying to lead his staff out of the pocket on foot and the Germans took 650,000 prisoners. They now fell victim to what would become standard Soviet practice when abandoning cities. Before departing Kiev, the Russians had booby-trapped any building or utility likely to be useful to the invaders. Large factory buildings that would be ideal as billets for housing troops, and hotels and government buildings that could be used for formation headquarters or offices for the staff, had explosive charges hidden in them to be detonated either by timing devices or by remote control by stay-behind parties (the Germans blamed Kiev's Jews). Such was the destruction caused by these explosions and the subsequent fires that Hitler ordered that in future cities and towns were to be bypassed and reduced to rubble by aerial bombing and artillery fire – an order which was generally ignored as the army needed the infrastructure of the cities for its own administration.

Although Hitler, in his directive Number 34 dated 12 August, agreed that the advance on Moscow could be resumed once the Kiev pocket had been eliminated, many German generals after the war blamed Hitler's decision to halt Army Group Centre's advance on Moscow and send Guderian's armour south as the decision that lost Germany the war. In support of this argument, they said that, had the drive on Moscow continued immediately after Smolensk, the weather would have been much more favourable to the attackers, and Stalin would not have had time to deploy the forces for the defence of Moscow that he did in due course deploy. On the other hand, the formations of Army Group Centre had by the end of August almost run out of ammunition, rations and fuel, and did need and, because of Hitler's interference, did indeed get a lengthy pause for replenishment and to allow their largely horse-drawn logistics units to come up. On this occasion, in a strange twist, the soldiers were thinking like politicians – capture the enemy capital – whereas Hitler was thinking like a soldier – destroy the enemy's armies. To this author at least, Hitler's decision seems perfectly sensible, and, while there is some evidence to suggest that a

German capture of Moscow in the autumn of 1941 might have been the catalyst for the anti-Stalin factions (and there were many) to coalesce and depose him, whether that would have led to a Soviet government that would have opened negotiations to end the war – and whether Hitler would have accepted an end before his armies got to the Urals – is a moot question.

In the meantime, it soon became apparent to OKH and OKW – as it had been to Army Group North for some time – that the forests and swamps around Leningrad were totally unsuitable for armour, and so the reduction of that city would now be entrusted to the infantry. Hoth's Panzer Group 3 was restored to Army Group Centre and von Leeb's own armour, Hoepner's Panzer Group 4, would also come under the command of Army Group Centre, which now had three panzer groups, or the bulk of the German armoured and motorized units on the Russian front. The plan for Case Typhoon – the attack on Moscow – envisaged another great envelopment battle. Panzer Groups 3 and 4 would encircle Moscow from the north and Panzer Group 2 from the south, meeting east of the city and closing the ring. Altogether, von Bock disposed of 2 million men in seventy-eight divisions and three panzer groups with 14,000 artillery pieces and over 1,000 tanks, supported by 1,400 aircraft of the Luftwaffe. Opposing him were ninety-six Soviet divisions of various types with around the same number of tanks (although only a few were of the latest type), about half as many guns and about 1,000 aircraft. The operation began on 2 October and almost immediately led to the annihilation of four Soviet armies at Vyazma, 125 miles west-south-west of Moscow, as Panzer Groups 3 and 4 closed behind them, and two more as Panzer Group 2 broke through to Orel and Bryansk, 150 miles south of the capital.

Despite Typhoon starting a month later than the army would have liked, the situation in late 1941 still appeared very favourable for Germany. In a series of brilliantly conducted battles of manoeuvre, German armies had killed or taken prisoner over 2 million Russians and wounded another 690,000. They had advanced 700 miles as the crow flies, and about 1,500 miles as the tank drives; they were poised to take the Caucasus and the Crimea in the south, Leningrad in the north and Moscow in the centre. In the Ukraine, Germans were being welcomed as liberators from the hated communists, and not just by those of German origin, planted there by Catherine the Great in the eighteenth century. But there were worrying signs. As the Luftwaffe had discovered in its initial bombing offensive in June 1941, the range of its bombers was insufficient to reach beyond Moscow, and so industrial plant east of that city could not be attacked and its removal farther east could not be prevented. The number of prisoners taken indicated that many Russian soldiers were only fighting half-heartedly for Stalin, yet fight they did, and, however many Russian armies were destroyed, more always seemed to appear from somewhere. And as early as 23 June the new Russian tanks, the KV-1 and the T-34, had begun to appear. There were very few of them and they were badly handled, but the standard German anti-tank gun, the 37mm, could do nothing against them, and even the Mk IV tank with its short gun was not a match for either.

At the outset of Barbarossa the Germans were poised at the narrow end of a large funnel, and as they advanced farther into the USSR, so that funnel widened out, and more and more troops were needed to cover it. The armoured units had performed wonders, but by the beginning of October the German army in the East had lost around 50,000 soldiers dead and 2,000 tanks, including 215 Mk IVs. Replacement tanks amounted to 999, including 128 Mk IVs, but, even when 122 captured tanks of various sorts were painted with iron crosses and taken into German service, the replacement rate was still only 50 per cent. All this notwithstanding, if Moscow could be taken before the onset of winter, the war could still be won in 1941. But then, on 6 October, the first snow fell.

6

THE ASIAN WAR

SEPTEMBER–DECEMBER 1941

On 14 November 1928, in a display of pomp and pageantry that was in part age-old tradition and in part copied from what court officials had seen of the coronation of George V in London in 1910, the twenty-eight-year-old Michinomya was crowned as Emperor of Japan, taking the name Hirohito. He had spent the previous night in the holiest of Shinto shrines, supposedly taking counsel of his direct ancestor the sun goddess, and from the moment of his coronation was divine. He now sat at the apex of a nation that was still unsure what it wanted. On the one hand, there was the liberal intellectual faction, influenced by the West and anxious to join the club of developed nations, while at the other extreme were the ultra-nationalists determined that Japan should be the superpower of the East and wanting to cast out all traces of Western influence and ideology. Meanwhile, at the very bottom of Japanese society were the peasants and manual workers, exploited as they always had been, but now by the industrialists and their allies in the army and the navy.

Even today, the personality of Emperor Hirohito is an enigma. After the war it was in the interests of the Americans and British to believe, or pretend to believe, that the emperor had been but a ceremonial figure, only able to act on the advice of his ministers, and with no responsibility for the horrors that his soldiers and sailors had unleashed on his unfortunate neighbours. As the Western Allies needed Japan as a counterweight to the USSR during the Cold War, this was a convenient way to retain Japanese support rather than alienate it by hanging their emperor as a war criminal – which many believed he was. From the little we know of the personality of the man whom in later years the West saw as a stooped, mild-mannered marine biologist, peering shyly at the world though thick, old-fashioned spectacles, Hirohito would probably have preferred peace to war, but there was an inevitability about his country's road to conquest.

Japan was still inclined towards the West in the aftermath of the First World War, but faith in the goodwill of the Americans and the British was fading fast. The Washington Naval Treaty of 1922 had stipulated a naval tonnage ratio of five for each of the UK and the USA to only three for Japan. American intercepts of Japanese communications revealed that three was the lowest ratio the Japanese would accept without walking out of the conference, but, although this was twice the 1.5 allowed to the French and Italians, the Japanese navy considered they had been sold out by the politicians, and all thought they had been let down by the British. In 1924 the United States Congress passed the Exclusion Act banning Japanese immigration, and in 1925 the British, largely under American pressure, had declined to renew the Anglo-Japanese treaty. The collapse of world trade consequent upon the onset of the Depression only strengthened the hand of those who thought that Japan should cut herself off from all Western ties and develop an economic strategy of her own. Japanese industry was efficient and modern; the problem was that there was now nobody to sell to, and it was totally reliant on imported raw materials. For some time it had seemed to those who held the real power in Japan – the industrialists, the generals and the admirals – that Manchuria might provide the source of raw materials, the market and the self-sufficiency that Japan needed.

Manchuria is that portion of the Chinese mainland that bordered on Korea to the south and the USSR to the north and east. Both Russia and Japan had long harboured designs on Manchuria, the land of the Manchus, the Mongolians who had invaded and conquered China in the seventeenth century and established the Qing dynasty in 1636. Early twentieth-century China was in nearly all respects a failed state. As with previous Asiatic invaders, the Manchus were absorbed and by the 1920s were indistinguishable from the Han Chinese, although the Japanese tried to justify what they did by maintaining that the occupants of Manchuria were still Manchu. Over the centuries, Qing emperors had been stripped of real power, which was instead wielded by an assortment of warlords, courtiers, eunuchs, generals and administrators, all to a greater or lesser degree corrupt and nearly all incompetent. As had happened many times before in Chinese history, when a dynasty had run out of steam, China had fragmented into a patchwork of semi-independent fiefdoms ruled over by bandits of varying degrees of viciousness and with a number of foreign concessions and treaty ports. To all Chinese, however, Manchuria was an inalienable province of the motherland, albeit one ruled by a semi-independent warlord, while to Japan it was the equivalent of the Wild West – ungoverned or ill-governed and there for the taking. Since 1905, Japanese troops had been in Manchuria to protect Japanese investments and interests there, but the deposition of the Qing emperor in 1912 and the establishment of government by the Kuo Min Tang, a nationalist movement intent on re-establishing control over the whole country, including Manchuria, threatened Japanese interests. Increasingly, Japanese army officers were ignoring the instructions of the home government and plotting a complete takeover of Manchuria.

The Asian war started on 18 September 1931, when a bomb went off in the railway station in Mukden, the Manchurian capital. It was almost certainly planted by the Japanese army and did very little damage, but it allowed the army to claim that Japanese property was under attack and to embark on a campaign to take control of the whole province. In Tokyo the civilian prime minister was horrified. He had no wish to go to war but he had no control over the army and navy ministers, who while they sat in his cabinet did not report to him but directly to the emperor in the latter's guise as Commander-in-Chief. Hirohito's advisers, nervous of upsetting the armed forces and mindful that they risked assassination if they did, advised the emperor not to interfere, and the prime minister resigned. After a six-month campaign, Manchuria was subdued. The army declared it an independent nation and installed the last Qing emperor, Pu Yi, as a puppet ruler. China objected and complained to the League of Nations, which set up a commission to investigate. The commission was chaired by the British representative, Lord Lytton, the son of a viceroy of India and a former governor of Bengal. An unlikely Tory, he was an advocate of temperance and votes for women. Although in Britain there was much sympathy for the Japanese – who were at least clean and orderly, compared to the filth and squalor that was the norm in China – and the French member of the commission was openly pro-Japanese, Lytton's report was a model of fairness. It accepted that Japan had legitimate grievances in her dealings with China, but found that Manchuria was unquestionably Chinese and should be ruled as an autonomous province of China. The League adopted the report and Japan left the League. Once again the white races were ganging up on Japan.

The new prime minister tried to scupper the army's plans to make Manchuria an independent state – in fact a Japanese colony. He complained to the emperor, to no avail, and was duly assassinated, probably by naval officers. In Shanghai, which was not part of Manchuria but housed a Japanese concession, scuffles between Chinese troops and Japanese marines led to intervention by the Japanese Army. It would be only a matter of time before the Japanese Army would take on the rest of China too, and this was accelerated by Manchuria not proving the economic salvation that Japan had hoped for. The conquest of Manchuria was hugely popular in Japan, and huge sums of Japanese money were poured in to build roads and factories in Manchukuo, the land of the Manchus, as Manchuria was now named, but it led to little. Manchukuo could not absorb Japanese exports, and goods manufactured there were not of the quality to replace goods hitherto imported from the West. At home the ultra-nationalist factions were gaining ground. An attempted coup in 1936 by a faction of the army claiming to want to remove the corrupt advisers surrounding the emperor was suppressed, but only at the expense of strengthening the power of the military: henceforth all cabinet posts were to be approved by the army and navy ministers, themselves serving officers. The prime minister was still for the moment a civilian, but entirely at the beck and call of the military. The defence budget was increased and in 1936 Japan signed Hitler's Anti-Comintern Pact.

The conservatives around the imperial throne were not yet ready to support an all-out war with China, and, as the current prime minister, Hirota Koki, could not control the army, the bureaucracy appointed one of their own, who they thought could. Prince Konoe Fumimaro was the scion of an old aristocratic family and the emperor's regular golfing partner. He had Balfour as his political idol, sent his son to Princeton, and was fiercely anti-communist, an extreme believer in Japanese racial purity, with good connections in the military, and, crucially, opposed to war with China. Despite his birth and connections, he too was unable to control the army, which continued to do what it liked. The next phase of the Asian War began with the so-called China Incident of 7 July 1937 when a Japanese private soldier stationed in Peking urinated in the street and went for a walk. He got lost and was posted as missing, and the Japanese demanded that they be allowed to search the area where he had been last seen. That area was supposed to be out of bounds to troops and a suggestion by the Chinese that they should undertake the search, or that it be done jointly, was considered an insult. It was no worse a reason for starting a war than was Captain Jenkins's ear in 1739, but any excuse would do, and although Japan never declared war on China – preferring to let it remain an 'incident' – war was what it was. The

Japanese took Shanghai after bombing it and, while casualty figures were hugely inflated (pro-Chinese elements claimed 250,000 Chinese deaths), it was none the less a major battle. Until now, the Japanese had reinforced the Kwantung Army, which had previously been stationed in Manchuria, via Korea, a Japanese colony since 1910, but in November 1937 there was a further Japanese landing in the bay of Hangchow, south of Shanghai, and Japanese forces began to advance on Nanking.

Nanking – 'Southern Capital' in Chinese, Peking being 'Northern Capital' – was the headquarters of the Kuo Min Tang forces, led by General Chiang Kai-shek,* who became leader of the party in 1937. The Rape of Nanking is probably the most notorious atrocity in a war of many atrocities. The Japanese army took the city in December when Chiang withdrew across the River Yangtze with the survivors of his army and those citizens with sufficient influence or money to go with him. Around half a million people were left in the city, a mixture of Nanking inhabitants, refugees from the countryside and army deserters in civilian clothes. Having marched into the city, the men of the Japanese Central China Army were told to mop up and their commander, General Iwane Matsui, instructed that no act which would stain the honour of the Japanese Army was to be tolerated, along with much other sanctimonious guff about maintaining discipline and securing the trust of the Chinese people. The army paid absolutely no attention and embarked upon a six-week orgy of plunder, rape and massacre, ignoring the occasional messages from Matsui about obedience to military law and good behaviour. Any Chinese of military age who ventured on to the streets was liable to be shot, and Chinese of any age were used for bayonet practice or shot out of hand. There were recorded instances of groups of Chinese being tethered together, taken to the bank of the Yangtze and machine-gunned. Anything in a skirt was raped, regardless of age, and even the pupils of girls' schools were not spared. Chinese were murdered and whole streets set on fire for no other reason than it seemed like fun at the time; anything portable was looted and anything liquid was drunk.

All armies do go off the rails from time to time. Soldiers are aggressive and trained to be so and are a lot less squeamish about blood and slaughter than their civilian counterparts. During the Peninsular War the British Army

---

*Chinese names have the family name first followed by the forenames; hence the general would be addressed as 'Chiang' by his superiors and 'Kai-shek' by his friends.

frequently and regularly misbehaved in captured cities, but this rarely lasted more than a couple of days before exhaustion and the provost restored order. Rape is not uncommon after a period of intense fear and danger. In Nanking, however, what happened was far more than a temporary loss of control. Nobody really knows how many Chinese civilians were killed: the war crimes trials held in Tokyo after the war claimed a quarter of a million, a figure which is almost certainly far too high, but the killings and the rapes went on for far longer than might be excused in an army seeking instant relief from the strains of fighting. In the Russo-Japanese War the Japanese army had been scrupulous in adhering to the laws of war, and it is most unlikely that the Japanese government instructed the barbarity of Nanking to happen – Konoe and his ministers were still sensitive to world opinion, and even the pro-Japanese German embassy described the behaviour of the conquerors as 'bestial'. The commander, Matsui, was either unable or unwilling to rein his men in, despite his platitudes,* and it is quite possible that junior officers encouraged the soldiers' excesses in order to teach the Chinese a lesson and discourage future resistance. That could happen with any army but once again it would not be long before hangovers, moral qualms and a realization that what was going on was contrary to law intervened to stop it. British and American, Italian and German soldiers might misbehave – indeed did misbehave – but not for any length of time, not as a corporate body and not with the approval, tacit or otherwise, of their superiors. The Japanese private soldier was an uneducated peasant or manual worker from a background that was harsh and unforgiving, and served in an army where he was brutalized and brainwashed, with physical beatings by officers and NCOs for minor infractions of the norm. Feelings of racial superiority are found in many societies, and hatred of the foreigner is the more intense the further down the social scale the hater is. Anti-Semitism in Germany was particularly virulent amongst the erstwhile have-nots, and today's British National Party is largely a lower-working-class movement. There had always been a belief amongst the Japanese that they were a superior race (there still is), and army propaganda had emphasized and reinforced this. The Chinese were subhuman, worthless, treacherous, corrupt and criminal, and the victorious and divine Japanese could treat them as they liked with utter impunity.

---

*He did at least have the grace to resign afterwards and take himself off to a Buddhist monastery. After the war he was hanged as a war criminal by the Allies nevertheless.

Prisoners were a nuisance as they had to be fed and guarded, so it was easier not to take any. It was a harbinger of what was to come.

The only concession the Japanese army made to protests about its behaviour in Nanking was to accept that rapes offended Chinese sensibilities, and henceforth army-run brothels would be provided, staffed by 'comfort women', Koreans, Chinese and a few Europeans, some working willingly but many more coerced. The Japanese army continued to ignore the home government and got itself more and more entrammelled in China: it took the ports of Foochoy, Amoy and Swatow, and Fukien and Canton provinces, the latter bordering on the British colony of Hong Kong; it pushed ever inland, forcing Chiang Kai-shek to move his capital to Chungking in the interior, but, while it won all the battles, it was capturing ground, not destroying Chinese armies, which took a beating, withdrew to lick their wounds and then popped up again somewhere else. It was costing Japan a great deal of money and mounting casualties. World opinion, particularly American opinion, which was well informed about Japanese atrocities, began to turn against Japan.

Within the ranks of the Japanese army, officers were divided. All were in favour of expansion and conquest; the only question was in which direction. Most generals, admirals and politicians favoured heading into South-East Asia, with its rubber, iron ore and oil, while many in the Kwantung Army in Manchukuo belonged to the 'Strike North' faction and wanted to attack the Soviet Union and take eastern Siberia. The Japanese had beaten and humiliated imperial Russia; they could surely do the same against the Bolsheviks. Neither the emperor nor his advisers had any wish to go to war with Russia, but, as had happened so often in recent Japanese history, it was the army, often at quite a junior level, that decided what to do and did it, regardless of cautionary strictures from home. In the summer of 1938 skirmishing broke out on Manchukuo's eastern border with Russia. The Red Army deployed aircraft and tanks, while the Japanese relied on the spirit of *bushido*. Fighting went on for two weeks with heavy casualties on both sides for no decisive result. Then in May 1939, on Manchukuo's western border with Mongolia, a republic of the USSR, full-scale fighting broke out, initiated, unwisely as it turned out, by the Japanese. The Russians had fifty-two divisions, or half a million men, with several thousand aircraft and 2,200 tanks in the area, and their forces, commanded by General Georgi Zhukov, who was later to become the Red Army's Chief of Staff, dealt the Japanese a serious blow. By the time a truce was signed on 15 September, the Japanese had taken around 50,000 casualties, of which around 8,500 were killed. That was the end of the Strike North concept, its demise emphasized by the Molotov–Ribbentrop Pact, about which the Japanese had no warning from Germany and which threw the government and cabinet (which resigned) into confusion.

* * *

Japan, lacking raw materials, had taken Formosa from China in 1895 as a source of sugar; she could obtain iron ore from Manchukuo and coal and timber from China, but she was entirely dependent on imported oil, rubber, nickel and other essential minerals. If Japan were to seek economic self-sufficiency by expanding southwards, then she would need oil from the Dutch East Indies, rubber, nickel and tin from Malaya, and rice and cotton from Burma. Between the Japanese mainland and those tempting riches lay the 7,000 islands of the Philippines, not in themselves attractive to Japanese expansionists but which, if left unoccupied, would act as a Trojan horse right in the centre of their defensive ring. The Philippines had been Spanish for 300 years until ceded to the USA after the Spanish–American War in 1898. She had an American governor general, a small American garrison and some local politicians more interested in the trappings of power than in responsibility but who were well aware that the United States had promised full independence in 1946. The defence of the Philippines against an aggressor – and there could only be one potential aggressor and that was Japan – was covered in Plan Orange, which envisaged the US Army and local forces withdrawing to the Bataan peninsula, west of Manila on the island of Luzon, and holding out for up to six months until reinforcements arrived from Hawaii. When Douglas MacArthur was Chief of Staff of the US Army from 1930 to 1935 he reviewed Plan Orange, declared it unworkable in relation to the Philippines, an area he knew well, and announced that, if war were imminent, his immediate reaction would be to send reinforcements in the form of two American divisions. As the US Army only had three divisions, this was clearly also unworkable, and MacArthur's suggestion did nothing to enhance his standing amongst his peers.

In 1935 President Roosevelt offered MacArthur the post of Governor General of the Philippines, which would mean his resigning from the army and would, the president intended, neutralize him politically. At the same time the head of the Philippines government, Manuel Quezon, an old acquaint-ance of the general's from his previous service there, asked for MacArthur as the head of the American military mission to his country, which would effectively make MacArthur the commander of the embryo Filipino Army. As Quezon's offer would allow him to continue as an American general, MacArthur accepted. On arrival in the Philippines, accompanied once more by Major Dwight D. Eisenhower as his assistant military adviser, MacArthur set about trying to produce a realistic defence strategy. He hoped to do this by creating a small regular Filipino Army and a huge part-time popular militia. The regular army plus the American garrison supported by aircraft and PT (motor torpedo) boats would oppose any landing, and, if that failed, the militia would wage a guerrilla war. At this stage, MacArthur (and his American staff) thought the Japanese army a joke and considered that Japan would never go to war against the United States.

Two years later MacArthur's view had changed. By then Japan had invaded China and was looking very aggressive indeed. MacArthur bombarded Washington with requests for more aircraft, more ships and more American troops, all of which were refused. His plan for Filipino military expansion was falling apart because the Philippines could not afford the expense and the United States would not. MacArthur, already the subject of some ridicule for accepting the rank of field marshal from Quezon and designing his own uniform to go with it, became increasingly an irritant to Washington and in 1937 he was summoned home. Considering this an insult both to himself and to the government of the Philippines, he resigned from the United States Army on 31 December 1937. He remained in command of the Filipino Army, but this time as a Filipino, not an American, officer, increasingly convinced of Japanese evil intentions towards his adopted land and, as he was no longer an American general, increasingly unable to do very much about it, nor to influence the posting of mediocre American officers to his staff. The ambitious Eisenhower, now promoted to lieutenant-colonel, stuck it out for nine months and then, with war declared in Europe and convinced that the United States would eventually become involved, decided that his career demanded the unhitching of his star from MacArthur and asked for a posting back to the United States. President Quezon, perhaps realizing that Eisenhower was the one stabilizing influence on MacArthur, pleaded with him to stay and asked him to name his own salary, but he insisted on going: 'I want to be there if what I think is going to happen actually happens.'[42]

MacArthur continued to try to cobble some sort of defensive posture together for the Philippines, having to weave his way through the convoluted maze of local politics and the problems of running a conscript army with no money. Back home, Washington now considered that war with Japan would come, but, as the president had already decided, although not announced, that Japan would take second priority to Germany, and as the Philippines would be independent in 1946 anyway, there was no point in sending substantial reinforcements or in spending US dollars on her defence. In June 1941, with war in Asia seemingly inevitable, General George C. Marshall, since 1939 the army's Chief of Staff and now at sixty-one the president's chief military adviser, realized that some gesture must be made to the Philippines. He had served there and in China himself, and considered that for all MacArthur's character faults he was the only man with the experience and the public profile to command in the Philippines. MacArthur was reinstated in the United States Army with the rank of lieutenant-general and would command all forces, American and Filipino, in that country. He would have little time to prepare.

* * *

The Dutch East Indies covered a vast area some 2,350 by 1,200 miles and included the islands of Java and Sumatra, most of southern Borneo, Dutch New Guinea, the Celebes, West Timor and the Moluccas. The population was around 71 million, which included 1 million Chinese and 250,000 Dutch, the latter there as colonial administrators, soldiers and businessmen, and spread around the islands was a garrison of around 100,000 men of the Royal Netherlands East Indies Army, mainly native troops with Dutch officers. Primarily intended for keeping order internally, they were poorly equipped for modern warfare. Their South-East Asian colony was hugely important to the Dutch, as it generated around 15 per cent of the national income, producing not only oil in large quantities (59 million barrels in 1940) but also rubber, copra, tin and bauxite. When the German army overran Holland in 1940, the East Indies administration pledged its loyalty to Queen Wilhelmina and the Dutch government-in-exile in London, rather than to the Reichskommissariat Niederlande set up by the Germans, and, when in January 1941 the Japanese foreign ministry made a reference to the Dutch East Indies as being included in the 'Greater East Asian Co-Prosperity Sphere', the Japanese term for territories it had grabbed, was grabbing or intended to grab to be exploited in its search for economic self-sufficiency, the colonial administration in Batavia, the People's Council, protested vigorously. It also refused Japanese demands for fishing rights and unrestricted use of its ports, and, while it did increase its exports to Japan, although not by the amount demanded, in August 1941 it followed the Americans and the British by banning the export of oil to Japan. It was a brave, but in the event futile, display of independence.

* * *

India was, of course, the jewel of the British Empire in the Far East, but the Empire also included Burma, Malaya, Singapore, Hong Kong, British North Borneo (now Sabah), Sarawak and Brunei, myriad Pacific islands among which Fiji, Tonga and Samoa were the more important, and, while not Asiatic but nevertheless in the area, the self-governing white Dominions of Australia and New Zealand. Japan's economic ambitions in 1940 did not then include India or Australasia (although the Japanese would make use of anti-British feeling amongst some Indian would-be politicians) but they certainly did include Malaya – for its raw materials – and Singapore – for its naval base. That Malaya produced 38 per cent of the world's rubber and 58 per cent of its tin makes British neglect of her defences all the more disgraceful. Successive governments had found other priorities and any excuse to avoid spending money in the Far East was eagerly seized upon, regardless of what, from the end of the Washington Naval Conference at least, was staring them in the face. In 1925 the Chancellor of the Exchequer, Winston Churchill, opposing the naval estimates, said that there was no possibility of a war with a first-class navy for at least twenty years, and that 'It is inconceivable that in our lifetime and in that of our children, Japan could pose a threat to the security of the British Empire in the East.'[43] Even as late as October 1939, when war had broken out in Europe and he was once more First Lord of the Admiralty, Churchill wrote: 'Consider how vain is the menace that Japan will send a fleet and army to conquer Singapore, which is as far from Japan as Southampton is from New York... do not let us worry about this bugbear... there will be no attack in any period which our foresight can measure.'[44] So much for the far-sighted statesman.

The population of British Malaya, which then included Singapore, was around 5.5 million. Just over half were Chinese who lived in the towns and ran the businesses, while the Malays provided the sultans and owned the land.

In addition, there were 750,000 Indians of various races, who manned large parts of the civil service, and 100,000 'others'. The peacetime defences of the Malayan peninsula rested in the regular Malay Regiment, two battalions of native soldiers with British officers, and four battalions of part-time volunteers. The governance of Malaya was unwieldy, some said ramshackle. Technically it comprised the Straits Settlements of Singapore, Penang, Malacca and Labuan (an island off North Borneo), which were ruled directly as colonies, and the Malay states, a patchwork of fiefdoms where the British had opted to rule indirectly through their sultans. The British had tried to persuade the rulers of these states to join together into one nation, but all they had managed to do was to create a loose federation of some, while others remained outside it. The Governor – properly the Governor of the Straits Settlements and High Commissioner to the Malay States – was an experienced colonial administrator, Sir Shenton Thomas. Known to the Malayan civil service as Tom-Tom because of his long service in Africa, he had been in post since 1934, and had the war in Europe not erupted would have retired in 1939 at the age of sixty. A perfectly decent man, he was faced with the near-impossible task of persuading the states to cooperate in defensive measures, but lacked the force of personality and the ruthlessness to achieve unanimity. He was the titular Chairman of the Defence Committee of which the three service chiefs were members and had little success in either gaining their respect or in preventing the all too common inter-service bickering.

The Commander-in-Chief Far East from October 1940 was Air Chief Marshal Sir Henry Brooke-Popham. Originally an infantryman, a pioneer of military aviation and a former governor of Kenya, Brooke-Popham was responsible for the defence not only of Malaya but of Burma, Hong Kong and various obscure islands too. Despite his title, he did not command the Royal Navy, which reported direct to the First Sea Lord in London, and he could not order civilian administrators to do anything. They continued reporting to their ministers in London in a leisurely fashion, and in many cases cooperated only reluctantly with his requests for the construction of barracks, roads and defences. His pleas for reinforcement and money fell on the generally deaf ears of a home government far more concerned with what was happening in Europe, but by the summer of 1941 the garrison of Malaya and Singapore was augmented by Lieutenant-General Sir Lewis Heath's III Indian Corps of two Indian divisions and one independent brigade, and an Australian division commanded by Major-General Gordon Bennett.

In May 1941 Lieutenant-General Arthur Percival was appointed General Officer Commanding Malaya. Percival had served in Malaya as a colonel from 1936 to 1938 and had expressed concern then as to the vulnerability of the territory to attack by the Japanese, who, he thought, would land in Thailand and advance southward towards Singapore. His paper outlining the risk and asking for more funding for defence was lodged in the War Office, drawn to the attention of the minister and forgotten. After the first war, British admirals had wanted Singapore to be developed into a base for a Far East fleet – one which could defend the sea routes to India from the east and to Australia from the north, and deter any Japanese ambitions – but the navy had been starved of funding and in any case now had few ships in the area, most having been withdrawn for service in the North Atlantic or the Mediterranean. Defences on the landward side were inadequate, as it was considered in London that no military force of any size could advance for any distance through the Malayan jungle. Contrary to the accepted myth, however, the guns of the shore batteries could certainly be pointed inland: the problem was that the ammunition with which they were equipped was armour-piercing and designed for taking on ships, not targets on land.

There was a plan for the defence of Malaya and Singapore. It presupposed that ships of the Royal Navy would intercept any Japanese convoy and destroy it. True, there were now not many ships, but in that case air power would suffice to stop any landing. Unfortunately, demands for more aircraft went unheeded and Malaya's sole air power consisted not of the 500 Hurricanes and Spitfires which Brooke-Popham had asked for, but 158 obsolete Brewster Buffalo fighters and two squadrons of even more obsolete Vickers Vildebeest torpedo-bombers, no match for the Japanese navy's Zero fighters and the army's Oscars. There was not a single tank in the country. As the best landing places in the event of Japanese attack were over the border in Thailand, Operation Matador saw the British crossing the border and establishing defensive positions in Thailand. This would, of course, mean invading a neutral country, but needs must. When on 22 November 1941, certain that a Japanese offensive was on the way, Brooke-Popham asked London for permission to implement Matador, the Cabinet got frightfully worked up and, as politicians do, procrastinated. Eventually, on 5 December, permission was granted. By then, however, it was too late.

* * *

Hong Kong, the British trading post at the mouth of the Pearl River, was the last British possession on the mainland of China. The British had withdrawn their small garrison from Shanghai under Japanese pressure, but Shanghai was an international city, not British sovereign territory, like Hong Kong. Hong Kong was never going to be defensible. It was only 400 square miles in size, and but twenty miles from the border to the southern tip of Hong Kong Island. Since October 1938 the Japanese army had been just north of the Chinese border and British officers popping across to Shum Shun (now Shen Zen) for a drink might rub shoulders (literally) with Japanese officers patronizing the same crowded bars. It was impossible to prevent Japanese intelligence from finding out exactly where the British garrison was stationed, how big it was and what it might do if attacked. The Hong Kong Police Special Branch had ample warning that an attack was coming, but all that the Commander British Forces, Major-General Christopher Maltby of the Indian Army, could do if it came would be to hold on and delay the enemy as long as possible. That was what the British government had instructed the governor, Sir Mark Young, to do in the hope that a stout resistance in Hong Kong, albeit one which would ultimately end in defeat, would buy time for the rest of the Empire in the East and avoid the damage to British prestige that would inevitably be attached to a speedy, even if realistic, surrender. To carry out his mission, Maltby had two British, two Indian and two Canadian infantry battalions, the Hong Kong Chinese Regiment, an infantry regiment recruited locally, and the Hong Kong Volunteer Defence Corps, a part-time unit of expatriate Britons unkindly referred to by many as a uniformed drinking club. In support were some Royal Engineers and the artillery of the Hong Kong and Shanghai Royal Artillery, a flotilla of one destroyer and a dozen motor torpedo and gunboats, and a tiny RAF contingent based at Kai Tak airport. One of the British infantry battalions, 2nd Royal Scots, had been diverted on its way home from India after seven years there and was in a state of near mutiny, and the other, 1 Middlesex, was actually a machine-gun battalion.* The two Canadian

---

*In 1915 medium machine-guns had been removed from infantry battalions on the formation of the Machine Gun Corps, which allowed the weapons to be concentrated and used to better effect than by parcelling them out to battalions. After the war, during the contraction of the army to its peacetime strength, the Machine Gun Corps went, but as the concept still held good a number of infantry battalions were turned into machine-gun battalions, which also had the advantage of protecting the tribal instincts of the infantry where the retention of a cap badge was more important than tactical development.

battalions, 1st Winnipeg Grenadiers and 1st Royal Rifles of Canada, had been rushed there in late 1941 and were scantily trained. Maltby's plan was to defend along the twelve-mile 'gin drinkers' line' in the New Territories, that part of the colony north of Kowloon leased to Britain in 1898, and then to withdraw back to the Island, making the attacker pay dearly for every inch gained. It was a perfectly practical, if in the event hopelessly optimistic, operational plan.

* * *

French Indo-China – Cambodia, Laos and what is now Vietnam but was then Annam, Tonkin and Cochin China – had a population of 25 million Buddhists and around 40,000 Europeans. Apart from Cochin China, which the French ruled directly as a colony, the imperial power governed through local kings, who were subject to the direction of a French governor general. By 1940 the garrison was around 100,000 strong, a mix of locally enlisted soldiers with French officers, Frenchmen of the Colonial Army and 20,000 of the French Foreign Legion. Once Hainan Island had been taken from China by the Japanese in February 1939, the threat to Indo-China was obvious, and, as it was the world's third-largest producer of rice, it could not but be attractive to proponents of Japanese expansion. After the French surrender to the Germans in 1940, Japan demanded that the railway from Haiphong in north Vietnam to Yunnan province in China, a line that was a main supply route for Chiang Kai-shek's nationalist Chinese forces, be closed.* The French Governor General, General Georges Catroux, was inclined to surrender to *force majeure* but the Vichy French government thought otherwise and replaced Catroux with Vice-Admiral Jean Decoux. Decoux tried to maintain the independence of the French empire in the East without provoking the Japanese, and put down nationalist risings with great severity. In the end, however, he had to compromise: there were a number of skirmishes when Japanese troops 'accidentally' attacked the French Army and then said how sorry they were; the use of bases was granted and in July 1941 the Japanese occupied Saigon and sent troops into Cambodia. By the autumn of that year there were 35,000 Japanese in French Indo-China, which carried on under its French administration but was now effectively controlled by the Japanese.

---

*It provided around 48 per cent of Chiang's supplies, mainly from the USA.

* * *

At 262,000 square miles, Burma is the largest country on the South-East Asian mainland. Its terrain ranges from 20,000-foot-high mountains in the north to swamps, huge rivers and a dry central plain. It is malarial, subject to an annual monsoon, short of roads and generally difficult to fight over. One million of its population were mountain tribes, the Chins, Kachins and Nagas, 4 million were Karens and 2 million were Shan, all of whom were generally pro-British if only because the British had prevented the Burmans from persecuting them. A legacy from Burma being governed from India until 1937 was the presence of around a million Indians, who largely staffed the civil service. The rest, around 10 million Burmans, were better educated and more politically aware than the rest, and some of their leaders were liable to intrigue against British rule and to conspire with the Japanese in the hope that they might thereby obtain independence. In fact, there was a considerable amount of democracy in Burma, with a legislative council elected by a fairly wide franchise, although defence and foreign affairs remained the prerogative of the Governor General, Sir Reginald Dorman-Smith. As the world's largest producer of teak and provider of 10 per cent of the world's tungsten, as well as oil, rice and rubber, Burma was attractive to the Japanese while occupation would provide flank protection for an attack on Malaya and Singapore. A major irritant, from the Japanese point of view, was the existence of the Burma Road, which had been opened in 1938 and ran from the railhead at Lashio for 350 miles eastwards into China. Once the Japanese had browbeaten the administration of French Indo-China into closing the railway line to China and had persuaded Stalin to close his link, the Burma Road remained Chiang Kai-shek's only supply route from the outside world. The Japanese protested to Britain and the British, somewhat cravenly, did close the road in July 1940 until, having screwed up a little more courage, they reopened it in October.

The standing garrison in Burma consisted of the Burma Frontier Force of six infantry battalions formed from the old Burma Military Police and manned mainly by Gurkhas with some Sikhs and Punjabi Mussalmans, and four battalions of the Burma Rifles recruited from Chins, Karens and Cochins, with a stiffening of Gurkhas. All had British officers seconded from the Indian Army, and Burmans were not recruited, being viewed as unreliable and not soldier material. As the storm clouds gathered, these regiments were expanded: more battalions were raised and the ban on Burmans was relaxed. By 1941 there were eleven battalions or battalion-sized units of the Burma Frontier Force, and twelve battalions of Burma Rifles, all at various stages of training. There were no tanks and artillery support came from a part-time artillery regiment, while the Burma Royal Naval Volunteer Reserve manned a motley flotilla of river craft. In 1941 there was a hurried augmentation in the shape of the Indian 17 Division, a regular division which had been intended for North Africa but was diverted to Burma instead.

* * *

In Japan the militarists were firmly in the driving seat by 1941. Political parties, never very influential anyway, were abolished in 1940 and replaced in the Diet, the parliament, by the Imperial Rule Assistance Association and from 1939 the army vice-minister and then minister was Lieutenant-General Hideki Tojo, a hardliner who had commanded the Kwantung Army's *Kempeitai* or military police, one of the nastier parts of a nasty army. It was Tojo who pushed for troops to be sent into French Indo-China in July 1941, which led to the USA adding to its existing ban on the export of oil and scrap metal to Japan by a total trade embargo. In March 1941 the foreign minister, Matsuoka, went to Berlin, where both Hitler and Göring urged him to take Singapore. The minister was evasive; he still hoped to avoid widening the war, and, despite discouragement from Ribbentrop and a warning from the Japanese ambassador in Berlin that Germany would soon attack Russia, he moved on to Moscow and signed a neutrality pact with Stalin. Germany's attack on the USSR in June 1941 strengthened the war party in Tokyo – even if Stalin had no intention of keeping to the pact, Japan need not now fear attack from the rear if she expanded southwards. In September 1941, as relations with the Western powers deteriorated even further, an imperial conference decided, on Tojo's recommendation, to go to war with the UK and the USA if the situation could not be resolved by October. The prime minister, Konoe, unable to repair relations with the West, resigned in October and the emperor asked Tojo to form a cabinet, which he did, becoming prime minister and also taking the posts of army minister and home minister. In November the American Secretary of State, Cordell Hull, delivered a note to the Japanese government saying that trade could only be resumed if Japan withdrew from China. There was no mention of Manchukuo or of Korea, but the Japanese chose to take the note as an ultimatum.

Japanese war aims were partly racial – the white races had humiliated the Japanese and would now be chased out of Asia – and partly economic – the establishment of the Greater East Asia Co-Prosperity Sphere that would make Japan self-sufficient. There was also the heady attraction of imperialist aggrandisement, pure and simple. The British were only just hanging on in the West, they could do little in the East, and the Dutch were already beaten. Because the Philippines could not be bypassed to leave a potential threat in the centre of the new empire, war with America could not be avoided. Yet opinion was still divided, even amongst Japan's military leaders. The navy was wary about going to war with America. Admiral Isoruku Yamamoto, the commander of the Combined Fleet upon which the burden of naval activity would fall, had been a student at Harvard and later a naval attaché in Washington, and he well knew the economic potential of the USA and had openly and stridently opposed going to war with her. Indeed, so vociferously had Yamamoto expressed his views as navy vice-minister that he ran the risk of assassination if he stayed on land, and his minister had given him a command, that of the fleet, at sea. The navy minister himself pointed out to the cabinet that America vastly out-produced Japan in steel and coal, and that she could build both more ships and more aircraft. Crucially, he emphasized, Japan was now subject to a total oil embargo and had stocks for only two years, or eighteen months of military consumption; he opposed war, but, if it was inevitable, then it had better be soon and it had better be over swiftly. Even the more warlike service, the army, did not speak with one voice. There were those who wanted to attack the USSR via Siberia now that Germany had launched Barbarossa, those who wanted to strike both north and south, and even those who would prefer not to go to war at all. Tojo, seen in hindsight as the prime mover of aggression and hanged for it in 1948, was particularly concerned that, if Japan did go to war, the normal courtesies should be observed – war should be formally declared: a surprise attack without warning would be dishonourable.

In the event, faced with a problem that had numerous possible solutions, Japan shut its collective eyes, jumped headlong and hoped for the best. The decision-makers knew what they wanted, but they also knew that, while they might win a war with the British, who would be knocked out by Germany before they could react to a threat to their Asian territories, and the Dutch, who were already conquered, they could not win a long war with the United States. However, it was Yamamoto, who had so strongly opposed war with

America, who was the driving force behind the eventual Japanese plan. Given that war could not be avoided, not least because Japan could not comply with American proposals that she should withdraw from China, where she had already suffered 160,000 dead, then only by a surprise attack which removed at a stroke the United States' war-making potential in the Pacific could Japan hope to seize the areas producing the raw materials she needed and establish the ring of bases necessary to defend them. By the time America recovered, the Greater East Asian Co-Prosperity Sphere would be a *fait accompli* that she would have to accept. Even then, Yamamoto was not entirely happy: he said that he was confident that Japan could win the battles for the first year, but that after that he was 'not sure', which for a Japanese raised in the samurai tradition is as near as it is possible to get to saying: 'Don't do it. We can't win.'

The plan eventually agreed to and made law by the fixing of the emperor's seal was, after all, for a surprise attack. The Anglo-Saxons were encircling Japan and attempting to strangle her by economic boycott: national survival was at stake and, even more important, Japanese self-esteem. It was better to go to war, even if that ended in defeat, than back down now. Phase One would entail six simultaneous surprise attacks on Thailand (then Siam) in order to provide a secure base for operations against Malaya and Burma; a landing in northern Malaya to obtain a jumping-off point for the attack on Singapore; the seizure of the American islands of Guam and Wake and the British Gilbert Islands to block the American sea route to the Philippines; the capture of Hong Kong; and, vitally, the destruction of the American Pacific Fleet with one mighty blow. Once Japanese flanks were thus secured, a landing would be made in the Philippines. Phase Two would eliminate resistance in Malaya and capture Singapore, establish air bases in southern Burma and occupy the northern Dutch East Indies and the Bismarck Archipelago. Phase Three would take Java, Sumatra and Burma, whereupon the land-grabbing would end and consolidation and exploitation would begin. The Japanese empire would cover a vast area of 4,000 miles from north to south and 3,000 from miles east to west – from Manchukuo to Java and from the Indian Ocean to New Guinea.

The United States Pacific Fleet was based in Pearl Harbor in Hawaii, and, if it could be eliminated, America would be unable to intervene. It would be an extraordinary gamble. The only way the fleet could be attacked was from the sea, and, if a straightforward ship versus ship battle – one Japan would not necessarily lose but which might prove expensive for her – was to be avoided, the attack would have to be delivered without warning, which meant from the air. The Japanese strike force would have to sail across the Pacific to within aircraft range of Hawaii without being detected, and the American fleet would have to be in harbour at the time. The Americans expected any Japanese attack to come from the south-west, from the Japanese Marshall Islands, so the Japanese naval staff determined to attack from the north. This would mean sailing to the Kuriles, 1,000 miles north of Tokyo Bay, and then over 4,000 miles to a location 800 miles north of Hawaii that would be the jumping-off point. From there, the fleet would have to sail undetected to 200 miles from Pearl Harbor before it could launch its aircraft. The route decided upon would take the fleet into the stormy latitudes above 40° north, where few civil vessels ventured in winter, and would require cold-weather clothing for the men and anti-freeze precautions for the machinery and equipment. Assuming the fleet was able to launch its attack, the damage would be inflicted by bombs and torpedoes. The bombs held by the Japanese naval aviation units were designed to explode on impact and so would do little damage to armoured decks: what was needed was a bomb that would penetrate armour and then explode, and so the Japanese, even then masters of improvisation, took armour-piercing shells designed to be fired from naval guns and turned them into bombs. As Pearl was a shallow harbour, the standard torpedo dropped from the normal height would simply hit the seabed, and so pilots had to spend many hours practising dropping their missiles at wave-top level. The code name for the attack was Operation Z, an intentional reference to Admiral Togo's victory over the Russian Fleet at Tsushima in 1905 when, taking a leaf out of Nelson's book (and the Japanese navy had been trained by the British and knew all about the Nelson touch), he raised the Z flag and signalled the fleet: 'On this one battle rests the fate of our nation. Let every man do his utmost.'

The original plan for Operation Z envisaged four aircraft carriers with escorts, but the captains of Japan's remaining two carriers complained so vehemently that Yamamoto relented and allowed them to come along as well. The attack group would therefore consist of six carriers, two battleships, two heavy cruisers, a light cruiser, eight destroyers, three tankers and a supply ship. Also heading for Hawaii, although on a different route, would be twenty-seven submarines: these would be deployed partly for reconnaissance and scouting purposes but also to deliver five midget submarines that would be unloaded from their parent vessels off Pearl Harbor. Radio silence would be maintained for the entire journey and any merchant ship met on the way would be sunk. On the carriers would be 396 aircraft: 81 fighters to protect the bombers and strafe targets on land, 135 dive-bombers, 140 conventional bombers and 40 torpedo-bombers. The force would be under the command of Vice-Admiral Chuichi Nagumo, a fifty-four-year-old torpedo specialist. In late November the ships began to assemble in the Inland Sea, between the islands of Honshu and Kyushu.

That Japan was going to attack American and British possessions in the East was no surprise to the more perspicacious of those that were there – the signs had been evident for years – but in London the British government, preoccupied with other matters, chose to ignore them. At a War Cabinet meeting on 20 October 1941, the prime minister, Churchill, persisted in his wishful thinking and told the meeting that he did not foresee an attack in force on Malaya, and even on 3 December he insisted that war with Japan was 'a remote possibility'.[45] Even on the ground, where the evaluation of Japanese capabilities should have been better than that made in London, there were misconceptions. That many Japanese were apparently short and bandy-legged, bespectacled and with buck teeth, was taken as evidence of their military incompetence; they were said to be unable to operate at night and to be incapable of handling modern technology; and the sight of Japanese army officers tripping over the swords that they insisted on carrying in battle and the sloppy and ill-fitting uniforms of its men with their 1905-pattern rifles lent the service a faintly ridiculous air, at least to those more accustomed to Blanco and polish. To many, it was inconceivable that Japanese pilots could take on British or American aircraft in a fair fight, and in any case the Japanese would never embark on a war that they were bound to lose.

In Washington, too, there were all sorts of indications that war was coming. The China lobby in the USA was a strong one, and most Americans failed to see the violence, corruption, cruelty and incompetence endemic in Chinese politics and instead idealized them as naive children who needed protection from the rapacious Japanese (and, come to that, from the British). The Secretary for the Interior, Harold Ickes, suggested to President Roosevelt that, as public opinion was strongly pro-Chinese and anti-Japanese, warlike moves by Japan might give the USA an excuse to get into the war without seeming to be an ally of communist Russia.[46] The United States Navy, on the other hand, concerned that it was becoming more and more involved in the North Atlantic in protecting convoys to Britain, wanted hostilities in the

Far East delayed as long as possible. On 26 July 1941 the United States had frozen Japanese assets held in America, followed by the UK and the Dutch government-in-exile. What the Dutch did was almost immaterial, but the American and British action was not. On 25 November the US chief of army staff and the chief of naval operations sent signals to all American commanders abroad, including MacArthur in the Philippines and Major-General Walter C. Short, commanding in Hawaii, that war with Japan was increasingly likely. In both locations, little attention was paid.

In October 1941 the German general staff had produced a paper on the Japanese position. It said that in the war in China time was on China's side. Her inexhaustible supply of manpower and vast area were the country's strengths, and this, coupled with the scorched-earth policy followed by Chinese armies, had forced Japan's campaign to grind to a halt. It would be helpful to Germany if Japan were to attack the USSR, but, as this would do nothing to help Japan's search for economic self-sufficiency, it was unlikely to happen. On the other hand, any action against the British would give Germany more room for manoeuvre in Europe, and an attack on America would discourage that country from getting involved in the European war. Hitler had assured the Japanese ambassador in Berlin that, if Japan found herself at war with the British and the Americans, Germany would come to her assistance, and on 29 November the Japanese government informed Germany that hostilities were likely and that war would come 'sooner than anyone dreams'. By now the Japanese had decided that X-Day* would be 8 December in the East, which would still be 7 December in the USA, on the other side of the International Date Line.

On 26 November the ships of Operation Z began to slip individually out of the Inland Sea and make their way north to a rendezvous in the Kuriles. On 7 December in the West and 8 December in the East, Japan struck the first blows in the final phase of the Asian War, and shortly afterwards she declared war on Britain and the United States; on the following day the United States, Britain and the British Empire, the Dutch and Yugoslav governments-in-exile, the Free French and several opportunistic South American states declared war on Japan. On 11 December, Germany, Italy and Romania declared war on the United States.

---

*The Japanese equivalent of D-Day, *J-Jour* and *A-Tag*.

7

THE MEDITERRANEAN WAR

JUNE 1941–AUGUST 1942

The German attack on the Soviet Union in June 1941 came as a relief to the British prime minister, Winston Churchill, who had always hoped that the two dictators might fall out. Churchill had long been a scourge of the Bolsheviks: in 1919 he was one of the strongest supporters of military aid to the White Russians and in 1929 he threatened to resign from the Cabinet in protest against the Anglo-Soviet trade agreement. His well-developed powers of rhetoric were often ranged against the USSR, the 'foul baboonery of Bolshevism' and a 'pestilence more destructive of life than the Black Death or the Spotted Typhus' being among his milder comments. But in this matter at least, if in few others, Churchill was a realist. 'Russia's danger is our danger,' he said, and, if Hitler should invade Hell, he would at least make a favourable reference to the Devil in the House of Commons. There was an instant announcement of support for the USSR and the speedy conclusion of a mutual assistance pact promising that neither the UK nor the USSR would make a separate peace. Supplies of war materiel were promised, but it would be some time before that could be provided; raids on Germany by the RAF would be increased, and, while Stalin's demand for a landing on the French coast was entirely beyond British capabilities at this stage of the war, commando-type raids would be increased – although, realistically, they would have little, if any, effect on Barbarossa. Stalin was highly suspicious of the British – with good cause – and requests by the British embassy for information were referred to the published official communiqués, which were usually works of pure propaganda.

For the British, Barbarossa, the attack on Russia, provided a breathing space: there were fewer air raids on British cities as Germany's main efforts were directed eastwards, and there would now be less interest in supporting Rommel and his Afrika Korps in Libya. Not everyone in Britain was as cheerful as Churchill on hearing the news. The War Office thought that Russia could not possibly hold out for long and that, with the Red Army defeated and Russia conquered, the Germans would then be able to throw their full might against the British. Meanwhile, Churchill's blandishments of the USA were having an advantageous effect. Roosevelt still had to tread very carefully not to go too far in advance of public opinion, which even by 1941, while generally sympathetic to Britain, did not support direct American involvement, but in his State of the Union speech to Congress on 6 January 1941 he warned of the dangers to America of a victory by what he termed the 'Dictator Nations' and promised American support for those who resisted aggression in Europe and, tellingly, in Asia. In April 1941 he was able to order American naval and air patrols to extend as far as Iceland and instruct them that they were to inform the British of any sightings of German warships. In July he ordered American troops to reinforce (and eventually replace) the British garrison that had occupied Iceland since the fall of Denmark, its owner, in May 1940. Then, in the initially highly secret Placentia Conference, which was held from 9 to 12 August, Roosevelt and Churchill met for the first time when the prime minister and his advisers on the battleship HMS *Prince of Wales* rendez-voused with the president and his team on the heavy cruiser USS *Augusta* off the coast of Newfoundland.

Churchill and Roosevelt had already been communicating for some years by letter and telegram, and, while diplomats on both sides feared how the two prima donnas would react to each other, they need not have worried. Both men preferred personal diplomacy. To the irritation of their professional diplomats, they established an excellent working relationship and the result was the Atlantic Charter, which purported to set out the two nations' war aims (even though the USA was not in the war). The British regarded the unity of the Empire as sacrosanct; the Americans had no interest in maintaining British imperial power. The Americans wanted the freedom of the seas to be guaranteed in peace and war; the British would not forego their traditional weapon of the blockade. The result was much weasel-wording but excellent propaganda, even if what it said came back to haunt both powers later on. The main points of the Charter said that neither Britain nor America had any territorial ambitions and nor did they intend boundary changes without the consent of the affected inhabitants; all peoples had the right to choose their own governments; equality of access to world trade would be guaranteed along with raw materials for all; there would be improved labour standards, economic advancement and social security; a lasting peace would give every nation the means of dwelling safely within their own boundaries; access to the high seas would be unhindered; and, finally, all nations would abandon the use of force. In short, it was sanctimonious claptrap.

On 4 September the United States moved a step further towards war when the American destroyer USS *Greer*, on the way to Iceland, assisted an RAF aircraft by following a German submarine, U-652. The aeroplane dropped depth charges which the U-boat's captain, Captain-Lieutenant Georg-Werner Fraatz, assumed were from the destroyer and so, not unreasonably, he fired two torpedoes at her. They missed, but it allowed Roosevelt to announce that henceforth American ships would attack any German or Italian submarines that they found in the West Atlantic and to persuade Congress to extend the provisions of Lend-Lease to the USSR. From mid-September the still officially neutral United States Navy took on the task of escorting UK-bound convoys as far as Iceland, where the Royal Navy took over. In October, after much rumbling, Congress, which remembered that a similar move had served as a prelude to entering the First World War, authorized the arming of American merchant ships, and on 31 October the first American battle casualties of the war occurred when the destroyer USS *Reuben James* was sunk by a U-boat off Iceland while on convoy escort duty and 100 sailors died.

The subsequent attack by Japan on American possessions in Hawaii and the Far East in December 1941 was once again greeted with relief by the British: Churchill had always hoped to bring the New World to the rescue of the Old and his whole war policy was based on hanging on until America could come in. Hitler did the British a favour by declaring war on the United States – presumably on the grounds that, as America was bending the laws of neutrality to breaking point in Britain's favour and would come in eventually, he might as well get it over with. Now the British Empire was no longer alone, although it would be some time before that would be expressed by troops on the ground. In the meantime, the only theatre where the British could fight the Axis on land was in North Africa.

* * *

On paper at least, Operation Battleaxe, which was intended to push the Germans and Italians back beyond Tobruk, should have worked. A fast convoy to Alexandria had delivered 240 tanks, giving the British a numerical superiority over the Axis. Unfortunately, they were the wrong sort of tanks:

the British were still thinking in terms of infantry and cruiser tanks and the Matildas, for the infantry, were far too slow, while the Crusaders, the new cruisers, possessed a good turn of speed but were under-armoured and mechanically unreliable. Wavell wanted time to build up his forces, train them, amass reserve stocks of supplies and sort out the tanks, but Churchill wanted a quick victory to compensate for the loss of Crete and Wavell was forced to attack on 15 June 1941 against his better judgement. The operation failed for the usual reasons: unreliable tanks, lack of training in infantry–tank cooperation and insufficient logistic support, but also because the Germans made skilful use of concealed anti-tank guns, particularly the 88mm anti-aircraft gun in the ground role, and demonstrated their customary ability to react swiftly and to outmanoeuvre the pedestrian British. At this point Churchill finally lost patience with those who would not pander to his flights of fancy. He never had much time for Wavell, a man with far more integrity and considerably more intelligence than him but one who never bothered to explain his position to those he thought incapable of understanding it and who was constantly surprised and disapproving when politicians did not behave like gentlemen. Wavell had advised against the totally unnecessary Greek adventure, although he eventually acquiesced, and he opposed Churchill's insistence on troops being sent to Iraq and Syria. Churchill now demanded that Wavell be replaced, and decided that he should change places with General Sir Claude Auchinleck, Commander-in-Chief India. In a typical piece of Churchillian mean-spiritedness, Wavell was not even permitted two weeks' leave in England, in case his dismissal might give Churchill's opponents an opportunity to coalesce around him.

Aged fifty-six in 1941, Auchinleck was seen as the rising star of the Indian Army – although, to be absolutely accurate, as Commander-in-Chief in 1941 he had already risen. Called to the UK in 1940 when the British Army was desperately short of competent corps commanders, he was resented by officers of the home army over whose heads he was promoted, and he particularly infuriated them when, sent as a mountain warfare expert to Norway, he recommended withdrawal and described British troops there as 'callow and effeminate' (as indeed they were). As General Officer Commanding Southern Command in June 1940, Auchinleck had the misfortune to have the thoroughly disloyal acting Lieutenant-General Bernard Law Montgomery as a corps commander under him, and his promotion to general and return to India as Commander-in-Chief in January 1941 must have come as a considerable relief. He was succeeded at Southern Command by Montgomery, who immediately, quite unnecessarily and deliberately, reversed almost all of Auchinleck's perfectly sound policies.

In the twenty-two months since Britain declared war on Germany, the British Army had not shone. Whereas the Royal Navy had rescued it from Norway and from France in 1940, and the RAF had made the Dunkirk evacuation possible and had then won the Battle of Britain, the army had been roundly defeated in Norway, in France, in Greece, in Crete and now in North Africa. The only victories it had won had been against second-class foes – the Italians and, with some difficulty, the Vichy French – but, as soon as Germans appeared, the army could not stand against them. This was not entirely the fault of the army or of its generals. Sailors have to know how to sail and maintain a ship, and pilots have to know how to fly, so there is a minimum standard beneath which the navy and the air force cannot be allowed to fall before the whole edifice comes apart, and does so very visibly. The army, on the other hand, can trundle along in peacetime without anyone noticing very much what it can or cannot do, and politicians can get away with repeated cuts in funding, delays or cancellations in procurement programmes and the rundown of reserve stocks. The British Army between the wars was very much the neglected child of the defence family, and, when it had to expand massively, it simply could not instantly produce officers and NCOs of the right calibre or experience, provide up-to-date vehicles and equipment, and develop the tactical doctrine that would allow it to take on the Germans – the best soldiers in Europe since the time of the Great Elector – on equal terms. Within the army there was, by 1941, an expectation of failure, not helped by the resurrecting of old saws about the British always losing every battle but the last (not true: in previous wars they had started to win pretty quickly) and about Germans being automatons only able to react to orders (arrant nonsense: the Germans had proved themselves to be far more flexible than the British). The generals knew the weaknesses: they wanted time to develop the tactics, build up the supplies, train the units in all-arms cooperation, go very steadily and carefully, taking on only limited objectives until they had honed an army that could go on the offensive and know that it was going to win.

Churchill did not understand this. He was under pressure in the House of Commons and he needed a victory, and he would get rid of anyone who told him that one was not possible just yet. Auchinleck knew all this and was under no illusions that if he did not toe the Churchill line he too would be for the chop, but he was not prepared to compromise his professional integrity, and, when Churchill, in a characteristic display of his style of micro-management, tried to dictate the composition of the garrison of Cyprus, Auchinleck told him firmly to wind his neck in. As for an immediate attack in the Western Desert, he replied by signal to the prime minister's urgings: 'I must repeat that to launch an offensive with the inadequate means at our disposal is not, in my opinion, a justifiable operation of war.'[47] He was subsequently summoned to London to explain why he considered an immediate attack on the Germans and Italians in North Africa was not a good idea. His grasp of statistics and his sound common sense convinced the Chiefs of Staff but not Churchill, and Auchinleck was sent back to Egypt under orders to mount an attack in October 1941.

Certainly, in terms of men and equipment Auchinleck would start from a better baseline than did Wavell. Tanks and artillery pieces arrived in relative plenty and, with Iraq and Syria pacified, more troops would be available in Egypt. The Western Desert Force, also known as XIII Corps, was now to be named Eighth Army and Auchinleck, as overall Commander Middle East, selected Lieutenant-General Sir Alan Cunningham to command it. Cunningham, fifty-four years old in 1941, had made his name in East Africa, where he had shown an aptitude for mobile operations with forces of mixed nationalities and had taken the surrender of the Duke of Aosta in May. The plan for the offensive, codenamed Operation Crusader, was selected by Cunningham from a number of options suggested by Auchinleck and saw the infantry pinning the Germans and Italians in their own defences on the Libyan frontier, while the armour would make a wide sweep from the south, destroy the Axis armour, relieve Tobruk and occupy Tripolitania. After that advance of 1,000 miles, the army would exploit westwards depending on the situation at the time. On the surface, it looked as if at last the British might make an impression: they had more tanks, about the same number of aircraft and for once a reasonable stockpile of ammunition, fuel and rations. There were, however, snags. Auchinleck himself did not know and was not known by many officers of the British Army, and there was still resentment about someone from the Indian Army being appointed to a plum command. He had not won the favour of his staff when he ordered the move of Headquarters Middle East Command from the fleshpots of Cairo into the desert, and then, when it became apparent that only Cairo could provide the communications required, moving the headquarters back into the city but setting up his own tactical command post in the desert, with consequent liaison and communications difficulties between the two HQs. He did not establish a comfortable relationship with the Australian General Sir Thomas Blamey, who held the non-job of Deputy Commander Middle East. The problem was partly Blamey's touchiness on the matter of command of Australian troops, and his readiness to appeal to the Australian government over Auchinleck's head, and Blamey's somewhat colourful private and business life, but, as he was one of the few senior Australian officers with regular army, as opposed to militia, experience, he could not be dismissed.

Cunningham should have been just the man to command the Eighth Army but he had no experience of the desert, which was quite different from the terrain in Somaliland and Eritrea whence he had come less than three months before Crusader (reluctantly allowed by Churchill to be delayed by a month) was to begin. He had no experience of armoured warfare and, not unnaturally, deferred to those of his subordinates who had. At this time the British armoured doctrine still held that cruiser tanks could operate on their own, and Cunningham organized Eighth Army accordingly. Lieutenant-General Norrie's XXX Corps would be armour-heavy with 7 Armoured Division and 1 South African Infantry Division and 22 Guards Brigade, while XIII Corps, commanded by Lieutenant-General Godwin-Austen, another general whom Churchill disliked, would have the bulk of the infantry with the New Zealand 2 Division and Indian 4 Division, supported by 1 Army Tank Brigade with Matilda and Valentine infantry tanks. Norrie was a cavalryman but without any of the supposed aversion to mechanization of that arm. He had served with the Tank Corps in the first war, had overseen the process of mechanization when commanding what began as 1 Cavalry Brigade in 1937 and became 1 Armoured Brigade in 1938, and was then briefly Inspector Royal Armoured Corps before being sent to Egypt in November. Apart from having hardly any time to get to know his new command, he was clearly the most competent armoured officer available to command the corps, and at only forty-eight he had the vigour of youth to add to his considerable experience. Commanding 7 Armoured Division was Major-General William 'Strafer' Gott, who was not an armoured officer but an infantryman and none the worse for that. Much has been made of the fact that Cunningham was a gunner and so did not understand armour, and that Auchinleck, who came from an Indian Army which in 1941 had no tanks, was equally ignorant. This is, of course, nonsense. While up to the rank of lieutenant-colonel officers command troops of their own arm, the syllabus at the Staff College is and was the same for all, and from the rank of colonel and above officers were required to understand the handling of all arms of the service, and this was emphasized at the Imperial Defence College. For Auchinleck and Cunningham to listen to the advice of officers with more experience of armour than they had was sensible, but to claim that they did not understand its handling is not. Auchinleck, Cunningham and Gott were every bit as knowledgeable about armour as the vast majority of British generals, and they, like the vast majority and including the armoured experts, were trapped in a doctrine – armour could act independently – that turned out to be faulty.

During the planning stage it became evident that the allocation of all the armour save the infantry tanks to XXX Corps was not greeted with universal approval, particularly the deployment of 4 Armoured Brigade Group. This was an armoured brigade but with its own integral motorized infantry and artillery and was commanded by Brigadier 'Alec' Gatehouse. Commissioned into the Northumberland Fusiliers in 1915 and transferring to the Tank Corps in 1916, Gatehouse had commanded a battalion of tanks in the last great British offensive of 1918, and was still commanding a battalion of tanks in 1939, having followed the normal career path of regimental and staff appointments in between. Regarded as one of the foremost practitioners of armoured warfare, he commanded his brigade seated comfortably in an armchair strapped to the top of his command tank. Gatehouse's brigade had originally been allocated to XIII Corps, but was then transferred to XXX Corps. Its task in Crusader was to protect the southern (left) flank of the infantry while keeping in touch with the right flank of XXX Corps. When the infantry divisional commanders expressed unhappiness about being asked to advance blindly into the wide sand-coloured yonder, where there were known to be German and Italian tanks, without any armoured support other than the slow-moving infantry tanks, they were told not to worry as 4 Armoured Brigade would be on their flanks. What would happen, asked Major-General Freyberg, commanding the New Zealand Division, if 4 Armoured were to be called away for another task by XXX Corps? It was a question that was never answered.

The Eighth Army was the best-equipped army that the British had yet fielded in this war, and with 708 tanks had more than twice as many as the Axis with 320 (and half of those were Italian light tanks that were no better than the worst of the British vehicles), and there were another 120 tanks inside Tobruk. By itself 7 Armoured Division had 453 tanks and it was this very number which posed a problem that the Germans had already solved but the British had not. Received wisdom says that the German army's reorganization of the armoured composition of the panzer divisions from 280 tanks in four battalions to 140 tanks in two battalions after the Battle of France was done to increase the number of armoured divisions overall, and standard German practice was indeed to create new formations by splitting one existing division into two and then making up the shortfall with recruits, but that was far from the whole story. There is a limit to the number of men that one man can control, and to the number of units that can properly be commanded by one headquarters. Four armoured battalions with 280 tanks were just too many to handle. Gott now had to control even more than the number of tanks that the Germans, with their vastly superior training in armour, had found unwieldy. Gott's infantry, 1 South African Division, had done well in Abyssinia, but as soon as they arrived in Egypt they were employed in refurbishing the frontier defences, which had been allowed to fall into disrepair after O'Connor's great thrust into Libya earlier in the year. Humping sand bags and coils of barbed wire is excellent physical exercise but it is no substitute for training for desert warfare, of which the South Africans had no experience. Their casualties in Abyssinia had been only partially replaced, and those who had come were only just out of recruit training. Reconstituting his division into two brigades instead of three, the South African commander, Major-General George Brink, told Cunningham that he was not happy about the manning or the state of training of his division. He was told to get on with it.

The troops moved out into their concentration areas in complete secrecy, thanks to the RAF and the South African Air Force, which had not only spent the previous days plastering any German or Italian position they could find, but kept the skies over the concentration areas clear of enemy aircraft. It was as well that they did, for in most units the move was a shambles. There had been insufficient driver training and many wheeled vehicles snapped axles and smashed differentials trying to negotiate the rocky surface in the dark, not helped by appalling weather which flooded stream beds, washed away what few tracks there were and reduced visibility to a few yards. Thanks to a deception plan by Auchinleck's intelligence staff, Rommel was convinced that the British were intending to invade Persia, to give some help to the Russians and safeguard the Persian oil fields, and that anything that they might do in the Western Desert would be no more than a feint to distract the Axis. Rommel was in any case intending to launch a major attack to capture Tobruk, which he had been besieging since the British retreat in April.

Operation Crusader was launched on 18 November 1941. Berlin's eyes were very much on Moscow, where it began to look as if Barbarossa might stall, and there were no reinforcements for Panzer Group Africa, as the combination of the DAK and the Italian forces was now named, and whose commander, Rommel, now General of Panzer Troops, had been ordered to remain on the defensive. At first the British achieved complete surprise: the infantry of 4 Indian Division took on the German and Italian frontier defences and the armour hooked round the southern flank deep into Libya. By last light on Day One, 7 Armoured Division was a third of the way to Tobruk and the three armoured brigades were at the points of a triangle around Gabr Saleh, where Cunningham had expected a 'clash of armour'. Then it began to go wrong. The panzer divisions had no intention of clashing where the British wanted them to clash, and next day, instead of the three armoured brigades keeping in touch with each other, they were allowed to operate independently, searching for Axis armour to destroy. But Rommel's armour did not sit around waiting to be found and all the British armour could see were reconnaissance vehicles withdrawing. When 22 Armoured Brigade, on the left of the division and heading for Tobruk, discovered the Italian Ariete Armoured Division at Bir El Gubi, off to the left of the advance, instead of fixing them in position – which could have been done by detaching two squadrons – and carrying on with their main task, they decided that it would be rather jolly to destroy the Italians. They duly lined up their relatively speedy but thinly armoured Valentines and, in a manner that would have been perfectly acceptable had they been on horses at Waterloo, they charged the Ariete and, just like the French cavalry in 1815, they were slaughtered. What they thought were Italian tanks lined up, waiting to be blown away, was actually an outpost line which withdrew, drawing the British on to well-dug-in and concealed tanks, which proceeded to take out the Valentines. By dusk 22 Armoured had lost half their tanks and the Italians still held Bir El Gubi. The excuse, then and since, is that the three regiments of the brigade, 3 and 4 County of London Yeomanry and the Royal Gloucestershire Hussars, were Territorials who knew no better. That may wash for the Other Ranks but cannot excuse the commanding officers of the regiments, who should have known better, the brigade commander, who assuredly did know better, or Gott, who allowed them to do it. The County of London Yeomanry seemed to have learned little from the debacle as, combined into one regiment and under a commander who had been a squadron commander at Bir El Gubi, they behaved equally stupidly at Villers Bocage in Normandy three years later.

Things went a little better the following day. The armour had been told to capture the two airfields of Sidi Rezegh* and El Adem, which were twenty-five and twenty miles respectively from Tobruk, and situated on the escarpment above the port. When 7 Armoured Brigade got there it found aircraft lined up on the ground. It attacked, and took the airfield, and, although three aircraft took off and attacked the tanks at low level, the British captured nineteen and rendered them unusable by slashing the tyres, holing the fuel tanks and smashing up the instruments. It was at this point that Rommel decided the British offensive might be more than a diversionary feint, but, as his troops had been positioned to attack Tobruk, they were equally well placed to defend it. On 19 November he sent Colonel Stephan with a battle group of eighty-five tanks, a mixture of Mk IIs, IIIs and IVs, two batteries of 105mm field guns and four 88mm anti-aircraft guns in the anti-tank role to see what was going on. Stephan ran into Brigadier Gatehouse's 4th Armoured Brigade Group at Gabr Saleh and in the first tank-versus-tank battle of the campaign, fought in a dust storm of its own making and confusing to both sides, 4 Armoured ended the day with eleven tanks that were not repairable compared to Stephan's three. Many more on each side were knocked out, but on the German side their superb recovery system could repair damaged tanks *in situ* on the battlefield, whereas the British had to recover theirs to the rear first.

On 20 November a running battle continued and the British were led astray somewhat by the RAF's reporting of columns of vehicles heading west. These were almost certainly resupply columns going back to replenish, but it was reported to Cunningham as the Germans and Italians in retreat. On 21 November the garrison in Tobruk was ordered to break out and link up with 7 Armoured Division's lead elements at El Duda. Led by thirty-two

---

*Sidi is a title of respect. Mr Rezegh was a prophet and his tomb was on a hill in the area, hence the name.

Crusaders and sixty-nine Matilda infantry tanks, they attempted to do so, but, instead of Italians holding the perimeter as they had thought, they ran into Germans, some of the tanks strayed off the axis and ended up in minefields, and their Matildas were unable to keep up with the lead infantry battalion, Second Black Watch, who decided not to wait for their support but to do it by themselves. The battalion did get part way to El Duda, fifteen miles south-east of Tobruk, but lost sixty-five dead in so doing. The British tanks were unable to join with the Black Watch because the Germans were able to sit back and with their superior range knock out the Crusaders long before they could fire back. Even when they could reply, the two-pounder shell fired by the British tanks would simply bounce off unless it could hit at exactly the right angle, which it rarely did. Seventh Hussars lost all their tanks, and, although only twenty all ranks were killed, the large number of wounded, mostly from burns, and the loss of almost all its vehicles meant that the regiment was effectively wiped out and it was not seen in North Africa again.*

Confusion and misunderstanding were not confined to the British, and on the night of 21/22 November the DAK pulled back, as Lieutenant-General Ludwig Crüwell was concerned that the British had many more reserves than they actually had. On 22 November the German armour attacked Sidi Rezegh, and by last light they had the ridge back again – the British tanks simply could not stand up to the German machines – but could not recapture the airfield as they ran out of ammunition and had to withdraw into defence on the ridge. The Germans did, however, manage to capture 4 Armoured Brigade's headquarters, a loss compensated for by the British capture of DAK headquarters, although again the corps commander and his chief of staff were away. Such incidents were typical of war in the Western Desert: it was not uncommon for units to laager up at last light and then wake up in the morning to find an enemy camped right beside them.

Next day was the last Sunday before Advent to the British and *Totensonntag* to the Germans, when they pray for the souls of their dead. It was a critical day for both sides: German armour followed up by infantry in troop carriers attacked the South African division and wiped out one of its brigades, but at heavy losses to themselves. *Totensonntag* was also the day when Cunningham began to lose his nerve. Initial euphoria as he and his

---

*Although it was re-formed for service in the Far East.

staff thought a great victory was in the offing turned to dismay when it started to become apparent that it was not. He transmitted his worries to his two corps commanders and asked them whether they should not break off Operation Crusader. Both demurred: XXX Corps had taken considerable casualties in tanks, but Norrie was convinced that he could carry on, and Godwin-Austen's XIII Corps had hardly been used at all. Cunningham decided to refer the matter to C-in-C Middle East, Auchinleck, who flew up to consult, his chief of staff having been warned by Cunningham's own chief of staff, Brigadier 'Sandy' Galloway, a fiery-tempered Cameronian who was rather more robust than his master, that a visit by the C-in-C would be helpful. Auchinleck had great inner strength and limitless resource; he was a strong-minded man who had the ability to allay fears and instil confidence and calm reflection by his mere presence. By this time Cunningham knew about the disaster that had befallen 5 South African Brigade and was even more depressed by it all. Auchinleck arrived that evening and, having listened to Cunningham's concerns and his advice that the operation should be called off and Eighth Army withdrawn to Egypt to defend the Canal, he pointed out that, while things certainly looked bad at present, the enemy had their problems too and were in no state to push into Egypt. He insisted that the offensive should continue, and he does seem to have restored the army commander's nerve somewhat. Cunningham now instructed Godwin-Austen to push the New Zealand Division westwards, that Norrie's armour should protect the flanks and that the attempt to link up with the breakout from Tobruk should continue.

Rommel had now come to the conclusion that the British were definitely a nuisance and decided to do something about it. He concluded that the Eighth Army were spread out over a wide area and that they had taken considerable losses. A thrust by the DAK towards the frontier would alarm and confuse the British and would cut them off from their supply lines. Unable to wait for the corps commander, he took command of 21 Panzer Division himself and led them on a headlong dash for the Egyptian border with 15 Panzer following. It was certainly a shock for the British administrative units through which the panzers burst: there was much panic as kit was thrown on to vehicles, or simply abandoned, as drivers, signallers, storemen, clerks and staff officers tried to escape the armoured torrent. Cunningham himself was nearly snaffled: he was in 7 Armoured's headquarters when it was suddenly shelled, and had to be rushed away by the Corps Commander

Royal Engineers to an airstrip and flown back to army headquarters, the experience doing little for his morale. By 1600 hours on 24 November, Rommel was at the wire defences of the frontier, but his troops were spread out over fifty miles behind him, and had many broken-down vehicles, unable to keep up with their commander's mad rush. Rommel had been able to witness the chaos and confusion in his wake, but he had not seen that the initially disorganized British had re-formed behind him rather more quickly than anyone thought they could.

On returning to his headquarters, Cunningham found written instructions from Auchinleck laying out the options: calling off the offensive and going on the defensive to hold the ground already gained, or carrying on. Auchinleck dismissed the first course as it would be seen as an Axis triumph and it would do nothing to relieve Tobruk, and concluded that Norrie must continue to press the attack relentlessly 'to the last tank'. He was to recapture Sidi Rezegh and link up with the Tobruk garrison, keeping as his immediate objective the destruction of the enemy armour. Cunningham now had to implement a policy with which he fundamentally disagreed. That same day, the movement of 15 Panzer Division, which was actually looking for a breach in the frontier wire, was taken as being an attack on Eighth Army headquarters and Auchinleck was unceremoniously whisked away to the airstrip and flown out of the battle area. On the flight back to Cairo he had much time for reflection. It was clear to him that Cunningham had indeed lost his nerve and in any case it was unfair to expect him to pursue vigorously a policy in which he had no faith. Auchinleck decided that there was no option but to replace Cunningham as Commander Eighth Army. The difficulty was with whom? He himself could fight the battle better than anyone, but his bailiwick was not just North Africa but the whole of the Middle East, from Persia in the north to Eritrea in the south.

Normally the vacancy created by an army commander being replaced or rendered *hors de combat* would be filled by the senior corps commander, but in this case both corps commanders were in the middle of a series of battles and to move one of them now could cause delay in pressing on. It is, however, unusual, almost unheard of, to remove an army commander in the middle of a battle, and Auchinleck's choice to replace him was equally unusual. Major-General Neil Ritchie was originally commissioned into the Black Watch and as a colonel had been Brooke's Chief of Staff in II Corps in the Battle of France, where he did well. He commanded the reconstituted

51 Highland Division after the original had surrendered at St Valery on 12 June 1940 and was now Deputy Chief of the General Staff in Cairo. To put a man who had never commanded a corps, and a division only briefly, in command of an army was taking a huge punt, and that the two corps commanders were not only senior to him in rank but four years (Norrie) and eight years (Godwin-Austen) older than him was not going to help. That said, he would, of course, only be there as a temporary army commander with the local rank of lieutenant-general until someone better qualified could be brought out from the UK, and Auchinleck would keep a close eye on him.

As it happened, Ritchie was not the man for the job, but perhaps there was no one else immediately available at the time. On 26 November, Cunningham was relieved and admitted to hospital in Cairo under an assumed name, although there cannot have been many working there who did not know who he was. While this author has been unable to trace Cunningham's medical documents (which may well no longer exist), it is clear that he must have been very tired, under almost intolerable strain, and had suffered what the layman would now term a nervous breakdown. Generals spend their whole adult lives training for and preparing for war, and, while they are not subject to formal psychiatric examination on their upward path, mental robustness and performance under pressure are certainly scrutinized in a process of continuous evaluation which will decide promotion prospects (or lack of them). That said, Cunningham's learning curve had been very steep indeed and commanding in East Africa was very different from commanding the armour-heavy Eighth Army. Surrounded as he was by men of strong personality and equally strong opinions, it would seem that he was put into a job that was just too big for him. Amongst the many accusations subsequently levelled at Auchinleck by lesser men was that Auchinleck was a bad judge of men, but it did not seem so at the time and Cunningham came to him with a high reputation. In any case, Cunningham was not exactly plucked from a cast of thousands.*

On 27 November Rommel, having spent an uncomfortable night lost near the wire and having to be rescued by Crüwell's command vehicle, decided that hanging about around the frontier was achieving little and

---

*High Commissioner in Palestine 1945–48, Cunningham had the thankless task of trying to contain an anti-British revolt by Jewish terrorists, when he had a run-in with Montgomery, then a field marshal and CIGS, who showed himself completely incapable of understanding the nuances of the Palestine question.

pulled the DAK back towards Tobruk, capturing 5 New Zealand Brigade's commander and his staff on the way. On the morning of the same day, the New Zealand Division recaptured the ridge of Sidi Rezegh and pushed on towards El Duda. The breakout force from Tobruk launched itself across the four miles separating them from El Duda and by midday the Tobruk corridor was joined. There was not very much that could be done through it, and it only lasted a day before the Germans attacked the New Zealand Division and cut the corridor on 28 November, but it gave a short-lived boost to morale at the time. The British had almost scored a major success on the 27th when they caught 15 Panzer Division strung out on the line of march heading west, but they then followed their normal procedure of breaking off at last light and pulling back well into the desert for the night.

Up to now, the Germans and Italians had won all the tactical encounters and had inflicted many more losses in vehicles, and marginally more in men, than they had suffered, but their supply line was a tenuous one running back to Tripoli and then across the Mediterranean to Italy. The Royal Navy and the RAF between them meant that Rommel could never rely on getting such reinforce-ments and supplies that Berlin could send – and North Africa was very far down OKW's list of priorities. He was now short of fuel and ammunition and many of his tanks were off the road, more as a result of mechanical breakdown than British anti-tank rounds. The British, on the other hand, might have fielded inferior tanks, and 7 Armoured Brigade had been withdrawn to Egypt and would not appear again, but they were able to replace them, and very quickly the tank delivery organization had provided over 100 cruiser and Stuart light tanks to XXX Corps. Before Ritchie could continue the offensive and restore the Tobruk corridor prior to relieving the port, Rommel, well aware that he was over-extended and needing to shorten his lines of communication, withdrew at his own pace back to Gazala, twenty-five miles west of Tobruk on 6 December, which coincidentally was the day that the United Kingdom reluctantly and under pressure from the USSR declared war on Finland, Hungary and Romania. Ritchie now planned to attack the Gazala position with D-Day being 19 December, but Rommel outsmarted him again and on the night of 16/17 December slipped away 270 miles to El Agheila, thus giving up most of Cyrenaica. The few feeble attempts the British made to cut him off failed with more tank losses. On Christmas Eve the British occupied Benghazi, to encounter a grumpy population which had not appreciated being bombed by the RAF for the past two months.

* * *

Meanwhile, in London, Churchill was once again sacking or trying to sack those who would not conform to his fantasies. He had already tried and failed to dismiss Air Marshal Sir Arthur Tedder, Air Officer Commanding in Chief Middle East, who had the complete confidence of Wavell and then Auchinleck. Churchill, who considered most RAF officers to be oily mechanics, could never be made to understand that it took more than the pilot to look after an aircraft. Highly complex machines need to be maintained, repaired, refuelled and rearmed, and there were inevitably far more ground crew than aircrew. When Tedder refused to slash RAF numbers to the extent that Churchill wished, on the very sound grounds that if he did the pilots would starve and the planes crash, the prime minister tried to do with him what he had already done with General Wavell. Very quickly, senior RAF officers made it known that they would refuse the post if offered, and the Chief of the Air Staff, Air Chief Marshal Sir Charles Portal, left the prime minister in no doubt that, if Tedder went, then so would he. Churchill backed down.

The prime minister next turned his ire on the Chief of the Imperial General Staff, General Sir John Dill. Dill was the son of an Ulster bank manager from Lurgan in Northern Ireland. Educated at Cheltenham and Sandhurst, where he only just scraped in, he was originally commissioned into the Leinster Regiment, which as a southern Irish and Roman Catholic regiment was an odd choice for a northern Protestant. His military career was almost all spent on the staff, and he was clearly what is tactfully known as a late developer since, having been only just up to the required academic standard at school and at Sandhurst, he found his metier in staff work. A student at the Staff College in 1913, brigade major (chief of staff) of 25 Infantry Brigade in 1914 and a temporary brigadier-general in the operations branch of Field Marshal Haig's General Headquarters in 1918, he was regarded as a ferociously hard worker and began to acquire the description 'intellectual'. After the war he was an instructor at both the Army Staff College and the tri-service Imperial Defence College, then successively Commandant of the Army Staff College, Director of Military Operations in the War Office, GOC British Troops Palestine and from 1937 General Officer Commanding in Chief Aldershot Command. He was certainly intelligent, although perhaps not really intellectual, and his ability to see the essentials of a problem and to explain it succinctly left a lasting impression on those who knew him. Surprisingly for someone who had risen so high, he had no military enemies that we know of. Both Auchinleck and Brooke were students under him at the Staff College and thought him a man of genius, of modesty, of boundless enthusiasm. Now, and to a large extent then too, officers being considered for higher positions in the service would be expected to have followed a career balanced between command and staff appointments. Dill obviously had the staff experience, but he had not commanded a battalion or a division, and only for a very short time a Territorial brigade (in 1923), when he was appointed to command I Corps of the BEF on the outbreak of war in 1939. Most of his contemporaries thought that he would none the less be made Chief of the Imperial General Staff in 1937, and in army circles he was considered the man most fitting for that post when, in a disgraceful piece of political chicanery, Field Marshal Sir Cyril Deverall was removed suddenly from office in 1937.*

The appointment of CIGS, as with the most senior posts in the other two services, is a matter for the royal prerogative, but in practice is a governmental decision. In deciding whom to appoint, the Secretary for War would normally have consulted the outgoing holder of the office as well as senior serving and retired officers. Whether the process was followed in this case is doubtful, but in any event the job went to Viscount Gort, who had risen from being an acting lieutenant-general in September 1937 to substantive general by Christmas, and who at fifty-one was the youngest ever incumbent of the army's most senior post. Gort then fell out with the Secretary for War, Leslie Hore-Belisha, and in order to get him out of the War Office he was made Commander-in-Chief of the BEF, instead of General Ironside, who became CIGS instead. Dill went to France as one of the two corps commanders (the other being Brooke). It was an extraordinary way to manage the senior command level of an army about to go to war. When Ironside began to fall out with the then First Lord of the Admiralty, Churchill, largely because he was equally confrontational, Dill was brought home to fill the newly created post of vice-CIGS in April 1940 and then became CIGS when Ironside found he could not work with Churchill as incoming prime minister.

---

*Deverall was a proponent of modernization, mechanization and preparation for a war in Europe. The Cabinet had little stomach and less money for a continental commitment and Leslie Hore-Belisha, the very unpleasant secretary of state for war, advised by the even more unpleasant Basil Liddell Hart, decided to remove Deverall, who arrived in his office to find a note sacking him.

Dill and Churchill were temperamental opposites. Churchill wanted derring-do, finest hours, glorious adventures and swashbuckling offensive action. Dill well knew that the British Army was in no state to buckle a swash and refused to be browbeaten by the prime minister's flights of strategic fancy. In hindsight, Dill's advice was sound in every respect. It was clear, unambiguous and backed up by impeccably marshalled facts, none of which the prime minister wanted to hear. What particularly incensed Churchill was that every scheme which Churchill insisted upon, but which Dill advised against, turned out to be a shambles, the Greek involvement being the obvious example. Politicians accept personal abuse as being a normal adjunct to discussion: army officers do not, and Churchill's unkindness and rudeness – he nicknamed Dill 'Dilly-Dally' – and his constant rejection of the CIGS's advice, coupled with personal difficulties – Dill's then wife was probably bonkers and he should never have married her in the first place – took their toll. At last, in November 1941, just as Crusader was getting under way in North Africa, Churchill saw his chance to get rid of a man who had the confidence of the whole army but who would not compromise his integrity by agreeing to policies that he knew to be wrong. The prime minister, who was also the minister of defence, introduced a new rule that said that the CIGS must retire at the age of sixty, and Dill would reach that age on Christmas Day 1941. This was arrant cheek of the highest order as Churchill would be sixty-seven by Christmas, and he had abused his body to a far greater degree than had the relatively abstemious Dill, but in the United Kingdom the political, however unfair, stupid or unnecessary, has primacy over the military and Dill had to go, being replaced by General Sir Alan Brooke, a dour Ulsterman who had commanded II Corps in the Battle of France. Brooke claimed to have felt deeply for Dill, whom he admired, but obviously not deeply enough to refuse the offer of replacing him. When commanding II Corps, Brooke had had as one of his divisional commanders Major-General Bernard Law Montgomery. Brooke consistently looked after his own, and this would soon have a major impact on the future conduct of the Mediterranean War.

* * *

Operation Crusader ended on 16 December 1941. In that the British were left in possession of the field, that the siege of Tobruk had been lifted and that Panzer Group Africa had withdrawn west of Benghazi, it might be – and was –

trumpeted as a British victory, but hardly the devastating and decisive one that Churchill had wanted. Despite the code-breakers in Bletchley Park keeping Auchinleck, Cunningham and Ritchie reasonably well informed of what the Germans and Italians were saying to each other by radio, the British, even when attacking, were nearly always on the back foot, reacting to what Rommel did rather than unbalancing him. When battle was joined, usually on ground of the Axis' choosing, the British had still not mastered the techniques of all-arms cooperation and neither of the two corps was a balanced force. German anti-tank guns were able to knock out British tanks before the latter got within range, and far too often the British armour outran their artillery and attacked without any infantry support. Read armoured knight for tank and archer for anti-tank gunner and the lessons of Crécy, Poitiers and Agincourt were repeated over and over again, but this time the British were the mounted knights. When Panzer Group Africa did withdraw in order to fall back on its logistic supply line, it did so at a time that suited it and the British pursuit was too cautious and too slow. The British had lost 2,900 dead, or 2.5 per cent of their total, and the Axis 2,300, or 1.9 per cent. As the attacker, the British would be expected to have more casualties, although when wounded, missing and prisoners are added up, the butcher's bill was slightly in favour of the British. That only a small number of the Eighth Army dead were actually British was an embarrassment for some, but as it was in the infantry where men, rather than vehicles, got killed and as the majority of the armour was British but most of the infantry was from the Empire, this was to be expected.

Far more worrying was the effect on the Eighth Army's morale. The war in the Western Desert is often held up to have been great fun, conducted in a gentlemanly way and the one to be in if you had to be in a war at all. In fact, at this stage of the war at least, life in North Africa was very far from comfortable. It was stiflingly hot during the day, and not far above freezing at night: rations did get up but were sparse and monotonous; water was always short and anyone who had any connection with a vehicle spent much of the day extricating it from being bogged down in sand or having cracked a sump on rock, and most of the night maintaining and refuelling it. In most areas it was impossible to dig trenches and instead sangars – firing posts created by building a circular wall of rocks, which had to be at least two feet thick to stop small arms fire – had to be constructed, a laborious and lengthy task for the infantry whenever they halted for any length of time. The only plus points about the desert were that there were few civilians to get in the way, and as the air and the soil, dust and sand were reasonably clean, wounds tended not to go septic. But worse than the physical discomfort which the troops had to put up with was the disappointment. The newspapers at home had told them they were going to win a great victory, the prime minister had told them so, their own leaders had told them so, and yet their own experiences indicated that the German soldier was better, more flexible and more efficient, and so was German equipment. While this was not entirely true, to many of the soldiers of the Eighth Army their hero was not Churchill, or Auchinleck, but Rommel, who seemed to them to be able to run rings round the ponderous British.

Under normal circumstances, if war can ever be normal, the Eighth Army would now regroup, replace its casualties, repair its damaged vehicles, take delivery of replacements, disseminate the lessons of Crusader and prepare for the next great leap forward – and the objective was still Tripoli. Unfortunately for Auchinleck, the events of 7 December, when Japan entered the war, just a week before Crusader began to wind down, were to place major restrictions on what he could now do. The British had learned at least one of the lessons from the Greek debacle, and troops would not be taken away from Eighth Army to go to the Far East, but troop reinforcements that Auchinleck would have received were diverted and he could not now expect any more tanks or anti-aircraft guns; indeed, he was prevailed upon to send an armoured brigade and some field artillery eastwards. Furthermore, 17 Division and fighter and bomber aircraft squadrons on the way to the Middle East would now be sent to India and the Indian 17 Division, which had been intended for Iraq, would now remain in India. Auchinleck was also concerned about the leadership available to him:

> If we add to inferiority in material an apparent inferiority in leadership, then we shall be in a bad way and not deserve to win...
> I have a most uncomfortable feeling that the Germans outwit and outmanoeuvre us as well as outshooting us... if it is true then we must find new leaders at once... commanders who consistently have their brigades shot away from under them, even against a numerically inferior enemy, are expensive luxuries, much too expensive in present circumstances.[48]

Despite the calls of the Far East from now on, the supply situation for the British in North Africa would in fact begin to improve, while that for

Panzer Army Africa (as it became in January 1942, with Rommel promoted to colonel-general) would decline. More and more, the British would throw vehicles, guns, stores into battles of attrition while the Axis, constantly short of everything, would try to rely on flexibility and tactical acuity, but before British material superiority could begin to tell, Rommel had one more offensive card to play. The RAF and the Royal Navy had sunk numerous supply convoys, but the Italian merchant marine showed great courage, ingenuity and persistence to get at least some deliveries through and on 5 January 1942 a convoy bringing much-needed rations, ammunition, replacement vehicles and – critically – fuel did arrive at Tripoli. Rommel was now operating on short lines of communication, while the British were overstretched on theirs. Rommel was convinced that one more push would take him to Cairo, despite the recently appointed Commander-in-Chief South, Field Marshal Albert Kesselring of the Luftwaffe based in Italy, making it plain that he did not believe the supply situation could possibly support such an escapade. On 21 January 1942 Rommel attacked with 117 German and 79 Italian tanks and burst though a much strung-out British front line, which for once had fewer tanks (141) than him. The British retreated to the Gazala line and Rommel followed and then halted to bring up supplies. Throughout the spring, both sides glared at each other from opposite sides of minefields and built up their stocks.

Berlin now began to take more interest in Rommel than hitherto, when he had been regarded as a mere sideshow. Grand Admiral Raeder, Commander-in-Chief of the German navy, pointed out that British involvement in the Middle East was much more about oil than any imperial designs in the area. If the British could be deprived of their oil in the Middle East and Persia, then their ability to wage war would be severely limited. A double envelopment with Rommel striking east combined with a drive south from the Caucasus would achieve this and would incidentally sever the British route to India. To do this Rommel would have to receive massive resupplies and reinforcements, which would necessitate achieving at least air parity in the Mediterranean in order for the convoys to Tripoli to have a chance of getting through. Part of the RAF threat to the Italian convoys carrying supplies came from airfields in Egypt, but a particular source of air attacks was the British colony of Malta, not only an unsinkable aircraft carrier in the Mediterranean but also with a fine natural harbour for Royal Navy surface ships and submarines. During the month of April 1942 Malta was subjected to constant air raids by Luftflotte 2, with around 12,000 tons of bombs falling on the island. Much damage was done, but an efficient air-raid warning system and plentiful shelters dug into the rock greatly limited the civilian death toll. However, the raids on Malta not only allowed more convoys than usual to get through to Rommel but also increased Churchill's demands for an immediate attack by Eighth Army.

As part of a plan hatched in Berlin, which as its first phase would see Rommel driving the British as far as the Egyptian frontier while Malta was invaded, Panzer Army Africa moved on 26 May. Rommel's plan was for a classic German encirclement, by outflanking the British line from the south, and, although this eluded him, he did provoke a tank battle in what became known as 'the cauldron' in the middle of the British front line, one in which the British lost around 400 tanks. By mid-June, the last effective British armoured brigade had lost over a third of its tanks and the British were once again forced into retreat. In what uncharitably became known as the Gazala Gallop, Ritchie began to extract his units and move them rearward as fast as they could go. London, Headquarters Middle East Command and Head-quarters Eighth Army all had different views, which did not help. Churchill in London could not understand why the British were retreating at all and demanded that whatever happened Tobruk, must be held; Auchinleck ordered that the Eighth Army hold west of Tobruk while Ritchie was insistent that the earliest a stand could be made was the Egyptian frontier. Auchinleck had to accept Ritchie's view but under pressure from Churchill did put a garrison into Tobruk under the command of Major-General Klopper with his own 2 South African Division, 11 Indian Infantry Brigade, a Guards brigade and 4 Royal Tank Regiment, augmented by various odds and sods who were unable to keep up with the rapidly retreating main body.

Ritchie realized that holding at the frontier with insufficient tanks (and much of the British armour had been lost) was not a realistic proposition as Rommel would simply outflank the infantry, and his plan, agreed by Auchinleck, was to make a stand 170 miles east at Mersa Matruh, with the infantry of X Corps, arriving from Syria, and XIII Corps supported by 1 Armoured Division's 150 tanks, while what remained of XXX Corps went back to refit and prepare positions where Auchinleck considered the enemy could realistically be stopped, at El Alamein, a mere seventy miles west of Alexandria. The need to besiege Tobruk would delay the Axis advance and give Eighth Army a much-needed opportunity to get itself sorted out at Mersa Matruh. It was to get no respite, for, after a siege of only one week, Klopper surrendered Tobruk on 21 June 1942 and Rommel became a field marshal, at fifty the youngest in the German army.

Klopper was hardly a charismatic leader, but in fairness to him the defences of Tobruk had been neglected since the last siege had been lifted in the previous December. Wire had been snaffled by local farmers, trenches and anti-tank ditches had silted up and mines had shifted. Long before the Gazala Gallop, Auchinleck had told the Chiefs of Staff in London that Tobruk could not and should not be held if the British had to withdraw again, and this had been accepted at the time, but not now. Not all of Klopper's troops accepted his orders to cease fighting. Second Battalion the Cameronians fought on for twenty-four hours before agreeing to surrender, and Second Battalion 7 Gurkha Rifles saw no need to surrender at all and broke out through the perimeter, intending to fight its way back to Egypt. It took an entire Italian corps and several weeks to round the Gurkhas up, some having got as far as Sollum on the frontier. One enterprising *havildar* (sergeant) somehow obtained a camel and Arab clothing and walked 400 miles all the way back to Egypt to rejoin Eighth Army. It is probably unnecessary to say that Gurkhas do not look at all like Arabs; nor do they speak Arabic.

Tobruk was, in fact, only of use to the British if it was behind their lines and could be used as a port for resupply. If it lay behind the German lines, the RAF could make it of little use as a supply point for the Axis, and it was only held because Churchill insisted on it. When the news came through that it had fallen with 25,000 men taken prisoner, Churchill was in America and he took it very badly. The only compensation was that Roosevelt felt so sorry for him that he promised to send him the first batch of 300 of the new M4 tank, known to the British as the Sherman, and 100 self-propelled 105mm artillery pieces by fast US ships to Egypt.

Auchinleck now had to sack another Commander Eighth Army. He flew up to Mersa Matruh on 25 June, looked at Ritchie's dispositions, heard his plan for the coming battle, decided that both they and he were not going to work and sent Ritchie back to Cairo.* As there was no one else obviously

---

*Unlike previously removed generals, and those yet to be removed, Ritchie did not sink into obscurity. He was a protégé of Brooke and Brooke was now CIGS. All sorts of excuses were manufactured, mostly blaming Auchinleck, and Ritchie was successively given command of a division in September 1942, promotion to lieutenant-general and a corps in December 1943, which he took to Normandy in 1944, and a knighthood at the end of the war. He became General Officer Commanding Scotland and then, as a full general, Commander-in-Chief Far East Land Forces from 1947 to 1949. God bless the Old Boy Network.

available to replace him, Auchinleck assumed command of the Eighth Army himself. Ritchie's dispositions were certainly faulty: his forces were too spread out with large gaps between units, which would not have mattered had there been sufficient anti-tank guns or mobile formations to cover the gaps, but there were not. More serious was Ritchie's intention to fight a defence to the last man and the last round. Auchinleck knew that what mattered was not a bit of useless desert but the Suez Canal and the Persian oil fields. He only had one army and if he broke it there would not be another. Mersa Matruh was to be a delaying battle while proper defensive positions were prepared farther back, and then units were to be extracted intact for the real battle at El Alamein.

Auchinleck had little time to prepare for battle at Mersa Matruh. What he wanted to do was send all troops without integral transport back to Alamein or to the Nile Delta, which meant that the only non-motorized infantry that could be retained would be that which could be transported by the trucks of the Royal Army Service Corps which were not needed for supplies – not many. The battle was to be fought by battle groups, each a mix of motorized or vehicle-borne infantry combined with tanks and artillery and each of roughly battalion size. How many of these could be created from each brigade would depend upon the artillery and armour available. It was a totally sensible idea, and it is the way we fight now with a battle group consisting (usually) of two infantry companies, two squadrons of tanks and a battery of guns, but in 1942 it was far too far ahead of its time. Divisional, brigade and even battalion commanders disliked splitting their formations up and even – heaven forfend – having their men commanded by some frightful outsider from the Royal Armoured Corps or the reverse, a grubby infantryman. Even the normally sensible Freyberg, commanding the New Zealand Division, announced that he would appeal over the head of Auchinleck to the New Zealand government, as if a politician sitting in Auckland on the other side of the world could possibly pronounce on orders of battle of the Eighth Army.* In the event, the matter became one of merely academic interest as on 26 June Rommel ordered the DAK forward, hoping to use its armour to push the British tanks away to the south, using the Italians to distract the defenders by advancing from the west and south, while 90 Light

---

*It was also a bit of a cheek as Freyberg was, after all, a British general. As New Zealand had always been one of the more cooperative Dominions, her government would probably have backed Auchinleck.

Division of motorized infantry attacked along the coast and took Mersa Matruh. While Rommel's plan did not work out as he planned, he sowed considerable confusion amongst the British, particularly in the case of Gott, now commanding XIII Corps, who misinterpreted 21 Panzer moving south to avoid British armour as a flanking move that had annihilated the entire New Zealand Division, and ordered his corps to withdraw. As Gott was convinced that the New Zealand Division had ceased to exist, they were left without any armoured support and had to break out alone, which they did with considerable skill, getting back to the south of the Alamein position. With the premature withdrawal of XIII Corps, X Corps was left to fend for itself and another chaotic retreat ensued, this time made worse by the corps communications breaking down. It was fortunate for the British that anyone got back at all, largely because the movement of the DAK was almost as chaotic. British and German columns were all moving in the same direction and all trying to avoid each other, and the situation was hardly improved by the Axis using large numbers of captured British vehicles and the fact that both sides' uniforms looked very much the same at night. The RAF bombed British columns and German machine-gunners fired on their own troops.

The Battle of El Alamein is associated in the public mind with Montgomery and the battle of that name fought from 23 October to 4 November 1942, but there were two battles of El Alamein and arguably the first, fought by Auchinleck, was the more important, for it was that battle that stopped the Axis advance towards the Nile, and marked the farthest east they ever got. Rommel's plan was to arrange a diversionary move to the south and then burst through the junction of the two British infantry corps with his 90 Light Division followed by his armour, which would then fan out north and south behind the British and either destroy Eighth Army piecemeal or panic it into retreating headlong for the Nile, whereupon Panzer Army Africa would follow and be in Alexandria by the end of the week. It didn't happen. Despite the chaos of the British withdrawal and the fact that some British units were still moving into position when Rommel launched his attack on 1 July, Auchinleck had placed his remaining troops in a series of brigade boxes, each with armoured support and integral artillery, through which even the men of the DAK could not break. By evening the infantry of 90 Light had not broken through and were digging in as fast as they could wield their shovels, with darkness bringing a blessed relief from the British shelling. Now Rommel, realizing that he had a new opponent, recast his plans. The breakthrough and bomb-burst plan became a combined infantry and armour attack due east making for the coast and at first light on 2 July the infantry formed up to try again. The panzers had suffered a bad night, however, for their replenishment columns had been bombed and scattered by the RAF and the refuelling and rearming, normally done under cover of darkness, had now to be done by day, and tanks would not be ready to move before mid-afternoon. When they did move, they found that the British, instead of their usual hunter chase tactics of a blind headlong charge, were holding back at the extreme range of their tank guns – and the British now had sizeable numbers of American Grant tanks with a 75mm gun – and were coordinating the tank fire with that of the artillery. It had taken a long time, but the British were beginning to learn, spurred on by Auchinleck – that Indian soldier who could not possibly understand the requirements of modern warfare. To the south, the one Italian formation in which the Germans had a certain amount of faith, the Ariete Armoured Division, was caught in one flank by the New Zealanders and in the other by concentrated artillery and anti-tank fire and was virtually wiped out. On 3 July, Rommel made one last effort to break through. But superb soldiers that the men of the DAK were, short of fuel and short of men, they could do no more. Just before midnight Rommel halted the offensive and ordered his men into defensive positions. First Alamein was over and this time there could be no doubt that it was an unqualified British victory. Auchinleck had roundly repudiated those who thought he should never have removed Ritchie, and calmed the panic behind him. The Royal Navy had hastily evacuated Alexandria and in Cairo 1 July became known as Ash Wednesday owing to the number of official papers being burned to prevent them falling into the hands of the Axis should Egypt fall. Destruction of documents gives all sorts of unintended opportunities and, while many of the files consigned to the flames might well have been of use to the enemy, many were the pending courts martial that did not happen as all the necessary paperwork was gone.*

Auchinleck now decided that what was needed was not the seeking out of Rommel's strongest formations – the Germans of the DAK – but instead the concentration on his weakest units – the Italian infantry. In a series of limited operations and raids, the British managed to knock the Italians, who

---

*This author recalls being stationed next to a famous British infantry battalion due to have its annual inspection, when accounts would be audited and stores counted. Lo, on the evening before the inspection there was a mysterious fire in the quartermaster's stores. Very little damage was done, but all the quartermaster's ledgers were destroyed. It is very difficult to burn ledgers.

were holding the front while the DAK rested farther back, off balance and on one occasion even penetrated to within a few miles of the headquarters of Panzer Army Africa, and on 15 July, despite a failure of the tanks to support the infantry, they captured the vital ground of the Ruweisat Ridge. Field Marshal Rommel was now forced to accept that the supply and manpower situation in Panzer Army Africa precluded any more offensives and that he would be fortunate to be able to hold the ground that he had won. On the evening of 21 July, Auchinleck launched a major offensive designed to break through the German defences and destroy the DAK. Alas, while the British were slowly learning the lessons of a successful defence, they had not yet absorbed the principles of attack. The armour failed to support the infantry, and when it did it reverted to the tactic of lining up and going as fast as it could; the infantry failed to properly clear minefield gaps, thus losing more tanks, and relations between the British, Australian and South Africans and between everyone and the armour were almost at breaking point, with all blaming each other and the mysterious 'they' for what was going wrong. Auchinleck knew what had to be done, but he simply did not have enough professional subordinates to carry it out. For the moment, Rommel could do nothing because he had no supplies, and Auchinleck could do nothing because he had insufficient men.

Auchinleck had saved the Eighth Army and the Suez Canal, but that was not the way Churchill saw it. Relations between the two men had been steadily, and occasionally, when Churchill sent a particularly offensive signal, unsteadily, declining since the spring, and Auchinleck's report after First Alamein that he would not be able to go on the offensive until mid-September enraged the prime minister, who now decided that he would personally go out to Egypt with the CIGS before they flew on, as arranged, to consult with Stalin in Moscow. He and Brooke arrived in Cairo on 3 August 1942. It was the beginning of what came to be known as the Cairo Purge, an episode that would not reflect well on either Churchill or Brooke.

8

THE RUSSIAN WAR

OCTOBER 1941—NOVEMBER 1942

By October 1941 the German army was poised to take Moscow in the centre, was well into the Crimea and about to break into the Caucasus in the south, and was besieging Leningrad in the north.* Despite the inability of the Replacement Army† to fully compensate for the losses of men and materiel, delays in the conversion of the Russian railway to German gauge and the ominous signs of the approach of winter, most German commanders thought, or convinced themselves they should think, that the war could still be won swiftly. Already, however, they were building up problems in the rear areas that would plague them for the rest of the Russian war. The Germans had overrun huge swathes of territories from which much of the population had not been removed and they had taken nearly 2 million Russian prisoners of war. Not all of the captured soldiers were enthusiastic about fighting for Stalin, and many of the civilians thought the Germans would release them from the burden of communism, particularly from the generally detested collectivization of farming. Within the German armed forces and the civil administration that followed them, there were divided opinions. All realized that pacification of the rear areas was essential to allow the Wehrmacht to move deeper into the USSR and to supply itself as it did so; the disagreement was in how that should be achieved. One school of thought – mainly, but not exclusively, in the army – held that humane treatment of prisoners and

---

*It is sometimes pointed out that Napoleon got to Moscow in two months whereas it took the Germans nearly five, but the German army was six times larger than Napoleon's, and Napoleon was making for Moscow and not Leningrad and Kiev and the Caucasus as well, and only had to fight one major battle on the way (at Borodino). That said, German infantry divisions and field artillery were, like Napoleon's, reliant on horse power.

†That organization in Germany responsible for making up losses in men and materiel.

the civilian population could turn them away from communism and, if not persuade them to actively support the invaders, at least keep them quiescent. The other school held that the way to keep the peace was to ensure that prisoners and civilians were too terrified to step out of line and that brutality should be the tool to ensure it. The latter viewpoint coincided with the desire of NSDAP party officials to carry out racial cleansing, and it was their policies that prevailed. It is unclear how much the army participated in what were termed atrocities at the post-war trials. At Nuremberg and in their memoirs, the generals denied that they had anything to do with illegal executions, blaming the party or the SS, and many of the records, if records were kept, have been lost or destroyed, but there can be little doubt that, while some units steadfastly refused to become involved in what officers considered to be conduct that stained the honour of the German army, there were also some that participated with varying levels of enthusiasm in the killing of political commissars and the rounding up of Jews.

Some of what went on can be understood, if not excused. Numbers of Russian soldiers were shot when trying to surrender, but that happens in any war and on any front and there were reports of Russians pretending to surrender and then carrying on fighting once their potential captors had lowered their guard. It was sometimes difficult to distinguish between partisans – armed civilians taking part in the fighting – who may legally be executed, and bypassed groups of cut-off soldiers, who may not. It was claimed that some commissars were removing their brassards and pretending to be ordinary prisoners, which led to the shooting of all sorts of people who just might be commissars but usually were not. The Germans were particularly concerned about women soldiers, of whom the Red Army had a great many, and at one stage there was an order (later countermanded) saying that all female prisoners of war were to be shot.* The German army found itself with far more prisoners of war than it ever thought it would have to look after. Prisoners need to be got away from the battle area and into detention camps well behind the lines, and the original intention was for them to be transported back to camps in occupied Poland or East Prussia in otherwise empty lorries going back to collect supplies. This rarely worked

---

*There are a good many people in the British Army who think that we should not be allowing women in the combat area, but they would probably draw the line at shooting them.

because commanders of transport units refused to carry prisoners on the grounds that they would infest their vehicles with lice, and prisoners had to march, often for hundreds of miles and taking weeks to get to the very basic accommodation made available to them. Many died on the way and those who did not found that the ration supplied was barely sufficient to keep them alive. Inevitably, in the primitive conditions of the camps into which they were eventually put, disease, particularly typhus, took its toll and medical arrangements, if provided at all, were of the most basic kind. Had the war been won as quickly as the Germans thought it would, then the brutality option would have worked, but as it was the treatment of prisoners and the civil population fostered a deep hatred of the Germans and acted as an excellent recruiter for partisan activity, something that would cause more and more trouble for the Germans as they drove deeper into the USSR. It was not, of course, a one-way street. The Russians shot prisoners and treated the captured at least as badly as the Germans; in Poland the Red Army set out to deliberately exterminate anyone who might lead a rising against them – priests, army officers, intellectuals. It is impossible to say who started it, but the Germans might at least have been expected to have known better.

The opening moves of Operation Typhoon, the attack on Moscow, had gone very well for the Germans. By 7 October they had captured Orel and Bryansk south of Moscow, cutting off yet more Russian armies and bagging 85,000 prisoners, while at Vyazma to the west they had taken another 600,000 when Stalin refused to permit a withdrawal until it was far too late. In the Soviet version of the war, much is made of the heroic fighting of the armies in the Bryansk and Vyazma pockets and of their undying glory, which rather calls into question why so many surrendered. Already there were captured Russians who were quite prepared to collaborate, and even the occasional unit whose commander took them across to the Germans. A number of generals, including three army commanders, captured by the Germans told their captors that the peasants and workers had been badly let down by the broken promises of the Communist Party, and that, if the German government made a public announcement that it would establish a Russian state where the farmer could tend his own land and the worker could have a say in the running of his factory, then they would certainly fight for the Germans and they thought that others still serving would too. The Reich was not prepared to make such a statement, and it was an opportunity missed. By the time the Germans set up the Russian Liberation Army under General

Vlasov, who commanded an army in the defence of Moscow and who was captured by the Germans in 1942, it was too late.

The Germans now assumed that the Russians had no reserves to mount an effective defence of Moscow, and were fearful that the Red Army would abandon the capital and retreat into the vast interior to regroup. In order to prevent that happening, and also to avoid the necessity of having to fight through the streets of Moscow if the Red Army, contrary to expectations, did defend it, the plan for Typhoon was recast. Hoth's Panzer Group 3 would now drive towards Kalinin, 100 miles north-west of Moscow, to relieve the Soviet pressure on Army Group North. Panzer Group 4 would hook round to the north of Moscow, and in the south Guderian's Panzer Group 2, now renamed Second Panzer Army, would split into two prongs: one would head north-east and slip round the south of Moscow while the other would drive south-east for Kursk. Von Bock was unhappy; he thought that this would disperse his troops more than was wise – and Second Panzer Army's units would be 200 miles apart – and he wanted to delay until he had finished mopping up the Bryansk and Vyazma pockets, but he was overruled. It was now that things began to go wrong.

With the autumn rains came what the Russians call 'the time with no roads'. The existing roads turned to mud and became heavily rutted, then froze with the early frosts and then thawed back into mud again. The speed of German advance slowed and the Luftwaffe found it increasingly difficult to use the primitive Russian airstrips it had captured. (The alternative was flying from airfields in Germany and Poland, which meant that the time aircraft could spend over their targets was greatly reduced.) Nevertheless the Germans did advance, and, when the bulk of USSR governmental functionaries were evacuated to Kuybyshev on the River Volga well behind the lines, there was panic and looting in Moscow. Order was swiftly restored by NKVD troops by the simple expedient of shooting anyone caught misbehaving, and quite a few who were not but would serve as object lessons. On 10 October, Colonel-General Konev, who had taken over as Commander Western Front from Timoshenko on 15 September, and Marshal Budenny, Commander Reserve Front, both ex-Tsarist NCOs, were relieved of their commands and both Fronts amalgamated into one Western Front to be commanded by General Zhukov. Konev was allowed to stay on as Zhukov's second-in-command and Budenny, an old friend of Stalin's, similarly escaped the usual penalty for failed generals. In Moscow itself, every able-bodied man, and woman, was pressed into digging anti-tank ditches and trench lines, and 40,000 were incorporated into so-called Peoples' Guard divisions with what equipment could be scraped together and some very rudimentary training. Plans to destroy factories and plants that might be useful to the Germans were drawn up, and those archives that could not be transported to the rear were burned. Huge efforts were made to bolster the defences of the city: thirteen rifle divisions and five armoured brigades were moved from the interior and, another 250 tanks were found from somewhere; Zhukov issued a stirring appeal to every Soviet soldier to do his duty in defence of the motherland, adding that 'cowards and panic-mongers' were to be shot on the spot as traitors. The Russians still could not identify where a German attack might come, and when the armour of Panzer Groups 3 and 4 burst through the defences of the 1812 battlefield of Borodino on 18 October and Colonel Sbytov, commanding the Moscow region Red Air Force, reported that his reconnaissance aircraft had seen German units also moving on Kalinin to the north and on Tula to the south, he was threatened with prosecution by the NKVD for scare-mongering.

On 14 October the Germans captured Kalinin, and the Russians formed a new Kalinin Front, commanded by Konev, and having at last recognized where the German thrusts were aiming for, and throwing everything they had at them, they managed to halt Guderian's northern prong at Tula on 29 October. Around Moscow the roads were being demolished and barricades of barbed wire and timber, covering anti-tank obstacles and minefields, were being erected. The Germans paused to wait for the weather to improve and to bring up supplies and repair their tanks. Their intention was to wait for that brief window between the ground freezing permanently, when the armour could move, and the coming of the heavy snows, when it could not, and make one last attempt to capture Moscow before the worst of the winter set in. Then Stalin, against the advice of Zhukov, ordered counter-attacks against the German north and south wings. They achieved nothing except to add to the already staggering Russian casualties. In Moscow the departure of the elite for safer pastures in the east had not gone unnoticed, and the NKVD firing squads were kept busy dealing with smugglers, looters, enemy spies, *agents provocateurs*, defeatists and anyone who happened to be in the wrong place at the wrong time. Political prisoners, including the wives of executed generals, were taken out and shot as the secret police dealt with their enemies now, just in case the regime did collapse. Stalin did not leave

Moscow, and insisted that, despite the Germans being but a couple of hours' drive away, the traditional (if something only twenty-four years old can be called traditional) military parade in Red Square should take place on 7 November, the anniversary of the 1917 revolution. It was a fast ball for the Moscow Garrison Commander but he did manage to rustle up clerks, storemen, militia and a band, as well as some regular troops supported by a few tanks called back from the front for the occasion. As it began to snow just before the parade started, participants and spectators at least knew that they were safe from German air raids.

The same day, 7 November, was also the first of the permanent freeze, and the Germans thrust forward again. Seven Panzer Division of Hoth's Panzer Group 3 pushed across the Moscow–Volga canal and penetrated as far as fifteen miles north of the capital, from where the men could see the onion domes of the old city twinkling in the frosty air. This caused great excitement in Berlin but rather less at the front – the soldiers knew that it could not last, and it was as close to Moscow as the German army would ever get. By mid-November, with the weather getting progressively worse and German divisions at about half their established strength and at the end of an increasingly unreliable supply chain, the Russians could muster eighty-four divisions and twenty brigades, supported by 700 tanks in and around Moscow. Every time units of the Red Army met the Germans, they were defeated, sometimes resoundingly so, but somehow the Russian supreme command, the Stavka, kept finding more units to throw in. By 1 December, Operation Typhoon had ground to a halt, and Field Marshal von Bock recommended to OKH that the offensive be called off. OKW (actually Hitler) refused to accept von Bock's assessment and insisted that the operation continue until Moscow had been captured. The attacks continued, but they made little progress. There were far more defenders than German intelligence had calculated, winter arrived unexpectedly early and by 4 December the temperature was down to –35°C. There were no Arctic lubricants; vehicles would not start; artillery breeches froze shut and rifle bolts would not open. Behind the lines, German railway engines running on converted Russian tracks constantly broke down as their boilers, never designed for such low temperatures, froze, and there were 100,000 cases of frostbite in December alone. In the north von Leeb was no nearer capturing Leningrad, and in the south von Rundstedt had captured the critical city of Rostov but had insufficient reserves to hold it and had pulled back. Hitler ordered him to reverse his decision to withdraw and, when the field marshal indicated that he would resign rather than countermand what he knew to be a correct military decision, Hitler accepted his resignation on 28 November and replaced him with the fifty-six-year-old Field Marshal Walther von Reichenau, one of the very few senior army officers who had openly supported Hitler and the NSDAP. Reichenau initially cancelled the withdrawal order, then realized that Rundstedt had been quite right, withdrew to Rundstedt's intended defensive position and then told Hitler he had done it, prefacing the signal with 'in anticipation of your concurrence…' He got away with it but was not to remain in post for long.

The Germans were holding a front of 1,200 miles. It was a vast, almost unimaginable distance to the soldier on the ground, and the Soviet regime had not collapsed, Moscow had not been captured and it was now clear that the war would go on into 1942. The German army would have to spend the winter in defence in the open, but they were in absolutely the wrong place to do so. The Staff College solution in such a situation is to withdraw to positions that can be defended, and which may already have been prepared for defence, shorten the line, replenish and wait for the weather to improve. Alas for the Germans, there were no prepared positions behind them, the priority for supply had been fuel and ammunition and there were no defence stores – timber, wire, cement, aggregate – to build any defences, nor were there the stores to build accommodation for the troops, nor was there any winter clothing, except for the Luftwaffe.

Then, on 4 December, the Russian counter-offensive began over a 300-mile front. Zhukov had husbanded his reserves, refusing to commit them in the defence of Moscow, and they not only had winter clothing but also the first few sub-machine-guns of the war. Russian commanders had little experience of offensive tactics and their lack of modern communications precluded the sort of wide encircling sweeps practised by the Germans. Their soldiers were uneducated, many had received only rudimentary basic training and most were appallingly bad shots. They were, however, stoical, tough and very brave, whether from genuine patriotism or the knowledge that a firing squad awaited them and their families if they were not. As most Russian attacks at this stage of the war were simple and frontal, the answer was to equip the infantry soldier with a weapon that did not need complicated machine tools to manufacture, was simple to operate and maintain, and would produce a high volume of fire at short range. Hence the introduction of the PPsh-41, known as the Shpagin after its inventor, which would eventually become a standard weapon of all arms of the Red Army. Although it would not come into full production until well into 1942, a few were manufactured in Moscow in late 1941 and issued to the troops for the December counter-offensive. Provided that supplies of ammunition could be maintained, it was the ideal weapon for a peasant army fighting at close quarters.

The Russians advanced through snow that was three feet deep, supported by plentiful artillery and the feared Katyushas, multiple rocket-launchers mounted on trucks. The Germans lacked air support because the cold made starting aircraft engines a long and laborious process, and, even when aircraft did finally get into the air, the impact fuses on German bombs would not detonate in the snow, whereas those on Russian artillery shells would. The wings of the German encirclement were pushed back – they would not now meet behind Moscow – and in the centre the men of the Wehrmacht retreated stubbornly. In Hitler's eyes a retreat was unnecessary: the German army should stand its ground where it now was. When the generals disagreed, the sackings continued: on 12 December, Field Marshal von Bock was relieved of his command and replaced by Field Marshal Günther von Kluge; on 19 December, Field Marshal von Brauchitsch, worn out by interminable arguments with the Führer in which his professional judgement was constantly disparaged, resigned as Commander-in-Chief of the German army, and Hitler appointed himself to replace him – not bad for an ex-lance corporal. On Christmas Day, Colonel-Generals Guderian and Hoepner, commanders of Second and Fourth Panzer Armies (as all the panzer groups were now titled) were told to clear their lockers – Hitler particularly had it in for Hoepner, who had withdrawn despite the Führer's orders not to, and wanted him cashiered from the army without pension. It was soon clear that the army would not stand for that and Hoepner got his pension.

In his capacity as Commander-in-Chief, Hitler insisted that the army stand its ground and defend where it now was. The advice of the military was that the front had to be shortened to defend against another expected Soviet offensive. Hitler, however, maintained that a limited offensive by the Russians to drive the Germans back from Moscow was one thing, an attack right along the whole front was quite another and, anyway, the Red Army was in no state to launch it. So the German army started to dig in – impossible in the frozen ground without explosives – and back at home the propaganda minister, Goebbels, launched a winter relief campaign to collect warm clothing for the troops. The populace responded with a will and huge amounts of garments were collected. Inevitably perhaps, the better items were siphoned off by rear-area troops and the quantities reaching the fighting troops were barely adequate.* It was unfortunate for the German army that in the event Hitler was right and, despite the difficulties and the suffering, the no-retreat order was the correct one. Hitler, of course, had been right about the Ardennes offensive in 1940, against the advice of his closest military advisers, and being right again in the winter of 1941–42 only convinced him that his instincts were a better guide to the conduct of war than the professional opinions of his generals. In many instances, Hitler would be proved right again, but far too often he would be disastrously wrong, to the extreme detriment of his soldiers' chances of survival. The expected Russian offensive all along the front did, however, come.

The success of the defence of Moscow – in that the Germans did not capture it and were forced to withdraw – now encouraged Stalin to believe that the tide had turned and to order attacks all along the front, from Leningrad in the north to the Crimea in the south. In vain, Zhukov protested. Stopping the Germans and pushing them back over a front of 300 miles when they were on the end of a very tenuous supply chain and the Red Army could call on virtually the whole of the air force to support it was one thing, but launching an offensive over a frontage of 1,200 miles with a largely untrained army was quite another. Stalin, however, had his way and on 5 January 1942 the advance began. It quickly ran into trouble. In the north, a new front, the Volkhov Front, was formed, commanded by General Meretskov, who had been arrested, imprisoned and tortured by the NKVD in January 1941 and then, as no one could remember what he had been arrested for, released and restored to his former rank in September. In an attempt to lift the siege of Leningrad, where Soviet historians claim that half a million of the inhabitants died of starvation and disease during the winter, the Twenty-Sixth Army was renamed Second Shock Army. Shock armies were supposed to have extra artillery and be trained as storm troops to carry out sudden and devastating attacks, and Second Shock Army did succeed in driving a salient deep into Army Group North. The trouble about salients is that they are all too easy to nip off, and this is exactly what Army Group

---

*This author recalls his fury when reporting to a brigade headquarters from a particularly uncomfortable field location where the infantry were lucky to have a blanket and a groundsheet each, only to find all the storemen in the Brigade Administrative Area with sleeping bags and camp beds.

North did in March, just after Meretskov had sent his deputy, Andrei Vlasov, in to assess the situation in the salient. In May, once the thaw had finished and the mud had dried up, the Germans attacked the surrounded Soviet army, which surrendered at the end of June.

In the centre, the temperature fell to −25°C in January. The fighting was intense and even insignificant hamlets became the scenes of major battles as both sides struggled for anything that would give them some shelter from the weather. Russian horsed cavalry units broke through the German lines and penetrated far to the rear, where they remained a nuisance until the spring, and two Soviet armies, Twenty-ninth and Thirty-Third, also succeeded in driving through the German defences, but they were surrounded and cut off, then eliminated once the weather improved. Fortunately for the Germans, the weather hampered the Soviet air force too and the few roads the German engineers managed to keep clear of snow were hardly ever attacked. For its part, the Luftwaffe was hard pressed to provide support to the army and could mount only token air raids on Moscow; it was also unable to attack the railway convoys taking Russian industrial plant off into the interior. Inevitably, some German units were themselves cut off but managed to hold out, supplied by the Luftwaffe, until after the thaw. Such success was welcome, but it only encouraged the Germans to believe that their air force was capable of much more than it actually was. Supplying six divisions under General Walther von Seydlitz – a direct descendant of Frederick the Great's general – as they held out for two months was one thing. Supplying an entire army, as the Luftwaffe would have to do at Stalingrad, would prove quite another.

Meanwhile, in the south, Field Marshal von Reichenau went for a run on 12 January 1942, returned to his headquarters, suffered a massive heart attack and died on 17 January. He was replaced by the now rehabilitated, albeit only briefly, Field Marshal von Bock. Also in Army Group South, Colonel-General von Schobert, commanding the Eleventh Army, had been killed on 12 September 1941 when his Storch reconnaissance aircraft crashed in a minefield. General of Infantry Erich von Manstein, previously commanding LVI Armoured Corps in Army Group North, took over and was promoted to colonel-general on 1 January 1942. Ordered to take Rostov and to clear the Crimea, he persuaded von Bock that he could not do both. Rostov was now made the objective of Colonel-General von Kleist's First Panzer Army, which, with Eleventh Army, was told to take the Crimea. Apart from the usefulness of the Crimea as a base from where the Luftwaffe could destroy or neutralize the Russian Black Sea Fleet, Hitler considered it to be the 'German South' of the expanded Greater Germany. It was to be cleared of its existing population, Russians, Ukrainians and Tartars, settled by ethnic Germans and linked by autobahn to Germany proper as Gau Gotland. By the end of September 1941 Manstein had captured the Perekop, the narrow isthmus connecting the Crimea to the mainland, and by the end of October he had destroyed two Soviet armies, taken 160,000 prisoners and was besieging Sevastopol, the Soviet naval base on the south-west corner of the Crimea. In his memoirs Manstein recalls sheltering behind a British grave marker on the Balaclava heights from the 1854 British siege of the port. Manstein hoped to take Sevastopol in December but the Russians mounted an amphibious landing on the Kerch peninsula, on the extreme east of the Crimea, and he had to divert troops to contain that. He held the Russians along the neck of the peninsula while still maintaining the siege, but it was a close-run thing. In May 1942, once the weather made movement possible, he launched a surprise attack on the Soviet forces in Kerch and, well supported by the Luftwaffe's Stuka dive-bombers, routed two armies, taking 170,000 prisoners. Now he could concentrate on Sevastopol.

The optimists in the German high command could be reasonably satisfied as they surveyed the military situation in the East in the spring of 1942. They had not taken Moscow, nor had they captured Leningrad, and they had suffered a defeat when they took and then lost Rostov on the River Don in November 1941, but they had taken the Crimea and survived a winter that they had neither expected nor prepared for, and they had stopped a Soviet offensive all along the front, inflicting yet further huge casualties on the Red Army. On the debit side, their logistics chain had only just held. The Germans had a bewildering plethora of load-carrying vehicles, all needing different spare parts and with different servicing schedules, but, with the better weather, resupply would become much easier. Losses had not been made good, however. On 21 April, at a conference in Berlin to discuss plans for 1942, Colonel-General Halder pointed out that, between 1 November 1941 and 1 April 1942, the *Ostheer* (German Army in the East) had lost 900,000 men, killed, wounded, missing and sick, but had received only 450,000 replacements. Between 1 October 1941 and 15 March 1942, 74,183 wheeled vehicles and 2,340 tracked vehicles had been destroyed or rendered useless, while only 7,441 wheeled and 1,847 tracked vehicles had been delivered. Of the horses, 179,000 had been lost and only 20,000 received.[49] The pessimists also noted that the United States was now in the war, and the longer that the war went on, the more her industrial might would be brought to bear. They were, of course, to be proved entirely correct.

* * *

The increasing viciousness of the war in Russia was to be mirrored by developments in Germany itself. On 20 January 1942, the day the Soviets launched their counter-attack in the Ukraine, a conference was held in Wannsee, a Berlin suburb, chaired by SS Obergruppenführer Reinhard Heydrich, the head of the RHSA, an amalgam of the German criminal police, the Gestapo and the security services. Heydrich appeared to be the archetypical Aryan German: tall, blond, blue-eyed, an excellent horseman and a qualified pilot, he was aged thirty-eight in 1942. Too young for the First World War, Heydrich had joined one of the *Freikorps* in 1919 and then the German navy in 1922. He was considered a promising young officer but his naval career was cut short in 1931, when he was required to resign for 'conduct unbecoming an officer and a gentleman'* after he was reported as having been more than just good friends with the daughter of a shipyard owner, without having the slightest intention of making an honest woman of her. Heydrich then joined the NSDAP and the SS. Himmler was impressed by him and his rise was rapid, particularly after his participation in the Night of the Long Knives when the SS removed the threat to the party and the armed forces posed by Röhm's SA.

The purpose of the Wannsee Conference, attended by fourteen senior civil servants and police officers, was to decide upon a Final Solution to the Jewish Problem. Anti-Semitism in Germany, and indeed Europe, was longstanding, but once the NSDAP came to power in 1933 it became government policy. Beginning with the boycott of Jewish shops and professionals, by 1940 it had escalated to the removal of citizenship and then forced 'resettlement' in the East. Hitler said that 'citizenship is determined by race: a Jew cannot be a German', but there were problems of definition here: a Semite is a member of an identifiable race, which includes Arabs, whereas Judaism is a religion. Some Jews are certainly Semitic, but very many are not and, in twentieth-century Europe, were not. Jewishness is conferred through the mother

---

*The same offence exists in British military law, but it is a sad reflection on our social decay that the words 'and a gentleman' were removed some years ago.

(a woman knows with certainty who her children are – a man does not) and the conference spent much time debating who was a Jew and who was not. Was someone who had one Jewish parent a Jew? Or one Jewish grandparent? What about someone who had married a Jew? Did someone with obvious Aryan physical features but who was a Jew by religion qualify? Could conversion to Christianity absolve one from being a Jew? And so on and so forth.

No reference was made in the minutes of the meeting to the killing of Jews – rather, euphemisms such as 'resettlement' and 'work camps' were employed – but there can be little doubt that, even if a deliberate policy of extermination was not specified at Wannsee, the likelihood that many Jews would die as the result of forced labour was accepted without question. In practice, of course, Wannsee formalized the killing of Jews. The Germans calculated that there were 11 million Jews in Europe to be dealt with, although some of those, such as the estimated 334,000 in Britain and Ireland, were beyond their reach, at least for the time being. There were 5 million in the USSR and, apart from the 3 million in the Ukraine and a few in the Baltic States, the rest would have to wait until Russia was defeated. There were 58,000 in Italy, yet despite Mussolini's instructions that they were to be handed over to the Germans, the Italian Army was deliberately obstructive, and the 9,000 in Spain and Portugal were safe, at least until Franco entered the war, which he never did. The Danes and the Dutch were reasonably successful in hiding or disguising their Jews, whereas the Vichy French regime was all too willing to hand over its own (there were 700,000 in unoccupied Vichy France, compared with 165,000 in the occupied part of the country).[50]

As it turned out, the Germans were to prove remarkably successful in eliminating such European Jews as they could get at, and while the statistics are uncertain, a conservative estimate is that they probably did away with 5 million and, as figures for the USSR are even more vague, it could be many more. In less than ten years, the Germans under Hitler had moved from boycott to mass murder, a grim progression that had an inevitably brutalizing effect on all who, actively or passively, were connected with it.

* * *

Regardless of what was, or was not, formalized at Wannsee, the Russian war had not been brought to a satisfactory conclusion in 1941 and so the plans for it now had to be re-examined. Both OKH and OKW were convinced that it would be in the East that the war would be won. Although Hitler still maintained that the capture of Leningrad, Moscow and the Caucasus remained objectives of the war, he accepted that all three could not be prosecuted simultaneously. In his Directive Number 41, issued on 5 April 1942, he ordered that the aim now was the destruction of the defence capabilities of the Soviet Union and the removal of her sources of energy.

The first priority of Case Blue, as the 1942 campaign was titled, was to break into and take the Caucasus, which would enable Germany to exploit the oil fields there and deprive the Russians of them. The Caucasus is that neck of land 500 miles from west to east and 1,000 miles north to south that lies between the Sea of Azov and the Black Sea to the west and the Caspian Sea to the east. Today, the southern border of the Russian portion of the Caucasus borders on Azerbaijan and Georgia, but in 1942 those republics and Armenia to their south were part of the USSR and the border was with Persia (now Iran) and Turkey. In the area north of the Caucasus between the Ukraine and Kazakhstan, both now independent republics but then part of the USSR, flow two mighty rivers, the Don and the Volga. The Don rises 150 miles south of Moscow and flows south through Voronezh and Pavlovsk before turning south-east and east until it is sixty miles from the Volga and Stalingrad. It then flows south for 120 miles before finally turning south-west and flowing into the Sea of Azov near Rostov. It is that great bend in the Don that provides the jump-off area for an attack south into the Caucasus and/or an attack east towards the Volga and Stalingrad. The Volga rises in the interior of Russia and flows 500 miles east of Moscow and then west-south-west to Stalingrad, where it switches course ninety degrees, flowing south-east until it empties into the Caspian Sea at Astrakhan. Army Group South was ordered to annihilate the Soviet forces on the north and west sides of the river Don and then capture or at least bring under artillery fire the important industrial and communications centre of Stalingrad so that its factories were rendered ineffective and river traffic along the Volga halted. Having thus created a jumping-off line, the army would turn south into the Caucasus and take the major oil fields around Maikop, Ordzhonikidze and Baku on the Black Sea, whence before the war came 75 per cent of the USSR's oil.

The operation would be secured in three phases, using the now standard German tactic of encirclement and destruction. Phase One would involve an armoured pincer movement from south of Orel eastwards for 100 miles to Voronezh on the River Don; Phase Two would see the Army Group split into two, Army Groups A and B, and an armoured thrust from Kharkov east to the Don (Army Group A) which would link up with the armour and motorized units coming down the Don from Voronezh (Army Group B); Phase Three would be a gigantic pincer movement on Stalingrad by an advance down the Don to the eastern extremity of the bend, to link up with the southern thrust coming from north of the Sea of Azov along the southern stretch of the Don that would also secure Rostov, at the western end of what would become the jumping-off line for the advance to the Caucasian oil fields. The two pincers would cross the Don at the point nearest to the Volga, push up to that river and deal with Stalingrad. When that had been done, Army Group A would push south into the Caucasus. Army Groups Centre and North would reinforce Army Group South and its successors, A and B. There the panzer divisions would be brought up to their full establishment of three tank battalions, whereas in the other army groups they would have but one. In total, there would be fifty-three infantry, eight panzer and seven motorized divisions for the offensive, but, impressive though this appeared to be, there was no armoured reserve, and the three Waffen SS motorized divisions, *Leibstandarte Adolf Hitler*, *Das Reich* and *Totenkopf*, were withdrawn back to Germany to be refitted and trained as panzer divisions. It was at this stage, it should be noted, that the German navy was advocating an even more ambitious advance, through Persia and on to the Suez Canal to coincide with an attack on Egypt by Panzer Army Africa.

Tactically, Case Blue made a great deal of sense, and the Operations Sections of OKW and OKH were in favour – they had, of course, produced the original plan which, even after Hitler's tinkering, they felt was sound. Others were not so enthusiastic. Some of the field commanders, notably Colonel-General Georg von Kuchler commanding Army Group North, recommended a thrust against Leningrad instead, but as Leningrad was in his bailiwick his views were not surprising. More seriously, Colonel-General Friedrich Fromm, Chief of Army Ordnance and commander of the Replacement Army, the officer responsible for providing both equipment and men to replace losses in the East, Major-General Wagner, the Quartermaster General, and Admiral Wilhelm Canaris, Chief of Foreign Intelligence, all doubted whether the army was strong enough or had sufficient mobility to take all of the Caucasus. Paradoxically, the oil crisis was receding somewhat owing to strict rationing and imposed economies at home and a lower than expected consumption of fuel by the Wehrmacht due to its having lost a great many vehicles. There were also other problems to be considered. If only the northern oil fields were taken, the single realistic way of getting the oil to Germany was by ship across the Black Sea and failure to take the whole of the Caucasus would leave some Black Sea ports in Russian hands, thus making transportation difficult. Despite these doubts, nobody was able to come up with a better plan, other than trying to make peace, as some thought advisable, or withdrawing, shortening the front, and going on the defensive, neither of which was remotely acceptable. Hitler's view, which was surely right, was that centres of production – like those in Moscow – could be rebuilt or relocated, whereas raw materials – like the oil in the Caucasus – would be irreplaceable once lost. At this stage, Stalingrad was a secondary objective. The Volga was an important means of moving goods and men by river transport, Stalingrad was an important centre of armaments production and major railway lines ran through the city. To put those facilities beyond Soviet use would be convenient and helpful, and would improve the security of the German left flank for the thrust into the Caucasus, but it was by no means essential.

Although the staff of Foreign Armies East, that department of the army high command which looked at the structure and capabilities of enemies and potential enemies, had underestimated both the ability of the Red Army to raise new formations and the number of men of military age in the USSR, it was well aware of the disparity in the manpower available to both sides. German losses so far had been enormous. Of the 209 divisions of the *Ostheer* in June 1941, 64 per cent were classified by OKH as fit for any offensive operations. On 30 March 1942 the frontage had expanded but the number of divisions had shrunk to 162 and only 5 per cent were classified as fit. While this percentage was expected to – and did – improve greatly before the onset of the summer campaigns, the losses in men could not be made up entirely by Germans, and so Germany turned to her allies. In 1941, when Barbarossa was first launched, German propaganda had made much of the participation of allied units, with newsreels showing Dutch, French, Danish, Croatian, Slovakian, Hungarian, Romanian, Spanish and Italian soldiers marching east. Apart from the Romanians and Italians, however, these contingents were tiny, drawn from various fascist or quasi-fascist organizations, and of no military significance, even if they were politically useful in that they emphasized the extent of the European Crusade against Bolshevism. In 1942, even though the additional manpower provided by Germany's allies might not have met the exacting standards of her own army, these troops could at least be used in support and in rear areas, thereby releasing German formations for offensive operations.

In June 1941 Italy had provided the Italian Expeditionary Force in Russia (CISR) of three infantry divisions and a cavalry group supported by an air force of eighty-nine fighter and reconnaissance aircraft, a total of 60,900 men, 5,500 vehicles and 4,650 horses. Now Mussolini offered to make this up into an Italian army, with the addition of three infantry and three mountain divisions, which would total nearly a quarter of a million men with 16,700 vehicles, 960 guns, fifty-five light tanks and 20,000 mules for the Alpine Corps. Mussolini's motives were straightforward enough: he wanted Great Power status for Italy and to secure her territorial claims in the Balkans and in the sea routes between the Black Sea and the Mediterranean – and the only way to obtain these, he believed, was to play a significant part in the German victory in the East. The Italian Chief of Army Staff, Marshal Count Ugo Cavallero, was opposed to the expansion, on the grounds that one Italian army would make little difference to the result of the war in Russia, whereas it might make all the difference in North Africa. The Commander CISR, General Giovanni Messe, was also opposed, on the grounds that the Italian Army was not up to coping with the conditions on the Russian front, that its equipment was sub-standard, that its tanks were useless and that relations with the Germans, on whom they would have to rely for resupply, were not good. Mussolini insisted, however, and the Italian Army in Russia was created, although his suggestion for its commander – Crown Prince Umberto of Savoy – was vetoed by OKH, which insisted on a professional, getting General Italo Gariboldi, an ex-governor of Libya.

The largest allied contingent in 1941 had been the Romanians, who provided four infantry divisions, three mountain brigades and two cavalry brigades as part of the German Eleventh Army. Now that was to be increased to two armies of twenty-seven divisions in their own Army Group, with the agreement that Germany would provide rations and medical services. Again, the motives for the Romanian dictator Marshal Antonescu were political. Permanent recovery of the provinces lost to Russia in 1939 could only be ensured by a German victory, and it was not only manpower that Romania provided, for, until the Ukraine and the Caucasus could be thoroughly exploited, Romania was a major source of oil and cereals for Germany. In contrast, Hungary had managed to avoid a major contribution to the German war effort so far. Unlike the leaders of other countries in the German camp,

Admiral Miklós Horthy, the Hungarian acting head of state and regent, had to pay some attention to his parliament, which was much more anti-Romanian than it was anti-Russian. After much negotiation by the German foreign minister, Ribbentrop, and the chief of OKW, Field Marshal Keitel, Hungary at last agreed to provide nine infantry divisions, an armoured division and seven security units – these latter being second-class divisions that would be used to maintain order in the rear areas.

In the north, there was not a great deal that could be expected of Finland, which was still a parliamentary democracy, albeit one operating under some wartime restrictions. Marshal Mannerheim, the president and Commander-in-Chief of the army, was not interested in the racial and ideological aspects of the German war, but simply wanted to win back territory lost to the USSR in the Winter War. Although he had signed the Anti-Comintern Pact in November 1941, he had no treaty of assistance with Germany and attempted to fight a parallel war, hoping not to offend the Western Allies. He was somewhat perturbed when the UK declared war on him in December 1941 and even more so when the United States, traditionally a friend of Finland's, made it clear that, once she entered the war against Germany on 11 December 1941, she was henceforth an ally of the Soviet Union. Finland would fight on, but the more grandiose schemes for cooperation with Army Group North would not now take place.

Spain had not joined the war, and nor would she, but she did provide the Blue Division, which fought as 250 Division as part of Army Group North's reserve. As we have seen, Franco constantly promised Hitler that he would join the war, but not before the British were defeated. When this became increasingly unlikely, Franco saw a way of repaying Hitler for his assistance during the Spanish Civil War, of keeping his claim to French Morocco and Gibraltar alive in German eyes and of getting rid of his more extreme Falange youth. At the same time, and despite the popular support for Germany and detestation of Russia amongst the majority of the Spanish people, Franco had no intention of sending more than a token force. Initially, this was to be from the Falange Militia, but the regular army dug its heels in and insisted that, while the Militia might have been perfectly adequate for fighting other half-trained Spanish Republican militias, it could not possibly be expected to perform against the Soviets, and the army must have its say. Eventually, it was decided that the force would be called the División Española de Voluntarios, or DEV, and it would be 18,000 strong. Two thirds of the second lieutenants and sergeants would be from the regular army, the remainder from the Militia, and all officers of the rank of lieutenant and above and all specialists (heavy weapons operators, signallers, drivers, technicians) would be from the regular army. If the Falange could not fill the junior ranks, then regular soldiers would be permitted to volunteer. As commander of the division Franco selected an old comrade, Major-General Muñoz Grandes, acceptable to all as while a regular officer he had at one point commanded the Falange Militia. He had a reputation as a competent and brave officer; indeed, British Intelligence considered him 'one of their best and most resolute generals'.[51] He was also well known to the Germans, having been involved with them in the planning of the abortive Case Felix, the capture of Gibraltar.

Recruiting for the DEV, which was to be drawn from all over Spain, was patchy. In strongly Nationalist areas, recruiters were overwhelmed, and many reserve officers joined as private soldiers. In others, particularly areas that had been Republican during the Civil War, only committed Falangists joined and the balance had to be made up from regular soldiers, supposedly volunteers but, in some cases, pressed men. Initially the uniform was exotic – red berets, blue shirts, khaki trousers and black boots, with officers wearing a khaki tunic with blue cuffs and collars. It was this preponderance of the Falange colour of blue that gave rise to the name – the Blue Division. During negotiations with the Germans, it was agreed that the Spanish volunteers would be paid, uniformed, rationed and armed by the Germans, and that, once they left Spain, they would wear standard German army uniform with a shoulder title of *España* and a red and gold shield, Spain's national colours, on the arm of the jacket. The need for the Blue Division to change its organization from the Spanish standard four regiments to the German three was managed eventually, and the only sticking point was that of rations. The egalitarian German army issued the same ration for all ranks, whereas in the Spanish Army officers' rations were superior and more plentiful. The Spanish had to agree, with rather bad grace, that not only would they have to accept the same amount and quality for everybody, but, as the Germans had no intention of providing a different ration for every national contingent, they would have to put up with sausages, sauerkraut and German bread, rather than the hoped for fresh meat, vegetables and light bread. The Blue Division duly joined Sixteenth Army in Army Group North, where it saw action in the fighting around Leningrad in October 1941. While the Spanish government would, for the time being at least, maintain the division at its established strength, and would provide so-called Blue Squadrons of aircraft operating under Luftwaffe command, it would make no increase in its contribution.

Other sources of manpower were ethnic Germans or those the Germans considered to be Germanic (for example, the Flemish, Dutch and Scandinavians), all of whom were enlisted into units of the Waffen SS, while non-Germanic volunteers (such as the Spanish, and also the French and Croats) were incorporated into the army. It was specifically forbidden to enlist Czechs and Russians, except for a few individuals with certain specialities. Later this would change, although by then it would be too late.

From the Russian point of view as well, matters in the spring of 1942 seemed a lot less gloomy than they had in the autumn of the previous year. The Germans had not captured Moscow, Soviet industry had largely been relocated eastwards and was again in full production, and the first trickles of vehicles and equipment from the Americans and the British were beginning to come through. The foreign minister, Molotov, had been to England. Travelling under the name of Mr Brown, he had flown to Scotland, been met by the Foreign Secretary, Eden, and conducted to London by train. Stalin had instructed Molotov to persuade the British to sign a treaty recognizing the borders of the USSR as those existing in 1941 before Barbarossa. As this would have given legitimacy to Soviet occupation of East Poland and the Baltic States, the British were not going to fall for that one; nor would they promise a second front in 1942, but a treaty saying nothing about boundaries was signed and a second front was promised 'as soon as possible'. Molotov and his entourage stayed at Chequers – where the bed-making staff were somewhat taken aback to find a loaded revolver under every pillow – and he enjoyed amicable late-night discussions with Churchill before departing happily for the USA, where he was similarly well received by Roosevelt.

The Russians now disposed of around 6 million men – German intelligence thought 5 million – facing around 3.25 million Germans. The Soviet divisions were full of inexperienced junior officers terrified to show any initiative lest it led to their being taken out and shot, and they had all sorts of manning and logistical problems, but the Red Army was still in being despite the horrific losses in men and equipment of the previous year, and it still had manpower as yet not mobilized – indeed, during the course of 1942 it would create another 134 divisions. The German was a far better soldier, he was better led and, so far at least, was equipped with better weapon systems, but there were precious few reserves and extra manpower could only come from stripping the garrisons at home in Germany and in the occupied countries. From the point of view of Hitler and the OKW, 1942 was all or nothing.

Russian intelligence, such as it was, predicted that the German objective for 1942 would be Moscow, and Stalin concurred. The movement of German troops getting into position for the advance on Voronezh, Phase One of Case Blue, was interpreted as preparations for an outflanking movement north-east to get behind Moscow and cut it off, which the Russians thought would coincide with a thrust from Orel towards the city. The logical conclusion was that the Germans would have weakened their south to bolster up their centre – exactly the opposite of what had been done. On 12 May, Marshal Timoshenko, commanding the South-Western Front with the future prime minister of the USSR, Nikita Khrushchev, as his chief commissar, launched an attack to retake Kharkov, completely unaware of the pending German attack from that area. With 640,000 men and 1,200 tanks supported by 900 aircraft, the Russian attack came out of a salient to the west of the River Donets and south of Kharkov, and by 19 May its main thrust had penetrated about thirty miles and leading Soviet armoured units were forty miles from the headquarters of Army Group South. While that operation was taking place, a smaller attack, across the Donets farther north, got within ten miles of Kharkov. The Germans were initially alarmed but then realized that the Russians still had not learned and were obligingly pushing deeper and deeper into a pocket, which on 17 May the Germans took steps to nip off when von Kleist's First Panzer Army struck north through the Russian flanks. By 23 May the German armour had made contact with Sixth Army to the north of the pocket, and by 28 May resistance inside the pocket had ended. The best part of four Russian armies, twenty-two rifle and seven cavalry divisions, and fifteen armoured brigades, were wiped from the Soviet order of battle; 1,200 tanks, 2,000 artillery pieces and 540 aircraft had been captured or destroyed and 239,000 prisoners taken – it would have been more had the Germans not run out of fuel.

This was a further stunning victory, but German commanders could see a little dark cloud on the horizon. Despite another error by their high command, the Russians were improving – as General of Panzer Troops Eberhard von Mackensen, commanding III Armoured Corps of von Kleist's army, noted: '[the Red Army's conduct of operations] is more fanatical, more ruthless and more solid [than in 1941]... the Red leadership is risking everything. It generally takes clear decisions and employs everything to implement them. Field commanders and troops execute its decisions far more resolutely than last year…'[52] Yet the Red Army still suffered from the oppressive supervision of the political commissars, who had joint responsibility with the military commander but in many cases had little or no military experience and viewed any backward move as treasonable, and anything other than constant and repeated frontal attacks as evidence of incompetence. Eventually, in October 1942, Stalin curbed the influence of the commissars, who could no longer overrule the military commander, although they could, and did, sneak to Moscow on a general they disliked or disapproved of. As a result of the fate of the armies trapped on the west side of the Donets while trying to retake Kharkov in May, and those in the Crimea, it was beginning to come home to Stalin and the Stavka that refusing to allow commanders to pull troops out when it was tactically necessary only led to their being surrounded, cut off and wiped out. From now on, while 'No Retreat' orders were still read out to the troops, withdrawals would be permitted. The difference is a fine one: both involve going backwards, but a withdrawal is something that the commander decides to do, whereas a retreat is forced upon him.

Case Blue proper was to start on 28 June, but before that von Manstein, having destroyed the Red Army's attempt to recapture the Crimea from the Kerch peninsula, launched his final attack on Sevastopol. On 3 June a devastating artillery bombardment began, followed by an attack by the infantry supported by Stuka dive-bombers of the Luftwaffe's VIII Air Corps commanded by General of Flyers Baron Wolfram von Richthofen, a fourth cousin of the first-war air ace Manfred, the Red Baron. The defence was fanatical – and with their backs to the sea and no hope of relief, the Russian soldiers had little option – but by 3 July it was all over with the destruction of two Soviet armies and the capture of yet more guns, tanks, aircraft and 90,000 prisoners. Manstein, with an infantry army, had done a brilliant job, without excessive casualties, and was duly promoted to field marshal, but, instead of sending his Eleventh Army to one of the southern army groups, A or B, where it could have made a real difference, Hitler sent it off to Army Group North, to assist in the capture of Leningrad. In fact, Leningrad was of little strategic significance and did not need to be captured – for, if it was, the Germans would then become responsible for the population, which was already near to starving – and, besides, Army Group North was already doing a perfectly good job of neutralizing the city.

Case Blue was very nearly compromised before it was launched when, on 19 June, the pilot of an aircraft carrying a staff officer of 23 Panzer Division, Major Joachim Reichel, became lost, strayed over the Soviet lines and was shot down. With Reichel were the complete operational orders for Blue, which were passed on to the two Red Army front commanders, Timoshenko and Golikov, and ultimately to Stalin. Inevitably, on the German side there was the most almighty fuss that escalated rapidly from division to corps to army to army group and back to Berlin. Should the operation be rewritten or even cancelled altogether? In the event, nothing changed and the Germans proceeded with Case Blue as planned, not least because any redeployment of troops would take so much time that it would risk running into winter. Meanwhile, both Red Army commanders and Stalin remained convinced that the main German objective for 1942 was Moscow, and that Blue was either a feint, a diversionary attack or deliberate misinformation, a view reinforced by deceptive measures carried out by Army Group Centre, under the not very originally named Case Kremlin, which were designed to make the Russians think that it was about to attack Moscow frontally. The wretched Reichel was beyond the reach of German military justice, but the divisional commander, the corps commander and his chief of staff were not, and they eventually found themselves accused of breaching security regulations and playing the starring role at a court martial presided over by Reichsmarschall Göring. The divisional commander, Major-General Baron Hans von Boineburg-Lengsfeld, was found not guilty, but the commander of XXXX Motorized Corps, General of Panzer Troops Georg Stumme, and his chief of staff were found guilty and sentenced to five years' fortress detention (imprisonment). As a result of representations by the army group commander, von Bock, they were both pardoned, and Stumme was sent off to North Africa to command the DAK.

In June 1942, when Case Blue was duly launched, the German army worldwide had 234 divisions of various types. Of these, 179, or just over three quarters, were on the Eastern Front and, of the twenty-six armoured divisions, nineteen were on the Eastern Front. In late June 1942 Colonel-General Halder, Chief of the General Staff of the German army (although, unknown to himself, for only another three months), received a paper on the Red Army from Lieutenant-Colonel (General Staff) Reinhard Gehlen, who headed Foreign Armies East in OKH. Gehlen's department relied on air reconnaissance, interrogation of prisoners, examination of captured equipment and data, analysis of operations and secret intelligence from disaffected Russians. In a remarkably frank report, Foreign Armies East predicted that the Red Army would attempt to preserve its combat strength into 1943 to permit American Lend-Lease assistance to become effective. Its elements would withdraw where necessary to avoid German encirclement and would deal with German advances by attacks on their flanks mounted from the Russian interior. As for manpower, whatever losses the Red Army might sustain in 1942, it could replace them by the winter by calling up those born in 1924. Even if Case Blue was entirely successful, thought Gehlen, the Russians' determination to resist would be unbroken, and, although still qualitatively inferior to the Germans, they would have considerable superiority in men and equipment. During the coming winter of 1942 the Red Army would try to so weaken the German army that it would be incapable of another summer offensive in 1943. It was a remarkably accurate, prophetic even, assessment and it appears that Halder, worn out with constant arguments and having to deal directly with Hitler without the buffer of a military commander-in-chief, never showed it to his Führer, despite agreeing with most of its contents. It would have made little difference: Case Blue had already started and Hitler was not going to be put off, whatever the army might say.

Phase One of the 1942 offensive was launched on 28 June as planned, by Group Weichs, commanded by Colonel-General Maximilian von Weichs with his own Second Army, Fourth Panzer Army and the Hungarian Second Army, which struck from north-east of Kursk towards Voronezh. This was what the Russians were expecting, albeit they thought it the preliminary to a drive to the east of Moscow, and the Bryansk Front had been massively reinforced. Reinforced or not, it initially made little difference. The spearhead of Group Weichs, Hoth's Fourth Panzer Army, advanced thirty miles on the first day with Second Army covering their left flank and the Second Hungarian Army their right. The Hungarians were initially in trouble owing, as Weichs said, to the inexperience of their commanders despite the bravery of their men, but by 4 July the Germans were over the River Don. Stalin ordered Fifth Tank Army to counter-attack. The number of the latest Russian T-34 and KV tanks now appearing was a worrying sign, but they were committed piecemeal and handled ineptly, and with the able support of the Luftwaffe the Germans were able to beat them off. By 7 July, Voronezh was in German hands, but this time the number of prisoners taken was far less than expected – the Soviets were learning, and pulling their men out before they could be surrounded. Now for Phase Two. On 9 July, Army Groups A and B became operational. Army Group A was commanded by the sixty-two-year-old Field Marshal Sigmund von List, and consisted of First Panzer Army, Eleventh Army (actually in the Crimea and on the way north, so not available) and Seventeenth Army (the Romanian Third Army with four German infantry divisions). The army group included three armoured and one motorized German divisions, the Viking Division of the Waffen SS manned by Danish, Dutch, Finnish, Flemish and – surprisingly perhaps, as they were not 'Aryan' – Walloon volunteers, the whole stiffened by Balkan Germans, and a Slovak motorized division. Field Marshal von Bock commanded Army Group B with Fourth Panzer Army, Second Army, Sixth Army, the Hungarian Second Army and, not yet operational but on the way, the Italian Eighth Army. In the army group were four armoured and three motorized divisions.

Now came more arguments between the men on the ground and OKH and Hitler in the rear. The original plan for Case Blue was to secure the jump-off line – Rostov to Stalingrad – before thrusting south into the Caucasus. Hitler now considered that the two could be done simultaneously, with Army Group B dealing with Stalingrad and the Volga while A, augmented by Fourth Panzer Army, headed south. Army Group B's commander, von Bock, was unhappy and was considered by Hitler to have got bogged down around Voronezh and to have been dilatory in sending Fourth Panzer Army (three armoured, one motorized, three German and four Romanian infantry divisions) to Army Group A. Von Bock had already ignored orders from on high and now Hitler had had enough. As he said to his army adjutant, Schmundt, he respected the field marshal but could only work with those who obeyed orders to the letter. Von Bock was persuaded to retire on health grounds on 15 July, being replaced by Colonel-General Maximilian Freiherr von Weichs, who was to clear the River Don and advance to the Volga and Stalingrad.

The problem now was that the German army in the East had been given a split aim – capture Leningrad in the north, and block the Volga, take Stalingrad and at the same time capture the Caucasian oil fields in the south. As the southern two army groups diverged – B west and A south – the German logistics machine was simply unable to supply both. Hitler decreed that priority was to go to Army Group A as the oil fields were more important than Stalingrad, and von Weichs found that much of his motor transport was taken away, and he only received fuel when the needs of Army Group A had been met. By the end of July the River Don had been mainly freed of Soviet units, except for three bridgeheads on the west bank which still held out, and OKH (actually Hitler) had decided to return Fourth Panzer Army for the thrust to the Volga. The bridgehead at Kalach, on the bend in the Don opposite Stalingrad, had to be cleared before the army could advance to the Volga, and Sixth Army was ordered to deal with it. Sixth Army had fourteen German infantry divisions, two armoured and two motorized divisions, three Italian divisions and a Croat brigade. It was commanded by General of Panzer Troops Friedrich Paulus.

Paulus had been von Reichenau's Chief of Staff when the latter had commanded Tenth Army in the invasion of Poland. He had then been Halder's deputy Chief of the General Staff at OKH, and, when in December 1941 von Reichenau had been appointed to the command of Army Group South, he had recommended Paulus as his successor at Sixth Army. Paulus had little experience as a commander, but he was a highly efficient and very effective staff officer. The original plan for Barbarossa, before it was watered down by OKH and tinkered with by Hitler, had been largely his, and in it he had been adamant that the Russians must not be allowed to retreat into the interior but must be cut off by encirclement and envelopment battles. These battles should, he added, include the capture of Moscow and be completed by October 1941, before the roads turned to mud. The German army had duly obliged, trapping one Russian army after another in pockets and effectively eliminating them. But the deadline of October 1941 set by Paulus had not been met, Moscow had not been captured, and the war in the East had not yet been won.

As it was, Paulus now headed for Kalach, although progress was slow for his horse-drawn infantry and made slower by the frequent halts his armoured units had to make as they waited for fuel to come up. In the first week of August, Sixth Army reached Kalach, and by 11 August it had roundly defeated the Soviet First Tank and Sixty-Second Armies but taken far fewer prisoners than had been the norm – the Russians abandoned their tanks and equipment, but the men escaped across the Don to be refitted and fight another day. Now Stalingrad and the Volga were only fifty miles away, but the army was exhausted and out of fuel. Meanwhile, on 23 July 1942, von List's Army Group A stormed Rostov on the Don and took almost a quarter of a million prisoners – the last time the Russians would allow such numbers to be encircled and captured – and then prepared to head for Baku and the oil fields. But even though he had priority for fuel, List faced all sorts of problems. After Rostov he had lost Fourth Panzer Army, which had been returned to Army Group B, and his remaining armoured formation, First Panzer Army, was down to 400 tanks. He had 750 miles to go from Rostov to Baku and he faced two Russian fronts and an increasingly effective Soviet air threat. Despite all this, and resupply difficulties which were only marginally less than those of Army Group B, progress was initially good. The infantry of Seventeenth Army covered thirty miles a day, in sweltering temperatures of 35°C. Of itself, this is not remarkable: a fit infantry soldier carrying the usual load of thirty or forty pounds' weight plus his weapon and ammunition can easily march thirty miles a day. What made this a near-incredible feat was the ability to get the impedimenta of an infantry army – stores, ammunition, rations, water, medical units and the like – to cover the same distance, which would be pretty good for a motorized army, never mind one moving on foot and in horse-drawn wagons. They crossed the Kuban River, and on 10 August captured Krasnodar, the regional capital, while Kleist's tanks penetrated as far as Maikop, an oil-producing region, to find that the Russians had set light to the wells and installations before withdrawing. On 22 August soldiers of XXXI Mountain Corps, part of First Panzer Army, raised the German flag on top of the 18,500-foot-high Mount Elbrus. Army Group A had advanced 300 miles from Rostov in under a month. It was as far as it would ever get.

On the day after the Reich standard first flew above the highest mountain in the Caucasus, the advance units of Fourth Panzer Army reached the suburbs of Stalingrad. Getting there had been a quartermaster's nightmare: vehicles bringing up fuel used most of it themselves just to get to the army, and even camel trains were pressed into service to get supplies up the two armies heading for the Volga. If the armoured and motorized units of the *Ostheer* had not been spread all over the Eastern Front, trying to achieve too much at the same time, then the Germans would have taken Stalingrad by the methods that they had trained for and had practised so well in the war so far – encirclement of the city by crossing the Volga north and south, cutting it off and starving it into submission. As it was, there were not sufficient mobile units to do this, and if the city was to be taken, then it could only be done by frontal assault. By September, when the Germans had closed up to the Volga, they were holding a front of 2,000 miles. In the north was Army

Group North, still besieging Leningrad; then Army Group Centre, which was on the defensive opposite Moscow and about 100 miles from it; then Army Group B, holding positions from north of Voronezh along the Don and then across to Stalingrad and down the Volga; and finally Army Group A, which had penetrated deep into the Caucasus. With such an enormous frontage, the Germans had no option but to make maximum use of the allied contingents, inferior to German soldiers though they might be. Army Group B's front had the German Second Army in the north, then, coming south, the Hungarian Second Army, the Italian Eighth Army, the Romanian Third Army, the Sixth Army and the Fourth Panzer Army opposite Stalingrad, and the Romanian Fourth Army.

The Russian defence of Stalingrad is often described as fanatical, although it might be more accurate to say it was determined come what may. The original commander of the garrison, General Lopatin, was convinced that the city would fall, so he was removed on 11 September. Commissar Nikita Khrushchev appointed General Vasily Chuikov to command the Sixty-Second Army in and around Stalingrad. In many ways the cartoon figure of a Russian officer, Chuikov was absolutely loyal to Stalin – thereby surviving the Great Terror – and obeyed orders to the letter; he consumed alcohol as if prohibition was just round the corner and, while not necessarily particularly intelligent, had all the cunning of the Russian peasant that he was. Stalin and the Stavka had not been impressed by the hasty defence of Rostov followed by a scuttle back to Stalingrad and various draconian orders were issued, threatening everything from the execution of the offender's relatives to permanent exile for those whose withdrawal was considered premature. The number of men transferred to penal battalions – essentially suicide squads used for everything from human mine-clearing to hopeless frontal attacks, and including naughty officers now serving as private soldiers – doubled and shootings by firing squads with or without sentence of court martial leapt up.

Stalingrad, originally Tsaritsyn, was renamed in honour of a Civil War battle in which the White Russians, spearheaded by a handful of British tanks, were defeated by the Bolsheviks supposedly directed by Comrade Stalin. It was a long, narrow industrial city on the west bank of the Volga, about eighteen miles from north to south and about three miles from west to east. In the centre and three miles west of the Volga was the airfield, and slightly south of that and a mile from the Volga was the main railway station. Running north from there were the Red October steel works, the Red Barricade ordnance factory and the Dzerzhinsky tractor plant (which actually made T-34 tanks). The first German assault took place on 13 September and stormed up the western slope of Hill 102 as Chuikov's headquarters hurriedly evacuated the eastern side. The railway station was captured and then lost to counter-attack and then recaptured. Over the next few days, the largely wooden residential buildings were destroyed by fires started by both sides' shelling, and fighting went on around the concrete buildings that survived, through cellars and amongst the rubble.

In Berlin, Colonel-General Halder had now finally had enough and resigned, being replaced as Chief of the General Staff by Major-General Kurt Zeitzler, the son of a vicar from Cossmar-Luckau in Prussia and, at forty-seven, eleven years younger than Halder. This was an extraordinary appointment to the most senior staff appointment in the whole German army: Zeitzler was an accomplished staff officer but his experience was limited to being Chief of Staff of a panzer army and very briefly in an army group headquarters, and, as a recently promoted major-general, he was far too junior to have the respect of the senior levels of the army. All this, however, suited Hitler very well. He had already browbeaten Field Marshal Keitel, the chief of OKW, into submission, and he wanted someone as chief of the general staff of OKH who would obey orders without question. Now the only senior officer in Hitler's entourage who was prepared to argue with him was General of Infantry Alfred Jodl, Director of Operations at OKW, and Hitler had plans to replace him with Paulus, just as soon as the latter had conquered Stalingrad.

On 14 October, Paulus attacked again, and after two weeks of savage fighting the Germans, headed by pioneers with flame-throwers and engineers with explosives to blow holes in walls and supported by precision bombing by the Luftwaffe, captured the tractor factory and cut what was left of Chuikov's army in two. At this stage, the Germans had captured most of the city and regular Russian counter-attacks, mounted from bridgeheads on the west bank of the Volga, were being as regularly beaten off. Despite the apparent successes, the army group commander, von Weichs, was unhappy that his army had been sucked into street fighting, always expensive in men, ammunition and water, and that the battle was going on for far longer than had been anticipated. He advised OKH to call the battle off and to concentrate on merely blocking the Volga. His advice was rejected. The battle had now become almost a personal one between Hitler and Stalin. Hitler did not need Stalingrad, and he had said that he had no wish for a 'Verdun on the Volga', but German soldiers were on the Volga and there they must remain; the city had been attacked and so it must be taken.

Paulus himself was still confident that he could take Stalingrad, despite all his logistics having to be delivered from a very long way away along one railway line. For the Russians resupply was equally difficult as the Germans had cut the only rail link from Stalingrad to Moscow, so reinforcements and supplies had to come the long way round via the Russian interior, but the Red Army was rapidly making up the losses of the winter of 1941/42 and of those divisions squandered in the offensives of the early part of 1942. The factories out of range of the Luftwaffe were churning out tanks – 2,000 a month by now – sub-machine-guns and aircraft, but, instead of feeding massive reinforcements into Stalingrad, the Stavka reinforced Chuikov – whose army was suffering terribly – with just enough to keep him fighting, while Zhukov and Rokossovsky created a massive reserve, so far uninvolved in the battle. The Red Army soldiers in Stalingrad fought from a mixture of hatred of the Germans, fear (NKVD troops shot those who were reluctant to go forward) and genuine patriotism, the Germans through professional pride, trust in their leaders and a belief, at least amongst the younger officers and men, that the Führer would provide ultimate victory. Paulus intended one final effort to complete the capture of Stalingrad before winter. Casualties so far had been heavy; the army was tired and rifle companies were down to around sixty men, but morale was still high and the men were in no doubt that with one final push they could do it. Paulus committed nine divisions and 180 tanks and on 11 and 12 November captured the Red October steel works.

Meanwhile, Colonel Gehlen and his intelligence apparatus in Foreign Armies East had picked up that something was going on behind the Russian front, and they were right. Zhukov and Rokossovsky had by now assembled over a million men, 900 tanks and 12,000 artillery pieces, supported by 1,200 aircraft. And on 19 November the first heavy snow fell.

9

THE ASIAN WAR

DECEMBER 1941–MAY 1942

Japanese coordination could hardly be faulted. Attacks 6,000 miles apart on Siam, Malaya and Hawaii all occurred within a period of one hour and forty-five minutes, and a further attack – that on Hong Kong – four hours later. The first blow fell on Malaya, where in August the British Commander Land Forces Malaya Command, Lieutenant-General Arthur Percival, had calculated that he needed forty-eight infantry battalions and two battalions of tanks, with associated engineer, artillery and anti-aircraft support, properly to defend his command, which included Brunei and British Borneo. What he actually had were thirty-six battalions: fifteen Indian, six British, six Australian, three Gurkha, five Indian State Forces (ISF)* and one Malay. He had a few armoured cars manned by the local part-time volunteer units but not a single tank. The British units had spent long years in garrison duty and had little chance to take part in all-arms training as part of a brigade or division, and in some cases had been in the Far East for many years. Because the Indian Army wartime expansion had been so rapid, its battalions in the Far East had been milked of experienced British and Indian officers and NCOs to man the units sent to North Africa, and while the Australian units had been in training for well over a year, most of their senior NCOs and officers had no experience other than as part-timers. The ISF and the Malay

---

*Not all of India belonged to the British. There was a plethora of supposedly independent states ruled over by maharajas, rajahs, nizams, ranas and sultans, some huge like Hyderabad and some little bigger than a few hamlets, which, provided they behaved themselves and took the advice of the British Resident, were allowed to get on with things in their own way. All had their own armies and could, if they wished, opt to join the Imperial Service Scheme, which meant that their armies were trained and equipped by the British and could be deployed in support of the British or Indian armies in the event of war.

battalions, although willing, were capable of little more than local defence. The best operational battalions were the Gurkhas, but there were only three of them and even they were short of many of their British and Gurkha officers, who had been extracted to manage the raising and training of new battalions. Nevertheless, the army in Malaya mustered a total of 88,600 men and should surely be more than a match for the Japanese, whose soldiers looked like a badly wrapped brown paper parcel.[53] The Royal Air Force too was considerably weaker than its commander would have liked. Altogether, there were 158 aircraft with the squadrons, and another 88, without crews, held in reserve. The fighters comprised sixty American Brewster Buffaloes, inferior machines with a top speed of only 295 mph, which made them 40 mph slower than the Japanese Zero. Of the bombers, only the twenty-four Vildebeest biplanes could carry a torpedo to launch against shipping but, unlike their Japanese counterparts, they were slow, lumbering and totally obsolete.

The Eastern Fleet, commanded by Admiral Sir Tom Phillips, consisted of one battleship, the *Prince of Wales*, one battlecruiser, the *Repulse*, three cruisers, four destroyers and a handful of gunboats and armed trawlers. The *Prince of Wales* and the *Repulse* had left England in October, and their arrival in Singapore on 2 December was intended to show the Japanese that the British meant business. The brand-new aircraft carrier HMS *Indomitable* should have arrived too, but she ran aground in the West Indies in November during her work-up, and the other ships sailed without her. The Eastern Fleet was therefore entirely reliant on land-based aircraft for air cover. Altogether, it was not an impressive display of British imperial might, but the priority was the defence of the United Kingdom and operations in and around the Mediterranean and there was little left over for the Far East. The only slight flicker of light in the whole gloomy situation was that six months' worth of reserve stocks – ammunition, rations, fuel – were held in depots around Malaya, and, if the Japanese did attack, reinforcements would surely arrive well within that time.

The conquest of Malay was entrusted to the forty-six-year-old Lieutenant-General Tomoyuki Yamashita's Twenty-Fifth Army. He had four divisions, but elected to use only three, as that was the maximum that he calculated he could supply through the Malayan jungle. Of these, 5 Division and 18 Division were stationed in China and were veterans of years of fighting there, and the elite Imperial Guards Division was in French Indo-China. Altogether, Yamashita would deploy 70,000 men, a lot less than the British had in Malay, but Yamashita also had 150 tanks – not very good tanks, as it happens, but they were a lot better than none, which is what his opponents had. Yamashita's plan was to effect landings at Singora and Patani on the east coast of Siam and at Kota Bharu on the east coast of Malaya. His men would then push south using the roads and tracks, take the capital Kuala Lumpur, and then advance on to Singapore. Some warning of the Japanese landings was received: reconnaissance aircraft flying in foul weather had identified Japanese troop transports moving down the coast of Siam on 6 December, but whether they were heading for Malaya or intended for a landing in Siam was not clear, and it was not until the afternoon of that day that Percival ordered General Heath's III Corps to stand to. In fact 5 Division, which would make the initial landings, embarked in nineteen transport ships at Hainan Island in the early morning of 4 December and, escorted by light cruisers and destroyers, headed down the coast.

At 1715 hours on 7 December 1941 Greenwich Mean Time, or 0045 hours on 8 December local time, the sepoys of 3/17 Dogras, part of 8 Brigade of 9 Indian Infantry Division, who were in position along the coast off Kota Bharu, suddenly found themselves subjected to severe shelling from ships offshore. Shortly afterwards Japanese troops began to land under cover of their own naval gunfire, and the defenders, unable to prevent the landing, began a fighting withdrawal. The RAF, reacting rather more swiftly than anyone else in the chain of command, did mount an attack on the Japanese ships, and did some damage, sinking one of the three transport ships and damaging landing craft. Useful for morale of the air crews though it was, this came too late to interfere with the landing. At 0400 hours Singapore experienced its first taste of what the Japanese could do when seventeen bombers, operating from Indo-China, appeared overhead and began their attack; the bombs were intended for the airfields but they fell in civilian residential areas too. Although British radar had given around thirty minutes' warning of the raid – information which was passed to all military units – the civil defence plan could not be implemented as the Air Raid Precautions headquarters was not manned, and hence the Japanese completed their mission with all of Singapore's street lights and commercial and domestic illumination shining brightly into the sky. Night fighters were on standby, but, as there was considerable (and justified) suspicion as to the ability of the anti-aircraft and searchlight teams to avoid shooting down friendly aircraft, they were not allowed to take off. No Japanese aircraft were hit.

Now, at last, the Governor of Malaya received permission from London to launch Matador, the pre-emptive invasion of Siam, which had hitherto been hung about with all sorts of caveats to ensure that the British could not be accused of invading a neutral country. By the time that all concerned had verified that the Japanese were actually landing in Malaya, and that they had or were intending to land in Siam, it was too late for Matador, which was scrapped, but a small detachment of two infantry battalions, named Krohforce, was sent off to take up a defensive position well inside Siam in order to block the expected Japanese advance from Patani. Confusion and muddle reigned, and it was after 1500 hours on 8 December when the force moved. Inside Siam they found to their consternation that the Siamese were not welcoming them as protectors from the Yellow Peril but had actually established roadblocks manned by the armed constabulary. It took time to deal with them and by the time Krohforce approached the area of the Japanese landings, they found the Japanese already in possession of the ground that they had hoped to turn into a blocking position. Krohforce tried to block the roads south but, when the Japanese began to attack with tanks and work their way round the British flanks, there was little option but to withdraw, with considerable casualties to both battalions, and, although some delay was imposed on the Japanese by blowing up bridges on the way back, the operation achieved little.

At Kota Bharu the RAF returned at first light, to find that the Japanese shipping had withdrawn and there were no targets to attack. Landing on the northern Malayan airfields to refuel, the British machines were then caught on the ground by Japanese aircraft which were now systematically attacking airfields in the area, to the extent that the RAF had little option but to withdraw all its machines to Singapore, hoping to use what airfields that might remain serviceable in the north for refuelling only. This was to have a serious effect on the Royal Navy's Force Z, HMS *Prince of Wales* and HMS *Repulse* which, escorted by three destroyers, had left Singapore Harbour as soon as they heard of the landings, in order to cut the Japanese supply lines to the beachheads. When it became apparent to Admiral Sir Tom Phillips, flying his flag on the *Prince of Wales*, that land-based air cover would not be available because the airfields in northern Malaya had been abandoned or rendered unusable, he decided to turn back, but, when he was told by radio that there were reports of more landings at Kuantan, on the east coast and about halfway between Kota Bharu and Singapore, he turned to investigate, yet, keeping radio silence, did not tell Singapore of his intentions nor ask for air cover (which might have been possible from Singapore). There were no landings at Kuantan, but the next day, 9 December, Force Z was sighted by a Japanese submarine, which then lost contact, only for it to be renewed by another submarine the next day. On 10 December a Japanese reconnaissance aircraft confirmed the position of the British ships, and now it was just a matter of time. From late morning the two capital ships were subjected to torpedo and bombing attacks from the air, and, when Phillips broke radio silence (it was unnecessary now) to ask for air cover from Singapore, it was too late. At 1233 hours the *Repulse* was sunk, and at 1320 hours the *Prince of Wales* followed her to the bottom. True to the code of the Royal Navy, Admiral Phillips went down with his ship, along with the 840 officers and men of both ships who lost their lives. The escorting destroyers, in a superb example of seamanship under fire, rescued over 2,000 survivors. This was the first time in the history of warfare that any capital ships at sea and under way had been sunk by air power alone, and with the loss of only three aircraft it was greeted with jubilation in Japan as a notable victory – as indeed it was. The sinking of the two ships came as a severe shock to the British public, not least because it had been executed with considerable skill by Asiatics, who were supposed to be poor pilots with even worse eyesight and to lack any understanding of complex technical matters such as bomb-aiming or synchronized torpedo attacks. It was a final confirmation, if any were needed, that the battleship was no longer the queen of the seas, and that ships without air cover were horribly vulnerable. Phillips knew that, as did most thinking naval officers, but Churchill was still living in the age of the dreadnought: the ships should never have been sent to the Far East without a carrier to accompany them and the idea of providing them with land-based cover was never going to work once the Japanese air force began its campaign to destroy the British airfields. As it was, Japanese land forces were now thirty miles into Malaya and seemingly unstoppable.

* * *

Six thousand miles away and one hour and ten minutes after the landings in Malaya, at 1825 7 December GMT and 0755 local time, the Japanese navy struck at Pearl Harbor, the main base of the United States Pacific Fleet. The commander of that fleet, Rear Admiral Kimmel, knew that a Japanese carrier force had sailed but had no idea where it was. Plan Orange, the war plan in the event of hostilities with Japan, required Kimmel to raid the nearest Japanese territory, the Marshall Islands, and as these were south-west of Hawaii that is where Kimmel concentrated his reconnaissance efforts. Admiral Nagumo, with four fleet and two light carriers, and their escort of two battleships, a destroyer screen and eight support ships, had sailed all the way across the Pacific to a point 275 miles north of Hawaii, without being detected. Strict radio silence, bad weather (or good, if you want to sail without being seen) and a route that was generally avoided by commercial shipping had all helped, but so had inter-service rivalry and general incompetence in Washington.

The Americans had broken some of the Japanese codes, including the one used to communicate with their spies in Hawaii, and had deciphered those asking for detailed descriptions of Pearl Harbor. This information was never passed on to Kimmel, and anyway American intelligence still thought that, if war came, the first move would be an attack on the Philippines, which had led to the transfer of most of Pearl's P-40 fighters to Wake Island and Midway, from where they could assist in attacks on targets in the Philippines. Kimmel himself was of the view that a conventional attack on Pearl Harbor was highly unlikely: the harbour was too shallow for torpedoes to run, and so no anti-torpedo nets were in place. In fact, as we have seen, the Japanese had taken note of the British success at Taranto – it had merely confirmed much of their own thinking – and modified their torpedoes. Some sort of submarine attack might be possible, however, and an American destroyer did detect a midget submarine near the entrance of the harbour and sank it an hour before the air attack came in, but no conclusion seems to have been drawn from this, and no heightened state of readiness was ordered.

The army commander at Pearl, sixty-one-year-old Lieutenant-General Walter Short, thought that the threat was from saboteurs, and so army anti-aircraft guns were not on standby, while on the ships only a limited number of AA machine-guns were manned and the ammunition for the larger guns was stored in locked magazines. Both commanders had seen no reason to alter the peacetime Sunday routine, whereby the officers played golf and/or had lunch parties, while the Other Ranks recovered from the previous night's excesses. A mobile radar unit, whose soldiers were under training in the use of their equipment, spotted the incoming raiders and reported unidentified aircraft approaching to their duty officer. That officer did nothing, as he was expecting American aircraft from the same direction, but, even if he had realized what the radar signal really presaged, there would not have been time to do anything about it.

Nagumo's first wave of 183 aircraft – forty-nine bombers, forty torpedo-bombers, fifty-one dive-bombers and forty-three fighters – approached Pearl Harbor in thick cloud, guided by the music being played by a local radio station. Then, just as they arrived over the island, the cloud broke, giving every pilot and bomb-aimer a clear picture of what was below. From now on they used the target grid map supplied by the Japanese consul-general's spies, and for thirty minutes the bombers attacked the ships below them while the fighters strafed the airfields. Then, after a pause of fifteen minutes, in came Nagumo's second wave of fifty-four bombers, seventy-eight dive-bombers and thirty-six fighters, which attacked the American ships before departing at 0915 hours local. In just one hour and twenty minutes the Japanese navy had sunk four battleships and badly damaged two more; they had sunk three light cruisers and three destroyers and sunk or damaged a host of lesser fry. It had either destroyed or badly damaged 292 American aircraft, nearly all caught parked up on the ground. Japanese losses were negligible; twenty-one aircraft, one submarine (out of the sixteen employed) and five midget submarines. It was a brilliant operation, although it could have been even better if Nagumo had launched a third wave (which he could conceivably have done) against the repair and fuelling installations, which would have put Pearl Harbor out of use as a naval base for a considerable time. Some of Nagumo's staff urged him to do just that, but, with his fuel levels running low and deciding that he had chanced his luck sufficiently for one day, he ordered the fleet to head for home.

Brilliant operation though it was, the attack did not achieve its aim: to destroy American war-making capacity long enough for the Japanese to conquer their Co-Prosperity Sphere, by which time the United States would negotiate a peace. It did not take out the Pacific Fleet's two aircraft carriers (and a third was on the way from San Diego) or the heavy cruisers, which were at sea; it only sank three destroyers out of the twenty-nine moored in the harbour; it had not touched the dry dock; and it failed to take into account the speed at which the American ship-building industry could repair and replace when it really had to – three of the battleships were back in commission by the end of the month. That said, Pearl Harbor did come as a great shock to the American people, psychologically as much as militarily, and it did unite them behind their president in declaring war against Japan.

Technically, the attack was part of a 'Day of Infamy', as Roosevelt put it, having been carried out without a declaration of war. The Japanese embassy was supposed to deliver a declaration some hours before the attack, but delays in deciphering the message from Tokyo and further delays as the Japanese ambassador waited to see the American Secretary of State meant that it was not delivered until Admiral Nagumo was on his way home. Numerous investigations during the war and a Congressional inquiry after it all blamed Kimmel and Short, while carefully ensuring that none of the blame stuck to the president or to the administration. Both men were relieved of their commands, reduced to their substantive ranks of rear admiral and major-general respectively and compulsorily retired.* Years later, a Congressional committee, set up under the Clinton administration in 1999, exonerated Kimmel and Short, saying that they had been denied intelligence available in Washington, and restored them to their held ranks. As both men were long dead, this was rather akin to the efforts of the Richard III Society in absolving Richard of the murder of the Princes in the Tower, but it was a nice gesture.

On the same day that Pearl Harbor was bombed, a task force under Rear Admiral Kajioka Sadamichi attacked the United States' most westerly Pacific base, Wake Island, but with rather less success. The defenders, men of the US Marine Corps, manned anti-aircraft guns and shore batteries while a squadron of fighters repulsed an attempted landing, sinking two Japanese destroyers. With the support of two carriers returning from Pearl Harbor, Sadamichi tried again on 23 December 1941, and this time he did succeed in taking the island, but at considerable cost, the tiny garrison accounting for four Japanese ships, twenty-one aircraft and around 900 men.

* * *

Three hours and forty-five minutes after Nagumo's second wave of aircraft had turned away from Pearl Harbor, at 2330 hours on 7 December GMT, or 0800 hours on 8 December local time, the British crown colony of Hong Kong became the next target for the Japanese, as Lieutenant-General Tadayoshi

---

*Largely because of Congressional meanness with money, American officers were almost never given substantive promotion above two stars (rear admiral and major-general) and if in an appointment meriting three, four or, exceptionally, five stars they held acting rank, which gave them the pay but not the pension, which remained that of their substantive rank.

Sano's 38 Division of the Japanese Twenty-Third Army, hardened by years of fighting in China and desensitized by years of butchery of Chinese civilians, hurtled across the Shum Shun river. Here the governor, Sir Mark Young, and the Commander British Forces, Major-General Christopher Maltby, were well aware that they would not be reinforced and were going to be defeated, although bellicose statements by some civilians and soldiers not in the know that Hong Kong was impregnable were difficult to refute without lowering morale. Malaya and Singapore would hold out, but Hong Kong could not, although its garrison had to resist for as long as possible, and do as much damage to the attacking Japanese as it possibly could.

There had been ample warning of Japanese intentions and from 5 December Maltby was deploying his troops to their battle positions, with a covering force of one company of 2/14 Punjab Regiment supported by armoured cars forward on the frontier, with the aim of identifying any incursion and then delaying the enemy's approach to the main defensive position, the so-called Gin Drinker's Line which stretched from Tsun Wan to Tide Cove, on the mainland north of Kowloon. By the time the news of Japanese landings in Malaya had been received by radio, all the troops in Hong Kong were at their stand-to positions, anti-aircraft guns were manned and the demolition of road and railway bridges in the frontier area had begun. As the Japanese infantry, led by local guides and supported by mountain artillery, with Chinese civilians pressed into service as carriers of ammunition, water and rations, crossed the frontier, the Japanese air force bombed Kai Tak airfield, destroying all five of the RAF's aircraft parked there. The covering force began to withdraw and scored a local victory at Tai Po, where they ambushed the Japanese tootling along in column of route and caused significant casualties. The Japanese advance was nevertheless faster than expected, largely owing to the excellence of their engineers, who were little inconvenienced by the demolished bridges and cratered roads.

In Hong Kong and amongst those who are or have been connected with Hong Kong, the defence of the colony has been talked up into a gallant and heroic defence carried out by brave and dedicated men who made the attackers fight for every inch of ground and were only defeated by overwhelming force. The truth is perhaps a little different. The Royal Scots, the First of Foot, acquired the nickname of the 'Fleet of Foot' or the 'First and Worst', having supposedly run away from the Gin Drinker's Line back to Hong Kong Island. They did not run away, but they did not defend the left-hand portion of the line with any great enthusiasm, and when the Japanese captured the Shing Mun redoubt, the lynchpin of that part of the line, their commanding officer declined to counter-attack it. When the Scots eventually gave way, the Indian battalions in the centre and right could not stay where they were and had to withdraw to conform. Maltby ordered a withdrawal to Hong Kong Island, and after a number of delaying actions by the Indian battalions the troops were taken off, an operation not assisted by the desertion of the Chinese crews of the ferries, and further complicated by panicking defenders opening fire on the cargo vessel shifting the garrison's store of explosives from Green Island; the ship promptly blew up, severely depleting the ability of the Engineers to create obstacles on the island. By 13 December, Kowloon and the mainland had been abandoned to the Japanese.

* * *

The last of the initial Japanese strikes was on the Philippines, when at 0500 hours on 8 December GMT, 1230 hours local time, an air raid from Formosa caught most of General MacArthur's air force on the ground at Clark Field and destroyed eighteen B-17 bombers, fifty-six fighters and a host of miscellaneous aircraft. It is difficult to excuse this, although MacArthur, unlike his colleagues at Pearl Harbor, got away with it. He had ample warning, having been told of the Pearl Harbor attack nine hours before, at 0330 hours local. By his own account, General Louis Brereton, commanding the USAAF Far East Air Force, immediately asked permission to launch an attack on Japanese air bases in China but was refused by MacArthur. MacArthur denied this, and said later that, even if the raid had taken place, the heavy defences of Japanese air bases and the lack of American fighter cover for the small bomber force would have rendered any such action suicidal. Brereton's version of events is the more credible, however, and MacArthur did authorize a raid much later, when it was too late. Had the raid been authorized immediately, the bombers would have been in the air rather than parked on the ground when the Japanese arrived. It seems that MacArthur still hoped that the Philippines would somehow remain neutral and avoid being attacked, whereas a glance at the map would have shown him that the Japanese had no choice but to take the Philippines once they embarked on their planned expansion.

In the teeth of overwhelming air superiority, Brereton now withdrew most of his remaining aircraft to Australia and to Java, in the Dutch East

Indies, leaving MacArthur with only a handful of fighters. The US Navy too decided to withdraw, when the sixty-four-year-old Admiral Thomas Hart, commanding the American Asiatic Fleet, learned of the fate of his friend Phillips in the *Prince of Wales*. Hart was an innovator in using air power against ships and knew full well that, with the removal of USAAF aircraft and the preponderance of Japanese air power, to leave his ships where they were would invite destruction. He ordered his ships to the Dutch East Indies, to the anger and consternation of MacArthur, who signalled Washington, demanding that aircraft carriers be sent out to strike a blow against the Japanese. But Washington was not terribly interested in the Philippines, or in MacArthur, and was certainly not going to risk valuable carriers in the defence of somewhere the US Navy had already written off. MacArthur now knew that with the withdrawal of the navy his small American army and fledgling Filipino militia would have to fight alone and that eventually they would run out of supplies. Dispersed landings by small bodies of Japanese troops had begun on 10 December, but MacArthur realized that these were intended to make him split his forces and declined to move. As with every other Western possession in South-East Asia, it would now be only a matter of time before the Philippines too succumbed.

* * *

On 11 December 1941, while the Americans were still clearing the rubble of Pearl Harbor, the *Prince of Wales* and the *Repulse* had been sunk, the evacuation of Kowloon was in full swing and MacArthur was wondering what to do now that the US Navy had gone, Germany and Italy declared war on the United States of America. It was a decision taken by Hitler alone, without consulting his military advisers, and was preceded by the hasty signing of an agreement by Germany, Italy and Japan that none would seek a separate peace. Hitler did not have to declare war on America, the agreements with Japan were consultative and defensive, and the whole point of including Japan in the Tripartite Pact of September 1940 was to deter America from entering the war. He accepted that war with the United States was inevitable eventually, but he wanted to delay it as long as possible, and ideally until the war in Europe was won. Now that Britain was, contrary to German expectations, still fighting on, Hitler had been encouraging Japan to attack British possessions in the Far East, and after June 1941 to attack Russia, but had advised her not to attack

America. Things had changed, however. By the autumn of 1941 it was clear that the war would not be won by a short, sharp stroke – Germany must prepare for a long war. Barbarossa had failed in the sense that it had not brought a result before the winter of 1941; the United States was providing far more support to Britain than a neutral nation should, and she had amended her Neutrality Acts to extend Lend-Lease to the USSR. American ships were reporting the position of German ships to the British, were depth-charging German submarines and would come into the war very shortly. If this were unavoidable, then Hitler would prefer to be the initiator rather than the recipient of a declaration of war.

To the British, the Japanese attack on Pearl Harbor was a delightful Christmas cake, and the German declaration of war was the marzipan on it. Churchill had always hoped that the United States would come into the war, and his whole war and foreign policy was predicated on this assumption. Many conspiracy theories have grown out of Pearl Harbor. It has been suggested that Roosevelt and his advisers knew about the Japanese intention to attack the Pacific Fleet's base and deliberately let it happen to allow the president to bring America into the war. Another theory has it that the British knew of the attack from intercepts long before it happened and did not tell the Americans. (A particularly entertaining theory posted on a website some time ago and now, sadly, removed had it that the attack on Pearl was actually carried out by RAF aircraft with Japanese markings.) It is probably unnecessary to say that there is not a shred of evidence to support any of these suggestions.

In the week immediately following the outbreak of war with Japan, Churchill and President Roosevelt met in Washington at the Arcadia Conference to discuss a joint strategy. For Roosevelt and the American planners the question now was what policy to adopt. Most American military activity so far was in the Atlantic, and most Americans had become accustomed to following the war there, in Europe and in the Mediterranean. To concentrate against Germany would therefore dovetail into what was happening anyway. To those on the west coast of the United States, however, Hitler's Germany, while undoubtedly a thoroughly nasty regime, did not pose an obvious threat to the United States, whereas Japan clearly did. To concentrate equally against both enemies east and west would stretch American military strength, even though this was now swiftly increasing, so a decision had to be made. The British view was that, despite the imminent loss of large chunks of their Asian empire, the long-term threat was from Germany, not Japan, and this was the side of the argument favoured by Roosevelt, against the advice of the US Navy, which wanted to go for Japan first and then turn on Germany. Field Marshal Sir John Dill, who had just handed over to Brooke as CIGS, accompanied Churchill to Washington and remained there as liaison with the United States Chiefs of Staff. He would establish excellent relations with them but, despite his best efforts, there was some suspicion of the British in both political and military circles. Because two nations speak a version of the same language, and because many of the citizens of one of those nations originate from the other, does not mean that each has the same agenda, and the Americans often tended to give the British far more credit for deviousness and subtlety than was perhaps warranted, seeking for hidden motives when one was not always present – although to be fair it often was: the British, as a nation old in the art of duplicitous diplomacy, conduct their foreign and defence policy in accordance with what they see as the national interest, and not along the lines of some abstract idea of freedom or fairness, although they would, if pushed, subscribe to both. From the American point of view, far too many of the British that they encountered seemed supercilious and arrogant, and the natural British reserve was interpreted as disdain. The Americans saw the British as class-ridden, and men like 'Vinegar Joe' Stilwell, the American military adviser to Chiang Kai-shek, and Stanley K. Hornbeck, a political adviser in the State Department, were particularly scathing in imitating the way British officers spoke and their obsession with tea. As one of the less scurrilous efforts circulating in Washington at the time put it:

> To lunch they go at half past one –
> Blast me old chap, the day's half done
> They lunch and talk and fight the Jap
> And now it's time to take a nap
> The staff study starts at three fifteen
> Such progress here you've never seen
> They're working now as you can see
> But blast me down, it's time for tea...[54]

Indeed, many Americans were conscious that in 1776 they had opted out of empire, and had little sympathy for – and, in many cases, some real antagonism towards – the British Empire. In some instances this stemmed from a genuine belief that the American system of democracy should be enjoyed by all the peoples of the world; in others it was the realization that America's chief trade rival was Britain and her Empire – as Admiral Benson, US Chief of Naval Operations from 1915, had explained when trying to persuade Congress to fund a massive ship-building programme. 'The British,' Benson had said, 'have always gone to war with their trade rivals eventually, and they have always won.' Nobody seriously thought that Britain and America would go to war, but even as late as 1941 many Americans thought that it was the Royal Navy that was the greatest barrier to American control of the world's oceans, rather than the Germans or Japanese.

Meanwhile, for many of the British who worked in the United States as diplomats or military liaison officers, the Americans were far too prone to emotion and exaggeration; they wore their hearts on their sleeves, were naive and, while criticizing the existence of British colonies, were quite happy to oppose the granting of independence to the Philippines. Some Britons questioned whether fifty clapped-out destroyers was a fair price for the UK base facilities granted to the United States (it wasn't, but the British had to have those destroyers), and Vichy France was a serious sticking point. The Vichy regime was a legal government: it was not established by coup or imposed by the Germans, but created by vote of the French parliament giving supreme power to Marshal Pétain, who then negotiated a surrender in June 1940. It was recognized by Britain until Vichy broke off diplomatic relations after the attack on the French fleet in Mers el Kebir. Most of the British Dominions and the United States maintained embassies there in Vichy, and the American view was that only by being nice to Vichy, or at least treating it seriously, could a post-war liberal democratic France in the Western orbit be assured. The British, on the other hand, saw Vichy as being devoid of any credibility and promoted Charles de Gaulle, difficult to deal with as he was, as the only man who could unite all Frenchmen and keep the spirit of French glory and pride alive. The Americans were particularly irritated when de Gaulle's Free French, egged on by the British, seized some French islands off the coast of Newfoundland in late 1941, and the question of the leadership of anti-German French elements was to be a constant source of disagreement throughout the war.

Given the differences in perspective, in national character and in ambitions for the post-war shape of the world, the fact remained (and still remains) that the British (and their white Dominions) and the Americans had more in common with each other than with any other country. Both were democracies, both were governed by the rule of law and both shared ideals of fair play and essential decency. As the war went on, the British would have to accept that more and more they would become the junior partner, and that they could not bring the war to a conclusion they could accept without the United States. Fortunately there were enough men on each side to ensure a generally harmonious relationship, despite occasional personal rivalries and disagreements on strategy. For the moment, the Royal Navy despatched an aircraft carrier to the Pacific to serve under the command of the US Pacific Fleet, and agreement was reached to set up a joint American, British, Dutch and Australian (ABDA) command for the Far East to be commanded by General Archibald Wavell, whose appointment was an American recommendation.

* * *

In Malaya, British forces continued to fall back under relentless Japanese pressure. It was now apparent that the Japanese could operate off roads, that their eyesight was every bit as good as anyone else's and that they could also operate perfectly well at night. The British were now down to ten serviceable aircraft in north Malaya, while the Japanese disposed of 150 flying from airfields just over the border in Siam. The withdrawal of ground crews from the forward British air bases was a shambles, rapidly taking on the characteristics of a disorganized rout. When the RAF was admonished for failing to destroy fuel and stores, thus handing the enemy a useful bonus, it blew up everything it could not move at RAF Alor Star but failed to tell the army. As Alor Star was behind the British front lines, the loud bangs caused considerable consternation amongst the soldiery, who not unnaturally assumed them to indicate Japanese penetration behind the lines.

The next attempt to hold northern Malaya was at Jitra, some thirty miles from the Siamese border, when the Indian 11 Division tried to hold a frontage of fourteen miles with only four battalions. If the whole area had been rice paddy, as some of it was, this might, just, have been feasible. But much of it was jungle, where visibility is twenty yards on a good day, and, when on 12 December the Japanese began to work their way round his right flank, the divisional commander, Major-General David Murray-Lyon, asked permission to withdraw, a request denied by Percival. As the day wore on, muddle and confusion reigned. There were reports that a particular battalion had been wiped out, that another battalion had withdrawn without orders, and that the Japanese had encircled the division. All were subsequently found to be false, but panic was beginning to set in amongst inexperienced and barely trained troops and eventually Murray-Lyon received permission to withdraw if he considered it essential – which he did. The withdrawal, to a position fifteen miles back, began at 2200 hours on the night of 12/13 December and was chaotic. Withdrawal, especially at night, is a difficult operation of war in any circumstances, and, for the badly shaken troops trying to move back along the only road in torrential rain with the Japanese snapping at their heels, it was a harrowing experience. Some units got the order to withdraw too late, others never got it at all, and guns and vehicles had to be abandoned when a bridge was blown prematurely. Had it not been for the efforts of two Gurkha battalions as rearguard (the third, 2/1 Gurkha Rifles, was by now reduced to one company, having had to fight its way out of a Japanese encirclement earlier in the day), the whole division might well have been lost. Although at the time the Japanese seemed to be present in overwhelming numbers, we now know that 11 Division was being attacked by just two battalions of infantry and a company of tanks but such was their speed of movement and determination that they gave the impression of far greater strength.

They tried to hold on to the Sungei Kedah,* the main river in the Sultanate of Kedah, but, once the Japanese closed up to the river, it was obvious that this could not be held and the division withdrew another twenty miles, to Gurun, on the night of 13/14 December. Here the positions had not been prepared for defence, and, as soon as the exhausted troops arrived, they had to set to with pick and shovel to try to entrench before the Japanese fell upon them. Sure enough, at first light on 14 December, Japanese infantry supported by tanks and mortars appeared. The tanks were a surprise as it was hoped that the bridge demolitions and cratering of the road would hold them up for several days, but the British had again failed to take into account the ability of the Japanese Army's engineers to be well forward to effect speedy repair of roads and throw bridges across rivers. Here the division should have taken charge of sixteen Marmon-Herrington armoured cars, recently arrived in Singapore and sent up by road. Sadly, not only had the

---

*Sungei means river in Malay.

cars arrived without mounts for the machine-guns, but their drivers, having never seen such vehicles before, and having to travel against the stream of retreating columns, had managed to write off most of them on the way up, and only three actually appeared.

On the night of 15/16 December, the division withdrew again, this time south of the next river line, the Sungei Muda. The rapid withdrawals brought problems both diplomatic and military. The Sultan of Perlis, the northernmost of the Malay states adjacent to the border with Siam, pointed out angrily that his treaty of accession to the British federation stipulated that British troops would always be available to defend his sultanate – they had gone: when were they coming back? Meanwhile, the withdrawals exposed the island of Penang, off the west coast, to Japanese attack. Penang had valuable port facilities and stores depots, and the defence plan for Malaya included the detachment of two battalions and anti-aircraft guns to defend it. There could now be no question of depleting the already seriously under-strength 11 Division by detaching men or guns, and, when Penang was subject to air raids from 16 December onwards, it was decided to evacuate the existing modest garrison, patients from the hospital and all European residents. Those stores that could not be removed must be destroyed. Asian residents would not be evacuated – there was insufficient transport, Singapore was overcrowded already and they must take their chances with the Japanese. It was unfortunate that the destruction of stores and installations did not include the broadcasting station, which was used by the Japanese for the rest of the war to disseminate anti-British propaganda, nor the civilian shipping, deserted by its crews, which came in very useful for Japanese coastal work thereafter.

The withdrawal continued, with Heath, the corps commander, and both his divisional commanders urging that a clean break must be made, rather than moving back in short bounds and never being able to shake the pursuers off. The troops were by now not much more than automatons, unable to get any sleep during the day, snatching a few minutes' rest where they could or in the back of vehicles as they withdrew, only to have to get digging as soon as they reached their new position. By 20 December the Japanese had repaired the British north Malayan airfields and were using them, Zero fighters and Mitsubishi bombers roamed the skies almost at will and on 23 December the airfield at Kuala Lumpur, after several Japanese air raids, was evacuated. The Public Works Department was ordered to arrange for defensive positions and anti-tank ditches to be dug which the troops could withdraw to, but the officials of that organization were either unable to muster sufficient labour, or were incapable of organizing it. General Percival was well aware of the problems of III Corps, but his priority was the security of the naval base – Singapore – and, as Japanese naval supremacy meant that a landing there could be attempted at any time, he dared not despatch any of the Singapore garrison to reinforce the troops farther north. Reinforcements from the UK, the Middle East, India and Australia had been asked for, and were on the way, but all available aircraft had to be retained in Singapore to ensure the safe arrival of the convoys. Percival had to keep the Japanese as far away from Singapore as possible and that meant III Corps, for all its problems, had to delay them for as long as they could. On Christmas Day seven RAF bombers arrived from Egypt – it should have been eighteen, but all the rest had crashed or gone unserviceable on the way.

The British next attempted to hold the Japanese along the Slim River and once again lack of coordination during the withdrawal meant that, by the time the rearguard Gurkha battalion got to the river, most of the bridges had been blown. Then, Gurkhas were not good swimmers* (there are very few places to learn to swim in the mountains of Nepal) and a number of men were drowned trying to get across. The troops had now withdrawn 180 miles in three weeks and 11 Division at least was in little state for any further fighting. The action on the Slim River was a disaster, and when the Japanese took the last remaining bridge on 7 January 1942, there was no alternative for the British but to withdraw once more into Johore, the southernmost of the Malay states and the last opportunity to keep the Japanese away from Singapore. By now 11 Division was militarily ineffective: 4/19 Hyderabad Regiment was down to three officers and 110 men; 5/2 Punjab to one officer and eighty men; 2 Argyll and Sutherland Highlanders to four officers and ninety men.[55] Of the three Gurkha battalions, the most effective units in the corps, 2/1 Gurkha Rifles had ceased to exist and 2/2 Gurkha Rifles and 2/9 Gurkha Rifles amounted to about one battalion between them.

On 11 January the Japanese entered Kuala Lumpur, capturing vast stocks of stores that the British had been unable to destroy in time, and by 13 January

---

*They are now, when the army teaches them to swim, and have won numerous military swimming competitions.

all the British troops that could get away were in Johore, a state with a more developed road system than the rest of the country and hence more difficult to defend against a fast-moving enemy. The defence of Johore was largely in the hands of the Australian 8 Division, commanded by Major-General Gordon Bennett. This division had been well trained and was reasonably fresh, but it was to little avail. They did succeed in killing a considerable number of Japanese in local actions and ambushes as they slowly withdrew into Johore, but, with Japanese reinforcements landing along the coast and rapidly depleting British air power, there was little that they could do to stem the tide. Command changes had been put in place and reinforcements were now beginning to arrive, however. On 23 December, Lieutenant-General Sir Henry Pownall, lately Vice-Chief of the Imperial General Staff in London and previously Chief of Staff to Lord Gort in the Battle of France, took over from Air Marshal Brooke-Popham as Commander-in-Chief Far East and, on 3 January, 45 Indian Infantry Brigade arrived, unblooded, full of recruits who were barely trained and short of officers and NCOs. The brigade's existence was to be but a short one. Air reinforcements trickled in, mainly of obsolete bombers, but at last, on 13 January, fifty-one crated Hurricane fighters arrived, and were hastily unboxed, assembled and dispersed for airworthiness tests. There were only twenty-four pilots with them, but it was hoped that the British now had something that could seriously inconvenience the Japanese. Alas, it was not to be. The Hurricanes were more than a match for the Zeros above 20,000 feet, but at lower levels they lacked the manoeuvrability of the latter and in any case there were not enough of them. In the same convoy came 53 Brigade of the British 18 Division, one anti-tank and two anti-aircraft regiments.

Meanwhile, the attempted defence along the Rivers Maur and Segamat was falling apart and, on 3 January, 45 Brigade and an Australian battalion were surrounded and cut off. Attempts to rescue them, not always pressed with the determination that they might have been, were unsuccessful and the brigade commander, having had all equipment and weapons not man-portable destroyed, ordered his men to break out in groups. Only 500 Australians and 400 Indians managed to do so, and the brigade commander and all three of the Indian battalion commanding officers were killed. Air raids on Singapore were now increasing, civilian labourers were refusing to work in areas under attack and the Chiefs of Staff in London, who had little knowledge of the Far East and few of whose staff had ever been there, were sending increasingly unrealistic instructions to Wavell and to Percival as to how the defence should be conducted. How Wavell kept his temper when reminded by London that road and railway bridges on the approaches to Singapore should be demolished, and how Percival kept a civil tongue in his head when London reminded him not to allow valuable stores to fall into Japanese hands, can only be marvelled at.

On 22 January a convoy with 44 Indian Infantry Brigade and 7,000 individual reinforcements for the Indian units in country arrived, but as the latter were almost all recruits who had completed only the scantiest of basic training, they could not be despatched to their battalions immediately and had instead to be held in Singapore for continuation training. They were at least disciplined and amenable, which was not the case with the 1,900 Australian individual reinforcements who arrived on 24 January; the latter had not even completed basic training (some had not been given any weapon training) and had no concept of military discipline. This was at least partly compensated for by the arrival in the same convoy of a well-trained and competent Australian machine-gun battalion. As it was considered that the collapsing defence of Johore was not conducive to the deployment of this battalion, it was set to digging defensive positions on the north coast of Singapore. Then on 27 January came another disaster when the Commander 9th Indian Division, Major-General Arthur Barstow, was killed in a Japanese ambush and one of his brigades, 22, was surrounded, cut off, ran out of ammunition, failed in an attempt to break out and had to surrender.

By now it was absolutely clear to everyone, except perhaps to Churchill in London, who was still breathing fire and brimstone and advocating fierce resistance and scorched earth in Johore, that the mainland could not be held, and so Percival, with Wavell's and Pownall's concurrence, ordered a withdrawal to Singapore. The troops fell back via a series of stop lines, and on the night of 31 January 1942 the rearguard crossed from Johore into Singapore and the Sappers and Miners* blew up the causeway. As it was 1,200 yards in length and thirty yards wide, this was a considerable demolition problem, but a bridge was demolished, a lock destroyed and another twenty-yard gap created. The last chapter in the dismal story of the defence of the Malayan peninsula was about to begin.

*The Indian Army's equivalent of the Royal Engineers.

* * *

It was never the intention to defend Britain's two colonies and one protectorate on the north Borneo coast and there was only one regular battalion in the whole island, 2/15 Punjab, whose job was to destroy oil installations in Miri, in north Sarawak near the border with Brunei, and then to withdraw to defend the airstrip in Kuching, also in Sarawak but 300 miles south-west along the coast. The Punjabis dealt with Miri on 14 December 1941, and, when the Japanese landed there that night and at Labuan on 1 January, the battalion had gone and the invaders faced no opposition, as the local forces had been ordered to maintain internal security only – anything else would have been suicidal. On 8 January the Japanese were in Jessleton (now Kota Kinabalu) and when they reached Sandakan, the capital of British North Borneo on the 19th, the governor surrendered. Having declined the Japanese offer to continue to administer the colony under their supervision, he and his staff were interned.

On 23 December a Japanese convoy was spotted heading for Kuching, and as bombing of airfields in Dutch Borneo had made the strip at Kuching irrelevant, the Punjabis cratered its runway and prepared to hold the Japanese up for as long as possible. Now began one of the very few examples of really professional soldiering displayed in the whole sorry saga of the loss of South-East Asia. The Punjabis inflicted considerable casualties on the Japanese landing parties and then, when it became apparent that the town of Kuching could not be held, they withdrew into Dutch Borneo. Two companies were cut off in the process but, although surrounded, the four British officers, eight Viceroy Commissioned Officers and 220 Indian Other Ranks fought on.* One platoon succeeded in breaking out and rejoining the battalion; the rest were never seen again. By 30 December the remains of the battalion had reached the Dutch airfield of Sinkawang, on the north-west corner of Borneo, and on 31 December they received an air drop of rations and ammunition from Singapore and prepared to defend the airfield with the existing Dutch garrison. Bad weather held up the Japanese but on 26 January they attacked and again the battalion withdrew. Again the rearguard, of two

---

*An Indian infantry company had two British officers, the company commander and a subaltern who was learning his trade. The company second-in-command and the platoon commanders were men commissioned from the ranks and holding a commission from the viceroy, as opposed to the king.

platoons this time, was surrounded and, of two officers and seventy men, only three got away. The rest were either killed or, when they had fired their last round and surrendered, executed on the spot by the Japanese, who were furious that the sepoys had killed or wounded over 400 of their comrades. Eventually, after an epic march of 500 miles along tracks through largely unexplored jungle, what was left of the battalion reached Sampit, on the south coast, only to have to lay down their arms when the Netherland East Indies surrendered on 8 March.

* * *

In Hong Kong, General Maltby placed his most experienced battalions, 2/14 Punjab and 5/7 Rajput, respectively in defence along the north-west and north-east coastlines of Hong Kong Island, while the willing but inexperienced and as yet unblooded Winnipeg Grenadiers and Royal Rifles of Canada took post on the south-west and south-east sides. The Middlesex manned machine-guns in pill boxes all along the coastline. The Royal Scots were supposedly in reserve on the Peak, but, although they had suffered only a handful of deaths in the fighting on the mainland,* they were now a busted flush from whom little could be expected. On the morning of 13 December a launch flying a white flag put off from Kowloon, and landed at the Star Ferry landing stage on the Island. In it was a Japanese staff officer with a letter from Lieutenant-General Takashi Sakai, commanding Twenty-Third Army, inviting the garrison to surrender on pain of artillery and aerial bombardment. The offer was refused and the bombardment duly began. Fires were started and casualties amongst the civilian population were inevitable. Although the Chinese were generally stoical, enemy fifth columnists were active, as were robbers in the air-raid shelters. To counter these, the governor formed an unholy alliance with the Triads, illegal criminal gangs who were nevertheless loyal to and generally controlled by Chiang Kai-shek's regime in Chungking. On 15 December the defenders beat off a Japanese attempt to cross the harbour, and a second offer to surrender, brought by two Japanese officers in launches, was refused. Maltby and the governor concluded that the repeated offer was motivated by a Japanese wish to secure a quick victory before they were attacked in the rear by Chinese

---

*2 Royal Scots had seven killed in the fighting in the New Territories and eighty-nine killed up to the surrender.

Nationalist forces – constantly promised by the one-legged Admiral Chan commanding the Chinese liaison team in Hong Kong, but they not only failed to attack but made no effort to do so.

By 18 December conditions on the island were critical. Bombing and shelling had collapsed buildings in Central District, roads were blocked by fleeing civilians and a pall of heavy black smoke hung over the whole coastline from North Point to Lei U Mun as oil-storage tanks burned. That night, under cover of heavy artillery fire, the Japanese effected landings on the north-east corner of the island, getting through the wire which had been cut by Chinese collaborators and falling upon the Rajputs, all of whose officers, British and Indian, were killed or wounded. The Rajputs fell back, although a mixed force of wounded Middlesex soldiers and members of the part-time HKVDC held out in the power station until well into the afternoon of 19 December. Over the next few days the Japanese landed more and more troops, and, although the defenders did their best – especially the two Canadian battalions – it was just a matter of time before the outnumbered British would have to concede defeat. Once the Japanese managed to cut the defence of the Island in half, the British could not recover the ground lost, despite repeated counter-attacks, including those by the Royal Scots, who had recovered their courage and hung on grimly to a shrinking perimeter west of Wanchai Gap. By Christmas Day only the area west of Wanchai and the Stanley and West Bay peninsulas were still in British hands, although isolated small groups were fighting on elsewhere, and the commanding officer of the Royal Rifles of Canada was adamant that his men could do no more. That officer's views applied to the whole garrison: under constant artillery and aerial attack, with little rest, dwindling ammunition, few guns still capable of action, scanty rations and mounting casualties, it was now obvious that the much anticipated Nationalist Chinese relief force was not coming (in fact, it had not started) and there was no hope left.

On Christmas morning a British officer and a civilian appeared with a white flag. They had earlier been captured and had now been sent to advise Maltby to surrender. The Japanese would observe an armistice until noon. Malby's inclination was to refuse, but, after consultation with his subordinate commanders and after the Japanese, ignoring their own armistice, had made further inroads, he decided that there was no hope of any further effective resistance. That evening, at the Peninsula Hotel, the departure point for peacetime P&O steamers heading for England, Sir Mark Young and General

Maltby signed the instruments of unconditional surrender to General Sakai. The total British and Empire battle casualties up to 25 December are estimated at around 4,400, of which perhaps 800 were killed. After the surrender, the remaining 7,500-odd became prisoners of war. The Japanese admitted to 675 killed and 2,079 men wounded.

The news that Hong Kong had fallen after only eighteen days' fighting came as a major blow to the government in London. Although all had accepted that the colony could be neither reinforced nor held for ever, it had been expected to resist for rather longer than it had. The reasons for the swift collapse were many. The overwhelming air superiority of the Japanese – although British officers were still convinced that the planes were being flown by Germans – the preponderance of the attackers' artillery and the failure of mainland demolitions to slow up the advance were major factors, but so too was the inescapable fact that the soldiers of the Japanese infantry, only marginally more numerous than the defenders, were more experienced, better trained and better motivated than their opponents, who had either been too long as garrison troops or were inexperienced and, in some cases, barely trained. Finally, Japanese intelligence, provided by Japanese living and working in Hong Kong and Chinese fifth columnists, allowed the attackers to know exactly where the defences were sited, and where the vulnerable points were. Churchill claimed after the war that the garrison of Hong Kong had, by their heroic defence, won themselves 'lasting honour', but then he could hardly say anything else.

* * *

The northernmost island of the Philippines is Luzon, with the capital, Manila, at the southern end of it. On 22 December, three days before the Hong Kong surrender, 20,000 Japanese troops landed at Lingayen Gulf, about halfway down the island's west coast and about 150 miles from Manila, and on 24 December another 7,000 came ashore at Lamon Bay, on the east coast this time and also about 150 miles from Manila. MacArthur had no ships or aircraft to stop the landings and the Japanese expected him to defend Manila on the plains of Luzon. MacArthur knew very well that, if he tried to do this, his men would be defeated, and instead, as the two Japanese columns advanced in a pincer movement to take Manila, he declared the capital an open city and prepared to withdraw to the Bataan peninsula, west of Manila, where he hoped to be able to hold out until relief arrived. In what General of the Armies John J. Pershing – 'Black Jack', who had commanded the American Expeditionary Force in the First World War and who normally had little time for MacArthur – called one of the greatest moves in all military history,* MacArthur had the northernmost of his two little armies, commanded by Major-General Jonathan 'Snowy' Wainright, occupy a defence position across the Japanese line of advance and then, when the Japanese had massed to attack it, withdraw ten miles or so and do the same thing again, and so on, thus delaying the Japanese without actually having to fight – which, given the Japanese superiority in the air, would have been calamitous. This tactic allowed MacArthur's southern army to withdraw without interference, and for Wainright's army to follow. Called armies for political and morale reasons – they amounted to about four divisions between them – MacArthur's men withdrew slowly. Blowing bridges behind them, by 6 January 1942 both armies were in the Bataan peninsula, with MacArthur and President Quezon on the island of Corregidor, just off the tip of Bataan. Including the troops not in the two armies, there were now 5,000 American and 65,000 Filipino soldiers in Bataan, along with a great many civilian refugees.

While the retreat had been competently and efficiently executed, stores and rations had not been moved from their pre-war dumps into Bataan. MacArthur had originally intended to use sea power and air strikes to stop the Japanese landings, and stores dumps had been positioned accordingly. With the departure or destruction of aircraft and ships, he had to recast his plans and the stores were not moved. Given the string of Allied failures that had marked the Asian war so far, it is not surprising that the Siege of Bataan was trumpeted as an example of heroism against insuperable odds, and in fairness it was far less shaming than events in Malaya or Hong Kong. MacArthur showed tremendous personal courage, refusing to wear a helmet and frequently visiting the front line, and then tarnished his image by issuing bombastic and patently untrue statements about massive reinforcements of ships, men and aircraft on their way from the United States. His Filipino soldiers never lost faith in him, but his Americans, 'the Battling Bastards of Bataan' as they liked to be known, called him 'Dugout Doug' in the (mistaken) belief that his headquarters on Corregidor was a lot safer than the trenches on Bataan. After President Quezon was persuaded not to seek terms from the Japanese and to allow himself to be evacuated to Australia, the siege went on, with rations being increasingly reduced and with mounting casualties.

---

*Hardly, but it was well conducted all the same.

President Roosevelt had agreed the Germany First strategy, and there were no resources to help the Philippines. Some rather feeble attempts were made to ship in some supplies, but Japanese submarines ensured that none reached Luzon.

Then Roosevelt had a change of heart. Having written off MacArthur, whom he still saw as a dangerous demagogue, he decided that to allow a senior American commander, an ex-chief of staff of the army, to fall into Japanese hands would be to hand them a propaganda victory that they would make much of. On 23 February he ordered MacArthur to hand over his command to Wainright and leave the Philippines. Wainright was to negotiate the surrender of his Filipino troops as he thought necessary, but the Americans were to fight on to the end. MacArthur was incensed. Much of the subsequent MacArthur legend was based on his refusal to leave until repeated direct orders from his president, but all the evidence indicates that MacArthur genuinely was prepared to die in battle leading his men from the front. Eventually, and after much protest, MacArthur and his wife and child, having declined to board a submarine (he suffered from claustrophobia), left by Patrol Torpedo (PT) boat* and were delivered 700 miles away to Mindanao, the island south of Luzon and as yet uninvaded, whence he was flown by the Royal Australian Air Force to Darwin in northern Australia. On arrival he made the speech that was to pass into the lexicon of Second World War legend. He had left the Philippines, he said, to organize resistance to the Japanese, but 'I shall return'.† On 9 April 1942 the defenders of Bataan surrendered, many of the soldiers by now not much more than walking skeletons, while Corregidor held out until 6 May. Wainright and his troops had done well: one could not have blamed them had they accepted the hopeless situation they were in and surrendered earlier, although, in view of what was to happen to them, many must later have wished that they had fought to the death.

Somewhat to the surprise of the American hierarchy, but not, one suspects, to the man himself, MacArthur was hailed as a hero, in a war that was so far singularly lacking in heroes, or at least any not wearing riding

*A fast, shallow-draft boat with a crew of about a dozen and armed with torpedoes and machine-guns – the PT boat was the American equivalent of the British MTB and MGB and the German *Schnellboot*.

†The US Army's public relations department tried to persuade MacArthur to change the wording to 'We shall return' but he refused.

boots and with a 'von' in front of their names. Brigadier General Lord Gowrie, the Governor General of Australia, who had won the Victoria Cross in 1898 in Kitchener's Sudan Campaign, was much taken by MacArthur and conveyed his admiration to Churchill, who was always ready to give time to a swashbuckler. As the unkind might say, it takes one mountebank to recognize another. But if you have a hero, you might as well make use of him, and, rather than MacArthur being pensioned off (he was sixty-two), in April he was given command of South-West Pacific Area, with very few troops, no ships and not much in the way of air support. Those who assumed that MacArthur would be content to remain in what was effectively a non-job, however, would be proved wrong.

* * *

Prior to the withdrawal from the mainland, very little had been done to prepare Singapore island for defence. The plan had been to defend this vital naval base and Britain's richest colony in the East by holding the enemy on the Malay peninsula, and, when it became obvious that this could not be done, there were issues of morale amongst the civilian population and difficulties in recruiting civilian labour in preparation for a battle for and on the island itself. Singapore is twenty-seven miles from east to west and thirteen from north to south. It is separated from the mainland by the Strait of Johore, which varies from 2.5 miles wide at its eastern end to about 600 yards at the causeway. The town of Singapore itself is on the south of the island, while the naval base was on the north, five miles east of the causeway that crossed the Strait at its narrowest point. Singapore city had a peacetime population of around half a million, but this had been swollen by refugees to nearly twice that number, all of whom had to be fed and watered. Those fixed defences that did exist were mainly located along the southern coast as an attack from Malaya had not been considered likely. Those who insist that the fixed coastal defence guns sited around the naval base could not fire across the Strait have not looked at a map: the guns could fire at the Johore mainland but the majority of the ammunition was armour-piercing, designed to get through a ship's armour belt before exploding – the main threat was considered to be from a fleet – so when fired at a target on land they would drive deep into the ground before detonating to little or no effect. Six of the 9.5-inch guns did have high-explosive shells, but only thirty rounds per gun, not sufficient to deal with a determined attack across the Strait. There were four airfields on the island: three in the north which could be shelled from across the water and one in the south which, while safe from artillery fire, could be bombed and, as it was built on marshy ground, required more time than usual to repair bomb craters. It was planned to create temporary airstrips that could be used, but, as the civil labourers regularly (and possibly not unreasonably) deserted when subjected to air raids, nothing very much had been done. Wavell, from ABDA command, got into trouble from Churchill when he ordered all aircraft save a token force of eight Hurricanes and eight Buffaloes to depart for Sumatra in the Dutch East Indies, but to leave them where they were would only have resulted in their destruction, given Japanese superiority in the air.

General Percival considered that he could hold Singapore for a three-month siege, and for the battle he had 85,000 men. Fifteen thousand of those were administrative troops, but even so, when the last of the reinforcements arrived under heavy air attack on the night of 4/5 February, he had forty-five battalions of infantry – fifteen Indian, thirteen British, six Australian, four ISF, three Straits Settlement Volunteer Force (SSVF), two Gurkha and two Malay – supported by field artillery and two British machine-gun battalions and one Australian. All this was considerably more than the Japanese would throw against them, but many of the battalions were under-strength, many were packed with recruits who had undergone but the briefest of basic training, and those that had fought on the mainland were badly in need of rest and recuperation, which they could not get. Although the main threat was obviously from the Malayan mainland, the possibility of a seaborne landing to the south could not be neglected, and so Percival disposed his troops in three groups to cover the whole coastline. Northern Area, which ran from the Causeway fifteen miles east to just short of Changi, was the responsibility of the Indian 11 Division and the British 18 Division under Lieutenant-General Sir Lewis Heath; Western Area under Major-General Gordon Bennett with the Australian 8 Division and the Indian 44 Brigade ran from the Causeway west all the way round to the mouth of the Sungei Jurong on the south coast, a distance of about twenty miles; and Southern Area, twenty-five miles from the Jurong to west of Changi and including Singapore city, was defended by Fortress Command under Major-General Keith Simmons, who had been Commander British Troops Shanghai until the British withdrawal, with two Malay brigades and the Straits Settlements Volunteers Brigade, or three British, two Indian, two Malay, one ISF and

Emperor Hirohito

Adolf Hitler

Benito Mussolini

Joseph Stalin

Winston Churchill

Franklin D Roosevelt

Field-Marshal Wilhelm Keitel

Grand Admiral Erich Raeder

Reichsmarschall Herman Göring

General of Artillery Franz Halder

General of Infantry Erich von Manstein

General of Fliers Albert Kesselring

Grand Admiral Karl Dönitz

Field-Marshal Erwin Rommel

General Dwight D Eisenhower

Lieutenant-General Omar N Bradley

General Douglas MacArthur

Lieutenant-General Mark Clark

General Sir Alan Brooke

General Harold Alexander

General Sir Bernard Montgomery

General Sir William Slim

Admiral Chester W Nimitz

Admiral Sir Andrew Cunningham

Admiral Sir Bruce Fraser

Air Chief Marshal Sir Arthur Harris

Marshal of the Soviet Union Georgi Zhukov

Marshal of the Soviet Union Ivan Konev

Admiral Isoruko Yamamoto

General Hideki Tojo

Vice Admiral Chuichi Nagumo

General Tomoyuki Yamashita

three SSVF battalions. The Force Reserve was 12 Indian Infantry Brigade of one British and two Indian battalions, and in addition to the main defences some of the small outlying islands were occupied.

Civil labour was now virtually impossible to recruit and so the infantry had to dig trenches, create anti-tank obstacles and erect beach defences to prevent landing craft from coming ashore. Morale was not improved when the soldiery realized that most of the RAF had gone and the navy was in the process of departing, destroying all civilian small craft as it went. Rumour was rife, not least amongst the Chinese population, who were concerned that the island might not be defended at all and naturally worried about the prospects of a Japanese occupation, to the extent that Percival found it necessary to have a stirring call to arms published in the local papers, assuring the readership that the Japanese would be driven off. Percival now found himself inundated with messages from the Chiefs of Staff in London, who, urged on by Churchill, were trying to micro-manage the battle from 8,000 miles away. One of their more encouraging instructions was that Percival must deny Singapore to the enemy, but, if that were not possible, then a scorched-earth policy was to be implemented. Percival pointed out – again, one is amazed how he kept his temper – that it was not possible to do both: scorched earth would destroy what he needed to deny the island, and, as both he and the governor, Sir Shenton Thomas, felt somewhat guilty about having left the non-European population of Penang in the lurch, Percival was not prepared to destroy the water, electricity and sewage infrastructure. He did his best to destroy military facilities, not always successfully, and much of the reserve stocks of field-gun ammunition was eventually captured by the Japanese – they could not use it in their guns, but then neither could the British.

Air attacks increased, as did shelling from across the Strait. It was soon apparent that Japanese intelligence was well aware of the British dispositions, and on one occasion Radio Tokyo actually advised that an Australian field hospital be moved the following day. It was duly moved, shortly before the buildings in which it had been were shelled. The oil tanks at the naval base had been partially emptied into the rivers but, when set on fire by bombing, they retained enough oil to create a blinding black pall of smoke, adding to that from the burning rubber in dockside warehouses. Air reconnaissance was not possible and the only knowledge of Japanese dispositions came from observation and from patrols sent across the Strait. As the artillery stocks were limited, Percival restricted them to twenty rounds per gun per day, far insufficient to counter the Japanese gun positions.

General Yamashita's plan for the conquest of Singapore was for his 5 Division and 18 Division to force a landing on the north-west corner over a frontage of 4.5 miles, avoiding the naval base, where he considered the defences were strongest, using sixteen battalions with another five in reserve plus a tank battalion that would be ferried across the Strait on pontoons, while the Imperial Guards Division would create a diversion to make the British think that the attack would be against the Changi area to the north-east, following across twenty-four hours after the main attack. In the preceding days the Japanese, with the aid of an observation balloon, directed intense artillery fire on the island, mainly on the Causeway and areas other than the ones to be attacked. During the day of 8 February it was the turn of the north-west corner to be shelled, mainly in the area of 22 Australian Brigade. By nightfall most of the telephone wires had been cut and after a short lull the bombardment continued, now even more intensely. The defenders were completely bamboozled: they assumed that the fire would soon switch back to the Causeway and the north-east, where they had convinced themselves that the attack would come, and British artillery was not called upon to shell the likely assembly areas and forming-up places that the Japanese would have to use for a crossing. At around 2230 hours landing craft were seen approaching but there were no communications to the defenders' guns and so the landings were not immediately shelled. By the time the Australian infantry had been able to use prearranged Verey light signals to bring down defensive fire, it was too late and far too little.

The Australians put up a stout resistance but were vastly outnumbered and out of communication with the rest of the force. More Japanese landed, following the first wave, the defenders fell back and at 2200 hours on 9 February the Imperial Guards Division began to cross in the Causeway area; engineers immediately began to repair the damage done by British demolitions and were soon able to begin transporting tanks and more troops across it. The defenders fell back and by evening on 9 February the Japanese were firmly on the island and were not going to be dislodged. In the confusion one Australian brigade withdrew when it should not have done, allowing the Japanese to outflank and force the withdrawal of the rest of the division. On 10 February, General Wavell flew in from Java, was unhappy at what he saw, ordered immediate counter-attacks on the Japanese lodgements and, after instructing Percival that his men were to fight on to the last, flew out again. With him went the last of the Hurricanes and the one surviving Buffalo – their airstrips were increasingly under fire and fifth columnists had even managed to pour rubber latex into some fuel tanks. In fact, none of the units in the line was capable of carrying out a counter-attack: only fresh troops could have done it and there were none. The Australian division, with some honourable exceptions, was not far off collective insubordination and, when General Bennett tried to organize a counter-attack, faulty communications and the obvious hopelessness of the task only made matters worse. Percival ordered a withdrawal to a last-stand position around Singapore City and the remaining airfield. By the morning of 12 February, despite stubborn resistance by 2/9 Gurkhas and Australian anti-tank gunners, Japanese tanks had penetrated as far as Bukit Timah, where they captured large stocks of British ammunition, rations and fuel and were now only five miles from Singapore City. By this time discipline in some units was beginning to break down, and gangs of deserters were reported in the town, hiding out in abandoned buildings and looting houses whose occupants had fled, forcing themselves on board ships leaving for safer harbours or locking themselves in liquor stores for one last gigantic beano. The Australian prime minister, John Curtin, hearing from his civilian representatives in Singapore that large numbers of deserters had forced themselves on to ships leaving for Sumatra and well aware of the punishment laid down by military law for the offence of desertion in the face of the enemy, sent a telegram to Wavell insisting that no Australian soldiers were to be executed without the agreement of the government of Australia. None was. There were far too many miscreants for the Royal Military Police to control and the matter has rather been skated over in post-war official accounts, but it would appear that the rot started with men of the 1,900 individual reinforcements who arrived from Australia on 24 January, some with only two weeks' training and some with none at all, and with members of British and Australian administrative units based around the docks and in the city. It is, of course, a lot easier to desert from a stores depot or a reinforcement camp than from an infantry battalion in the field.

By the morning of 13 February it was clear to Percival that, despite the rantings of the prime minister in London, any prolonged resistance was out of the question. His reserve ammunition was in Japanese hands; the water-pumping station had been put out of action; fires were raging throughout the city; the Australian troops were convinced that they could do no more; swollen by refugees, the population in a three-mile radius from the town was over a million and civilian casualties had reached a stage where they could not be properly cared for. That day and the next the Japanese made further gains and on the morning of the 15th General Percival sent a deputation of the brigadier administration, the colonial secretary and an interpreter who walked through the British and Japanese lines with a white flag. They returned saying that the Japanese were prepared to discuss terms and that they would do so with General Percival at 1630 hours at the Ford Factory at Bukit Timah. During the interval Major-General Gordon Bennett brusquely informed a startled Brigadier Cecil Callaghan, his Commander Royal Artillery, that he was now in command of the Australian Imperial Force, departed for the docks, commandeered a junk and arrived in Australia twelve days later. He claimed that it was essential to take the lessons of Singapore and Malaya back to Australia to be incorporated in future training; his men considered that he had ratted on them. He never held a field command again.

Even today, sixty-seven years later, no Briton can look at the photograph of Percival's party walking to meet General Yamashita without a feeling of shame. It was not Percival's fault that he looked liked a frightened rabbit, with his buck teeth and knobbly knees, but he, accompanied by one officer carrying a Union Flag and another a white flag, all three exhausted, defeated, hopeless and helpless, broadcast an image from which the British Empire in the East never recovered. Percival signed the terms of unconditional surrender of all British troops in Malay and Singapore and, at 2200 hours on 14 February 1942, the fighting stopped. It was the biggest surrender of British troops in the whole of that nation's long military history, and it had been achieved in just thirty days – a third of the time that General Yamashita thought would be the minimum needed. In the whole campaign, including the fighting on the mainland, the British and Empire forces lost around 7,500 killed while eight of their generals, thirty-four brigadiers and around 120,000 others became prisoners of war. Japanese losses were said to be 3,500 killed.

At the time and subsequently it was easy to blame General Percival for the disaster. He was not an attractive figure and by making him the scapegoat no mud could stick to the politicians or the Chiefs of Staff. In fact, Percival was a competent and efficient soldier, by no means the desk-bound staff officer that his detractors claimed (he had won an MC in the first war and the IRA had put a bounty of £1,000 on his head, a huge sum in 1920); before the war he had protested that the defences of Singapore were inadequate and nobody listened. Once the *Prince of Wales* and the *Repulse* were sent out without carrier escort and as a direct result sunk before they could interfere with the Japanese invasion fleet in any way, the campaign was lost. In the fight for the Malayan peninsula the Japanese were just too good: experienced and battle-hardened, they easily outfought the raw recruits and the garrison troops that the British could put against them – reinforcements arrived too late and had no time to acclimatize or train for the conditions; the Japanese used tanks to great effect as mobile gun platforms, while the British had not a single tank; British aircraft were markedly inferior to those of the Japanese and, when some Hurricanes did arrive, it was far too late. Only by holding Johore could Singapore be defended, and there were insufficient shelters, a civil defence organization that did not work and faulty communications on the island. It is doubtful whether any other general could have done better: you simply cannot repair years of neglect, parsimony, overconfidence and lack of interest in a few months. The loss of Malaya and Singapore was and is a national disgrace and there is no point in pretending otherwise.*

* * *

With the fall of Hong Kong, good progress in the Philippines and the Malayan campaign well under way, the Japanese high command could now turn its attention to the Netherlands East Indies, that rich treasure house of raw materials desperately needed by Japanese industry. The task of capturing the vast archipelago was given to Lieutenant-General Hitoshi Imamura and his Sixteenth Army based in Saigon, in French Indo-China. His plan was to 'island hop' through Mindanao, the east coast of Dutch Borneo, the Celebes and Timor on one flank and Sumatra on the other, until the main island, Java, could be attacked. Despite heroic actions by the British, American, Australian and Dutch navies, Imamuru's plan proceeded much as he intended: the first landings on the east coast of Dutch Borneo and the Celebes took place on 11 January 1942 and by 20 February the Japanese were on Sumatra and Bali and it was obvious that an invasion was imminent. The Dutch had 25,000 regular troops on Java, but their equipment was antiquated and they were short of heavy weapons. The British contingent was B Squadron 3 Hussars with twenty-five light tanks, two experienced and

---

*So were the surrenders of Calais and Tobruk, but not on the same scale.

well-trained Australian infantry battalions fresh from the Middle East and three anti-aircraft artillery regiments. In addition, there was an American field artillery regiment.

On 27 February a combined British, American, Dutch and Australian striking force of two heavy and three light cruisers and nine destroyers under the command of the Dutch Admiral Doorman met the Japanese Admiral Takagi's two heavy and two light cruisers and fourteen destroyers. In the Battle of the Java Sea the Allies were convincingly defeated, with only four American destroyers, sent off to rearm in Australia, surviving. Admiral Doorman went down with his ship, and for all the loss of men and ships the Japanese invasion was delayed by only twenty-four hours. The next night the first Japanese landings took place on the east and west of Java. On 8 March the Dutch governor and commander-in-chief surrendered all Dutch forces in the Netherlands East Indies. The commanders of the British and American troops had little choice but to surrender too, which they did on 12 March.

* * *

By 6 May 1942 the Japanese had captured Hong Kong, Wake Island, all of Malaya and Singapore, the British colonies on Borneo, the Philippines and the Dutch East Indies. They were occupying Indo-China and Siam, had caused huge damage to the US Pacific Fleet at Pearl Harbor, had undertaken raids far into the Indian Ocean, sinking two British heavy cruisers and a light carrier off Ceylon (now Sri Lanka), and had killed, wounded or captured over a quarter of a million British and Empire, Dutch, American and Filipino soldiers, sailors and airmen and huge numbers of civilians and non-combatants, and they had done it all in a mere five months. Now the only place where Allied troops were still fighting the Japanese on land was in Burma, which had been invaded on 11 December 1941, and things there were not going at all well for the British.

10

THE MEDITERRANEAN WAR

AUGUST 1942–MAY 1943

On 3 August 1942, Churchill landed in Cairo to see at first hand what was happening in the North African theatre. With the prime minister were General Sir Alan Brooke, CIGS since December 1941, travelling in a different aircraft, and to confer with him at various meetings were Generals Wavell, who had flown in from India, and Auchinleck, who had come back from the Libyan Front, Vice-Admiral Sir Henry Harwood, Commander-in-Chief Mediterranean Fleet, Mr Richard Casey, Minister of State for the Middle East, and Field Marshal Jan Smuts, the prime minister of South Africa. Harwood, although only a junior rear admiral, had been promoted to vice-admiral and appointed to take over in the Mediterranean from Admiral Sir Andrew Cunningham, who had been sent off to Washington as the British naval representative at the Anglo-American staff talks. Harwood was a favourite of Churchill's who knew him from his time as Assistant Chief of Naval Staff at the Admiralty, and like so many of Churchill's personal appointments was not a success and would be removed in January 1943, when Cunningham again took up the command. Smuts was another chum of the British prime minister's. Originally a Boer leader, after the South African War he realized what side his bread was buttered on and became a staunch (and, to be fair, probably genuine) ally of the British. He first came to the attention of David Lloyd George, British prime minister during the First World War from December 1916. Lloyd George had been one of the most vociferous of the pro-Boer faction during the South African War and after it he took to Smuts as a fellow amateur strategist, using him as an alternative source of military advice and bringing him into the War Cabinet in 1917. Churchill too was attracted by Smuts, who had been South African prime minister from 1919 to 1924 and again since 1939; he had him made a field marshal in May 1941 and frequently sought the advice of this crafty politician. Considering that Smuts's military experience was limited to guerrilla skirmishes and German East Africa, he had an influence over British government thinking far beyond his abilities or experience, but this was all part of Churchill's method of running the war by kitchen cabinet, instead of leaving it to people who knew what they were about.

Politically, Churchill was in trouble. The Russians and the Americans were pressing for a second front and there was a strong lobby within the Labour Party that felt not enough was being done to help the USSR. The performance of British arms in Malaya, Singapore and Hong Kong contrasted unfavourably with the American performance in Bataan, which, while also a defeat, had a considerable tinge of glory and none of disgrace attached to it. In Burma the British were in headlong retreat, and the Indian Congress Party was demanding independence now. There had been a motion of no confidence in the running of the war in the House of Commons, and, although it was easily defeated, the fact that the subject had been debated at all was a worrying sign. Even Conservative MPs were muttering that the government was in trouble and would not survive another defeat or the defeat of the USSR. Churchill desperately needed a victory – any victory – and in North Africa, in the one theatre where one might be possible, the general in command was saying that no offensive action could be taken at this time. If Auchinleck would not budge, then he had to go and another general be found who would give Churchill what he wanted and needed.

Churchill and the British Chiefs of Staff had managed to persuade the Americans that an invasion of Fortress Europe in 1942 was not remotely possible: there were not enough men, not enough landing craft and no indication that the landing of four British divisions at Cherbourg, one option being canvassed, would lead to anything other than their annihilation. A cross-Channel raid in force against the port of Dieppe was being planned for later in August, but the British cannot have had much faith in its success, other than to show the Russians that they were doing something and reinforcing the impossibility of invasion in 1942 to the Americans. Instead Churchill had pressed hard for the Mediterranean to be the main focus of Allied efforts. Here would be the second front, here could Churchill's favourite ploy of attacking the 'soft under-belly' be implemented in the form of clearing the Axis forces from North Africa, and then invading Italy via Sicily. The Americans, still at this stage willing to accede to British experience, reluctantly agreed to go along with the Mediterranean option and the result was a plan named Operation Torch – Allied landings in French North Africa which, combined with an offensive along the Libyan coast, would squeeze the Germans and Italians into Tunisia and defeat them.

Torch could not happen, however, without the guarantee of an attack from Libya, one which should happen as soon as possible, but Auchinleck and his staff, backed up by the cold logic of ration strengths, ammunition returns, vehicle states and movement tables, insisted that an attack could not be mounted for at least six weeks, despite the prime minister's pleading. Churchill having decided that Auchinleck must go, Brooke acquiescing, the discussions centred around possible replacements. Auchinleck had sacked Ritchie and was commanding Eighth Army himself, as well as being Commander-in-Chief Middle East, and this situation could not continue – as Auchinleck readily accepted. To command the army, the obvious successor was 'Strafer' Gott, who had gone from command of a battalion to that of a corps in three years and had a reputation throughout Eighth Army for competence and originality. Brooke was unsure: he said that Gott was tired – he had been in the Western Desert since 1940 – and advanced the merits of his own protégé, Montgomery, who had been a fellow instructor at Staff College and had commanded a division under Brooke in the Battle of France, and was now in England as the commander designate of the British contingent for Operation Torch. Churchill, sure that a man with a nickname like 'Strafer'* must be just the chap to command an army and give him a victory, insisted and Gott was duly sent for. After talking to Gott on 5 August, Churchill was convinced and Gott was duly appointed. Gott looked at the ground, identified the Alam Halfa position as critical in the coming battles, embarked on an aircraft to fly back to Cairo, was shot down by the Luftwaffe and died. Brooke now got his way and Montgomery was sent for from England. We can discard Montgomery's typically ungenerous comments about Gott in his memoirs published in 1958,[56] in which he says that Gott's appointment would have been a disaster and that Gott was tired, worn out and needed a rest, a view supported by Brooke,[57] who thought Gott's death was 'the hand of God'. In fact, Gott was a man of great ability and perspicacity, humane and humorous and having the confidence of the whole army. Tired he may well have been, but with his desert experience he would surely have avoided making the mistakes in the use of armour that marked Montgomery's handling of the

---

*It came from the German *Gott strafe England*.

Second Battle of Alamein and would have established far better relations with the Americans than Montgomery ever could.

In discussions with Brooke, Auchinleck was agreeable to Montgomery taking over Eighth Army rather than Gott (or at least Brooke claimed he was – Auchinleck wrote no memoirs and published no diary) but Brooke claimed that he thought the two could not work together, and it seems very likely that Brooke's agreement to Churchill's sacking of the Auk (as Auchinleck was known) was to ensure a clear run for Montgomery. After toying with the notion of putting Brooke in as C-in-C Middle East, it was decided that Auchinleck's replacement was to be General the Honourable Sir Harold Alexander, who was, like Montgomery, of Irish extraction but, unlike Montgomery, a gentleman, a Guardsman, an Old Harrovian, as was Churchill, and, at fifty, one of the younger full generals in the British Army at that time.* That Brooke agreed so readily to Auchinleck's dismissal, egged on by Montgomery, who having got the job proceeded to blacken the Auk in every way he could, was fuelled largely by Brooke's propensity to advance the careers of his inner circle – those who had served with him or under him – but also by British Army resentment of their Indian Army contemporaries.

To be accepted for the Indian Army, an officer had to pass out of the Royal Military College Sandhurst in the top twenty or thirty in the order of merit, depending upon how many officers the Indian Army needed in a particular year. The Indian Army had no recruiting problems, was not plagued by the regular run of petty disciplinary offences to which the British soldier was prone and was almost continually on active service on the frontiers of India. An officer could live very well on his pay in India, and, as there were far fewer British officers in an Indian unit than in a British one, responsibility came much earlier than it would at home. Although it was perfectly normal for an officer of the British service to command an Indian division or corps, or even, like Wavell, to be Commander-in-Chief India, many British officers objected when the tables were turned and an Indian Army officer – such as Auchinleck – was appointed to a senior command that included British formations. Montgomery had desperately wanted to be commissioned into the Indian Army, but had not done well enough at Sandhurst (where he was back-termed for bullying) and had to settle for the Royal Warwickshire Regiment instead.

---

*Of whom, and of whose background and abilities, see Chapter 11.

Churchill suggested a splitting of Middle East Command, giving the Auk Persia – where an Indian Army expedition had occupied the oil fields to forestall any German attempt to seize them should their Caucasus attack succeed – and Iraq. Auchinleck declined – he knew very well that this was but a face-saving sop, and he considered it beneath the status of an ex-Commander-in-Chief India – and returned to India, for the moment unemployed. Fortunately for British arms, he would not be idle for long. While it cannot be disputed that the public face of a military command, the commander-in-chief of a major theatre of war, must be acceptable to the government of the day, politicians have no business in interfering with the workings of the military machine below the top level. That Churchill was allowed to order the sacking of Lieutenant-General Thomas Corbett, Auchinleck's Chief of the General Staff, acting Major-General Eric 'Chink' Dorman-Smith, the Deputy Chief of Staff, and Lieutenant-General William Ramsden, the commander of XXX Corps, was nothing short of a disgraceful abrogation of responsibility by Brooke. Corbett was an officer of the Indian Army whom Brooke had met once and to whom he had taken an instant dislike, and, although Dorman-Smith was not an Indian, he had served there and was a friend and confidant of Auchinleck. What cooked Dorman-Smith's goose was that, while a student at the Staff College in Camberley, he had fallen out in a big way with Montgomery, then an instructor, and had ostentatiously burned the notes from Montgomery's lectures immediately on completing the course. Brooke was well aware of that and now it was payback time. There was little sympathy for Dorman-Smith: he was largely responsible for Auchinleck's successful plan for First Alamein which had saved Egypt but if you are cleverer than your contemporaries and superiors it is as well not to let them know that, and Dorman-Smith could not resist poking fun at those with less intelligence than himself. Ramsden would eventually go for no greater sin than being disliked by Brigadier 'Freddie' de Guingand, former Director of Military Intelligence and now about to become Montgomery's chief of staff, who told Montgomery that Ramsden was useless, which he wasn't.

Alexander arrived in Cairo on 8 August and the formalities of the handover of the commander-in-chief's post were quickly concluded, with as much tact as the situation required. Churchill and his entourage departed for Moscow, and four days later Lieutenant-General Montgomery arrived and good manners went out the window. Montgomery was rude and dismissive to Auchinleck, who, as the changes in appointments were not due to take effect until 15 August, was still his superior in the chain of command as well as, of course, in rank and seniority. Montgomery then went off to the front, announced that he was not waiting until 15 August to take over but would do so immediately – a piece of staggering discourtesy – sent an ostentatious signal to Cairo ordering the immediate destruction of all withdrawal plans and went to sleep 'with an insubordinate smile… I was issuing orders to an army that someone else reckoned he commanded.'[58]

Along with de Guingand, whom he had known and liked in previous postings, Montgomery now began to recast the plans for the defence of the Alamein position and informed Alexander and London that he hoped to be able to go over to the offensive at the end of October, a month after the date that Auchinleck had been sacked for insisting upon. While the troop movements and thickening of the minefields to create a solid front in place of the series of defended boxes was going on, Montgomery embarked on a tour of his command to impress his personality on the army. He initially wore an Australian bush hat, on to which he affixed a variety of unit cap badges, and, when someone plucked up the courage to tell him that he cut a ridiculous figure so attired, he took to wearing a tank corps black beret with two badges, one of the general staff and one of the Royal Tank Regiment. To the former he was entitled, to the latter he was not. His tours of units became the stuff of the Montgomery legend. He would stand on the bonnet of a jeep, tell the men to gather round, take their hats off and relax and then harangue them with assurances that the days of retreat were over and that they were going to knock Rommel 'for six, right out of Egypt'. To the listeners the idea that the army commander should take them into his confidence was a novel concept and his visits generally went down well, but one soldier who was at the receiving end of several of Montgomery's pep talks said: 'it might have impressed the wartime-only boys, but we regulars could see right through him.'[59] To officers and in his written despatches to London, Montgomery unfailingly criticized all that had gone before him, and here was evident the beginnings of the egotism, vanity and ungenerous treatment of anybody not a Monty sycophant that was to become more marked as his life went on. He began to surround himself with a coterie of uncritical and admiring subordinates whose loyalty was unquestioned, many of them young and good-looking. It is inconceivable that Montgomery could have been a practising homosexual (then a serious offence in both civil and military law) but he may well have been a suppressed one, and it is noticeable that his liking for the handsome de Guingand declined markedly once the latter got married.

In strengthening the front all along its line rather than having a series of defended localities from which mobile forces would operate, Montgomery was probably right: Panzer Army Africa was far better at manoeuvre than the British and Montgomery hoped to make use of the perceived traditional ability of the British soldier to stick it out, even if those supposed qualities had not been displayed in any great measure in Hong Kong or Singapore. On 30 August, Rommel made one last attempt to reach the Nile Delta by hooking round to the south of the British line to cut the coast road – as Dorman-Smith had predicted. The thrust was beaten off by infantry and armour dug in on Alam Halfa Ridge, as Dorman-Smith had said it should be. Now Rommel had run out of options: his command was not being reinforced; he had lost air superiority to the RAF; rations had been cut; dysentery, scabies and lice infestation were rife and the sick rate was rocketing, even amongst the Germans. He was short of everything from bullets to socks to petrol; rations of food and water had been reduced and Berlin had effectively written him off while forbidding him to withdraw. Worse, nineteenth months of desert soldiering had caught up with the *Generalfeldmarschall* and he was evacuated to recuperate in Germany via Rome, where he was assured of immediate improvements to his logistic problems, and Berlin, where Göring assured him that, contrary to what he may have thought that he had seen, the Luftwaffe and not the RAF ruled the skies. The only person who listened to what he had to say was Hitler, who promised him some ferries that had proved relatively immune to torpedo attack, some of the new Panzer Mk VI (Tiger) tanks and more artillery. Rommel was then unwise enough to announce at a public meeting that his army stood but fifty miles from Alexandria and that they had not come all that way only to go back again. In temporary command of Panzer Army Africa was General of Panzer Troops Georg Stumme, fresh from commanding a motorized corps in Russia and being court-martialled over the loss of the Case Kremlin plans.*

For Montgomery, on the other hand, things could only get better. With the double layer of Alexander and Brooke to protect him from Churchillian interference; with men, supplies, aircraft and vehicles including the new

---

*See Chapter 8.

Sherman tank arriving almost daily, he was able to build up Eighth Army and prepare it to take the offensive. By the middle of October the British had reorganized Eighth Army into three corps: X Corps consisting of two armoured divisions, XIII Corps of one armoured and three infantry divisions and a Free French infantry brigade, and XXX Corps of five infantry divisions and an armoured brigade. This amounted to 220,476 men in three armoured divisions and an armoured brigade group, seven infantry divisions (three British, one including a Greek brigade, one Indian, one Australian, one New Zealand and one South African) and a Free French brigade, 1,348 tanks, 856 artillery field guns and 1,403 anti-tank guns.[60] Opposed to them were 112,000 men (50,000 Germans and 62,000 Italians) in three armoured and eight infantry divisions with 560 tanks, 500 field guns and 850 anti-tank guns. Of the Axis tanks, only 220 were German and of those only thirty-eight were Mk IVs with a 75mm gun, whereas the British had 246 American Grants and 285 Shermans, all with 75mm guns.

The plan for Second Alamein – or the Battle of El Alamein as it became known, First Alamein being conveniently forgotten as not being Montgomery's – was for XIII Corps in the south to mount diversionary attacks to prevent the Axis from moving troops to the north, where the main British effort would be. There XXX Corps would attack on a four-division frontage and clear two corridors through the mines to allow the armour of X Corps to come through and to deploy to protect XXX Corps's infantry as they cleared the German and Italian infantry positions. Once that had been done, the British armour would move against the Axis tanks and Eighth Army would then move over to pursuit. The battle would start with a night attack during the full moon, and would be preceded by a massive artillery bombardment.

Montgomery was not an original thinker and his tinkerings with Auchinleck's plan were more cosmetic – to indicate his disapproval and contempt for all that had gone before – than substantive, but he had the ability to explain the most complicated plan in simple terms. By 24 October, D-Day for the battle, all his subordinates knew exactly what they had to do – even if some did not approve. Major-General 'Cal' Renton, commanding 7 Armoured Division, thought the proposed employment of his tanks in the southern battle was wrong and told the newly arrived XIII Corps commander, Lieutenant-General Brian Horrocks, just that. Horrocks was another of Montgomery's favourites, brought out to North Africa at the army commander's behest, and Renton was given an almighty rocket and told to get on with it. No doubt his subsequent sacking after the battle was nothing at all to do with his being proved right.

At 2145 hours on the night of 23/24 October 1942, Operation Lightfoot began with eighty-two field and medium guns opening a bombardment that must have reminded the older soldiers on both sides of the Western Front in the last war. Augmented by RAF bombers dropping high explosive on German and Italian positions, the bombardment became a creeping barrage behind which the infantry moved out to cross the minefields and take up position for the engineers to clear the armoured corridors before first light. At first the advance went well, particularly in the northern sector, the responsibility of the Australians, but soon difficulties became apparent. Navigating officers – subalterns with compasses – were killed, map-reading in the featureless plain became difficult; visibility despite the full moon was reduced to a few yards by the dust kicked up by exploding shells; there were arguments as to what was the British artillery barrage and what was Italian or German defensive fire; and traffic congestion ensued as follow-through battalions and heavy weapons tried to come up. The Australians got to pretty well where they should have been except for the extreme northern flank; the Highland division took most of their objectives but at very heavy cost; the New Zealanders got well beyond their stop line and then had to come back through their own artillery; the South Africans were held up by particularly accurate artillery fire but did reach their objectives on the extreme south of the line. The infantry had done reasonably well but had fallen behind schedule, and there were delays in getting corridors open for the tanks. The Axis troops held a forward outpost line but had their main defensive positions well back, out of range of the immediate fire support available to the attackers. Well-organized counter-attacks pressed home with determination and minefields that had not been detected all militated against the British, and, while infantry could survive at the bottom of a forward slope if they could dig in before daylight, tanks would be sitting ducks. When Major-General Gatehouse, commanding 10 Armoured Division, objected to being told to advance unsupported through a minefield against a German anti-tank screen that had not yet been cleared, he was told to get on with it and his leading regiment was virtually wiped out. After the battle he was sacked, as eventually was his corps commander, Lieutenant-General Herbert Lumsden. Arguing with Monty did not pay. A cavalryman who had played a major part in the mechanization of that arm between the wars, Lumsden had ridden in several

Grand Nationals and had won the Grand Military Gold Cup in 1926. An Old Etonian of independent means, he saw no need to kow-tow to Montgomery and frequently argued with him. He had particularly offended the army commander by voicing his objections to Montgomery's entirely unauthorized and unearned wearing of the black beret of the Royal Tank Regiment, and this alone would have got him his cards eventually.

Despite the British plan not going exactly as intended, the artillery bombardment had destroyed large numbers of German and Italian guns and much of their communications, although the death of General Stumme early on in the battle when he ventured too far forward to see what was happening and ran into Australian machine-gun fire did not have the traumatic effect that it might have done in a British formation – German staff officers were trained to cope with dead or missing commanders. Perhaps if Rommel had been there the British would have had a lot more difficulty than they did, but by the time he arrived, on the night of 25 October, Eighth Army had established itself inside the Axis defended area and was not going to be dislodged. Ultra transcripts of Axis radio traffic told Montgomery exactly what Rommel intended to do next and it was soon obvious that, pedestrian and unimaginative though the British might be, they ruled the skies, had no fuel shortage and hugely outnumbered their sick and logistically impaired opponents.

The British attacked again on the night of 29 October, this time on a one-division front, and then again on the night of 1/2 November in Operation Supercharge, a major offensive led by the New Zealand Division with 1 Armoured Division in support. To deal with those mines not yet cleared, the advance was preceded by thirty-two Scorpions, old Matilda II infantry tanks with flail drums attached in front. The drums revolved and the flails – lengths of chain – struck the ground in front, exploding the mines. The idea was a good one, and applied to Churchill tanks in Normandy later in the war worked well, but here the tanks were just too old and too unreliable and many were blown up when they broke down or the flails failed. There were communication difficulties between the infantry and the tanks, navigational failures and traffic gridlock, but by 2 November Rommel had come to the conclusion that the overwhelming British superiority in materiel gave him no choice but to withdraw. By this stage the DAK was down to twenty-five tanks and the army had lost 50 per cent of its German infantry and 40 per cent of its artillery. OKW in Berlin at first tried to get him to stand fast but eventually relented and Rommel began to disengage. The British began a cautious pursuit and on

4 November the commander of the DAK, General of Panzer Troops Wilhelm Ritter von Thoma, was captured with the rearguard.

Once the Alamein battle was over, Eighth Army lost one of its better divisions when the Australian prime minister, John Curtin, concerned as to the approaching Japanese, requested its return to Australia. In addition, the South African division was pulled out to be converted to armour, and by the end of the year two British divisions, 8 Armoured and 44 Infantry, would be disbanded when the logistics tail, getting longer and longer as the British moved westwards, was unable to supply them. The men would be used as reinforcements for formations still in being.

Alamein was duly trumpeted as a great British victory and Montgomery was promoted to full general and received a knighthood. Church bells were rung in Britain and Churchill talked about the end of the beginning. As it was, the British had consistently been beaten by the Germans, in Norway, in France, in Greece, in Crete. The Dieppe Raid on 19 August 1942 had been a disaster: 6,000 Canadian and British troops had been deployed and less than 2,000 returned, leaving all their tanks and most of their heavy equipment behind, and, despite much rubbish being talked then and since about it being a necessary rehearsal for the invasion of Europe in 1944, the raid achieved nothing except to prove that any such invasion could not happen in 1942; in Hong Kong and Singapore the performance of British troops compared unfavourably with that of the Americans in Wake Island and in the Philippines. Alamein was a British victory, but it almost stalled in the first twenty-four hours, had to be rethought and only just succeeded. Eighth Army could only produce results in a tightly controlled and well-rehearsed set-piece operation. For all that, it was the only British victory for many a long day, even if the success of ten British divisions against eleven Axis was not the turning point of the war, as many have claimed. Alamein and Stalingrad were happening at the same time, and the turning point of the war was surely determined by the twenty German divisions fighting seventy-five Russian at Stalingrad.

Now, however, was the time to cut Rommel's forces off, trap them in Egypt and destroy them. Unfortunately for the British, it was not to be. They were far too slow; their attempts to hook behind the retreating Panzer Army Africa were too hesitant; a break in the weather brought driving rain and low cloud and restricted flying, prevented vehicles from moving off roads and disrupted radio communication. Above all, Rommel might have been beaten but he still had an army in being, bruised and battered though it was, and its withdrawal was conducted with skill and determination. On the morning of 8 November, Rommel's troops were closing up to the Halfaya Pass at the Egyptian border and, although the weather had improved sufficiently for him to be subjected to regular air attacks, there was still no sign of the pursuing Eighth Army. Then, that same day, 2,000 miles to the west, British and American troops began landing at Casablanca, Oran and Algiers in Morocco and Algeria, both colonies loyal to the Vichy regime.

The Allied landings in French North Africa, successively named Gymnast, Super Gymnast and finally Torch, were the result of a not altogether happy compromise between American and British strategic aims. From April 1942 the planners of the two nations had been endeavouring to produce a common, coordinated strategy that would ensure no dispersion of effort. All agreed that this was needed; the problem was that both parties had different ideas as to how it should be achieved. The Americans, having accepted the Germany First policy, despite the reservations of Admiral King,* now wanted to get on with it, and proposed a landing in northern France in 1942, possibly around Boulogne. This would take pressure off the Russians – and at the time the proposal was first made it looked as if the Russian front might collapse – and attacking German-occupied Europe head-on was the obvious thing to do. For their part, the British knew very well the most that the Allies could land in 1942 would be six divisions, at least four of them British, and that with over twenty German divisions in Western Europe such a lodgement could not possibly be sustained nor expanded. There were insufficient landing craft to get even six divisions ashore in one lift, and in any case after September the weather in the Channel would make any large-scale adventure there very risky indeed. The Americans thought that the lack of landing craft was a mere excuse – this was a technical problem which could easily be overcome – but as the troops involved would be mostly British (there were as yet insufficient American troops in England for them to take the leading role) they had, unwillingly, to acquiesce. Eventually, in what was

---

*Admiral Ernest J. King, at this stage combining the posts of Commander-in-Chief US Fleet and Chief of Naval Operations and a member of the Combined Chiefs of Staff Committee, never actually said that he disagreed with the Germany First policy, only that the Pacific was being neglected because of it. A man of great ability and considerable influence, albeit intolerant and with a weakness for other men's wives and alcohol, he was considered unnecessarily Anglophobic.

known as the Marshall Plan, both sides signed up to an intention to land in Europe in 1942 if possible (Operation Sledgehammer) and, if that were not achievable, a landing in 1943 (Operation Roundup) with thirty US divisions and eighteen British, supported by 6,000 aircraft.

Despite agreeing to the plan as a statement of intent, and no doubt crossing their fingers behind their backs as they signed, the British were in fact much more concerned with the shores of the Indian Ocean and the Mediterranean: the US Navy's victory at the Battle of Midway in early June, when four Japanese carriers were sunk for the loss of only one American, was good news for the Asian war, but at this stage things in Burma were going from bad to worse, the situation in North Africa was giving cause for concern and the British had given vague hints to the Russians about a second front in late 1942, while stressing that there were no promises. In July 1942 Churchill informed Roosevelt that, despite their best intentions, the British could not take part in a proposed landing in Cherbourg and the Channel Islands in 1942, or anywhere else in Europe that year, although he held out hopes of one in 1943. This caused a major crisis in Anglo-American relations: the British, despite their protestations, were reneging on the common strategy agreement; their performance so far was unimpressive and General Marshall and Admiral King unsuccessfully pressed their president to leave the British to it in Europe and the Mediterranean and concentrate on the Pacific.

In the summer of 1942 the Allied generals, admirals and air marshals were not helped in their planning by Churchill's flights of fancy, which ranged from simultaneous landings in Denmark, Holland and Belgium to an invasion of northern Norway or, if an invasion of northern France was decided upon in 1943, a series of landings all around the coast, with the intention of forcing the Germans to disperse their resources to defend multiple locations. The planners were horrified – this would force the Allies to disperse their resources too, and it made no operational sense. Another matter that sowed distrust was the development of atomic fission. The British had been working on this for some time and, by the summer of 1942, the scientists involved were confident that a weapon of enormous power could be developed. The expense of building the necessary plant to produce such a weapon was, however, going to be so enormous that it was decided to pool knowledge with the Americans, who had also been undertaking research in the field but lagged behind the British. Under the codename of 'Tube Alloy', the British work to date was handed over to the Americans and a facility to develop a bomb was built in the Nevada desert. To begin with, despite the agreement to develop jointly, the Americans would not divulge details of the project's progress, citing various laws which restricted the passage of military information to a foreign power. Eventually, in late 1943, the matter was resolved to British satisfaction, but the atomic relationship was not one to foster mutual trust.

The British accepted that, while they had persuaded a reluctant Roosevelt and Marshall that no major cross-Channel offensive could take place in 1942, they nevertheless had to be seen to be doing something, particularly under pressure from Marshall, who wanted US troops to gain some battle experience. Churchill had always favoured Operation Gymnast, a plan for a landing on the north-west coast of Africa, considered but never implemented, and he now resurrected this as Super Gymnast. The Americans were suspicious: was this all about British imperial ambitions to control the Mediterranean? Was it an excuse to avoid doing anything in Europe? They were not interested at first, but as they realized that the British were not prepared to get involved in anything else in 1942, they reluctantly went along with it, eventually having to accept that, if Gymnast, now renamed Torch, happened, then that ruled out a major landing in Europe for 1943 as well – which the British knew very well. While Torch did favour British interests over Allied ones, the British were right to veto a landing in Europe in 1942, and in 1943 as well. In the interests of Allied solidarity and to keep the USA on side, they had to make some show of being interested in the Marshall Plan, but the British had considerable experience of opposed landings – much of it disastrous – and any attempt to invade Europe in 1942 or 1943 with the troops and landing craft available at the time would have risked a massive military and propaganda defeat, and, once they were thrown back into the sea, there could be no knowing when the Allies would be ready to try again. General Sir Alan Brooke was not always right in his strategic appreciations, but this time he surely was.

Operation Torch would coincide with an attack – a successful attack, it was hoped – by Eighth Army from Egypt, as this would ensure that Axis eyes were looking east and not towards the other end of the Mediterranean. There would be three landing areas, West Task Force at Casablanca on the Atlantic coast of Morocco, Central Task Force at Oran in Algeria and East Task Force at Algiers. Here arose a major disagreement between the Americans and the British: the British wanted to land near to Tunis in order to give Rommel and the Axis as little room for manoeuvre as possible, whereas the Americans were concerned that German and Italian submarines would make any landing east of Algiers too risky. The American view prevailed, although in hindsight the Royal Navy could almost certainly have got a task force ashore somewhere in the Tunis area. The Western Task Force would have 35,000 American troops commanded by Major-General George S. Patton, last seen chasing Bonus Marchers out of Washington, and would be mounted from Norfolk, Virginia, and escorted by the US Navy; Central Force troops would also be American, 37,000 men commanded by Major-General Lloyd Fredendall, mounted from the UK and escorted by the Royal Navy; and Eastern Force, also mounted from the UK and under the care of the Royal Navy, would consist of 10,000 Americans and 10,000 British troops, initially commanded by the American Major-General Charles Ryder, who would hand over to the British Lieutenant-General Kenneth Anderson. These somewhat unusual command arrangements were necessitated by the belief that the French were unlikely to oppose American troops, whereas they almost certainly would fight hard against their traditional enemy, who had moreover attacked their fleet in 1940. Once the assault landing by the Americans had succeeded, the British would then take over. The overall commander would be an American, the now Lieutenant-General Dwight D. Eisenhower, currently commander of all US troops in the European theatre, which consisted of those of the continuing build-up of American troops in Britain, codenamed Operation Bolero, with Major-General Mark Clark as his deputy and Brigadier-General (major-general from December 1943) Walter B. Smith (always known as Bedell Smith) as his chief of staff, both Americans. The overall naval commander would be Admiral Sir Andrew Cunningham RN and the air commander Air Vice-Marshal Welsh RAF, with Brigadier-General Doolittle commanding the USAAF component.

In Berlin, German intelligence had been picking up rumours about an Allied landing somewhere in the Mediterranean and Eisenhower's promotion to lieutenant-general in July 1942 was taken as a prelude to a second front somewhere. In August, General Juin, the French Commander-in-Chief North Africa, dismissed rumours that a landing would be made in his bailiwick, and various intelligence reports suggested Portugal, Spanish Morocco, Dakar or between Tripoli and Benghazi in Libya. In the same month General Vigón, now Spanish Minister for Aviation and an old chum of the Germans from the days of their joint planning to take Gibraltar, said that he expected a landing in Tunis or Algeria, probably in October. For its part, the German navy concluded that the likely objective would be the Libyan coast, while the

Italians worried that any landing might be aimed directly at them, and the German army assumed that the increased British convoy traffic was intended to reinforce Malta. But the source that got it right was one in the Vatican, who in September told the Germans that there would be a landing in Algeria between mid-October and mid-November.

Allied intelligence about the likely reaction of the French was mixed. The Free French, ever the optimists, claimed that the French colonial administrations were only waiting for an opportunity to declare for de Gaulle, whereas British intelligence was less sure, citing the French tendency to obey whoever was in charge. The Allies put little faith in de Gaulle and he was not told of the operation until after the landings had begun, largely because his Free French organization leaked like a sieve with very large holes: anything told to the Free French got to the Germans eventually, not through deliberate betrayal but through a general lack of security, loose talk in bars and clubs, and in letters that evaded the censor. In the event, despite the approach of over 300 warships, including a number of the new escort carriers, merchant ships converted into small aircraft carriers by the addition of a flight deck, and 370 transports carrying over 100,000 men, local surprise was complete, but the French did not roll over and invite *les Anglo-Saxons* to tickle their collective tummy. Pétain had made clear to Roosevelt in a telegram that the French would fight if attacked, and those few French officers who tried to take their men over to the Allies were quickly disarmed and arrested. With the exception of Algiers, where resistance was quickly overcome, fighting was fierce with around 1,400 Americans and 700 French being killed, and the French battleship *Jean Bart* in Casablanca harbour being badly damaged by Allied gunfire. On 10 November, General Juin agreed to a ceasefire but insisted on referring the proposal to Admiral Darlan, the Commander-in-Chief of all French Armed Forces, who was in Algiers in a private capacity to see his son, who had contracted polio. After some negotiation, Darlan agreed to a truce but his decision was repudiated by the French government, and, when he tried to cancel the ceasefire arrangements, he was promptly arrested by the Americans. Despite not being convinced of the success of the Allied landings, the Germans reacted swiftly, moving troops into the hitherto unoccupied part of France and airlifting 17,000 German and Italian troops into the French protectorate of Tunisia, where the French minister-resident, Admiral Estéva, interpreted Pétain's claim that French troops would fight if attacked as applying only to the Allies and not to the Germans, with whom his administration cooperated wholeheartedly. Meanwhile, Germany made another unsuccessful attempt to persuade Franco to bring Spain into the war, the Italians occupied Corsica and Vichy France broke off diplomatic relations with the United States.

Admiral Darlan now considered that, with the German occupation of Vichy France, he no longer owed any loyalty to the Pétain regime and declared for the Allies.* His efforts to persuade the French fleet in Toulon to come over came to naught, although the admiral in command did at least scuttle his ships before the Germans could take them over. The Allies then set up a client French regime in North Africa headed by Darlan as high commissioner, but the admiral was promptly assassinated on Christmas Eve 1942 by a French student who may or may not have been an agent of de Gaulle's Free French and has been claimed by some conspiracy theorists to have been put up to it by the British. Whatever the truth of the assassination, the trial and execution of the perpetrator were carried out in remarkably quick time and General Henri Giraud, always the Americans' preferred candidate for leadership of the Free French, became high commissioner and Commander-in-Chief. With the Allies safely ashore, the British took the port of Bougie, 120 miles east of Algiers, by an unopposed seaborne landing on 11 November and Bône, another 120 miles east, by a combined sea and parachute landing on 12 November. The British 78 Division began to disembark at Bône on 15 November and the Americans relieved the British at Bougie on the 17th. Now for the push east, as the various task forces coalesced into First Army, commanded by Anderson and containing the US II Corps commanded by Major-General Lloyd Fredendall, the British V Corps commanded by Lieutenant-General C. W. Allfrey and the French XIX Corps commanded by Major-General Marie-Louis Koëltz. The immediate task was to defeat the Axis forces in Tunisia and then to squeeze the retiring Panzer Army Africa between Eighth Army and themselves.

History has not treated Kenneth Anderson kindly. He had served on the Western Front in the first war and had seen considerable active service between the wars before commanding a brigade under Montgomery in the Battle of France and then a division and a corps in the UK. His command of First Army was fraught with difficulty: Fredendall did not like the British and nor did his

---

*His difficulties were added to by his hatred of the British, who had killed his great-great-grandfather at Trafalgar in 1805.

eventual replacement, Patton. Koëltz also disliked the British, perhaps with more reason, and refused to accept any orders from Anderson unless they had been cleared though Juin first, and Juin insisted on clearing everything through Giraud. His American troops had no battle experience, his French troops were lacking modern equipment and had only just turned their coats from being loyal Pétainistes, and his British troops had been sitting around on anti-invasion duty in England. The Supreme Commander, Eisenhower, was in Algiers and his representative in Tunisia, Major-General Lucian Truscott, established himself so far away from Anderson that it took a minimum of four hours to get from one headquarters to the other. Anderson's main problem, however, was not the chaotic command arrangements, eventually rectified at the Casablanca Conference in January 1943 when he also got a second British corps, but his fellow army commander, Montgomery. When serving under Montgomery, Anderson had obviously not tugged his forelock sufficiently hard, for Montgomery did all he could, in letters to Brooke and in comments to visitors, to disparage Anderson, an exercise he continued when the North African campaign was over and subsequently in his memoirs. One can only assume that Montgomery's paranoia was now such that anyone who might possibly be a rival must be destroyed: any glory going was to be his and he was not prepared to share it with anyone. The commander of V Corps, Lieutenant-General Allfrey, would also eventually suffer, although he would last until Italy before being sacked in March 1944 on Montgomery's departing recommendation.

Despite the swift German response to the Torch landings, OKH in Berlin were inclined to accept that North Africa was a write-off, and Field Marshal Albert Kesselring, Commander-in-Chief South, thought that the Italian navy should be used to evacuate all Axis troops to Italy. Hitler, on the other hand, having initially been relatively uninterested in African adventures, now decided that Tunisia was 'the cornerstone of our conduct of the war on the southern flank of Europe'[61] and he took note of Mussolini's concerns that an Axis defeat in North Africa would mean unfettered Allied control of the Mediterranean and hence an invasion of the Italian mainland. The main focus of German strategy would remain the Russian front but Tunisia must be held 'at all costs' – a form of words frequently sent down from on high and one which is particularly depressing to soldiers because it usually means that they are destined to be killed or to spend a considerable time in a prison camp. The Axis troops in Tunisia were to be formed into Fifth Panzer Army, under Colonel-General Hans-Jürgen von Arnim, with, unusually, because

German doctrine did not include such appointments, Lieutenant-General Heinz Ziegler as his second-in-command. In fact, it would not be much more than a corps, with one German armoured division (10 Panzer), and two divisions of infantry, one German and one Italian. That it was named an army and commanded by an officer of a rank normally found in command of three or four times as many troops was pure propaganda. It did include a company of the latest German tanks, the much-feared Mk VI Tiger, but, despite the rapid initial build-up, it could only be reinforced with great difficulty, anything sent from Italy having to run the gauntlet of Allied naval vessels and air strikes.

On 25 November, Anderson's First Army began to push east in three columns, using 78 Division augmented by tanks from the US 1 Armoured Division, and that day met the Germans at Medjez El Bab, about twenty-five miles from Tunis, while an American tank column penetrated as far as the airfield at Djedeida, only fifteen miles from Tunis, before being forced to withdraw when German anti-aircraft gunners using their 88mm guns in the anti-tank role began to pick them off. The Germans withdrew skilfully by groups and began to defend along what they called the Tunisian Bridgehead, centred on Djedeida airfield. On 28 November, Kesselring visited Tunis, decided that the bridgehead was too small and ordered that it was to be expanded using the arriving 10 Panzer Division. At 0705 hours on the morning of 1 December sixty-four German tanks, including two Tigers, moved off. Supported by low-flying aircraft, they punched east out of Djedeida airfield and by 10 December they had pushed the Allies back east of Medjez el Bab, where they encountered stiff resistance from American armour and British infantry. The size of the bridgehead was now considered sufficient; von Arnim and his deputy arrived in Tunis that day and Fifth Panzer Army now went into defence along a 100-mile line from the north coast through Djefna south-east to Pont du Fahs to Gabes on the east coast. The north was held by a German infantry division, the centre by 10 Panzer Division and the south by the Italian Superga Division. For the time being, the Allies concentrated on reinforcing their army and positioning troops and guns for a major attack intended to capture Tunis. The attack was originally intended for 16 December but the weather broke on that day and Anderson postponed his D-Day until 24 December. As that date approached, however, Eisenhower decided to hold on the Tunisian front and concentrate instead on Eighth Army's operations in Libya.

Eighth Army had been making its plodding way along the North African coast. Four times Montgomery attempted to cut Rommel off and four times when the trap closed there was nobody in it. Experienced desert hands recommended wide and deep flanking movements before then closing in to the coast, perhaps as far away as Tobruk, but Montgomery would have none of it. He had got his victory and he was not going to risk throwing it away. On 11 November, Eighth Army reached the Egyptian border and on the 13th entered Tobruk once more; on 15 November the advance units were pushing towards Derna and on the 20th they occupied Benghazi, last seen by the British when they were chased out of it in April 1941. On 23 November the British had got as far as El Agheila, but now they had outrun their supply lines and had to halt to allow the logistic units to catch up. Rommel was ordered by the *Commando Supremo* in Rome to hold this position, shown on Axis maps as the Marsa Al Borayquah line. Rommel was well aware that this was not a practical proposition. Of his original three Italian corps, X Corps of three divisions no longer existed, XXI Corps was down to one infantry and two artillery battalions, and, of XX Armoured Corps's one motorized and one armoured division, one regiment with no tanks remained. Of the DAK, there was not much left. The armoured units could provide one weak regiment between them; 90 Light Division could muster but one and a half battalions; 146 Infantry Division had two battalions of infantry (out of an original nine) and two batteries of artillery, and the Luftwaffe Parachute Brigade had lost half its men and all its heavy weapons. Rommel was being told to defend the indefensible against 420 British tanks, when out of an original establishment of 371 he had but thirty-five left. On the night of 22/23 November he flew to Hitler's headquarters in East Prussia and told the Führer bluntly – 'too bluntly' he later said – that the situation was untenable. He was subjected to a tongue-lashing, including the accusation that Panzerarmee Afrika had thrown away its weapons, and told that North Africa must be held, 'for political reasons'. Fortunately for Rommel, the British halt to allow supplies to catch up lasted a lot longer than Rommel would have allowed his own army, and when Montgomery was ready to move again, with preliminaries on 12 December and the main offensive beginning on the 14th, Rommel disposed of eighty-eight tanks, and had prepared a defence line at Buyarat further west to which he could withdraw. Once again, Rommel was bombarded with 'resist to the last' calls from the Duce in Rome, but, as these were usually combined with appeals not to risk the Italian infantry,

Rommel was able to justify what he knew was his only option – to withdraw tactically causing as much delay to the British as possible. When the main British attack came in, it found only mines and barbed wire – Rommel had slipped away once again.

By 18 December what was left of Panzerarmee Afrika was in the Buyarat line, which had been prepared by 164 Division and several hundred Italian labourers. Minefields and wire obstacles there were, but the number of men and armoured vehicles to cover the forty miles considered essential to avoid encirclement were pitifully few, and Rommel began to withdraw his Italian infantry, followed by his armour, back to the Tarhuna-Homs area once the British attack developed. When the British duly turned their attention to Tarhuna-Homs on 19 January, Rommel again delayed as long as he could and then withdrew to Tripoli. When on 23 January German reconnaissance confirmed that Eighth Army was embarking on a sweep to the south to encircle him, Rommel abandoned Tripoli that night and fell back towards the Mareth Line. The Mareth Line dated from the first war, and, although its defence works had been largely destroyed by the Italians, they were now being put back into a habitable condition. There, with the sea to his left and the mountains to his right, Rommel could realistically expect to fight a delaying action to stop Eighth Army from getting into Tunisia. As he had only 500 lorries, a mix of Italian, German and captured British vehicles, it took ten days to ferry the Italian infantry back, but he was helped by Montgomery ordering another halt and a victory parade after the occupation of Tripoli, which Churchill visited on 3 February. On 15 February, Panzerarmee Afrika was firm in the Mareth Line and the long retreat from Alamein was over.

Churchill's visit to Tripoli came as he returned from the Symbol Conference, which was held in a cordoned-off and depopulated suburb of Casablanca from 14 January 1943. There, Churchill and Roosevelt met to discuss Allied strategy after the fall of North Africa. Stalin was invited but declined owing to what was happening on the Volga as the Battle for Stalingrad rose to its climax. Present were the British and American Chiefs of Staff and Generals Eisenhower and Alexander, with Admiral Lord Louis Mountbatten as a recent addition to the British team. Included in the British Chiefs of Staff, to the irritation of the other members, as Chief of Combined Operations at Churchill's behest, Mountbatten was regarded with great suspicion, then and later. With tenuous royal connections of which he made much, and a tendency to drive any ship he commanded into a collision with something else afloat, Mountbatten had undoubted personal courage and this, combined with his tactical rashness and flair for publicity and self-aggrandizement, made him just the chap to appeal to Churchill, who arranged instant promotion from commander to commodore and then to vice-admiral, lieutenant-general and air marshal at the age of forty-two, giving him some clout in all three services and infuriating their more conservative senior officers.

At Casablanca the arguments over priorities were once again thrashed out: Admiral King for the Pacific, General Marshall for France; General Brooke for Sicily, Admiral Mountbatten for Sardinia. In the teeth of American suspicion that British imperial interests were driving the discussions, as indeed they were, Churchill and Brooke got their way, and it was agreed that the next step would be an invasion of Sicily as a prelude to landing in Italy. Meanwhile, the build-up of American troops in the UK would continue with a view to a landing in France in, almost certainly now, 1944. Perhaps as a sop to the Americans for agreeing to Sicily, Churchill proposed an American overall commander for North Africa. As there were twelve British divisions in North Africa and only three American ones, the suggestion of Eisenhower as Allied commander-in-chief soothed any ruffled transatlantic feathers. Once Montgomery made contact with First Army in Tunisia, 18 Army Group containing both armies would come into being, commanded by Alexander, who would report to Eisenhower. The thorny problem of the French was also addressed: the intention had been for the conference to reconcile de Gaulle and Giraud, but de Gaulle initially refused to leave London, and was only persuaded by a fear of being sidelined by Giraud. The British found de Gaulle difficult to deal with: he spent more time scheming to ensure that he governed France after the war than helping to win it, and Giraud, who had won renown at home by escaping from a German POW camp, had always been the Americans' preferred candidate. Giraud and de Gaulle were bitter rivals: de Gaulle had the better political antennae, while Giraud was even more arrogant. At Casablanca they agreed to work together, becoming joint chairmen of a French Committee for National Liberation, but there was never much doubt that de Gaulle would outmanoeuvre his rival and by the end of the year Giraud would resign and lapse into well-earned obscurity.

The subject which raised most hackles publicly at the time, and has often been raised since, was a statement made at the closing press conference, when Roosevelt said that the Allied aim was unconditional surrender of both

Germany and Japan. Unconditional surrender means exactly that: there are no conditions, no deals, no assurances; the defeated party places himself absolutely at the mercy of the victor. The objections to it came from those who believed that there was an anti-Hitler movement within the German armed forces and civil service that would depose Hitler and end the war if reasonable terms could be assured. Quite what these terms might have been is a matter for conjecture, but they might have included recognition of the Austro-German union, German ownership of the Polish Corridor and Danzig and retention of the Sudetenland, or everything Germany had obtained up to 1939 and a bit of what she had taken in the Polish campaign. A post-Hitler regime would presumably also have insisted on no occupation, no indemnity and no war crimes trials by outside parties. With the announcement that only unconditional surrender would be accepted, so the argument goes, the anti-Hitler movement had no incentive to act, and nothing with which to persuade the population, and particularly the Wehrmacht, to make peace: they might as well keep on fighting to the end as the terms they would get then would be no worse than if they sued for peace now – exactly the same argument as the British deployed for rejecting German overtures in 1940. There are several flaws in this argument. Firstly, whatever has been claimed in post-war Germany, there was no anti-Hitler movement of any significance, and, even if there had been, it is very doubtful whether the bulk of the army, whose soldiers and junior officers had been thoroughly indoctrinated with NSDAP ideology and belief in Hitler, would have followed it. Secondly, both British and American soldiers and statesmen remembered what had happened in 1918, when Germany had been granted a conditional armistice. The legend of the 'stab in the back' was fostered, extreme nationalism was allowed to continue to grow and twenty years later the Germans were at it again: this time there would be no armistice, no terms, no concessions, no understandings. No trace of fascism (or Japanese warmongering) would be allowed to survive.

It has often been said that Roosevelt's statement was a spur-of-the-moment throwaway line, and that Churchill was taken by surprise yet had to be seen to agree with his partner. In fact, Roosevelt had always intended to say it, and Churchill before the conference had put the question to the War Cabinet in London, whose only comment was that they thought unconditional surrender should be applied to Italy as well as to Germany and Japan. The conference over, and Allied strategy for the coming year agreed, Churchill took himself off to Turkey, to try to persuade her president to bring his country into the war on the Allied side. Having backed a loser in the last war, the Turks were in no hurry to get involved in Great Power politics again and declined, whereupon Churchill departed for Tripoli and Montgomery's victory parade, then to Algiers for some relaxation and discussions with Eisenhower, somewhat to the latter's horror, and finally back to London, where he promptly went down with pneumonia and, forbidden cigars and brandy, was his doctors' most cantankerous patient while he recovered.

The war went on. As First Army had failed to take Tunis in the early stages of the campaign, the aim now was to push through to the central Tunisian coastline in order to split the two Axis armies in North Africa. Rommel, withdrawing into the Mareth Line in Tunisia, and von Arnim were well aware of this, and, when von Arnim launched an attack on the French divisions holding the Tebessa mountains south-west of Pont du Fahs in mid-January, they broke and retreated in disarray. Allied views that tanks could not operate in the mountains were proved wrong, and by the end of the month von Arnim's troops were holding the eastern ends of all the passes through the mountains. The Allies calculated that von Arnim would attack again, but a misreading, misunderstanding or mistranslation of Ultra transcripts led Anderson to think that the attack would come in the north, and that is where he placed the bulk of his reserves. To cover the pass through the mountains at Kasserine farther south was a small American force of one infantry battalion, an artillery battalion, a tank destroyer (anti-tank) battalion and some field engineers, with a French artillery battery attached. Rommel was settling into the Mareth Line and he calculated that he had time to strike a blow at First Army before Montgomery would be ready to attack him. On 14 February he and von Arnim cooperated to launch an attack, not on the north but on the Kasserine Pass. Two panzer divisions, 10 and 21, the latter late of Rommel's DAK, from Fifth Panzer Army attacked through Sidi Bou Zid and Bir el Hafi, while a detachment of the DAK struck through Gafsa. During the night, the American battle group was reinforced by a tank battalion of the US 1 Armoured Division and the force, commanded by Colonel Robert Stark, managed to hold off the Germans on 19 February but thereafter his command degenerated into order, counter-order and disorder. Despite reinforcements of American armour and the British 16/5 Lancers, who were using the new Sherman tanks for the first time, Stark lost over 100 tanks and thirty artillery pieces. Rommel forced his way through the pass and pushed the Americans back forty miles. Now his intention was to crack on along the Tebessa road, a main supply route for the Americans, which not only would allow him to interrupt the supply line but also would split the US II Corps in the south from the rest of the Allied army to the north.

Rommel could no longer enjoy the relatively free hand that he had in Libya, however, and, as Tunisia, too, was an Italian theatre, he had to obey orders from the *Commando Supremo* in Rome to disengage from the Tebessa road and strike towards Le Kef, to the north, where the British armour was. Rommel obeyed, but knew very well that he could not sustain an operation so far from his supply base, despite capturing large stocks of aviation fuel at Kasserine. By 22 February, Allied resistance had hardened, and Rommel withdrew back through the Kasserine Pass, unmolested, and returned to the Mareth Line. The debacle at Kasserine came as a severe shock to American morale in North Africa and at home, but the Americans were only learning the same lessons that the British had already been taught in 1941 and 1942. Eisenhower sacked the corps commander, Fredendall, replacing him with Patton, and the Americans took on board the lessons of the defeat. As even Montgomery admitted, 'They learn faster than we do.'

On 18 February, 18th Army Group came into being, despite there not yet being any physical contact between the two Allied armies. On 23 February the Axis too reorganized its command arrangements when Rommel's Panzer Army Africa and Fifth Panzer Army were combined into Army Group Africa. Panzer Army Africa was renamed the Italian First Army, reflecting its composition of the DAK and two Italian corps, and was to be commanded by General Giovanni Messe, fresh from command of the Italian corps in Russia. Colonel-General von Arnim would continue in command of Fifth Army and Rommel would command the army group.

Now that Tripoli was available to the Allies, the supply lines were considerably shortened and, despite the best efforts of the Luftwaffe, around 3,000 tons a day were being unloaded. More divisions were brought up from Egypt and the French Général de Brigade Philippe Leclerc* appeared, having marched his largely Senegalese brigade overland from the French colony of

---

*He was that unusual creature, a well-bred French army officer, in reality the Viscomte de Hauteclocque who took the pseudonym Leclerc to protect his family still in France, a subterfuge which probably fooled the Germans for about five minutes. A forty-year-old captain in 1940, he had been promoted by de Gaulle, who sent him off to Africa to rally the garrisons there to the Free French.

Chad, west of the Sudan and south of Libya. Then, while Montgomery was preparing for his stately assault on the Mareth Line, refusing to be hurried by Alexander's calls for him to take the pressure off the American corps of First Army, Messe carried out a spoiling attack on Eighth Army at Medenine on 6 March with nearly 100 tanks and half-tracks. Initially they made progress in an early-morning mist, but then ran up against a strong British anti-tank screen and were forced to withdraw. The first British anti-tank guns in the desert war had been two-pounders, incapable of doing much damage to German tanks and generally ignored by them. Now the two-pounders had gone, to be replaced by the much better six-pounders, and there were even some of the new seventeen-pounders, a truly formidable anti-tank gun capable of taking on even a Tiger, if the wind was in the right direction. In this battle too were a troop of captured German 88mm guns, operated by the New Zealanders, and even a few 3.7-inch heavy anti-aircraft guns used in the ground role.*

On 9 March, Rommel flew to Berlin to try to persuade OKW and Hitler that the Mareth Line, despite running for twelve miles from the coast westwards to the Matmata Hills, being well supplied with concrete bunkers, minefields and wire, and possessing a natural anti-tank ditch in the form of a dried-up riverbed running in front of it for most of its length, was not an ideal defensive position as it could be outflanked. Far better would be to withdraw back to the Wadi Akarit, where a reasonable defence could be maintained. Surprisingly, for a war leader who by now was increasingly opposed to withdrawals of any sort, Hitler agreed that the marching infantry could be moved back, leaving a screen of mobile troops at Mareth which could then be extricated when the British attacked. Permission was duly signalled to von Arnim, who issued the orders to the units of the army group, only to have them overruled by the *Commando Supremo*, who would brook no withdrawal west of Mareth. Rommel was ordered not to return to Africa. He had been warned as early as February that he was to be relieved and now

---

*This author, albeit a simple infantryman, has never understood why the British did not make far more use of the 3.7-inch as an anti-tank gun, the way the Germans did with the 88mm. When questioned, numerous gunner friends have given all sorts of reasons for not having doing so, most of them unintelligible and ranging from the difficulty of moving the gun to problems with the sighting mechanism and the risk of the rivets popping out at low elevation. I suspect that the real answer was a then prevalent cult of conformity.

was an opportune time. OKW knew that defeat in Tunisia was unavoidable eventually, and a German field marshal must not be captured. Von Arnim would now command Army Group Africa and do the best he could to delay the inevitable.

Montgomery planned to attack the Mareth Line on 20 March. Although the French insisted that the ground to the west of the Matmata Hills was impenetrable, the Long Range Desert Group, a battalion-sized unit raised for reconnaissance and raiding behind the lines, had found a navigable route, and the intention was to launch the main attack frontally along the coast with three Indian divisions, 50, 51 and 4, supported by most of the armour, which would break through and then roll up the Axis position from east to west. The New Zealand Division with an armoured brigade and Leclerc's French would go left, flanking to the west of the hills in order to cut off a withdrawal. It was hardly an imaginative plan, a fact brought home on the night of 16/17 March when an attempt to straighten the intended jump-off line went badly wrong and the defending 90 Light Division inflicted 300 casualties on Sixth Battalion Grenadier Guards, among them its CO and thirteen other officers. Preceded by a massive artillery bombardment and air support, the attack still went in as planned on 20 March, the infantry with scaling ladders and the tanks carrying bundles of fascines to cross the anti-tank ditch. Fighting was fierce: by 23 March the British had still not broken through and the battle had stalled. Montgomery, having originally said that the Americans were to be 'kept out of my way', now appealed for an attack by Patton's US III Corps but this was vetoed by Alexander as putting that corps at too much risk. A rethink was essential, and with much talk of reinforcing success, and claims that the original plan was working, Eighth Army reinforced the New Zealand Division on the left flank with 1 Armoured Division and there eventually began to make some progress. Messe, realizing what the British were trying to do, withdrew forty miles to the Wadi Akarit position and Eighth Army wearily followed, for what would be their last major battle in North Africa.

The Wadi Akarit position covered what was known as the Gabes Gap, actually about ten miles north of Gabes, and was the last position from where, if it held, von Arnim could prevent the two Allied armies joining up. The gap ran for five miles inland to the Roumana Hills, which ran south-west to another line of hills, Hachana, Fatnassa, Meida and el Beida, on the west side of which were salt marshes generally impassable to vehicles except by the road running north-west to Gafsa, sixty miles away and held by the US III Corps. Along the gap from east to west ran the Wadi Akarit, a dried-up riverbed, linked in to anti-tank ditches, minefields and wire, and with craters blown on both the Gafsa road and the road from Gabes to Sfax that ran from south to north through the middle of the gap. None of the hills was particularly high – about 500 feet above the plain – but they dominated the gap and were strongly held by the Italian Spezia and Pistoia Divisions, with German units interspersed amongst them. The gap itself was held by the Young Fascist Division on the east and the Trieste Division on the west. Behind and in reserve to deal with any break-in were the German 15 Panzer Division and a panzer grenadier (motorized infantry) regiment.

Montgomery's plan was, after the usual lengthy build-up of fuel, ammunition and spare parts, to attack in overwhelming strength straight up through the gap with 51 Highland Division and the armour, while the Indian 4 Division would take the heights of Roumana to prevent interference from the flank. The problem was that Roumana was not the highest hill feature and was overlooked by Fatnassa and parts of Hachana, from where fire could be brought to bear on anyone on or attacking Roumana. Unusually, for Montgomery did not normally brook any criticism of his plans nor any modification that could not be thought to come from him, he did allow himself to be persuaded to change his mind by Major-General Francis 'Gertie' Tuker commanding the Indian 4 Division. Tuker was an officer of 2 Gurkha Rifles and he was commanding that regiment's first battalion on the outbreak of war. (Fortunate he was that it was the First Battalion, as what was left of the Second Battalion had gone into the bag at Singapore in February 1942.) He was convinced that a frontal assault on Wadi Akarit would be a disaster, and suggested that his division should swing round much farther to the west and instead take the Fatnassa feature. This was the highest ground in the area and would allow the British to dominate the gap and render the Axis defence positions untenable, and also allow them to open up the route to the Americans at Gafsa. Montgomery did not believe such an operation was possible, particularly when Tuker suggested a night attack, but Tuker had two Gurkha battalions in his division, including the one that he had been commanding only four years previously, and he knew that in the mountains and at night no troops in the world could equal the Gurkhas. Despite Montgomery's prejudice against the Indian Army, he could see the sense of Tuker's proposal and the plan was duly changed.

On the night of 5/6 April the Gurkhas set off, climbed the escarpment and broke into the first enemy position on the top. It was too dark to fire rifles safely in such close quarters and the initial killing was done by kukris. Second Gurkhas were followed by 1/9 Gurkha Rifles and well before first light, when the main attack went in, the high ground had been secured by the Gurkhas, the Royal Sussex had also come up (they should have been guarding the Gurkhas' right flank but had got lost), the machine-guns of the Rajputana Rifles were in position to support them and the division had forced a crossing of the anti-tank ditch between Hachana and Roumana. Now was the opportunity to encircle Messe's army and perhaps end the campaign: at 0845 hours Tuker spoke to his corps commander and urged that, if the armour of X Corps moved now and thrust through the gap created by his Division, it could get well into the enemy rear before the latter could disengage and withdraw. Montgomery agreed, but, thanks to typically pedestrian Eighth Army staff work, it was twenty-four hours before the tanks could move. Nevertheless, once the Gurkhas had taken Fatnassa, it was obvious to Messe that he could not stay where he was; German reserves came up to stiffen the Italians and on the night of 6/7 April the Axis withdrew in good order. That same day, a Gurkha patrol in a jeep headed up the Gafsa road and made the first contact between Eighth Army and First Army when it met an American patrol, even if the Gurkha *jemadar** did not entirely understand being greeted as a 'good ole limey'. Tuker got little credit for the victory, while Montgomery made much of the success of 'my' plan and how he had deployed 'my' Gurkhas.

Army Group Africa could now only delay, and, fighting as they now were in the mountains, they were able to hold out for well over a month. Eighth Army continued its advance up the coast and took Sfax on 10 April and Sousse two days later. It was at this time that Montgomery embarked upon another of those point-scoring exercises that to him were merely amusing but which infuriated those against whom they were directed. Many British officers' messes then and since had a wagers book – 'Lieutenant Merk bets Captain Crump two glasses of port that he can jump his polo pony over the village well'† – and Montgomery was fond of making minor bets on

---

*Indian Army Viceroy Commissioned Officers were *jemadar* (usually a platoon commander), *subadar* (usually a company second-in-command) and *subadar-major* (only one in a battalion and the senior native officer). For a full explanation of how the Indian Army rank system worked, see my *Sepoys in the Trenches* (Spellmount, Staplehurst, 1999).

†This actually happened in this author's regiment. Merk lost, killing himself and his pony in the process.

everything from the weather tomorrow to the results of inter-regimental football games. At a meeting between Montgomery and Eisenhower's chief of staff, Lieutenant-General Walter Bedell Smith,* Montgomery had said that he hoped to have captured Sfax by the middle of April. Smith, who did not think it possible, said jokingly that, if that happened, he would give Montgomery a B-17 Flying Fortress plus crew. The Boeing B-17 was a four-engined bomber, protected by armour plate and a large number of .5 calibre Browning machine-guns, but it was also occasionally used as a long-distance transport aircraft. Smith duly forgot about the bet, but it was entered in Montgomery's wagers book, and, when Sfax fell on 10 April, Montgomery sent a signal to Smith asking for his winnings. Smith tried to treat the whole thing as a joke, but when Montgomery sent a second signal, making it clear that he expected to be paid, Smith had to confess all to Eisenhower. Eisenhower was furious, but Montgomery got his B-17 and an American crew for his personal use for the duration of the war. It was just one more example of Montgomery's arrogance and inability to understand the feelings of others – Brooke thought it 'crass stupidity' on his part – and it did nothing to dispel an increasing climate of mutual antipathy, dislike and distrust between Montgomery and the Americans that would only become worse as the war went on.[62]

Montgomery attacked again on 19 April, but this time he was trying to break through the Zaghouan range, hills 3,000 feet above sea level with spurs running down to the coast and impossible to outflank. Eighth Army was stalled after only three miles, and First Army too, attacking from the west, could make no progress. At this stage Alexander's 18th Army Group disposed of ninety-six British, Indian and Gurkha, thirty-eight French and twenty-two American infantry battalions and about 1,200 tanks. Army Group Africa had ninety under-strength German and Italian battalions and 140 tanks. Alexander now decided that Eighth Army was to hold the line against which First Army would drive the Axis. Accordingly, two armoured divisions, 1 and 7, the Indian 4 Division and a Guards infantry brigade were transferred from Eighth to First Army, which on 5 May attacked towards Tunis. On 9 May burning fuel dumps and desperate rearguard actions indicated that von Arnim could not hold out much longer. On 10 May the commanding officer

---

*He had risen from being a forty-six-year-old major in March 1941 to lieutenant-general in January 1943.

of Second Gurkhas, Lieutenant-Colonel Lionel Showers, was going forward on a reconnaissance about forty miles south of Tunis when from a hilltop he saw a German staff car flying a white flag. In it was a staff officer who explained that General von Arnim, whose headquarters was nearby, wished to discuss terms of capitulation. Showers and his orderly got into the car and were taken to see von Arnim. German staff officers said that they were most anxious to surrender to the British, and not to the French, and a letter in English was despatched to General Tuker:

> Since my troops have fired their last round I am ready for the surrender of those under my immediate command. I trust that the conduct of my soldiers who have done their duty to the utmost in this battle will have earned the respect of my opponent. I have instructed the handling of the details of the surrender to Colonel (General Staff) Nolte, Chief of Staff of German Afrika Korps, and to Colonel Stoltz, commander of the troops. I have given these officers full powers. You may rely upon their honour as soldiers.
>
> (signed) von Arnim, Colonel-General

On 12 May the German and Italian forces surrendered. The war in North Africa was over.

11

THE ASIAN WAR

DECEMBER 1941–NOVEMBER 1942

The astonishing success of Japanese arms all across South-East Asia and the Pacific in the winter of 1941 and the spring of 1942 came as a surprise and a shock to most British, American and Dutch commanders and politicians. It was followed by an orgy of savage and bestial behaviour which to anyone who had been following events in China should not have been either a surprise or a shock. On Christmas Day 1941 in Hong Kong the Japanese overran a British field hospital in the grounds of St Stephen's College on Hong Kong Island. Clearly marked with Red Cross flags, it was undefended and full of wounded soldiers being tended by unarmed military medical officers, orderlies and female nurses. The Japanese infantry stormed into the buildings and began by rounding up the nurses who were then gang-raped, over and over again. Next came the wounded and the medical staff, who were first tortured to amuse the soldiery and then killed, over sixty of them being despatched by the bayonet, presumably to avoid wasting ammunition. After the surrender it was the turn of the local Chinese females. Nobody knows how many of them were casually raped by Japanese soldiers but some sources put the number as high as 100,000 over the three years and eight months of occupation. On 14 February 1942 in Singapore the Japanese rampaged into the Alexandra Hospital, rounded up and raped the nurses, then bayoneted them and dumped the bodies in the under-growth. Next was the turn of the patients and orderlies, many of whom were also bayoneted, including the bed-ridden. Those who survived the first onslaught, about 200 walking wounded and staff, had their hands tied behind their backs, were roped together in groups of eight and were marched away from the battle area. Anyone who collapsed on the way was cut loose, bayoneted and left to die. Those who survived were locked in three small rooms for the night, left in their own filth with no food or water, and next day taken out in batches and bayoneted. One officer and four Other Ranks survived.

Elsewhere, in Bataan the Japanese wanted to remove the American and Filipino soldiers who had surrendered in April to clear the area for the attack on Corregidor. The intention was to move the 12,000 Americans and 65,000 Filipinos to a prisoner-of-war camp at Camp O'Donnell, which involved an initial march of around fifty-five miles to a railhead that was expected to take two days. After the prisoners' personal possessions, particularly watches and money, had been taken by the Japanese soldiers, the Death March, as it became known, took five days for the fit and twelve days for the wounded and less fit, all of them herded along like animals in temperatures in the nineties and with 100 per cent humidity by Japanese guards who shot or bayoneted anyone dropping out. One American officer who was caught with a few Japanese yen was beheaded by a Japanese officer with a sword. Of the 10,000 Americans who started the march (2,000 had died or had been executed before it began), less than half survived it. We do not know what the death rate amongst the Filipinos was but it cannot have been less.[63]

Leaving aside the specific question of the treatment of prisoners for the moment, ill-treatment, including rape and murder, can occur in any operation of war, and British and American soldiers too have been guilty of atrocities. The difference is that in Western armies it was specifically forbidden and individual misbehaviour was swiftly dealt with once discovered. In the case of the Japanese, mass cruelty and barbaric behaviour was normal, common and not just condoned but permitted and in many cases actually encouraged. The Japanese refused to recognize the International Red Cross and executed its representative (and his wife) in Borneo when he tried to protest against the treatment of prisoners. Those who try to find excuses for Japanese behaviour during the war point to the background of poverty and ignorance from where the vast majority of the troops were recruited: their behaviour, while regrettable, was thus understandable. This argument is nonsense: poverty and ignorance do not automatically lead to deliberate cruelty, and Japanese society, while autocratic and oppressive, did not glorify rape, torture, murder and mutilation. Even if there was some truth in the argument that the soldiers knew no better, there can be no excuse for the officers, who assuredly did know better, being educated and raised on standards of honourable behaviour and whose orders for the burning of all 'souvenir' photographs of beatings and beheadings shortly before Japan's final surrender in 1945 would indicate that they knew very well that what they had been doing was wrong.

In regard to prisoners of war, Japanese commanders insisted that, while Japan had signed the 1929 Geneva Convention, she had never ratified it and therefore was not bound by its provisions. This is true, but is legalistic semantics: ordinary rules of decency would say that you do not starve a prisoner to death, you do not beat him for no reason, you do not put him to work which you know will kill him and you do not permit cavalier torture and execution for minor offences or none, and in any case Japan had signed and ratified the Hague Convention of 1907, of which the Geneva Convention was only an update. The Hague Convention laid down that, while non-commissioned prisoners could be given work, it was not to be war-related and must not be of a life-threatening nature, and that rations and medical cover were to be of the same standard as that of the captors' own soldiers. Japanese military law had been amended in the 1920s to make surrender an offence: soldiers were expected to fight to the death rather than allow themselves to be taken prisoner and anyone who did give in forfeited all honour. The forfeiture of all honour, which the Japanese insisted applied not just to themselves but to all combatants, cannot, however, mean that the prisoner can be treated with deliberate cruelty. The Japanese treatment of military prisoners and the civilian populations of lands conquered by them was simply appalling.

As it was, because the Americans and the British wanted the Japanese as a post-war bulwark against the USSR in the Far East, the unconditional surrender condition was modified and, while the emperor was obliged to renounce his divinity, far greater leniency was shown than to the Germans. War crimes trials were fewer and conducted with less publicity than in Germany and what had happened was officially forgotten as soon as possible. Unlike in Germany, where the entire population was browbeaten into feeling guilty for the treatment of the Jews and for the ravages of yet another war that Germany had initiated, a stigma that has affected German foreign and defence policy ever since, the Japanese were never forced to face up to what their soldiers and administrators had done in their name. Even today, young, educated Japanese with whom this author has discussed Japan's wartime behaviour find it almost impossible to come to terms with it. Most simply say that it never happened, it is all a fiction of Allied propaganda; others claim that, while there might have been isolated cases of misbehaviour, it was not systemic; and all insist that the emperor could not possibly have known anything about it. The fact remains, though, that the Japanese had not always been like this. In the Russo-Japanese War, they had been assiduous in behaving properly to prisoners and civilians in occupied areas. One can only posit that the rise of extreme nationalism and emperor worship with the inculcation of a belief in Japanese racial superiority developed and nurtured during the 1920s and 1930s led them to behave in the way that they did, and to take an especial joy in seeing the white races humbled.

* * *

The capital of Burma and its only major port was Rangoon, twenty-five miles up the Irrawaddy delta from the Indian Ocean and with a pre-war population of around half a million. Its significance to both the Allies and the Japanese was that it was to Rangoon that American supplies, weapons and equipment for Chiang Kai-shek's Chinese Nationalist government in Chungking came by sea, to be offloaded and transported overland by road and rail 350 miles north to Lashio, the beginning of the Burma Road. If Rangoon was lost, then so was the main route for aid to China. Like all developed parts of the Empire, Burma was expected to fund her own defence, although military equipment was supplied by Britain at cost. As no one before 1940 ever expected Burma to be attacked, her defence budget was small, and, when minds in India and Whitehall began to consider the possibility that Burma might be a target, there were few military assets in the country and very little with which to reinforce them. Expansion of the indigenous forces had been at the expense of the two British battalions in the country, First Battalion the Gloucestershire Regiment and Second Battalion the King's Own Yorkshire Light Infantry, which had provided officers and training cadres, being reduced to two companies each by the outbreak of hostilities. Burma was the responsibility of Wavell's ABDA Command, which was far more concerned about Malaya and Singapore than it was about Burma, whereas the Indian authorities realized that, with the Japanese in control of Siam, Burma was an obvious next step, and Burma was the route to India. For the first time for centuries, the threat to India was not from the north-west but from the south-east. Eventually, when the Asian war broke out, responsibility was split: operational command remained with ABDA, while responsibility for administration, supplies and reinforcements went to India. It is never a good idea to divorce operational from administrative command.

If Japan was to make use of her control of the airstrips and roads in Siam to attack Burma, then she would do so through Tenasserim, the narrow spit of Lower Burma that runs along the east coast of the Bay of Bengal and peters out at the top of the Kra Isthmus and is bordered to the east by Thailand (then Siam). The first Japanese action against Burma was on 14 December 1941, when an infantry regiment of the Japanese 55 Division captured Victoria Point, on the southernmost tip of Tenasserim, and put the tiny garrison of local troops to flight. Now air reinforcement of Malaya from India was blocked. Then, on 23 December 1941, the Japanese air force raided Rangoon. They did little damage to installations but there were heavy casualties to the civilian population who gathered in the streets to watch rather than taking refuge in the air-raid shelters. As there was not a single anti-aircraft gun in the country, the defence was undertaken by a squadron of RAF Buffaloes and one of the American Volunteer Group's marginally more useful P-40 fighters that had been lent to Burma by Chiang Kai-shek. The most serious result of the raid, however, was the mass defection of most of the dock labour force, whose Burmese members took refuge in the jungle outside the city, while its Indian members headed for India on foot. A second raid on Christmas Day saw the departure of the remaining dock labourers and the beginning of a mass trek to India by the many Indian workers in southern Burma. These refugees blocked roads and bridges and were a constant source of interference with British military movement.

Reinforcements for Burma had begun to arrive on 9 January, in the shape of the Indian 17 Division, commanded by Major-General J. G. 'Jackie' Smyth VC MC. Smyth had won the VC as a subaltern with 15 Sikhs on the Western Front in 1915, and was one of the Indian Army officers brought back to England to command British formations at the beginning of the war (he commanded a British brigade in the Battle of France in 1940) before being posted back to India with the acting rank of major-general. His command of 17 Division was in many ways a poisoned chalice in that it had been raised in July 1941, intended for the Middle East, and was still short of technicians and some heavy weapons. Two of its original brigades had been sent to Malaya in December 1941 and lost, while all of its regular battalions had been severely milked of British and Indian officers, NCOs and sepoys as cadres for the raising of new battalions. Even the Gurkha battalions had each lost 250 British and Gurkha officers and riflemen, whose replacements were just out of the training centres and had never seen a hand grenade, still less used one; there were none for training as the limited stocks had gone to equip battalions going to North Africa. There had been no opportunity for formation training and such unit training that had taken place in between digging defences and humping stores had been for war in the desert, not the jungle.

The General Officer Commanding Burma, Lieutenant-General Thomas Hutton, who had been appointed in December 1941 having previously been Chief of the General Staff India, decided that the only realistic course of action in the event of a Japanese attack on Burma was to conduct a fighting retreat. His reputation, and his career, suffered for it but, given the paucity of his troops, the few aircraft, the lack of armour and heavy weapons, and the state of training of most units in theatre, his decision was absolutely correct in the circumstances. He ordered Smyth to fall back using the Rivers Salween, Bilin and Sittang to delay the Japanese and cause as much damage to them as possible, but to keep his division intact for the eventual defence of Rangoon. On 11 January 1942 a Japanese battalion crossed the border and captured the town and airstrip of Tavoy, putting to flight the garrison of two companies of 6 Burma Rifles and a volunteer artillery battery whose defence collapsed once the commander, a regular officer of 7 Gurkha Rifles, was killed. With the capture of Tavoy, the third airstrip in the south, Mergui, could not be held and its garrison was withdrawn by sea. The Japanese could now use these three airstrips to support their operations farther north, and a few days later two divisions advanced towards Moulmein, the provincial capital, across the Dawna mountain range from Siam. By now it was quite clear that a major Japanese offensive was under way and 17 Division was spread out over 400 miles, trying to maintain a presence astride the major routes into Burma proper.

On 18 January the advance guard of the Japanese 55 Division hit two companies of 1/7 Gurkha Rifles of 16 Brigade at Mayawaddi on the frontier with Siam. Contact with them was soon lost – the battalions had only one radio, the rear link to brigade, and companies were reliant on flags and heliograph – and, as the Japanese infantry were probing through the bamboo jungle to find the gaps and the Japanese air force was in complete control of the skies, the brigade was ordered to withdraw to defend Moulmein, the provincial capital. All non-essential stores were to be destroyed, and when one vehicle drove on to the ferry at Kyondo, to cross a tributary of the River Gyaing, and promptly sank it, the vehicles that had not crossed were destroyed as well, still in their desert camouflage. Some of the trucks still had ammunition on board, which blew up when the vehicles were set on fire, causing many a mule to stampede and disappear into the jungle, and one burning vehicle carrying bleaching powder caused a gas alert when it emitted a huge white cloud of vapour. The only bright spot in an otherwise depressing scenario was the arrival of the two cut-off companies of Gurkhas, who had fought their way out on foot and reported with all their weapons and equipment less their vehicles, which they had abandoned.

On 30 January the Japanese attacked Moulmein, which was defended by a brigade of Burma Rifles with one Indian battalion as stiffening, and, as they fought their way closer and closer to the centre of the town, Smyth ordered the brigadier commanding the defence to withdraw, which at 0800 hours on 31 January he did, using a fleet of river steamers. The last troops, of 12 Frontier Force Regiment, embarked at 1000 hours with the brigade headquarters and, as they steamed across the estuary of the River Salween making for Martaban, the Japanese arrived at the jetty. In the meantime, the RAF were attacking the Japanese headquarters and the airport in Bangkok, using six Blenheim light bombers – the raids did little damage but they were good for British morale – and the bulk of the reserve ammunition and stores in Rangoon were being moved by rail to Mandalay, 400 miles north. Having withdrawn the brigade from Moulmein, Smyth now pulled out of Martaban and tried to hold along the Salween, as ordered by Hutton, but with a frontage of 100 miles he could not possibly cover all the likely crossing points, and, when on 13 February it was obvious that the Japanese were crossing and liable to infiltrate to the rear of his division, he ordered a withdrawal to the next practical obstacle line, the River Bilin. Here he intended to make a stand, and, as far as Commander ABDA was concerned, he should have done so before now. Wavell signalled Hutton: 'I do not know what considerations caused withdrawal behind Bilin river without further fighting. I have every confidence in judgement and fighting spirit of you and Smyth but… time can often be gained as effectively and less expensively by bold counter-offensive…' That was all well and good, but the numbers, standard of training and mobility of Smyth's division were simply not such as to allow bold counter-offensives. Fighting at the Bilin was ferocious, as the Japanese tried to cross and 17 Division tried to stop them. The Bilin was hardly an insuperable obstacle; it was easily fordable at numerous points and the defenders were always liable to be turned by a sea landing to their southern, right, flank or through the myriad of jungle tracks to their north. On the night of 17/18 February, elements of the Japanese 215 Regiment forced a crossing in the centre and attacked 8 Burma Rifles; on 18 February the Japanese 143 Regiment crossed the Bilin estuary by boat, landed at Zokali and pressed inland behind 17 Division's positions. That night it reached Tungale and was being held off by a company of 2/5 Gurkha Rifles. To the north, two battalions of 215 Regiment had crossed the Bilin on 17 February and were in action against the British division's extreme left-hand battalion, 1/4 Gurkha Rifles.

By 19 February, Smyth's men had held the Japanese off for four days and had forced them to slow up and deploy most of their units. The time bought meant that 7 Armoured Brigade, on its way by sea, could land at Rangoon. That formation was equipped with the American Stuart tank – the Honey to the British – armed with a two-pounder gun, a weapon that would have been more useful than it was had there been any high-explosive ammunition for it. Unfortunately, the only rounds available were armour-piercing solid shot, which was fine against Japanese tanks but of no use against infantry. Other assistance was also arriving from China, in the shape of two Chinese armies that would move into the Shan States and the British end of the Burma Road. These latter were somewhat of a mixed blessing: the so-called armies were in fact rather smaller than British divisions, they lacked modern equipment and had no logistic services, being accustomed to living off the country. Although Chiang Kai-shek had agreed that these armies would be under the command of GOC Burma, in practice they would do nothing without the agreement of the Chinese headquarters in Chungking, and any orders to them or to their subordinate units had to be delivered by the commander personally or in writing and signed by him – there was no concept of a staff officer acting for his commander. Equally, by 19 February it was clear to Smyth that, if he did not withdraw at once, he would be most unlikely to be able to withdraw at all, and this view was reinforced when a patrol sent north found a large Japanese force ignoring 17 Division completely and heading west as fast as it could go, presumably intending to cut 17 Division off from the Sittang. Orders went out for a withdrawal and at 2330 hours that night Smyth issued the codeword to implement it.

The Sittang was, and is, a mighty river – between 1,200 and 1,800 yards wide, fast-flowing and subject to a violent tidal bore. In February 1942 it had one remaining bridge over it, a railway bridge of eleven spans which Smyth had ordered to be decked to allow vehicles to cross. Upstream of the bridge was a ferry, and all boats belonging to locals had been commandeered, paid for and then destroyed to prevent the Japanese using them. If the British were to be able to defend along the Sittang, then they needed that bridge to get west of it. Conversely, if the Japanese wanted Rangoon, then they too needed that bridge as the Sittang was the last major obstacle before the capital. It was unfortunate that at some time on 18 or 19 February the plan for the withdrawal was passed by radio in clear – that is, it was not encoded. The official history is coy about which unit sinned in this way, but it was probably one of the three brigade headquarters as battalions passed the orders verbally. Inevitably the message was intercepted by the Japanese, who sent two battalions round to the north of the British to head for the Sittang bridge. The bridge was guarded by 3 Burma Rifles, whom Smyth knew would not stand if attacked in force, so he sent a company of Second Battalion the Duke of Wellington's Regiment, recently arrived as a reinforcement, to bolster them up. Seventeen Division managed to break contact and withdraw from the Bilin on 20 February. There was a metalled road to within fifteen miles of the Sittang bridge, and a dirt track thereafter. The troops marched along the road with as much of their impedimenta as they could take with them, flank guards moving parallel through the jungle, and vehicles ferrying the marching troops forward. To begin with, the Japanese left them alone – they too had their problems and had far outrun even their meagre resupply chain. Then on 21 February the Japanese air force appeared, bombing and strafing the columns of transport. Vehicles trying to get into cover off the road overturned in drainage ditches, mules panicked and dashed off into the jungle carrying infantry mortars, and the situation was made worse by the arrival of aircraft of the RAF and the AVG whose pilots thought the columns of troops and vehicles were the Japanese and attacked them, causing even more chaos and delaying the withdrawal to the bridge. Late that afternoon, the advance guard of the division, a battalion of Indian infantry and some sappers and miners, got to the bridge to find little had been done to prepare to defend it. The sappers and miners began to prepare the bridge for demolition while the infantry began to site defensive positions on the east bank. The plan was for the division to withdraw over the bridge with one of the brigades acting as rearguard and then for that brigade to withdraw, after which the bridge would be blown.

By now the Japanese had caught up with the retreating British. That night 17 Division, whose main body was approaching the bridge, received a signal from Rangoon saying that there was a risk of a Japanese *coup de main* on the bridge using paratroopers – there was no evidence that the Japanese had parachute troops in Burma but they had recently used them in the Netherlands East Indies and that information must have put the wind up the intelligence staff in Rangoon. No paratroopers appeared, but it was now urgent to get the division across the bridge, a task made more difficult when in the early hours of 22 February a vehicle went off the decking of the bridge and jammed in the girders. The blockage was not cleared until 0630 hours, and in the meantime traffic was closing up on the east side. A Japanese attack on the bridge from the north-east at 0830 hours put 3 Burma Rifles to flight and destroyed the river ferry, but a counter-attack by Indian troops restored the perimeter. By now the Japanese were attacking the flanks of the columns, ambushing withdrawing battalions and generally causing chaos. That day the sappers and miners completed preparation for the demolition of the bridge, but there was only sufficient explosive to blow the three central spans. This would produce a gap of 150 yards, which was quite sufficient, but there was also a shortage of fuse and initiator cable, which meant that, instead of the firing point – the location from which the bridge would be blown – being dug in and well back on the west bank, it had to be on the west side of the bridge itself, which meant that, should the Japanese get close enough to shoot at the bridge, the sappers could not guarantee to be able to set off the demolition in daylight.

During the night of 22/23 February, Brigadier Hugh-Jones, commanding 48 Brigade and the bridgehead commander, became more and more concerned about his ability to hold the bridge under increasing Japanese attack, both by infantry and from the air. The direct route to the bridge was blocked by Japanese troops and the only approach was from the south. As units and bits of units straggled in, it seemed that no unit of the division was intact. He had no communication with either of the other two brigades and only a very poor link with Smyth's headquarters. Eventually he reported to Smyth that he did not think he could hold the bridge much longer, and certainly not for the following day. Smyth was in an unenviable position. If he blew the bridge now, the bulk of his division would be cut off and destroyed; if he did not blow it and the Japanese captured it, then the road would be open for them to take Rangoon, and his division would still be cut off. Smyth told Hugh-Jones that he had authority to blow as he felt necessary. At 0530 hours on 23 February there was an almighty bang as the bridge went up. As it did so, the bulk of two brigades were still on the east side of the river.

Every man on the wrong side of the river could not have failed to realize what had happened. Their backs were to the river, if they could fight their way to it, and there was no way across except what they could improvise. Bamboo was cut and brought to the bank, as were empty petrol cans, tree trunks, any piece of equipment that might float. Men were set to building rafts and the first priority was to get the wounded across. Then the strong swimmers set out in small groups but even some of those could not breast the current: some were swept out to sea, many were drowned. The men were at least fortunate in that the Japanese did not press too hard that day and the next – there was little point now that the bridge was gone – and they too had problems in resupplying their troops and caring for their own wounded. The non-swimmers – and there were many, particularly amongst the Gurkhas – either learned to swim very quickly, tried to cross using improvised flotation aids or headed north into the jungle to try to cross the river higher up. Not many made it, and those that did reached the other side barefoot, exhausted and without weapons or indeed anything except what they stood up in. Counting heads on the west bank on 24 February told its own story. When 1/7 Gurkha Rifles left Bilin it was 550 strong – now it mustered 300; the third battalion of the same regiment had been reduced from 600 to 170, and its losses were not the worst. Of the twelve infantry battalions of the division, only eighty officers and 3,404 Other Ranks paraded that evening, and only 1,200 of those still had their personal weapons. The remnants of 17 Division made their way painfully back across rice paddy or along the railway track, for there was no road, to the railhead at Waw, from where they were taken by train to the divisional concentration area at Pegu.

Inevitably, after such a disaster heads had to roll, although, unlike some belonging to the men taken prisoner by the Japanese, not literally. Major-General Smyth had given the order to blow the bridge and he had to take the blame. That he had always pointed out the deficiencies in the equipment and training of his division compared to the Japanese was forgotten; that he had consistently recommended withdrawal to a position that could be defended properly, rather than having to fight a series of delaying actions, was immaterial; that whatever decision he came to on the night of 22/23 February was probably going to be wrong mattered not a jot; that his division had no opportunity to train together, or to train at all, and that it was very largely composed of recruits led by emergency commissioned officers would have no bearing. He was in command and he must take the rap. Smyth was relieved of command, ostensibly on health grounds, reduced to his substantive rank of brigadier and retired from the army. Ever afterwards, Smyth felt he had been unfairly treated, and so he had been. While he can be criticized for not forcing his division, which was admittedly dog-tired and short of water, to the bridge a day earlier than he did, his command was perfectly competent in the circumstances, but there had to be doubt as to whether any soldier would ever have had confidence in him again: he had blown a bridge when most of his division was on the enemy side and the justification and the factors influencing his decision would have been forgotten. Brave, decent and honourable man that 'Jackie' Smyth undoubtedly was, it was right that he was sacked (although a kinder regime might have let him keep his rank and the pension that went with it). He was replaced by his chief of staff, Brigadier (now acting major-general) David 'Punch' Cowan, a forty-seven-year-old Sixth Gurkha.

Nor could Hutton, General Officer Commanding Burma, escape censure. He had told Wavell that what was needed was a corps headquarters, and, now that 7 Armoured Brigade was in station and 1 Burma Division was relieved from static defence, he would get one. The newly formed Burma Corps would be commanded by acting Lieutenant-General William Slim, and Hutton would return to India as Secretary to the War Resources and Reconstruction Committee. He was replaced by General Sir Harold Alexander, who became Commander-in-Chief Allied Forces Burma. It is one of the more unfortunate assumptions propounded by British class warriors that, because someone is well bred, has been to a decent school and speaks properly, he is therefore foppish and incompetent. Alexander's reputation, at least among the general public, is that of a bear of little brain. Born a younger son of the fourth Earl of Caledon in the Irish peerage* and educated at Harrow, the Honourable† Harold Leofric George Alexander was commissioned into the Irish Guards in 1910 and in his twenties commanded his battalion and 4 Guards Brigade on the Western Front in the First World War.

---

*His forbears had been in trade and the second earl had bought the notorious 'rotten' borough of Old Sarum for £43,000 in 1802.

†For those who do not have *Debrett's* instantly to hand, the eldest son of an earl holds his father's junior title of viscount, and succeeds to the earldom, while the other sons and daughters are 'the honourable', usually abbreviated to 'hon'.

In 1919 and 1920 he served in the allied intervention force against the Bolsheviks and commanded a Polish brigade of ethnic Germans. His personal courage and leadership proven, he showed intellectual ability too by passing the examination for the Staff College and, later, by being selected to attend the Imperial Defence College before he became a brigadier in 1935 and the youngest major-general in the army in 1937 at the age of forty-six. He was a competent divisional and corps commander in the Battle of France and the last general officer to be evacuated from Dunkirk. A lieutenant-general from December 1940, he was knighted and promoted to full general in January 1942. Fluent in German, Russian and Urdu, he was a man of considerable charm and, as he was to prove in North Africa and Italy, well able to smooth ruffled feathers, and it is largely due to Montgomery's bagging all the credit for North Africa and Alexander's association with the secondary campaign in Italy that history has not placed him in the top rank of military commanders. In his short period in Burma there was little he could do except try to manage the retreat and do his best to help the army get back to India without it disintegrating, and he did that as well as anyone could have.

The disaster at the River Sittang did at least delay the Japanese, who had two options: cross the Sittang and capture Rangoon, or turn north-east and take on the Chinese. In the end it was the precarious state of their logistics chain that forced the decision: only by the capture of a sizeable port could sufficient supplies to keep the Japanese Fifteenth Army in the field be delivered, and on 3 March the Japanese crossed the Sittang and headed for Pegu, on the road and railway link to Rangoon and forty miles north of it. Alexander, egged on by Wavell, initially intended to hold Rangoon. As the fighting in and around Pegu intensified, it became clear that to attempt to hold Rangoon would only lead to his troops being cut off from India and defeated in detail, and on 6 March he ordered the port installations and any stores that could not be moved to be demolished and the garrison to move north-north-west to Tharrawaddy, on the Prome road and on the direct route back to India. Rangoon's docks were soon blanketed by a pall of smoke as oil installations and stores depots were fired; Lend-Lease vehicles that could not be driven away by the troops were disabled, and as there would now be nobody to guard and look after them, the prison was opened and the occupants released, and the residents of the lunatic asylums turfed out on the streets. The cages of the animals in Rangoon zoo were opened, and a story did the rounds that a chaplain of the Gloucesters, the garrison's British infantry battalion, decided to have a rest on a conveniently placed log only to find that it was a sleeping crocodile.*

Alexander was lucky, for his original decision to hold Rangoon and the delay in withdrawing that resulted very nearly lost him a large part of his army. The Japanese had cut the road to Tharrawaddy and it was only a misapprehension by their divisional commander, who thought that the British intended to fight for Rangoon, that persuaded him to withdraw his troops from the road in case their presence gave away the Japanese axis for their attack. After deploying for an attack to clear the road from the south, the British discovered that there were now no enemy on it, and pushed on to Tharrawaddy. When the Japanese marched into Rangoon on 8 March, they found to their astonishment that no one was there – Alexander and his staff had left just six hours before them.

Concurrent with the abandonment of Rangoon, the British evacuated the Andaman Islands, 200 miles south-south-west of Rangoon in the Indian Ocean and with good all-weather airstrips and ports that could be used to police the sea routes from Malay to Burma. With Rangoon gone, the Andamans could no longer be supplied or supported and the garrison, one Gurkha battalion, was withdrawn. The loss of Rangoon meant that links with China were severely curtailed, for it was through the port there that Lend-Lease equipment was provided. Burma was hardly defended at all before the war, and even after December 1941 very few people thought that Malaya would not be held, and, even if it could not, Singapore surely could. Once Singapore went, Burma was sure to follow, even if the command structure – the country was initially part of Far East Command, then placed under Indian responsibility, then transferred to ABDA but with India remaining responsible for administration, and finally given back to India – had been consistent, which it was not. There was little to reinforce Burma with. At one stage it was proposed to divert the battle-experienced 7 Australian Division, on its way back from North Africa, but this was very sensibly vetoed by the Australian government. Even if Rangoon could have been held for long enough to receive the division, itself doubtful, it would have been unable to tip the balance and would almost certainly have been cut off and destroyed.

Safety lay in Imphal, in Assam, 600 miles north as the crow flies and through terrain that might kindly be described as inhospitable at best. The

---

*And as the Great Duke (of Wellington) said, if you believe that…

terrain was difficult anyway – few roads, mountainous ridges, steep valleys and wide, fast-flowing rivers – but would get far worse once the monsoon broke in May. The army not only had to contend with the pursuing Japanese but also with the Japanese-sponsored Burma Independence Army under the aegis of the Burmese communist leader Aung San. Having been educated by the British at Rangoon University, Aung drifted into ultra-nationalist politics and at the age of twenty-five formed the Thakin or Masters party, dedicated to the overthrow of British suzerainty. He was a thoroughly nasty piece of work, and one of his more endearing tactics was to have Burmese villagers welcome British and Indian stragglers, feed them and give them somewhere to sleep, and then either cut their throats themselves or summon the Japanese to kill them. Very soon it became an absolute rule in Burma Corps that wounded were never to be left in the care of local Burmans. The BIA had been armed by the Japanese and told by Aung that they were immune to bullets. Great was their surprise when they discovered that they were not, but they never lost faith in Aung, who would not only get rid of the British but allow them to revert to the traditional Burmese pastime of enslaving and murdering Chins, Nagas, Kachins, Karens and other indigenous tribespeople – who even in the worst days of defeat remained steadfastly loyal to the British. Not only did the retreating army have to cope with the jungle and Burmese traitors but also with endemic malaria and ticks carrying scrub typhus, not to mention those constant companions of retreating armies in a hostile landscape, cholera and dysentery. Very soon the RAF aircraft had to be withdrawn to India, and those of the AVG to China, and, while the RAF continued to evacuate wounded from makeshift jungle strips, the Japanese ruled the skies.

Any reasonably competent general can manage a victory, and it is unusual for a man to become a general unless he is reasonably competent, at least in Western armies, but it takes a great general to manage a defeat, and a lucky one to manage a defeat and survive. Bill Slim was that general. If Montgomery was arrogant, boastful, careless of the feelings of others and unwilling to give credit to his subordinates, then Slim was just the opposite: modest, unassuming, caring and always deflecting plaudits on to those he commanded rather than taking them for himself. If Montgomery was respected for his professional dedication and eye for detail, Slim was loved for his readiness to share the hardships of his men and for his determination never to let them down.

William Slim came from modest roots: his father was a wholesale ironmonger but the family had little money and Slim went to a grammar school in Birmingham and was employed as a teacher and a clerk while belonging to an Officer Cadet Training Unit of the Territorial Force.* Mobilized in 1914 and commissioned into Ninth Battalion of the Warwickshire Regiment, he was wounded at Gallipoli but was impressed by his neighbouring battalion, 1/6 Gurkha Rifles, and after the war transferred to the Indian Army and that regiment. No doubt part of his motivation was the ease with which an officer of the Indian Army could live on his pay, and Slim was always short of cash, but soldiers and British officers alike took to him and admired his no-nonsense ways, his humanity and his uncluttered intelligence. In the interwar years Slim progressed steadily if unspectacularly up the promotion ladder. He was a student at the Indian Staff College at Quetta, commanded a battalion of 7 Gurkha Rifles, attended the Imperial Defence College and in 1939, at the age of forty-eight, was appointed acting colonel and Commandant of the Senior Officers School in India. In his own eyes at least, he had little hope of further promotion. But the war gave him his chance. Commander of the Indian 10 Infantry Brigade in Eritrea, where he was wounded, and subsequently of the Indian 10 Division in the Iraq rebellion, the Syrian campaign against the Vichy French and then in the Anglo-Soviet occupation of Persia, he was asked for by Alexander to command Burma Corps in March 1942.

It was hardly a corps. Seventeen Division had been badly mauled in the retreat from lower Burma and its losses on the Sittang had not been completely replaced, while 1 Burma Division was composed of very shaky Burma Rifles battalions (albeit mainly composed of members of hill tribes and with very few Burmese) stiffened with a few British and Indian battalions. Slim had 7 Armoured Brigade, still relatively unscathed, and another British infantry battalion, First Royal Inniskilling Fusiliers, flown in from India. There was insufficient air transport to provide corps signals and logistic units, however, and these had to be put together by milking units and formations already in Burma, a thoroughly unsatisfactory state of affairs. Slim was lucky, however, with his divisional commanders. Major-Generals 'Punch' Cowan and Bruce Scott were not only of Slim's regiment but they had all three served in the same battalion, 1/6 Gurkha Rifles, and knew well

---

*The forerunner of today's Territorial Army.

and trusted each other. Not only did Slim have to extricate Burma Corps from his headquarters in Prome, 150 miles north of Rangoon, but there were also the peacetime impedimenta to consider. British regiments and some of the British-officered Burma battalions had their wives and children in station with them. Children had mostly been evacuated when Rangoon fell, and those wives who stayed behind were inducted into the Women's Auxiliary Service Burma, or Wasbies, and employed in rear areas as nurses, clerks and drivers, but moved well away from the front lines and the Japanese. First Gloucesters, stationed in Burma since 1938, had the problem of what to do with their mess silver and when it could not be sent to India for safe keeping, it was eventually buried in the jungle.*

Burma Corps moved back, and on 3 April the Japanese bombed Mandalay. Law and order broke down, with panic, riots and looting, an unwelcome diversion for the army that now had to police the city as well as getting its troops back more or less intact. As the Japanese advanced up the Irrawaddy River, the British employees of the Burma Oil Company strove desperately to destroy the oil installations before they fell into enemy hands, while Burma Corps fought a delaying action at Kyaukse, south of Mandalay, to allow 7 Armoured Brigade time to get its tanks across the Irrawaddy. Viper Force, formed in February by Royal Marine volunteers manning an assortment of motor launches and river boats in the Irrawaddy, harassed the Japanese at every opportunity, and collected British and Indian stragglers where they could, but they were far too few to have any major effect. Once the troops, the tanks and as much equipment and as many vehicles as could be shifted were across, the Ava Bridge, the longest in the world at that time, was blown at 2359 hours on 30 April 1942 and any British pretence to rule Burma was gone. The Japanese routed Chinese armies sent to Lushio by Chiang Kai-shek to defend the Burma Road and cut the only overland route to China. From now on, all supplies for the Chinese would be delivered by air, flying from India over the Hump, a spur of the Himalayas between Assam and China. Two Chinese armies (equivalent to divisions) led by the American Lieutenant-General Joseph Stilwell marched into India, where their administration became the responsibility of the Allies.

---

*Alas, when an officer returned to dig it up after the war it had gone. In the late 1960s an officer of the regiment while serving in Malaya found some of the items for sale in a bazaar in Singapore. He bought them and returned them to the regiment.

Stilwell, fifty-nine in 1942, had been a corps commander in California until war broke out, when he was sent off to be Chiang Kai-shek's Chief of Staff as well as commander of all US troops in China, India and Burma. The wartime commander with perhaps the trickiest appointment of all, he found Chiang to be duplicitous and far more interested in amassing equipment and supplies to take on Mao Tse-Tung's communists than in waging war against the Japanese, which he was quite happy to let the British and the Americans do for him, while most of the Chinese generals spent more time intriguing amongst themselves and against each other than in waging war. Even when Chiang did agree to commit his armies, he was constantly changing his mind, with the result that any deployment involving them took far longer than it need have. Chinese armies were always short of equipment – only two thirds of their men were armed, the rest being used as porters. Nevertheless, the Chinese had manpower resources that the Allies did not, and had to be tolerated and pandered to. Stilwell had a reputation, possibly deliberately fostered, for rudeness and abrasiveness – he was nicknamed 'Vinegar Joe' – and for being anti-British. He claimed to be unable to understand Alexander's accent – which was odd, as Alexander spoke King's English, as did just about every other British officer, and Stilwell seems to have had no problems with understanding the Chinese generals, many of whom barely spoke English at all (although, to be fair to Stilwell, he did speak some Mandarin). Slim, on the other hand, liked Stilwell and found him, in private at least, to be tolerant and utterly reliable.

The British having crossed the Irrawaddy, the last obstacle before Imphal and relative safety was the River Chindwin, over which there were no bridges, only ferries that were inadequate for the task. Here more of the few vehicles and heavy equipment left to the corps were rendered unusable and dumped, and on 11 May the first units of Burma Corps began to arrive at Tamu, on the Assam–Burma border, just as the American and Filipino survivors of Corregidor were being rounded up. On the border was IV Corps of the Eastern Army (in peacetime Eastern Area), charged with receiving Burma Corps and with defending India against Japanese incursions. This corps was commanded by Lieutenant-General Stephen Irwin, who disliked Slim intensely and was prepared to give only the barest minimum of support to him and his beaten corps. Units arriving at the end of that long and desperate retreat, exhausted and short of everything from razor blades to socks, were directed to hastily erected tented camps on the plains of Imphal, with little drainage to protect them from the monsoon rains that began as the last soldiers of the corps trickled in on 17 May, a few days after Stilwell and his headquarters had arrived, having also evacuated Burma on foot. Slim went to see Irwin to complain, and found to his astonishment that, in failing to provide proper care for Burma Corps, Irwin was allowing his professional duty to be affected by personal feelings. Irwin was an officer of the Essex Regiment and, when Slim commanded 10 Indian Infantry Brigade in Eritrea in 1940, First Battalion the Essex Regiment was in his brigade, along with two Indian battalions and one Gurkha. At one point the Essex broke, and Slim, perfectly properly, sacked the commanding officer, who was a personal friend of Irwin's. Things got better, but, as Irwin would shortly assume command of Eastern Army, it would be some time before it did.

It was not only the British and Indian Armies that suffered in the retreat to India. Once the army had pulled out of Northern Burma and the Arakan, the Burmese fell with glee on the long columns of refugees, Indians resident or employed in Burma who had fled before the advancing Japanese. Many Burmese – perhaps most – did not want the British in their country and, while, apart from assisting the Japanese and encouraging those Burmese in the Burma Rifles to desert, they could not directly attack the British, they could attack their unarmed lackeys – the Indians – and murder, robbery and rape of those unfortunates were commonplace once the British administration was withdrawn.

The British Army is no stranger to retreats. The retreat to Corunna in 1808–09 lasted twenty days and cost 8,800 casualties (killed, wounded, missing and prisoners of war), around a quarter of the force, and the commander, Lieutenant-General Sir John Moore, was killed; the retreat from Mons in 1914 lasted twelve days and cost 10,000 casualties or one sixth of the force, and the commander, Field Marshal Sir John French, was ultimately sacked; the retreat from Burma lasted 125 days and cost 12,000 casualties (including 3,000 Burmese deserters) or around half of the force. Worse, while prisoners taken by the French or the Germans could expect decent treatment, those taken by the Japanese could expect to be humiliated, starved, tortured, worked to death or all four. This was undoubtedly the worst retreat in British military history, but fortunately the commanders – Alexander at the top and Slim at ground level – survived and Slim would ultimately lead that same army to victory and the defeat of Imperial Japan.

* * *

In March 1942 the British Chiefs of Staff decided that Madagascar was the next likely objective for Japanese expansion and that the island should be occupied by the Allies before this could happen. Madagascar is an island in the Indian Ocean lying 250 miles east of what was then the Portuguese colony of Mozambique. It is 1,200 miles from north to south and 300 miles east to west, or rather larger than Great Britain, and was under the control of the Vichy French. While Japanese occupation of Madagascar, and particularly of the naval and air base at Diego Garcia (now Antsiranana), could undoubtedly interfere with shipping in the Indian Ocean, and even make the route round the Cape to the Suez Canal very dangerous indeed, it is unlikely in the extreme that the Japanese ever intended to go there, or that, if they did, they could have sustained a force so far out of their defensive ring of captured territories. The suggestion that the British should take Madagascar was first discussed in December 1941, when de Gaulle* was a strong advocate, deliberated upon again in March 1942 and finally approved in April. By then the Royal Navy was not in favour – they would have to find the ships from resources already overstretched – and Brooke, the CIGS, was worried that the Vichy government, which had recently installed as prime minister Pierre Laval, who was even more anti-British than his colleagues, might react by handing over French ships and colonies to the Germans, or by bombing Gibraltar.

Despite the doubts, it was decided to go ahead with Operation Ironclad. The ships would be found from Force H, responsible for the Straits of Gibraltar and the Western Mediterranean, and the United States Navy was persuaded to increase its presence in the Atlantic while Ironclad was under way. The troops would be 29 Brigade Group, which had been trained in amphibious operations and consisted of four regular infantry battalions, an army commando† and supporting light tanks, artillery and engineers, and 17 Brigade Group, comprising three regular and one Territorial battalions, with artillery, engineers and a field ambulance unit. Later on, 13 Brigade, part of 5 Division and intended as a reinforcement for India, was added, and

---

*Described by Brooke during the discussions as 'an unpleasant specimen'.

†A recent concept, commandos were intended as raiding forces, in order, as Churchill put it, 'to leave a trail of German bodies behind them'. They were manned by volunteers from the rest of the army and were quite separate from Royal Marine Commandos, who belonged to the Royal Navy and had a similar purpose.

the whole would be supported by a squadron of light tanks. The mounting base would be Durban, and, when the various elements of the force arrived there, they were lobbied by Smuts, the South African prime minister, who did not agree that taking Diego Garcia would lead to the inevitable collapse of French rule in Madagascar and wanted the expedition to take other ports on both sides of the island as well. As the British did not want to delay in Madagascar but needed to get the operation over with and the troops sent on to India as soon as possible, this suggestion was put on hold for the time being.

Covered by naval gunfire and attacks from carrier-borne aircraft, the landings took place an hour and twenty minutes before first light on 5 May 1942 and at first all went well. A radio message was broadcast inviting the French commandant of Diego Garcia to surrender and when this was refused, as expected, British troops began to advance on the town. After some hours, a captured French officer was sent back into town with another message to surrender. He carried not only a message inviting surrender, however, but also his own observations as to how many troops the British had, what they were equipped with and where they were. The French defence now stiffened. Four British tanks were knocked out, there were problems finding a beach on which the British artillery could be landed and hence delays in fire support, two more tanks were disabled and the crews captured and by last light on 5 May the attack had stalled. A dawn attack on 6 May failed and it was not until the Royal Navy landed fifty Royal Marines behind the French defences in support of a night attack that Diego Garcia was finally captured at 0300 hours on 7 May. On 8 May the local commander surrendered. So far 100 British had been killed and 300 wounded, while the French admitted to 150 killed and 500 wounded. Wavell as Commander-in-Chief India was now urging that a South African garrison should be installed and the British troops released for the defence of India, but both the intransigence of the French governor of Madagascar, who was not of course bound by the local surrender in Diego Garcia, and large numbers of cases of malaria and dengue fever amongst 13 Brigade – which could not now be used anywhere – militated against him.

On 23 May the French governor opened negotiations with the British from the capital, Tananarive, in the centre of the island, and the Royal Navy, having sunk three French submarines and destroyed twenty French aircraft at little cost, prepared to reduce their presence. Then, on 29 May, the navy suffered its first serious loss in the campaign, but not from the French. A force of five Japanese submarines had crossed the Indian Ocean and launched midget submarines, which, with considerable skill and bravery, torpedoed the battleship HMS *Ramillies* and an oil tanker. The tanker sank but *Ramillies* managed to limp back to Durban for repairs. The Japanese were chased off by depth charges and air attacks, but their presence was seen by some as a justification for Ironclad. Five submarines do not amount to an invasion force, however: the Japanese foray was a raid launched in the hope that it might catch some shipping in Durban, and, when none was found, the Japanese had sent up a reconnaissance float plane which had duly spotted the British warships off Madagascar.

Negotiations with the island's governor were long and tortuous, hinging on what arrangements could be made to safeguard the honour of (Vichy) France and the integrity of the army. It was made very plain that de Gaulle's solution, whereby the island would declare for the Free French and be run by them, was completely unacceptable to the administration and to the officers of the French garrison (many of whose soldiers were Senegalese) and soon it became plain that the governor was playing for time, hoping to spin out negotiations until the rains came, when military operations would become very difficult, not least because the movement of vehicles would be impossible. The British had no option but to restart operations while continuing to negotiate. On 23 August the French declared the capital an open city and withdrew south, and on 29 September the British made a series of landings in the south, eventually hemming the governor and his troops into the southernmost part of the island. At last, on 6 November the governor surrendered on very much the same terms as had been offered and rejected when Diego Garcia had been captured. What was hoped would take a few weeks had lasted for six months and had achieved little, except rendering two brigades (for 29 Brigade had also succumbed to malaria) unfit for operations from India for some time.

* * *

What was now needed in India was a period of consolidation, retraining and re-equipping from a defensive position along the border. The Japanese were at the end of a very long supply chain, had large numbers of sick which they could not evacuate by roads since these had been washed away by the monsoon, were short of even their standard, basic rations of rice and vegetables and were in no condition to attack India just yet. That the army in India was not left alone for a period of recuperation and preparation was due to Churchill's insistence on constant aggression, without his having any real idea of conditions on the ground, hence the First Arakan Battle. It was certainly true that British prestige was at an all-time low – not just in the Far East but worldwide – and a victory would do much to restore morale in the army and show the world that the British were still a force to be reckoned with. As Slim pointed out, however, it is better to let a victory speak for itself rather than predict one with the inevitable consequences when it doesn't happen.[64]

The Arakan is that coastal province of Burma that lay immediately south of India (now of Bangladesh) and included the Mayu peninsula that runs down to the island of Akyab, which is about ninety miles south of what was then the Indian border and separated from the mainland of Burma by a narrow channel. The mainland of Arakan had few roads and was divided by steep ridges running north to south interspersed with narrow, cultivated valleys and streams. The aims of the first Arakan offensive were limited and seemingly attainable, even given the state of the army in India at the time. It was modest in scope and intended simply to clear the Mayu peninsula of Japanese and capture the island of Akyab along with its airstrips that could be used to attack India. Intelligence said that there were only four Japanese divisions in Burma and of those only one regiment was in the Arakan. At this stage Eastern Army had two corps covering the Indian border: to the north-east IV Corps of two divisions, 17 Indian, which had still not recovered from the disastrous retreat, and 23 Indian, and XV Corps, now commanded by Slim after the disbanding of Burma Corps, with the Indian 14 Division and 26 Division. In front of the army was the newly formed V Force, of British officers with local knowledge and languages commanding small bodies of loyal tribesmen whose job it was to gather intelligence. Irwin, now commanding Eastern Army, decided that the offensive would be carried out by Major-General Wilfred Lloyd's newly formed 14 Division, but, instead of his reporting to XV Corps, Irwin decided that he and Eastern Army would control 14 Division direct, an unusual departure from the normally accepted system of command and control. Slim thought this most irregular, but, in the event, by being cut out of the chain of command he was untainted by the disaster that followed.

* * *

At the time of Pearl Harbor, the US Army had but one operational division. By the end of the war it would have ninety, but for the moment there was no means of hitting back at the Japanese save by air or by sea. Despite the damage done to the US Pacific Fleet on 7 December 1941, the carrier fleet of the USS *Enterprise, Lexington* and *Saratoga*, now reinforced by the *Yorktown* from the Atlantic, had escaped destruction, along with many cruisers and destroyers, and almost immediately it began to harass Japanese island bases by air attack whenever it could. None of this was anything more than a pinprick, of little concern to the Japanese and generally ignored by them, particularly once they had put the *Saratoga* out of action by torpedoing her on 11 January 1942, but in April of that year came an American raid which did little damage but had huge consequences. A force of sixteen US Army Air Force B-25 Mitchell bombers was loaded on to the recently built carrier USS *Hornet* and on 18 April they were launched in the teeth of a gale 650 miles east of Japan. Three of the bombers dropped incendiary bombs on Nagoya, Kobe and Osaka, while the other thirteen, led by Lieutenant-Colonel James Doolittle, bombed Tokyo itself. Although the B-25s could take off from a carrier, it was doubtful if they could land on one, and in any case to return to the launch area would be to risk running out of fuel. The surviving aircraft – and, as it turned out, this meant all sixteen – had therefore been instructed to fly to China and land at friendly bases there. In the event, one aircraft landed at Vladivostok, four landed at airstrips held by the Chinese and the crews of eleven, unable to find an airstrip, bailed out, some over Japanese-held territory. Three men were captured and executed out of hand (illegally) but most of the rest got safely to Chungking. Although the raid accomplished little in terms of the killing of Japanese and the destruction of property, it provided a great fillip to the American public, which had so far had to live with an uninterrupted string of defeats, and worried the Japanese, who had been assuring their people that the mighty Japanese armed forces and the divine emperor would protect them from anything the effete and defeated Westerners might try to throw at them.

As it was, with the initial, and spectacular, success of their expansion plan, the Japanese had next decided to widen the scope of their defensive ring and cut Australia off from America. To do this, they would need bases in northern Papua, taken in early 1942, and the Solomon Islands, which they began to capture in March 1942. The next step was Port Moresby, on the south-eastern coast of New Guinea and only 400 miles from the coast of

Queensland, in northern Australia. Three Japanese convoys were assembled in the Carolines and New Britain, one each to take the Louisades Archipelago, south-east of Port Moresby, and Tulagi Island in the Solomons, while the main one would attack Port Moresby. There would be two naval task forces to support the invasion, the covering force of one light carrier, four heavy cruisers and a destroyer, and the strike force of two fleet carriers, two heavy cruisers and six destroyers. By now the British were able to decipher Japanese naval codes, through the Ultra organization, and knew of the Japanese intentions. An Allied naval force of two US fleet carriers, the *Lexington* and the *Yorktown*, and a mix of American and Australian cruisers was assembled to counter them. What came to be known as the Battle of the Coral Sea was the first naval battle to be fought entirely by aircraft, with none of the ships involved on either side able to see their opponent. The numbers of aircraft were equal – around 120 on each side, although the Japanese aircraft were better – and inevitably there were errors by both navies: ships mistakenly taken for carriers were attacked; ships sailed off in the wrong direction; and erroneous assumptions were drawn from air reconnaissance reports. But on 7 May the Japanese light carrier was sunk and the Port Moresby invasion force withdrew to wait and see what would happen next. The next day, both sides located the other's main fleet and launched their aircraft into the attack. The Japanese sank the *Lexington* and the Americans so badly damaged the two Japanese fleet carriers that they were out of action for months. In terms of tonnage of ships sunk, the Japanese won the Battle of the Coral Sea, and they did succeed in taking Tulagi Island, but the battle ended the Japanese attempt to take Port Moresby from the sea, and the albeit temporary loss of two fleet carriers was to have a significant effect on the much larger naval encounter which took place the following month. The Battle of Midway, which was fought from 4 to 7 June 1942, was to be the first decisive defeat that the Japanese suffered in this war. While luck was certainly on the side of the Americans at Midway, so was good intelligence and superior equipment in the form of radar, something that the Japanese had not yet fitted to more than a few of their ships and aircraft. The battle would tip the balance of naval power in the Pacific against the Japanese and they would never be able to regain it.

After the first initial and startling – except perhaps to the Japanese – successes of 1941 and 1942, argument had once more broken out in Tokyo as to what to do next. Options were to move north against the Soviet Union, west against India and Ceylon, south against Australia or east towards Hawaii. The army vetoed attacking the USSR on the very sensible grounds that taking on two world powers at a time was quite enough without adding a third; the navy favoured going for India and also Australia, while Admiral Yamamoto, Commander-in-Chief of the Combined Fleet, considered that the capture of Hawaii would force the Americans to a negotiated peace. The result was a compromise – Australia and Hawaii. The former resulted in the Battle of the Coral Sea and the removal of two carriers from the Japanese order of battle. To achieve the latter, Yamamoto planned to lure the US Pacific Fleet into a battle when the superior Japanese fleet could destroy it, and he intended to do this by threatening Midway Island, America's most westerly Pacific base and the most northerly of the Hawaiian chain. Japanese intelligence suggested that one of the three remaining American carriers, the *Yorktown*, had also been sunk in the Coral Sea battle and that the other two were nowhere near the intended battle area, giving Yamamoto ample time to deploy his forces before they could arrive. In fact, the *Yorktown* had been damaged, not destroyed, but the other two were indeed in the South Pacific and, if not forewarned, would certainly take time to get anywhere near Midway.

Yamamoto's plan was to mount a diversionary raid on the Aleutian Islands while landing a marine expeditionary force on Midway once it had been comprehensively bombed by carrier-borne aircraft. Vice-Admiral Nagumo, the hero of Pearl Harbor, would be following up with a strike force of four carriers with 261 aircraft, and two battleships with associated escorts of cruisers and destroyers. Further back-up would be provided by Admiral Yamamoto himself, flying his flag in the *Yamato*, one of the two biggest battleships ever built (the other was her sister, the *Musashi*), with two other battleships and their escorts. Altogether, the Japanese force totalled some 800 ships of various types including the troop transports and a submarine screen that would be positioned on the approach to Midway, with the four carriers serving as the weapon with which Yamamoto would defeat what remained of the US Pacific Fleet once its two remaining carriers appeared to defend their last base before Hawaii. It might well have worked had not Allied code-breakers discovered the plan, the routes and the fact that the main objective was to be Midway. The garrison of the island was reinforced and its complement of aircraft boosted by transfers from Pearl Harbor. The *Hornet* and the *Enterprise* were recalled to Pearl Harbor and sailed from there under Rear Admiral Raymond Spruance on 26 May; the damage to the

Yorktown was repaired in the astonishingly short time of two days and she, along with her escorts, sailed on 30 May under Admiral Frank Fletcher. The three carriers rendezvoused on the afternoon of 2 June and the whole fleet under Fletcher moved to the north of Midway, well before Yamamoto's submarines could get in position. The Americans had 230 carrier-borne aircraft, less than those of Nagumo, but they could also call on land-based air cover from Midway, which the Japanese could not.

On the morning of 3 June, an American reconnaissance aircraft spotted the approaching Japanese and land-based B-17 bombers took off to attack the transports. Japanese anti-aircraft defences were neither as plentiful nor as sophisticated as those on Allied ships, and on this occasion their crews did not begin firing until the bombs were splashing into the sea around them; even so, little damage was sustained by either the Japanese ships or American bombers. Then, at first light on 4 June, Nagumo's carrier-based bombers attacked Midway. They destroyed many of the buildings on the base and set the oil installations on fire, but they did not put the airstrip out of action and the lead pilot radioed to Nagumo that a second attack wave would be needed. Meanwhile the torpedo-armed aircraft from the American carriers were attacking the Japanese carriers with little success, taking huge casualties from Zero fighters. The accepted version of what happened next is that Nagumo began to rearm his aircraft with bombs, to attack Midway once more, but changed his mind and began instead to arm them with torpedoes, to attack the enemy ships whose presence he had now detected. At 1020 hours, all his aircraft were armed, on deck and about to take off, and it was now that the American SBD Dauntless dive-bombers arrived overhead and hit three Japanese carriers in less than six minutes. Had the Americans arrived five minutes later, so goes this account, then Nagumo would have launched and destroyed the American carriers and the war would have taken a very different turn. That, at least, is the version propagated by the Japanese and accepted by nearly all Western historians since.[65] Recent scholarship, however, suggests that this is not so and that what really happened was that the decks of the carriers had been kept clear to enable the ships' defensive fighters to be launched or recovered and that the torpedo-armed aircraft had not yet been brought up from below. The process of lining aircraft up for a launch was estimated to take at least forty-five minutes, and in all cases the last launch or recovery of fighters was but fifteen minutes before the dive-bombers arrived.[66] There was therefore no possibility of a successful counter-stroke being delivered, even if the Americans had not arrived for a further twenty minutes, never mind the five of legend. As it was, the crews of three Japanese carriers, the *Akagi*, the *Kaga* and the *Soryu*, had to abandon ship and the *Kaga* and *Soryu* sank that evening. The burning hulk of the *Akagi* was sunk next day by a Japanese submarine. The fourth Japanese carrier, the *Hiryu*, initially escaped the dive-bombers and launched her aircraft against the *Yorktown*, damaging the American carrier to the extent that she had to be taken under tow, to be finally sunk by a Japanese submarine on 7 June. *Hiryu* herself was then attacked by dive-bombers from *Enterprise* and *Yorktown*, set on fire and, when she could not be recovered, was sunk by a Japanese cruiser on 5 June.

Despite having lost all of his carriers, Yamamoto still hoped to lure the Americans into a trap where the firepower of his battleships could be brought to bear, but Admiral Nimitz, commanding the Pacific Fleet, would not be tempted and, on 7 June, Yamamoto accepted the inevitable and ordered the remnants of his fleet home. The Battle of Midway was the turning point of the Asian War. Never again could the Japanese navy operate out of range of land-based aircraft; American industry could easily replace her losses in ships and aircraft while Japan's could not; America's huge educated population and her technical educational institutes could replace the mechanics and aircrew lost, but for Japan it would be far more difficult. As the British Official History put it: Coral Sea checked Japanese expansion, Midway stopped it.[67] Midway was the Stalingrad of the East and after it Japan could not win the war, although it would take much hard fighting to convince her of that.

12

THE RUSSIAN WAR

NOVEMBER 1942–JUNE 1944

All summer, refugees had been pouring into Stalingrad from the west, some driving their animals in front of them, some on bicycles, some on horses, some, mainly party administrators, in cars and lorries, but most on foot. By the time the Germans had closed up to the Volga, the population within the city had swollen to an estimated 1.5 million from a pre-war total of 400,000 and Stalin forbade the Red Army from evacuating them, a stance he did not reverse until the late summer, when he accepted that the presence of useless mouths that had to be fed was an intolerable burden on the defence of the city. All through the summer and autumn, the Red Army had been building up its strength from the vast and seemingly inexhaustible pool of manpower that was the Russian population, and by the summer the enormous losses of 1941 had been all but replaced. These new brigades and divisions were not fed into Stalingrad, however, where Chuikov received only the reinforcements necessary to prevent a complete collapse, but instead they were trained and equipped for the massive counter-blow that the Stavka had been planning.

The Germans had little warning of what was to come. Some indications that the Russians might attempt an attack on the Romanian Third Army on Sixth Army's left flank were countered by stationing XXXXVIII Panzer Corps behind it, but this was a corps in name only: its two German armoured divisions had just seventy-seven tanks between them and the forty-one belonging to 22 Panzer were unreliable because, during the period of immobility due to severe fuel rationing, mice had got inside the vehicles and chewed through their electrical wiring. The corps's other division, the Romanian 1 Tank Division, had 103 tanks but 40 of them were Czech light tanks and virtually useless against Russian armour. The Germans had bitten off far more than their available manpower could chew, and the launching of the drive into the Caucasus before Stalingrad was taken, the inability of

Hitler to listen to military advice and sanction a closing down of the attack on Stalingrad, the vastly over-extended supply lines, the demands of Leningrad, the need for security in the rear areas and a failure by German industry, efficient though it was, to replace vehicle losses all conspired to put the German Eastern Front in a precarious state as the winter of 1942/43 approached.

With four Army Groups, North, Centre, A and B, the Germans were trying to hold nearly 2,000 miles of a front that ran from Leningrad in the north to Stalingrad on the Volga, then south and west across the Caucasian front to the Black Sea at Novorossiysk. Sixth Army opposite Stalingrad had twenty divisions, six of them supposedly armoured or motorized, but most of their tanks and many of their other vehicles had been removed on the grounds that, as the taking of Stalingrad was now a matter of street fighting by the infantry, the vehicles were not needed and not having to provide fuel for them eased the logistic problem. Sixth Army's southern neighbour, Fourth Panzer Army, was down to two German and two Romanian divisions, and again they had few tanks, and those formations that were sent up to add some depth and stiffen the defences behind Sixth Army were soon sucked into the fighting for the city. Rifle companies in Sixth Army infantry battalions were down to forty men, not much more than platoon strength, and at one stage Paulus ordered that tank crews should be used as infantry – he was deaf to protests that to waste these highly skilled men, who could not easily be replaced when the time came for tanks to be manned again, was counter-productive. In October formations had been ordered to reduce their staffs by 10 per cent to boost front-line units, but attempts to use surplus Luftwaffe ground troops to increase combat strength failed when, instead of being used as individual reinforcements for existing infantry divisions, the Luftwaffe insisted that they form their own divisions commanded by Luftwaffe officers and NCOs, none of whom had any experience of or training in ground warfare.

Like Churchill, Hitler desperately needed a victory, and this became more urgent after the success of Operation Torch in the Mediterranean, when even in Germany the legend of the Führer's invincibility was beginning to wear a little thin. Like Alamein to Churchill, Stalingrad had become a symbol to Hitler. He had claimed over and over again in public speeches and in discussions with his allies that the Germans were on the Volga to stay and that Stalingrad would soon be taken – 'fragments to be mopped up' was an expression used – and he could not now disengage.

In normal circumstances, the Germans would never have placed the allied armies in the front line along the Volga and the Don, yet, with all the German formations fully committed, there was no alternative. North-west of Sixth Army was the Romanian Third Army, covering a length of 100 miles with fourteen divisions, which on the face of it seems not unreasonable, but they were very short of modern equipment and had only sixty 75mm anti-tank guns for the whole army, the rest being horse-drawn 37mm weapons firing rounds that would simply bounce off Russian T-34 tanks. The Romanians had not been able to close up to the River Don completely, and there was a forty-mile strip on the west bank that was still held by the Russians and which allowed the Red Army to go back and forth across the Don under cover of darkness or smoke. On the Romanian Third Army's left was the Italian Eighth Army of ten divisions, which, like the Romanians, had never been equipped to German army standards despite the promises made. South of Fourth Panzer Army was the thirteen-division Romanian Fourth Army, again covering a frontage of about 100 miles but with only thirty-four effective anti-tank guns. German intelligence about the forthcoming attack was sketchy. The army Chief of the General Staff in Berlin thought it unlikely that the Red Army would be able to launch anything like the offensives of the previous winter, while Hitler, with that extraordinary intuition that just occasionally proved him right and his professional advisers wrong, thought that the outbreak of bridge-building over the Don in front of the Romanian Third Army might indicate a major thrust in the direction of Rostov, and he ordered a stiffening of the Romanian front by German divisions – but there were very few German divisions available to send. As it turned out, Hitler was correct to expect an attack, but wrong in failing to draw the obvious conclusion and withdraw Sixth Army to a more easily defended and shorter line. Instead, he still hoped to capture Stalingrad before the Russians moved.

Operation Uranus was the Russian name for the counter-attack to be launched by the new armies raised during the summer. It was intended to take the Germans on at their own game and carry out a massive encirclement of Sixth Army by driving through the weakest points of the German front north and south of Sixth Army and Fourth Panzer Army and meeting at Kalatsch fifty miles west of Stalingrad. For Uranus, the Red Army had amassed over a million men, 900 tanks, 12,000 artillery pieces and 100 multiple rocket-launcher batteries, supported by 1,200 aircraft. On the morning of 19 November 1942 in a thick fog the Russian artillery opened up on the forward positions of the Romanian Third Army. The Russian artillery controllers could not see their targets but, having checked the ranges in the weeks and days before the attacks, they did not have to. After an hour and twenty minutes, the artillery and the rockets switched to targets farther back and the 300 T-34 tanks of I and XXVI Tank Corps of the South-West Front, which had crossed the Don under cover of a smoke screen during the bombardment, advanced. In parts of the front, the Romanians fought hard and well, but mostly there was panic as the soldiers tried desperately to get away from the seemingly unstoppable Soviet tanks. After the tanks came the infantry of First Guards Army and within a few hours the Russians were through. An attempt by Lieutenant-General Ferdinand Heim's XXXXVIII Corps to seal the breach failed when he lost contact first with the Romanian Army, whose communications were never very good, and then with his own Romanian tank division, and finally when dwindling fuel forced him to halt and pull back. The preponderance of aircraft that the Russians had been able to concentrate and the snow that began to fall that day cancelled the superiority the Luftwaffe had enjoyed hitherto, but until well into the afternoon Sixth Army staff to the east thought the Russian attack was merely a local offensive, a 'side effect' of their own attacks on what was left of the city, and it was only at Headquarters Army Group B that suspicions of the Russians' real intentions began to surface, a view that was reinforced the next day when another Soviet spearhead of Fifty-First and Fifty-Seventh Armies with 220 T-34s launched itself out of the mist to the south and drove through the Romanian Fourth Army. Now it was clear that the Russians were attempting an encirclement, and both Army Groups A and B began to move such mobile units that they had to try to prevent it. Increasingly heavy snow, iced-up tracks, shortage of fuel and the inability of the Luftwaffe to provide either air reconnaissance or ground support meant that all these measures were far too late, and by the evening of 20 November the Russians had penetrated to a depth of forty miles behind the front. On 21 November an attempt by XXXXVIII Corps to relieve the increasingly desperate situation west of Stalingrad failed and 25,000 Romanians were killed or captured. On 22 November the Russians cut the Stalingrad to Rostov railway line, the main supply route for Sixth Army and in some senses its lifeline, and on 23 November the Soviets closed the ring when 45 Armoured Brigade from the South-West Front's IV Armoured Corps moving east met advance elements of the Stalingrad Front going west at Kalatsch.

Inside the ring were the whole of Sixth Army, elements of Fourth Panzer Army that had not managed to move in time and stragglers from both Romanian armies. The corps commanders of Sixth Army assumed they would now break out, something they could still have done relatively inexpensively before the Soviets had time to reinforce the ring, but Paulus demurred. Hitler's instructions had been to stand still, and he intended to do just that and carry on with attempts to take the city. The wretched General Heim, having quite properly withdrawn what was left of his corps to avoid being cut off, now found himself placed under arrest on Hitler's direct orders, accused of failing to stop the Soviet advance, flown to Berlin and flung into Moabit Prison, where he languished until April 1943 before the Führer relented and allowed him to retire from the army.* That this could happen indicates the grip Hitler had by now succeeded in imposing upon the Wehrmacht – even two years previously the army would never have allowed one of their own to be treated in such a way.

Hitler refused the recommendation of Colonel-General von Weichs, Commander Army Group B, that Sixth Army should break out; it must now defend and wait to be relieved. Along the front facing the Volga and running through Stalingrad defence positions already existed, although they had been constructed as jump-off lines for attack rather than defence, but across the wide expanse of steppe to the army's rear nothing other than scattered alarm posts had been constructed, as it had not been thought necessary to defend against an approach from that direction. The soldiers dug in as best they could, an activity that became increasingly difficult as the temperature dropped and the ground froze. The army's winter clothing was held in supply depots outside the perimeter and the men had only temperate-climate uniforms, leather boots and one blanket per man. Straw and old newspapers became prized to stuff boots and to pack inside jackets, whereas the Russian soldiers were well equipped with felt boots, sheepskin jackets and fur hats. When the ring closed around them, Sixth Army held fuel and rations for one week and, if not replenished, would have only three options: starve, surrender or break out, and the second implicitly and the third explicitly had been ruled out.

It was now that Reichsmarschall Göring, Commander-in-Chief of the Luftwaffe, inserted his baton into the pot: the Luftwaffe would keep Sixth

---

*He was reinstated after the Normandy landings in 1944 and commanded the Boulogne garrison, before being captured by the Canadians in September of that year.

Army supplied by flying in what it needed – perhaps not the 500 tons demanded by Paulus but certainly 350 tons. The professional flyers were aghast: the workhorse of the Luftwaffe's transport fleet was the Junkers Ju 52 (fondly called *Tante Ju* or Aunt Ju) which, depending on the version, could carry a maximum load of around 4.5 tons. Other transport aircraft in the fleet were the Ju 86 (just over 1 ton), the Ju 290 (4.5 tons), the Heinkel He 111 (4.25 tons) and the Focke-Wulf Fw 200 (5.25 tons). The only aircraft capable of carrying any greater amount of freight was the Messerschmitt Me 323, which could carry 10 tons, but there were very few of those, and to be of any help they would have to operate from the Ukraine. Altogether, by denuding other theatres and taking aircraft from training units, the Luftwaffe assembled 500 transport aircraft for the Stalingrad operation, mostly Ju 52s and including some from North Africa, to operate from two airfields about 100 miles from the pocket. As fighter cover would be essential, a squadron of Bf 109s was flown into Pitomnik, the only airstrip within the pocket suitable for such aircraft. Theoretically, if all the transports were Ju 52s and they maintained a standard rate of 30 per cent operational readiness when not being either repaired or serviced, 350 tons a day could be supplied, but only if all the aircraft were indeed Ju 52s, there was no interference from the Russians, the weather allowed flying, and more airstrips could be constructed inside the pocket. Quite apart from the inconvenient facts that not all the aircraft were Ju 52s, that the Russians did interfere and that the weather was not kind, the original calculations were totally wrong. Paulus as an experienced officer knew perfectly well, without looking at his staff tables, that the minimum requirement for his army and the 300,000 servicemen and Russian labourers for whom he was responsible was 1,500 tons per day. He actually asked for only 500 tons per day, hardly enough to supply one corps. As Paulus ended up as a Russian prisoner and subsequently lived and died in what was then communist East Germany, we do not know what his thinking was, but it may be that, as he had supplies for one week, he calculated that 500 tons a day would top him up for the short period before he was relieved and the Russian ring destroyed. Alternatively, he may have known that the absolute maximum the Luftwaffe could fly in was 500 tons and that there was no point in asking for more – an odd attitude for a senior general to take.

By 23 November all Hitler's advisers – Keitel and Jodl from OKW, Zeitzler from OKH, Colonel-General Hans Jeschonnek, the Chief of Staff of the Luftwaffe, von Weichs from Army Group B and Paulus from Sixth

Army, the latter having changed his mind – were united in recommending that Sixth Army break out to the south-west. He now turned to the man whose tactical acumen he valued above all others and ordered Field Marshal von Manstein to take over the battle. He would form a new army group, Army Group Don, run by his Eleventh Army staff and taking under command Fourth Armoured Army, Sixth Army and the Romanian Third Army, leaving von Weichs and Army Group B to care for Second Army and the Italian Eighth Army, the latter being even more unreliable than the Romanians. Manstein had only just returned to the Eastern Front, having buried his son, killed by a Russian shell outside Leningrad, and then taken leave to break the news to his wife in Liegnitz. Hitler's orders to Manstein were that he was to 'bring the enemy's attacks to a standstill and recapture the position previously held by us'. Manstein knew very well that at this stage it was no use his also recommending a breakout: Hitler would never agree. He also knew from a Luftwaffe officer who had just flown out of the pocket that ammunition was down to between 10 and 20 per cent of the normal scale of issue, enough for one day's intensive fighting, and that fuel was sufficient only for minor local movements. He did not believe, therefore, that Sixth Army actually could break out, and that, even if it did, it would reach the Don with no ammunition and very little to back it up.[68] If, on the other hand, the breakout failed and the Sixth Army had to fight it out on the open steppe and was destroyed, then the whole German southern wing in the Caucasus would be in danger of being cut off. Having taken over the battle on the morning of 27 November, Manstein initially told OKH that he intended to break in, create a corridor to resupply Sixth Army and then attack and push the Red Army back across the Volga. He said that he would recommend a breakout 'only as a last resort'.[69]

In planning for the relief of Sixth Army, Manstein had to assume that the forces to break through to Stalingrad would be provided by OKH, as there was nothing available to his command. These forces were promised: four armoured divisions, four infantry divisions and three Luftwaffe field divisions, some from Army Group A and some from Germany, all to arrive by 5 December. These forces might be enough to create a corridor to Sixth Army, but they were nowhere near enough to restore the original front.

In the meantime, the Luftwaffe was attempting to supply Sixth Army. The routes that could be flown were of course well known to the Russians, who placed large numbers of anti-aircraft guns along the thirty miles or so that they occupied, and Soviet fighters were constantly on the lookout for the incoming Junkers. On some days, the weather was so bad that no flying could take place; on others, the temporary airstrips in the pocket iced up. Soon flying by day became just too dangerous as more and more German aircraft were shot down, and as the airstrips were not equipped for night flying, loads instead had to be parachuted in. Sixth Army had insufficient fuel to move the containers dropped, which meant that the contents had to be manhandled to where they were needed, and in any case nothing like the quantities promised were ever delivered. In the first week of the airlift, 23–29 November, only 277 tons (193 of fuel, 70 of ammunition and 14 of food) were delivered, less than 10 per cent of that promised, which was itself far less than what was needed. In the second week, 30 November to 6 December, there was an improvement to 503 tons, still only 20 per cent of that promised. The Luftwaffe's best day was 31 December when, using 146 aircraft, it delivered 200 tons, but it never got anywhere near the amount Göring had rashly promised and which Colonel-General Baron von Richthofen, commanding Army Group B's affiliated Fourth Air Fleet, had warned everyone who would listen was impossible.[70] The Luftwaffe's officers and men did their best. The Germans lost 480 aircraft and around 1,000 aircrew killed in the attempt to keep Sixth Army in being, and they managed to fly out 24,627 wounded, but it was never going to be enough: even if every transport aircraft the German armed forces possessed had been available, it was an impossible task, and even Göring must have known it.

Within the pocket, rations were reduced for combat units to eight ounces of meat (from killing and butchering artillery and transport horses), eight ounces of bread and one ounce of cheese per man, with half that for rear echelon soldiers. It was nowhere nearly sufficient to keep a man healthy and active in temperatures of thirty below zero, but, as long as the hope of swift relief was there, morale remained high. The besieged soldiers knew that Manstein had taken over a new army group – 'Manstein will get us out' was the cry – and Manstein had signalled Paulus, assuring him that he would do all in his power to relieve him and his army. It took two weeks for Army Group Don's promised reinforcements to arrive, and even then they fell short of what had been promised and all the while the Russian rings round Stalingrad grew stronger. Colonel-General Hoth's Fourth Panzer Army got 17 Panzer Division from Army Group Centre, 23 Panzer from Army Group A in the Caucasus and 6 Panzer from France. The need to find troops to occupy all of France after the Torch landings, the risk of an Allied landing in the south of that country and the requirement to send more troops to Tunisia combined to ensure that there were few spare formations to send to Manstein.

In the same way that the Battle of the Somme in 1916 cannot be considered in isolation from what was happening simultaneously at Verdun 120 miles to the south-east, so Stalingrad must be looked at in the light of what was happening at Rzhev on the Upper Volga and 600 miles north-west of Stalingrad. Rzhev was the tip of a German salient that the Germans had held since 1941 and from which they still threatened Moscow, which was 150 miles south-east of it. There, on 25 November, two days before Manstein took command of Army Group Don, General Ivan Konev's Western Front with 800,000 men in eighty-three divisions and 2,350 tanks fell upon the defensive positions of the German Ninth Army in Operation Mars. Mars was originally intended to be launched in tandem with Uranus, but the winter freeze was late in that area and Mars was delayed until the rivers and streams froze to allow the tanks to cross without bridging. With seventeen infantry and six armoured divisions, Ninth Army, commanded by Colonel-General Walter Model, was the strongest army that the Germans had on the Eastern Front; it had already beaten off numerous Soviet counter-attacks, some of them in very fierce fighting, and it knew its area well. Initially the Red Army broke through and the Germans formed 'hedgehogs', a system of all-round defence in the villages that dotted the steppe. Fighting in the snow was ferocious and there were no divisions to send south to Manstein. The Soviets poured through, the Germans shelled their flanks, counter-attacked, eventually cut off huge numbers of Russians and by 15 December had stabilized the front. The Red Army lost around 400,000 men killed, wounded, missing or taken prisoner and lost 1,700 tanks. By then, however, it was too late to send help to Manstein.

Manstein's plan to rescue Sixth Army – and by now he was determined to take them out of the pocket rather than simply reinforce them – was in two phases. Phase One – *Wintergewitter* – envisaged Hoth's Fourth Panzer Army driving a corridor through the encircling Russians. Once he had made contact with Sixth Army, which would advance to meet him when he was within twenty miles (Sixth Army had hoarded sufficient fuel for only that distance), a convoy would follow through with 2,000 tons of fuel, for without it Sixth Army could not move any further. That fuel would fill the petrol tanks of a Sixth Army convoy that would be ready and loaded with wounded and would drive out through the corridor to the west and return with 4,000 tons of fuel, rations and ammunition. Once Sixth Army had been replenished with fuel and ammunition, Phase Two – *Donnerschlag* – would begin, with the army withdrawing to safety through the corridor, although, as far as Hitler and OKW were concerned, it would be a relief operation only, with Sixth Army continuing to hold Stalingrad.

Hoth's armoured spearhead attacked the Russian ring on 12 December with 260 tanks. Then, on 19 December, the Soviets launched Operation Little Saturn north-west of Stalingrad and fell upon the Italian Eighth Army and what was left of the Romanian Third. They broke. The Russians poured through, tearing a huge gap in the German front, posing a real risk of the whole of Army Group A being cut off in the Caucasus. Manstein had no option but to detach Hoth's strongest armoured division, 6 Panzer, to deal with the new threat. Hoth had now only thirty-five tanks and, although the men could see the flares over Stalingrad and the parachute loads falling over the city, there was no chance of reaching it. When the Russians overran one of the two German airfields supplying Stalingrad, most of the aircraft got away and it was recaptured in a counter-attack, but not before the Russians had destroyed all the stockpiled stores and air traffic control equipment.

What happened next is still argued over. Field Marshal von Manstein in his memoirs says that he now ordered Paulus to attempt to break out over the twenty miles or so separating the Sixth and Fourth Armoured armies, but that, while Paulus was willing to have a go, his chief of staff, Major-General Arthur Schmidt, persuaded him to decline and insisted that all that was needed was a sufficient airlift of supplies. Other authors, including Manstein's ADC,[71] say that Paulus begged to be ordered to break out and that Manstein said that he could not give that order but that he would back Paulus up if he decided to do so unilaterally. The fact is that Sixth Army could not have broken out as an army with all its vehicles and equipment – it simply did not have the fuel to do so – but it might well have been able to get the men out on foot by divisions, or even by battalions and companies, before its small arms ammunition became exhausted and starvation began to set in. Officers within the pocket were quoted as saying better for six divisions to get out than twenty to be lost, but nobody was prepared to risk giving the order: Hitler was adamant that Sixth Army must stay put as the springboard for a great offensive that would end the war in 1943, and there was still hope now that Field Marshal Milch of the Luftwaffe had arrived to resolve the chaos at the airfields, where many of the ground crew, recently transferred from North Africa, had no idea about cold-start procedures nor much experience of loading drills. Milch did indeed improve matters, but the air bridge remained incapable of delivering anything like the quantities needed.

On 21 December, Sixth Army reported its first deaths of starvation, although the death certificates read 'death from exhaustion'. By 23 December, Hoth's remaining panzers had advanced twelve miles but were still a very long way from making contact with Sixth Army. They could do no more, and, as Manstein manoeuvred desperately to restore the Don Front, Fourth Armoured Army was forced to pull back. It would never get any nearer to the beleaguered city and soon the word began to spread inside the pocket that the attempt to get Sixth Army out had failed. Farther north, the Russians now attacked the Hungarian Second Army – never the most enthusiastic of Germany's allies, the Hungarians would have been much happier fighting the Romanians than the Russians, and, armed as they were with Austro-Hungarian equipment from the Great War, they could not stop the T-34s. When the Red Army overran some of the airfields behind the Hungarians from where Stalingrad was being supplied, the German airlift became even less effective since it now had to operate from 200 miles away. But the important thing was to repair the rupture in the German front: Stalingrad and the Sixth Army must take their chances.

As the siege went on, rations were cut again and medical supplies ran out. The wounded had to be left lying in the streets and were finally forbidden rations at all: food was to be issued only to those capable of fighting. First the main airstrip in the pocket was lost, then the last remaining. Sixth Army was pushed back into the ruins of the city and, on 9 January, Paulus refused a call from the Russians to surrender. As ammunition ran out and the last remaining cats, rats and pieces of horseflesh were eaten, it was obvious to all that the end was near. On 28 January, Russian tanks cut the pocket in half and Hitler promoted Paulus to field marshal; his badges of rank and baton were dropped by air into the area still held by the Germans.* It was presumably intended to stiffen his resolve – no German field marshal had ever surrendered or been captured, and the implication was that Paulus had

---

*He had been promoted to colonel-general only two weeks previously.

better shoot himself before the city fell. Next day, all hope, ammunition and food gone, Paulus surrendered his part of the pocket, and the last remnants of Sixth Army ran up the white flag on 2 February 1943.

The Battle of Stalingrad, from September 1942 to February 1943, tore the guts out of the German army – destroyed it, wrecked it, devastated it – and yet it went on fighting for another two and a half years. No other army in the world, then or now, could have done that, and yet Stalingrad was the turning point of the whole Second World War. It was not just the loss of Sixth Army and the damage done to the flanking armies; it was not just the 120,000 dead German soldiers of Sixth Army and the 90,000 who spent years in Russian prison camps, most of them dying before the remnants were released in 1955; it was not just the 474,400 dead in the rest of the *Ostheer* between November 1942 and February 1943[72] (it had already lost 400,000 dead, including 13,000 officers, since the start of Barbarossa), more than twice as many as the British or the Americans lost in the whole of the second war; it was not just the exposure of the Luftwaffe's inability to perform as more than airborne artillery; it was not just the effect on a German population accustomed to an unbroken string of victories, although it was all of those too. The real significance of Stalingrad lay in the realization by both Germany and Russia that the Red Army not only would resist, but could resist, and that Russia was just too vast to be conquered without far more armoured and mobile units and far more men than even the Germans could produce. There could not now be a swift victory over the Soviet Union, or indeed anything other than a stalemate at best. It need not have been so. Had the German army not frittered away its strength in the summer of 1942 by trying to do far too much at the same time; had it retained Manstein's Eleventh Army in the south after the fall of Sevastopol; had it put everything into achieving a secure jump-off line before diving into the Caucasus; had von Weichs been given another Panzer Army – First – then Stalingrad might have been encircled and captured in July 1942. Even as it was, once it became clear that the Russians would continue to hold Stalingrad, had the German army gone into defence along the Volga and then gone for the Caucasus, it might still – just – have snatched something from the debacle.

Stalingrad and the offensives associated with it cost Germany's allies heavily too. Of the 250,000 men in the Hungarian Army, over half were either killed or captured, and the Italians lost 114,520 killed, captured or wounded, to the extent that their Eighth Army could not be reconstituted and the remnants were recalled to Italy in March. Of the 49,000 Italian prisoners, 28,000 died in captivity. One Romanian army was destroyed and the other badly mauled. Of course, Stalingrad cost the Russians too. They did not publish their casualties at the time but they cannot have been less than half a million, of which perhaps 200,000 might have been killed. Tactically, the only service that Sixth Army's stand did provide was to hold down seven Russian armies and give Manstein time to restore the front. A faster capitulation might have allowed the Soviets to cut off and annihilate Army Group A as well as Sixth Army and have allowed them to begin their final advance to Berlin a year before they actually did.

After the war, with Hitler dead, the German generals placed most of the blame for Stalingrad on him, insisting that they could not disobey the order for Sixth Army to stand fast. In fact, while officers who did disobey Hitler's orders were sometimes flung into jail, as we have seen they were nearly always released and reinstated fairly soon afterwards, and generals who disobeyed or refused to carry out an order that they thought was wrong were not executed but placed on Führer Reserve, a euphemism for retirement, and even then often recalled – Rundstedt more than once. Indeed, in September 1942, Hitler had sacked Field Marshal List as commander of Army Group A, largely for arguing with him and failing to advance into the Caucasus swiftly enough. That his supply lines, now augmented by camel trains, had provided insufficient fuel for him to move any faster was ignored, and Hitler, whose previous experience of military command had been of a section of ten men twenty-five years previously, took over command of the army group himself. He did not move to the front but remained in East Prussia while List's erstwhile chief of staff, Lieutenant-General von Greiffenberg, did the actual work. In due course this command arrangement was seen even by Hitler to be impracticable, and Colonel-General Ewald von Kleist, previously Commander First Panzer Army, was appointed on 21 November, while the Red Army was breaking though the German flanks at Stalingrad.

Now, however, with the disintegration of the Hungarian and Italian armies to the north of Stalingrad, there was a 200-mile gap in Army Group B's sector of the German Eastern Front through which poured troops of the Red Army's Voronezh and South-Western Fronts, led by Lieutenant-General Popov with four tank corps totalling 924 tanks and self-propelled guns with their associated infantry and field artillery. Ignoring his flanks, Popov moved as fast as he could, hoping to get to the River Dnieper before the spring thaw made the ground impassable to vehicles. Farther south, opposite Army Group Don, the front was now only 150 miles from Rostov on the River Don, a town vital to Army Group A because through it ran the only railway line and the main supply route. If the Soviets could break though and get to Rostov, then the whole of Army Group A in the Caucasus would be in danger of being cut off. For the moment, the latter threat had been averted, but Popov's advance threatened the whole southern wing of the German army in the East, for, if the Red Army could get to the River Dnieper, and all the indications pointed to that being their objective, then Army Groups A, Don and much of B would be in deadly peril. Manstein asked for a free hand, and, surprisingly, Hitler eventually gave it. The field marshal would fight the sort of battle the German army were so good at, a mobile battle of manoeuvre, not the static unyielding defence that Hitler seemed to favour. Taking Army Group A under command as well, Manstein had available for mobile operations First and Fourth Panzer Armies, the former from Army Group A, and First Army. In addition he was given Obergruppenführer Paul Hausser's SS Panzer Corps of three panzer grenadier divisions, which had recently been moved from France and which were up to strength in men and vehicles. Manstein's first action was to order Army Group A to withdraw from the Caucasus Front; Hitler resisted the move for reasons both of morale and of economics, but eventually agreed to it.

Popov crossed the River Donets and on 14 February entered Kharkov. Kharkov lies in the Ukraine and was the first Soviet city to be retaken by the Red Army. It had been held by II SS Panzer Corps, which had been ordered by Hitler to hold the city. Hausser, on his own authority, although supported by Manstein after the event, withdrew as Popov's tanks approached. Hitler was not pleased but Hauser got away with it – you could disobey, as long as you were subsequently proved right. The Russians too were disappointed – they had hoped and expected that the city would be defended and intended to surround it, bypass it and mop it up later in a smaller-scale repetition of Stalingrad. When the Red Army entered Kharkov, it found that, of a pre-war population of nearly a million, only around 400,000 remained. Many had, of course, fled in advance of the Germans, but, once more underlining the stupidity of a policy that alienated a people who, if treated decently, might well have forsaken communism and Stalin, the Allgemeine SS and NSDAP bureaucrats following the army had executed around 30,000 Jews, Communist Party officials and anyone suspected of helping the partisans.

Many had died of starvation, as the priority for food produced locally was for it to be exported to Germany, and many of the able-bodied had been deported to Germany as forced labour to replace Germans conscripted into the Wehrmacht. The Russians had no sympathy for those who were left and the NKVD took over the building formerly used by the Gestapo and began to execute those suspected of collaborating with the Germans, and many who had had nothing to do with the Germans but were denounced by fellow citizens in the settlement of old scores.

On 19 February, Popov's leading tanks were only ten miles from Zaponezhe on the Dnieper, and then Manstein struck. In a masterly example of what war should be, he sent his tanks hammering into the Russian flanks with the Luftwaffe once more doing what it did best: acting as reconnaissance and airborne artillery and knocking out Soviet tanks from the air. The motorized infantry followed and in four days Manstein had completed a classic double envelopment of the Russian forces, now strung out and having huge problems in resupplying themselves so far from their start point. On 14 March, Kharkov was recaptured by the *Leibstandarte Adolf Hitler* Division of the SS and by 24 March the battle was over. The Red Army had abandoned 6,000 square miles of newly captured territory, had lost around 23,000 killed with 615 tanks and 354 artillery pieces captured or destroyed. By now all Russian soldiers knew the likely fate of becoming a prisoner of the Germans, and only 9,000 prisoners were taken this time – many soldiers tried to make their way back to the Russian lines as individuals or small groups and many perished in the attempt. With the failure of a Soviet attack on Army Group Centre, halted on 18 March with the Luftwaffe's ground-attack aircraft again playing a leading role, the front was now stabilized, and, although the Germans had withdrawn from the Caucasus and abandoned Rostov, and Army Group Centre had abandoned Rzhev, it had also been considerably shortened, throwing up some German formations to create a mobile reserve.

Army Groups B and Don had now been subsumed into Army Group South, commanded by Manstein. Elsewhere, in Army Group North's area, the Russians had managed in January to force a land corridor about six miles wide through to Leningrad, along which they swiftly built a railway. Leningrad had never been entirely cut off from the USSR, as there was now a pipeline across Lake Lagoda, but, although the corridor was within German artillery range, it did allow sufficient supplies to be brought in to the city to enable it to continue to withstand the German siege. In short, the Eastern

Front was now back more or less where it had been before the summer offensives of 1942, although north of Voronezh the Russians had driven 200 miles into the German lines and created a salient 100 miles from north to south around the town of Kursk. Here would be played out what is often claimed to have been the greatest armoured battle in history, and what was the last opportunity for the Germans, if they could not now win the war on the Eastern Front, at least to create a climate where a negotiated peace – or, as Manstein put it, a draw – might be achieved.

As major movements by either side drew to a halt in the mud of the spring thaw of 1943, the German planners knew that strategically they were in trouble. Tunisia was not expected to hold out much longer, and, once that went, a landing in Europe was a certainty. Despite increased use of forced labour in Germany and the combing out of men in reserved occupations, the armed forces were nearly a million men short of establishment. If a landing in Europe took place, then the obvious place to reinforce that theatre from was the East, but troops could not be taken away from there as long as the threat of a major Soviet offensive remained. Colonel-General Guderian had just been appointed Inspector General of Panzer Troops with a brief to rebuild and re-equip that arm, and he recommended a defensive posture on the Eastern Front while the reconstitution took place, but despite the shortening of the front there were not enough formations in the East to maintain static defence. Manstein for his part suggested a mobile defence, the sort of operation that the German army was good at, with localized attacks to keep the Red Army from massing the troops needed for a major offensive.

In the end, the decision was part political and part military. Hitler badly needed a victory to reassure his now very wobbly allies, and the Wehrmacht needed to destroy the Soviets' ability to mount a major offensive so that troops could safely be released for the expected Anglo-American landing in Europe. From the German viewpoint, the Kursk salient was not only a threat as the obvious place from which the Soviets could launch an offensive against Army Group South, but also an opportunity: if it could be bitten off, then not only would very large numbers of Red Army men and equipment be destroyed, but the front could also be straightened, thus reducing the number of men needed to defend it. The important thing was to do it quickly, for the window between the ground drying up sufficiently to allow armour to move and the likely date of an invasion of Europe was small. The Germans were not, of course, to know that under British pressure the Allies had abandoned plans for a landing in France in 1943 and were intending to go for Sicily and Italy instead.

The Russians, too, were well aware of the significance of the Kursk salient, and even before the thaw ended they were bringing up troops to launch an offensive from it as soon as the ground dried up. Then, as their own intelligence, reports from partisans moving between the lines and information from the British (the Russians were not told that this was from Ultra, nor even that Ultra existed), indicated that the Germans were intending to attack the salient, the Russian generals argued with Stalin that to take the Germans on in a mobile battle by trying to get the Russian offensive in first would be futile: what the Red Army should do, argued Zhukov, would be to let the Germans attack and wear down their armour in a battle of attrition, and then, when their panzer and motorized divisions were exhausted, go over to the offensive against a fatally weakened enemy. Stalin agreed.

The original German plan, *Fall Zitadelle*, or 'Case Citadel', was largely Manstein's, although it was soon taken over by OKH and Hitler. It had Army Group Centre's Ninth Army, commanded by Colonel-General Walter Model and with four panzer and fourteen infantry divisions, nipping out the northern end of the salient's neck, while Manstein's Fourth Panzer Army and Army Detachment Kempf,* with altogether five panzer, ten infantry and four panzer grenadier (three of them Waffen SS) divisions, would deal with the south. In total, there would be 2,700 tanks and assault guns available and in support 1,800 aircraft, fighters, bombers and dive-bombers, for it was essential that the Luftwaffe obtained early air superiority to allow the armour to move. Had the operation gone ahead in May, which it could well have done, then it might have turned into another great Manstein triumph, but delay followed delay, as more armour was moved up and new vehicles designed to counter the Russian T-34s and to deal with enemy strongpoints, a lesson learned from Stalingrad, were brought into service. Among the new vehicles were 200 of the new Mk V Panther, a tank specifically designed to counter the T-34, and 104 of the Mk VI Tiger, itself a heavy tank that had originally been designed for defence. The Panther had a 75mm gun, sloping armour and wide tracks to cope with snow and mud, while the Tiger boasted

---

*An army detachment was a group of units equivalent in size to an army but put together for a specific operation, rather than being a permanent formation. It was usually named after the commander, in this case General of Panzer Troops Kempf.

an 88mm gun, one adapted from the highly successful anti-aircraft gun often used in the anti-tank role, and sufficient armour to stop anything except a high-velocity round at point-blank range. There were also a variety of new assault guns and self-propelled anti-tank guns, and the SS even had one company with captured Russian T-34s. All in all, it was the most powerful force the Germans had ever assembled for a single operation.

Within the salient, the Russians had two fronts – Central and Voronezh – consisting of nine armies and two tank armies, and these were backed by a third reserve front – the Steppe – of another five armies and a tank army. In accordance with their plan to wear down the German armour, they constructed a series of concentric defensive belts, extending for up to 100 miles behind the front lines. Huge numbers of civilian labourers were drafted in to dig trenches, construct anti-tank ditches, create concrete bunkers and lay mines. The idea was to use the minefields, a mixture of anti-tank and anti-personnel devices, to channel the German armour into killing areas where they would be taken on by 6,000 anti-tank guns supported by 20,000 field artillery pieces and mortars and over 900 Katyusha rocket batteries as well as dug-in machine-gun posts to take on the supporting German infantry. Each position was supported by at least two others and the emphasis was on defence in depth, so that, if the Germans broke through one belt, they would immediately run up against another. The 3,500 Russian tanks and assault guns would either be dug in as static anti-tank guns or held back for counter-attacks when the time was ripe. They would be supported by the Red Air Force with 2,700 aircraft.

As time wore on and more and more delay was imposed on a start date for *Zitadelle*, both Model and von Manstein, whose idea it first was, began to doubt the wisdom of the operation. They knew that they could not conceal the build-up of troops and vehicles north and south of the salient, and that the Russians had had ample notice to reinforce and prepare their defences. When Hitler ordered the attack to begin on 5 July, the Russians were ready and their own artillery opened up before the German preliminary bombardment, which did not begin until 0430 hours, an hour later than intended. In the north the attack was led by the infantry, in the south by the armour, and initially all went reasonably well with the Germans breaking into the first line of defence and Russian counter-attacks being beaten off. In the air the Luftwaffe kept the Red Air Force at bay, the Stukas acted as airborne artillery and the fighters destroyed numbers of Russian vehicles on the ground. Then, as the Russians had planned, combat drag began to tell as the German tanks penetrated the minefields. The mines did not destroy many tanks but by blowing off a track they immobilized them, and, although the Germans were very good at swift field recovery and repair, the momentum slowed down as the numerical superiority of the Red Air Force began to tell. When German armour faced Russian armour in the open, the Germans won, largely because their guns had a greater effective range, but after the first day the Russians did not expose their armour and left it to the mines and the anti-tank screen to do their work for them. Casualties of men and vehicles on both sides began to mount, and the enormous quantitative superiority of Russian artillery – 20,000 tubes against half that number – began to tell. By 12 July, Model's northern prong had penetrated twelve miles into the salient but was now bogged down; it was still twenty-five miles from Kursk and casualties were mounting. Worse, on that same day, 12 July, the Russians launched an offensive of their own against the Orel salient, a mirror image of that at Kursk and just fifty miles north of it. Model had to rapidly detach one of his panzer divisions to bolster the defences of Orel and could do no more against Kursk. In the south Manstein had made better progress. He had pushed twenty-five miles into the salient and had got through the last Russian defensive belt. He was still forty miles from Kursk but he was now engaging the Russian mobile reserves. While his own losses in both men and armoured vehicles were high, he had inflicted massive casualties on the Russians and was optimistic about the outcome. The next day Hitler summoned von Manstein and Model to his East Prussian headquarters. The Führer was rattled: the Allies had landed in Sicily, Germany's southern flank was in danger and all the evidence was that a major Russian offensive was in the offing. When OKH reported that von Kluge was adamant that Army Group Centre could not continue to attack south owing to the Soviet push against Orel, Hitler accepted that *Zitadelle* was finished – although, true to form, he used the phrase 'suspended' rather than 'at an end'. The German armour had done its best, but too much reliance had been placed on the Panther tank. It was beautifully designed but had been deployed far too early, before full troop trials had evaluated it, and many of them broke down or overheated. The Tigers had done rather better but were not well suited to offensive operations and the Russian decision to go for a wearing-down operation relying on mines and anti-tank guns had overcome the Germans' ability to manoeuvre and had brought the Wehrmacht to a halt, despite Manstein's advice that the battle should continue. It was the last occasion on which the Germans held the initiative on the Eastern Front.

* * *

Despite the failure of *Zitadelle*, the German army in the East was still very much in being: Russian claims of the numbers of German tanks destroyed were hugely exaggerated and the Red Air Force did not by any means have it all its own way. The panzer divisions were not annihilated and while the Germans lost around 650 tanks and self-propelled assault guns at Kursk, these were replaced from German factories relatively quickly and at the end of the month there were still around 2,000 tanks in the *Ostheer*. But the Germans could not increase that number: they could not match Russian industrial production, helped by Western aid, and the Russian ability to replace their enormous losses in manpower. Particularly menacing was Soviet artillery. At the beginning of the war, this had been a badly handled arm with out-of-date equipment; now it was not only competently handled and increasingly sophisticated technically, but there was masses of it and the number of guns and batteries continued to increase at a rate that far outstripped the Germans. Even so, when the Russians launched their diversionary attack on the Orel salient, they came up against solid defences that the Germans had had plenty of time to prepare, and, although the two armies defending it, Ninth and Second Panzer, could not hold, they were able to withdraw westwards at their own pace, inflicting massive casualties on the attackers, who took Belgorod on 4 August and Orel on 5 August, by which time Ninth Army had established itself on the Hagen Line, previously prepared defensive positions along the north–south road east of Bryansk. For once, Hitler had not objected to the withdrawal of Ninth Army – indeed, by withdrawing II SS Panzer Corps to be redeployed to Italy, he accelerated it. Manstein's view, according to his ADC, was that to defend Italy was nonsense: what the Germans should do was to withdraw all forces from Italy and go into defence in the Alps, thus freeing up more divisions for the East.[73]

Now began the battle for the Ukraine in the south, where von Manstein, insistent that the army must be in secure well-prepared defensive positions before the winter, finally received permission to abandon the Donnets basin and withdraw to the River Dnieper, while Army Group Centre slowly gave ground and in the north the Germans held out south-east of Leningrad against the attempts by two Guards armies to rupture the front. On 13 August the Russians were in the suburbs of Kharkov and Manstein's efforts to fight a mobile defence were blocked by Hitler's insistence that the city must be held. The six German divisions defending Kharkov inflicted horrific losses on the attackers, who had resorted to human wave frontal assaults, but in the end numbers told and on 22 August, when it was clear that the Red Army intended an encirclement of the city, Manstein ordered a withdrawal on his own authority as he then (rather unfairly) sacked the army commander, General Kempf. On 15 September, Army Group South began its withdrawal to the Dnieper and on Army Group Centre's front the Russians took Smolensk on 24 September, again at frightful cost. As both army groups pulled back, handing the Russians off with local counter-attacks, a scorched-earth policy was instituted. Anything that could possibly be of value to the advancing Russians was removed or destroyed. No buildings could be left for them to use as billets or as forming-up places, roads and airfields were cratered and crops still standing burned. As the Russian policy was to conscript all men and most women of military age once they recovered an area, the population too was removed. Manstein in his memoirs claims that this was done in as humane a manner as possible, and Major-General von Mellenthin, Chief of Staff of XXXXVIII Panzer Corps, is adamant that, although the very survival of the army group was at stake, the policy was carried out with as much decency as the situation allowed.[74] Other sources suggest that those Jews and party members not killed out of hand by the SS were deported as forced labour. In areas where the Germans, going the other way, had executed large numbers in 1941 or 1942, efforts were made to destroy the evidence and in some cases mass graves were dug up and the bones scattered. As this sort of work was thought to be too distressing for even the General SS *Einsatzgruppen*, much of it was delegated to locally employed Russians, some of whom were then despatched by a bullet in the back of the head so that they could not tell of what they had done.

Once Army Group South had withdrawn west of the Dnieper, the Crimea, occupied by Seventeenth Army, was cut off. The Germans evacuated the Kuban peninsula, across the Strait of Kerch, but they hung on in the Crimea itself – it had well-developed airfields from which the air defence of the vital Romanian oil fields could be mounted and could be supplied by the German navy across the Black Sea. A Russian airborne assault to the south of Kiev failed when the attacking troops were dropped into the middle of a German division of which the Red Army was unaware, but on 6 November the Germans evacuated Kiev and the Russians took Zhitomir and Forosten and cut the rail link between Army Groups South and Centre. A counter-attack by Manstein with XXXXVIII Panzer Corps, of whose men there were few left who had been serving with the formation a year before, restored the situation but Fourth Panzer Army's attempt to retake Kiev failed. Hitler suspected that Fourth Panzer had been too cautious, and, when Manstein ordered that army to withdraw from a salient south of Kiev to avoid being cut off, Hitler took the opportunity to sack its commander, Colonel-General Hoth, who was replaced by General of Panzer Troops Hermann Balck.

With the capture of Kiev, the Russians were now firmly established in the Ukraine, and, while the Germans were still much better at manoeuvring, they had precious little to manoeuvre with. By Christmas 1943 the Germans had around 2.5 million men on the Eastern Front but were desperately short of infantry. With 151 infantry divisions between the three main army groups and Kleist's small Army Group A, there were only 341,000 combat infantrymen, less than 20 per cent of authorized establishment, and there were very few reinforcements arriving – indeed, there were very few available to be sent. Facing them were nearly 2 million Red Army combat infantrymen. The situation in armour was even worse: out of about 2,000 tanks and assault guns in the East, the Germans mustered 686 that were operational – many that would have been available were lost when the advancing Russians overran German armoured workshops – compared to the nearly 8,000 available to the Red Army. By now the German Panzer Mk V Panther had had most of its teething troubles ironed out and was technically a much better tank than the T-34 – some authorities think it was the best tank of the war – but quality can only defeat quantity up to a certain limit, and the Russians had gone way past that limit.

As it was, the Soviet offensives continued with the main point of effort against Manstein in the south, and with Hitler once more reverting to his 'not an inch' philosophy. While he could eventually be persuaded to change his mind, it was often far too late and soldiers were sacrificed needlessly when they could instead have been pulled out from pockets to fight another day. In January 1944 the Red Army reached the old Russian–Polish border and German generals were becoming increasingly unhappy about the command arrangements on the Eastern Front. It was an OKH theatre – that is, the army high command was responsible for it – but there was no overall commander in theatre since the actions of the various army groups were being coordinated by Hitler, who was the army's Commander-in-Chief and paid little attention to the counsel of his chief of the general staff, Zeitzler. Manstein attempted to persuade Hitler that he should give up command on the Eastern Front and appoint a commander-in-chief (presumably Manstein himself, under whom, according to his ADC, Field Marshals von Kluge, von Kleist and Rommel* were prepared to serve), but the Führer would not budge. Many of the generals could not see how the war could be won, although many were convinced – or said they were – that the Russians could not keep on attacking and must run out of men soon. Manstein still thought that, given complete operational freedom, he could effect a stalemate that would allow political negotiations to end the war. He seems, however, to have been living in a fool's paradise, for it is inconceivable that the USSR, the USA or the UK would have entered into any negotiation with Hitler or an NSDAP government, and in any event Hitler would not, now or at any time, give Manstein that operational freedom he wanted.

The German line now ran from Leningrad in the north, south to the west of Smolensk, through the Pripet Marshes, down to the west of Kiev and then along or behind the elbow of the River Dnieper to the Black Sea. Behind it, the only obstacle barriers left were the Rivers Bug and Dniester, after which the Germans would be defending on Romanian soil in the south and back in Poland in the centre. In the north, massive attacks on Army Group North at last lifted the siege of Leningrad when the Soviet Second Shock and Forty-Second Armies of the Baltic Front crashed through the German defences on 19 January 1944. South of Kiev, the Germans still held a sector of the east bank of the Dnieper west of the town of Cherkassy, but the two northernmost German corps, belonging to Eighth Army, were becoming increasingly liable to encirclement as the Russian salient round Kharkov continued to expand. Forbidden to withdraw, the corps commander began to stockpile rations and ammunition, despite protests from the Luftwaffe that they could supply him by air. Sure enough, on 24 January 1944 the Red Army's First and Second Ukrainian Fronts under Generals Nikolai Vatutin and Ivan Konev began their attempt to encircle this enticing morsel, and on 28 January, against stiff German resistance, they succeeded in closing what became known as the Korsun Pocket, with 60,000

---

*As Rommel was only on the Eastern Front for a health cure and had no command appointment there, his views were of little practical import.

German soldiers inside. Initially, all went well for the Germans. The Luftwaffe managed to deliver between 150 and 200 tons a day, which with the stockpiles already there was sufficient; a Russian lieutenant-colonel appeared with a flag of truce inviting surrender and was taken to General Wilhelm Stemmerman, the senior German officer in the pocket, who gave him a glass of champagne and sent him on his way. Then the Russians began to put more and more fighters overhead and more and more anti-aircraft guns on the routes in and out of the pocket. At this point, Manstein recommended a breakout. Hitler would have none of it, instead insisting that Gruppe Stemmerman's situation would enable its Red Army attackers to be themselves cut off and allow the Germans to recapture Kharkov, even as he completely failed to realize that the units he intended to achieve this with were so under-strength that such a bold move was totally impossible. As it was, Manstein launched a counter-attack that at first made considerable progress, pushing the Russians back against the river and getting within a few miles of the pocket. Then the spring thaw came early, with the ground turning to mud under the snow by day and freezing again by night, taking away the German advantage in manoeuvre. The counter-attack ground to a halt and Manstein ordered Stemmerman to break out the last five miles with his own resources. The retreat from the pocket was very nearly a total disaster: the wider tracks of the Russian tanks spread their weight better and allowed them to move when German tanks could not and the American Lend-Lease trucks and jeeps were far more reliable and performed better in mud than the collection of captured and cobbled-together vehicles the German army was reduced to. Russian tanks machine-gunned the horses of ambulances and drove over the wounded; a Belgian brigade of SS Division Viking was wiped out; General Stemmerman was killed and, with vehicles bogged in and abandoned, the troops retreated on foot through the snow by companies and platoons. Through their own efforts and a sterling performance by Manstein and Eighth Army's two panzer divisions, contact was finally made with the pocket, and by 16 February 35,000 men were extricated. To the surprise of all, Hitler approved Manstein's decision in retrospect. Had the Russians been tactically more nimble, they might have ruptured the German line and poured through, but, as it was, the shortening of the line allowed Manstein to plug the gap just in time. General Konev was none the less promoted to Marshal of the Soviet Union.

As this was going on, all army group commanders on the Eastern Front and a selection of senior officers from all three services were summoned to Hitler's headquarters in Rastenburg to be subjected to a diatribe by the Führer on the subject of loyalty – a move probably sparked off by rumours that some of the officers captured at Stalingrad had been induced to agree to broadcast anti-Nazi propaganda. Most members of the audience were highly offended; how dare they be spoken to like this? Had they not already sworn a personal oath to Hitler? Manstein was particularly displeased and said so. A second summons came on 19 March to all field marshals, who were required to line up at the Berghof in Obersalzburg and sign a declaration of loyalty that was then read out by the senior field marshal, von Rundstedt. This time, the trigger was the formation of the National Committee for Free Germany formed in Russian captivity by General von Seydlitz, a corps commander captured at Stalingrad, who was calling for the overthrow of Hitler.

Meanwhile, the German defences along and behind the Dnieper were now in tatters, and the westward withdrawal went on. On 23 March 1944 the Red Army encircled First Panzer Army, which since October 1943 had been commanded by the one-armed General of Panzer Troops Hans Hube, on the River Bug, and once again Hitler issued his 'to the last man and last round' order. An incandescent Manstein flew to the Berghof and threatened to resign. Hitler relented, Manstein ordered a breakout and Hube got his army away, for which he was promoted to colonel-general.* It was the last time Manstein would argue with Hitler. On 30 March he and Field Marshal von Kleist, commanding Army Group A, were summoned to Obersalzburg, where they were presented with the swords with oak leaves of the Knight's Cross and relieved of their commands. Hitler thanked both men for their services and told them that the time for operations was over, now there could only be defending. Manstein would be replaced by Walter Model, a field marshal since the beginning of the month, and Kleist by Colonel-General Ferdinand Schorner.

Now Army Group South would be renamed Army Group North Ukraine, despite its not having anything left of the Ukraine to cling to. In April 1944 the Red Army invaded the Crimea from the north, and in May the German navy began to evacuate Seventeenth Army, after Hitler had

---

*He had been a divisional commander at Stalingrad, and was flown out of the pocket and given command of XIV Panzer Corps in Sicily. When the Germans withdrew from Sicily in August 1943, he was appointed to command First Panzer Army on the Eastern Front. After his promotion to colonel-general, he was also awarded the diamonds to his existing Knight's Cross with oak leaves, which Hitler presented to him personally. On his way back to the Eastern Front, his aircraft crashed and he was killed.

sacked its commander, Colonel-General Erwin Jaenecke, for pointing out that the position was untenable. The Russians now had all the Ukraine and the Crimea, although it would take time to restore peace in the teeth of furious opposition from Ukrainian guerrillas who had no wish to return to the arms of Mother Russia and who killed the Commander First Ukrainian Front, Colonel-General Vatutin, in an ambush. The NKVD would also be kept busy deporting to Central Asia 200,000 Crimean Tatars (virtually the entire Tatar population), who were considered to have collaborated with the Germans.

Then, on 6 June 1944, the British and Americans landed in Normandy. Germany would now have to fight on three fronts.

13

THE ASIAN WAR

JUNE 1942–AUGUST 1944

In the India of 1942 General Wavell not only had to defend against the external threat from the Japanese; he also had to worry about the threat from within. The British could rely on the loyalty of the non-political classes, whence came the police and the soldiers of the Indian Army. The vast majority of the rulers of the nominally independent princely states backed the British as their shield against democracy and the mob, and the professional classes employed in the judiciary and the administration were also trustworthy. Not only did they rely on the British for employment and advancement, but most could see that the only time when India was united was when she came under British rule, and they could genuinely appreciate the benefits of the rule of law and of an administration that, while it did not always do what they would like, was at least incorruptible, a rare quality in the East. This outlook was not shared by all, however, and one of the results of the import of universal education and the opening of the professions to Indians was a wish for more political power than the British were prepared to give. Prior to the abolition of the East India Company, a Royal Proclamation of 1858 had declared Indians to be 'equal citizens of the British Empire' and successive British governments accepted that India would certainly be ready for Dominion status, like Canada or Australia, at some point, but that point tended to be a lot farther off than politicized Indians would have liked. The largest and oldest Indian political party, All India Congress, had supported the British unequivocally in the First World War, and felt that it had got little reward. By now there was a strong 'Quit India' movement which, having failed to get the British to agree to 'Swaraj' or Home Rule, demanded that they leave India altogether, and attempted to advance its aims by (mainly) non-violent protest such as stopping rail travel by lying down on the tracks,* marching around and sitting down in the streets, and generally being a confounded nuisance.

The inspiration for the 'Quit India' movement was one Mohandas Karamchand Gandhi, seventy-two years old in 1942 and a high-caste Hindu who had been educated in London and called to the Bar of the Inner Temple in 1891. After a short and generally unsuccessful career as a lawyer in the Bombay courts, he took a post as a lawyer for an Indian trading company in South Africa in 1893, which led him into agitation for Indian rights in South Africa, including the organization of an Indian ambulance unit which served on the British side during the South African War. Returning to India via London (where again he organized an Indian ambulance corps in 1915), he was awarded a gold medal by the (British) Indian government, but once back in India he came to the conclusion that the British Raj must be overthrown, not because it was intrinsically bad or because he disliked the British but because it was materialistic and detracted from what he thought India should be – largely rural, self-reliant and with only minimal government, a land where all races and religions could live peacefully together. To the British, that was all very well in time of peace – Gandhi and his adherents could be locked up for a short period and then released when they had seen the error of their ways – but it posed a real threat in time of war when other, more sinister, elements piggy-backed on Gandhi's probably genuine moral principles.

Already there were those amongst the political classes who were prepared to back the Japanese, believing, or pretending to believe, that the Japanese meant what they said and that the implementation of the Co-Prosperity Sphere would lead to Indian self-rule unfettered by Japan. One of these, a Bengali, Subhas Chandra Bose, another high-caste Hindu, born in 1897 and educated in English schools in India and then at Cambridge and secretly married to an Austrian, was, unlike Gandhi, a believer in getting rid of the British by force. He had been the leader of the Bengal Congress, the mayor of Calcutta, briefly the president of the All India Congress and in and out of jail for various acts of violence in the 1930s. In January 1942 he fled Calcutta and entered Afghanistan, whence by a roundabout route he reached Berlin, where he tried to set up the Indian Legion, recruited from Indian prisoners of war captured in North Africa. In February

---

*As the blockers of the rail or road were often of high caste, one way to shift them instantly was to line up Gurkha or Sikh soldiers and threaten to have them urinate on the protesters.

1943 a German submarine handed him over to a similar Japanese vessel and he arrived in Tokyo, where he persuaded the prime minister, Tojo, to let him set up an Indian government-in-exile and to reinvigorate the Indian National Army, which the Japanese had already tried and failed to organize, from Indians captured in Malaya and Singapore. Much pressure, often including torture and beatings, was applied to persuade prisoners to join, and it is to their very great credit that the vast majority refused.* Those that did join did so from a mixture of motives: fear, disillusionment, a belief that the British were indeed beaten, the hope of an improvement in rations, release from imprisonment – all played a part, and, in the case of the few Viceroy Commissioned Officers who signed up, promises of promotion and status were undoubtedly persuasive. The INA, when it was eventually deployed against the British, was a complete disaster. The men either went to ground and avoided fighting, or deserted to the British, to the great embarrassment of those few King's Commissioned Officers with political ambitions who had agreed to serve in the hope of rapid advancement in the army of an independent India. Bose himself died as the result of an aircraft crash in Taiwan in August 1945, but for many years there were those who believed that, like some Indian King Arthur or Drake, he would return when his country needed him. As he has yet to materialize, we may safely assume that he did indeed die of burns in 1945.

Despite the risk of protesters blocking the rail and road lines to the north-east and preventing supplies and reinforcements from reaching the front, the Quit India movement did little to impede British military operations in and from India – those who led the movement were interned when necessary – but it did harden opinion, both in India and in the United Kingdom, and meant that complete British withdrawal sometime after the war, assuming that Britain won the war, became inevitable, as did partition and the bloodshed associated with it, and the tensions that continue to this day to bedevil relations between the two successor states to the Raj.

* * *

One of the most extraordinary aspects of the Second World War is not that the United States was able to take a tiny regular army that was unloved, ill-equipped and inexperienced in 1941 and turn it into the largest army in the

---

*Not a single Gurkha joined, despite being subjected to appalling brutality, and some were executed for non-compliance.

West and the most technologically advanced in the world – money, population and industry could do that in time – but that they managed to do it so quickly, for by mid-1942, and despite the gloom, doom and despondency in Allied circles about the progress of the war as a whole, in a mere twelve months after being dragged into it the Americans were already making their presence felt. By June 1942 there was an American division in New Caledonia, 900 miles north-east of Brisbane, Australia, another in the New Hebrides, 300 miles north-west, another in Fiji, 600 miles east, a Marine Regiment (a brigade in British terms) in Samoa, still further to the north-east, and there were two US divisions in Australia itself, bolstered by the arrival of the Australian 7 Division from the Middle East. American engineers were constructing airfields in the northern New Hebrides, Australia was now relatively secure from Japanese attack and the Americans could begin to think of embarking on limited offensives of their own.

It was now that argument arose. Both the Americans and the British were agreed, at least at this stage, that Japan herself must be conquered and forced into surrender. As Britain had few forces to spare from the defence of India and the eventual reconquest of Burma, the burden of any offensive against Japan would, at least to begin with, fall to the USA. There were two ways to get near enough to the Japanese mainland to mount an invasion: the Americans could either go via the Dutch East Indies, Borneo, the Philippines and Taiwan – the southern route – or by way of the islands and atolls of the Pacific, the Solomon, Gilbert, Marshall and Mariana Islands – the northern route. Unsurprisingly, given his emotional attachment to the Philippines, MacArthur favoured the southern route. This had some roads and airfields that could be used, but there were also large Japanese garrisons to consider. For its part, the US Navy, in the form of Admiral King, who was concerned about American carriers and battleships having to operate where they could be subject to attack by land-based aircraft, favoured the northern, island-hopping route. Eventually, after a great deal of special pleading and inter-service bickering, the decision was made in Washington and it was that both approaches would be used. It is probable that MacArthur was right, although perhaps for the wrong reasons, as, should an invasion of the Japanese home islands become necessary, then only by the southern route could a base be established for an army large enough both to mount a successful invasion and be supplied once ashore. It might be argued that the northern arm of the advance was therefore unnecessary, and entailed much loss of life in a succession of assaults on well-dug-in Japanese positions in order to capture barren rocks. That said, the two-pronged strategy did confuse the Japanese as to American intentions and prevented them from concentrating their naval assets. What was inexcusable militarily was the refusal to appoint one overall commander in the Pacific. Instead, MacArthur was to command the recapture of the occupied Japanese territories or southern route while Admiral Nimitz with a separate command would mastermind the island-hopping or northern route. This led to dispersion of assets, fierce arguments between the various service commanders and, in some cases, unnecessary casualties and wasteful duplication. MacArthur, interminable self-publicist though he was, was surely right when he described the decision not to appoint one supreme commander as one that 'cannot be defended in logic, in theory, or even in common sense... The handicaps and hazards unnecessarily resulting were numerous and many a man lies in his grave today who could have been saved.'[75] MacArthur felt so strongly that the command should not be divided that he offered to serve under Nimitz, despite being senior in rank, but the prospect of that enormous ego satisfactorily serving under anybody else rather defies belief.

The plan was for the navy to clear the Solomon Islands and, once that had been done, for MacArthur to secure Papua New Guinea from any more Japanese adventures by capturing New Britain Island, north of Papua, where the Japanese had a major base at Rabaul, on the north of the island. Two things now intervened to upset the planning: the Japanese landed on Guadalcanal in the Solomons and began to build an airfield, from which they could severely disrupt the coming operation, and they also landed on the north-west of Papua with the aim of taking the capital, Port Moresby, their previous attempt to do so having been frustrated by the Battle of the Coral Sea in May. From their landing area at Buna, the Japanese force of two regiments had 250 miles to go to reach Port Morseby and would have to cross the 6,000-foot-high and jungle-covered Owen Stanley range of mountains. Japanese intelligence thought that there was a road across the mountains, the Kokoda Trail, which could take motorized traffic but this was in reality no more than an overgrown jungle track – a fact that did not hinder the Japanese for more than a few moments. Pushing aside a few Australian troops that were lurking near the beachheads, they cracked on and took Kokoda, on the top of the range, on 27 July, and, although hampered by supply problems caused by the terrain and the climate and by sheer exhaustion, they got to within twenty-five miles north of Port Moresby before a combination of the arrival of Australian and American reinforcements and the situation on Guadalcanal forced them to withdraw and consolidate around their beachheads on the north coast.

The Solomon Islands, then divided between those islands taken from Germany after the first war and governed by Australia under a League of Nations mandate and the British Solomon Islands protectorate, are a string of islands that run roughly north-west to south-east for about 600 miles. They are only sparsely populated since their climate is unpleasant, being wet, hot, humid and malarial throughout the year, and the terrain is mountainous jungle or covered by lallang grass, which is tough, fibrous and liable to cut the unwary traveller. Guadalcanal is the southernmost island of the Solomons of any size, and, if the Allies wanted to invade New Britain and its surrounding islands, then they would have to clear the Solomons, beginning with Guadalcanal. On 7 August 1942, under the tactical command of Vice-Admiral Fletcher USN, a composite division of the United States Marine Corps effected landings on the north of Guadalcanal, near the Japanese airfield in the making, and on Tulagi and its associated islets twenty miles to the north, where the Japanese had established a garrison just before the Coral Sea battle. The Marines were supported by five American and three Australian cruisers and eleven destroyers, as well as by aircraft from three American carriers and by bombers from MacArthur's Army Air Force. The landings on Guadalcanal were unopposed and the next day the Marines had the almost completed airstrip, to be named by them Henderson Field. On Tulagi, the Japanese were not caught napping and the Marine Regiment landed there met violent opposition. Nevertheless, the Marines captured the island in twenty-four hours with the loss of 108 killed, while of the Japanese garrison of 500 men nearly all fought to the last, refusing to surrender and committing suicide rather than be captured, as their military code demanded. On the neighbouring islands of Gavutu and Tanamdogo, the 500 Japanese went to ground in caves, some natural, some man-made, and had to be blasted out by grenades or flame-throwers. Only fourteen were captured, all the rest being killed, committing suicide or crawling into cover and dying of their wounds.

From the Japanese headquarters 600 miles away at Rabaul, New Britain, reaction was swift. On 7 and 8 August, Japanese land-based aircraft attacked the American fleet off the landing areas, and the troops on shore. Thirty-three

Japanese planes were lost to twenty-two American. The following day, on 9 August, a force of seven Japanese cruisers and a destroyer caught an Allied task force steaming through the ten-mile-wide channel between Guadalcanal and Savo Island and sank four cruisers, three American and one Australian, and damaged three other warships, at trifling cost to themselves; 1,270 Allied sailors were killed in explosions, drowned or perished in the shark-infested waters, for thirty-four Japanese deaths. On the evening of that same day, the ships supporting the landings, too vulnerable to attack from the air, withdrew away to the east, leaving the five Marine battalions on shore horribly exposed. With their seaborne supply chain interrupted, Marine rations were cut in half and work began to complete the airstrip. Although the US Marines were now unable to obtain the building materials that should have been landed with them, the Japanese engineers and their Korean labourers who had been working on the airfield had left most of their equipment and materials behind, and the Marines had the airfield completed and able to receive aircraft in two days – although it took another two weeks before any were available. The Japanese had seriously underestimated the size of the American force and, when two weak battalions of around 900 men – they had been landed by five destroyers twenty miles east of the American lodgement on Guadalcanal on the night of 18/19 August – attacked frontally two days later, they were massacred by American artillery and machine-guns and recently arrived fighters and dive-bombers. The Japanese commander, Colonel Kiyono Ichiki, went back to his makeshift command post, burned his regimental flag and shot himself.

Now that American aircraft were on Guadalcanal and their transport ships were vulnerable, the Japanese took to landing more men from destroyers. Warships are not designed to carry passengers, and each destroyer could only carry 150 men, but by nightly dashes by six or seven destroyers, which took around ten hours and were known to the Americans as the 'Tokyo Express', the Japanese were able to assemble a force of around 6,000 men to the east of the American perimeter. The campaign now became one of successive overland attacks by the Japanese supported by naval bombardment and accompanied by clashes between the two navies. Imperial Headquarters in Tokyo ordered a shutdown of the attempt to reach Port Moresby until Guadalcanal had been cleared of Americans, and continued to land troops on the island. At one stage, with the *Saratoga* put out of action and the *Wasp* so damaged that she had to be scuttled, the Americans had only one operational carrier in the South Pacific, but the Japanese navy suffered too. On 11 October, in the confused – and confusing – Battle of Cape Esperance a Japanese task force of three heavy cruisers, two destroyers and two seaplane carriers landing tanks and heavy artillery was eventually seen off by the US Navy and its commander, Admiral Goto, killed. When the remnants got back to Japan, Goto's second-in-command was sacked. On 14 October two Japanese battleships bombarded the airfield with 900 shells, setting fire to ammunition dumps and fuel tankers and destroying fifty parked aircraft. Although the battleships were eventually chased away by American PT boats, their 14-inch shells had churned up the runway so much that it could not be used for several days. This was probably the nearest the Americans ever came to losing Guadalcanal, and the Japanese landed another 4,500 men the following night, using transports this time, bringing the total to 22,000 or only slightly less than the American invaders turned defenders.

The American position around Henderson Field, which was well dug-in and protected by barbed wire and covered by artillery, was not at risk from even 22,000 Japanese, but the Marines were tired, still on short rations and beginning to go down with malaria, whereas the Japanese troops were reasonably fresh. This was not to last. A Japanese offensive on 23 October turned into a bloodbath. The approach march to get within striking distance of the Americans was along thirty miles of mountainous jungle path and in the event took eight days. Each soldier had to carry an artillery shell as well as his own weapon and equipment, and light artillery pieces were dragged along by the men. The weather was atrocious and the path, such as it was, quickly turned into a quagmire. Heavy weapons and equipment had to be abandoned, the engineers had to expend all their efforts in constructing a track along which the ten light tanks could move, the men went on to half-rations and zero hour for the attack was postponed several times. A diversionary attack went in a day early, the commander not having received news of yet another postponement, and resulted in 650 Japanese dead for no purpose. When the main attack did go in on the night of 25/26 October, the light tanks were easily disabled or destroyed and 900 Japanese were killed, shot down on the American wire.

The Japanese garrison in Guadalcanal would now be expanded by the bulk of Eighteenth Army, commanded by General Hyakutake, who would launch a fourth, and it was hoped final, attack on Henderson Field and the American lodgement. Thirteen and a half thousand troops with 10,000 tons of ammunition and supplies were concentrated at the mounting base in the north-western Solomons. The plan was to ship the men and supplies to Guadalcanal in eleven troop transports escorted by battleships and cruisers and covered by Zero fighters from carriers cruising to the north of the Solomons and land-based bombers from Rabaul. The force left Shortland, one of the Solomon Islands, on 12 November and in negotiating The Slot – the Solomon Islands channel – ran into an American task force of five cruisers and eight destroyers. There was pandemonium as the Japanese rushed to replace the high-explosive shells intended for a bombardment of Henderson Field with armour-piercing shells for use against warships, and as aircraft tried to identify which ships were Japanese and which American. Despite being caught unawares, the Japanese inflicted heavy damage on their opponents, killing two admirals and sinking three cruisers, largely because the American destroyers fired their torpedoes too early, but were nevertheless crippled themselves. Between then and 14 November one Japanese battleship, the *Hiei*, was sunk and seven of the troop transports were sunk in The Slot by American bombers, although destroyers picked many of the men up from the water and returned them to Shortland, while the Japanese continued to bombard Henderson Field, dashing off before they could be attacked.

On 15 November the three remaining Japanese troop transports were run ashore and beached, and the 2,000 Japanese soldiers still aboard were landed on Guadalcanal. Off shore, one American battleship, the USS *South Dakota*, whose radar had broken down, was caught by the Japanese, badly shot up and driven off, while another, the USS *Washington*, so seriously damaged the Japanese battleship *Kirishima* that she had to be scuttled by her crew. Far from being able to launch a major offensive, the Japanese were now on the defensive, short of ammunition, rations and medical supplies. Only prodigious efforts by Admiral Tanaka to provide at least some supplies by the Tokyo Express, parachute air drops and the lashing of containers to rafts launched from submarines, allowed the troops to exist at all, while on the other side of the island the very tired and now malaria-riven 1 Marine Division was withdrawn and replaced by fresh troops. At last reality began to dawn on the Japanese high command, and this despite their navy's success on 31 November and 1 December when, for the loss of only one destroyer, they sank three American cruisers and set two on fire, with only the USS *Honolulu* escaping unscathed. When Admiral Tanaka was badly wounded on 12 December, the impetus went out of the supply effort and, after bitter argument in Tokyo, which saw army and navy officers coming to blows as each blamed the other for the situation in Guadalcanal, the order went out to withdraw. The orders were slow in getting there, and by mid-January 1943 the Japanese were confronted by 40,000 American troops under the fifty-four-year-old Major-General Alexander 'Sandy' Patch.* Then, on 19 January, Patch's men went on the offensive along the island.

Patch knew that the only way to defeat the Japanese infantry was to kill them, preferably by blowing each man into very small pieces, so his advance was slow, methodical and exceedingly detailed. After a heavy artillery bombardment, the US Marines would advance over the ground that had been shelled, deal with any Japanese who survived and then stop and dig in. Another stretch of ground would be shelled and the process would be repeated. On the night of 1/2 February the Japanese evacuation began once a fresh battalion had been landed to act as rearguard. By 8 February 12,000 men had been taken off, and when the Americans closed in they were opposed only by snipers, hidden in trees, who would not surrender and had to be hunted down and killed. By 10 February there was no resistance anywhere. Guadalcanal had been a disaster for the Japanese. A campaign that both sides expected to last little longer than a week at most had cost the lives of 30,000 Japanese soldiers and sailors: half killed in action or dying from their wounds, and half dead from disease or malnutrition. The Imperial Navy had lost twenty-three warships and sixteen transports, 100,000 tons in all, and over a thousand Japanese aircraft had been shot down or had crashed into the sea. The American casualties amounted to 5,000 navy and 1,592 army dead, and 15,000 wounded or sick. The US Navy had lost twenty-five warships and three transports sunk. The significance of Guadalcanal, however, was far greater than the simple arithmetic of the butcher's bill: the confidence of the Japanese in their ability to continue a string of uninterrupted victories was badly shaken; the navy's and army's dislike and distrust of each other – already there, if usually muted – was exacerbated, and the Americans had obtained a secure base and staging area for their island-hopping strategy that would eventually lead to Allied control of the entire South Pacific. Henderson Field, the objective of the furious Japanese land, sea and air assaults, was now transformed into a major all-weather complex, and it was from there that on 18 April 1943

---

*Patch Barracks in Stuttgart, Germany, headquarters of the United States Forces in Europe, is named after him.

eighteen American P-38 Lightning fighters took off. Thanks to information garnered from US naval intelligence decrypts, they duly intercepted two Mitsubishi 'Betty' bombers and their escort of six Zeros over Bougainville, some 500 miles to the north. Both bombers were shot down, and one of them was carrying Admiral Yamamoto, the architect of Japan's naval victories, even if he never really believed that they would not be overturned. Yamamoto's body was found the next day.

Meanwhile, on Papua, MacArthur's force of one Australian division, one Australian division less one brigade and one American regiment was closing up on the eleven-mile-long Japanese lodgement on the north coast. Since late September 1942 this force had been commanded by an Australian, General Sir Thomas Blamey, who was fifty-eight and a man of distinctly dubious character. The son of a cattle drover, Blamey obtained a rare commission in the tiny Australian Staff Corps, a cadre of regular instructors who oversaw the part-time militia, attended the Indian Staff College and served in the first war with the Australian Imperial Force at Gallipoli and on the Western Front, both as a staff officer and in command of a battalion and then a brigade. After the war he continued to serve on the staff in Australia and as the Australian representative on the Imperial General Staff in London. He left the permanent force in 1925 and was appointed Commissioner of Police for the state of Victoria, while also a major-general of militia. Blamey was knighted in 1935 but after a series of scandals involving abuses of authority by him* he 'resigned' in 1936 and became a journalist. With the outbreak of war in 1939, Blamey was recalled to the colours and commanded first an Australian division and then, on promotion to lieutenant-general, the Australian Corps in Palestine. A corps commander in the Greek caper, he got out at the very end in the last RAF flying boat, giving the last remaining seat to his son, a major on his staff. Given the non-job of Deputy Commander-in-Chief Middle East, he became a thoroughgoing nuisance, referring anything he did not like concerning the deployment of Australian troops to the Australian government and being considerably more of a hindrance than a help to Wavell and Auchinleck, to both of whom he was thoroughly disloyal. On the recall of Australian troops from the Middle East,

---

*These included being caught in a police raid on a brothel and, upon discovering that the 'Don't you know who I am' approach cut no ice, later denying that the person with Blamey's police identity badge and claiming to be Blamey was actually him.

Blamey, now promoted to general, went too and became Commander-in-Chief Australian Military Forces and Commander-in-Chief Allied Forces South-West Pacific, under MacArthur.

Blamey got his men over the Owen Stanley range, mainly on foot in appalling conditions but with a flanking force inserted north of the mountains by air. Supply was by Papuan porters and air drops, with the wounded being evacuated on stretchers carried by porters. Again, as happened so often when fighting Japanese troops in defensive positions, the operation took far longer than had been hoped. Blamey replaced his original Australian troops by fresh units flown in, and the Americans increased their contribution to a complete division. The Japanese attempted to supply their men around Buna using destroyers, but Allied air power made this a very risky business and only a tiny proportion of food, medicines and ammunition got through. Conditions were atrocious, with the ravages of weather, disease and terrain affecting Allied and Japanese alike, the difference being that the Allies could evacuate their wounded and supply their troops, whereas the Japanese could not. All that said, the Japanese continued to fight stubbornly to the last, although it was clear to even the most junior soldier that the situation was hopeless. Finally, fighting through each individual Japanese position in driving rain, the Australian and American troops got the upper hand, and by the last week in January 1943 Papua was completely cleared of the Japanese, who reported 9,390 dead. It was the end of another six-month campaign and had cost 5,700 Australian and 2,800 American casualties, of which around a quarter were deaths by enemy action or disease, but now both Guadalcanal and Papua were free of Japanese and any residual threat to Australia was gone.

With the loss of both Guadalcanal and Papua, the Japanese were determined not to lose Lae, a somewhat precarious base farther up the coast on New Guinea, nor their other bases along the northern coast. Their attempt to reinforce Lae with 6,900 troops and a number of crated Zero fighters sent by sea from Rabaul in eight transports escorted by the same number of destroyers led to the Battle of the Bismarck Sea, when on 2 March 1943 Allied aircraft spotted the convoy. The result was a massacre as over the next three days more and more fighters, bombers and dive-bombers were summoned to attack ships the Japanese could only muster a handful of Zeros to protect. A new Allied technique of skip bombing, a variation of which would be employed two months later by the RAF against the Mohne Dam in Germany, proved especially effective. Bombs were dropped from masthead height so that their forward motion bounced them along the surface of the sea into the less well-armoured sides of the ships. Once crippled by the bombs, the ships were finished off by PT boats. By the end of the battle, only four destroyers made it back to Rabaul; they and two submarines had managed to rescue 2,734 soldiers and sailors from the water but around 6,000 others had drowned or been killed, including those machine-gunned in the water by aircraft and PT boats.* The loss of the convoy to Lae was a further blow to Japanese pride and Imperial Headquarters forbade the sending of any more convoys to New Guinea: from now on, the bases there would be supplied by submarine or barges with a shallow draught under which torpedoes would pass without exploding (or so the theory went).

In Tokyo the emperor was displeased – he thought the convoy destroyed in the Bismarck Sea should have been aimed much farther up the coast of New Guinea, where it might have been able to land its troops without interference – and Imperial Headquarters demanded a show of strength. This took the form of a series of air raids on Allied positions on Guadalcanal and Papua New Guinea, including one on MacArthur's headquarters in Port Moresby, which, while a nuisance, had little effect and only incurred further losses of Japanese aircraft that could not be made good. Between June and September 1943 Australian and American forces were landed, some of the latter by parachute drop, east and west of Lae and by 16 September Lae and its associated base of Salamaua had been taken. The surviving Japanese, 7,500 of them, withdrew north, making for Sio on the coast. It was only fifty miles away but such were the terrain and the weather that it took them a month to get there, by which time the Allies were already planning to attack there too. Between December 1943 and January 1944 the Allies, mainly the Americans now, were established on the southern tip of New Britain and on the opposite coast of New Guinea, thus controlling the Straits of Vitiaz and cutting Japanese communications between Rabaul and New Guinea. When Australian troops supported by tanks advanced against Sio, the garrison there, augmented by the fugitives from Lae, had little choice but to embark on

---

*This was totally contrary to the Law of Armed Conflict and a war crime. Some years ago, this author interviewed a British sailor on an MTB or motor torpedo boat (the equivalent to a PT boat) who described shooting shipwrecked Japanese soldiers and sailors who were trying to climb on board and pleading to be rescued. His view was that, if he had allowed them aboard, such was their fanaticism that they would have attempted to take over the boat and might well have succeeded. He was probably right.

another jungle safari, this time to Madang, 250 miles up the coast. This too was a desperate ordeal and of the 12,000 men who began it, 2,000 died en route from disease, accident and starvation. Their commander, now Major-General Hatazo Adachi, was not with them – he had escaped from Sio by submarine.

Another Japanese foothold on New Guinea was the mountainous island of Biak. If Papua New Guinea looks like a turtle, then Biak is just to the north of the turtle's neck, and on 27 May 1944 12,000 US troops landed there, expecting to deal swiftly with a few hundred Japanese. To their dismay, Allied intelligence had got it wrong and the garrison was around 10,000 strong, and determined to sell their lives dearly. The Japanese commander, a colonel, decided to allow the Americans to land and to advance inland, when they would then come up against his men dug in at the base of cliffs and in dug-outs scattered all over the mountainside. The American advance was slow and MacArthur sacked the commander and replaced him with the fifty-eight-year-old Lieutenant General Robert L. Eichelberger, who had masterminded the assault on Buna. Finally, but not until August 1944, Biak fell.

Nevertheless, by the spring of 1944 the situation of the remaining Japanese on New Guinea was perilous: to the north was the sea, now controlled by the Allied navies, to the east were the Australians and the Americans, to the west were the Americans, and to the south was inhospitable mountain and jungle, while in the skies above the Allies had complete air superiority. The American two-pronged strategy was working, but they were still a very long way from Japan and the Japanese would never be driven out of their toeholds in New Guinea and its offshore islands: their army and navy commanders would only accept the inevitable when the Japanese emperor and government surrendered to the Allies in September 1945, and even then they took a week to make up their minds.

* * *

In India, General Irwin's plan for the reconquest of the Arakan went through several versions. In the end, there were insufficient ships to allow a series of amphibious landings; the terrain was thought unsuitable for flanking movements and there were insufficient aircraft to land a brigade behind the Japanese, so it was decided to make a straightforward advance down the peninsula. On 21 September 1942, 14 Division began its advance south from Chittagong. It had to make frequent stops to construct its own communications route and bring up supplies as it went and by 14 December the division had advanced 180 miles, or just over two miles a day, which even in thick, roadless jungle is poor going. Another pause to regroup and resupply gave the Japanese time to reinforce and by 6 January 1943, when the advance began again, resistance was severe. For the first time, the British encountered the Japanese bunker, their standard method of defence in the jungle.

A bunker was a hole dug in the ground then roofed and faced with tree trunks, over which was four or five feet of packed earth. It might hold anything from five to twenty men, and these were usually well supplied with machine-guns and light mortars. Bunkers were well camouflaged, very difficult to locate except at very short range and sited where they could support each other. Packed earth has the capability to absorb enormous shock, which is why it is a far better protection than, for example, concrete and these bunkers could often withstand a direct hit from an artillery shell with little if any damage to the occupants. When attacked, the Japanese would disappear into their bunkers and bring down massive artillery and mortar fire on their own positions, a tactic against which the men of 14 Division, attacking over open ground or through jungle with no overhead cover, had no answer.

Now the advance became even more tortuous and slow, with attacks on the tip of the Mayu peninsula being unable to penetrate the Japanese defences. Irwin sent more troops to reinforce Lloyd, and at one stage 14 Division, organized and staffed to command three or at most four brigades, was trying to command nine. Still Irwin would not allow Slim's corps headquarters, which was structured to command two to four divisions, to get involved. Slim was ordered to send one troop of Valentine tanks to Lloyd, to be used as bunker busters, and his objection that a troop was far too small a unit to be effective was overruled. A troop was sent, and all its tanks were lost.

It was now clear that the Arakan offensive had ground to a halt, and Wavell had to decide what to do with his Long-Range Penetration Brigade, 77 Brigade, which had been organized and trained to be inserted behind enemy lines in support of a conventional offensive. The conventional offensive had failed here, and the options were to send in 77 Brigade anyway, to salvage something from the Arakan battle even if this meant revealing its existence to the Japanese, or to keep it until it could be used as part of a wider operation later. The brigade's commander was in no doubt – he wanted to go and to go now. Brigadier Orde Wingate, forty years old in 1943, was one of those odd characters that the British military establishment throws up from time to time – 'Chinese' Gordon and T. E. Lawrence spring to mind – and who are regarded as dangerous lunatics or cutting-edge visionaries depending on one's viewpoint. Wingate's father, an army officer, was a member of the Free Presbyterian Church of Scotland and his mother belonged to the Plymouth Brethren, and their non-conformism in matters of theology was reflected in their son's frequent refusal to conform to accepted military standards. Wingate was commissioned into the Royal Artillery in 1923, and his service in Palestine in 1937–38 turned him into an ardent Zionist when most British army officers, and most Foreign Office officials, were Arabist. When an Arab revolt directed against the British and the increasing number of Jewish immigrants settling on Arab land broke out, Wingate threw himself wholeheartedly into the operations of the Special Night Squads, composed of Jewish junior ranks recruited locally commanded by British officers and NCOs, and who aimed to out-terrorize the terrorists. Here he came to the attention of the General Officer Commanding in Palestine, Wavell, who always had a sneaking admiration for the unorthodox and protected Wingate from the consequences of his rudeness to those who had ideas other than his and his firm belief that he and only he knew how to conduct clandestine operations.

Shortly after the outbreak of war, Wingate, now a major, raised and commanded Gideon Force, made up of Abyssinian guerrillas commanded by British officers, during the campaign in Italian East Africa. He did well, but his arrogance and refusal to credit anyone else at all with any ability made him many enemies, and, when he returned to Cairo after the Italian capitulation, he attempted to cut his throat with a Bowie knife in a hotel bedroom. An officer in the room next door found him and had him taken to hospital, where his life was saved. Normally a failed suicide would not be permitted to remain in the army, particularly not an officer,* but Wavell, despite describing Wingate as a very prickly subordinate, saved him and when Wavell was rusticated as Commander-in-Chief India, he sent for Wingate, who as an acting lieutenant-colonel began to press the merits of special operations behind the enemy lines. The result was 77 Brigade and the rank of acting brigadier for Wingate. His troops were the unpromising Thirteenth Battalion the King's Liverpool Regiment, a Territorial battalion raised at the

---

*After all, if you can't kill yourself, how can you possibly be expected to kill the enemy?

outbreak of war and which had been on coastal security duties in England before being sent to the Far East, 2 Burma Rifles (Karens, Kachins and Chins with a few Gurkhas), and a company of army commandos, the whole being stiffened by Third Battalion 2nd Gurkha Rifles.

Wingate's plan was to infiltrate his brigade – now to be known as the Chindits for the mythical Burmese beast, the Chinthe, that they adopted as their formation sign – in eight-company- or two-company-sized columns into northern Burma, 300 miles north-west of the Arakan front, to get behind the Japanese lines and cause as much mayhem as possible. They would travel light, carry mortars and radio sets on mules, be supplied by air drop and call upon RAF bombers in lieu of artillery. The daily ration per man was to be twelve ounces of biscuit (*shakapura** for Indians and Gurkhas, hardtack ship's for the British), two ounces of cheese, one ounce of milk powder, nine ounces of raisins, three quarters of an ounce of tea, four ounces of sugar, one ounce of sweets or chocolates, half an ounce of salt, twenty cigarettes and a box of matches. This was not exactly a balanced diet, and it was hoped to supplement it by fish or meat bought or trapped in country and with an occasional air drop of bully beef, but the medical establishment reckoned that men could remain physically fit on it for up to three months.

In February 1943 Operation Longcloth was launched from Imphal, 300 miles north-east of the Arakan; the columns crossed the Chindwin, moved into northern Burma and began to blow up Japanese railway lines and attack and ambush isolated Japanese supply columns and bases. The concept of supply from the air worked up to a point and in lightly held northern Burma the Chindits' operations were mostly successful, but once Wingate took his columns east of the Irrawaddy River, the now aroused and very grumpy Japanese began to take notice. Eventually Wingate had to split his columns into small parties of 'dispersal groups' and order them to make their way back to India independently. Four months later, the last groups returned to Imphal. A quarter of the brigade had been lost, killed or, captured or had died of wounds or disease; they had only received their already sparse rations around half the time; they had perforce to abandon their heavy weapons and mules, and morale of the troops was not enhanced by the necessity of leaving their wounded behind in the care of locals, who might or might not hand them over to the Japanese. They had marched around a

---

*A cold chapatti.

thousand miles and, while they had proved that, with proper preparation and enough air support, units could be maintained behind the Japanese lines, they had achieved nothing of strategic value and such damage as they had caused was quickly and easily repaired. To Churchill, however, always attracted by the maverick, here was something that could be trumpeted to balance the uninterrupted run of British defeats in Asia, and Wingate was summoned home and accompanied Churchill to the Quadrant Conference held in Quebec in August 1943. Quadrant was mainly devoted to discussions about a cross-Channel invasion in 1944 and atomic weapons policy, including a secret agreement signed by Roosevelt and Churchill whereby each promised not to use an atom bomb against the other, but the conference also heard Brigadier Wingate expound on his theories about long-range penetration in Burma. The Americans, anxious to reconquer northern Burma in order to open up the overland route to China and bring Chiang Kai-shek's assets fully into the Allied campaign against Japan, were sold and Wingate was promised massive American air support and equipment in his next venture.

Argument still rages amongst soldiers and historians as to the merits or otherwise of the Chindits. On the one hand, they achieved very little for the time, energy and assets devoted to them; on the other, they had at least inflicted some damage on the Japanese and could be held up as a success story amid all too many failures. What is incontrovertible, however, is that the reports of the doings of the Chindits, suitably embellished, did act as a tonic both at home and in the United States and did publicize the doings of an army that, in Mountbatten's words, was not so much forgotten as positively never heard of. Wingate returned to India and was promoted again – he had now moved from major to major-general in just over two years – with a brief to expand the Chindits to divisional size. With his elevated status and the confidence of the prime minister, his eccentricity knew no bounds. He grew a bushy beard, rode around on a grey horse, took to holding conferences stark naked except for a pith helmet and would attend a gathering of his elders and betters in Delhi with a large alarm clock set to go off in half an hour. (At least he was now clothed.) If when the clock rang a decision had not been reached, he would walk out. He stopped washing, on the grounds that it harmed the natural oils of the skin, and became more and more impatient, dismissive of his superiors and disregarding of the chain of command, sending missives direct to the prime minister (who had to be talked out of making him an army commander) and to the Secretary for

India. It is difficult not to draw the conclusion that the man was stark raving mad,* and the frequent comparison of him to various messianic Old Testament prophets, who in their dealings with burning bushes, angels, devils, flying carpets and ladders that reached to heaven can also be presumed to have been stark raving mad, tends to support that contention. That said, like many lunatics, he was certainly able to inspire many of those who worked with and for him, if not those above or distant from him.

There were other changes in the command structure emanating from Quadrant. The new post of Supreme Commander South-East Asia Command was created, to be filled by Lord Louis Mountbatten, while Wavell, raised to the peerage as a viscount, would succeed the Marquis of Linlithgow as Viceroy and Governor General of India, with General Sir Claude Auchinleck brought back from gardening leave as Commander-in-Chief India and Slim appointed to command Eastern Army, to be renamed Fourteenth Army. Mountbatten, now an acting admiral with the honorary ranks of lieutenant-general and air marshal, and in the view of many of his contemporaries grossly over-promoted, established a staff largely of his own nominees and far larger than his post required firstly in Delhi and then, after April 1944, in Ceylon. (That he imported as his personal barber an employee of Trumper's in London and enlisted him in the RAF as a sergeant was, for example, thought to be just a wee bit over the top.) The new Supreme Commander was frustrated in his wish to direct operations personally – he had experts from all three services to do that – but he did have to persuade British, Americans and Chinese to work harmoniously together and in that the famous Mountbatten charm was generally successful, except in the case of Stilwell, who saw straight through him.

* * *

In the Arakan, on 18 March 1942 the Japanese, having beaten off every attempt to penetrate their defences, turned to counter-attack and 14 Division began to collapse. Irwin sacked Lloyd, took over the division himself, then ordered Major-General Lomax and 26 Division from Calcutta to replace 14 Division. By now the Japanese were infiltrating behind the British, and on

---

*Although it can be argued that madness is not necessarily a bar to military competence – General James Wolfe, the hero of Quebec in the Seven Years War, was widely considered to be mad, and at one stage King George suggested that it might be a good thing if he were to bite some of his other generals.

14 April Irwin ordered Slim and XV Corps to take over the battle. Slim quickly realized that trying to hold on to any part of the Arakan was not a practical proposition and began to organize a withdrawal. By 11 May the army was back where it started. Morale was severely dented, more equipment and vehicles had been lost, and, while battle casualties had been few, the sick list had grown alarmingly, largely from malaria. Only the onset of the monsoon stopped the Japanese from pressing them any harder. The remnants of Burma Corps knew that they had been out-fought, out-manoeuvred and out-generalled. Tactically they had not been anywhere nearly as competent as the Japanese, and spirits were at a very low ebb indeed. It was now up to the commanders of the army in India to rebuild, retrain and re-equip their men to go back into Burma, and particularly to restore their confidence in their ability to beat the Japanese. General Irwin was now a busted flush as Commander Eastern Area; he had tried to dismiss the one British general in the Far East who really knew how to fight the Japanese – Slim – and, when Wavell refused to countenance it, Irwin did at least have the grace to send Slim a signal: 'You're not sacked – I am.' Wavell, promoted to field marshal in February 1943, asked for General Sir George Giffard to succeed Irwin.

Giffard was in many ways an unusual British general. He had commanded a British battalion, but most of his service had been in Africa with African troops. In one of his brief incarnations in the wider army, he had been on the staff of 2 Division in Aldershot from 1933 to 1936, when Wavell had commanded the division, and it was that experience that convinced Wavell to ask for Giffard to come out to India. Wavell's instinct was right: Giffard was a robust, no-nonsense commander who knew that the priority was to restore morale, and he began to institute better medical arrangements and measures to maintain health in an unhealthy climate, an improvement in rations and in the way that they were prepared and a shake-up of the army's organization so that what we would now call human resources problems were better dealt with. Tactically, he examined how troops could best be supplied by air and insisted on resources and assets being devoted to ensuring that this could be done. One of his great strengths, much appreciated by those under him, like Slim, was that, once he was convinced that a subordinate knew what he was about, Giffard would back him to the hilt.

As regards future strategy, Wavell as Commander-in-Chief India had become embroiled in one of those nasty little spats between allies that are not only unnecessary but usually a product of too much testosterone and individuals' overweening ambition. In 1942 Wavell and Stilwell had discussed a joint offensive into Burma in 1943 with between fifteen and twenty Chinese divisions, or up to 140,000 troops, advancing from Yunnan Province and five to seven British and American divisions, plus the two Chinese divisions in India, advancing from Assam, with a landing at Rangoon. The two thrusts would converge at Mandalay, and, as air cover and protection against Japanese naval manoeuvres would be essential, this would be provided by a combined British and American fleet of several battleships and up to eight aircraft carriers. In the meantime, the Americans would increase supplies to China to enable the promised divisions to be equipped for the campaign, and the British would work on providing an all-weather road from India into Burma. When in November 1942 the British announced that the fleet could not be made available as most of the ships earmarked for it were needed in the Mediterranean, notably to support the Torch offensive, and it was becoming obvious that the first Arakan offensive was not going as well as had been hoped, Chiang Kai-shek insisted that the British had broken their promises, citing Churchill as having promised such a fleet earlier in the year. Churchill (correctly) denied this, saying that his remarks were an aspiration, not a promise. Chiang now threw his teddy bear in the corner and announced that, if the British did not provide the fleet, then he would take no part in the coming offensive, which he claimed his troops were assembled and equipped to undertake.

There were also disagreements within the American command structure. Brigadier-General Claire Chennault, who since April 1942 had been in command of all United States Army Air Force units in China,* was in disagreement with General Stilwell as to the proper role of his air force. Chennault thought that Japanese supply lines, always tenuous, could be attacked from the air, and that, given the relatively primitive state of Japan's industry, this would do far more damage than an expensive land offensive into Burma. General Stilwell, claimed Chennault, was deliberately starving the air force of aviation spirit in favour of bringing in army supplies for the forthcoming offensive, and soon Chennault's men and machines would be

---

*He had been a regular officer of the USAAF, and regarded as somewhat of a loose cannon, until 1937, when he retired on medical grounds and became air adviser to Chiang Kai-shek, training the Chinese air force in American aircraft and organizing the airlift over the Hump. He was reinstated in the USAAF in April 1942.

grounded. It also soon became clear that, contrary to Chiang's bellicose statements, his divisions were not ready to undertake an offensive and that complaints about British bad faith were a cover to allow him to refuse to play. Eventually, after the Casablanca Conference had reinforced the decision that the war against Germany had priority over that against Japan, and after much to'ing and fro'ing between Washington, Chungking and Delhi, and with the failure of the First Arakan, it was decided that the Allies should endeavour to recapture all of Burma in one dry season – November 1943 to May 1944. As control of the Bay of Bengal would be essential to prevent the Japanese landing reinforcements in Burma, no major forays should be made before that, although aggressive patrolling could be undertaken and jump-off positions along the Chindwin established. Meanwhile, work would continue on the construction of an all-weather road from Ledo that would replace the Burma Road and once again enable the Americans to run supplies overland into China, and when the advance began Wingate's Chindits would be inserted behind the opposing lines, by air this time.

As time went on, it became increasingly apparent to Wavell and then to his successor Auchinleck that an invasion of Burma in 1943 as originally envisaged was going to be very difficult, if not impossible. Some discussion centred around bypassing Burma and landing instead on Java and Sumatra, which were closer to the Japanese homeland. This might succeed in breaking the Japanese defensive ring and also offered an opportunity to cut off Japanese shipping between the South China Sea and the Bay of Bengal, but the plan foundered on a lack of naval resources. British warships were needed most in the Mediterranean and to combat the U-boat menace in the Atlantic, and, anyway, supplies and equipment were not arriving from the UK in sufficient quantity to support the requirements for the planned expansion of the Indian Army, the building of airfields in Assam and the needs of Indian industry, never mind an offensive as well. There was also the risk of further political dissent within India which had not yet begun to affect the loyalty of the army but might do in the future. The enormous expansion programme had necessitated enlisting men from classes not previously considered suitable, and the commissioning of British and Indian officers who, unlike the pre-war regular cadre, had not had the time to acquire the understanding of the language and culture of their men.

Another real problem was famine, which struck Bengal in the aftermath of severe tropical storms in the autumn of 1942 that had flooded huge areas of rice-growing paddy. The peasant farmers had had to eat both their surplus and seed rice, rather than planting the latter in the winter, and so the 1943 crop was far smaller than usual. This would have been bad enough in itself, but the population of Bengal had increased hugely in the previous fifty years, the normal supply of imported rice from Burma had been cut off, there had been a poor wheat crop in the Punjab and a scorched-earth policy had been adopted along the Assam–Arakan border. As a result, there was simply not enough food available to feed the people. The Bengal provincial government was unable to cope; the British government had enough problems feeding its own population and in any case was unwilling to release shipping from the Mediterranean. By the summer of 1943 large numbers of Bengalis were starving, and with starvation came disease. By October people in Calcutta were dying at a rate of 2,000 a month (compared to a 'normal' death rate of 600 a month) and in the countryside things were worse, with men, women and children dying at the roadside or in their huts. Cholera was rampant and the crowds of refugees headed for the cities only made matters worse. The provincial government was composed of Indian politicians, many of whom had cornered the market in what rice was available and sold it at exorbitant prices, but it was advised by British officials and the provincial governor was British. If incompetence and corruption were among the reasons for the failure to provide relief measures, which they were, the British must shoulder the ultimate blame.

At last it dawned on the British government that, if steps were not taken, and taken swiftly, to relieve the plight of the people of Bengal, then the implications for the security of India would be immense. Already Chandra Bose in Singapore was offering to supply rice from Burma, and this was trumpeted across India by Japanese radio broadcasts. The loyalty of its population was essential were India to be the base for operations against the Japanese, and so the War Cabinet in London reluctantly agreed to release the shipping to send food aid from the UK. That, and the realization by the new Viceroy, Wavell, that the civil administration was incapable of organizing and implementing famine relief measures and his instructions to the army to take over that responsibility, saved the day. Army convoys went to the outlying villages, army food distribution points were opened in the cities, camps were set up for the destitute and teams from the Royal Army Medical Corps and the Indian Medical Services fanned out to deal with sickness and disease and to enforce preventative measures, particularly in regard to sanitation and the provision of clean water. The famine was quickly overcome, but it was a close-run thing that cost many lives and could, and should, have been prevented in the first place or at least alleviated far sooner than it was.

On 31 November 1943 a limited Allied offensive into Burma began. In the Arakan, XV Corps was to establish a firm baseline from the small, but usable, port of Maungdaw on the west coast, along the track – which it would convert into a road – running east from there across the Mayu mountain range to Buthidaung on the River Kalapanzin. In the centre, IV Corps would advance from Assam towards Tamu and Tiddim, while Stilwell's American and Chinese force was to move out from Yunnan to capture Myitkyina. Wingate's greatly expanded Chindits, with better rations, more radios and a plethora of American-supplied weapons, was to support Stilwell's and the Assam fronts, with two thirds of his columns being flown in and the others infiltrating on foot. Fighting was intense, and as usual the Japanese defended their bunkers, caves and dugouts tenaciously until they were winkled out by a combination of tanks firing armour-piercing solid shot at the bunkers to cover the infantry attacking them from the flanks or rear.

Slim had always predicted a Japanese counter-attack, but when it came it was a surprise. From the Japanese viewpoint, the one thing that the first Chindit expedition had done was to convince Lieutenant-General Kawabe Masakasu, commanding the Burma Area Army, that to prevent another, and possibly larger, infiltration they should seize the likely mounting areas in India – Imphal and Kohima. This was approved by Imperial Headquarters in Tokyo and it was agreed that the necessary reinforcements could be moved using the newly completed railway that ran from Siam to link up with the existing rail network in Burma. Built between July 1942 and November 1943, a month ahead of schedule, the railway cut through 260 miles of mountainous jungle in what is probably one of the unhealthiest climates in the world. The Japanese used 60,000 prisoners of war and up to 200,000 Burmese, Siamese, Tamil, Malay and Javanese civilian labourers to build the railway and regarded this labour force as entirely expendable. Fed a meagre diet, or often nothing at all, and beaten unmercifully for the slightest attempt to rest from a pace that was unceasing, 9,000 British and Australian, 2,500 Dutch and 350 Americans died of disease, malnutrition or beatings, as did probably around one third of the civilian labourers.

Once permission from Tokyo had been obtained and the necessary reinforcements agreed, the plan became rather more than just the capture of

British mounting bases in Assam. Kawabe, egged on by his subordinate commanders and with the encouragement of Bose, the leader of the Japanese Indian National Army, thought that the offensive could be expanded into an invasion of India: once Imphal was taken, the units of the British Indian Army would desert en masse to the INA, there would be revolution in India and the 'March on Delhi' could begin. The 40,000-strong INA was moved up to the Burma front and Japanese soldiers were issued with guidance advising them not to eat cows once they reached India and not to treat Indian females as 'comfort women' in the way they had in all the territories conquered by them so far. Kawabe did not have the logistic support, artillery or air cover to embark on such an ambitious scheme so relied on the usual Japanese tactics of speed and surprise. If he could capture Imphal quickly, he could use the British supply depots to feed and fuel his army, and he had a large contingent of gunners without guns who would operate captured British artillery pieces. Experience had told the Japanese that, once British units were cut off from their supply lines by a Japanese hook to their rear, they would attempt to fight their way back and could be annihilated while so doing. The first phase of the operation would be a diversionary attack in the Arakan, aimed at the rear of XV Corps, and particularly the administrative area, or admin box, of the Indian 7 Division, the left-hand or easternmost division of the corps. This would be Operation Ha-Go, which would force the British to commit their reserves and distract them from the far larger Operation U-Go against Imphal.

Despite Slim's conviction that the Japanese would counter-attack, when Japanese troops suddenly appeared behind Lieutenant-General Christison's XV Corps and threatened his administrative area, Fourteenth Army had no prior warning and had to react very swiftly to prevent disaster. The British practice had been to fight backwards towards main supply routes, but now XV Corps stood fast and the 7 Division administrative area was reinforced and told to defend itself. When the blow fell against Imphal, Slim flew two divisions in by air and the position held. When Kohima, north-east of Imphal, was also attacked and the main supply route from Dinapur cut, Slim refused to panic and ordered all concerned to stand firm. The fighting, much of it hand to hand, was ferocious, and at one stage the opponents blasted each other from either side of the tennis court of the Deputy Commissioner's bungalow. In a prodigious effort, the RAF's Third Tactical Air Force succeeded in resupplying all the beleaguered units while its fighters destroyed more and more Japanese aircraft. Time was not on the side of the Japanese. The INA proved useless, unwilling to fight and unhappy about having to eat Japanese rations, and the arrival of the monsoon in May made what were already scanty logistic arrangements almost unworkable. As it was, the road to Dinapur was reopened and, on 18 July, Kawabe was forced to admit that the operation had failed and ordered a withdrawal back across the Chindwin. Now the Chindits, instead of being a support for a main advance elsewhere, found themselves harrying and disrupting a beaten army as the Japanese reeled back.

Wingate himself had been killed in an air crash during the deployment of his force in March 1944 and immediately the legend-makers went into action. Perhaps it was well for Wingate's reputation that he died in action: as with those of General Gordon and T. E. Lawrence, his methods and ideas might not have stood up to cold scrutiny had he survived. His successor in command of the Chindits was Brigadier Joe Lentaigne, an officer of the fourth Gurkhas who, although he had commanded one of Wingate's brigades, had never absorbed the Wingate ethos, considering his ideas and tactics to be fundamentally flawed. Inevitably, the Wingate deification lobby has accused Lentaigne of being the man who grievously misused the Chindits after Wingate's death, whereas in fact he was simply reflecting Slim's view that long-range penetration was an adjunct to more conventional operations and not an end in itself, and should not be allowed to denude the army of all its best men and assets.

Although neither side realized it just yet, the failure of U-Go and Ha-Go was the beginning of the end for the Japanese in Burma. The British and Indian units were very different in outlook, skills and equipment from those that had been defeated so comprehensively a year before. Training and leadership had given them the confidence to hold out against a determined Japanese assault, and now they had shown that they could do that and win. For the Japanese, it was their first taste of defeat by the despised British, Indians and West Africans; of the 85,000 Japanese combat troops committed to battle, 35,000 were killed or missing and the rest were starving, disease-ridden and exhausted. It is certainly true that Fourteenth Army outnumbered the Japanese both in the Arakan and in Kohima and Imphal, just as it is true that the British were able to resupply by air whereas the Japanese could not and that the British were able to evacuate their wounded while the Japanese had to be left to die. All this notwithstanding, the Japanese were able to achieve local superiority in some areas, they did surprise Slim and his intelligence staff, and they did fight ferociously, tenaciously and with real courage. Slim has been accused of using a sledgehammer to crack a nut – some nut.

Furthermore, what had previously been sheer fear of the Japanese had now been replaced by hatred: most of the soldiers of Fourteenth Army had heard of the atrocities committed in Hong Kong and Singapore, but few had actually experienced them. The overrunning of a field hospital in the Arakan in February and the pointless massacre of the British and Indian medical staff and the patients brought it home just how inherently bestial their enemy was, and little mercy would be shown from here on. While this had the laudable effect of galvanizing the individual soldiers, it had less desirable results too, and Indian soldiers who captured members of the INA took to shooting them out of hand, partly because they were associated with the Japanese and partly because they had let down the Indian Army. While the soldiers who had remained loyal no doubt considered that they were only anticipating the results of subsequent courts martial, the shooting of prisoners, however understandable, is and was unquestionably illegal.

* * *

While Slim and Fourteenth Army were giving the Japanese a bloody nose in Burma and the Americans were preparing for Phase Two of their two-pronged strategy in the South Pacific, the Americans were also engaged in a battle rather closer to home. In June 1942, as part of the manoeuvres that led to the Battle of Midway, the Japanese had landed on Atu and Kiska, two of the Aleutian Islands. The Aleutians are a string of small and generally inoffensive islands that run from the tip of the Kamchatka peninsula in Russia to the tip of the Alaskan peninsula. Running in the other direction from Kamchatka, and part of the same geological feature, are the Kurile Islands that run for 700 miles to northern Japan. Atu and Kiska are 1,700 miles from Alaska but they are American territory and raised an old bugbear, one that dated to well before the first war, of invasion of the USA by the Yellow Peril. The Japanese had no intention of trying to invade continental America and had only occupied Atu and Kiska in case the Americans thought of invading Japan by way of the Aleutians and the Kuriles, but American public opinion demanded that they be removed and on 11 May 1943 an American division was landed on Atu. The Japanese garrison of 2,650 fought to the last man – 2,622 were killed and the remaining 28 too badly wounded to kill themselves – and it was not until 29 May that resistance ceased. The next step was to take Kiska, and 30,000 American and 5,000 Canadian troops were assembled in Alaska for this purpose. The Japanese, realizing that they could not reinforce in the teeth of American naval superiority, decided to evacuate the garrison, and in a brilliant little operation in July, carried out in thick fog, Japanese destroyers embarked the entire garrison and Japanese civilians – 5,000 in all – and slipped away unseen. When the American expeditionary force came storming up the beach on the night of 15/16 July in driving rain, they found nobody there. The operation to reclaim the Aleutians was entirely unnecessary and the Japanese garrisons could well have been left to wither on the vine, as the official history puts it, and the troops put to far greater use elsewhere, but in a democracy military common sense often has to come second to political necessity, and this was one of those times.

In the South Pacific, MacArthur and his combined Australian and American forces had by now taken most of New Guinea, while Nimitz continued his island-hopping advance along the Solomons. In February 1943, the Russell Islands, the next stepping stone up from Guadalcanal, fell, and in June New Georgia was taken. This was followed by Vella Navella in August and by October American troops were poised to land on Bougainville, the most northerly island in the Solomons of any consequence. Both MacArthur and Nimitz followed similar strategies. An island or a base would be taken, and immediately converted into an airstrip from which land-based fighters and bombers could cover the move to the next base or island. Japanese land-based air support grew less and less as the nimble Oscar and once much feared Zero were now being bettered by more modern Allied fighters, and increasingly Japanese carriers risked destruction if they ventured out of range of land-based air cover. From September 1943 the Japanese were on the defensive and Imperial Headquarters decided that defence should be based on a smaller perimeter than that conquered in 1941 and 1942. The line from the Bonin Islands through the Marianas to the Carolines across the most westerly tip of New Guinea and via the Dutch East Indies to Burma would mark the new perimeter of the Greater East Asian Co-Prosperity Sphere, while the Gilbert, Marshall and Solomon Islands and all but the west of New Guinea would be abandoned. Yet these outlying garrisons would be expected to fight, even if they were going to be abandoned, and fight they did, with no thought of surrender. The death toll was enormous but the Allies' ability to replace ships sunk and aircraft downed at a far faster rate than the Japanese could ever match ensured that by the spring of 1944 the Japanese tide was going out. It would not come in again.

14

THE EUROPEAN WAR

MAY 1943–AUGUST 1944

By the summer of 1943 the war situation for the Allies was very different from that of a year before. The Axis had been completely cleared from North Africa; the balance was beginning to tip against the U-boats in the Atlantic; the Russians had decisively defeated the last major German offensive on the Eastern Front at Kursk; the bombing of Germany by the RAF and the USAAF was intensifying; and in the Far East the Americans were fighting their way up the Solomons and the Australians were holding the Japanese on Papua New Guinea. None the less, once it had become apparent in the spring of that year that the Axis surrender in North Africa could not be long in coming, Allied differences as what to do next had resurfaced. The Americans were very reluctant to do anything that might detract from landings in North-West Europe, while the British were still in favour of the 'soft under-belly' approach as advocated by Churchill. Two Allied conferences, one in the United States and one in Casablanca, had agreed that a cross-Channel invasion would be the priority and, after much debate, that the next move would be to take Sicily. The British saw this as a prelude to an invasion of Italy, while the Americans preferred to reserve their position in this regard, and an agreement to invade Italy after Sicily had been taken was not arrived at until the Trident Conference in May. Even then, it was hedged around with all sorts of caveats that would contribute greatly to the muddle and confusion of the subsequent campaign.

What the Allies could not allow was a stalemate: Churchill was quite clear that, now that Panzer Army Africa was dealt with, North Africa must be 'a springboard, not a sofa'; Stalin was unhappy that there was to be no second front in 1943 and even more unhappy that Lend-Lease convoys had been suspended during Operation Torch and had only just been resumed. So, with the surrender of 250,000 German and Italian troops in Tunisia in

May 1943, planning for Operation Husky, the invasion of Sicily, went into high gear. The strategic aim agreed by both Americans and British was to knock Italy out of the war and tie down the maximum number of German divisions to divert them from the Eastern Front: that the British, or at least their prime minister, had a subsidiary hope of opening a Balkan Front was regarded with great suspicion by the Americans, who saw it as nothing more than a furtherance of British imperial ambitions to control the Mediterranean.

The overall plan for Husky was to reduce Sicily's defences by air bombardment supported by naval gunfire and then to mount a seaborne assault. Fighter cover would be essential and, as Malta, no longer under siege, could not of itself provide all the airfields needed, Eisenhower decided to take the Italian islands of Pantelleria and Lampedusa, both of which had hardened aircraft shelters and good airstrips, and could interfere with shipping from Tunisia to Sicily if left unoccupied by the Allies. On 9 May 1943, five days before the Axis surrender in Tunisia, air raids were mounted on Pantelleria, thirty miles east of Tunisia and seventy-five miles from Sicily, and on Lampedusa, 100 miles to the south-south-east of Tunisia and 125 miles from Sicily. On 13 May the air raids were augmented by naval bombardment, and, when a British brigade landed on Pantelleria on 11 June, 11,000 Italians surrendered. The following day, the 4,600-strong Italian garrison of Lampedusa surrendered, initially to the pilot of an antiquated Fleet Air Arm Swordfish that had crash-landed on the airfield.

From the German perspective, the days of lightning war and sweeping advances were over. German strategy now was aimed at holding the enemy as far away from Germany proper as possible, and relied on the hope that some sort of compromise peace could be made when the Allies fell out amongst themselves or became exhausted. Sicily and, of course, Italy were nominally Italian theatres, under the direction of the *Commando Supremo* in Rome, but already the Germans were suspicious of Italian intentions – with good reason, for there were those in the Italian government and armed forces who had come to the conclusion that Germany was going to lose the war and had made unofficial approaches to the Allies to see what might be salvaged for Italy. The German Commander-in-Chief South was still Field Marshal Kesselring, who deferred to Mussolini and then proceeded to do what he thought to be best, and who had correctly predicted that an Allied landing directed at Italy was a certainty after the collapse of North Africa.

He had stationed one German division in Sardinia, a brigade in Corsica, a division in Calabria (the toe of Italy) and two divisions in Sicily, and by June he was moving a further four German divisions into the south of Italy. Sicily itself was held by the Italian Sixth Army, commanded by the sixty-six-year-old General Alfredo Guzzoni, recently recalled from compulsory retirement after accusations of incompetence in Albania in 1941. Sixth Army disposed of four field divisions, or about 60,000 men in all, and six coastal divisions, or around 40,000 men, made up of soldiers of lower medical category and lacking much basic equipment. Theoretically under Guzzoni as his German liaison officer and commander of German troops in Sicily but in fact reporting direct to Kesselring was Lieutenant-General Fridolin von Senger und Etterlin, a Rhodes Scholar at Oxford in his youth and son of the German First World War general who had given the British so much trouble in East Africa. Under von Senger were 15 Panzer Grenadier Division and, at two infantry and two tank battalions, the seriously under-strength Hermann Göring Luftwaffe Field Division. These German units were held as a mobile reserve which could reinforce where needed.

Although the British had mounted a disinformation operation – one involving the well-known Man Who Never Was* – to conceal the actual objective, by June Kesselring was reasonably certain that it would be Sicily and instructed the German commander that an Allied landing should be countered on the beaches, but that, as movement by day would be impossible because of Allied air superiority, the counter-attack units should move into position by night. Although the number of defenders was impressive, there were problems. The estimated daily tonnage of supplies needed by the troops and the civilian population was 8,000 tons, whereas only 2,000 were actually coming across the Straits of Messina from the mainland; communications were poor, with the Germans – probably wisely – refusing to give their codes to the Italians and the only contact von Senger had with Kesselring was via a Luftwaffe undersea telephone cable, and the procedures of the Luftwaffe and the Italian air force were not compatible, meaning that separate systems of air traffic control and target allocation had to be maintained.

---

*The British dressed the body of a tramp who had died of pneumonia, a disease with similar symptoms to drowning, in the uniform of a Royal Marines officer and dumped it off the coast of Spain. When the body was washed up, the Spanish found operational instructions that indicated an attack on Greece and Sardinia, which they duly passed on to the Germans.

The Allies intended to invade Sicily with two armies: the British Eighth commanded by General Sir Bernard Montgomery with seven divisions (one of them Canadian) and the American Seventh with six divisions commanded by Lieutenant-General George S. Patton. In support would be an Allied fleet including six British battleships, two British aircraft carriers, ten British and five American cruisers, seventy-one British and forty-eight American destroyers, and twenty-three British submarines, and the aircraft of the North African Tactical Air Force consisting of the RAF's Desert Air Force and Middle East Tactical Bomber Force and the USAAF XII Air Support Command. Under Eisenhower, the naval elements would be commanded by Admiral Sir Andrew Cunningham RN, the land forces by General Sir Harold Alexander and the air forces by Air Vice-Marshal Sir Arthur Coningham.

Planning was marked by acrimony and inter-service and inter-Allied sniping, and, as Alexander tried to keep the peace between the two prima donnas, Montgomery and Patton, he had frequently to call upon Eisenhower to mediate. At last a plan of attack was agreed: after an air and naval bombardment, the two armies would land side by side, the British on the south-east coast and the Americans on the south-west. D-Day was to be 10 July and on the previous night three American parachute battalions and a British glider-borne air-landing brigade would take out key installations, gun positions and the bridge over the River Anapo delta, the Ponte Grande, which had to be in Allied hands to allow an advance up the east coast. It was to be a massive amphibious landing, putting 115,000 British and Empire and 66,000 American troops ashore to face an island-wide garrison of 315,000 Italians and, ultimately, 50,000 Germans.

The airborne phase of the operation was a disaster. The air-landing brigade of 1,200 men were to be delivered in 144 gliders, a mix of American Wacos, which could take fourteen men and their equipment, and British Horsas, which could carry thirty. The towing aircraft were 109 USAAF C-47 Dakotas and thirty-five Albermarles of the RAF. The RAF pilots of the towing aircraft all had considerable experience of training with gliders, and the British Glider Pilot Regiment crews (two to a glider) had practised the operation over and over again in the UK. Unfortunately for their passengers, many of the Waco pilots had not completed their training, while the C-47 pilots had little or no experience of glider operations and some had done little night flying. During the night the weather worsened and the wind got up to 40 mph. The defenders were fully alert and, as the airborne armada approached, their anti-aircraft guns opened up.

A military glider has the aerodynamic properties of a brick: once it is released from its towing aircraft, the only way is down, although turns to right and left, and even complete circles, are perfectly possible. What is critical is that the towing pilot releases his glider at the correct distance from the target, and this depends on the height at which release takes place. Also critical is the ability of all gliders to 'stream', that is to arrive at the landing ground from the same direction, which is achieved by the towing aircraft flying in formation to the release point. It was not easy to tow a fully laden glider at night while being shot at and to many of the inexperienced USAAF pilots it was just too much. Sixty-nine gliders were released too soon and crashed into the sea; fifty-six were released in the wrong place and did make landfall, but scattered all along the coast. Only twelve, all towed by RAF pilots, landed where they should have done, and, when the main assault came in across the beaches, eight officers and sixty-five soldiers of Second Battalion the South Staffordshire Regiment and a mix of glider pilots, Royal Engineers and members of the brigade headquarters defence platoon held the Ponte Grande and the rest of the gallant band had taken a nearby coastal battery. The 2,700 American paratroopers fared equally badly: forced to take a complicated approach route to avoid the shipping lanes, many of the pilots got lost, others could not see the dropping zones that had been obscured by fires started by the preliminary bombardments, and the men were dropped all over Sicily or in the sea. Some consolation came from the fact that the Italian defenders were unable to work out exactly where the main point of the attack was supposed to be.

H-Hour for the main force was 0245 on 10 July and, despite the increased swell and sea sickness amongst the troops, the landings did take place, with Italian gun batteries that started to shell the beaches being knocked out by naval gunfire. To the west, the Americans were exposed to the full force of the wind; there were delays in launching the landing craft, and some units were not able to land until after First Light (0415 hours, British double summer time or GMT + 2) but despite the difficulties all were ashore by 0630 and by 1000 tanks and vehicles were being landed and both armies had secured their lodgement areas and were beginning to push inland and, in the case of the British, along the coast to the Ponte Grande. The intention now was for Patton's Seventh Army to cover Montgomery's left flank, while Eighth Army sent XIII Corps up the coast to Catania, to seize the port and then press on to the Straits of Messina and cut off the Axis line of retreat to Italy, while XXX Corps made for Leonforte and Enna, the centre of the island and location of the German main force headquarters, with the aim of cutting the island in half.

The British moved cautiously – those who had fought in North Africa knew that they could not beat the Germans in a battle of manoeuvre and thus relied heavily on artillery and air bombardment before moving forward – and failed to prevent 15 Panzer Grenadier Division from withdrawing towards the east of the island. An attempt to capture bridges over the River Simeto at Primasole on 13 July by a British parachute brigade emplaned in North Africa ran into trouble when Allied warships mistook their aircraft for the Luftwaffe, failed to see recognition signals and opened fire on them. This forced them off course over the no-flying zone above ships unloading at the beachheads and these also opened fire, provoking more diversions that brought many of the planes over German-held territory and into more flak. Of the 126 aircraft containing paratroopers, nineteen returned to their base without dropping their troops, fourteen were shot down, twenty-seven got hopelessly lost and dropped their loads over the sea or on the slopes of Mount Etna, many miles from their objective. Only thirty-nine aircraft managed to drop their sticks within a mile of the bridge, which was at last captured by one officer and fifty men.

In the opinion of both Guzzoni and von Senger, once the Allies were ashore Sicily was lost: to add to the garrison was pointless and the island should be abandoned with the main battle fought in Italy. Hitler did not agree, however, and from 12 July reinforcements began to arrive in the form of the one-armed Colonel-General Hans Hube, late of the Russian front, whose XIV Panzer Corps took over the existing two German divisions and brought with them 29 Panzer Division and 1 Parachute Division. Hube knew that he had to delay the Allies as long as he could and established three lines of defence running from Catania on the east coast north-west to San Stefano on the north coast.

By 16 July, Patton was unhappy about what he saw as a subsidiary role to Montgomery and protested to Alexander, who agreed to let him off the leash. In a lightning dash Patton got to Palermo on the north coast on 22 July. It looked good and captured a lot of Italians but in fact did little to shorten the campaign and was the scene of Patton's career hiccough when on two separate incidents he accused soldiers in hospital with psychiatric problems of being cowards, slapped them across the face and ordered that they be sent back to the front. Those journalists who saw or heard of the incidents agreed to cover them up but one, Drew Pearson, then a radio reporter and later infamous as a muckraker (when admittedly there was much muck to rake), reported them and Patton was ordered by Eisenhower to apologize in public to the units of the men involved.

Eventually, on 23 July, Eighth Army captured Leonforte and Bradley's corps of Seventh Army cut the island in two, too late for it to have any effect. One of the principles of amphibious operations was the need to capture a port or ports as early as possible, as it was not considered possible to supply an army over open beaches for longer than a few days. Catania held out, and would not be taken until 5 August, but the Allies were fortunate in that there is almost no tide in the Mediterranean, the weather had improved and the arrival of a quantity of DUKWs, amphibious trucks, allowed supplies to be offloaded out to sea and delivered inland.

Meanwhile, momentous happenings were under way in Italy. Mussolini had been seduced by the prospect of easy pickings after a short war, and his declaration of war in 1940 was purely pragmatic. Italy's economy was never capable of withstanding a long war, and by 1943 harsh reality had begun to make itself felt. Rationing had been introduced and food consumption reduced by 25 per cent; soap, coffee and tobacco were luxuries; bread was being sold at eight times its pre-war price; there was a thriving black market, and in Rome little old ladies were wondering where their pet cats had disappeared to, as the less well-off ate them. The German alliance had never been popular but with no oil of her own Italy was dependent on imports of German coal, which decreased as Germany needed it for her own use. Steel production had fallen, and Italian industry was barely capable of replacing the outdated weaponry of the country's armed forces, let alone of manufacturing sufficient numbers of the modern fighter aircraft the Regia Aeronautica desperately needed. And as the British and Americans stepped up air raids on Italian targets, production declined yet further. Workers began to strike in protest at increases in working hours and in the armed services chaos reigned as generals were shuffled about and Mussolini made pointless appeals to Italian soldiers to die at their posts. The Duce himself was not well; an old ulcer had flared up, he was subject to violent mood

---

*It has been suggested that this was the result of syphilis caught in his youth. The same has been said about Napoleon, who also vacillated wildly from elation to depression.

swings* and he was unable or unwilling to curb the ambitions of his young mistress, Clara Petacci, who was thirty years younger than him and openly solicited favours for her numerous relations. While he was well aware that the Italian population was now equating fascism with shortages, hunger and air raids, he refused to consider telling Hitler that the Italian people could not take much more. However, a number of individuals who mattered – the king, Victor Emmanuel of the House of Savoy, Marshal Badoglio, the onetime Chief of Staff of the army until Mussolini sacked him, the dictator's son-in-law Galeazzo Ciano, the former foreign minister who was now ambassador to the Holy See and a longtime opponent of the German alliance, other disillusioned former fascist functionaries – and one very influential institution, the Vatican, had all concluded that it was time for Mussolini to go. The final straw was probably an Allied air raid on Rome on 19 July that killed over 1,000 people, and on 24 July the Fascist Grand Council passed a vote of no confidence in Mussolini's leadership and called for him to be replaced as head of the armed forces by the king. The next day Victor Emmanuel dismissed him as head of government, had him arrested and swore in a new government headed by Marshal Badoglio. Badoglio appointed soldiers and technocrats to his government, while those unreconstructed fascists who were unable or unwilling to turn their coats headed for Germany. The public generally supported the new regime but demonstrations demanding social reform were put down firmly, even brutally, with many of the agitators locked up.

The new government did not attempt to leave the war, or at least not just yet. It made secret approaches to the Allies while still professing eternal solidarity to the Axis, but the Germans, from Hitler in Berlin to Kesselring in Rome, could see the writing on the wall and Hube was ordered to withdraw towards Messina while the Allies attacked either side of Mount Etna. In a skilful operation on the night of 11/12 August, the Germans evacuated 60,000 Italians and 40,000 Germans with all their weapons and most of their vehicles and equipment across the straits to Italy. The Allies, who were too busy squabbling amongst themselves, did little to oppose it and their amphibious operations designed to prevent it failed. There was now an unseemly race to Messina, the British from the south and the Americans from the west, which was won by the Americans, to Montgomery's fury, on 16 August. Operation Husky cost the Allies 31,000 casualties, of which around half were from malaria (probably contracted in North Africa), the Germans about the same (but none from malaria) and the Italians 132,000, mainly deserters and prisoners of war. The Axis had lost 1,800 aircraft to the Allies' 400 and, although the efforts of the Italian navy had been minimal, the Allies did lose twelve vessels, none of them capital ships.

Now would have been the time to strike across the Straits of Messina, drop an airborne division on Rome, accept an Italian surrender, trap the German forces in Italy and free up the whole of the Italian mainland as an air base from which to bomb Germany. It was not to be. Inter-Allied argument and dissension, muddle and confusion, political wheeling and dealing all contributed to a three-week delay before the terms of Italian surrender were agreed and the Allies were ready to cross the straits. In agreeing that they would invade Italy, the Allies never expected to have to fight all the way up that country. Kesselring had other ideas, however, and every intention of exploiting the defensive qualities of the peninsula, and, while the Allies were indulging in secret haggling with the Italian government over the terms of surrender, the Germans moved sixteen divisions into Italy and honed their preparations for the long-suspected Italian defection. In the meantime, AMGOT, the Allied Military Government of Occupied Territories, set up a civilian administration of Sicily composed of local worthies, who turned out to be the Mafia in suits.

During the negotiations between the representatives of Badoglio's government and the Allies, which took place in Lisbon and Tangiers, much delay was caused by differences as to exactly what the Italian exit from the war would mean. The Allies had stated at Casablanca that only unconditional surrender would be accepted, whereas the Italians saw themselves as joining the Allies in the fight against Germany. Further delay was imposed by the conflicting requirements for landing craft: the Americans were insisting that the cross-Channel invasion in 1944 – now codenamed Overlord – was the absolute priority, while the British pressed the claims of the Far East, where Wavell was planning an advance into Burma supported by amphibious landings. Eventually an agreement was hammered out and signed on 3 September. The Allies would mount an attack on southern Italy, with three seaborne landings – one at Calabria on 3 September followed by one at Taranto and one at Salerno on 9 September – and would drop an airborne division on Rome. At the same time the Italian surrender would be announced and the Italian government would demand that the Germans leave. In the event, the Italians were unable to guarantee the security of the drop zone for the airborne operation, which was cancelled.

The landing on Calabria, Operation Baytown, would be carried out by the British Eighth Army, which would put two divisions, 1 Canadian and 5 British, across the Straits of Messina on 4 September. Operation Slapstick would send another division, the British 1 Airborne, across to Taranto from North Africa by sea the following day. The Salerno landings, with their objective Naples, thirty miles to the north-west, would be the responsibility of Lieutenant-General Mark Clark's American Fifth Army, which had been formed in January 1943, originally for the defence of Algeria and Morocco. As it was seriously under-strength, it was augmented by British troops and now consisted of the US VI Corps of four divisions, the British X Corps of two infantry divisions and one armoured division, three American Ranger battalions and two British army commandos. All landings would be supported by naval gunfire, mainly by the Royal Navy as the Americans withdrew shipping in the build-up for Overlord, and in the case of Calabria by massed artillery firing across the straits. As bomber squadrons were being withdrawn from the Mediterranean, the air support was less than ideal, and indeed Air Marshal Tedder considered it to be inadequate. As it was, the British landings on 4 September were carried out with little opposition, the German regiment covering eighteen miles of coastline very wisely withdrawing in the face of the overwhelming artillery bombardment, and by 8 September the toe of Calabria was firmly in Allied hands. The landings at Salerno, Operation Avalanche, were a different matter.

Although Marshal Badoglio's accredited representatives had signed the instruments of capitulation on 3 September, it was agreed that they would not be made public until 1830 hours on 8 September, when Eisenhower and Badoglio would both broadcast the news. Badoglio then asked that the announcement be delayed until after the Allied invasion. As the Allies had no intention of telling the Italians when the invasion was to come, Eisenhower insisted that the terms could not be varied and at 1830 hours, when the invasion forces for Salerno and Taranto were at sea, he broadcast the news that Italy had surrendered. An hour later Badoglio announced over Italian radio that Italy had left the war. Within the Italian armed forces and administration there was chaos. Hardly anyone knew of the intention to rat, and even the Chief of Staff, General Mario Roatta, was taken completely by surprise. Having been told nothing, most units of the Italian Army stayed in barracks and did nothing. A few turned on the nearest Germans, many conscripts took the opportunity to desert and go home, and in the Balkans some joined the partisans, but the vast majority were bewildered and without orders – no one had told them what to do in such an event and only the navy acted in accordance with the armistice terms, sailing to Malta and losing one battleship, the *Roma*, sunk and another badly damaged by the Luftwaffe on the way. The Germans reacted swiftly. Within an hour of Badoglio's announcement, Kesselring had issued the code word *Achse* – Axis – for the disarming of the Italians and the seizing of Rome. Reinforcements poured in over the Brenner Pass, brushing Italian roadblocks aside, government buildings were occupied, Italian troops disarmed and coastal defences taken over. Those few Italian troops who were prepared to fight for the Germans were retained; over 600,000 were disarmed and sent to prison camps in Germany.

On the day that Italy surrendered, another of Churchill's pet schemes was unveiled when General Sir Maitland Wilson, now Commander-in-Chief Middle East, was persuaded against his better judgement to despatch troops to the Aegean to capture Rhodes and other islands in the Dodecanese. It was a totally misguided attempt to persuade Turkey to enter the war on the Allied side, as well as being part of Churchill's dream of a Balkan Front, was strongly objected to by the Americans, failed to take Rhodes and achieved nothing except the surrender of five British battalions and the loss of 113 aircraft and eighteen vessels of various types when the Germans retook the subsidiary islands in October 1943.

At Salerno, the landings on 9 September began at 0330 hours under naval cover that included four battleships, seven cruisers and forty destroyers of the Royal Navy and four cruisers and seventeen destroyers of the US Navy. As Salerno was at extreme range for aircraft operating from Sicily, 150 miles away, most air cover would be provided from seven Royal Navy carriers. The initial waves got ashore, and then it all started to go wrong. The area was the responsibility of General Hube's XIV Panzer Corps and when X Corps landed on time and began to make some progress in getting off the beach, they were met by 3 Panzer Division, while 16 Panzer Division stopped the Americans and prevented them from even getting off the beach. For three days the situation was desperate. The German build-up was happening faster than that of the Allies and, although the British managed to capture Salerno port and Montecorvino airfield, they were unable to push the Germans back far enough for them to be able to be used. When the German Tenth Army mounted a counter-attack on 12 September, it looked at one stage as if the landing was about to be pushed into the sea. Only by committing all his reserves and by throwing every man who could hold a rifle – clerks, cooks, drivers, bandsmen and storemen – into the battle was Clark able to hold. Eventually, but not until the arrival of 1,500 British reinforcements rapidly moved by three cruisers from Tripoli, the dropping of three battalions of the American 82 Airborne Division into the beachhead, the addition of two British battleships and the diversion of almost every aircraft in the Mediterranean capable of dropping a bomb, the situation was stabilized and on 16 September the Germans withdrew at their own pace to take up a defensive position north of Naples. On the same day the Americans made contact with Eighth Army making its way up from Calabria, and on 1 October the Allies entered Naples.

The latter stages of Operation Avalanche saw one of the few mutinies of British troops during the Second World War. Mutiny is the worst of all military offences for it strikes at the very basis of discipline; it is a collective offence, that of deliberate and wilful defiance of lawful authority, and was defined in the Army Act applicable at the time as 'collective insubordination to resist or to induce others to resist lawful military authority'. Many of the 1,500 men sent out from Tripoli at the height of the battle included men in reinforcement camps or returning from leave or recovering from wounds, and the idea was that they should be fed in as individual reinforcements to units. As it transpired, they arrived on the beaches when the worst of the crisis was over, but some of them, mainly men of the 51 Highland Division and 50 Tyne Tees Division, were unhappy that they were being sent to battalions other than the ones into which they had originally been conscripted. The British Army takes the regimental system very seriously, and in law a soldier cannot be ordered to change his cap badge, but it has always been accepted that in an emergency men can be drafted to whatever unit has need of them, even if they are returned to their parent regiment when the moment passes. Of the 1,500 men who arrived, three sergeants, sixteen junior NCOs and 170 privates refused to move and join the units to which they were allocated.* In due course they were brought before a court martial in Bizerta that, after an exhaustive inquiry, found them guilty

---

*They may, of course, have been simply 'windy' and seeking an excuse not to go into the line, but cowardice, also an offence under the Army Act, is notoriously difficult to prove in court.

of mutiny – indeed, it is difficult to see how the verdict could possibly have been otherwise. Mutiny was a capital offence* and the three sergeants were sentenced to death (suspended on review), with the others receiving prison sentences of between five and ten years (also suspended). While we do not know what passed through the minds of the confirming authorities who decided that the sentences should be suspended, no doubt the existing shortage of manpower, the fact that the men were conscripts, and a fear of what the press might say (no executions had yet been carried out in this war) were persuasive. Whatever the mitigating circumstances (and there appear to have been few in this case), there can never be any excuse for mutiny, particularly in the middle of a war and in the circumstances of the critical situation pertaining to the Salerno landings. That the men concerned were clearly a thoroughly bad lot is evidenced by the fact that over 40 per cent of them subsequently deserted when returned to their parent units.

It was during the Salerno battle that the Germans decided to 'rescue' Mussolini from his arrest and detention in the Hotel Campo Imperatore, 7,000 feet up in the Apennine ski resort of Gran Sasso, seventy miles east of Rome. It was a daring and spectacular affair with German troops landed by glider and Mussolini removed in a two-seater Fieseler Storch short take-off and landing aircraft on 12 September, the whole under the command of SS-Sturmbannführer Otto Skorzeny. As the Gran Sasso was accessible via a perfectly good chair-lift and as the Germans by now controlled most of Italy, one can only assume that the method of rescue was intended as a public relations coup – as indeed it was – and Mussolini was soon on his way to Venice, where the Germans were firmly in control. Skorzeny was promoted to SS Obersturmbannführer and awarded the Knight's Cross of the Iron Cross.

Prior to the Calabria and Salerno landings, Hitler and OKW had believed that, in the event of an Italian defection and an Allied landing, southern Italy should be abandoned and the German defence concentrated in the north. Kesselring had held the opposite view, and the Salerno battle had proved him right; the whole of Italy could be defended and from now

---

*Until 1998, when the death penalty was abolished in British Military Law – inadvisably in this author's view. 'Go forward and you may be shot, refuse and you will be' is persuasive: 'Refuse and you will be put in jail and there will probably be an amnesty after the war' is less so. You don't want to shoot your own, but you should retain the threat of doing so, at least for a conscript army.

on it would be. Kesselring based his plan on a series of lines which would make the most of the Italian mountains and were already being prepared for defence. The German army would delay, harry and generally make life difficult for the advancing Allies and then withdraw back to the next prepared defence line. Kesselring was confident that he could hold Italy and the Balkans almost indefinitely, giving up ground only slowly and only when he had to. Winston Churchill, who was convinced that Italy was the 'soft under-belly', had obviously never consulted a map, or at least not a map with contours, for in Italy the mountains run east to west from a central spine, and the rivers run in the valleys created between those spurs. That means that anyone wanting to fight their way up Italy has to fight over a succession of mountain ridges, having first got over the rivers in front of them. The geography of the country is ideal for defence and the Germans, with their usual ingenuity and professionalism, were going to make full use of it. That the Allies were still fighting in Italy up to May 1945 tends to prove the point.

The first main position for the German defence of Italy was the so-called Gustav Line, which ran roughly from Minturno on the west coast to Ortona on the east across the narrowest part of the Italian peninsula and had as its dominating feature the 1,700-foot-high Monte Cassino, a craggy mountain crowned by a medieval Benedictine monastery that dominated the landscape for miles around and overlooked the Liri Valley and Route 6, the approaches to Rome. The ground made digging impossible and the Germans had blasted artillery positions, machine-gun nests and troop bunkers out of the rock; they had turned every village into a strongpoint and had carefully sited positions which covered the Rivers Garigliano and Sangro that ran south of the Line. With the British advancing up the east side and the Americans the west, the onset of the autumn rains soon reduced the few roads and tracks to muddy streams; wheeled vehicles could not move off the roads and there were few wide-open spaces for the tanks to manoeuvre. Although the Allies had complete air superiority, this was of less help in the narrow defiles of the hills and valleys than it had been in the open wastes of North Africa. Once the two armies had got over the rivers in front of the Gustav Line, there were to be four battles of Cassino and a long and costly four months of attritional warfare before they could move on.

The Allies did not, of course, expect to fight four battles. Alexander, commanding 15th Army Group, intended the American Fifth Army to attack the Monte Cassino area which, he hoped, would force Kesselring to move his reserves south. When that happened, an amphibious landing would be made on the west coast north of the Gustav Line behind the Germans. With the Allies north and south of them, the Germans would have no choice but to withdraw, abandoning the Gustav Line and Rome. Eighth Army would then hook across Italy and take Rome – and the Fifth Army operation orders were entitled 'The Battle for Rome'. There were a number of flaws in this plan. Firstly, Allied intelligence had concluded that the German troops, having fought their way back up Italy from Salerno, must be exhausted and close to collapse, and that morale was low. Unfortunately, however, wishing that something is so does not make it so, and, while the Germans were certainly tired and most units were under-strength, they were well led, well motivated and confident that they could make the Allies fight for every bit of ground before withdrawing at a time of their choosing. Secondly, any amphibious landing would have to happen before mid-January 1944, as after that there would be insufficient landing craft to move enough troops for a landing that could beat off the inevitable counter-attacks and survive. The landing craft were originally to be withdrawn in December, as part of the build-up for Overlord, but after pleading from Churchill the Americans had reluctantly agreed to a postponement, and this meant that the battle would have to be fought with the minimum time for preparation and rehearsal, and regardless of the weather, which in winter made low-level bombing extremely hazardous and thus reduced the effects of Allied air power.

On 12 January 1944 the Free French Corps, comprising two divisions, one of Moroccan and one of Algerian troops commanded by French officers and part of Fifth Army, attacked in driving snow to the north of Cassino. It made some progress and was then held up by the men of a German mountain division. The French Corps commander, General Alphonse Juin, lately Commander-in-Chief Vichy French Forces in North Africa, was convinced that just one more division would allow him to get through the defences and round behind Cassino, but Clark was not convinced and the French had to go on to the defensive where they were. On 17 January the British X Corps, reinforced by 5 Division from Eighth Army, crossed the River Garigliano near the west coast and established bridgeheads from which it was hoped to outflank Cassino, but swift reaction by the Germans brought a counter-attack by two panzer divisions from Rome on 21 January and the advance was halted. Although X Corps could get no further, it had drawn at least some of the German reserves on to its front, which Clark hoped would assist the next phase of his attack, which would see the British 46 Division making a diversionary attack across the Garigliano farther north while the American II Corps attacked across the River Rapido just north of Cassino. This would happen on 20 January and would precede the seaborne landing on 22 January, which was to be at Anzio, a port and town sixty miles up the coast from the Gustav Line. The attack by 46 Division was a failure: the fast-flowing river washed assault boats away or overturned them, the engineers were unable to get a bridge across, and German minefields and a stout infantry defence forced abandonment, with those few infantrymen on the other side of the river left to their fate. Without a diversion, the II Corps attack went in anyway, spearheaded by 36 Division of the Texas National Guard.* Starting at 2200 hours, the Texans were required to cross the river and then attack the German fixed defences. The approach to the river was overlooked by Monte Cassino, all stores and boats had to be manhandled through the mud, and minefields on the opposite side covered by German mortars meant that when, on the second day, 36 Division did manage to get two battalions across, they were pinned down and unable to move. Two foot bridges that the divisional engineers managed to put in place were quickly washed away and efforts to lay a Bailey bridge across to take armour had to be abandoned. The attack stalled, and by the afternoon of 22 January all those who had been on the enemy bank were dead or prisoners. That night the seaborne force landed.

The Anzio landing, Operation Shingle, took place at 0200 hours on 22 January when the US VI Corps put one British and one American division, a British commando brigade, an American Ranger battalion and an American parachute regiment ashore. The landings took place to no opposition and the corps commander, the fifty-four-year-old Major-General John P. Lucas, had every reason to be pleased with himself and began to bring ashore tanks of the US 1 Armoured Division. In hindsight, if Lucas had cracked on as soon as he had landed, and pushed inland to the Alban hills, he might have achieved something, but as it was he waited to land the rest of his corps, consolidate his position and stockpile rations and ammunition. By 24 January his lodgement was fifteen miles wide and seven miles deep. Unfortunately for Lucas, the delay gave the Germans time to assemble six divisions to lay siege to the beachhead. Major-General Lucian Truscott, one of Lucas's

---

*In peacetime the part-time National Guard comes under State control. Its nearest equivalent is the British Territorial Army but with a lot more money spent on it.

divisional commanders and who would eventually take over from him in command of the corps, was soon to comment that the Anzio situation bore grave similarities to Gallipoli, with the same amateur (Churchill) being its inspiration.

Now the need to break through the Gustav Line became urgent if VI Corps at Anzio was not to be snuffed out, and the Germans handed a massive propaganda coup. Clark renewed his assaults, with all three corps, the British X, the US II and the Free French, attacking, but, although they got into the outskirts of the German defences in some places and on 7 February men of 34 Division's 168 Infantry Regiment got to within a few hundred yards of the monastery on Monte Cassino, they could get no farther. The German defence was just too good, and that afternoon Clark ordered his men to pull back and he closed the battle. The Gustav Line was still intact. Meanwhile, at Anzio, Lucas, now reinforced by the American 45 Division, at last attacked out of his beachhead on 30 January, one day before a planned German attack on him. Initially VI Corps made some progress, with the British 1 Division gaining a mile and a half in two days, but the Germans were able to reinforce, and, when Tiger heavy tanks arrived on 1 February, Lucas could only accept that the advance had ground to a halt and he ordered his men to dig in and defend where they were.

While 15th Army Group was gearing itself up to deal with the Gustav Line, major command changes had taken place in the Mediterranean. General Eisenhower and General Montgomery were recalled to England, the former as Supreme Allied Commander and the latter as Land Forces Commander for Overlord, the cross-Channel invasion. General Sir Maitland Wilson, chosen as much for his diplomatic skills as for his sound military common sense, replaced Eisenhower as Supreme Allied Commander Mediterranean, and Lieutenant-General Oliver Leese, late of the Coldstream Guards and previously an armoured division and corps commander in North Africa and Sicily, replaced Montgomery at the head of Eighth Army.

By the end of January the Gustav Line still barred the way to Rome: Fifth Army had put all its divisions into the line and all had taken considerable casualties, while on the east coast a combination of determined Germans, difficult terrain and foul weather had halted Eighth Army too. Alexander now considered that, as Kesselring's reserves had been deployed to deal with the Anzio landing, Clark could now be reinforced by three divisions from Eighth Army, 2 New Zealand, 4 Indian and 78 British, to be formed into a corps which, as it was to be commanded by Lieutenant-General Bernard Freyberg VC, would be named the New Zealand Corps. Clark's plan for the Second Battle of Cassino was essentially a rerun of the first, with the New Zealand Division attacking the town and 4 Indian Monte Cassino and the monastery area. Neither Freyberg nor Major-General Tuker, commanding 4 Indian Division, thought that this stood any chance of success and protested to Clark. Tuker, with three Gurkha battalions in his division, was convinced that the sensible thing to do would be to reinforce the French in the mountains and push on with them, getting behind Cassino and into the Liri Valley, and Freyberg concurred. It was unfortunate that Clark did not welcome Freyberg's presence. At forty-eight years old, Clark was the American army's youngest three-star general and had made his name as a superb staff officer and administrator. He was very conscious of public relations and reluctant to allow anyone else to share any glory that might be going. He had a reputation as a commander who lacked tactical originality and always conducted operations conventionally. Freyberg was older, had been a general for longer and had considerably more operational experience, while Tuker was an officer of an empire of which many Americans disapproved. The two men's objections were listened to and rejected. Tuker then asked that, as his line of advance was overlooked entirely by the monastery, the building should be bombed. This caused a problem. The Germans had announced a 300-metre neutrality zone around the monastery and had always insisted that they would not use it for any military purpose. American reports suggested that this was not true, and when Tuker asked for it to be bombed, Freyberg, Clark, Alexander and finally Wilson agreed on the grounds of military necessity, although fully aware that they would be accused of cultural vandalism.* On 15 February the monastery was duly reduced to piles of rubble by Allied bombing, an operation which killed a number of Italian refugees who had taken shelter there, and with their neutrality zone now breached, the Germans

---

*According to an officer of 15 Panzer Grenadier Division, interviewed by this author in 1967, the Germans had helped the monks to remove all paintings and other religious valuables to safety in Rome before the battles, and at no time were any soldiers, equipment or weapon systems placed in the monastery, although small parties of Roman Catholic soldiers in civilian clothes did visit the monastery on sightseeing tours. General von Senger himself was a lay member of the Benedictine order.

swarmed into the cellars and built positions amongst the ruins. Nothing had been achieved and, when 4 Indian Division attacked, it was observed every foot of the way, and not even the Gurkhas could get to the top. When the New Zealand Division attacked the town, nestling at the bottom of the hill, it was a similar story, and on 18 February Clark accepted defeat.

Meanwhile, at Anzio, Colonel-General Heinrich von Vietinghoff's Tenth Army had launched its counter-attack against Lucas's VI Corps on 17 February. At first they forced the American and British defenders back almost to their original beachhead, but then Allied artillery, naval gunfire support and massive air bombardment began to tell and by 20 February both sides were utterly exhausted and settled down, the Allies to defend and the Germans to contain. Lucas was now removed from command, not before time in the opinion of some, and returned to the USA, being replaced by Major-General Truscott, who had hitherto been commanding 3 Division.

Alexander was convinced that the pressure must be kept up on the Germans and the Third Battle of Cassino was a holding operation while stocks and troops were assembled and prepared for a truly mammoth smashing assault on the Gustav Line. The Third Battle would be almost a repeat of the Second, and again it would be the responsibility of the New Zealand Corps, with 4 Indian Division attacking the monastery and Monte Cassino, and the New Zealand Division Cassino town. Freyberg insisted that he would not attack until there had been three clear days without rain, to allow vehicles and tanks to move, and at last on 15 March the attack began with carpet-bombing of the town. This provided no advantage, except to the Germans, as ruins are far more easily defended than undamaged buildings. The plan was to support the infantry with a mixture of British and American armour, but the bombing had blocked every route into the town and any attempt by the engineers to shift the piles of rubble immediately drew shell and mortar fire from the Germans, and the attack achieved little. Simultaneously, 4 Indian Division went for the monastery, but, apart from a small group of Gurkhas who captured Hangman's Hill, a few hundred yards below the summit, they too could achieve nothing. The battle went on, with the British making occasional gains but unable to reach the summit or to break through the German lines. On 20 March, Freyberg threw in his third division, the British 78 Division, but it too could do little, and on 23 March Freyberg withdrew his men from their exposed outposts, consolidated what little he had gained and closed the battle down.

The Fourth, and as it happened the final, Battle of Cassino, Operation Diadem, was much better prepared for than any of the others, and here Alexander took over the planning personally, with the intention of bringing the maximum amount of firepower on a twenty-mile front between Cassino and the sea. The inter-army boundary was changed and Eighth Army now took over the Cassino sector, moving the bulk of its troops to the west, leaving only enough men in the eastern, Adriatic, sector to hold the front. Alexander's plan was for Fifth Army to push up the west coast to link up with the US VI Corps at Anzio, which, now reinforced by two more divisions, would break out, and then the whole would swing inland to cut off the retreat of the German Tenth Army. The Free French Corps would attack to the south of Cassino, break through and then wheel right into the Liri Valley, while the British XIII Corps of the British 4 Division and the Indian 8 Division would attack to the north and wheel left. The monastery and Monte Cassino itself would be attacked by the Polish Corps of two divisions, supported by a Polish armoured brigade. Ready to exploit the breakthrough once it occurred would be the Canadian Corps of the Canadian 1 Infantry Division and the Canadian 5 Armoured Division, and the British 78 Division and 6 Armoured Division.

At 2300 hours on 11 May 1944 over 1,000 field, medium and heavy guns of 15th Army Group began a ferocious bombardment of the known German positions, and the US II Corps began its advance along the coast behind a creeping barrage and supported by naval gunfire, while the French launched their Berber tribesmen against the southern hills. That same day General Leese ordered the Polish Corps to attack with both divisions, but it was too early; the Germans were not in the slightest ruffled and, although they had taken casualties from the artillery bombardment and continued to suffer from air attacks, they repelled the Poles, who by evening were back where they started. The French made excellent progress, however, and on 13 May they had got through the hills and were looking down into the Liri valley behind Cassino, while on the Fifth Army axis German resistance had stiffened and Clark was making only moderate progress. The fighting became more reminiscent of the battles of the first war, with the attackers inching forward and the advantage always with the defender, but weight of artillery, air power and superior numbers began at last to tell, and when at 1800 hours on 16 May the Poles attacked again with one division the defences began to crumble, and, when the second Polish division was sent forward at first light the following day, the Germans realized that they could no longer hold and withdrew from Monastery Hill. The heights were in Allied hands, but the fighting would go on as the Germans withdrew to previously prepared positions about ten miles back – the Hitler Line. The US VI Corps was ordered to break out on 23 May and, after two days of intensive fighting, it at last linked up with Fifth Army. On the Hitler Line, the German Tenth Army held the Allies up for another two days and then began a fighting withdrawal. Now was the time for Mark Clark's Fifth Army to close the door and cut off the withdrawing Germans, but in an astounding piece of rank disobedience, which even some of the American generals thought was very bad form, he made for Rome instead, while his astonished troops watched Tenth Army pull back along Route 6, which was kept open by the Hermann Göring Division. Fifth Army, led by its commander, Mark Clark, entered Rome on 4 June 1944, and Clark's public relations team made much of his getting there before the British. As it happened, the British could not have cared less who got to Rome: what mattered was the destruction of the German Tenth Army, something which was prevented by Clark's failure to do what he had been told. Had Clark been a British general, or Alexander an American one, Clark would have been sacked on the spot, but one of the difficulties in making war in a coalition is that it is almost impossible to get rid of one's partner's incompetents and Clark survived.* The four battles of Cassino cost the Allies 31,000 casualties, killed, wounded, taken prisoner and missing, and they were as yet barely halfway up Italy.

* * *

If we discount the 700,000 men transported by Darius the Great in his expedition against the Scythians in 511 BC and the crossing of the Hellespont by Xerxes with 2 million men in 481 BC as exaggerations (the entire population of the Persian Empire was only around 4 million), then Operation Husky, the invasion of Sicily on 10 July 1943, was the largest single-phase amphibious operation in history, but, when follow-up troops and equipment are included, Operation Overlord, the invasion of Normandy on 6 June 1944, dwarfs them all. On this occasion, 8,000 aircraft, 1,200 warships and nearly 3 million men all combined to land over 133,000 soldiers and their tanks, vehicles and equipment on a fifty-mile stretch of beaches in the bay of the River Seine on one day, and by

---

*It has recently been suggested that Clark was actually acting on Roosevelt's orders.

the end of June that force had swollen to 850,000 men, 150,000 vehicles and half a million tons of supplies.

The British had never really wanted to invade North-West Europe, not least because they had bitter first-hand experience of amphibious operations that had gone wrong: Churchill had never forgotten the Gallipoli campaign of the first war and Dieppe had been a disaster dressed up as lessons learned. (At this stage, Anzio was still to come.) From the British point of view, an ideal solution would be for the Germans and the Russians to fight each other to a standstill, after which the Allies would enter Europe almost unopposed and dictate a peace that would keep the Soviets as far away from Western Europe and the Balkans as possible. The Americans took a much more uncomplicated stance: Germany should be defeated as soon as possible and this could only happen with a cross-Channel invasion. There was much inter-Allied suspicion; the British suspected the Americans of being prepared to grant concessions to the USSR in Europe in exchange for help in the Pacific, while the Americans suspected the British of pursuing their own imperial interests by pressing the claims of a Mediterranean and Balkan strategy rather than a European one. There was much truth in both attitudes, while the Soviet Union, which had been doing most of the fighting against the Germans since 1941, was interested in nothing other than a second front in Europe as soon as possible, to draw German forces away from its own. After much argument, discussion, pleading and horse-trading, the Casablanca Conference of January 1943 directed that planning begin for a cross-Channel invasion no later than 1944. The British now had to accept that they would be going across the Channel – for, if they did not agree wholeheartedly, the Americans might well switch the bulk of their efforts to the Pacific and let Europe look after itself – and set out to make the best of it, without abandoning hope that operations in the Mediterranean might yet pre-empt such an invasion. In March 1943 a joint planning staff was set up under the British Lieutenant-General Sir Frederick Morgan, who was titled Chief of Staff to Supreme Allied Commander and told by the CIGS, Brooke, who at that stage did not really believe in Overlord, that despite its improbability he had to get on and make it feasible. Morgan was hampered by not yet knowing who the supreme commander was to be, and thus he had only his own, fortunately sound, military judgement to go on.

The major considerations that would influence the planning for Overlord were: where should it be; when should it be; and how many men and ships would be available? The where presented a choice of 2,000 miles of coastline in German-occupied Europe, from northern Norway to the Franco-Spanish border. Apart from the difficulties of geography, invading Norway would put the troops too far away from Germany, and in any case the Germans had always feared a British landing in Norway and maintained a large army there to counter it. A landing in the Biarritz area with its scantily clad young ladies on the beaches, even in wartime, might have been attractive to the younger soldiers but again was too far away from the main target. What was needed was a beach or beaches long enough to land three divisions (the maximum that Morgan then thought could be transported), reasonably sheltered from the weather, with good routes leading inland, within fighter aircraft cover from the UK and near a port that could be captured very shortly after landing. The Pas de Calais was the shortest distance from the UK, but that was also the most obvious; it was where the Germans expected a landing and where the defences of their Atlantic Wall were strongest. Eventually, Morgan came up with the bay of the Seine, between Cherbourg and Caen in Normandy. It was, just, within fighter cover, had three beaches long enough to take a division apiece, had good roads leading inland and lay between two ports, Cherbourg and Caen, which could be captured on or shortly after the first day.

The when would depend on tides and weather. The construction of the Atlantic Wall, begun by the Germans in 1942, had included the placing of obstacles on all beaches that might be used for a landing and these included mines, steel spikes designed to tear the bottom out of a landing craft and concrete blocks intended to obstruct the movement of tanks. If the landings took place at high tide, the troops would have less open beach to cover once leaving the landing craft, but the obstacles would be covered by the sea and so could not be seen. If the landings were at low tide, the opposite applied and the troops would be unloaded short of the obstacles which could then be neutralized by engineers, and naval gunfire could perhaps keep the defenders' heads down for long enough to get the troops off the beach. Added to this were the wishes of the army to land at first light, having the cover of darkness for the run-in to the shore; of the parachute elements for a full moon; of the air forces for clear and calm weather; and of both the navy and the air forces for two hours of daylight before the landings to be sure that their final bombardments actually hit their designated targets. Taking all these factors into consideration, the decision was made to land at the time of the full moon when low tide was two hours after first light, with the flanks of the landing being secured by the insertion of airborne troops the previous night.

The number of troops that could be landed would depend upon the number of landing craft available, and, when Morgan was drawing up his plan, which was then approved in principle by the Quadrant Conference in Quebec in August 1943 that laid down a target date of 1 May 1944, it appeared that the most that could be transported in one lift was three divisions, with the craft then returning and bringing in a second lift. When, in January 1944, Generals Eisenhower and Montgomery began to look at Morgan's plan, they both felt that three divisions in the first lift would not be sufficient to ensure that the lodgement could be held against all-comers while preparing to capture a port and break out at the earliest possible moment. It was therefore decided to land five divisions on the first lift and to increase the airborne element from one division to three. This meant finding another two beaches, as the nominated three to the west of Caen – codenamed, from east to west, Sword, Juno and Gold – were only large enough for one division apiece, and more landing craft. Two more beaches – codenamed, from east to west, Omaha and Utah – were found, albeit with a sizeable gap of twenty miles between Omaha and Gold, and the date of 1 May was put back to June to allow more landing craft to be built. The Americans would land on the two westernmost beaches, Utah and Omaha, as it was intended that they would eventually be supplied direct from the United States, and the British on the three easterly ones. When all the variables of weather and tide were factored in, the only suitable dates were 4, 5 and 6 June 1944 and the target date was now set at 5 June.

A disinformation and obfuscation scheme was put into operation to disguise from the Germans where the landing was to be. The largely British (the Americans thought that the British, being a devious people, were rather better at this sort of thing than they were) Operation Fortitude involved double agents, dummy ships, blow-up rubber tanks and guns, wireless operators pretending to be the divisional, corps and army headquarters of a non-existent United States 1st Army Group commanded by Patton (who was paraded ostentatiously around England) ready to invade Boulogne, and a British army in Scotland waiting to invade Norway. The RAF and the USAAF were directed to destroy the French road and rail system and to attack the fortifications of the Atlantic Wall, but, for every bomb dropped in Normandy, three were dropped elsewhere. Concurrent British arrangements to preserve secrecy included banning all embassies apart from those of the USA, the USSR and Free Poland from using their national ciphers to communicate;* imposing restrictions on envoys entering and leaving the country; stopping all visitors from entering a ten-mile-deep coastal strip; landing small beach recce parties by submarine on beaches far from Normandy, some of whom were in fact captured and interrogated;† and the stopping of all traffic between Britain and Eire.

The Germans were convinced, except possibly for Hitler, who thought it was all some sort of gigantic bluff and remarked at a conference in Berlin in April 1944: 'The whole thing the British are performing looks like theatre to me. The news about blockade measures, the defensive movements and so on, normally one doesn't do that when planning an operation like that… I can't help feeling that the whole thing is an impudent charade.'[76] While OKW were convinced that the landing would be across the Pas de Calais, Hitler was not and he instructed Rommel, now commanding Army Group B in the west, to check the beach defences and fortifications in other areas, including Normandy, which resulted in an armoured division (12 SS) being sent to Caen, some improvement in the beach defences and a hastening of the erection of anti-glider poles.

At the beginning of 1944 the German army fielded 304 divisions, of which 187 were on the Eastern Front, twenty-two were in Italy, twenty-six in the Balkans including Greece, sixteen in Norway and Denmark and fifty-three in the west – Germany, France, Belgium and Holland. The Commander-in-Chief West was Field Marshal von Rundstedt, recalled (again) from retirement in March 1942 and now sixty-eight years old. Under him were two army groups (A commanded by Colonel-General Johannes Blaskowitz and B under Rommel), Panzer Group West and Colonel-General Kurt Student's First Parachute Army. The command arrangements for the panzer group (equivalent to an army) were unnecessarily complicated and in the event did not work. General of Panzer Troops Geyr Freiherr von Schweppenburg was responsible for their training and administration but OKW insisted that Rundstedt retained

---

*The USA and the USSR because they were allies and in any case the British had broken their ciphers; the Poles because the British were unable to break their cipher and reckoned that, if they couldn't, then neither could the Germans.

†The members of these clandestine parties did not, of course, know where the real landings were to be, and if captured anything they said under interrogation added to the German conviction that the landings would not be in Normandy. The intelligence staffs well knew that they were throwing men's lives away, but the sacrifice of a few would save many.

operational control with Schweppenburg as his adviser. In March 1944, after a disagreeable conference with OKW in Berlin, Rommel was given command of three panzer divisions, while the remaining three panzer divisions and one panzer grenadier division were held in a central reserve under OKW – actually Hitler's – control. Responsibility for the Normandy area was vested in Army Group B with Seventh Army (Colonel-General Friedrich Dollmann) and Fifteenth Army (Colonel-General Hans von Salmuth). In the immediate area of the landings, the coast was originally held by three static coastal defence divisions, and according to Major-General Rudolf-Christoph Freiherr von Gersdorff, who commanded XXV Corps in Brittany, these divisions were largely made up of men who were unfit for service on the Russian front, fathers of large families, unreliable foreigners or individuals who were medically downgraded. In many cases, they were equipped with out-of-date or foreign weapons, and, as the pick of the staff officers were on the Russian front or in Italy, the staff in the west was composed of older or less talented officers.[77] If Gersdorff is right, one shudders to imagine what might have happened had the landing been opposed by first-rate German troops.

Rommel and Rundstedt held diametrically opposed views as to how a landing, if it came, should be opposed. Rundstedt, supported by Schweppenburg, had no faith in the Atlantic Wall – and, in that it presented a formidable appearance but had little depth behind it, he was right – and was convinced that the armour should be held well back out of the range of naval gunfire until the Allies were ashore and had begun to move inland and then, when the Allied thrust line had been identified, launched in a concentrated counter-attack. Rommel, with his North African experience, insisted that, as the Allies would have total air superiority, armour could not move by day and must be held well forward so that an invasion could be met and destroyed on the beaches. In a sense, they were both right: armour forward would have permitted instant reaction, whereas holding back would have allowed the Germans to fight the sort of battle – one of mobility and manoeuvre – they were good at and the Allies bad.

As it turned out, Allied air power was not going to destroy the German armour in Normandy and subsequent claims that it did are not borne out by squadron war diaries: indeed, bad weather, the difficulty of telling friend from foe and the lack of guided weapons all made it very difficult to knock out armoured vehicles from the air. What air power did do was to hinder armoured movement by demolishing bridges and rendering roads and railways unusable, although in general German tanks seem to have been able to move relatively safely, unless caught in convoy on a road or in a defile where they could not spread out. And, anyway, by the time the armour was eventually deployed against the landings, it was too late.

Overlord was the most complex operation of war ever carried out, and the planning to get every man and every ship to the right place and at the right time and with the right kit was nothing short of extraordinary, far harder than the actual fighting when it came and much larger and more complicated than anything attempted before or since. The credit should have gone to Morgan and his staff, but of course they got little recognition once Montgomery bagged the plaudits for himself. On the days and nights leading up to 4 June, infantrymen filed aboard troopships and paratroopers made final adjustments to their equipment while the Royal Navy, which provided most of the shipping, prepared to escort the convoys and batter the German coastal defences. Then the unreliable Channel weather intervened. It was too windy for the gliders and the paratroopers and too cloudy for the aircraft, and the sea was too rough for the amphibious tanks and the flat-bottomed landing craft. Eisenhower took a considerable gamble, based on the opinion of one junior meteorological officer of the RAF, who thought things would improve in the early hours of 6 June, and postponed the invasion for twenty-four hours. If the weather was still bad, the invasion would be in serious trouble as the next suitable combination of moon and tides would not be for several weeks and it would be almost impossible to conceal what was happening from neutral Swedes in London, who would tell the Germans, or the Free French, who would talk about it in pubs; nor could the troops be expected to maintain their edge if they were confined aboard ship for much longer. The gamble paid off: during the afternoon and evening of 5 June things began to improve, and from midnight men began to drop from the sky or land in gliders over Normandy.

The role of the three airborne divisions inserted during the night of 5/6 June 1944 was to secure the flanks of the landing from interference, to capture bridges over the rivers to allow the Allies to break out once they had landed, and to deal with particularly difficult shore batteries that the air forces or the navy could not reach. Although the weather had improved markedly from the day before, it was still cloudy and windy, and, although the German navy had stayed in port on the grounds that the weather was still so bad that nobody would attempt an invasion, and although many of the coastal defence units were caught napping, the anti-aircraft batteries were not, and, as the Allied aircraft crossed the coast of France, they were fired upon and this, combined with the difficulty of seeing anything in the cloud, caused the aircraft to lose formation and drift off course. Of all the airborne troops dropped or launched by glider that night, over three quarters took no part in the fighting; they were dropped in the wrong places and landed miles away from their objectives or, if they were really unlucky, in flooded meadows or even in the sea. Extraordinarily enough, this did not matter too much: airborne operations are always planned to use far more troops than are actually necessary, on the assumption that some will always end up in the wrong place or injure themselves on landing. Furthermore, as in Sicily, the appearance in all sorts of unlikely locations of parachutists and dummies with firecrackers attached made it extremely difficult for the Germans to work out just what their objectives were. In the event, nearly all the objectives were secured, albeit often by people other than those who were supposed to be securing them. Men in airborne units were specially selected and were supposed to have more initiative and drive than the average, so, once those – not many of them, but enough – dropped in the wrong place had managed to work out where they were, they simply headed for the nearest objective and attacked that.

As the Germans had not expected a landing in Normandy, nor indeed a landing anywhere that night, many of the commanders were not at their posts. Rommel was on leave for his wife's birthday and Seventh Army staff were at Rennes on a study day to review anti-invasion measures. As the tide flows from west to east up the Channel, low tide on the American beaches was earlier than on those of the British, and H-hour for them was to be 0630 hours. On Utah Beach the US 4 Division landed virtually unopposed: they had in fact drifted east and landed in the wrong place, where the Germans had only scanty defences on the grounds that the area was flooded and had only one route off the beach, so no one would land there. Accepting that they were where they were, the division got on with it and by evening had all its men and vehicles ashore and was pressing inland. It was a different story on Omaha. This was always going to be a difficult beach: it was longer than any of the others, it was more exposed to the weather and it was overlooked by a long low ridge,* but the planners thought this would be compensated for by its being defended by 716 Division, a static formation that included conscripted

---

*Ridge = Bluffs, in American accounts.

Poles of German origin and Russian volunteers who, it was assumed, would not fight with great enthusiasm for their masters at this stage of the war. How wrong the planners were.

On 15 March 1944 the German 352 Division, commanded by Lieutenant-General Dieter Krais, had moved into the area to bolster up 716. Although described by Lieutenant-General Omar N. Bradley, commanding the American landings, as 'one of Rommel's crack field divisions',[78] 352 was hardly that: it had been formed in 1943 from cadres of units destroyed on the Eastern Front in the Battle of Kursk and brought up to strength with men born in 1926 and conscripted at the age of seventeen, and 50 per cent of its officers had no combat experience; 30 per cent of its NCO positions were unfilled; its troop-carrying transport drivers were French; it had only two infantry battalions per regiment rather than the normal three; training had been hasty; and its non-combat support elements contained 1,500 Russians. Nevertheless, it had a hard, tough commander, a highly competent chief of staff and a leavening of veterans of the Eastern Front. Allied intelligence had failed to spot its move until the last minute, still putting it at St Lô, twelve miles inland, and not placing it on the beaches until after the invasion force had sailed. When the American 1 Division and its follow-up 29 Division, the Virginia National Guard, landed at 0630, they met fierce resistance, not helped by most of their amphibious tanks being launched too far out and going straight to the bottom. At first it looked as if the landing might have to be aborted, but at last, thanks largely to suppressive fire from two destroyers of the Royal Navy, the Americans had their beachhead and an exit from it, although the area they held was very narrow and well short of what had been planned.

On the British beaches the landings at 0730 hours went more or less as planned, except for the centre beach, Juno, where the landing flotilla was late because of an offshore reef and 3 Canadian Division lost ninety of its 306 landing craft to beach obstacles or German artillery. That excepted, up to now all had gone well, but the plan to capture Caen – never a realistic proposition anyway – came unstuck owing to over-caution on the part of the British infantry units sent to probe towards it. Once the opportunity on that first day was lost, it would be another month before Caen was taken, but by last light on 6 June 83,115 British and 73,000 American troops had been landed and the Allies were firmly ashore and preparing to enlarge the bridgehead. Allied casualties had been remarkably light – far less than expected. Estimates vary but calculations by the Museum and Record Office in Portsmouth, from where many of the troops sailed, show a total of 10,000 killed, wounded, missing or taken prisoner. Of these, the Americans lost 1,465 dead, 238 in the two airborne divisions and most of the remainder on Omaha, while the British lost 1,326 dead, including Canadians and airborne troops.* So far, although individual units on the ground had resisted strongly, German reaction had been muted: Berlin did not accept that this was anything more than a diversion and only released the armour piecemeal and after long delays. Had a panzer division been in the St Lô area, as Rommel and Dollmann wanted, then it might well have been able to tip the balance at Omaha, and, had that beach not held, Utah could have been isolated and eliminated, and the remaining three British beaches may well not have been a large enough lodgement to hold. All this is speculation, but political interference in what was more properly the business of the German generals was to increase as the campaign went on. When the German armour finally moved, on 7 June, it inflicted a very bloody nose on the Canadian 3 Division trying to take Carpiquet airfield, west of Caen, but it failed to reach the beaches. By 9 June all the British beaches had been joined up, and on 12 June Omaha and Utah had joined with each other and with the British: now the Allies could set about capturing a port, Caen for the British and Cherbourg for the Americans. But by this stage the Germans had finally accepted that the landings in Normandy really were the main cross-Channel invasion and resistance hardened, and, although the Allies had total air superiority, this was often offset by bad weather and limited time over targets until airstrips in Normandy could be captured. Several British attempts to capture Caen failed, including a quite disgraceful performance at Villers Bocage when a weak tank company of the Waffen SS brought an entire British armoured division to a halt and forced its withdrawal. Despite local successes, however, the Germans were prevented from fighting their sort of war by Hitler, who refused to countenance the giving up of ground. When Rundstedt, exasperated by OKW and Hitler's constant interference, told Field Marshal Keitel on 1 July that the only thing they could do now was to make peace, he was awarded the oak leaves to his Knight's Cross and sacked yet

---

*The US National D-Day Memorial Foundation disputes these figures and puts the American dead at around 2,500 and the British and Empire at 1,915 – still well within acceptable limits.

again, to be replaced by Field Marshal Kluge, who had been recovering from wounds received on the Eastern Front. When it was obvious that the Cotentin peninsula was about to be nipped off by the Americans, the defenders were refused permission to withdraw to fight another day, instead being told pointlessly that Cherbourg was a fortress to be held to the last. The Americans took Cherbourg between 28 and 30 June and the British finally took Caen on 9 July. The facilities in both ports were so badly damaged by Allied shelling and bombing that they could not be used and the Allies had to continue to relay on Mulberry, two floating harbours brought across from England and established off Omaha and Gold beaches, although after fierce storms in late June only Mulberry B off Gold was still operational.

On 17 July, Rommel was badly wounded when his staff car was shot up by an RAF fighter. He was evacuated to Germany and command of Army Group B was assumed by Kluge, who combined it with the post of Commander-in-Chief West. On 18 July the Americans captured St Lô and the second phase of Overlord could begin – the breakout. The plan was for the British to draw the German armour on to their front – Operation Goodwood – so as to allow the Americans to strike south – Operation Cobra – and in that Goodwood did draw the German armour over to the east and the Americans did break out it succeeded, but Montgomery's hopes that he might break out too, with objectives set miles inland, were dashed and the subsequent cover-up, with Montgomery claiming that all had gone to plan when it clearly had not, only served to dent his reputation and increase American exasperation with his manner and dislike and distrust of him. Air Marshal Tedder, Eisenhower's British deputy, recommend that Montgomery be sacked, and, although this did not happen – indeed, by now his fame as a great British hero was such that he was fireproof – it scuppered any chance he had of continuing as overall Land Forces Commander once the battle for Normandy was over. By August the Allies were advancing across Brittany and south into Normandy, and it became obvious that the German Seventh Army was in danger of being encircled and cut off. The obvious thing to do was to withdraw that army and pull it back to a river line – possibly the Seine – where it could defend properly and impose maximum delay on the Allies, but this was not going to happen.

On 20 July a group of disgruntled army officers had attempted to assassinate Hitler by exploding a bomb in the conference room of his headquarters in East Prussia. It failed to kill the Führer and only intensified his by now paranoiac suspicion that everybody was against him. Post-war Germany has made much of the resistance to Hitler, painting the German people as victims of Nazism rather than its enthusiastic supporters. All this is, of course, nonsense – in reality there was very little resistance, organized or otherwise, to either Hitler or the NSDAP regime. The attempt to remove Hitler only arose because he had stopped giving Germany victories. Those very few officers who were involved in the bomb plot were far from being liberal democrats – rather they were firm believers in aristocratic rule and in German hegemony – but, now that Hitler no longer seemed able to guarantee that hegemony, they hoped to engineer a peace with the Western Allies that would preserve German polity and allow them to turn their full attention to countering the Russian menace. One of the results of the bomb plot was the inevitable rounding up and execution of anyone remotely suspected of sympathizing with it, including Rommel, who was given the option of suicide and a state funeral and a pension for his widow, or going on trial, and Field Marshal Kluge, who was relieved by Field Marshal Model in both his appointments, summoned back to Berlin and took poison on the way. (The likely truth is that both Rommel and Kluge took the attitude, 'If it works, count me in; if it doesn't, then I know nothing about it.'*) Another result was an absolute refusal by Hitler to countenance the withdrawal of even a company, thus preventing the generals from fighting the war of movement that alone might have allowed them to salvage something from the campaign.

With the failure of *Fall Lüttich*, an attempt to counter-attack through to Mortain and destroy the American thrust down the west coast of Normandy, and, when it was obvious that the entire Seventh Army was likely to be surrounded in the Falaise pocket in the middle of August, Model was unable to persuade Hitler that only a withdrawal before the pocket closed could save the army from annihilation. Even SS Obergruppenführer Sepp Dietrich, commanding I SS Panzer Corps, an old chum of Hitler's from the early days and one of the very few of Hitler's intimates to argue with him

---

*Rommel remains somewhat of an enigma. Far from the most competent of German generals, he is the only second-war one to have a barracks, a regiment and a ship named after him by the present Federal Republic of Germany, largely through the post-war manufacture of the Rommel legend, which maintains that he was always anti-Nazi. That he blatantly exploited his association with Hitler to gain swift promotion was conveniently forgotten. The best that might be said is that he was politically naive.

(he had protested several times to Hitler about the killing of Jews), remarked when asked to intercede with the Führer that to do so would be the quickest way to get himself shot. When Model finally persuaded Hitler to agree to his withdrawing the army on the premise of concentrating for a counter-attack (one he had no intention of making), it was too late. The gap closed when the British from the north met the Americans from the south at Montormel on 19 August and, although 1 SS Panzer Division *Leibstandarte Adolf Hitler* managed to hold open a few routes to allow some 30,000 men to escape east, they had to abandon nearly all their tanks, guns and vehicles. Ten thousand German soldiers were dead, 50,000 were taken prisoner and 500 tanks and 700 guns were destroyed or captured. It was the end of the German Seventh Army. The Normandy campaign was over and the road to Paris was open.

15

THE SEA AND AIR WAR

Most of this book concentrates on the land war, but it would be folly in the extreme to think that the war was fought and won solely, or even primarily, by armies. Navies were vital to its prosecution too, and for obvious reasons. Naval forces operate in both offensive and defensive roles. Offensively, they can destroy enemy ships, deliver troops to effect amphibious landings, provide shore bombardment, blockade enemy ports, interfere with enemy trade and supply arrangements and project air power in areas where land-based aircraft cannot operate. Defensively, they can protect trade routes, defend territorial waters, escort convoys, lay and clear minefields and guard aircraft carriers. They can also, and usually by deploying submarines, carry out reconnaissance and sabotage missions, gather intelligence and facilitate clandestine landings.

Britain has been a maritime power since at least the time of Alfred the Great. As an island nation, she could survive without an army; without a navy, however, she would long ago have fallen into the hands of European adventurers. For much of Britain's history the British Army has been, in the words of Admiral Sir Jackie Fisher, a missile fired by the Royal Navy. Without a navy there could have been no Dynamo and no Ariel, the operations that brought home 400,000 British and Allied troops from Europe in 1940, and without Dynamo and Ariel it is questionable whether Britain could have stayed in the war. It was largely fear of the Royal Navy that convinced Hitler, like Napoleon before him, that an invasion of England in 1940 or 1941 was not a starter. Equally, Britain, as a net importer of food and raw materials, would soon have starved without a navy, and operations in the Mediterranean could never have been mounted and supported without a fleet. The United States, too, was a sea power and the fighting in the Pacific would simply not have been possible without the US Navy and the ability of America's shipyards to build warships at a rate that would have seemed impossible before the war.

Although the London Naval Agreement of June 1935 allowed Germany to build up to 35 per cent of the total Royal Naval tonnage, and up to 45 per cent in submarines, when war broke out the Royal Navy was, at least on paper, far superior to the German and Italian navies combined. Only in submarines did the Axis powers outnumber the British. If the French fleet is added to that of the British, the numerical superiority is overwhelming, and, even after the removal of the French from the equation following their surrender in 1940, the total of British warships still compared favourably with the Germans, Italians and Japanese put together. But the figures were deceptive: lack of funding between the wars meant that many of Britain's warships were obsolescent, even obsolete, and the recognition by most naval experts that the aircraft carrier had replaced the battleship had been opposed vehemently by, among others, Churchill, who as Chancellor of the Exchequer in 1927 cut the Naval Estimates so that the seven carriers that had been planned to be built were reduced to three. The German navy had lost all its capital ships at the end of the First World War, when they had been interned at Scapa Flow while the victorious Allies argued as to their disposal,* and it now really only had to worry about coastal defence (although it did have wider ambitions, supported by the building of pocket battleships and heavy cruisers intended for commerce raiding); the Italians had no interests outside the Mediterranean and the Gulf, and the Japanese had only to look to the Far East. The Royal Navy, however, had worldwide responsibilities even if the Far East had been almost abandoned, and, although sizeable, the fleet in Alexandria could not guarantee the protection of merchant shipping in the Mediterranean in time of war. It was fortunate that the ambitious German naval expansion programme was predicated on war not breaking out before 1944. One of the few advances in British naval preparedness was actually a reversion, when the responsibility for naval aviation was returned to the navy from the RAF, where it had occupied a very low priority for the air marshals, who were more concerned, understandably, with the defence of the United Kingdom than with the projection of power overseas.

Like the British Army, the Royal Navy suffered from Churchill's delusion that he was not only a great exponent of land warfare but a great naval strategist

---

*An argument that was resolved, if not entirely to the Allies' satisfaction, when the German crews at Scapa succeeded in scuttling their ships in 1919.

as well. Having been First Lord of the Admiralty (the minister responsible for the navy) twice, he knew how the Admiralty worked, and in the early days of the war took with great glee to moving individual ships around the world, usually to the detriment of the war effort. Once he became prime minister as a result of the Norway debacle, for which he was largely responsible, he had less time to interfere with the minutiae of naval operations, but still took to sending stirring and impractical signals to individual naval commanders. In Admiral Sir Dudley Pound, Churchill had a First Sea Lord (the professional head of the navy) who was unable to stand up to him* or to prevent him appointing old chums to important posts – for example, the sixty-seven-year-old retired Admiral of the Fleet the Earl of Cork and Orrery as Flag Officer Narvik; the sixty-eight-year-old and nine years retired Admiral of the Fleet Sir Roger Keyes as Chief of Combined Operations; and the very dubious Captain Lord Louis Mountbatten, with his accelerated promotion to commodore (and eventually to vice-admiral, lieutenant-general and air marshal), to succeed Keyes. Nor could Pound prevent him from insisting on the despatch of the *Prince of Wales* and the *Repulse* to Singapore without air cover, with fatal results. Churchill did come up against tougher opposition from individual commanders, and the navy generally closed ranks to block his more lunatic fancies; he could never have got away with a naval equivalent of the Cairo Purge (when the supine acquiescence of the CIGS allowed Churchill to sack three generals). Admiral Sir Andrew Cunningham in particular suffered from Churchill's attempts to manage the war in the Mediterranean from Whitehall, and had no qualms about dealing with him in the manner of General Seydlitz's words to Frederick the Great at the Battle of Korndorf: 'After the battle Your Majesty may have my head, but in the meantime kindly allow me to use it' – so much so that, when Pound died and Cunningham was his obvious replacement, Churchill did his best to appoint a less robust officer. As the admirals' trade union refused to cooperate, Cunningham was appointed.

In the first war, the Royal Navy had been able to deploy one of its primary weapons – the blockade – to considerable effect, and by 1917 the civilian population of Germany was not far above starvation level and the German army was starved of vital raw materials such as rubber. In this war a blockade would have far less effect. Up to June 1941 Germany was able to import what she wanted from Russia, and even after that the length of coastline controlled

---

*It later transpired that he was suffering from a brain tumour which killed him in 1943.

by or sympathetic to Germany and the extent of German conquered territories largely negated the effects of any blockade, always assuming, of course, the Royal Navy had possessed the assets to mount one. Of the many naval campaigns of this war, the most critical, after the removal of the army from Europe to fight elsewhere, was the protection and preservation of the sea routes to and from Britain, particularly that from North America. Known as the Battle of the Atlantic, the fight to keep the trade routes open went on for virtually the whole of the war. If it had been lost, Britain could not have stayed in the war and, if Britain had left the war, she would not have been available as the springboard for eventual re-entry into Europe, and the United States may well have written Britain and Europe off as a lost cause and concentrated on Japan. Hitler's Germany knew, as had the Kaiser's Germany in 1914–18, that the only way in which Britain could be defeated was by starving her population of food, her industry of raw materials and her armed forces of armaments.

The Battle of the Atlantic was the single longest campaign of the war and was fought between German submarines and a few surface ships on the one hand and British and ultimately American surface ships and aircraft on the other. Initially, the British were more concerned about surface raiders than about submarines. The Germans deployed warships disguised as merchantmen and warships proper, which by June 1941 had sunk 900,000 tons of British and Allied shipping. The British had forced the pocket battleship *Admiral Graf Spee* to scuttle herself off Montevideo, Uruguay, in December 1939, but the first major naval engagement of the war came in May 1941 when the battleship *Bismarck* and the heavy cruiser *Prinz Eugen** on a raiding mission sank the battlecruiser HMS *Hood* – there were only three survivors – and damaged the brand-new battleship HMS *Prince of Wales*. Although there were all sorts of excuses, and although the *Bismarck* was sunk by the Royal Navy a few days later, it was a severe jolt to British morale.

The real threat, however, was to come from submarines, and the first sinking by a submarine came only hours after the declaration of war on 3 September 1939 when, 400 miles north-west of Ireland, the U-30 sank a passenger liner, the *Athenia*, outbound from Glasgow for Halifax, Canada, causing the deaths of 118 passengers, of whom twenty-two were American

---

*Named after Prince Eugen of Savoy (usually anglicized to Eugene), the Austrian general who was a staunch ally of the British and co-belligerent with John Churchill, Duke of Marlborough, against the French in the War of the Spanish Succession.

citizens. The German navy was under strict orders to obey the Hague Convention, which forbade the attacking of passenger ships without first surfacing and allowing the crew and passengers to take to the lifeboats, and, to be fair to the captain of the U-boat, he genuinely thought he was attacking an armed merchant cruiser. As it was, the Germans denied all knowledge, saying it was a British plot to stir up anti-German feeling, while to the British it was a gift, winning them sympathy and increased support in the United States. The British now instituted anti-submarine measures, including the convoy system, but even so to begin with the Germans seemed to be winning. From the outbreak of war until May 1940 German submarines sank 562 British, Allied and neutral (but bound for Britain) ships, totalling 1.75 million tons; from then until February 1941, with the whole of the French and Norwegian coasts at their disposal as bases, the German submarine fleet sank 1,377 ships and over 5 million tons, including twenty-one out of thirty and twelve out of forty-nine of the ships in two east-bound convoys following behind each other in October 1940. Over the next four months, from March to June 1941, it accounted for 582 ships and over 2 million tons. Losses were now exceeding new builds and between September 1940 and June 1941 the British merchant fleet was reduced from 18 million tons to 15 million, and, although some of this could be made up from chartered or seized foreign shipping, total imports into the UK dropped sharply. Before the war, the British had calculated that their normal peacetime imports were between 50 million and 60 million tons, and that in time of war they needed 47 million. In fact, imports fell from 44 million tons in the first year of the war to 31.5 million in the second year and to 23 million in 1942. Food rationing, the ploughing up of golf courses and the disappearance of luxury goods from the shops made this bearable, but it could not go on.

One of the problems was that Royal Navy escorts could only take the convoys across the Atlantic as far as 300 miles west of Ireland before they had to either turn back for the next convoy or take over one coming the other way, and with the deployment by the Germans of the Fw 200C Condor, a long-range reconnaissance bomber, the convoys were vulnerable beyond that range. Counter-measures besides the building of more escort vessels included the arming of merchant vessels, the conversion of some into aircraft carriers by the fitting of a flight deck and others given a catapult to launch a single Hurricane or Hurricat fighter which, having theoretically dealt with the Condor, would either land at the nearest friendly air base or ditch in the sea with the pilot being plucked to safety. (Those pilots who crash-landed in the (neutral) Irish Free State were interned in a camp near the border with (British) Ulster and the gate left ajar.) Fortunately, the Germans were slow to give priority to the building of submarines over and above other types of ship, only doing so in July 1940, but the measure had a significant effect: whereas the number of U-boats that could be at sea at any one time (although not all ever were) in January 1941 was twenty-two, in July of that year it was over sixty.

Once refuelling bases in Iceland had been set up, in the spring of 1941, Royal Navy escorts could take the convoys halfway across, to be handed over to the United States Navy, even before that country formally entered the war. The German response was the wolf pack, whereby submarines were spread across the likely shipping routes, and, when a convoy was sighted, submarines, which could move on the surface faster than the merchantmen, would mass to attack it. In early 1941 the British broke the German naval cipher sent on the famous Enigma machine, but then the Germans changed their cipher, added an extra wheel to Enigma and broke the British code that was used by all the Allies to marshal and control convoys. With over 100 U-boats now available, the German navy was able to attack American coastal shipping until the convoy system was introduced there too. November 1942 was a dreadful month for British shipping, the worst of the war, when over 700,000 tons were sunk by U-boats and German aircraft. This may have been less than the rate of 750,000 tons a month that, if sustained for a year, Admiral Dönitz claimed would force Britain to make peace, but British shipbuilders were unable to keep pace with the losses and the country became even more dependent upon the output of American yards (something which was to have a marked impact on Britain's economic woes after the war). The prospects for 1943 looked bleak.

Like the Royal Navy, the United States Navy suffered from a lack of resources and a reluctance to spend between the wars. America had only two oceans to worry about, whereas the British had three, and the American government managed to avoid a naval arms race (which she could have neither afforded nor persuaded Congress to finance) by the Washington Naval Treaty of 1922. There were many Americans who had been convinced by Colonel 'Billy' Mitchell's experiments with attacking ships from the air*

---

*These were very much staged experiments whereby obsolete unmanned ships moored in calm water in good weather were bombed, with predictable results. In fact, with reasonable anti-aircraft armament a ship that was under way and capable of manoeuvre was very difficult to hit from a conventional bomber – submarines and torpedo bombers had far more success.

that the days of large warships were numbered and that the available money would be better spent on aircraft and air defence. In the event, very little money was spent on either, and, when war broke out in 1939, the US Navy was smaller than the Royal Navy, even if it was none the less a formidable force. The US Navy knew what it might have to do in the Pacific – defend the Philippines – but was unsure of whether it might have any involvement in the Atlantic, and, although America maintained an Atlantic Fleet, her naval officers were very much looking west towards Japan rather than east towards Europe. There were, however, problems: a number of American battleships were either obsolescent or obsolete; there were insufficient oil tankers to keep a fleet at sea for long; transport and ammunition ships were woefully inadequate; most ships' crews were under-strength; there were few bases west of Pearl Harbor and those that did exist were very basic; and a policy of moving key officers after sometimes only one year in post meant that improvements or new developments were often not carried through. With war raging in Europe, Congress at last agreed to Roosevelt's request for funding for a naval expansion programme, but as Admiral Stark said, 'Dollars do not buy yesterday', and it would be some time before American shipyards could be geared up to produce the ships that were needed. None the less, by the time that Japan attacked the United States without warning in December 1941, Roosevelt had already proclaimed that the United States should be 'the Arsenal of Democracy' and that Britain should be given 'all aid short of war', American industry had cranked itself up far more quickly than anyone had predicted, and American ships were already escorting UK-bound convoys out into the Atlantic.

Gloomy though the prospects for 1943 in the Atlantic looked, that year was in fact the tipping point of the Battle of the Atlantic. The British cracked the new German cipher and changed their own; then the Germans cracked the new British code and for a time both sides could read each other's signals. Then the British changed their code again and, after a bad time in early 1943 when it looked as if the U-boats might indeed win, technology and tactics began to alter the balance. Improved underwater detection; a radar that could pick up submarines on the surface; more powerful depth charges and also the means to hurl these ahead of a ship attacking a U-boat rather than drop them behind it; the deployment of very long-range aircraft; direction-finding equipment that could locate submarines by the radio transmissions they made; the building of small escort carriers that could accompany a convoy and use their aircraft to detect and attack submarines: all increased the attrition rate of U-boats and in July 1943 for the first time the total Allied tonnage built since the outbreak of war exceeded that sunk.

The Germans had an average operational strength of forty-nine submarines in 1939 – that is, those available for operations, excluding those undergoing repairs or trials or being used for training – and the Royal Navy sank nine. In 1940 there was an operational strength of thirty-four and twenty-three were sunk. Then new builds began to overtake losses and in 1941 there was an operational strength of fifty, and thirty-five were sunk, rising to 137 in 1942, when eighty-eight were sunk. In 1943 new builds failed to keep up with losses and with an average of 208 operational boats there were 247 losses, ninety-six of them in the first five months and twenty-four in May alone.[79] Now, with more powerful escorts and roaming carrier groups, instead of the convoys being a target for the wolf pack, the wolf packs became a target for the convoys and their escorts.

On 23 May 1943 Admiral Dönitz ordered a withdrawal of his U-boats from the North Atlantic. It was supposed to be a temporary expedient but, although they continued to sink Allied shipping, and although to the end of the war the Germans continued to develop faster and more powerful submarines, the U-boats never again dominated the ocean, and they never again looked like bringing Britain to her knees. The Battle of the Atlantic was won by the Royal Navy, the Royal Canadian Navy and the RAF with the help of the US Navy. The interception of German naval codes certainly helped, but far more important was the closing of the air and sea gaps in mid-Atlantic.

Further north, the Allies ran perilous Arctic convoys to Russia. The British had tried to warn Stalin in 1941 that he was likely to be Germany's next victim, warnings that were largely ignored as being British disinformation designed to drive a wedge between the signatories of the Molotov-Ribbentrop Pact. When Barbarossa was launched, the immediate British reaction was to pledge all possible help to the USSR. That the Russians had provided Germany with essential war supplies when Britain stood in peril; that Radio Moscow had railed continuously about the linked evils of British imperialism and Wall Street capitalism; that the Communist Party of Great Britain had done its best to interfere with war work in factories: all was forgotten – it was in the British interest to do everything that could be done to keep the USSR in the war, even if it meant depriving their own forces. The first delivery, of mines for the Russian navy, was made at the end of July 1941 as part of a

A German Panzer Mark VI Tiger in Tunisia, April 1943.

The world's first purpose-built armoured personnel carrier, the German open-topped SdKfz 251, had crew of two and carried ten infantrymen in the back. This example was operating in Russia in 1943.

A 17-pounder anti-tank gun being manoeuvred into position at Salerno, 10 September 1943. The 17-pounder was the first British anti-tank gun capable of taking on any German tank.

German civilian dead from an Allied bombing laid out in a Berlin gymnasium, Christmas 1943.

German armour moves into position for a counter-attack on the Russian Front in the spring of 1944.

German infantry on the Russian Front in February or March 1944 drop to the ground and lie motionless while a flare illuminates the area.

Men of the Durham Light Infantry move through the ruins of Cassino, May 1944.

Canadian troops landing on Juno Beach, D-Day 6 June 1944.

'Somewhere in Southern England': Troops and vehicles wait to embark for Overlord, the invasion of North-West Europe, June 1944.

The Battle of the Bulge: SS (left) and Luftwaffe (right) infantry with a captured Allied armoured car in the Ardennes, December 1944.

Mogaung, Burma, June 1944. On the left, the thirty-one-year-old Brigadier 'Mad Mike' Calvert, commanding 77 Infantry Brigade, and on the right, Major Jimmy Lumley, 3/6th Gurkha Rifles, father of Miss Joanna Lumley, actress and campaigner.

A supply column of the 2nd Punjab Regiment moves up to the front in Burma.

American Marines come ashore at San José, Leyte Island, October 1944.

The centre of Dresden after the Allied air raids of February 1945.

A Führer briefing conference in the Reich Chancellery in Berlin in March 1945. Left to right, General of Artillery Wilhelm Berlin of OKW staff, General of Fliers Ritter von Greim commanding Air Fleet 6, Major-General Franz Reuß commanding a fighter division, General of Fliers Job Odebrecht commanding II Anti-Aircraft Corps, and Colonel-General Theodor Busse commanding Ninth Army.

The remains of a Japanese pill box during the fighting for Iwo Jima, February – March 1945.

The Imperial Japanese Navy's *Yamato*. At 64,000 tons standard displacement, she was the biggest battleship ever built. Seen here off Okinawa, she was sunk by US carrier aircraft on 7 April 1945 on what was effectively a suicide mission.

An American flame-thrower team takes out a Japanese bunker, Okinawa, April 1945.

HMS *Victorious* hit by kamikazes in the Pacific in May 1945. Because of her armoured flight deck, she was back in action much faster than the wooden-decked American carriers subjected to similar attacks.

Hiroshima after the bomb: August 1945.

then largely inconclusive but later totally successful attempt to interrupt German coastal shipping between northern Norwegian and Finnish ports. Thereafter, convoys escorted by the Royal Navy set off about every three weeks relatively unscathed until the end of the year. Once the Germans realized that they were not going to defeat Russia in 1941, however, they turned their attention to the convoys, which had to make the journey round the north of Norway to the Russian ports of Murmansk and Archangel by routes that could only be varied marginally. Never more than 300 miles from German air and submarine bases, in summer they sailed in perpetual daylight while the cover of perpetual darkness in winter was offset by the southern advance of the ice that restricted their routes even more.

Conditions on the Russian convoys were extreme: weapons and equipment that were never designed to operate in such low temperatures had to be modified; special winter clothing had to be issued to the crews, who knew that they could survive only a few minutes' immersion in the sea even in summer. Convoys were liable to attack from aircraft, U-boats and surface raiders. Altogether, from 1941 until 1945 there were thirty-four outward convoys, given a number with a prefix PQ until December 1942, when the prefix was changed to JW (return convoys were prefixed QP and then RA), involving 1,400 merchant ships, of which eighty-five were lost. Royal Navy losses were two cruisers, six destroyers and eight other escorts (corvettes, minesweepers and an oiler). Most convoys got through without too much damage, but the statistics are skewed by some severe losses, such as that of PQ 17, which left Reykjavik, Iceland, on 27 June 1942 with thirty-six merchant ships, of which two returned to port with engine trouble. Escorting the convoy were six destroyers and four corvettes. British naval intelligence thought (mistakenly, as it turned out) that the Germans were concentrating their heavy ships, including two battleships and a heavy cruiser, to attack the convoy, and, after three merchantmen had been sunk by German aircraft on 4 July, the Admiralty ordered the escort to withdraw and the convoy to scatter. Ten merchantmen were subsequently sunk by the Luftwaffe and ten by U-boats. The surviving eleven ships limped into Archangel over the next few weeks. Supplies intended for Russia that went to the bottom included 3,850 wheeled vehicles, 430 tanks and 210 aircraft.[80] On the day after PQ 17 had been ordered to scatter, a returning convoy, QP 13, of thirty-five merchant ships ran into a British minefield in the Denmark Strait and an escort minesweeper and five merchantmen were sunk. Controversy still rages over the fate of PQ 17 and no more convoys were run until that September.*

The Royal and Merchant Navies got little thanks for their freezing, unpleasant and often dangerous efforts to deliver aid to Russia (most American aid came through Persia or via the Pacific). In between his constant demands for a second front, Stalin continually grumbled that not enough was being supplied, or that it was the wrong sort or that the quality was poor. Facilities at the Russian ports were primitive and the Russians claimed that they could not provide fuel, so convoys had to take fuel for the return journey with them. Accommodation for the British handling teams at the ports was of the most basic nature, contact with Russian civilians was discouraged and liaisons with local girls were dealt with by the simple expedient of arresting the girls and locking them up. The Russians thought little of Allied tanks (12,700 supplied) – the British ones were too lightly armed and their tracks too narrow, whereas the American ones ran on petrol (the Russians called the US M3 the 'coffin for seven brothers' because of its tendency to explode and incinerate the crew when hit) – but they did like British tank engines, which were much more reliable than their own, so British tanks were used for training rather than in front-line units. The production line for the Valentine, long superseded in British service, was kept open until the end of the war solely for the Russians. What the Russians really did like, however, were Western wheeled vehicles, of which 51,500 jeeps and 370,000 trucks of various types were delivered. British radar, too, was an indispensable aid that allowed the Red Air Force to control its own operations right across the Front and to detect incoming Luftwaffe raids. Tempting though it must have been for the British and the Americans to leave the Russians to stew in their own juice, the USSR had to be kept in the war and there is no doubt that Allied aid and Lend-Lease enabled them to do so, reluctant though they still are to acknowledge the contribution of the factories of Detroit and the shipyards of the Clyde to victory in the Great Patriotic War.

* * *

---

*As a brown job, this author is wary of commenting on naval matters, but it does seem in hindsight that the decision might have been better left to the naval commander on the spot, who might not have withdrawn the destroyers. Certainly, the Americans thought so and said so forcefully at the time.

The Mediterranean had long been considered a British lake, and, as long as Italy, an ally in the first war, was considered friendly, that continued to apply. Once Italy joined the Axis, however, the balance began to shift, and, once she joined the war and France was defeated, German submarines and surface vessels, if they could get into the Mediterranean (which meant running the gauntlet of the British Strait of Gibraltar), posed a serious threat to British dominance. In general, the Italian surface fleet was manageable, having been fatally weakened on 11 November 1940 when twenty-one Swordfish, venerable torpedo bombers each flown by a crew in open cockpits with a torpedo slung beneath, took off from the aircraft carrier HMS *Illustrious* and attacked the Italian naval base of Taranto, sinking two battleships and damaging others, with all but two of the aircraft returning safely. It was the first major attack on a fleet in harbour by aircraft alone, and was studied with great interest in Tokyo. The Battle of Cape Matapan in March 1941, when in one night the Royal Navy sank three heavy cruisers and two destroyers, and that of Cape Bon in December 1941, when two light cruisers went down, persuaded the Italian navy to avoid fleet actions, but they were more successful with small boats and small numbers. Italian soldiers, sailors and airmen all seemed to be better at doing things individually or in small groups rather than in large, formed bodies. In the first war the Italian navy had achieved considerable success with motor torpedo boats: on 10 June 1918 one of its MTBs (cost: a few hundred pounds) had sunk the 20,000-ton Austro-Hungarian battleship SMS *Szent Istvan* (cost: millions of pounds). In this war, Italian midget submarines had penetrated Gibraltar and in an escapade of great daring human torpedoes got into Alexandria harbour in December 1941 and attached explosive charges to the hulls of the British battleships *Queen Elizabeth* and *Valiant*, sinking them both. As it happened, the harbour was shallow and, with the keels resting on the bottom, the superstructures were still above water, and the British managed to level both ships and pretend to enemy air reconnaissance that they were undamaged, but it was a time of considerable embarrassment, particularly as the other battleship in the Mediterranean, HMS *Barham*, had been lost only a few weeks before.

Indeed, the real threat in the Mediterranean was not from Italian human torpedoes or midget submarines but from the air and from U-boats. In 1940 the Luftwaffe had transferred 150 bombers to Sicily, at a time when there were but fifteen Hurricanes on Malta and only another eighteen delivered by *Ark Royal* in April 1941. The one carrier in the Mediterranean, HMS *Illustrious*, was so badly damaged by air attack in January 1941 that she had to be withdrawn for repairs in America. There was another carrier with Force H, the naval force stationed at Gibraltar whose role was to guard the Strait, but she could not be detached from that vital task and the replacement for *Illustrious*, HMS *Formidable*, sent out via the Cape, could not arrive before March. The Royal Navy transported British troops to Greece, then evacuated them from Greece and from Crete and, given that the Luftwaffe enjoyed almost complete air superiority, it suffered severely in so doing. The removal of a portion of the German bomber force from Sicily in preparation for Barbarossa lessened the threat from the air, but the undersea threat was increased with the despatch of twenty-six U-boats into the Mediterranean. In November 1941 U-331 sank HMS *Barham* and then U-557 sank the cruiser *Galatea*. In December the cruiser *Neptune* and a destroyer ran into a German minefield and sank and the Luftwaffe dropped mines in the Suez Canal. The army's advances and subsequent retreats along the North African coast would not have been possible without Cunningham's Inshore Squadron that delivered ammunition, fuel and rations, evacuated wounded and bombarded Axis positions on shore, but nevertheless the naval position in the Mediterranean at the end of 1941 was precarious.

The next year started badly for the British with the huge embarrassment of the Channel Dash, or Case Cerberus as the Germans named it, when the battlecruisers *Scharnhorst* and *Gneisenau* and the heavy cruiser *Prinz Eugen* with their accompanying escorts, all under the command of Vice-Admiral Otto Ciliax, left the French port of Brest at 2245 hours on 11 February and sailed up the Channel heading for Norway, where Hitler expected a British invasion. Despite having warning that the squadron was liable to come out, the British, through a combination of faulty planning, lack of liaison between the navy and the air force, signals jamming by the Germans and sheer disbelief that the Germans would actually attempt the Strait of Dover in daylight, were slow to respond, and, when they did, it was in a piecemeal fashion. All the ships involved reached German ports on 13 February, even if they did suffer some damage from mines laid by the RAF. As a *Times* editorial put it: 'Vice-Admiral Ciliax has succeeded where the Duke of Medina Sidonia failed... Nothing more mortifying to the pride of sea power has happened in Home Waters since the 17th Century.'*

---

*The duke commanded the Spanish Armada, of 131 ships carrying 17,000 soldiers (and 180 priests), which was scattered by a mix of the Royal Navy's seamanship and bad weather in 1588 with the loss of perhaps 25,000 Spaniards killed and drowned.

In the Mediterranean, the situation became critical by the summer of 1942 when Axis air attacks on convoys to the island of Malta were so severe that at one stage the submarine flotilla had to be removed and it looked as if the few aircraft stationed there might be grounded for lack of fuel. At last, in August, a convoy from the west, Operation Pedestal, succeeded in getting through, but at very heavy cost to the escorts and to the convoy: only five out of fourteen merchantmen got through but this included the vital fuels in the tanker *Ohio*, chartered from America with a British crew, her decks awash and lashed to a destroyer on either side. Eventually, with many of the Luftwaffe aircraft removed to the Eastern Front, the appearance of American warships to support Operation Torch, the landings in French North Africa and the removal from Axis hands of air bases in North Africa, the balance swung in favour of the Allies. The subsequent surrender of the Axis forces in Tunisia and the necessary build-up of naval forces for the invasion of Sicily and later Italy, then the surrender of Italy herself, meant that naval supremacy was finally restored.

* * *

From the late 1930s the British Admiralty had reluctantly accepted that a sizeable Far Eastern fleet could only be maintained in time of war if the French assumed responsibility for the Mediterranean, but with the French defeat and surrender in 1940 that option no longer existed. When Japan entered the war, there was no sound strategy to guide the Royal Navy and, even when a unified command to coordinate the efforts of the British, the Americans and the Dutch was established in Java under an American admiral, he had but a motley collection of ships that lacked balance as a force. With the sinking of the *Prince of Wales* and the *Repulse* there was nothing at sea to prevent the loss of Malaya, Singapore and Burma, and by March 1942 the Royal Navy had abandoned the South Pacific except for toeholds on Fiji, the New Hebrides and New Caledonia, which had to be held as staging posts on the route by which ships and men might travel from America to Australia. The efforts of the Royal Navy now had to be based on Ceylon, and a new Eastern Fleet of five battleships, seven cruisers and sixteen destroyers was assembled under Admiral Sir James Somerville, late of Force H in Gibraltar. On the face of it, this seemed a powerful force, but four of its battleships were old and slow and the Japanese carrier force could muster far more aircraft, so it was no match for Japan, which was now, if only temporarily, the regional naval superpower.

The British were very much on the defensive, at sea as well as on land. Port Darwin in Australia's Northern Territory had been heavily damaged by Japanese air attacks, but, when the Japanese carrier force and its escorts entered the Indian Ocean and attacked Colombo in Ceylon in April 1942, Somerville had withdrawn his fleet to the Maldives, the defences of Colombo held out and the Japanese were beaten off, and, although Japanese carrier-borne aircraft searched for the Eastern Fleet and sank two heavy cruisers on their way to join it followed by a light aircraft carrier, the *Hermes*, on 9 April, they failed to find the main fleet and withdrew. This was, in hindsight, the critical point in the Far Eastern sea war for the Royal Navy, for, had the Japanese succeeded in finding Somerville's fleet, they would surely have destroyed it and there would have been little to prevent them from landing on and capturing Ceylon with its vital naval bases of Colombo and Trincomalee. As it was, the Battle of Midway, in June of that year, meant that the Japanese could never again attempt to dominate the Indian Ocean and the Bay of Bengal, and the British hoped that they could begin to slowly rebuild their naval strength and prepare to go over to the offensive, although they had to accept that increasingly the Allied naval effort in the Far East would depend upon American, rather than their own, ships.

In the event, the American dominance of the eastern seas was even greater than the British expected. Far from Somerville's fleet being reinforced, he found himself having to detach ships for convoys to Malta, then for Operation Torch and again for the invasion of Italy, while still retaining responsibility for the protection of sea traffic from the Cape along the east coast of Africa to the Gulf. Although Admiral Nagumo's carrier force had been eliminated at Midway, the Japanese Combined Fleet remained a powerful threat, and an American request for a British carrier in late 1942 was to spark off another inter-Allied spat. The British agreed to provide a carrier to Admiral Halsey in the Pacific but pointed out that, as there would be no British land-based maintenance facilities within range, the carrier's aircraft should be American rather than British and the conversion of the ship's launching and recovery equipment, and the retraining of the aircrew, would take some time. Admiral King, never an Anglophile, took this as an indication that the British were unwilling to help and many harsh words were exchanged before HMS *Victorious*, with American aircraft flown by British Fleet Air Arm crews, appeared in the Pacific in May 1943. Once the Japanese were forced out of Guadalcanal, they could still spring unpleasant surprises but their merchant navy was never going to be big enough to support their extensive conquests, and, however many Allied ships they managed to sink, Allied, and particularly American, powers of recovery and replacement were always going to outstrip theirs. By mid-1943, although the Royal Navy presence was still little more than an anti-submarine escort force, the balance had shifted irreversibly and American naval task forces, which included British, Australian and New Zealand ships under command, were increasingly able to support the US Navy's island-hopping and MacArthur's more conventional strategy, and in particular to construct naval bases and anchorages as they went along.

* * *

Russia had not been a naval power since the Japanese had destroyed her Far Eastern and Baltic Fleets at the Battle of Tsushima in 1904. Then the Japanese had sunk seven Russian battleships, four cruisers and five destroyers and had taken the surrender of four more battleships and numerous smaller craft. Other Russian ships had run aground, collided with each other or been interned in neutral ports. The British-trained Japanese navy and its British-built ships lost three torpedo boats sunk, and eight other ships, torpedo boats and destroyers, damaged. The Japanese lost 117 sailors killed, the Russians 5,000. It was the most overwhelming naval victory since Trafalgar and the end of Russian naval pretensions to anything much more than coastal defence and control of the eastern Baltic, with a number of river flotillas. In the run-up to the Second World War, the Soviet navy was regarded as purely defensive, and, although in 1938 a naval expansion and building programme was ordered, few ships were actually built and those that were completed were of obsolete design and their crews, like those of the navy as a whole, badly trained. In the whole of the war, the total shipbuilding output of the USSR was but two light cruisers, nineteen destroyers, fifty-four submarines and around 800 torpedo boats and other small craft. But, although not a world power in naval terms, the USSR did have a sizeable minesweeping fleet and a significant merchant marine, and amongst the many aspects of Lend-Lease that annoyed the Royal Navy was the refusal of the Russian navy to sweep mine-free corridors for the Arctic convoys, or to enable its merchant vessels to carry some of the equipment being delivered. In naval terms, therefore, while Russian submarines sank a (minuscule) quantity of Axis tonnage, her surface fleet played little or no part in the war against Germany. None the less, after the shock the Japanese had received when they fought the

Russians in 1939, Tojo and his successors were careful not to antagonize the USSR, despite German requests. When the USSR eventually declared war on Japan on 8 August 1945, two days after the dropping of the first atomic bomb on Hiroshima, the Soviet Pacific Fleet played a major part in a series of amphibious and airborne operations by the Red Army that captured the ports of Darien and Port Arthur and occupied the Kuriles, southern Sakhalin and North Korea, in support of the Russians' concern that it should be they, and not the Western allies, who would control those areas when hostilities ended. While later, in the Cold War years, the Soviets would create a powerful blue water navy, it was their army and air force which fought and won their Great Patriotic War.

* * *

One of the few aspects of British defence policy that had received some attention and reasonable funding between the wars was the air defence of Great Britain. This was partly the result of a widely held view that aerial bombing would be far more effective than it actually turned out to be – 'The bomber will always get through' – and partly because many British policy-makers, or those who influenced policy, thought that air power would obviate the need for a costly and bloody campaign on land. Besides, aviation was modern and visible, there was general public support for aircraft rather than for ships and soldiers, and in any case, unlike ships, aircraft could be rolled off the assembly lines relatively quickly. All this meant that at the outbreak of war there were sufficient air defence aircraft (fighters) – just – to ensure that the Luftwaffe did not win air superiority over the Channel and hence could not produce the conditions for an invasion. When the Germans turned their attention away from airfields and aircraft production to cities – the Blitz – the limitations of the Luftwaffe were exposed: it didn't have enough bombers and those it did have couldn't carry enough bombs. The exponents of winning a war from the air were right when they said that a bomber could wreak unimaginable damage and terrify the recipients of its load of high explosive, but they were only right if that bomber was unopposed. Provide air defence in the form of radar detection, fighters, anti-aircraft guns and barrage balloons, and the power of the bomber was much reduced. Londoners (along with the residents of all the other British cities targeted) survived the Blitz not because they were plucky, determined, brave and patriotic – although of course many of them were – but because the Luftwaffe simply could not drop enough explosive on the right targets to bring economic and social activity to a halt, nor to kill or injure enough civilians to make the population demand a halt to the war.

With France out of the war, the end of the Battle of Britain and the Luftwaffe putting its energies into preparing for Barbarossa rather than air raids on England, the Royal Air Force could concentrate on four main roles: tactical support for the army on land; assistance to the navy with anti-submarine patrols; transport of men and materials including, later, gliders and parachute troops; and strategic bombing. Of all the principal combatants, only the British and the Americans had given the idea of strategic bombing much thought, and only those two countries had in production or on the drawing board aircraft sufficiently modern to carry it out. Strategic bombing might be defined as the attacking of an enemy from the air with the intention of destroying his economy, his communications, his industries, his morale, his ability to continue the war, or any combination of those aims. It is carried out independently, that is, it is not necessarily waged in conjunction with any land or sea campaign, although it may be planned to help or enhance the operations of the armies or navies. With the French surrender and the humiliating defeat of British forces in Norway, France, Greece and Crete, the only way the British could hit back at the Germans in their own country was by strategic bombing. The greatest difficulty was not getting to Germany – the RAF had aircraft that could go there and back – nor the lack of long-range fighters to escort and protect the bombers – that would be rectified in time – but that to damage or destroy an enemy's economy, industry, communications and the rest you have to be able to hit a precise target. Blowing up a railway bridge or a marshalling yard or an armaments factory by dropping bombs on it will do great harm to the enemy's capacity to make war. However, a bomb landing in the river beside the bridge, in a field alongside the railway yard or on a building a mile away from the factory may prove a considerable irritation, but is not why it is carried hundreds of miles over hostile territory, and the reality was that in the early days the RAF was very bad indeed at hitting point targets, or indeed at finding its way to anywhere near the target it was supposed to be attacking.

The problem was largely one of navigation; the early radio direction-finding aids were primitive by later standards and much map-reading was by dead reckoning and following landmarks – the coast, rivers, railway lines. Cities were blacked out and while a 'bombers' moon' – a full moon in a clear sky – helped navigation it also helped the air defence fighters sent up to intercept. One of the problems was that following bombers would use the explosions or fires caused by the aircraft in front of them as an aiming mark, and, as those often released their loads too early, there was a reverse creep whereby successive salvoes of bombs landed farther and farther from the target. The direction given to the RAF's Bomber Command varied as the war progressed. Once the Battle of Britain was over, it was ordered to concentrate on bombing synthetic oil plants, then the emphasis was switched to German commerce raiders in port, U-boats and U-boat pens, and, finally, to German military capacity, industry and civilian morale. In late 1940 the Commander-in-Chief of Bomber Command, Air Chief Marshal Sir Richard Peirse, calculated himself that for targets at short range one in three of his aircraft found it, and at longer ranges only one in five. Navigation for the bombers by day was, of course, far easier than at night but it was easier for the defenders too and very soon almost all bombing raids were carried out at night. For no real reason other than the problem of navigation, the RAF bombed military targets on clear moonlit nights, and cities on nights when the weather was such that only an area target could be attacked. German air defence – not just anti-aircraft guns and searchlights over the targets but also the radar-directed guns and fighter aircraft which harried British bombers all the way in from the coast of occupied Europe and all the way back to it – was robust and RAF losses were horrific, far worse than anything sustained by the army or the navy, and, when in the period 7 July to 10 November 1941 Bomber Command lost 526 aircraft for what seemed like little return, even the air marshals began to wonder about what they were doing.

The Butt Report, compiled by an Air Ministry civil servant, one D. M. Butt, merely made matters worse. Having analysed thousands of operational reports, aircraft logs, squadron war diaries and aerial photographs of targets attacked in the summer of 1941, Butt showed that on clear moonlit nights only one in four bombers had dropped their bombs within five miles of its target, and on nights with no moon only one in twenty. Not only did this demonstrate a lamentable inability to find the target, but also that within five miles might as well be within fifty miles if the target was a precise installation, bridge, building or railway junction. The War Cabinet ordered a halt to the bombing campaign while all took stock. Although the Butt Report went no lower than the Air Staff and commanders-in-chief, its findings inevitably trickled down, and, while men in uniform will do their utmost if their objective seems achievable, they are less ready to risk their lives if they appear to be accomplishing nothing. Much debate ensued between those who questioned the considerable resources of men, money and industrial capacity devoted to Bomber Command and those exponents of air power who insisted that, if the RAF was given the right aircraft and enough of them, Germany could be brought to her knees. The suggestion that the alternative was a long and bloody land campaign, reminiscent of the first war, was particularly persuasive in Churchill's eyes, and the bomber barons got their way. Peirse was duly sacked and replaced by Air Chief Marshal Sir Arthur Harris, more and better aircraft were planned and technical developments were accelerated. The War Cabinet's direction to Bomber Command was that its efforts were now 'to be focussed on the morale of the enemy civil population and in particular of the industrial workers'. That was unequivocal: if the RAF could not hit specific military point targets – because the technology to allow them to do so did not exist – then its aircraft would attack the cities, large enough targets for a bomb dropped anywhere to do damage.

Attacking cities meant dealing out death and destruction to men, women and children, the old and the infirm, soldiers and civilians alike. In 1939 the view in the RAF was that, if an attack on a target endangered civilians, then the target should not be attacked, and there were even arguments as to whether it was permissible to attack private, as opposed to government, property. These gentlemanly attitudes did not last long, and, while some service officers and politicians still had doubts as to the morality of the deliberate targeting of civilians, the Germans had set a precedent, although they may not have intended to. When the bombing offensive got into its stride, particularly with the advent of the Lancaster and Halifax four-engined bombers, better navigational aids, the use of Pathfinders – specially selected aircrew who marked the target for the following bombers – and bombs which contained 1,000lb of high explosive, the destruction wreaked seemed to be enormous.

The raids on Hamburg, Germany's second city and a major port, in July and August 1943, Operation Gomorrah, were intended by Harris to utterly destroy a city and its people, with the aim of persuading the Germans that, unless they sued for peace, the process would continue with other cities. The so-called Battle of Hamburg opened on the night of 24/25 July when 791 bombers of the RAF attacked the city, using for the first time 'windows' to confuse German radar.* Twelve aircraft were lost, a far better result than in the bombing offensive against the Ruhr that had just ended, 2,300 tons of bombs were dropped, much damage was caused to residential areas and fires were started all over the city. The following day 127 B-17 Flying Fortress aircraft of the American Eighth Air Force, based in the UK since 1942, set out to attack the Hamburg shipyards and an aero-engine factory. Smoke from the fires of the previous night and smoke screens laid by the defenders made it almost impossible to identify the targets, and, although 350 tons of bombs were dropped in the area of the shipyards, little damage was caused and the USAAF lost nineteen aircraft of the 114 that actually got to Hamburg.

The operations against Hamburg emphasized the different philosophies of the RAF and USAAF. The British, as we have seen, found that flying by day was too costly, but that precision targets were hard to hit by night and so had taken to attacking area targets – in effect, cities. The Americans thought that it would be more productive (and morally more acceptable) to attack precision targets and that their aircraft would allow them to do this by day by flying above the maximum range of anti-aircraft fire. Hence when both air forces worked together, the RAF operated by night and the USAAF by day.† As it was, on the night of 25/26 July Hamburg was left to burn and the RAF bombed Essen instead and then the USAAF mounted another day raid on Monday, 26 July, when it again tried to destroy the shipyards and aero-engine factory. Neither of these could be seen clearly, and so the American aircraft dropped 118 tons of bombs on an electricity-generating station instead, leaving half of the city without power. Then, on the night of 27/28 July, the RAF returned and 787 aircraft dropped 2,326 tons of bombs on the city. Humid weather and a brisk wind fanned the flames and created a firestorm, whereby a fierce updraught sucked the oxygen in from surrounding areas and the pillars of

---

*Windows ('chaff' to the USAAF, *Dupple* to the Luftwaffe) was strips of aluminium foil that were shovelled in huge numbers out of the flare chutes of bombers. German radar operators found it hard to distinguish between a strip of windows and a genuine bomber. The more experienced did, however, learn to spot the difference and subsequent use of windows was less effective.

†American bombers had been designed on the assumption that they would have to operate from the United States without fighter cover and therefore needed a longer range and heavier protective and defensive armament than British or European aircraft. It was, therefore, relatively safer for them to operate by day.

fire created spread to other buildings. The heat was so intense that those residents not burned died through lack of oxygen, and by the time the RAF came back again on the night of 29/30 July the fire and rescue crews were spread so thinly over the city that they were quite unable to cope, even if road access for fire engines had not been blocked by falling buildings, and the 2,000 tons dropped by 707 aircraft merely added to the carnage and the fires which raged out of control. A final attack on the city, by 740 RAF aircraft on the night of 2/3 August, was unable to achieve very much as bad weather prevented most of the bombers from reaching their targets.

The casualty bill for Hamburg is still widely debated. It is probable that up to 46,000 residents of the city, of whom 22,000 were women and 5,000 children, were killed, and around 1 million fled the city.[81] The results of the raids seemed and still seem appalling, and it is highly questionable whether the operation shortened the war to any appreciable extent. The Germans unsurprisingly imposed a news blackout and, with their usual organizational ability, got Hamburg's factories working again remarkably quickly: most of those who had fled returned within a week of the raid, and only about fifty days' production was lost.

Both the raid on Hamburg and the later assault on Dresden have given much ammunition to those who maintained at the time and still maintain that to attack innocent civilians was a war crime and that Harris and his crews were therefore war criminals. Quite apart from the fact that the Hague and Geneva Conventions, the relevant international law of armed conflict of the time, do not forbid aerial bombing (although Roosevelt had said in 1939 that he hoped belligerents would avoid it), the facts are that the only way to hit back directly at the German homeland from 1940 to 1944 was by bombing, and a government that refused to use Bomber Command for that purpose would have been censured, not least by those whose own homes had been destroyed by the Luftwaffe, and would have drawn even more opprobrium from Stalin, who was constantly demanding a second front, never mind the bombing of German cities. The exigencies of war could be pleaded for the Hamburg slaughter, but the attack on Dresden is cited as being unnecessary, coming as it did only three months before the end of the war. Dresden was attacked by 796 Lancasters of the RAF on the night of 13/14 February 1945 which dropped 2,700 tons of high-explosive and incendiary bombs, and on the days of 14 and 15 February and 2 March by 300 B-17s of the USAAF. The resulting firestorm destroyed the medieval centre of the city and may have killed 40,000 people, many of them refugees from the approaching Russians. Why, some asked then and others ask now, did this have to happen when the war was nearly over? The raid was questioned in the House of Commons, where Churchill, sensing that world opinion might not entirely approve of the policy of saturation area bombing, swiftly distanced himself from what had been his own policy. But, while we now know that the war would end less than three months later, nobody knew that at the time: fighting was still fierce on both European fronts; the Western allies had not yet got over the Rhine, and the Russians had specifically requested that Dresden be bombed. Beautiful medieval city it undoubtedly was but it was also a legitimate military target: it was a centre of road and rail communication through which German troops and supplies for the Eastern Front passed, it manufactured optical instruments, gas masks, aero-engines and artillery shells, and its military industries employed some 10,000 people. The USAAF has managed to avoid the opprobrium piled upon Harris and the RAF because of its policy of only going for military targets, but in practice it too found it almost impossible to hit precision targets, even by day, and dropped bombs on cities just as the RAF did, although it took twice as many aircraft to deliver the same weight of explosive.

It is sometimes asked why RAF Bomber Command failed to take action against the concentration camps, the theory being that, had the camps been bombed, the inmates could have escaped. Some would, of course, have been killed in the bombing, but then they were going to be killed by the Germans anyway. Against this, most of the camps were in Poland or in eastern Germany, which meant the bombers would have had to fly for a very long way over enemy territory to reach them, and it is unclear what the inmates were supposed to do once they had exited the camps. Dressed in prison clothing and weakened by minimal rations as they were, they could not simply have slipped back into the population at large: Poland was just as anti-Semitic as Germany and the locals would not have given them shelter. In any case, had the inmates been really determined, they could have effected their own escape; they vastly outnumbered their guards and in a mass breakout many would have succeeded, leaving behind no more dead than would have been caused by the RAF's bombing, and a lot less than would eventually go up the chimneys of the crematoria. The harsh truth is that the release of concentration camp prisoners, even if it could have been effected by Bomber Command, would have contributed nothing to winning the war and that there were other, far more important targets. Furthermore, perhaps the Jewish lobby would have been listened to more readily, in Britain at least, had its terror gangs not been killing British soldiers and officials in Palestine: even Churchill, who had been sympathetic towards the idea of a Jewish state, rather went off the idea when the Fighters for Israel's Freedom, the re-branded Stern Gang, murdered Lord Moyne, the Secretary of State for the Colonies, in Cairo in November 1944.

Protest about attacking civilians by bombing cities is strangely muted when applied to the Japanese. The USAAF deliberately targeted Japan's cities using incendiary bombs, which were particularly effective when dropped on conurbations containing so many wooden buildings. The fire-bombing of Tokyo alone may have killed up to 100,000 people and yet there is little criticism of it in the West. Perhaps this is explained partly by old prejudices about the Japanese, and partly by the feeling that, by their blatant disregard of the laws of civilized behaviour in war – laws to which they had signed up – they forfeited all claims to sympathy. It may, of course, be argued that it was the German and Japanese governments and their armed forces that were the enemy, and that their civilian populations could do nothing to influence them. This argument can be dismissed in short order: the Germans had voted the NSDAP into power in as democratic an election as Germany had ever had, and, while the Japanese system was not a democracy in the British sense, it governed with the consent and support of the people, who must therefore take responsibility for what they had spawned.

Argument still rages as to whether area bombing of cities shortened the war or could have shortened the war. There were those who insisted in 1942 that if other German cities were systematically subjected to the same treatment as Hamburg, and were reduced one by one, then the German government would be forced – by public opinion, if nothing else – to end the war. This line of debate has to be suspect: Hamburg was a special case in that, being a port, it was relatively easy to find; it was also a compact city and the destruction caused was helped by a freak weather pattern which might not be repeated elsewhere. In any case, the Allies did not have the numbers of aircraft needed to repeat the exercise on other German cities, and the suggestion that Berlin, a city of far greater expanse than Hamburg and surrounded by more anti-aircraft defences than anywhere else in the Reich, should be next was simply pie in the sky. The bombing offensive by the RAF and USAAF did not cause German morale to collapse, just as the Blitz had not caused British morale to collapse; nor was its effect on German industrial production as great as its advocates predicted. What it did do was to disrupt communications – roads, railways, bridges – to such an extent that, while Germany continued to manufacture large quantities of tanks and aircraft right up to the end, she could not get them from the factories to the front. It also – and this was crucial – forced the bulk of anti-aircraft defences, including the Luftwaffe fighter arm, back into Germany for the defence of the homeland, leaving very little to oppose the Allied air forces in the run-up to Overlord or later. This enabled the Allies to maintain complete superiority over North-West Europe in 1944–45, which meant that, unless the weather intervened, which of course it sometimes did, Allied units could move far more easily than could German ones.

Despite the fact they did not win the war from the air, Arthur Harris and the men of Bomber Command were in many ways the heroes of the British war effort. Night after night, in the cold and the dark, they set out over hostile territory facing enemy fighters, flak and weather, knowing full well what the consequences could be. With only 7 per cent of all British military manpower, Bomber Command suffered 24 per cent of all British military deaths, and they got precious little thanks for it. Embarrassed by criticism of civilian deaths, the British government pulled the carpet from under Harris and his men. There was a Burma Star and an Africa Star, an Atlantic Star and a Pacific star, but there was no Bomber Offensive Star, and alone amongst the commanders-in-chief Harris was not elevated to the peerage after the war. It was a disgraceful way to treat brave men, who were following the policy dictated to them by the War Cabinet and the prime minister, and it rankles still amongst the few ageing survivors of Bomber Command.

* * *

In the Far East, air power was critical. China was kept in the war – not that she did very much to help the Allies but at least she kept large numbers of Japanese troops tied down – by American pilots flying supplies over the Hump; the second Chindit expedition could not have been maintained without the delivery of troops and supplies by air; and at sea it was the American ability to build more carriers and produce many more aircraft than the Japanese that tipped the balance. Equally, air power was essential to Slim's reconquest of Burma and the Asian war was eventually brought to an end by the dropping of atomic bombs on two Japanese cities and the threat of more to come. The Allies would probably not have dropped the atom bomb on the Germans or the Italians, but, as with fire-bombing, the Japanese were seen as fair game. Indeed, it is very likely that without Hiroshima and Nagasaki they would not have surrendered without a full-scale invasion of the Japanese homeland, every inch of which they would have fought for, presenting the Allies with a huge death toll.

On the Eastern Front, Germany and Russia fielded very different air forces. In 1941 the USSR could deploy over 8,000 aircraft. Most units were intended to offer direct support for army formations, but there were also a few strategic bombers and some naval aircraft. The latter were, however, almost all land-based and used to protect the flanks of army fronts, with only a small percentage of their sorties being directed against enemy shipping. When the Germans attacked on 22 June 1941, they caught much of the Red Air Force on the ground and destroyed it: Russian aircraft and Russian pilots were no match for the highly skilled Luftwaffe crews, whose talents had been honed by lightning victories in Poland and France, and at least until Stalingrad the Germans had complete air superiority over the Eastern Front. Stalin's insistence in 1941 on evacuating Soviet factories to the east, out of range of German bombers, paid off, however, and even in the first six months of the war, from June to December 1941, although around 12,000 aircraft were lost, not only to the Luftwaffe but around 25 per cent to accidents and crashes due to pilot error or incompetent maintenance, Russian factories managed to build 7,000 replacements.

While Lend-Lease, starting in 1941, helped, the Soviets themselves began to replace their obsolete fighters and bombers with indigenous designs, many of which – the robust Yak-9 fighter, for example – were more than able to meet the Germans on their own terms. Between 1939 and 1945 the Russians built 158,000 aircraft of various types, building 18,000 in 1942 and reaching a peak of 31,000 in 1944, and received 14,800 from the Allies as Lend-Lease, including 2,800 Spitfires and 1,300 Hurricanes from Britain. As a comparison, between 1939 and 1945 the United Kingdom produced 103,000 aircraft and Germany 117,000. Even as late as 1944, however, more Soviet aircraft were lost to accidents than to the enemy; the priority was to get aircraft into the air, at the expense of pilot training. The vast majority of aircraft produced were fighters, for air defence, or ground support aircraft, and little attention was paid to strategic bombing. The Ilyushin Il-2 Sturmovik, a two-seater assault bomber or ground support aircraft with a top speed of 280 mph and armed with cannon, machine-guns and rockets, was manufactured in large numbers and particularly effective. From the summer of 1943, when the Germans were being pushed back on the Eastern Front, Soviet aircraft factories were completely safe from air raids and output – largely by a female workforce – increased accordingly. Although Soviet air power was not a critical factor in the German defeat on the Eastern Front, the inability of the Germans to follow up their initial complete mastery of the skies certainly was. Similarly, their neglect of roles other than that of direct tactical ground support, and a political failure to give clear and consistent direction to the air staffs as to exactly what roles they should undertake, combined to ensure that, excellent though the Luftwaffe's pilots were, there were never enough of them. Furthermore, its transport aircraft never possessed sufficient capacity to counterbalance the overwhelming numerical superiority of the Soviet ground forces.

The aviation industries of the main combatants produced an intimidating number of aircraft types that ranged from the excellent to the very bad and soon forgotten. The Soviet Union, as we have seen, recovered rapidly from the shock of invasion and, despite Stalin's fondness for imprisoning aircraft designers, went on to produce very capable aircraft such as the Petlyakov Pe-2 bomber and Lavochkin La-7 fighter. These were technically less sophisticated than their Western counterparts, but they were ideally suited to Russian pilots and to operations over the Eastern Front, being for the most part rugged, easy to maintain and repair, and reliable. In contrast, Germany's aircraft industry, although inventive and productive, suffered from a damaging duplication of design and manufacturing effort as well as an unnecessarily complicated procurement process. The Luftwaffe's principal fighters, the Bf 109 and Fw 190, proved stalwart and adaptable, but opportunities were frequently squandered. The Heinkel He 219 night-fighter was just what the Luftwaffe needed and could have cut a swathe through the British bomber stream, yet it was cancelled after only 288 had been produced, mainly because Field Marshall Erhard Milch, the Inspector General of the Luftwaffe, disliked the concept of such a specialized aircraft and was suspicious of the untested technology. Meanwhile, the development of many promising aircraft degenerated into a bewildering number of variants, and standardization on the production lines was rare, with the result that the German air force ended up with far too many sub-types of aircraft. German designers regularly conceived potentially war-winning aircraft, among them the world's first operational jets, but their efforts were frustrated by air ministry bureaucracy and infighting – not to mention, in the case of the

Messerschmitt Me 262, by the direct intervention of Hitler himself, who decreed this revolutionary jet aircraft should be used as a fighter-bomber rather than a fighter, thereby delaying its entry into service until it was far too late. At the war's end, the Allies were to capture blueprints for radical new concepts that would influence the thinking of British, American, Russian and French aircraft designers for years to come, and so it was perhaps fortunate that Germany's expertise in this field was so often thwarted.

In contrast, Italy never really had a wartime aircraft industry worthy of the name. Italian aeronautical design had flourished in the 1930s, but by the time Italy declared war many of her aircraft were either obsolete or obsolescent. Her pilots were generally good but, with few exceptions, their mounts left much to be desired. Later in the conflict, a trio of fighters – the Macchi MC 205, the Fiat G 55 and the Reggiane Re 2005 – proved themselves the equal of anything the Allies could put up against them, but they were built in pitifully small numbers and all three were powered by a licence-built version of a German engine. As for the Japanese, their own, comparatively small, industrial base was to cause them similar problems. In December 1941 Japan's army and navy air forces could call on a useful mix of modern fighters and bombers, but, even though there was no shortage of competent Japanese aircraft designers, replacing these machines with newer types often proved a challenge. The fate of the Mitsubishi A6M Zero fighter was perhaps typical. The Zero carried all before it in the early stages of the Pacific war, but unlike, say, the Spitfire, it had only limited development potential and by 1943 was in danger of being outclassed by its latest Allied opponents. Mitsubishi struggled to provide the navy with a new fighter in the form of the J2M Raiden, a good land-based interceptor that sacrificed manoeuvrability for speed, while another company, Kawanishi, produced an excellent all-round fighter, the N1K Shinden. But neither was produced in significant numbers and the Zero had to fight on until the very end – even in August 1945 its intended successor, the Mitsubishi A7M Reppu, only existed in the form of a handful of prototypes. The Japanese aircraft industry always struggled to build enough aircraft or to produce engines that were as reliable as they were powerful. The occasional earthquake didn't help, and, once American B-29 bombers could reach the homeland and hit its factories, that effectively meant the end of any significant Japanese aircraft production.

In any case, Japan could never realistically hope to compete with the awakened giant that was American industry, which in a very short space of time began to roll vast numbers of aircraft off its production lines, just as it did ships and tanks. The statistics tell their own story: in 1941 America produced 26,277 aircraft and Japan 5,088; in 1944 she produced 96,318 and Japan 28,180.[82] The United States' overwhelming superiority was not just a matter of numbers. In 1941 the country's front-line fighter aircraft were mostly rather pedestrian machines, but their replacements – the P-51 Mustang and P-47 Thunderbolt on land and the F6F Hellcat and F4U Corsair at sea – were anything but. As for America's heavy bombers, while later versions of the B-17 Flying Fortress and B-24 Liberator represented significant improvements over their predecessors, it was the entry into service in 1944 of the B-29 Superfortress that, although not without its problems, signalled a major advance in aircraft design. The B-29 was the first such aircraft to be pressurized for the comfort of its crew, its defensive armament was remotely controlled, it flew higher and faster than any of its contemporaries, and it carried 20,000lb of bombs, a payload only specialized variants of the British Lancaster could match. It was, in every sense, a very American aircraft, combining brains with brawn, high technology with hitting power.

Britain's aircraft industry could not compete with America's in terms of scale, but it proved innovative, robust and resilient. Inevitably, there were setbacks, failures and disappointments. The Spitfire's structural complexity meant that initially it proved difficult to mass-manufacture, and it took much sweat and toil to resolve the problem; the Manchester heavy bomber's single redeeming feature was that it led directly to the development of the Lancaster; and the Typhoon was to fall very short as a fighter even if it later found its metier as a ground attack aircraft and train-stopper. Withal, the British husbanded their resources well, designing and then assiduously developing some outstanding aircraft – the Spitfire and Hurricane, the Beaufighter and Mosquito, the Halifax and Lancaster – and producing them in substantial numbers. It was an impressive showing, and one that contributed significantly to the Allies' victory.

While historians have tended to concentrate on the war on land, and it was on land that the greatest contribution to the defeat of Germany was made, by the Red Army on the Eastern Front, without naval and air assets the British could not have stayed in the war beyond 1940, and the Americans could never have rolled back the Japanese expansion in the Pacific. The contribution of the Allied navies and air forces was immense and should not be underestimated.

16

THE AXIS RETREAT

AUGUST–NOVEMBER 1944

By the summer of 1944 the Germans and the Japanese were withdrawing on all fronts, but it was a controlled withdrawal, and by no means a rout. In Italy, the Germans were still tying down two Allied armies, giving up ground only slowly and as they chose, and by August were safely ensconced in the Gothic Line, the next major defence line across the Italian peninsula. On the Eastern Front, the Red Army had launched a major offensive against Finland, and, while at first the Finns were forced to pull back to a more easily held line, stubborn defence halted the Soviets, who themselves were forced on to the defensive. In France, the German Seventh Army had been destroyed in Normandy, while farther south 2 SS Panzer Division had massacred the entire population of the town of Oradour-sur-Glane in retaliation for British-inspired efforts by the Resistance to interfere with their movement to the front. In Asia, meanwhile, the Japanese had failed to capture the British Fourteenth Army's administrative base in Assam and was pulling back, pursued by Stilwell's Chinese–American force and Slim's British (or, more properly, British Empire) army and harried by the Chindits. In the Pacific itself, although both MacArthur and Nimitz were making progress towards the home islands, Japanese garrisons were defending as fiercely as ever, with no quarter given and no thought of surrender.

Up to now, the American approach to Japan via the northern route was by means of relatively modest hops, ensuring that each successive move was covered by land-based or carrier-borne aircraft and within reasonable distance of a logistic base. Now they would try the longest hop yet – the invasion and capture of the Marianas. The Greater Marianas, north of the Carolines and roughly halfway between Japan and Papua New Guinea, is a chain of fifteen islands but only three of them – from north to south, Saipan, Tinian and Guam – had any military significance. From the Allied point of view, the capture of the Marianas would provide yet another springboard on the way to Japan, and the plan, Operation Forager, was to land a combined US Army and Marines force on Saipan, then Tinian and finally Guam. Some 535 ships and 127,000 men were available for the task, but the logistic demands were formidable: Saipan was 1,000 miles west of the nearest American base in the Marshall Islands, the troops would be cooped up on board ship for some time and only carrier-borne air cover would be available. It was thought, however, that the overwhelming advantage in numbers would enable the islands to be captured relatively quickly.

For the Japanese, this was the greatest challenge yet to their position in the Pacific. Saipan was vital to their ability to hold their inner defence perimeter, and it was regarded as part of the home islands. Should the Americans be able to take and hold the island, then not only would communications from Japan to her South Pacific conquests and the Philippines be severely interfered with or even cut, but also the USAAF would gain a base from which it could bomb Japan itself. The garrison of Saipan was 22,700 soldiers under Lieutenant-General Yoshitsugo Saito and a coastal defence small-boat flotilla under Vice-Admiral Nagumo, the hero of Pearl Harbor and the loser of Midway. In addition, there was the First Naval Air Fleet, which was actually land-based in the Marianas under Vice-Admiral Kanji Tsunoda and possessed around 1,000 aircraft of various types. Once the Japanese realized that the approaching American fleet was heading for the Marianas, they made attempts to reinforce Saito but American submarines sank the troopships. As it was, at 0844 hours on 15 June 1944 two American divisions of the available five landed on eight Saipan beaches over a four-mile frontage and immediately came under Japanese artillery and mortar fire. The initial bombardment had not had anything like the effect hoped for and, despite massive naval gunfire support, the Marines could make but slow headway as the Japanese contested every inch and sent in repeated counter-attacks.

If the Japanese could not reinforce Saito with men, then they must aid him with ships, and the Carrier Force, now commanded by Vice-Admiral Jisaburo Ozawa, who had replaced Nagumo, steamed towards Saipan. On paper Ozawa was hugely outnumbered by the American fleet under Vice-Admiral Mitscher – there were nine Japanese aircraft carriers to fifteen American, five battleships to seven, thirteen cruisers to twenty-one and twenty-eight destroyers to sixty-nine – but Ozawa had the advantage of support from land-based aircraft, which the Americans did not, and the Japanese carriers, lacking the weight of extra armour plate and self-sealing fuel tanks, were faster and had a longer range, as did their aircraft. Finally, because of the prevailing wind, Ozawa could launch and recover aircraft while sailing towards the enemy, whereas the American carriers would have to turn away. On 19 June the two fleets clashed in what became the Battle of the Philippine Sea. It was the largest carrier battle in naval history and when it was over on 21 June the Japanese had lost their three largest carriers, numerous other smaller ships and 480 aircraft in what the Americans termed 'The Great Marianas Turkey Shoot'. When Ozawa finally accepted defeat and withdrew, he had only thirty-four carrier-based aircraft left. No American ships were sunk, although the Japanese shot down fifty aircraft and a number of others were lost when on 21 June they had to return and land on their carriers in the dark. The Japanese had taken massive losses in naval aviators in their defence of Rabaul and the Marshall Islands, and many of the crews sent up in the Philippines Sea battle had been speedily trained and just as speedily killed. From now on, with dwindling numbers of aircraft and experienced pilots the Japanese air forces had few tactical options open to them, and they would choose to make use of the most extreme – that of suicidal attacks.

On Saipan itself, numbers and firepower at last began to tell, and, as more and more of his infantrymen were being killed in charges led by sword-waving officers into the muzzles of American howitzers firing over open sights, Saito issued his final order of the day:

> Officers and men of the Imperial Army at Saipan… The barbarous attack of the enemy is being continued even though the enemy has occupied only a corner of Saipan, we are dying without avail under the violent shelling and bombing. Whether we attack or whether we stay as we are, there is only death… I will never suffer the disgrace of being taken alive, and I will calmly rejoice in living by the eternal principle. Here I pray with you for the eternal life of the Emperor and the welfare of the country, and I advance to seek out the enemy. Follow me… Banzai![83]

Saito and Admirals Nagumo and Tsunoda committed suicide and 8,000 soldiers and civilians, including women and children, followed suit, many of them leaping off cliffs to their deaths rather than surrender. On 9 July all resistance ceased – there was nobody left to resist – and the Americans counted the bodies of 24,000 dead Japanese soldiers and sailors, for a death toll of 3,426 of their own.[84] On 21 July, after a savage naval bombardment, the Americans landed on Guam, an American possession for forty years before the Japanese captured it, and this too was robustly defended, not falling until 12 August. (The last Japanese defender did not surrender until 1960.) In the interim, the central island, Tinian, was invaded on 24 July, when napalm* was used for the first time, and was in American hands by 12 August. The Marianas were now secure, and such was the blow to Japanese prestige and to her government's conduct of the war that on 18 July General Tojo and his cabinet resigned. There had been mounting criticism of Tojo's retention of the posts of prime minister, defence minister and chief of staff of the army, and of his conduct of the war. There were, in the way of the Japanese political process of the time, even plans to throw a bomb at his car, and had Tojo not resigned, he might well have been assassinated.

Tojo's replacement as prime minister was the retired general Kuniaki Koiso, a former governor of Korea, who was thought to be more amenable than Tojo had been to the idea of negotiating a peace. While Japan had often considered attacking the USSR, her attempts to do so in 1939 had met with failure and, despite German requests for Japan to attack Russia, Japanese diplomatic efforts thenceforth were aimed at keeping the USSR neutral, and on several occasions Japan proposed a German–Soviet peace, to be brokered by herself. This was simply wishful thinking: during the years of German successes on the Eastern Front there was no incentive for Hitler to seek a peace, and, now that the tide had turned against Germany, there was no incentive for Russia to do so. It was made clear to the German foreign minister, Ribbentrop, that the only circumstances under which Japan would enter the war against the Soviet Union were if the latter granted bases in Siberia to

---

*A very effective weapon of petroleum jelly delivered from the air, it ignites and flows into bunkers and dugouts, incinerating the occupants. The US used it extensively in Vietnam, eliciting much outrage from the usual protesters. The British were swift to claim the moral high ground, saying that they neither possessed nor would ever use it, until the Royal Navy and RAF were told to deal with a major offshore oil leak from a damaged tanker, the *Torrey Canyon*, and found that only napalm would do. Amazingly, nobody seemed to notice, or, if they did, they considered that owning napalm was a lesser sin than allowing an epidemic of oil-covered seagulls.

the Allies from which they could bomb Japan, and there was no sign of that happening. The German–Japanese scheme to effect a land link-up through the Caucasus to Persia and on to India and Burma was now in tatters, and, while many Japanese politicians, and even some military men, could see that Japan could not now win the war, anyone who was found putting out peace feelers ran the risk of being assassinated by one or other faction of the armed forces. The only solution seemed to be to continue to resist everywhere, kill as many of the enemy as possible, and hope that the Allies could be forced to negotiate.

On the American side, with the Marianas, from where bombers could reach the Japanese homeland, now secure, there was much debate as to where to go next. On the southern route, MacArthur had rightly decided that rather than incur heavy casualties by attacking them, he would let the Japanese garrisons in Rabaul and the surrounding islets wither on the vine: they were cut off, could not be reinforced and were incapable of supporting military operations elsewhere. He now wanted to go for the Philippines, whereas the US Navy's view was that, rather than get bogged down in a slogging match there, MacArthur's army should be subordinated to Admiral Nimitz and together they should go for Formosa (Taiwan), bypassing the Philippines altogether. MacArthur, who was a master of rhetoric and unafraid to deploy every emotional argument in his extensive armoury, argued that to leave the Philippines to its fate would be to betray the vast majority of Filipinos who had remained loyal to the USA and had suffered starvation, deprivation and ill-treatment as a consequence. After making personal appeals to Roosevelt, MacArthur was ordered to attack Mindanao, the southernmost island of the Philippines, while the island-hoppers would continue to push ever closer to Japan by going for Iwo Jima and Okinawa in the Ryukyu Islands, which were Japanese home territory and the last step before Kyushu, the southernmost island of Japan proper. MacArthur had got his way, and would have his own Sixth Army and Vice-Admiral Thomas Kincaid's Seventh US Fleet under command, but it is probable that the stark realities of America's war effort carried more weight in the councils than MacArthur's powers of oratory: the number of divisions considered essential to take Formosa would not be available until after the European war was over.

The Philippines consist of 7,000 islands that stretch for 1,200 miles from Mindanao in the south to Luzon in the north. Essential to any attempt to land on Mindanao was the capture of the Palau Islands, part of the Western

Carolines, and in September Marines landed on Peleliu. This resulted in some of the fiercest jungle fighting of the whole war: the island was rocky and riddled with caves and carefully camouflaged dugouts, all defended by Japanese who were not going to give in, come what may. In a month of fighting, the US Marines suffered over 1,100 dead, it took 1,500 rounds of ammunition to kill one Japanese* and only the use of flame-throwers that could be fitted to tanks enabled the Americans to winkle out the defenders or burn them alive in their caves. Having done all that the emperor could have asked of him, and with his men either dead or so badly wounded that they could fight no more, the Japanese commander, Colonel Kunio Nakagawa, committed suicide. Then Vice-Admiral William Halsey, double-hatted as commander of the US Third Fleet in the Pacific, and thus responsible for the Western Pacific Task Forces, musing over maps and charts in his cabin aboard the battleship USS *New Jersey*, suggested that, rather than land on Mindanao and work north, the objective should be Leyte, slap in the middle of the Philippine archipelago and with thirty miles of beaches along the Gulf of Leyte on the east of the island. MacArthur agreed and plans were rapidly amended.

In Japan there was much debate as to where MacArthur might land next and, after it had been concluded that it would be in the Philippines rather than Formosa, there was further debate as to how the archipelago might be defended. Previously, Japanese doctrine had espoused the destruction of invasion forces on the beachheads, but this had become increasingly unworkable because of the enormous firepower that American battleships could bring down for shore bombardment, and it was now proposed that landings should be allowed to take place; the attackers would be then defeated when they ran up against stout Japanese defences inland. In the Philippines, it was impossible to predict exactly where the Americans might land first (although Mindanao was an obvious choice), so rather than try to defend every island, the Japanese would concentrate their main force on Luzon while leaving strong subsidiary garrisons elsewhere. The capital, Manila, was situated here and there were also good roads, which made the

---

*This statistic is quoted in John Toland, *Rising Sun,* Cassell & Co., London, 1971. It is perhaps somewhat misleading as all rounds fired are not necessarily aimed directly at an enemy but used as covering fire for movement, or fired speculatively, and in any case wartime conscripts of any nation are not noted for their marksmanship. It remains indicative, nevertheless, of the fierceness of the fighting.

island easy to defend. Lieutenant-General Shigenori Kuroda, commanding Fourteenth Area Army responsible for the Philippines, was sacked on the grounds that he played too much golf* and replaced by the Tiger of Malaya, General Yamashita, who had been recalled from virtual exile in Manchuria: his popularity with the Japanese public after his capture of Singapore was such that he had been seen as a possible threat to Tojo and the army high command. Yamashita had little time to make his presence felt, for two weeks after he arrived the Americans landed on Leyte. He had wanted to abandon that island as being of no strategic significance but the thought of giving up any territory without fighting for it was unacceptable to Yamashita's superior, the sixty-five-year-old Field Marshal Count Hisaichi Terauchi, who had speedily removed his headquarters from Manila to Saigon.

Before MacArthur's men could land on the Philippines, it was essential to neutralize the Japanese air fleet based in Formosa, and from 12 October Admiral Halsey's Third US Fleet, using aircraft from nine fleet carriers and eight light carriers, began a devastating series of raids on Formosan air bases and support installations. In three days they destroyed 500 Japanese aircraft, either on the ground or in the air, and numerous freighters and small craft as well as oil depots, ammunition dumps and shore maintenance establishments. The Japanese aviators did their best to strike back, but could only cause slight damage to three ships; they did, however, shoot down seventy-nine American aircraft, albeit with considerable losses of their own. Inexperience and wishful thinking, however, led them to report that they had sunk eleven American carriers, two battleships and three cruisers and that they had shot down 112 American aircraft. In Japan a great victory was proclaimed, the emperor ordered a national celebration and the announcement that 312 Japanese aircraft 'had not yet returned' was glossed over. The high command briefly assumed that the invasion of the Philippines would not happen. They were to be swiftly disabused.

Leyte was held by 20,000 men of the Japanese 16 Division, an inexperienced formation of wartime conscripts hitherto regarded as suitable only for static duties, and initially all went well for the Americans. On 18 October all the little islands around the mouth of the gulf were secured and, on 20 October, Sixth US Army, commanded by Lieutenant-General Walter Krueger,

---

*And quite right too. As someone who as a small boy had to trudge round innumerable golf courses following a golfing father, this author would have sacked him long before.

began to land on the beaches, against no opposition. MacArthur waded ashore and broadcast to the Filipino people: 'I have returned.' MacArthur's progress from landing craft to beach had, in fact, to be re-enacted several times until the cameramen were sure they had caught it, and only then could MacArthur, the saviour of his people, climb into his Jeep and begin to accept the cheers and adulation of the islands' population. Despite these complications, by midnight on 20 October 132,000 men and 200,000 tons of supplies had been landed on Leyte.

The Japanese now realized that their victory celebrations had been premature, and Admiral Soemu Toyoda, commanding the Combined Fleet, decided on one last gamble that at best would annihilate the invasion force on Leyte, destroy the American fleet and halt the American advance towards Japan, and at worst might yet reduce the odds against Japan and grant her some breathing space. His plan was for Admiral Ozawa and his carriers to lure Admiral Halsey and his powerful Third Fleet with its battleships and carriers away from Leyte, leaving only the weaker US Seventh Fleet, which other Japanese naval formations would then pounce on and destroy. The American troops on Leyte would now be cut off from reinforcement and lack naval gunfire support, and the Japanese garrison could mop them up.

Nearly all of Japan's remaining warships were involved in the operation, and the resulting series of engagements fought between 23 and 26 October, known as the Battle of Leyte Gulf, was by a considerable margin the largest naval battle of the war. The Japanese almost succeeded. They changed their naval code just before the ships sailed and strict radio silence was enforced, thus eluding Allied intercepts and giving the Americans no warning of what was coming. Admiral Halsey was indeed persuaded to steam away to the north towards Ozawa while three Japanese striking forces attempted to converge on Leyte, leaving Admiral Kincaid's Seventh Fleet greatly outnumbered. The eventual result was, however, a shattering defeat for the Japanese. They simply did not have enough aircraft or well-trained pilots to protect their ships, their communications were poor and finally, when Vice-Admiral Takeo Kurita's First Striking Force did penetrate Leyte Gulf after losing a battleship, the *Musashi*, and two heavy cruisers sunk and one badly damaged, he threw away his advantage by ordering his remaining ships to attack individually rather than as a coordinated formation. For their part, the Americans benefited from greatly superior fire-control radar that allowed them to take on targets they could not see, especially by night, and they made skilful use of radar-equipped PT boats as an early-warning screen. They were also lucky: sudden rain squalls appeared just as Kincaid's light carriers were about to be blown into very small pieces by Kurita's battleships. None the less, when the surviving Japanese ships had retired, the United States Navy had lost three carriers to the Japanese four, but the Americans still had twenty-two left to the Japanese four. The US Navy lost no battleships, the Japanese three out of seven; the Americans and Australians lost no cruisers, the Japanese ten out of seventeen; and the Americans four destroyers out of eighty, the Japanese twelve out of thirty-seven. All the Japanese had managed to achieve was to land 2,000 army reinforcements on the west side of Leyte, but this was the last time they would seriously challenge the Allies at sea, and it also saw the first appearance of a weapon of last resort – the suicide bomber.

In 1274 and again in 1281 Japan had been under threat of invasion by huge seaborne Mongol armies and on each occasion a typhoon had dispersed the invasion fleet and sunk or dismasted the ships, forcing the survivors to turn back. It was the Japanese version of the Armada legend and the typhoons were referred to as divine winds or *kamikaze*. After the fall of Saipan in 1944 and the realization that Allied sea power was now such that an inexorable advance towards the Japanese homeland was inevitable, the commander of the Philippines-based First Air Fleet, Vice-Admiral Takijiro Onishi, suggested the formation of Special Attack Groups that would train pilot volunteers to dive-bomb their aircraft on to Allied ships. The idea was enthusiastically approved by Tokyo and volunteers were called for. There was no shortage of young men willing to give their lives for the emperor, however hopeless the cause might now be, and this applied not only to officers and NCOs from the recognized martial clans – the descendants of the samurai – but conscripted commoners as well. Initial volunteers were already pilots but it was swiftly realized that this was a waste of skill and soon volunteers who had never flown were given a one-week course, sent off in whatever aircraft were still available, as long as they could carry a bomb, and told to aim for the central deck lift (which brings aircraft up to and down from the flight deck) on a carrier and the base of the bridge on other craft. The aircraft that hit but failed to sink the HMAS *Australia* as she covered the landings on 21 October may have been the first kamikaze, but, even though it did succeed in killing thirty of the Australian cruiser's crew, this could have been an inadvertent crash rather than a suicide mission. What is not in doubt is that on 25 October there was an attack on the American carriers by six kamikaze and that one of them succeeded in sinking the light carrier USS *St Lô*.

The Japanese navy having failed to interrupt the landings on Leyte, it was left to 16 Division to inflict as much damage as they could. Good businessmen they may have been, as they were contemptuously referred to by Yamashita when he told them they were on their own, but they were pretty good soldiers too and soon MacArthur was bogged down in a dreary and bloody battle of attrition in the mud, and for a while it looked as if the advance was stalled as the Japanese continued to land reinforcements from fast runs by destroyers at night, another Tokyo Express. By this means they managed to land a further 45,000 troops in total, about twice the number that had been there in the first place, although still outnumbered by the US Sixth Army, but then on 11 November US Navy aircraft caught a large troop convoy from Manila, sinking a number of the transports and drowning around 10,000 soldiers. MacArthur eventually broke the impasse on 7 December by landing a division behind the Japanese at Ormoc, on the same beaches as their own reinforcements had come in on, and on Christmas Day 1944 fighting on Leyte, save for mopping up, was declared over. Mopping up actually went on until May 1945, as small groups of Japanese refused to surrender, but the bulk of the American land and naval forces could now concentrate on MacArthur's next move – a landing on the main Philippine island of Luzon, after which Nimitz and his island-hoppers would take Iwo Jima and Okinawa.

* * *

In Burma, while Slim was successfully resisting the Japanese attempt to supply themselves by capturing Kohima and Imphal, Stilwell's Chinese–American force, supported by the Chindits, were attempting to capture the major Japanese communications centre of Myitkyina, defended by Lieutenant-General Tanaka Nobuo's 18 Division. Stilwell was convinced that the British were not playing their part in Burma – 'only shadow boxing' as he put it – while the truth was that Slim's Fourteenth Army was fully committed at Kohima and the Chindits were supporting an attempt to take Mogaung. Mogaung, the first major town in Burma to be recaptured, was eventually taken by Brigadier 'Mad Mike' Calvert's Chindit Brigade, spearheaded by a spirited charge into the town by a Gurkha battalion on 24 June 1944 that unbalanced the defences of Lieutenant-General Hisashi Takeda's 53 Division.

The Japanese defence collapsed three days later. Stilwell now ordered Calvert to support his attack on Myitkyina, and, when Calvert refused, more petrol was flung on to the flames of Stilwell's dislike of the British. Calvert, however, broke through the barrier put up by Stilwell's staff, who were terrified of their master, and explained to him in person that no Chindit brigade was in any state to help anybody, and cited the medical statistics. Vinegar Joe forgave Calvert, while reserving his right to be rude about the British. The Chindits had in fact been in the field in their second expedition – Operation Thursday – for far longer than even Wingate when alive had thought they could be; John Masters, later a hugely successful writer,* then an officer of the Fourth Gurkha Rifles and in temporary command of one of the Chindit brigades, had his entire force of 2,200 men medically examined and only 118 were pronounced fit for duty – seven British officers, twenty-one British soldiers and ninety Gurkhas. This was fairly typical of the whole force and a product of Wingate's belief in mind over matter and a complete disregard of hygiene and preventive medicine. Water discipline was bad, rations were far below the minimum calorific value and it was a generally unhealthy environment where 60 per cent of all evacuations were of men with malaria – easily preventable with the issued Mepacrine if the men bothered to take it, which far too often they did not. The Chindits were withdrawn and on 4 August Stilwell's men captured Myitkyina.

As Slim's Fourteenth Army and Stilwell's Chinese–American force consolidated their front and mopped up preparatory to the next move, there was considerable debate between Mountbatten, GHQ India, Churchill, and the British and American Chiefs of Staff as to what that next move should be. While all agreed that the liberation (or recapture) of Burma was a priority, the British wanted to avoid a long struggle southwards (Operation Capital), preferring instead an air- and seaborne operation to capture Rangoon (Operation Dracula), thus cutting off the Japanese forces in Northern Burma and forcing their withdrawal or leaving them unsupported to be mopped up in limited actions. The Americans, opposed to any strategy that might risk communications with China, favoured Capital, particularly when it became clear that the resources to carry out Dracula did not exist and would not until after the 1945 monsoon. In the event, Mountbatten was instructed

---

*Whose wonderful *Bugles and a Tiger*, read by torchlight, under the bedclothes while at school, motivated this author to seek service with Gurkhas.

to proceed with Capital but to keep Dracula under review in case an early collapse of Germany should allow assets to be withdrawn from the European theatre and shifted to the Far East. A major problem, even without Dracula, was manpower. Many of the British units in 11th Army Group were seriously under-strength, particularly the infantry battalions, and it was clear that the reinforcement system could not keep pace with losses, particularly in view of the high casualties in the European theatre, which had priority, and the recently changed rules about repatriation whereby a British soldier previously entitled to be posted back to the UK after five years in the Far East was now due back after three years and eight months. Fourteenth Army had 134 infantry battalions of which fifty-five were Indian, thirty-one British (including four Royal Marine Commandos), thirty West African, fifteen Gurkha, two Rhodesian and one Nepali, and there was a shortfall of 10,000 British soldiers, mainly in those thirty-one battalions. A further complication was the perceived need for airborne and parachute troops for the Burma campaign which the War Office had made plain could not be supplied from the Middle East as had originally been hoped.

The solution arrived at was to reduce the troops on the North-West Frontier and those allocated to internal security in India, disband a number of light anti-aircraft and anti-tank regiments of the Royal Artillery and send the men to the infantry (which must have delighted them), and also disband the Chindits. This last drew some harrumphing from Wingate's apostles but in truth the achievements of their previous expedition did not justify the losses, and with the vast increase in Allied air power, more field and mountain artillery and a huge improvement in the standards of the ordinary infantry, there really was no role for them any more, and the manpower shortage was a convenient excuse to get rid of them. These measures brought the British battalions up to something approaching their authorized establishment and allowed the formation of an Indian airborne division of two brigades, each with one British, one Indian and one Gurkha battalion.

Changes came farther up the chain of command too. General Sir George Giffard, the commander of 11th Army Group, had always had a difficult relationship with the Supreme Allied Commander, Mountbatten, who thought Giffard was too cautious and constantly tried to interfere in matters properly the responsibility of the army group commander. Mountbatten sacked him, replacing him with Lieutenant-General Sir Oliver Leese, lately Commander Eighth Army in Italy. Leese, aping his patron Montgomery, arrived with a plethora of thirty staff officers from Eighth Army to replace the staff at 11th Army Group, who of course knew and were known by the staffs and commanders lower down. It was something that Slim had never done and never would do and it was not a happy handover: Giffard was held in high regard as the man who had rebuilt the army after the early defeats, and the appearance of senior staff officers who had no experience of the Far East and were unable to converse with Indian troops was not welcome. Leese too was taken aback by the opulence of Mountbatten's headquarters in Ceylon, which had by now swollen to over 7,000 bodies, many of whom seemed to have been selected on grounds of breeding and ability to make small talk at cocktail parties rather than for any military qualities. Another difficulty with the command arrangements was the position of Stilwell, whose Northern Area Combat Command of American and Chinese troops was at least nominally part of 11th Army Group, although as he also held the posts of Commanding General China Burma India (commander of all American troops in those countries), Deputy Supreme Commander South-East Asia (under Mountbatten) and Chief of Staff to Chiang Kai-shek, he was a very difficult chap to pin down and consistently refused to accept orders from the army group commander but only direct from Mountbatten. When Leese was selected to replace Giffard, Mountbatten argued strongly that the appointment must be agreed by the American Chiefs of Staff and Stilwell first. The CIGS in London demurred: this was a British appointment and not subject to the approval of anyone else. Mountbatten feared another outburst of disobedience by Stilwell, but in the event it was Chiang who cut the knot.

The relationship between Chiang and Stilwell had been on a knife edge for some time. Stilwell regarded Chiang as ungrateful, corrupt, incompetent and far more interested in his own political power than in fighting the Japanese, and in this Stilwell was unquestionably right. Chiang resented the fact that Stilwell would not involve himself in Chinese political skulduggery nor obey Chiang's orders when they were patent lunacy. He was suspicious of the two Chinese armies that had been trained in India and were not under his own, Chiang's, direct influence, and in October he asked Roosevelt to recall Stilwell as he had lost confidence in him. Stilwell returned to the United States on 27 October 1944 and his responsibilities were now divided between his erstwhile deputy, Major-General Daniel I. Sultan, who was promoted to lieutenant-general and took over the Northern Area Combat command and had no difficulty in taking orders from the army group commander, and by Lieutenant-General Albert C. Wedemeyer, until now Mountbatten's Chief of Staff, who became Chief of Staff to Chiang and was in turn replaced by Lieutenant-General Frederick 'Boy' Browning, rusticated from Europe as one of the scapegoats for the Arnhem disaster. Then, in November, the command structure changed with the setting up of Allied Forces South-East Asia instead of 11th Army Group. AFSEA, under Leese, would take direct command from Slim of XV Corps in the Arakan and Slim's lines of communication, which would allow Slim and Fourteenth Army to concentrate on the reconquest of central Burma without having to worry about the Arakan or their rear.

Meanwhile, at the front Fourteenth Army was now poised along the River Chindwin, and Northern Area Combat Command augmented by the British 36 Division was preparing to push south from Myitkyina. In order to supply the advance, roads were being built but this needed an enormous engineering effort in the monsoon weather and it was not unusual for a vehicle convoy to cover but five miles a day along corduroy* tracks, while railways to accommodate 'jeep trains'† were also being built. Even with these prodigious efforts to build roads and railways, the whole army could not be supplied by road once it advanced, but Allied air power would now allow at least one division to be supplied by air, and airstrips were being developed and stores stockpiled at Imphal to support the move. Once the monsoon was over, it was intended that most casualty evacuation would also be by air.

There were changes in the Japanese command structure too. Lieutenant-General Masakazu Kawabe, Commander Burma Area Army, had ordered his Fifteenth Army to hold along the Chindwin after its disastrous attack on Kohima and Imphal. Starving and riddled with disease, it was in no state to do this and Kawabe, suffering from amoebic dysentery, was relieved and replaced by Lieutenant-General Heitaro Kimura, who was left in no doubt by Field Marshal Terauchi that he could expect no reinforcements, no evacuation of the wounded and no supplies, but must live off the country. Kimura accepted the impossibility of holding the Chindwin and ordered his units to pull back behind the Irrawaddy, calculating that Slim would make

---

*A road surface created by laying logs across a bulldozed track.

†Freight carriages on railway lines pulled by a jeep with its normal wheels replaced by flanges.

for Mandalay, and as he did so the Japanese could sally out from behind the Irrawaddy and cut the British lines of communications, and then, if the British did not retreat, starve them to death or surrender. While this was what Kimura assured his superiors he was going to do, he was well aware that the most he could hope for was to delay the Allies as long as he could and to sell every Japanese soldier's life as dearly as possible.

Slim's plan, made before he knew of the Japanese withdrawal to the Irrawaddy, was to push two spearheads across the Chindwin and destroy the Japanese forces between the Chindwin and the Irrawaddy, after which he would advance on Mandalay and link up with Sultan's Chinese–Americans as they advanced from the north. Once Slim realized that Japanese troops were being pulled out of the Arakan to defend behind the Irrawaddy, he knew that his plans would have to change as, instead of meeting and defeating the Japanese south of Mandalay and taking the port of Rangoon before the 1945 monsoon arrived, he would have to switch his thrust east and might well have insufficient logistic support to keep all his divisions in the field. By pushing the 19 Indian Division across the Chindwin, Fourteenth Army linked up with the Americans on 16 December 1944 at Indaw. Northern Burma was now secure and the clearance of Central and Southern Burma could begin.

* * *

Stalin had promised that the Red Army would mount a major offensive in coordination with the Allied landing in Normandy, and on 22 June, once he was quite sure that the Allies were actually ashore and were not in danger of being driven back into the sea, he launched Operation Bagration,* pitting 2.5 million men supported by 5,000 tanks, 30,000 artillery pieces, over 2,000 Katyushas, 70,000 troop-carrying vehicles and 5,000 aircraft against Field Marshal Busch's Army Group Centre. Busch was holding a frontage of 400 miles in a bulge around Minsk with 580,000 men in four armies: Third Panzer, Fourth, Ninth and Second. Less than half the men were infantry and they had 9,500 artillery pieces and 900 tanks and were supported by 775 aircraft, of which around a third were operational at any one time. A clever piece of Russian disinformation had convinced German intelligence that the forthcoming offensive would be directed against Army Group North Ukraine, to the south, and most of the armour had

---

*After General Prince Pyotr Bagration, killed fighting the French at the Battle of Borodino on 7 September 1812 during Napoleon's advance on Moscow.

been sent there. Not only did the Russians outnumber the Germans in men, guns, aircraft and tanks, but they would use against them their very own tactics, something the Red Army could not have done even a year previously. Now with American four-wheel-drive Lend-Lease trucks, vastly improved standards of training, better communications and, perhaps above all, Hitler's refusal to allow the German army to fight a battle the way its generals wanted to, the Soviets were confident that they could inflict a shattering defeat and push the Germans back into East Prussia, the Baltic States and Poland. In the north, First Baltic and Third Byelorussian Fronts, coordinated by Marshal Zhukov, would drive deep into and behind the German positions; in the south, coordinated by Marshal Vasilevsky, the First Byelorussian Front would also penetrate the German front while the Second Byelorussian Front would pin the Germans frontally. The northern and southern pincers would link up at Minsk, and the encircled Germans would be destroyed in detail. It was a hugely ambitious plan, but, with the improved transport and Soviet tank and artillery factories in full production, the Russians were now not only able to outnumber the Germans in everything but also to move faster than they could. The concentration of artillery that the Russians brought to bear could reduce any stretch of countryside to a cratered wasteland, collapse any dugout and smash any city to heaps of rubble.

On the morning of 22 June, the third anniversary of Barbarossa, a hurricane bombardment of massed Russian artillery blasted the German forward defences, and armoured columns with infantry riding on the tanks thrust deep into the German lines supported by waves of ground attack aircraft. By the end of the first day, the Germans had been pushed back ten miles, and the Russian tactic of splitting German formations from each other and then encircling them was beginning to work. By 26 June the German Ninth Army had been effectively neutralized and Hitler sacked the army commander, General of Infantry Hans Jordan, and replaced him with General of Panzer Troops Nikolaus von Vormann. So far Busch had refused all requests from his army commanders to permit a withdrawal or to give up the so-called 'fortified places' concept whereby towns and cities of political importance were to be held by at least one division (and in some cases a corps) even if surrounded. The concept of leaving a powerful force behind enemy lines might have had some merit if the Luftwaffe could have supplied it, but those days were long gone. On the same day that Jordan was sacked, Busch flew to see Hitler to ask permission not for a general withdrawal but to make some adjustments by pulling back some of his formations to avoid encirclement, but, as he must have known, the order was to stand fast come what may. This is, of course, exactly what the Russians were hoping for: despite their greatly improved combat performance and overwhelming numerical superiority, they still did not want to take the Germans on in a war of manoeuvre.

On 28 June, Hitler sacked Busch and replaced him with Field Marshal Model, who would continue to command Army Group North Ukraine, although he delegated effective command of that formation to the chief of staff. Busch felt bitter: he had, after all, only been obeying orders, but a good general does not obey orders when he knows them to be pointless and that they will contribute to the loss of an army to no purpose, and there are plenty of examples where generals disobeyed Hitler's orders and got away with it – provided, of course, that what they did worked. By 29 June, Army Group Centre had lost 130,000 men killed and 60,000 taken prisoner, and had very few tanks left. On 1 July the Germans began to evacuate Minsk and shifted 8,000 wounded and 12,000 Russian auxiliaries westwards. Meanwhile, the German Fourth Army, trying to withdraw across the Dnieper and towards Minsk, deployed its one panzer division with seventy Mk V Panthers and fifty-five Mk IVs to hold the Red Army back, and, although they wreaked much havoc in the ranks of the Third Byelorussian Front, numbers eventually told. On 2 July, Hitler agreed that Minsk could be abandoned, but it was too late: Fourth Army was too far to the east and the armies either side, Third Panzer and the remnants of Ninth, were collapsing. On 3 July, Fifth Guards Tank Army entered Minsk and the pincers closed behind Fourth Army, which was now isolated. Fourth Army tried to break out, and tried again, but it could not and by 8 July had ceased to exist, with 60,000 men killed or wounded and most of the other 40,000 prisoners in Russian hands.

Now there were numerous pockets of Germans, all surrounded by the Red Army and far too numerous to be supplied by air, even if the aircraft existed, which they did not. Some commanders ordered their men to break out to the west in small numbers, and they were duly slaughtered by partisans. Other groups stood and fought, and were overrun by phalanxes of T-34 tanks and hordes of Red infantry. When Model finally managed to stabilize the front and Operation Bagration came to an end on 11 July, the Soviets had advanced over 400 miles to the River Vistula in Poland and were poised on the River Memel to drive into East Prussia. It was the greatest defeat the Germans had suffered on the Eastern Front; it destroyed Army Group Centre and cost them twenty-eight divisions, 350,000 men dead, wounded, missing and captured with the loss of 1,500 artillery pieces and around 250 tanks and assault guns. Amongst the Army Group Centre casualties in Bagration, eleven generals were killed in action, two committed suicide, two were missing believed killed and eighteen were taken prisoner. In contrast, in the whole war, seven British generals were killed and one died as a prisoner of the Japanese.*

On 17 July the Russians herded 57,000 German prisoners through the streets of Moscow, and on 21 July Colonel-General Zeitzler, the Chief of the German General Staff, having become increasingly disillusioned with Hitler's interference in military matters, resigned on health grounds and was replaced by Colonel-General Heinz Guderian.† Three days later, as a spin-off from the bomb plot against Hitler, and on Göring's suggestion, the Nazi salute was imposed upon the armed forces in place of the normal military salute. The order was greeted with ridicule by most of the army, and only grudgingly complied with in the presence of NSDAP officials or the SS.

* * *

There had been rumours in the West about German extermination camps, but they were generally dismissed as propaganda – after all, in the First World War there had been all sorts of stories about German soldiers roasting Belgian babies on the points of their bayonets, ripping open the bellies of pregnant women and raping nuns, all of which had turned out to be pure fiction – but then on 24 July 1944 the Red Army overran Madjanek near Lublin in Poland, and the full beastliness of the German racial policies was exposed. Madjanek was built in 1941 as a work, as opposed to extermination, camp where the inmates were supposed to be used for labour to help the war effort. In fact, due to administrative incompetence on the part of the Inspectorate of Concentration Camps of the SS Main Office of Economy and Administration, the government department responsible, there was very little useful work for them to do and inmates

---

*Even this is slightly suspect as it includes generals killed in motor and air crashes whilst in the battle area, including Major-General Willans, the Director General Army Welfare and Education, killed in a plane crash while on a visit to North Africa. Only three British generals were actually killed by enemy fire: Hopkinson by a sniper's bullet in Italy in 1943, Lumsden by a kamikaze attack on his ship in 1945 and Rennie by a mortar bomb during the Rhine Crossing in 1945.

†Hitler suspected that Zeitzler knew about the July bomb plot but did nothing to stop it (he almost certainly did not know) and in January 1945 dismissed him from the army and deprived him of the customary right to wear uniform in retirement.

were frequently paraded to move stones from one side of the camp to the other, or to dig holes and then fill them in again. Although not specifically for extermination, Madjanek had the facilities for mass killings if required, and prisoners who were unable to work were regularly herded into the camp's gas chambers and their bodies cremated. Of the estimated 500,000 people who passed through Madjanek, the largest groups were Poles, then Jews and finally Russians: 360,000 did not survive; 144,000 were shot or gassed, including 18,000 Jews; and 216,000 died of starvation, ill-treatment or disease. As the Germans retreated from the Eastern Front, the SS made great efforts to cover up the evidence of mass extermination and prisoners not killed and disposed of on the spot were marched away towards Germany and the camps demolished, in many cases trees being planted to disguise the mass graves of those not cremated. But with the rapid advance of the Red Army, the SS had not had time to cover up Madjanek, and the Russians found a shed piled high with pairs of shoes, the gas chambers labelled Bath and Disinfection, the crematoria and the hastily filled-in mass graves of those shot as the Death's Head units of the SS prepared to depart. The Russians, no strangers themselves to presiding over mass murder, made much of the gruesome discovery. The Soviet official newspaper *Pravda* ('Truth') devoted the whole of a front page to it, thus ensuring that the story was picked up by news agencies around the world. At the same time, claims that the Russians had come upon trainloads of Russian children about to be taken to camps and gassed were widely disseminated to the troops of the Red Army and, while almost certainly not true, were made to seem all too believable by the undoubted evidence of Madjanek.

In London the members of the Polish government-in-exile viewed the approach of the Red Army with mixed feelings. On the one hand they welcomed the imminent expulsion of the Germans, but on the other they had no diplomatic relations with the USSR (these had been broken off by Russia in April 1943 over the Katyn Forest massacre*) and were concerned

---

*In April 1943 the Germans discovered mass graves in the Katyn Forest in Eastern Poland containing the bodies of 4,400 Polish officers. All had their hands tied behind their backs and had been shot in the head. The Germans asked the International Red Cross to investigate and the evidence was overwhelming that this had been done by the Soviets after the occupation of their part of Poland in 1939. The Russians claimed it had been a Nazi atrocity, but in 1990 the Russian government admitted responsibility.

that they, and not the Soviets or the Polish communists, should decide the shape of post-war Poland. They concluded that the only way in which Free Poland could influence the USSR would be by themselves contributing to Poland's liberation, and the so-called Home Army was instructed to begin operations against the Germans. The Home Army was an amalgam of various resistance groups owing allegiance to the government-in-exile and was commanded by General Tadeusz Komorowski, a cavalry officer who took the name Bór as a cover. He was regarded by the Germans as such a threat that they put a price of £400,000 on his head, but he was never betrayed. The army itself consisted for the most part of ex-soldiers of the Polish Army who had not managed to get away to France and England, and a few Russians left behind when the Wehrmacht swept through in 1941, and was equipped with a mixture of Polish, Russian and captured German weapons along with others parachuted in by the Special Operations Executive, the British organization responsible for operations in occupied countries. With Moscow Radio calling for a rising and with the London Polish government's approval, Bór-Komorowski gave the order for a rising on 1 August, assuming that it would divert the Germans from their defence against the Russians and that the Red Army would soon be able to link up with the Home Army. In the event, the Russians were very happy for the Germans and the non-communist Poles to fight each other, made no attempt to come to their rescue and prevented the British and the Americans from dropping arms and supplies by refusing overflying rights to the RAF and the USAAF. The main action took place in Warsaw – the Warsaw Rising – and pitted around 37,000 Poles with about 1,600 small arms and numerous homemade petrol bombs between them against, eventually, 21,000 Germans armed with the full panoply of weapons including artillery, commanded by SS Obergruppenführer Erich von dem Bach-Zelewski, a former army officer who had joined the SS in 1931 and was now responsible for anti-partisan operations on the Eastern Front. The formation of Army Group Centre responsible for Warsaw was the reconstituted Ninth Army, which did not want to get involved in house-to-house fighting, so the battle was initially left to the SS, with some artillery and mortars lent by the army.

The SS had had some previous experience of street-fighting in Warsaw when demolishing the ghetto there in 1943. By then, of the 400,000 Jewish inhabitants before the war, 300,000 had been deported to concentration camps and about 60,000 were still in the city. Realizing that they were all doomed to extermination, they resolved that they might as well die with honour and perhaps set an example to Jews elsewhere. The resistance when the Germans attempted to demolish the ghetto and deport the remaining residents on 19 April came as a rude shock to SS Brigadeführer Jürgen Stroop and his 3,000 SS and police, and, although the Jewish leaders committed suicide on 8 May, resistance went on until 16 May. Fourteen thousand Jews had been killed and the rest were removed to Treblinka and Madjanek for 'processing'. Around 400 Germans were killed and the uprising did spark off minor (but unsuccessful) mutinies in some of the camps.

This time, the fighting was bloody and a far bigger problem than the Germans had expected. The Poles could move relatively freely through the sewers until Bach-Zelewski pumped gas into them, and initially any Pole captured was shot out of hand, mostly by the Kaminsky Brigade, otherwise 29 SS Grenadier Division of turncoat Russians, until Bach-Zelewski ordered it to stop. The Luftwaffe did its bit by dive-bombing those parts of the city held by the insurgents, completely unscathed by Russian anti-aircraft guns that were well within range but did not open fire. Despite the Germans' firepower, things were not going well for them until General von Vormann was replaced as Commander Ninth Army by General of Panzer Troops Smilo Freiherr von Lüttwitz, previously commanding XXXXVI Panzer Corps, who was more amenable to helping out the SS with the reduction of the Polish Home Army and placed his 19 Panzer Division at Bach-Zelewski's disposal. The Poles were driven more and more into smaller and smaller areas of the city, their buildings demolished by tanks and bombed by Stukas, and on 28 September Bór-Komorowski radioed Soviet Marshal Konstantin Rokossovsky – himself of Polish origin – that, if the Russians made no move within the next seventy-two hours, the Polish Home Army must capitulate. No reply came and so on 2 October Bór-Komorowski surrendered to Bach-Zelewski. The rising had gone on for sixty-three days and the fighters had drawn the reluctant admiration of the SS, so much so that Bach-Zelewski shook hands with Bór, congratulated him and ordered that he and his 15,000 survivors be treated as prisoners of war – in law he could have treated them as *franc tireurs* and had them shot. Around 15,000 members of the Home Army were killed, while the Poles subsequently claimed that 250,000 civilians had died, and the Germans that 17,000 of their men had been killed. Both claims are almost certainly exaggerated.

* * *

With the close of Operation Bagration, the centre of the Eastern Front settled down for a while as the Red Army turned its attention to the north. On 12 July the First Baltic Front ripped a fifty-mile hole between the German Sixteenth Army, Army Group North's southernmost formation, and Third Panzer Army of Army Group Centre. This was the beginning of an offensive against Army Group North when Marshal Koniev threw the Leningrad, Third, Second and First Baltic Fronts, 1.2 million men with 2,500 tanks, against Army Group North's 540,000 men with 300 tanks and assault guns. Army Group North had been commanded by Colonel-General Georg Lindemann, who had taken over from Field Marshal Model on 31 March 1944, but, having been refused permission to withdraw to shorten his line, he had been retired as being, according to Hitler, 'too old and too weak' (he was sixty) and replaced by Colonel-General Johannes Freissner.

The USSR was determined to regain the Baltic States. Although Estonians, Latvians and Lithuanians historically looked more to Germany than to Russia, both Tsarists and Bolsheviks considered the Baltic States to be within the Russian sphere of influence and Germany had conceded that in the secret protocols to the Molotov–Ribbentrop Pact of 1939. Now the roads were packed with refugees who had no wish to return to Russian subjugation, and the Latvian units in the German army in particular fought determinedly to keep the Red Army out. Despite their efforts, by 23 July, Army Group North had been pushed out of Estonia, was cut off from Army Group Centre and was holding a frontage of 500 miles in Latvia around the Gulf of Riga. When Freissner proved reluctant to order yet more pointless counter-attacks to restore the link with Army Group Centre, he was moved on 25 July to take over Army Group South Ukraine, exchanging places with Colonel-General Schorner, who now took over Army Group North. As long as the German navy had mastery of the Baltic, the situation of Army Group North was not (quite) as bad as it seemed on the map, and wounded and non-essential elements were already being evacuated through the port of Riga. On 16 August, General of Panzer Troops Erhard Raus's Third Panzer Army of Army Group Centre launched *Fall Doppelkopf*, designed to close the thirty-mile gap to Army Group North. The plan was for XXXX Panzer Corps of two armoured divisions, one motorized division and one infantry to attack east and hold off the Red Army, while XXXIX Panzer Corps would thrust up the coast and link up with Army Group North. XXXX Corps's inland advance ran into ten Soviet rifle divisions supported by four anti-tank brigades and three artillery divisions, but it did attract their attention, and much reduced the opposition that would have been met by XXXIX Corps when it launched its attack on 18 August. This was one of the rare occasions when the German navy was able to provide naval gunfire support for the army, and the heavy cruiser *Prinz Eugen* and a flotilla of destroyers were able to add to the corps's own artillery as the troops pushed up the coast. XXXIX Corps's spearhead made contact with Army Group North at noon, and a tenuous corridor eighteen miles wide was now open and convoys of supplies began to pour through. Now was the time to pull Army Group North out and back into East Prussia for the eventual defence of the Reich, but Hitler would have none of it. Concerned that Finland might be about to defect, he insisted that strong forces must be kept in the Baltic States to encourage (or possibly to threaten) the Finns.

Hitler was right to suspect the Finns, for one by one Germany's erstwhile allies were deserting her. The Romanian dictator, Antonescu, saw the Red Army rolling ever closer to his borders and for some time he, his government and the opposition had been seeking terms. All these feelers had foundered on the Allied insistence on unconditional surrender and Romania's demand for a guarantee of post-war independence from the Soviet Union. In the end, with Soviet troops on Romanian territory, Antonescu, as a soldier, could not abandon his German ally and, on 23 August, King Michael had him arrested and asked the Russians for an armistice, which was signed in Moscow on 12 September. Romanian units surrendered to the Red Army en masse and Army Group South lost its 400,000 Romanians and could no longer hold. Within a few weeks, Romania declared war against Germany and twenty Romanian divisions joined the Red Army. It did them little good: as soon as the war was over, they lost what little independence the agreement with the Russians had allowed them. In the German puppet state of Slovakia, a communist-inspired uprising broke out on 30 August but, as with Warsaw, Stalin refused to help and the rising was eventually put down by German troops. Bulgaria had never declared war on the USSR, but only against Britain and the USA, and her military contribution to the German war effort was limited to chasing partisans in the Balkans, but with the approach of the Red Army the Regent, Prince Cyril, severed diplomatic relations with Germany and then, as the Red Army steamroller burst into Bulgaria, a communist coup persuaded the Bulgarian Army to change sides. The regent did not profit from his treachery, and he would be shot by the NKVD in February 1945. A few days later, Finland did indeed leave the war: her troops had managed to hold the Red Army but

Marshal Mannerheim, who was now prime minister, was well aware that in time sheer weight of numbers would crush him and the whole country might be swallowed up. The Finnish government arrived at terms with the Soviets, informed the Germans that they were leaving the war, and asked that German troops leave her territory. German formations still in Finland withdrew back into Norway. Now only Hungary was left as a German ally of any importance but the Regent, Admiral Horthy, was already in discussions with the Soviets and had agreed to change sides, when the Germans, who knew very well what was going on, engineered a pro-German coup, arrested Horthy, installed a puppet government, took control of the Hungarian Army, began to recruit Hungarians for the Waffen SS and rounded up 437,000 Hungarian Jews and sent them to Auschwitz. Here was the cause of one of many shouting matches between Hitler and Guderian. Hitler insisted that the German army in Hungary be strengthened to keep her in the Axis and prevent the Russians from taking Budapest. For his part, the Chief of the General Staff argued that the next Russian offensive would attack straight through Poland and into Germany, and that all reinforcements should be concentrated there and not wasted in Hungary. But Hitler would not be moved, and his insistence would ultimately rob Germany of her last armoured reserves.

The corridor between Army Groups Centre and North did not stay open for long. On 5 October a massive Soviet offensive cut the link and pushed Army Group North into the Courland peninsula, where it held a 100-mile front with the Baltic behind and on each side. The Red Army was now preparing for the last great offensive of the Russian War, one that would take it to Berlin itself.

* * *

In Italy, Operation Diadem, the fourth Battle of Cassino and the breakout from Anzio, had represented the last chance for a quick victory. However, Clark's insistence on heading for Rome to secure a publicity coup before the British could get there, and in so doing allowing a gap to open up between his Fifth Army and Oliver Leese's Eighth, enabled the Germans to slip through and prepare to delay the approach to their next major defensive position. Originally named the Gothic Line by the Germans when they began work on it in April 1944, then renamed the Green Line by Hitler in June and called by the Allies the Pisa–Rimini line, it actually ran two thirds of the way up the Italian peninsula from just north of Lucca on the west coast for 200 miles north of Florence through the

Apennines to south of Pesaro on the Adriatic coast. Like the Gustav Line, it consisted of well-sited defensive positions with fixed concrete emplacements, anti-tank ditches, wire entanglements, minefields, cleverly concealed machine-gun positions with interlocking arcs and artillery and mortars that could dominate the approaches. As with all Allied pursuits in this war, the one from Rome was slow and ponderous, giving the Germans ample opportunity to pull back at their own pace. Kesselring now had nineteen German divisions, although most were seriously under-strength, with three in reserve and another three working on what for convenience we shall continue to call the Gothic Line. As for the Allies, there had been a continuing haemorrhage of troops and landing craft for Overlord, and now a further six divisions, including the North African mountain specialists of the French Corps, were withdrawn for Operation Dragoon, the landing on the French Riviera by the American Seventh Army supported by the Royal and United States Navies on 15 August and against which the British had argued strongly. On paper some of this loss of troops was made up by units of the reconstituted Italian Army supposedly now fighting the Germans, but, with the Allies having to provide them with logistic support and to clothe and equip them, not to mention their extreme reluctance to actually fight, the British at least found that the Italians could only be used as labour battalions or for static guards in rear areas.

The next objective for the British and Americans was Florence, and to slow them up German tactics involved deploying mobile battle groups of a battalion or so of infantry in commandeered trucks supported by a few tanks. They would take up a defensive position and force the Allies to deploy, hold their position for a day or so and then slip away before a main attack came in. This proved an excellent delaying tactic and it was not until 4 August that the Allies closed up to the River Arno with Florence on the other side and no way across as the Germans had blown all the bridges except one. The German commander on the spot was not prepared to go down in history as the man who wantonly destroyed the Ponte Vecchio, built in 1345, but he rendered it equally unusable by demolishing the buildings at either end and blocking the approaches and exits with rubble. The Germans did not attempt to fight on the Arno for any length of time, but the Allied need to bring up bridging companies and get bridges across the river that would take armour added to the delay.

North of the Gothic Line, Mussolini was attempting to establish a fascist republic run from Salo on Lake Garda. Its existence was entirely dependent upon German goodwill, and there was very little of that. Italian partisans, hitherto quiescent, were becoming bolder and murder of lone German servicemen and sabotage of roads and railways were becoming more frequent. The Germans were forced to take sterner and sterner measures to keep order, including the deportation of men of military age to Germany as forced labour and eventually the shooting of hostages and the burning down of villages where German soldiers had been fired upon. While there was not much else the Germans could have done, such measures inevitably provoked more murders and more sabotage. Mussolini and fascism had lost all credibility, even in the areas that he nominally controlled, while Allied troops were greeted by cheering crowds in the towns and villages that they entered, and the rate of Allied desertion duly went up. Desertion was an attractive option, with the prospect of sitting out the war in a remote village surrounded by Italian girls whose menfolk were interned in Germany and where the Chianti was cheap and plentiful, and, while there are no accurate figures as to how many American and British soldiers made up the bands of deserters, the situation was sufficiently serious for Alexander to demand the imposition of the death penalty for desertion, sanctioned by military law but not yet imposed in this war. Politicians, fearful of public reaction at home, refused.

Alexander's plan to breach the Gothic Line involved what he called the 'two-handed punch'. Eighth Army would attack through the Rimini gap on the Adriatic coast, covered only by foothills and where the British armour could be used to best advantage, and when Kesselring was forced to move his reserves, and possibly redeploy troops from his centre as well, Clark's Fifth Army would deliver the second punch, from Florence through the passes to Bologna. D-Day was to be 25 August, and, even though the move of Eighth Army to its concentration area on the east coast was a huge logistic task, involving 80,000 vehicles, prodigious road repair work by the Royal Engineers, including the construction of eighty Bailey bridges to allow tank transporters to operate a shuttle service, meant the whole operation was completed in fifteen days. For the second punch Clark had asked the American Chiefs of Staff for reinforcements for his severely depleted army. Italy had never been a priority for the Americans and it was even less so now. What Clark got was a regimental combat team* from an all-black division (the US Army was still segregated) and two battalions of the recently arrived Brazilian Expeditionary Force. Both these units and the one-third

---

*A small brigade in British terms.

under-strength US 1 Armoured Division were placed in reserve. Wilson and Alexander had also asked for reinforcement for the British units, and they too got little response – a Greek mountain brigade* and 4,000 Poles who had been captured in German uniforms in Normandy and were prepared to turn their coats and join the Polish Corps under British command in Italy.

The concentration of Eighth Army on the Adriatic coast came as a complete surprise to the Germans. Kesselring had nineteen divisions in and forward of the Gothic Line. To oppose them, Eighth Army had V Corps with an augmented armoured division, one Indian and three British infantry divisions; X Corps with one Indian and one New Zealand division, an armoured brigade and the Greek mountain brigade; and the Canadian I Corps with five armoured divisions and one infantry division and the Polish Corps. The American Fifth Army consisted of II Corps with two infantry divisions: IV Corps with a South African and an American armoured division, the black regimental combat team and Task Force 45, this latter a mix of American and British anti-aircraft and anti-tank gunners given some hasty infantry training; and XIII British Corps with a British armoured division augmented by a Canadian armoured brigade and one British and one Indian infantry division. Eighth Army attacked at 2300 hours from the River Metauro on 25 August in complete silence to maintain surprise, and met only slight resistance. By first light there were five divisions across the river; by 30 August they were over the River Foglia and into the advance positions of the Gothic Line and prospects were looking good. On 2 September, the Canadian Corps and V Corps advancing side by side were over the River Conca, and then it all began to turn sour. The German 1 Parachute Division, 26 Panzer Division and 29 Panzer Grenadier Division were strongly dug in on Monte Coriano and Gemiano, five miles to the south, and, when the British attacked on 4 September, they were not to be shifted. The impetus had now gone out of the Eighth Army attack and it was time to launch Fifth Army. On 8 September the Americans attacked, spearheaded by 8 Indian Division, and on 12 September they were overlooking the strongly fortified Futa Pass. Then the weather broke. The autumn rains, not normally due for another month, were nothing short of torrential, and in the mountains, combined with mist and howling winds, any operation of war was made exceedingly difficult and air support impossible. Some progress was made on the Adriatic coast where

---

*Which somewhat to the surprise of the British fought rather well!

aircraft could still fly and on 12 September V Corps and the Canadians between them took Coriano and three days later Gemiano fell to 4 Indian Division. On 20 September the Greeks entered Rimini but now the rains had turned the whole area back into the swamps from which it had been reclaimed in Roman times; glutinous mud prevented even tracked vehicles from moving off the roads, and there were precious few of those. Further operations in early October to get Fifth Army clear of the mountains succeeded but at terrible cost as the Germans withdrew at their own pace, making the Americans and their attached British units fight for every yard.

On 10 October, General Leese was transferred to take over from Giffard as Commander Land Forces South-East Asia. He was thought to be too methodical and too slow for the dash that was expected in the Italian theatre, despite the inescapable facts that the weather, the lack of troops and the Combined Chiefs' view of Italy as a backwater made it impossible for even the most dashing general – if one could be found – to employ methods other than those of slow, deliberate attrition. Leese's replacement was Lieutenant-General Sir Richard McCreery, a cavalryman who had fallen out with Auchinleck, was reinstated as Alexander's chief of staff after the Cairo Purge, was not thought highly of by Montgomery but survived to command X Corps at the Salerno landings. On the German side too there were command changes. Field Marshal Kesselring was badly injured when the staff car in which he was travelling collided with a gun and while he was in hospital Colonel-General Heinrich von Vietinghoff, who had been commanding Tenth Army, was temporarily in command of Army Group C. Neither change of command made much difference: the Allies were through the Gothic Line but exhausted and with a heavy bill of casualties who could not be replaced. Eighth Army had lost 465 tanks and was 7,000 infantrymen short of establishment, and McCreery had no option but to disband 1 Armoured Division, reduce 56 Division to a brigade and reorganize all infantry battalions into three rifle companies instead of four. The Germans too had not survived unscathed and of their ninety-two infantry battalions thirty had fewer than 200 men and only ten had more than 400.

In December, Alexander ordered a further offensive, which made little progress in appalling weather and was called off with the Allies still short of Bologna and their line running from the east coast along the River Senio, north of Firenzuola, south of Monte Vergato across to Viareggio on the west coast. The proponents of the Italian campaign could argue that they had kept twenty or so German divisions away from the Eastern Front or from North-West Europe, but as it had also tied down around the same number of Allied divisions, there would seem to have been little, if any, advantage. As it was, the winter put a stop to any major operations by either side, and the front would not move again until the spring of 1945.

* * *

With the virtual destruction of the German Seventh Army in Normandy, the Allies now had to prevent the Germans from establishing a defence line on the River Seine, something which the Germans were in fact unable to do, being ordered to fall back while destroying everything of military value as they went. Eisenhower had hoped to avoid having to fight for Paris, mindful of the problems of street-fighting and the subsequent responsibility for feeding a city of several million inhabitants, but despite de Gaulle's orders to the Resistance not to take military action, fearing as he did that French communists would seize control of the city, a general strike by Parisians on 18 August led to an armed rising the next day. General of Infantry Dietrich von Choltitz, Paris Military Commandant, had been ordered not to allow the city to fall into Allied hands except as a heap of rubble, but, with only around 20,000 mostly rear echelon troops, he could not have destroyed the city even if he had wanted to (which he probably did not). For political reasons, it was decided that Paris should be liberated by the French and so the Americans held back and von Choltitz surrendered the city to General Le Clerc's French 2 Armoured Division and representatives of the Resistance on 25 August 1944. There followed a spate of lynch law where old scores were settled and numbers of people shot as collaborators – which some of them undoubtedly were.

On 31 August the British seized the bridges over the River Somme at Amiens, on 3 September the Guards Armoured Division entered Brussels and on 4 September Antwerp fell to the British Second Army. On 1 September, Montgomery had ceased to command the Allied Land Forces when Eisenhower took on that responsibility in addition to his role as Supreme Allied Commander. It was only a recognition of the fact that the American Army had continued to grow, whereas the British were running out of manpower, and an acceptance that the American generals were increasingly critical of Montgomery, who, demoted to command of 21st Army Group, was promoted to field marshal as a sop. Eisenhower now had thirty-seven divisions – twenty-one American, twelve British, three Canadian and one

Polish – supported by 7,700 tanks, 6,000 bombers, 5,000 fighters and 2,000 transport aircraft, and one of the major problems was the supply of food, ammunition, fuel and spare parts, most of which was still coming in through the artificial Mulberry harbour in Normandy. The Allies badly needed a major port, as well as the smaller ones captured by the Canadians as they advanced up the Channel coast, and, although Operation Dragoon, the American landings in the French Riviera, had captured Toulon and Marseilles, these were simply too far away. Although the Allies now had Antwerp, they could only use it when the Germans had been cleared out of the Scheldt delta on either side. Until that happened, the logistic machinery could not support offensives by all five Allied armies, two in 21st Army Group and three in the US 12th Army Group.

Montgomery, supported by Bradley, urged that one northern thrust should be given maximum support to drive deep into Germany, take Berlin and end the war in 1944, with the added advantage of doing so before the Russians got too far into Europe. Eisenhower preferred a less risky strategy, envisaging a steady advance on a broad front, and in any case the American State Department was dismissive of London's fears as to Russian intentions, seeing only further evidence of British deviousness and imperial ambitions. It would also have been unthinkable to let the British undertake the final thrust that would presumably seal Germany's defeat while the American divisions were stuck in France. The result was a compromise: the role of 21st Army Group was now to advance through Belgium and Holland while Bradley's 12th Army Group was to strike east against the Siegfried Line, the defences protecting the border of the Reich itself. A subsidiary aim of the British advance was to take out the sites from which the Germans were firing their Vengeance weapons against England. They had started bombarding London and the South Coast with the subsonic V1, an early cruise missile carrying 1,800lb of high explosive, in June 1944, but the RAF and the Royal Artillery learned reasonably quickly how to shoot them down, although they did kill over 6,000 people. Much more serious was the supersonic V2, the first ballistic missile, which also carried a warhead of 1,800lb. There was no defence against the V2 other than destroying the launching sites, which were mobile, unlike those for the V1, which were fixed ramps. The first V2 attacks came in September 1944, and, although they came far too late to affect the result of the war, they were sufficiently worrying for the British government to cover up the fatalities caused by them – around 3,000 Londoners – until much later. Initially, the government reported the missile detonations as gas main explosions, and then as what they were but giving a location well beyond their actual point of impact. The Germans thus altered the range, causing the rockets to land well short of where they were aimed at. At one stage, this provoked Ernest Bevin, Minister of Labour in Churchill's government, to accuse the prime minister of deliberately decoying V2s away from the rich City of London and on to working-class housing in the East End. As it was, the missiles continued to fall on London (and on European cities too) until the last launching sites were overrun in March 1945.

On 30 August, Lieutenant-General Courtney Hodges's First US Army encircled and forced the surrender of six German divisions on the Franco-Belgian border and on 5 September Field Marshal Rundstedt was recalled yet again as Commander-in-Chief West, although there was little he could do to prevent Hodges driving his troops back to the German border at Aachen while Patton's Third US Army took Verdun. However, any idea that German resistance might collapse, as some on the Allied side thought and hoped, was misplaced: the closer German units were pushed back to Germany, the harder they fought, and Allied intelligence reports noted that young officers taken prisoner still believed in final victory.

And then Montgomery did something that was totally out of character: normally cautious, meticulous, painstaking, ponderous, he proposed a lightning thrust to bypass the West Wall, the German frontier defences and make it unnecessary to clear the Germans out of the Scheldt. He planned to drop airborne troops on 17 September to seize a series of bridges over rivers all the way from the Dutch border to the town of Arnhem on the lower Rhine – Operation Market – and then drive an armoured corps along a sixty-mile corridor through German-held territory to link up those bridges – Operation Garden. Having thus outflanked the West Wall, the British would then turn right and penetrate into the heart of the Ruhr, Germany's industrial heartland. Eisenhower approved the plan and gave Montgomery logistical priority for it. It didn't work: the American 82 and 101 Airborne captured their objectives but the British 1 Airborne landed too far away from the bridge at Arnhem and only one battalion got there; their second lift was too late; XXX Corps with its armour took far longer than was planned to get through the corridor and Allied intelligence had failed to pick up, or had ignored, the fact that two SS panzer divisions were refitting in the area. When it all ended in failure with the evacuation of the remnants of the British Airborne division on 25 September, 2,500 dead were left behind and 4,500 went into captivity.

Montgomery made sure that no stain attached to him, blaming Lieutenant-General Sir Richard O'Connor,* who was in command of one of the flanking corps, and continued to protect his longtime toady Lieutenant-General Brian Horrocks, commanding XXX Corps, to whom, after Montgomery himself, the blame should really have been attached. Montgomery then had O'Connor sacked in November, allegedly for not being sufficiently tough with the commanders of American units under his command. With Market Garden a failure – and it is difficult to see what it could have achieved even if it had succeeded – the Allies were still without Antwerp, and its clearance had been put back by several weeks.

On the German side, Rundstedt thought that, if he could only delay the Allies until the onset of bad weather, then there would be a chance to go on to the offensive again, while Hitler and many of the officers at OKW were convinced that the Anglo-American alliance with the Soviets could not last. Rundstedt was facing forty-eight Allied divisions plus the Free French over a front of 300 miles from the River Scheldt to the Swiss border, with his own panzer divisions able to muster only five or ten tanks each and with only eleven infantry and four motorized divisions up to strength and capable of offensive action. The West Wall had never been the obstacle that the Allies feared it would be, but now the Todt Organization, Hitler Youth and other party organizations were working on it under the supervision of the Gauleiters and local military headquarters. Additionally, towns that lay in the path of the Allied advance were declared fortresses, as were the Channel ports, to be held to the last, rear areas were being combed out for men who could be sent to the front, and stragglers were being rounded up and fed in as reinforcements.

Eventually, on 28 November 1944, the Allies were at last able to get a naval convoy into Antwerp, and, with the supply situation now eased somewhat, Eisenhower's next priority was to get a bridgehead across the Rhine. But the Germans still had a powerful shot in their locker.

---

*After being captured in North Africa, O'Connor had escaped from an Italian POW camp. Had he not been captured, he would almost certainly have commanded Eighth Army instead of Montgomery and much inter-Allied squabbling might have been avoided.

THE HOME WAR

After the war, it was in the interests of all those who had lived under German or Italian occupation to present themselves as having actively resisted, or at least not to have collaborated. The tongue-in-cheek comment that until 1944 in France there were 40 million collaborators and after 1944 there were 40 million resistance fighters is an exaggeration, but it makes the point that in most occupied countries the bulk of the population were concerned with surviving, with their own lives and with those of their families, and, whatever they may have thought of the occupiers, they tended to keep their heads down and stay out of trouble.

German occupation varied widely depending on the country: in general terms, it was fair but firm in the West and ranged from mildly brutal to utterly bestial in the East. The inhabitants of Western European countries were seen as either racially akin (Scandinavia, Holland, Flemish Belgium) or not so far removed as to fall into the racially inferior category (France, Wallonia). In Poland and the Soviet Union, however, the Slav populations were generally *Untermenschen* – 'subhumans' – to be exploited without regard to legal niceties, or indeed common decency, while active partisan activity in the Balkans meant that there too control measures were harsh. In large parts of the Soviet Union the Germans were initially seen as liberators from the hated Russian or communist yoke and as we have seen it was one of the major errors of the German government and Wehrmacht that they did not tap into this. They did employ large numbers of Crimean Tatars, Ukrainians and Latvians as military auxiliaries, although the Latvians and other citizens of the Baltic States who came into German employ were mainly of German ethnic origin. In Poland, ethnic Germans, now German citizens, were conscripted into the army like any other German, but large numbers of ethnic Poles were also employed, ex-soldiers to whom a uniform, pay and three square meals was vastly more attractive than languishing in a prisoner-of-war camp.

While the image of the Italians, at least in British minds, is one of harmless accordion-playing and Chianti-drinking military incompetents, their occupations were in fact remarkably harsh. In areas of Libya that had been overrun by the British and then reoccupied by the Axis, the Italian authorities shot large numbers of Jews (mainly Italian Jews but some French as well) and Arabs whom they suspected (often correctly) of driving Italian colonists off their land in British-controlled areas. Italian attitudes to Jews varied: in Libya they happily exterminated them, yet in the sliver of France occupied by Italy the Italians refused to hand over the Jews living there to either the *Milice Française** or to the Germans for deportation to extermination camps in the East. In Italy itself Mussolini did agree to deport his Jews but the machinery for doing so worked so slowly that very few actually went.

It is, though, the French Resistance that has attracted the most post-war coverage on the page and screen, but it has to be said that much of this is fiction. The fall of France in 1940 came as a mind-numbing shock to most French men and women, who thought that the British had left them in the lurch, had never heard of the obscure brigadier-general who broadcast to them from London and in the main pinned their faith on Marshal Pétain, the hero of Verdun who had been brought back from his post as ambassador to Spain to be deputy prime minister and then head of state and who negotiated the surrender. To many, perhaps most, Frenchmen, Pétain had maintained France as a nation, still with her empire, still with her fleet and still allowed an army of 100,000. It was true that the north-western *départements*, Nord and Pas de Calais, were governed directly by the German military administration in Belgium; that three fifths of the country, including the area around Paris and the coastal strip, was occupied by German troops; that the portion of Lorraine and all of Alsace that were German between 1871 and 1918 were annexed to the Reich with its men (generally not unhappily) conscripted into the German army, and that France was required to pay US$10m per day towards the occupation costs; but nevertheless nearly half the country was not occupied, the Church was not unhappy to see the demise of the anti-clerical Third Republic and Papa Pétain would surely ensure that all would be well in the end.

---

*The paramilitary security police of the Vichy regime, set up in January 1943.

Indeed, Pétain's government, based in Vichy, was not established by a coup nor forced on France by the Germans but was a perfectly legal government recognized by most of the world including the United States and most of the British Dominions and by the UK until Vichy broke off diplomatic relations after the British attack on the French fleet in Mers el Kebir in July 1940. Even then, unofficial contact was maintained and the British assured the Vichy regime that they would permit the French to retain their empire after the war, would not appropriate French colonies and would allow France to import food from her North African colonies through the British blockade. In return, Vichy promised not to attempt to recover the colonies that had gone over to de Gaulle and not to allow the rest of the French fleet to pass into German hands. The fiction that Vichy ruled not only unoccupied France but the occupied portion as well was maintained, and outwardly that was true in so far as the civil administration was concerned, but behind the scenes in occupied France gendarmes and civil servants who did not act as the Germans wished were swiftly removed.

Most Frenchmen assumed that Britain could not long outlast their own surrender: after all, if the Germans could beat the finest army in Europe – that of the French – how could the puny British Army possibly resist? The Royal Navy would be destroyed by the Luftwaffe and Britain would have to make what accommodation she could, and in fact around 20,000 Frenchmen volunteered for the SS, in either the Charlemagne Division or the French Storm Brigade. It was the French who first used the term collaboration, but, far from having the pejorative connotation attached to the word now, then it simply meant cooperation. In occupied France there were those – not all of them fascists – who welcomed a German victory, whose future depended on it and who worked enthusiastically to ensure it, as allowing a regeneration of France from the old corrupt and incompetent democratic regime, and who saw a future French nation as having a major part to play in a German-dominated Europe. In Vichy, while the fact of French defeat in war was accepted, collaboration only went as far as to ensure the survival of a French state, although as the war went on the little independence given to Pétain was constantly whittled away. Vichy France very quickly introduced anti-Jewish laws – and its ministers were at pains to point out that these owed nothing to the Germans – which were actually stricter than the Nuremberg Laws. The latter defined a Jew as someone who had at least three Jewish grandparents and who practised the Jewish religion, whereas Vichy's rule required only two grandparents and converts were not exempt. While Vichy did not run its own extermination programme, it cooperated wholeheartedly by rounding up Jews in the unoccupied zone and returning those who fled from the German-controlled areas.

Active, as opposed to passive, resistance to the Germans came only slowly, and, when it did, it was divided and expended more time in squabbles between the various groups than it did in opposing the occupiers. Up to June 1941 the French Communist Party, which was persecuted by Pétain's government but sizeable none the less, supported Germany in accordance with the Molotov–Ribbentrop Pact; thereafter, when it did start to organize anti-German resistance, its members were hunted down by the Germans and by Vichy. To begin with, the methods were simple: the writing of graffiti on walls, then the publication of clandestine newspapers and eventually the assassination of Germans waiting for a train or shopping, actions which inevitably attracted reprisals in the shooting of hostages, these latter drawn from the many communists already detained by the French government on the outbreak of war. In due course the communist groups coalesced into the *Front National*, but they were not the only organization. There were *Combat*, based in Marseilles and run by an ex-army officer; *Libération*, based in Lyons and headed by an ex-navy officer; *Franc-Tireur*, based in Avignon and made up of leftist Catholics; *Sabotage-Fer*, whose speciality was derailing German troop trains; and the *Maquis*, originally young men hiding from compulsory forced labour in Germany but whose numbers were swelled by officers of the Vichy army, disbanded when Germany occupied all of France after the Torch landings.

These were the main groupings but there were many others, some locally based, some centred on political parties or determined by religious or class affiliation. All were jealous of their own areas of expertise and of the territory in which they worked, lacked cohesion, were suspicious of each other and, initially at least, lacked structure and organization. Most were particularly contemptuous of any attempt from London to direct their activities, whether by British or American agents or by de Gaulle's Free French, and, despite the setting up of the *Conseil National de la Résistance* in London in 1943, it took another six months before the main resistance groups in France agreed to be part of it – and, crucially, to accept that it would be de Gaulle and his Free French who would form a French government once the Germans had been driven out. Despite the publicity given to acts of resistance at the time and since, it is probable that their military contribution was slight, although their attacks on roads and railways prior to and just after Overlord did hamper German movement up to a point. After the war, General of Artillery Walter Warlimont, who had been Deputy Chief of the Armed Forces Operations Staff at OKW, was asked what effect the Resistance had had on German military operations. 'What resistance?' was his reply. The achievement and legacy of French resistance, therefore, was in ensuring an agreed government of liberated France, rather than the civil war that many feared.

* * *

In the case of Denmark, the German invasion of the country in April 1940 did not involve a declaration of war by either side. A German ultimatum was presented, the Danish parliament spent four hours debating it and then accepted it. As there was no war, there was no surrender, and the fiction that German troops were in Denmark to guarantee that country's neutrality was accepted, at least on the surface. For the first three and a half years, it was a mild occupation: the king remained as head of state and rode around the streets of his capital without an escort conversing with his people; the Social Democrat (socialist in British terms) government continued to function almost as normal; the courts and the judicial system carried on; and, although the army was reduced from 7,000 to 2,000, the police remained Danish and were actually increased and given more weapons. Political parties were tolerated, including the communists, free elections were held (in March 1943 the Danish Nazis got 2 per cent of the vote), Danish Jews were protected or hidden and strict orders were given to German troops in regard to their behaviour towards Danes, whose honour they were not to impugn and whose women they were to respect. In return, Denmark, with a population of 4 million, exported enough food to feed 9 million Germans.

The fate of Denmark could be favourably compared to the rumours that were creeping back about what was going on in Poland, and 10,000 Danes joined the German army or the Waffen SS, including the government-sanctioned *Freikorps Danmark* that served on the Eastern Front with heavy casualties. Initially, all went well. Then, as the war went on, German requirements became more stringent, including the transfer of workers to German armaments factories, the suppression of the Danish communists and demands for the handover of Danish Jews. Minor acts of sabotage began, workers went on strike, and people began to boycott German goods. All this was stirred up and encouraged by SOE agents inserted by the British and in August 1943, after the Danish government refused to allow German troops to search for Danish saboteurs, the Germans imposed direct rule and took over the entire administration of the country themselves. This, not unnaturally, led to a reversal in public perception, hitherto still prepared to cooperate with the Germans in return for minimal interference, and now strikes became general and sabotage increased with the blowing up of bridges, the blocking of railway lines and the circulation of over 200 newssheets urging non-cooperation and resistance. When the Germans sent an SS Police battalion into Denmark in October 1943 to arrest and deport the Jews for extermination, the Danes slipped 7,000 across to neutral Sweden* and hid the rest. The Germans found fewer than 500. When the Germans began a round-up of those whom they suspected of organized resistance, in March 1945 the RAF mounted one of the most extraordinary raids of the war: using Mosquitos, it precision-bombed the Gestapo headquarters in Copenhagen, destroying its records section and allowing thirty-two of the thirty-eight prisoners held there to escape.

While German occupation of Denmark was benign for most of its tenure, that was not the case in Norway, where the German invasion had been resisted and the tiny, militia-based Norwegian Army had fought bitterly. At first, though, the Germans attempted a policy of peaceful cooperation – after all, the Norwegians, like the Danes, were Aryans and could surely understand that what mattered was the eradication of communism. The German concern was to control the long Norwegian coastline and there was a constant – and totally unfounded – fear of invasion that caused them to increase the occupation army from 100,000 to 250,000 in mid-1942. With a government-in-exile in London encouraging resistance, acts of sabotage increased, as did the killing of German soldiers and officials, leading to the inevitable reprisals and equally inevitable increase in acts of resistance. In January 1942 the formation under German auspices of a Norwegian government headed by Vidkun Quisling, a Norwegian National Socialist in whom very few of his countrymen had any confidence, and the elimination of the population of the village of Televaag in a reprisal for sabotage attacks finally killed any chance the Germans might have had in retaining at least a quiescent Norway.

---

*Sweden was neutral in favour of Germany, but that did not extend to handing over Jews.

About 6,000 Norwegians joined the SS, serving mainly in the Viking division, but most were unenthusiastic, particularly when America, where many Norwegians had relatives, entered the war.

The Dutch, a peaceful and deeply moral people with a strong strain of Calvinism who had stayed out of the First World War, were deeply offended by the German invasion of their country. They had given sanctuary to the Kaiser in 1918 and were linguistically and racially German – how dare this vulgarian Adolf Hitler behave as he had done? To begin with, the Germans trod carefully; they hoped that the Dutch could be persuaded to become allies, they released Dutch prisoners of war and they did not interfere with the machinery of government run by state secretaries who had been appointed before the Queen and her government had departed for London. Dutch factories worked happily for the German war effort and exports of food and raw materials to the Reich went on as normal. There was a Dutch National Socialist Party, led by Anton Mussert, but he had little support in Holland and was held in little regard by the Germans. When the Germans attempted a round-up of Dutch Jews in February 1941, there was a strike and a refusal by university staff to continue in office once Jewish lecturers had been dismissed. Then, after Stalingrad, everything changed. Germany was gearing up for total war and this meant the exploitation of all the occupied countries.

Attempts to Nazify the Netherlands, promote Dutch Nazis and carry out anti-Semitic measures caused widespread anger, and resistance encouraged by the government-in-exile increased. When the Germans attempted to arrest and re-intern previously released Dutch prisoners of war, there was a general strike, which was put down with great severity, but the Germans did stop the arrests. The execution of saboteurs caused particular outrage in a country where the death penalty had been abolished seventy years before and many young men went underground to avoid the forced labour introduced in 1943. In September 1944 the government-in-exile ordered a national rail strike to coincide with Operation Market Garden, a strike which continued for the rest of the war, and in retaliation the Germans banned the movement of foodstuffs by road or canal, with the result that perhaps as many as 15,000 Dutch died of starvation during the winter of 1944/45. To their great credit, the Dutch did their best to prevent their Jews being deported to the concentration camps, with mixed success. In a small country like the Netherlands everybody knew everybody else's business and concealing people on the run was not easy; nor was there a hinterland into which they could escape. The Germans deported 104,000 Dutch Jews to camps in Poland and eastern Germany, and around 36,000 were hidden in attics and allotment sheds or by being given false identities. Recruiting for the SS was admittedly more successful in Holland than in any other Western European country, but many of those joining did so in order to avoid being drafted to Germany as forced labourers, others because they believed in a pan-Germanic Europe which would give Holland the Flemish-speaking parts of Belgium. In all, 50,000 volunteers joined various SS units, including the Dutch Legion commanded by Lieutenant-General Seyffart, lately the Chief of Staff of the Dutch Army, whose tenure was short as he was promptly assassinated by one of the Dutch resistance groups. Another SS unit formed in Holland was the SS *Wachbataillon Nordwest*, which had six Dutch companies and one of Ukrainian volunteers, and accepted recruits up to the age of forty for duty as guards in concentration camps in Holland, whose occupants were largely uncooperative Dutch academics or suspected saboteurs.

Whereas the Dutch head of state and government had departed before the Germans arrived, Leopold, the King of the Belgians, insisted that it was his duty to share the sufferings of his people and as Commander-in-Chief of the army he demanded to be taken prisoner. The Germans obliged, confining him to his palace, Laaken Castle on the outskirts of Brussels, with a staff of twenty and 100 servants. Like Holland, Belgium at first complied and cooperated. Forty thousand Belgians joined the German forces, the Flamands the SS and the Walloons, who were not considered sufficiently Aryan, the German army, but they too were later incorporated into the SS. Despite the return to Germany of those frontier areas ceded to Belgium after the first war, the Belgian administration carried on with a relatively light German touch on the tiller now and then; Belgian industry worked happily for the Germans and exports of food and raw materials continued. Apart from the early stages of the war when there were food shortages (and a thriving black market), the civilian population was not greatly discommoded by occupation, at least to begin with. The Germans released Flemish prisoners of war (they kept the Walloons locked up), right-wing Belgian organizations, mainly Flemish, pointed out Belgian Jews for deportation and the churches were treated with respect and allowed to function provided sermons did not become too critical of German policies. Resistance grew but slowly, initially led by ex-army officers and, even before the German attack on the USSR, Belgian communists, but the imposition of the conscription of labour provided an increasing stream of recruits for the various anti-German organizations. While the Belgian resistance achieved little militarily, its running of clandestine escape routes for shot-down Allied airmen and its seizure of the port of Antwerp before the Germans could destroy the facilities were useful contributions to the war effort. At the end of the war, however, it was Belgium that put on trial a larger proportion of its population as having collaborated than any other occupied country in the West.

In the Channel Islands, the only part of the British homeland to be occupied, there was effectively no organized resistance. The Royal Navy had removed 30,000 civilians, including most able-bodied males to the mainland before the Germans arrived, leaving a population of 60,000 behind. Policemen and civil servants were ordered to stay at their posts, and were generally well treated. Many of those not belonging to the administration were not well treated, however, and endured a hungry and much restricted existence with fines and detention imposed for breach of the occupier's rules. Civilians found hiding Russian prisoners of war brought in to build defences were deported to Germany, as were a number of the islands' Jews. Even today, the part played by the local British administration in that deportation is contentious.

* * *

While the German occupation in the West, the conscription of labour (for which the labourers were paid) aside, was generally firm but reasonably fair if the inhabitant was not a Jew and did not attempt to oppose the conquerors, the same cannot be said of the East. In Poland those of ethnic German origin became German citizens and were subject to military service, Jews were put into concentration camps and many exterminated, and ordinary Poles were treated as the subhumans NSDAP ideology said they were. Resistance was inevitable and came to a head with the Warsaw Rising of 1944. In the Protectorate of Bohemia and Moravia, that part of the erstwhile Czechoslovakia that was not hived off to Germany or incorporated into the puppet state of Slovakia, the occupation was much less harsh than in neighbouring Poland, largely because the Germans were keen to make use of its agricultural and industrial potential, in particular Skoda, one of Europe's most advanced arms manufacturing firms. The Germans ruled through existing Czech administrative channels and resistance was very slow to appear and, when it did, was of little military value, although the intelligence it transmitted to London was to prove of considerable help. Student demonstrations in favour of Czech independence led to the closure of the universities and the shooting of the ringleaders, but the most obvious act of resistance was the assassination of the German governor, Reinhard Heydrich, in May 1942 by two Czechs parachuted in from England. Heydrich, best known as the architect of the Final Solution, may well have been a monster but he was no fool, and he fully understood the importance of keeping the Czech people if not actively onside then at least acquiescent, which was all the more reason for the Allies to have him removed. The assassination attracted brutal reprisals, including the complete destruction of two villages, Lidice and Lezaky, and the shooting of virtually all their inhabitants, which acted as a recruiting stimulus for the underground, such as it was. Later, a rising in Prague in 1945 as the Red Army approached did hinder the German defence and probably forced them to withdraw earlier than they otherwise would have done.

Resistance in Russia was almost entirely by partisan warfare, and warfare it undoubtedly was, with the partisans armed and directed by officers of the Red Army and engaged in attacks on German outposts, ambushes of convoys, sabotage of roads and railways and the killing of any German they could find. No mercy was shown by either side and the activities of the partisans meant that very large numbers of German troops were tied down guarding the lines of communication when they could have been used to far greater effect at the front. Despite the appalling treatment meted out to civilians in the path of their advance through the USSR, the Germans found many willing volunteers and auxiliaries from amongst the non-Russian minorities and ethnic Russians who had no love for the communist system, or who simply wanted to stay alive. Over 60,000 volunteers from the USSR served in the SS and up to 750,000 in *Hilfswilliger* or 'voluntary assistant' units of the German army: Russians, Byelorussians, Georgians, Azerbaijanis, Turcomans, Uzbeks, Cossacks and Ukrainians all served and suffered for it after the war, while volunteers from the Baltic States included 80,000 from Latvia, 25,000 from Estonia and 50,000 from Lithuania.

In the Balkans, the German occupation that followed Berlin's need to bail out the Italians met with much opposition and a civil war, and repressive measures were harsh. Even here, though, the Germans found men prepared to fight for them: 20,000 from Croatia, 10,000 from Serbia, and 7,000 from Albania. In what had been Yugoslavia, the Croat fascists – the Ustashe – set up a client state cooperating wholeheartedly with the Germans provided that they were allowed to slaughter anyone who was not Croat and Roman Catholic, while armed resistance was provided by the Cetniks commanded by the Serb Colonel Draža Mihailović, who wanted to return to a Serb-dominated monarchy after the war, and the partisans, commanded by Josip Broz, cover name Tito, the Croat head of the Yugoslav Communist Party, who wanted a communist republic allied to the Soviet Union. Both men were typical of their race: mercurial, murderous, treacherous and happy to shift their loyalty to whatever seemed temporarily expedient. With both the Italians and the Germans occupying their respective areas, the two resistance groups fought each other, the Germans and the Italians, or cooperated with Germans or Italians against each other. The Allies originally supported Mihailović but later, from September 1943, switched their support to Tito, on the grounds that he was killing more Germans. That Tito had negotiated with the Germans to jointly oppose a (mistakenly) expected British landing in the spring of 1943 was conveniently passed over, as by now Tito was fighting the Germans, the Italians and the Cetniks, while the latter seemed to be avoiding fighting anyone but waiting for an Allied landing. Despite being from time to time far too friendly with the Italians, and even the Germans, Mihailović did continue to look after Allied airmen on the run and never betrayed the British and American agents who came into his hands. He did not deserve to be executed after a show trial in 1946.

Across the border in Greece, there were a large number of resistance groups, as one might expect of the Greeks. Most were republican to a greater or lesser degree, ranging from those who would reluctantly permit the king to return if a majority plebiscite approved it, to by far the largest and most effective, ELAS, which was communist and unsurprisingly wanted to turn Greece into a communist republic. The occupying power was Italy, at least until its surrender, when the Germans took over, and resistance was military and largely restricted to the hills, where bridges were blown up and Axis troops ambushed. As the Germans could never quite make up their minds whether the Greeks were Balkan mongrels or the inheritors of the Glory That Was Greece, reprisals varied from the ferocious to the merely extreme. Much of the rural population survived at only just above starvation level, and after the war the British government estimated that 85 per cent of Greek children suffered from tuberculosis and up to 1,000 villages had been laid waste. The inability of the various resistance groups to agree the post-war governance of their country meant that the departure of German troops in November 1944 did not end the fighting, which went on until January 1945 and needed the removal of two British divisions from the Italian front to quell it. Even that was not the end of the story, for civil war flared again from 1947 to 1949, when the country was only saved from a communist takeover by military support and a massive injection of cash from Britain and the USA.

* * *

Active resistance everywhere was encouraged by the British to begin with and then by the Americans, but here there were conflicting agendas. Churchill, once prime minister, encouraged the setting up of the Special Operations Executive in July 1940, along with the renamed Combined Operations, which had been established a month earlier as Raiding Operations. Churchill said that SOE was 'to set Europe ablaze' and that Combined Operations was 'to leave a trail of dead Germans behind it'. All this rhetoric conflicted with the more traditional British foreign intelligence organization, MI6, from which SOE was a spin-off, which wanted a quiet Europe with sleepy policemen and lazy occupation troops, so that they could get on with collecting clandestine intelligence. The American equivalent of SOE, the Office of Strategic Services, was established in the summer of 1941 but not given that name until June 1942. Although SOE came under the direction of the Ministry of Economic Warfare, other organizations from the Chiefs of Staff, the Foreign Office, Bomber Command and local commanders-in-chief had an interest in what SOE was up to, which often restricted and infuriated its strong-minded and frequently eccentric members. Both SOE and OSS attempted to run agents in occupied countries, to arm, train and direct the various resistance movements where they existed, and raise them where they did not. Clandestine agents inserted into enemy-controlled territory were well aware of the risks they were taking: legally spies, they could perfectly properly be executed, as were German agents caught in the United Kingdom. The latter were shot by firing squad, usually in the moat of the Tower of London, having been first given the option of being turned and sending back false information provided by the British. Many of them did agree to cooperate with their new masters, although to their credit some, usually officers of the German armed forces, did not and they paid the price.

By 1944 SOE could field around 13,000 agents, of whom 3,000 were female, and was supported by 40,000 RAF air and ground crew, as the chief method of insertion, supply and extraction was by air. Its operatives were active around the world, except in the Soviet Union, where, although it had a liaison office, the NKVD told it nothing and permitted it to do nothing. Communications were usually by short-wave radio, which had the range to get back to the nearest Allied territory but could be pinpointed by radio direction-finding. Operators had to keep moving and keep transmissions short, and of those caught red-handed by the Germans or Italians most were radio operators. While the Germans were not good at foreign intelligence, they were very good at infiltration of Allied networks in occupied or neutral countries: most of the SOE (and OSS) agents they caught were betrayed by a member of a resistance cell who had been turned. In Holland, the German counter-intelligence Abwehr and the security service, the SD, penetrated the SOE and MI6 operation very early on and from March 1942 until November 1943 virtually controlled it as *Fall Nordpol* or *das Englandspiel*, capturing most of the agents parachuted into that country. Altogether, fifty-four SOE and MI6 agents and an unknown number of Dutch civilians were executed and around fifty RAF aircrew were killed when their aircraft were ambushed and shot down or caught on the ground. Probably the most useful act of sabotage by SOE was the destruction in February 1943 of a heavy water plant in Norway, essential for the control of a nuclear reactor, after a Combined Operations mission the previous year had failed.

Although the Combined Operations Directorate often worked with or cooperated with SOE, it was in fact an entirely separate organization and operated in a more conventional manner, mainly by undertaking small-scale amphibious raids on enemy coastlines, using Royal Marines and specially raised army commandos for the purpose. Many of these raids were spectacular and looked good in the press, but proved of little value to the war effort. Blowing up a fish-oil factory in Norway might irritate the Germans but was hardly likely to keep Hitler lying awake at night in a cold sweat wondering what was coming next. On the other hand, the destruction in March 1942 of the dry dock at St Nazaire, the biggest in Europe and the only one that could accommodate the *Tirpitz*, meant that the one remaining modern German battleship stayed in a Norwegian fjord and rarely ventured out for the rest of the war. Combined Operations' biggest raid was that on Dieppe in August 1942, involving 6,000 soldiers, mainly from the Canadian 1 Division, with naval and air elements. For all sorts of reasons, including faulty intelligence, bad security, lack of sufficient naval firepower and air support, and the inability of the tanks to get off the beaches, it was a disaster. Mountbatten, then Chief of Combined Operations with a seat on the Chiefs of Staff Committee, survived the fiasco, and Montgomery, who shared at least some of the responsibility, had gone to North Africa. The Dieppe Raid happened at a time when Stalin and the Americans were pressing the British for a second front on the ground in Europe, when the British knew very well that there were neither enough landing craft nor enough men to effect a landing that would have a reasonable chance of success. The cynic might wonder whether the British knew very well that Dieppe would fail but mounted it anyway to prove their point.

Combined Operations' raids were carried out by soldiers, sailors and airmen who were usually in uniform, and thus under the protection of the laws of war and entitled to be treated as prisoners of war, but in October 1942 Hitler ordered that any commandos captured in action were to be shot and, if captured otherwise, were to be handed over to the SD and then shot. What appears to have happened is that during the Dieppe Raid German prisoners had their hands tied, in contravention of the Geneva Convention. This angered the Germans, who ordered Canadians in German prison camps to be shackled as a result, whereupon the British duly replied in kind. Eventually, common sense prevailed and a mutual unshackling was brokered by the Red Cross. Then, in October 1942, in a raid on the island of Sark in the Channel Islands, the Germans claimed that four of their soldiers were snatched, had grass stuffed in their mouths to stop them alerting their comrades and their hands tied behind their backs. When they were being taken to the waiting British boat, three broke free and tried to escape. Two were shot and one knifed. All this, if true, was also a breach of the laws relating to the treatment of prisoners and Hitler's Commando Order was the result. It was actually hardly ever carried out, German soldiers being well aware of the rules of war, although it was followed in the case of the Operation Freshman raid on Norway in November 1942, when Combined Operations sent two glider-loads of Royal Engineers to Norway to blow up the Vemork hydroelectric plant, which produced heavy water. The gliders crashed and the survivors, despite the fact they were in uniform, were shot. If Combined Operations men were caught not in uniform, it depended upon who caught them. Capture by the Gestapo or by the French *Milice*, who usually handed such prisoners over to the Gestapo, normally meant a bullet and a quick trip to an unmarked grave, whereas capture by the German army meant there was a fair chance of survival, even if the law was not entirely clear: execution was permitted for saboteurs and spies, but escaping soldiers in civilian clothes were entitled to protection provided they carried no weapons.

Many of the operations launched under the aegis of successive Directors Combined Operations, Admiral of the Fleet Sir Roger Keyes, Vice-Admiral Lord Louis Mountbatten and Major-General Robert Laycock, seem to have been planned in the manner of a schoolboy who knows that his chum whom he has persuaded to lock the headmaster in his study is going to get six of the best for his trouble, but assures him that the fun will be worth it. There was often little thought given to the recovery of the raiders, nor the training that they might need in order to evade capture. Indeed, in Operation Freshman, the glider-borne sappers were supposed to meet local SOE agents, blow up the heavy water plant and then escape to neutral Sweden. Sweden was 200 miles away; the men had no training in skiing and did not speak Norwegian. Even if, against all the odds, they had got to Sweden, the Swedes at that stage of the war would have been far more likely to hand them over to the Germans, or at best intern them for the rest of the war, than allow them safe return to England.

Another occasion when the Commando Order was implemented was in December 1942, when Operation Frankton saw a group of Royal Marines, later popularized as the 'Cockleshell Heroes', being launched from a submarine at the mouth of the River Gironde, whence they were to canoe into Bordeaux harbour and attach limpet mines to a number of ships carrying war materials for Germany. Having done that, they were expected to escape across occupied France by a circuitous route into neutral but pro-German Spain, and then to Gibraltar, a distance of 1,500 miles. Only the officer commanding could speak any French, and, while they succeeded in placing their mines and doing considerable damage to shipping, of the twelve Marines involved, two damaged their canoe on launch and took no part, two overturned in the tidal race and were drowned, six were betrayed or otherwise captured and executed, and only Major Herbert Hasler and Marine William Sparks managed to get over the Pyrenees and reach safety in Gibraltar.

Except on very rare occasions, such as when they were attached to partisans in Italy or the Balkans, SOE agents, by the clandestine nature of their role, could not wear uniform and if caught were liable to torture and execution, particularly if they happened to be nationals of the country in which they were working. While SOE had many British agents who were fluent in the language of the country to which they were sent, and could get away with it if questioned casually by an Italian or a German, very few of them could fool a native speaker so bilingual operatives or nationals of the country to which they were sent were often preferred, once they had passed rigorous security checks. British agents in a European country had a reasonable chance of survival (of the 470 sent to France, 117 were killed or otherwise died[85]), but in Asian countries (Burma, Hong Kong, Malaya) they had to lie very low indeed. Only in Germany and Japan were SOE unable to operate – the population were firmly behind their leaders and their police, and the security forces were just too thorough. Not all agreed with what SOE were doing; the 'conventional' intelligence services were suspicious, at least at first, and Bomber Command was always reluctant to divert any assets away from its primary role of dropping very large amounts of high explosive on the German homeland. SOE was, however, unique amongst government departments in peace or war in that it showed a budget surplus when it was wound up in January 1946, largely by an operation which bought luxury watches in occupied France and diamonds from de Beers and then sold them in China at a huge mark-up, the justification being that it not only made friends with influential Chinese but provided the finance for other operations more directly concerned with the war effort.

Details of much of what SOE and its junior colleague OSS did were never written down, and of what was recorded some was destroyed after the war and some was not declassified until relatively recently. This lack of evidence in the public domain has given rise to animated debate as to what the results of SOE's operations were, and how much they contributed to winning the war. No one would claim that organizations such as SOE could win a war all by themselves; like guerrillas, they can only operate either against an enemy already fatally weakened or in support of a conventional force, but by tying down Axis troops that would otherwise be at the front in the guarding of ammunition dumps, railways, bridges and factories, by maintaining the fiction that an invasion of Norway was a possibility, by encouraging those who wanted to resist against occupation and by providing the weapons, the communications and the training to allow them to do so, the handful of men and women deployed around the globe amply repaid the investment in them.

* * *

It is part of the heroic myth of Britain in the Second World War that everyone pulled together, helped each other and was steadfast in their determination to beat the Nazis and fascists and stick it out, come what may. That vision was helpful at the time and has sustained Britain's perception of herself since, but it is far from the whole story. For the first time in her history, Britain embarked on total war – that is, with everything subservient to the war effort – from the earliest days. Unlike in the first war, conscription was introduced from the outset, and those too old, too young, too unfit or in civilian occupations considered essential to the war effort could join the Home Guard, the Air Raid Precaution service, the Observer Corps or any of the myriad voluntary organizations, many of which made no contribution whatsoever but allowed people to think they were doing their bit. While the television series *Dad's Army* is not entirely accurate, there is much truth in it, and Home Guard units varied from the hopelessly incompetent to the vaguely useful in their role of providing static guards against parachutists and saboteurs who never came. When war broke out, the Defence of the Realm Act (DORA) last used between 1914 and 1918 was wheeled out again, giving the authorities powers that the Gestapo would have welcomed. At first, only enemy aliens considered to be a security risk were interned; others were permitted to return to their home country or allowed to stay where they were.* After Dunkirk, invasion scares and fears of Fifth Columnists led to all such individuals being interned, in makeshift camps, mainly on the Isle of Man but with some being shipped to Canada and Australia. When this caused protests about over-reaction, common sense prevailed and a review led to a large number of the internees (many of whom were refugees from Germany or Italy in the first place) being released. Meanwhile, the imposition of food rationing, essential to a nation that imported a large proportion of its food, produced probably the healthiest generation of Britons ever, in that the ration was carefully balanced and contained what was needed rather than what was necessarily liked, but it also led to a thriving black market, hoarding and smuggling. Restaurants

---

*In this author's village, the proprietor of the local ice cream shop, a fat and jolly Italian who had been there for years but had never changed his nationality, was hauled off and locked up, to the dismay of the villagers. It was widely believed that this had been engineered by his brother, who had British nationality and wanted to take over the business.

and cafés stayed open and served meals, albeit with restricted menus, and gave rise to the claim that the rich could eat what they liked while the poor had to subsist on the ration.

The blackout in cities, where all street lights were extinguished, car headlights dimmed and windows covered to give no assistance to German bombers, inevitably led to an increase in traffic accidents, burglaries and what would now be described as muggings, with a commensurate decrease in the number of young, fit police officers to deal with them. Civil executions for murder went up from a total of forty-three in the five years 1935 to 1939, to sixty-three in the five years 1940 to 1944. The damage caused by air raids and the dispersal of the population into air-raid shelters provided ample opportunity for looting, which was hushed up as far as possible but punished in an increasingly draconian manner.* The existing criminal population, or that part of it which had not been conscripted, was swollen by those who did not see it as their patriotic duty to serve and had deserted, living in a shadow world but knowing full well that, whatever the Army Act said, they were not going to be executed. It has been estimated that, once the war got going, there were at any one time up to 20,000 deserters from the armed forces,[86] and, although many of these had left their units to solve a domestic problem, or to avoid punishment for some offence or were actually Absent Without Leave,† life as a genuine deserter was difficult: no ration book, no identity card, no possibility of legal employment, no benefits, and no going anywhere near home, where all police stations would have the man's description. Only if the fugitive could be absorbed by the existing criminal underworld would he be relatively safe: the black market in stolen or forged ration books and identity cards was buoyant. The use of firearms in the commission of a crime was relatively rare in pre-war England: now, with deserters often bringing their weapons with them, it increased. Deserters who knew their way into military vehicle depots were particularly valued by

---

*At a recent university seminar based on Angus Calder's *The People's War*, a mature student decried the 'blitz spirit' and asserted that her father had been in the London Fire Brigade during the war and had been jailed for stealing from bomb-damaged houses.

†A deserter absents himself with the intention of never returning; to be AWOL is a less serious offence where the offender does intend to return. A soldier miles away from his unit wearing civilian clothes and claiming to be a merchant seaman on leave would be odds on to be convicted of desertion. A soldier who walks out with a pass, gets drunk and falls asleep in a ditch and misses the next day's parade is AWOL.

the criminal gangs, as from the summer of 1942 the previously tiny ration of petrol for the private motorist was abolished altogether.

Class warfare has always been a popular British sport, and the policy of the evacuation to the countryside of children from inner cities vulnerable to German air raids forced the middle classes, who were in the main the recipients of the evacuees, to take a long, hard look at the lower working (or not working) classes who provided the bulk of them. Many of the children came from conditions of appalling poverty in rundown slums and were verminous, malnourished, infected with scabies and head lice, and in many cases had never seen or been put in a bath. As bad as the children were, some of the mothers who accompanied them were worse: ill-mannered sluts interested only in going to the pub while neglecting their children. These ragamuffins and slatterns were not the majority, but they were the ones who attracted publicity and criticism, and they split their hosts into two groups: those who wanted to pull up the drawbridge and have nothing to do with the mob, and those who realized that something must be done and who supported the Beveridge Report when it came out in late 1942. Sir William Beveridge was a civil servant, and later a Liberal MP, who had been directed to look at the way the state looked after, or did not look after, its citizens, particularly its needy citizens. His report was the foundation of today's British welfare state and, while many may feel now that it is no longer suitable for twenty-first-century society, it was revolutionary at the time, proposing a cradle-to-grave system of care with a free health service, enhanced unemployment benefits, sick pay, and old age and widows pensions. Allied to it was a raising of the school leaving age to fifteen and free secondary education for all. It was to be financed by a compulsory deduction from wages – National Insurance – and was to produce a standard of living 'below which no one should be allowed to fall', while politically it was being held out as a reward for the British people's efforts and hardships nobly borne. The prime minister and his immediate circle were uninterested – winning the war was all that mattered now, and in any case Churchill was suspicious of anything that smelled of socialism – but a large number of Conservatives and the entire Labour Party did support Beveridge, forcing Attlee to work very hard to prevent a split in the wartime coalition. The recommendations of the report were, of course, subsequently adopted as part of both parties' manifestos for the 1945 election, although many voters felt that the Conservatives were at best lukewarm towards it.

Most countries had a laidback attitude to broadcasting, either letting market forces rule or selling off wavelengths to the highest bidder. Two countries reserved the control of broadcasting to themselves: the Soviet Union and the United Kingdom. From the earliest days of broadcasting, the British government was determined to retain control of the airwaves and the BBC had an absolute monopoly of all radio (and television) broadcasting within the United Kingdom. The BBC carefully nurtured the belief that it always told the truth, regardless of how unpleasant that might be, and it had a huge influence not only in the UK but, particularly as London now housed the kings of Greece, Norway and Yugoslavia, the Queen of the Netherlands, the Grand Duke of Luxembourg and assorted governments-in-exile, in the occupied and neutral countries too – indeed, it might be argued that the BBC achieved more than SOE, OSS and Combined Operations all put together. The BBC did not, of course, tell the unvarnished truth, but it told fewer and smaller lies than Radio Berlin and was trusted more than any other belligerent's radio – including Voice of America.*

One might have thought that in wartime, where every piece of hardware coming out of the factory door could mean the difference between victory and defeat, industrial squabbles and trade union militancy might be put in abeyance for the duration, but this was to prove a vain hope. The shift to total war meant full employment and thus workers and their unions could afford to be more militant without the fear of the sack. In the five years before the war, 1935 to 1939, 10 million man-days were lost to strikes and go-slows; in the five years 1940 to 1944, 9 million were lost, and the most days lost in the whole of that ten-year period were the 3.7 million lost in 1944.[87] While Germany resisted a move to total war in its economy until 1944, the British directed labour from a very early stage, and, when it became apparent that there was a shortage of labour in the coalmines, one in ten of all conscripts was directed towards the mines – the Bevin Boys. While the system tried to send men who were already miners, or who were volunteers, down the mines, there were those who had no objection to putting on a uniform and wielding a rifle but were horrified at the thought of hacking at a coal face hundreds of feet underground. Similarly, by 1942 women between the ages of eighteen and forty were liable to conscription for war work, which led to an upsurge in volunteering for the women's uniformed services as preferable

---

*Although, according to this author's father, James Joyce (Lord Haw Haw) broadcasting from Germany got the English racing and football results out faster than the BBC.

to being directed into a factory. Inevitably, as the calls of home and factory conflicted, absenteeism was rife.

As always in wartime, promiscuity, venereal disease and illegitimate births rose. In an age when efficient contraception hardly existed and bastardy was a disgrace, casual sex other than the commercial variety was much scarcer than it is today, but the plea that the young man was going away and might be dead tomorrow was persuasive. Between 1940 and 1945 the number of illegitimate births increased by over forty percent from the pre-war period.[88] At the end of the war, divorce, far more difficult to achieve then than now, became more common as men who had been away for years returned to find their wives had taken up with other men, or had simply got used to fending for themselves and had grown apart from their husbands. The arrival of large numbers of foreign, Empire and American troops, many with more pay than their British equivalents, led to increases in prostitution, unwanted pregnancies (and illegal abortions) and considerable jealousy: a night spent jitterbugging with a gabardine-attired American and a present of a pair of silk stockings was rather more attractive than a visit to the pictures and a bag of chips with a British soldier in his hairy battledress.

If the British were not all pulling together and singing 'We're Going to Hang Out the Washing on the Siegfried Line', then at least the government knew what the trends of public opinion were. In an early and surprisingly sophisticated exercise in opinion polling, it used Mass-Observation, a commercial organization founded in 1937, to find out what people really thought and used that information to shape opinion or to at least nudge it in the desired direction. Press censorship and the use of cunningly, or often not so cunningly, disguised propaganda in the form of films, posters and radio broadcasts did help to keep the bulk of the population in favour of the war and broadly approving of the government's conduct of it, while an exaggeration of the threat – invasion, parachutists disguised as nuns, the importance of the Home Guard – sufficed to support a broad public consensus even if it only papered over the existing deep divisions in British society. While life for those at home was in many ways bleak – rationing, shortages, blackout, restrictions on movement, increased taxation – it was nevertheless preferable to defeat and occupation, and despite the cracks most people really did think that by fighting on they were doing the right thing, and could at least be united in blaming the war for all manner of problems, including those that had nothing to do with it.

* * *

Unlike Britain, the continental United States did not suffer air raids or mass blackouts, except along the East Coast, or suspension of the electoral process, but she did gear up for war production, and while Britain increased her industrial capacity fourfold and Germany twofold between 1939 and 1945, America increased hers twenty-five-fold. The Second World War finally got the US out of the grip of the Great Depression. In 1940 there were 8 million Americans unemployed, and by the end of 1942 there were virtually none; in 1939 the gross national product was $91bn and in 1945 it was $215bn. The ability of Americans to adapt and convert and improve was truly staggering. In 1940 the British ordered sixty cargo ships to a simple design from American shipyards. Known as Liberty Ships, the first few took 200 days to build – perfectly normal for that time – and then Henry J. Kaiser got involved. Kaiser was an industrialist who was better known for building dams and bridges rather than ships, but in 1942 he acquired shipyards in California, amended the Liberty design, introduced welding rather than riveting and cut the time down, first to forty days and then to an incredible twenty-four. By 1944 the Kaiser yards and others using his methods were turning out an escort carrier every week and the time for a Liberty Ship was down to seventeen days.

For American workers, for American factory owners and for American industry generally, the war came as an economic bonanza, and the United States was the only belligerent country where the standard of living of the population actually rose during the conflict. Farmers, badly hit by the Depression, found that they could sell whatever they produced and, although petrol rationing was three gallons a week for the private motorist, car manufacturers were able to turn their plants to producing Jeeps, DUKWs, trucks, tanks or aircraft. As in Britain, the return of full employment increased the powers of trade unions, and, although the major ones – the American Federation of Labour and the Congress for Industrial Organization – had signed a no-strike agreement, dissatisfaction with controls of wages (which were in reality generous) while profits soared led to 14,000 strikes, involving 7 million workers. However, as employers were doing very well indeed, most of these disputes were simply bought off.

Rationing was sporadic and initially varied by area (petrol was rationed on the East Coast but not in Texas), although it was eventually extended to the whole country. Shoes were rationed to two pairs a year, except for children,

carried by hand. The camps were surrounded by barbed wire, searchlights and armed guards, accommodation was basic and cramped, and ablutions, dining facilities and laundry were communal. In January 1943, however, the US Army announced that it would accept for enlistment *Nisei* volunteers, and 17,000 internees did join. No doubt their motivation was partly to escape the boredom and lack of freedom of the camps, but there was also a feeling that only by fighting for America could they prove their loyalty to their adopted country. Eventually, in December 1944, the Supreme Court ruled that to intern American citizens against whom there was no evidence to indicate disloyalty was unconstitutional and internees began to be released. Many found that their property and businesses had been sequestered by whites who had no intention of giving them back and the legal arguments went on for many years after the war. At the time, the internment of Japanese Americans was generally seen as an unfortunate military necessity, but later it was, and still is, denounced by many as being different only in degree to what the Germans were doing to the Jews.

Meanwhile, the American Civil War had not been fought for the emancipation of the slaves, whatever propaganda value that slogan may have had amongst northern liberals at the time, and on the outbreak of war Negroes, as they were then referred to, were very much second-class citizens and discriminated against in employment, housing, medical care and education. In 1940 there were two black officers in the United States Army and none in the navy. The army was strictly segregated, with separate black regiments with white officers being only rarely used as other than static guards and labour battalions, while the navy only recruited blacks as kitchen hands and mess stewards. More blacks were commissioned as the war went on, but they were rarely placed in command of white troops, and there was a disproportionate number of judicial executions of black soldiers for offences such as rape, still a capital offence in US law and regarded as particularly horrifying if committed by a black on a white. Although there were exceptions – there was a USAAF fighter group composed entirely of black pilots, the so-called 'Tuskegee Airmen', which was a highly commended bomber escort force in Italy – Americans both in and out of uniform were reluctant to see their black citizens involved in combat. The state legislature of South Carolina announced that the war was being fought for White Supremacy, and black emancipation made little outward progress during the war. Labour shortages in some industries did help black employment chances, but it was not until near the end of the war that President Truman ordered the armed forces to move towards full integration. It would not be until after the Korean War that it would be achieved.

* * *

Perhaps surprisingly for a nation where war was regarded by many as a normal extension of the political process, Germany was reluctant to interfere with the traditional norms of society, and a marked lack of enthusiasm for war in 1939 reinforced the government's determination to give the impression of business as usual. As the German strategy was one of short wars and swift victories, this made sense, but, even when it became apparent that a swift end to hostilities had eluded them, NSDAP ministers were reluctant to gear up for total war. A policy of bread and circuses was not confined to the Roman Empire and the NSDAP state made great efforts to encourage public entertainment, to the extent of conscripting actors, musicians, artists and entertainers of both sexes into the Actors War Service Office headed by Goebbels as Reich minister for culture, and keeping cinemas and theatres open. Much use was made of radio, not only for straightforward propaganda designed to keep public opinion behind the war, but in fostering a sense of togetherness by airing interviews with men at the front and by request programmes (one Prussian infantry regiment on the Eastern Front asked for the sound of the bells of Potsdam cathedral to be broadcast – they got it). Rationing was introduced at the start of the war but, as long as the pact with Russia held, there was no shortage of basic foodstuffs, and even after the onset of Barbarossa the British blockade was not as effective as it had been in the first war, not least because it had to cover a far greater area. Food was anyway imported into Germany from the occupied countries, and, once the Ukraine had been taken, its harvest of grain and sugar beet was used to supplement the rations of the armed forces on the Eastern Front. From 1944, however, with the advance of the Red Army and the loss of captured territories, much more severe rationing was introduced, the priority being the armed forces and then those involved in war production. For the rest of the civilian population, the basic ration comprised black rye bread, potatoes, vegetables and limited amounts of meat, usually pork. Those in rural areas fared better than their counterparts in the cities, and, while there was a black market in ration coupons, the introduction of the death sentence for its practitioners kept it under control. As the war went on, new clothes became almost impossible to obtain and new shoes could only be purchased if the old ones were handed in.

There was great reluctance to employ German women in war work – the NSDAP ideal of a racially pure, classless, structured society with the married woman at home producing lots of children rather militated against it – and women whose husbands were away at the front received a family allowance, abated by any money they might earn from employment. Initially women between seventeen and twenty-five who were not married and not in education were encouraged to join the *Reichsarbeitsdienst* or 'Reich Labour Service' for employment as carers for the sick and the old and as home helps, but, as the war went on and casualties on the Eastern Front mounted, women gradually became more and more involved, and in mid-1944 all women between the ages of seventeen and fifty were liable for conscription for war work. By then, in fact, women operated (one hesitates to use the term 'manned') most of the anti-aircraft defence systems within the Reich, as indeed they did in the United Kingdom. Also within the armed services, women were increasingly employed as clerks, radar and radio operators, telephone operators and, of course, nurses. The employment of three female pre-war stunt pilots, one of them being Hanna Reitsch, as flyers by the Luftwaffe was unusual and not repeated, and it was done more for propaganda purposes than because there was any real intention to employ women as combatants.

The dark side of the home war in Germany was the liquidation not just of Jews but of all those deemed useless or racially inferior stock, including the euthanasia of the severely disabled and the incurably mentally ill. The logic for the latter was the removal of the inferior or damaged genes from the breeding pool, but, as this could have been done under an existing German law (one still on the statute book) which required a certificate of medical fitness to marry, the aim could have been achieved without resort to judicial murder. How much the civilian population knew about all this is still debated, but given the number of people involved in the extermination industry, all of whom of course had friends and relatives, it is inconceivable that it was not widely known – the cleverness of the policymakers residing in their ability to convince the public that what they were doing was for the greater good of the nation.

The extraordinary fact is that support for the war, and for Hitler, was strong even up to the end, and it was not all imposed by the fear of being sent off to a concentration camp. Germans believed, and even when they were trying to scratch out a living amidst a heap of rubble, the Russians were coming ever closer, and the young boys and old men of the *Volksturm* were all that stood between them and complete disintegration, they still believed; the tendency was to blame the officials or the advisers rather than Hitler himself, and, even if they had doubts, 'Victory or Siberia' remained a powerful rallying cry. While the upper echelons of society had not been greatly changed by Hitler's Germany – the generals, the men of business, the bureaucrats, the landowners, the upper middle classes stayed much as they were – considerable opportunities had been created lower down. A commission in the army was no longer the prerogative of the aristocracy or the grammar school boy: a young man of humbler origins could now make a career for himself as an officer, and, while he adhered to the professional standards of the old army, unlike it he was politicized and loyal to the regime and to Hitler personally. In this war, unlike the last, there were no mutinies, no individual surrenders of units and no mass desertions, and this applied to the civilian population as much as to the armed forces.

* * *

Italy had neither the industrial base nor the financial muscle to engage in modern war. The bulk of the population had no desire to fight anyone but, if they had to, then, despite resentment over Italy's treatment after the first war, many would have preferred to have been on the side of the Allies. Had Mussolini been able to provide quick victories and obvious economic gains, then public opinion would no doubt have moved from coolness towards the war to wholehearted support for it. But fascist propaganda was unable to disguise a long series of Italian defeats and embarrassments, a pill made doubly difficult to swallow by the knowledge that only German intervention had prevented complete collapse in North Africa, Greece and Yugoslavia. Furthermore, while Italy's African adventures and intervention in the Balkans could both be presented as necessary for the reconstitution of a Roman Empire, few Italians could see any point in sending soldiers to the Russian front, particularly when by February 1943 75,000 had been killed and over 50,000 had been evacuated back to Italy with severe wounds, disease or frostbite.[89] The 11 December 1941 declaration of war on the USA, where large numbers of Italians had relatives, came as a severe shock while Italy's zones of occupation in France and Greece provided no advantages and only administrative headaches.

By European standards, Italy was a poor country even before the war. With a population roughly the same as that of Britain and France, in 1940 Italy's gross national income was one quarter of that of Britain's and one half of that of France. Such wealth that existed was unevenly spread, with poverty endemic in the south and in Sicily, while the higher standards of living in the industrial north did nothing to heal the traditional north–south divide. Corruption and profiteering were widespread, and while the government tried to stamp them out its efforts were dogged by incompetence, not assisted by Mussolini's habit of removing officials deemed to have failed and replacing them with functionaries even less capable. In March 1943 a series of strikes by factory workers protesting against inflation and wage control was bought off by the printing of money, which only increased inflation and did nothing to improve the ability, or inability, of Italian industry to support the war effort, made worse by the high costs of imported raw materials which had to be paid for by scarce hard currency. Once the Allies landed in Sicily, bombing of the Italian mainland, previously relatively light, increased, and, while it never approached the severity of the campaign against Germany, nor did it create anything like the same destruction, to a population unused to direct assault it had a much greater effect on public morale than the actual damage warranted.

Domestic opposition to fascism and to Italy's participation in Germany's war was limited and mainly amongst the communists and the clergy, although Mussolini's concordat with the Church stifled much of the latter, but it did increase once Italy left the war and, nominally at least, rejoined on the Allied side. There was in any case an inherent dislike of Germans, fanned by a suspicion that Germany had covetous eyes on those areas of the South Tyrol obtained from Austria after the first war, and Italians could never understand the German obsession with eradicating the Jews. Once fighting began on the Italian mainland, the lot of the population was slow to improve in the liberated areas, and a lot worse in those under German occupation, where the removal to Germany of large numbers of forced labourers (many of whom never returned) encouraged physical resistance, which, although exaggerated after the war for perfectly understandable reasons of Italian self-respect, did cause some problems for the occupiers, particularly in rural regions. The re-establishment of civil government as the fighting moved north was not helped by conflicting Allied views: the British wished to preserve the monarchy, while the Americans cared nothing for the king and wanted to devolve control to the liberal (and republican) political parties. There was also much Allied suspicion of the Vatican. The British, and even more so the Americans, were particularly incensed by Pope Pius XII's welcoming of a Japanese embassy and his request that black soldiers not be included in the units garrisoning Rome.[90] The Allies thought that he had condoned German expansion and had not taken a strong enough stance against the rounding up and killing of Jews. The Church's view was and is that open and outright condemnation would only have made matters worse, and might have led to similar persecution of Roman Catholics, that the pope did achieve much amelioration behind the scenes and that the Vatican was instrumental in hiding many Jews and in providing false papers for others. That may well be so, but the argument has not gone away, and has resurfaced recently with the implementation of the first steps towards the elevation of Pius to sainthood. That this is being done under the aegis of a German pope has done nothing to improve public perceptions.

* * *

Like Italy, Japan had few raw materials and lacked the industrial capacity to sustain a long war, but, unlike Italy, at least from 1941 onwards, her population had few doubts about the war until the very last few months. Japan had been at war since 1937, and so by the time she embarked on war with the West in December 1941 she had already stretched her resources. Many Japanese were not entirely happy with the China campaign, which seemed to be directionless and to have no end in sight, but with the exception of a very few the attack on Pearl Harbor and war with Britain and America were greeted with joyous approval. At last the humiliations, snubs and insults – some real, more imagined – from the whites could be repaid, and the string of seemingly unstoppable victories made it unnecessary for the population to be subjected to mobilization for total war. Rigid control of the press and radio meant that the checks to Japanese progress in New Guinea and the Solomon Islands in late 1942 could be concealed from the populace (and from many in government too) and in any case these could be counterbalanced by the successes in Burma. Even the USAAF's Tokyo raid in April 1942, while it came as a severe shock, could be explained away as American barbarity, and it was not until the reverses in the Aleutian Islands in May 1943 that the bulk of the population learned that not all was going Japan's way. To begin with, the regime at home, unlike that in Japan's conquered territories, was relatively benign, but, as the war turned against Japan and as American bombing increased, draconian control measures were introduced.

Prior to 1941 the Japanese had watched Hollywood films, enjoyed classical music and played baseball (although the American-English phrases used in the game were being laboriously translated into Japanese), but now the government embarked on a policy of 'overturning modernity', by which they meant purging the nation of anything remotely 'Anglo-Saxon'. German and Italian music could still be played and listened to but American and British films and books went; women were forced to wear traditional Japanese dress – although the (male) cabinet ministers and civil servants continued to sport morning suits and top hats – and a system of block leaders was introduced to ensure compliance with the much talked about 'Japanese spirit'. Anyone suspected of defeatist tendencies, or having relatives in the USA, was liable to be arrested on suspicion of spying and to undergo a painful interview with the secret police. Emperor worship, already extreme, intensified and, beginning in the primary schools, everyone was required to leap to attention at the mere mention of his name.

Rice had been rationed since late 1940, and all foodstuffs became scarcer as the Allies got closer and closer and as more and more supply routes were denied to Japan. American bombing in 1943 and 1944 was much less effective than that visited upon Germany, and had little effect on the morale of the civilian population, which was more concerned with shortages, disease* and the lengthening lists of military casualties, but from early 1945 bombing from the Marianas, from China and then, crucially, from Iwo Jima began to lay waste Japanese cities. The number of Japanese killed in the bombing offensive of 1945 is not known, but, as Japanese building techniques made much use of wood and rice paper, the fires started by the bombing made every Japanese city attacked another Dresden. In the summer of 1945 schoolchildren were being instructed to write to soldiers at the front telling them to 'die gloriously', while American and British aircraft from land bases and carriers wrought destruction in the homeland, and ships of the United States and Royal Navies shelled coastal towns in broad daylight. Even up to the very last minute, there was no effective popular resistance to government policy; partly this was due to rigid control of the media and an all-pervasive security apparatus, but more than that it was a fatalistic belief in Japanese superiority, conformity, deference to authority and a total abrogation of decision-making to the emperor that had been inculcated into a whole generation of Japanese which, allied to a lack of coherence in a government that decided policy as it went

---

*In the late 1930s there was an average of 140,000 cases of tuberculosis a year in the Japanese population. By 1943 this had risen to 170,000.

along, made the Japanese home front the starving and devastated environment that it eventually became.

* * *

Soviet Russia was a largely militarized society even before 1941, and it became even more so once the country was forced into the war. 'Everything for the Front' was the cry and the increase in industrial production outpaced Germany's almost from the beginning. Contrary to his behaviour before the war, Stalin only executed one general – G. D. Pavlov – and no ministers during it, but the thought that he might kept military and official minds wonderfully concentrated. Stalin turned out to be extraordinarily good at producing tanks, aircraft and artillery pieces, and industrial output quadrupled between 1941 and 1945, but, with the loss of two thirds of the country's agricultural land and the rank inefficiency of the collective farms that remained under Soviet control, it was remarkably bad at feeding its people, at least those in the towns. Lend-Lease delivered not only Jeeps and trucks, but canned food as well and the Russian townspeople got used to Spam, even if they never actually liked it. Food rationing was severe, and once the 'No Surrender' order was issued by Stalin to the Red Army, the families of Soviet prisoners of war had their ration books withdrawn and were left to beg or starve. Furthermore, unlike Germany, the USSR made full use of its female population. There were women signallers, drivers, tank crews, and fighter and bomber pilots in the Red Army and air force, and many of those working alongside former occupants of the gulag in factories and rebuilding roads were also women.

Radio and the press were subjected to absolute control and, while Stalin made only a very few broadcast speeches during the war, they all emphasized the patriotic* nature of the war and promised to wreak defeat and vengeance on the Germans in the end. Russian industry suffered less from air raids than did Germany's or Britain's, largely because of the inadequacies of the Luftwaffe, but the population of towns that could not escape, such as Leningrad and Stalingrad, suffered from constant artillery bombardment and dive-bombing attacks. No one knows exactly how many civilians died in Russia as a result of the war, but the figure was certainly in the millions and may even have been in

---

*The war against Napoleon was the Patriotic War in Russia, so now this one, initially the Great Fatherland War, quickly became the Great Patriotic War.

the tens of millions. Not all Russian civilian deaths were inflicted or caused by the Germans, however. As the Red Army began to recapture Soviet territory, Stalin ordered the deportation to the remote interior or to the far east of the USSR those that he considered had collaborated with the Germans or who had not shown sufficient loyalty to the Soviet system. Kalmyks, Ingushi, Chechens, various Balkan peoples and others were uprooted, packed into trains and abandoned in the middle of Kazakhstan to fend for themselves as best they could. The problems of these minorities still plagues Medvedev's and Putin's Russia today.

Organizationally, Committees of Defence were formed in each area. Consisting of representatives from the party, the local government, the army and the police, they had power over everything from conscription of recruits for the army to the output from factories. Much of the labour was drawn from the gulags, or concentration camps, full of so-called enemies of the regime, who laboured in appalling conditions on near-starvation rations. As the war went on, the advice of the professionals was listened to on military matters but the party remained supreme in all else. Knowing that he had to get the whole population behind him, whether by coercion or persuasion, Stalin did make some concessions. Persecution of the Russian Orthodox Church was eased, many writers, composers and musicians were released from imprisonment and encouraged to put on (politically correct) performances, and the impression was encouraged that, if only the people would put up with hardship until the war was won, then there would be considerable liberalization and a relaxation of many of the oppressive regulations that abounded in every corner of Russian society. It was not, of course, to be.

* * *

This war was the first in modern history to have a home front. Whether being bombed from the air in London, Tokyo, Berlin, Leningrad or Rome or eking out an existence on the bare minimum of food, whether working long hours in factories to turn out the sinews of war or hiding in the woods, steppes and mountains trying to keep resistance alive, the civilian populations of all the belligerents were fully a part of this war. Willingly or unwillingly, they fought too.

18

END GAME

By December 1944 the Allied advance in Italy had ground to a halt. Small-scale patrolling and raiding still went on but any idea of a major winter offensive was soon dispelled by a German counter-attack on 26/27 December against the black troops of the American Fifth Army's 92 Division; the division broke, allowing the Germans to storm through down the valley of the River Serchio towards the west coast. This was blocked by moving 8 Indian Division across from Eighth Army, but it served as a salutary reminder that the Germans were still capable of offensive action. Both Fifth and Eighth Armies were in fact exhausted, short of men, short of vehicles and tanks, and, with British artillery restricted to five rounds per gun per day, short of firepower too. Meanwhile, following the death in the United States of Field Marshal Sir John Dill in November 1944, there had been changes in the command set-up. General Sir Maitland Wilson was selected to replace Dill and promoted to field marshal, while Alexander, also promoted to field marshal, took over as Supreme Commander Mediterranean, with Mark Clark promoted to general and taking over as commander of the Allied Armies in Italy, which once more became 15th Army Group. He in turn was succeeded at Fifth Army by Lieutenant-General Lucian Truscott. On the German side, Field Marshal Kesselring would be summoned to the Western Front in March 1945 to take over as Commander-in-Chief West from von Rundstedt, who yet again would be sacked. Kesselring would be succeeded in Italy by von Vietinghoff.

Once again the Allies had to endure a cold, wet, northern Italian winter. With all thought of any offensive action before the spring now dismissed, the armies held the front with the minimum number of troops needed to deal with any German activity, and let the remaining formations rest, retrain and build themselves up for what all hoped would be the last campaign in

Italy. The American Fifth Army held a front of nearly eighty miles from the Ligurian Sea to Monte Grande, where it joined with the British, and now had a total of ten divisions: two armoured, including one South African, four infantry, one of black and another of Brazilian infantry, the newly arrived 10 Mountain and the Italian Legnano Group. An Italian group was a small division, in this case organized on the American model with two regiments each of three battalions, the whole amounting to about 8,000 men. During the winter Fifth Army was able to absorb reinforcements and get to grips with the new weapons and vehicles that were coming in from America, in contrast to the British Eighth Army, where morale amongst some of the British units was not high and made worse by the removal of the Canadian Corps to North-West Europe in February and the news that the three divisions from Greece and the Middle East, which had been expected in Italy, would now go to the Western Front instead. The only consolations were that XIII Corps had returned from Fifth Army and the arrival of new armour in the shape of amphibious tanks, bridge-layers, Kangaroo armoured personnel carriers and Crocodile flame-throwers. With a front of around thirty miles from Monte Grande along the River Senio to the Adriatic coast, Eighth Army disposed of one British armoured division, three British armoured brigades as well as one New Zealand and one Polish, two British, two Indian and two Polish infantry divisions and one from New Zealand, a parachute brigade, a Royal Marine Commando brigade, 43 Gurkha Independent Lorried Brigade, the Jewish Brigade and three Italian infantry groups.

The Jewish Brigade comprised men from all over Europe, many refugees from Germany or the occupied territories but also with Palestinian, Russian, Yemeni and Abyssinian Jews, and was officered by mainly British Jews. It had been raised in September 1944 when the British acceded to a request from the Jewish Agency, perhaps rather naively, as many of its soldiers, having received military training in the brigade, subsequently joined Jewish terror gangs in Palestine (thirty-five members of the brigade became generals in the Israeli Army), assisted in organizing illegal immigration into Palestine, and, after the war, formed revenge gangs who roamed Germany misusing their status to murder anyone they could find who might have been in any way responsible for the extermination camps or who had been in the SS.[91] While one might have some sympathy for their wish to exact vengeance, that they used British uniforms to do it illegally only reinforces the old adage that two wrongs don't make a right.

In addition to holding against the British and Americans in Italy, German formations were now trying to hold in the Yugoslav mountains and along the Franco-Italian frontier, while facing increased partisan activity behind their lines in northern Italy. In the spring of 1945 Colonel-General von Vietinghoff's Army Group C had five infantry divisions (including one Cossack division) and three divisions of Mussolini's Italian Republican Army on the frontiers, while available for the Allied front were one panzer and two panzer grenadier divisions, three mountain, two parachute and ten infantry divisions (including 162 Turcoman Division recruited from the Caucasus). The Allied air forces had done their best to destroy communications back to Germany and within the German zone of Italy, by bombing roads, bridges and railway lines, as well as destroying Italian factories engaged in producing war materiel, but, while the Germans were thus short of vehicles of all types, they had got their priorities right and were well stocked up with clothing, rations and ammunition, as well as having plenty of artillery pieces and mortars. Even at this late stage of the war, morale was high and the German staff were confident that they could make the Allies pay dearly for every foot of Italian soil they captured.

Clark, supported by Alexander, decided that he could make no offensive move before April, when warmer weather would improve matters for the infantry, the ground would dry out for the tanks and better visibility would allow Allied air superiority to have a major influence on the campaign, despite the fact that several American squadrons had been withdrawn to the West. The plan, which was intended to end the war in Italy, envisaged Eighth Army attacking across the Rivers Senio and Santerno and through the Argenta Gap towards Ferrara and the River Po, with Fifth Army then capturing, or at least isolating, Bologna and breaking into the Po Valley. This should split the German defence lines, enable the destruction of the German armies south of the Po and allow the Allies to capture Verona.

The Argenta Gap was a ten-mile neck of land with the town of Argenta at its centre between Lake Comacchio on the Adriatic coast and the Lombardy marshes. It was well defended by the Germans but, if the Allies could get through it, then they would be into the Lombardy Plain and the approaches to the Po and north-eastern Italy. The British intended to force a German withdrawal by a series of amphibious landings on the shores of Lake Comacchio that would outflank their defences and on 1 April Operation Roast saw the Royal Marines using a variety of boats to establish a beachhead to protect the British right flank. The artillery ammunition position had now improved to the extent that a massive artillery bombardment of German positions along the shore of Lake Comacchio could begin on 9 April, allowing the main offensive to begin with V Corps utilizing the recently arrived amphibious DD tanks and the few remaining landing craft to negotiate German mines and land on the south-west corner of the lake on 11 April, unbalancing the Germans' defences and forcing them to move 29 Panzer Division south from the Po. Another landing farther north by 24 Guards Brigade on 13 April gave the German armour no option but to withdraw, leaving only scattered and cut-off units defending the Gap and allowing 6 Armoured Division to storm through supported by Allied fighter-bombers. By 18 April the British were closing up to the Po, with the Germans still attempting to get back to that river. Furious attacks by the British V Corps and the destruction of the German pontoon bridges across the river by the RAF on 22 April gave the German LXXVI Panzer Corps no choice but to try to fight it out on the south bank. The battle raged all day on 24 April and long into the night, until by the morning of 25 April all coordinated resistance had ceased. That morning Lieutenant-General Gerhard Graf von Schwerin, the forty-six-year-old corps commander, surveyed the wreckage of his corps: burned out vehicles, abandoned tanks, loose horses and dead oxen littered the south bank of the river and, with hardly any soldiers capable of fighting, he surrendered what was left to the 27th Lancers, inviting them to take possession of his headquarters mess stocks of champagne.

Subsidiary operations on the west side of the Lombardy Marshes were the responsibility of the Polish II Corps, with 43 Gurkha Lorried Brigade under command. The Germans may have been on the run but they had no intention of giving up any ground without a fight. In this area a network of canals and rivers provided natural tank obstacles that could be held by a machine-gun and section of infantry long enough to force an attacker to deploy before the defenders then fell back to the next obstacle. The Gurkhas were ordered to establish bridgeheads over the rivers to allow the Polish II Corps to advance along the axis from the Speranza crossroads to Marochia and then to Medicina. The area was defended by men of 4 Parachute Division, experienced, well trained, well led and in no mood to roll over and die, whatever the overall situation might be. The only way for the brigade to take its objectives in the time frame required would be to act speedily, get the enemy on the back foot and bounce him out of his defensive positions. In many ways 43 Gurkha Brigade was the forerunner of a modern, twenty-first-century brigade: it had three Gurkha battalions, two armoured regiments, two field artillery regiments and one medium, an anti-tank battery, two field troops and an armoured field squadron Royal Engineers. Everyone was on tracks or wheels, the infantry in Kangaroos, with a crew of two and carrying ten infantrymen, or in Priests, self-propelled guns with the gun and ammunition racks taken out and carrying twenty infantrymen. Although the battles fought by the brigade were of little importance in the greater scheme of things, they anticipated British all-arms tactics by thirty years and so are worthy of closer examination.

On 13 April the brigade crossed the Santerno River by Bailey bridge erected by the engineers and by last light, after numerous skirmishes with retiring defenders, they reached La Ringhera. By first light on 15 April the infantry was poised to cross the River Sillaro, stoutly defended by men who well knew the tactical significance of the obstacle. At 1115 hours on 15 April, Second Battalion 2/10 Gurkha Rifles tried to establish a bridgehead on the northern bank, but, while they initially succeeded in getting across the river, they could not hold in the face of determined German infantry and fire from medium and heavy mortars. In the small hours of 16 April they tried again and this time they did succeed in establishing a precarious lodgement, closing up to Cesarina by 0430 hours, while 2/8 Gurkha Rifles, riding on 2 RTR tanks, reached Formasaccia. By 0700 hours the engineers had got a bridge across the river and now it was the turn of 2/6 Gurkha Rifles. With the Kangaroo-borne B Company and a tank squadron of 14/20 Kings Hussars in the lead, the battalion group pressed on. Around 1300 hours at Madonna del Silvaro they were held up by two German self-propelled guns (probably 88mm anti-tank guns) but these were disposed of and at 1500 hours C Company passed though B and hit the outskirts of Medicina at 1700 hours, just as it was getting dark. Medicina was, and is, a small medieval town with narrow streets and cellared houses, posing all the problems that operations in built-up areas bring. Fighting from building to building, dismounted from their Kangaroos, the Gurkhas fought their way into the town, ably supported by the tanks, which could blow holes in walls with their 75mm guns to allow the infantry to get in. Fighting in close quarters is always bloody and kukris and bayonets were used to good effect where ranges were too short for rifle fire. By 1800 the rest of the battalion group was in the town and by 2100 hours Medicina was secure. The next morning was spent in mopping up. Now the Polish Corps was across the Sillaro, its flanks secure and the advance went on. There were many one-day battles similar to that at Medicina, when a few companies or a battalion of infantry in armoured personnel carriers supported at close quarters by tanks and artillery fought to clear determined German defenders, who even with the end of the war only weeks away did their duty with little thought of giving up.

Meanwhile, the American Fifth Army, faced with a choice of attacking up the heavily defended Ligurian coast or trying to turn the German defences by a flanking movement through the mountains to the east, chose the latter, and from 5 April began preliminary moves to establish secure start lines for the main offensive, which was planned to start on 12 April. On 10 April the town of Massa was taken, and the River Frigido crossed, and Carrione was captured on the 12th. Now the disadvantages of the mountain route began to show: the Massa to Cassione road was under German fire and all supplies had to come by mule up narrow mountain tracks. Attempts to air-drop supplies were abandoned when they provisioned only the enemy or delighted villagers well away from the action or fell into ravines unreachable to the troops. Despite the difficulties, 10 Mountain Division managed to force the Germans to pull back under cover of their own smoke and artillery and then the main offensive was launched on 14 April – it had been postponed for two days because low cloud prevented flying. Despite progress along the coast and in the western foothills being painfully slow, the advance on the right made spectacular progress and by 18 April the Americans had cut the German lines of communication and forced them to withdraw once more – again at their own pace – to the River Panaro. At 0900 hours on 21 April the leading elements of 133 Infantry Division, riding on tanks, entered Bologna to find that they had just been pipped by a few hours by the Poles, advancing from the direction of Medicina.

The Germans were now in real trouble: the Allied air forces made road movement almost impossible by day, and, as von Vietinghoff's men retreated across the open plains towards the Po, many artillery pieces and vehicles had to be abandoned. The troops still fought well, however, particularly the parachute divisions and LI Mountain Corps, but, as time went on, it became increasingly apparent that even if the Germans could get most of their men back and across the Po – by improvised bridges or boats, for all the permanent bridges had been destroyed by Allied bombing – they were going to have great difficulty in mounting a coherent defence along it. As the days went on, the Allies overran more and more piles of burning stores, and took more and more prisoners from administrative units that could not keep up with the retreating infantry and tanks, including a paymaster who had just drawn his division's pay from a field cashier, and a field bakery where the bread was still warm. The Allies were not without their own difficulties: damaged roads made supply precarious, the British had fired off a quarter of the artillery ammunition in theatre and there was a serious shortage of bridging equipment, but by last light on 24 April Fifth Army had closed up to the Po and was holding a sixty-mile front from west of Parma to Felonica, where it linked up with Eighth Army's V Corps. With most of the German army group's vehicles and communications equipment abandoned south of the Po and many men having had to swim across that river with only the bare minimum of equipment, the last chance the Germans might have had of withdrawing to the Alps and fighting a defensive battle there had gone, despite Berlin's increasingly hysterical orders to fight to the last man.

Even with so many signs of an imminent German collapse, the Allies could not afford to take chances – beyond the Po was the River Adige and, if that had been prepared for defence, then there would be another fierce battle to get across it. Political factors now began to weigh: there were increasingly vociferous bands of Italian partisans operating in the liberated areas or in the areas abandoned by the Germans but not yet under control of the Allies; the communist Yugoslav partisans were claiming Trieste; the Red Army was approaching the Balkans. It was vital for the Anglo-Americans to occupy as much of north-eastern Italy as possible, and even to get into Austria, before the Russians or their surrogates got there first. The Germans had calculated that after the push to the Po the Allies would now do what they always did, and have a long pause to regroup and replenish, allowing defences along the Adige to be prepared. It was not to be. By straining every logistic sinew they had and by requisitioning every vehicle they could find, German, Italian, military, civilian, mechanically propelled or horse- or ox-drawn, both Allied armies pressed on. Now they were on a roll, and Fifth Army began to cross the Po on the night of 24 April against negligible resistance, Eighth Army following suit on the 25th. On 26 April the Americans had Verona and the British were across the Adige. On 29 April, Eighth Army captured Padua and Venice, Fifth Army took Milan and on the east coast the German 148 Division and the Italian Bersaglieri surrendered to the Brazilians, before the two Allied armies linked up at Treviso on 30 April. That same day, after fierce fighting around Lake Garda, the Americans were able to report that the towns to the north of the lake were secure, they took control of Turin from the partisans and made contact with the French on the Franco-Italian border along the west coast towards Nice, while the British 6 Armoured Division pressed on towards Caporetto, scene of the Italian debacle and great Austro-German victory of 1917. The Germans were given no chance of occupying a further defence line; they were being pushed back and given no chance to halt and consolidate, their transport by now was almost non-existent, communications were severed and the escape routes through the Brenner Pass and back into Austria were blocked.

Feelers for a possible surrender in Italy had been put out since February, tentative at first for, had Berlin known about them, the instigators would have been hauled before a court martial and quite possibly shot, and unofficial negotiations involving representatives of the British and American governments, Alexander's headquarters and the Germans had been conducted sporadically in neutral Switzerland under the codename of Operation Sunrise. On the German side the prime mover was Obergruppenführer und General der Waffen SS Karl Wolf,* SS Leader and Police Commander Italy, and on the Allied side Allen Dulles, head of OSS for the Mediterranean and later head of the CIA. Ostensibly, Wolf's line was that the war was lost and further bloodshed was therefore unnecessary, while his unwritten agenda was that a German surrender now would allow the Western Allies to occupy northern Italy and forestall a communist republic, and to get into the Balkans before the Russians. Negotiations stalled when the Russians heard of them and demanded to be represented, and again when Kesselring, Commander-in-Chief West, refused to agree. Eventually, after much discussion to and fro, an instrument of unconditional surrender was signed by Colonel-General von Vietinghoff in Caserta on 29 April. Even then, Kesselring would not accede to it until after Hitler's death on 30 April. The ceasefire was due to come into effect on 2 May, and on that day the Italian campaign officially ended, although it took some time for the message to get through to all German units and the fighting went on throughout the 2nd, with the British finishing up in Caporetto and finding Tito's Yugoslavs just down the road in Cividale.

With the end of the war in Italy came the end of Mussolini's rump state: on 28 April communist partisans stopped a convoy including Mussolini and

---

*As a reward for his help in securing a ceasefire, Wolf was promised by Alexander that he would be permitted to wear badges of rank and decorations as a prisoner of war, which, contrary to the Laws of War, was denied to other captives.

his mistress, Claretta Petacci, took them to Mezzegra and shot them both. The next day the bodies were taken to Milan and displayed hung upside down from the girders of an unfinished building opposite a petrol station which the partisans claimed was the site of a hostage shooting by fascists the year before. The bodies were spat at and abused. It was not the way to treat a head of state, however misguided he may have been. The Italian campaign had lasted for twenty months, had cost the Allies 312,000 casualties, including 21,000 British, 29,560 American and 7,000 Indian and Gurkha dead, with German casualties estimated at over half a million, 200,000 of this number killed. In many ways it has been a forgotten campaign, entered into reluctantly and always taking a lower priority to events in Western Europe, but it was a vicious, hard slog against a superb enemy, foul weather and unforgiving terrain, and, if its contribution to the winning of the war was slight, the achievements of the soldiers and airmen on each side can only be admired and wondered at.

* * *

By the end of 1944 the situation for the Germans on the Eastern Front was desperate. Twenty-seven divisions of Army Group North were bottled up in the Courland pocket in Lithuania, relatively secure as long as the German navy still controlled the Baltic, but fulfilling no useful purpose other than to obey Hitler's 'no retreat' order. South of that, the Front ran from the Baltic through Poland, Slovakia and Hungary to the Dalmatian coast. Army Group Centre had been destroyed, as had Army Group South Ukraine in Romania; all Germany's allies had deserted her except for the Hungarians; fuel was desperately short, particularly now that the Romanian oil had been lost; most of the Luftwaffe was grounded and the army even more dependent on horse-drawn transport, with what meagre fuel supplies that could be obtained reserved for the armour. The huge losses in manpower could not be made up, and in September the first conscription for the *Volksturm* had been ordered: over a million boys and men aged from sixteen to sixty and hitherto exempt from military service for all sorts of reasons were formed into battalion-sized units where they would be given the most rudimentary basic military training and sent off to defend the Fatherland. The extraordinary thing is that the vast majority of them did their duty willingly to the end. On paper, German strength on the Eastern Front in December 1944 was twenty-one panzer, eleven panzer grenadier and 106 infantry divisions, but the ration strength was far less. Hardly any divisions were more than 50 per cent manned, many far smaller, and the lack of fuel for troop-carrying vehicles and administrative transport meant that the infantry could only move as fast as a man or a horse could march. German industry, despite the constant attrition wreaked by the Allied bomber offensive, was still functioning, however, and tanks continued to arrive at the front. In December the Germans could field around 5,000 tanks and assault guns, but the Red Army faced them with 14,000.

The Russians now hurled their full weight at Hungary – for them the capital, Budapest, was a political symbol of great importance; for the Germans it was the last source of oil that they controlled and they would fight determinedly to keep it. The Soviet offensive to take Budapest began on 23 October, but with stubborn German defence and furious counter-attacks – and the *Ostheer* was still capable of stopping the Red Army and doing considerable damage in limited and local operations – it was not until 29 December that the Soviets were able to surround the city, now designated by Berlin as a fortress, inside which one German army panzer division and one infantry division, two SS divisions and a Hungarian division had been ordered to fight to the last man. And fight they did. Offered surrender terms on 29 December, they refused; the city was subjected to a three-day artillery bombardment and then the Soviets attacked, but it was not until 13 February, after bitter fighting with the Russians being driven back again and again but always coming on with even more forces, that the garrison was forced to accept defeat. Fifty thousand of the defenders were killed and 138,000 captured. Sixteen thousand men broke out but only 700 got back to their own lines. In the meantime, earlier than had been intended, Stalin had launched the Red Army's last major offensive, one that would drive to the Rivers Oder and Neisse, Germany's old borders, and then capture Silesia and Pomerania and Berlin itself. The reason for the earlier start was simple: on the Western Front the Germans had once again demonstrated that, however hopeless their situation might seem, they were not beaten yet.

* * *

After the heady advances though northern France and Holland following the Normandy battles, with some optimistic souls convinced that the war would be over in 1944, the realization that the Allies could not simply walk through the German's West Wall came as a shock and a disappointment. By the end of November 1944 the front ran from the Scheldt Estuary north of Antwerp, east to Nijmegen in Holland, roughly south-west of Roermond, east of Aachen, and then south-east through Luxembourg to the Lower Rhine and Strasbourg. In the north was Montgomery's 21st Army Group with Henry

Crerar's Canadian First Army and Dempsey's British Second; in the centre was Bradley's 12th Army Group with William Simpson's Ninth, Hodges's First and Patton's Third Armies, while in the south-west was Lieutenant-General Jacob Devers's US 9th Army Group, consisting of the US Seventh Army under Lieutenant-General Alexander Patch, which had landed in the Riviera in Operation Dragoon, and the French First Army under General Jean de Lattre de Tassigny. By now, Montgomery had accepted that his narrow thrust policy was not acceptable and was touting his theory that Eisenhower should revert to being Supreme Commander with a single Land Forces Commander under him – meaning, of course, himself – a proposition that he constantly put to anyone who would listen, and repeated in letters to Eisenhower. One of Montgomery's peculiarities was that he spent his time either in his relatively small tactical headquarters surrounded by admiring young sycophants, or out visiting formations in his own army group, and hardly ever went to coordinating conferences at Eisenhower's headquarters, claiming he was too busy and sending his chief of staff instead. It may, perhaps, have been that he had an inkling, even if only on a subconscious level, that he cut a somewhat ridiculous figure with his posturing and boasting. What is certain, however, is that his lack of contact with the other commanders and their staffs left Montgomery blissfully unaware of the effect his lobbying had on them, for the politics of the Anglo-American alliance were such that there was not the slightest possibility that, with forty-two US divisions in theatre compared to nineteen British, there could be an overall British commander – even if Montgomery was a reincarnation of the Duke of Wellington, which he palpably was not.

On the German side, Rundstedt, once more ensconced as Commander-in-Chief West, fielded Colonel-General Kurt Student's Army Group H in Holland and the Ruhr, Field Marshal Walter Model's Army Group B in central and west Germany and General of Panzer Troops Hermann Balck's Army Group G in Alsace,* while in the south there was newly formed Army Group Oberhein, commanded by Reichsführer SS Heinrich Himmler, who, being too young for

---

*After the war, General Balck was arrested and put on trial because in November 1944 he had found an artillery lieutenant-colonel drunk on duty and had him shot by firing squad (which seems a perfectly reasonable thing to do). The court claimed that the correct court martial procedures had not been followed and Balck was imprisoned. One wonders why, amongst all the quasi-judicial and extra-judicial death that was being inflicted, Balck was singled out.

the First World War, had no previous experience of military command whatsoever.

As Montgomery's plea for priority for a northern thrust had been rejected, the Allied plan was to attack on either side of the Ardennes, push on to the Rhine and, having reached that river, continue operations in accordance with the situation then prevailing. In an inexplicable failure to learn from events as recent as those of 1940, the Allies decided that there was little prospect of danger from the Ardennes, and this area was covered thinly and in the main by newly arrived or inexperienced divisions of the US First Army as the main weight of the Allied forces was shifted to the flanks.

While most German officers thought that the Eastern Front posed the most danger to the Reich and that it was there that available reinforcements and such armoured vehicles that German industry could produce should be directed, Hitler had different views. He had never believed that the unlikely alliance of democratic and capitalist Britain and America with the communist dictatorship of the USSR could last. If the Western allies could be dealt a short, sharp shock, a decisive defeat and perhaps even a second Dunkirk in the West, then German forces could be shifted to the East, and, while even Hitler now accepted that the German army could no longer defeat Russia, if the Red Army could be halted, some sort of a compromise peace might be arrived at. Since September, OKW operations staff had been looking at the possibilities of an offensive in the West, and these ranged from an attack west towards Aachen to break up the Allied divisions massing for an assault across the Rhine to a thrust through the Ardennes to capture Antwerp, and it was this latter, *Fall Wacht am Rhein* ('Case Watch on the Rhine'), that was decided upon. It was a bold concept, a typical Hitlerian gamble staking everything on one card. If it succeeded, then the Allies would lose their major port and be unable to supply their armies, and they would also be split in two, with the British 21st Army Group and the US First and Ninth Armies cut off from the American armies to their south and either forced to evacuate or be destroyed.

The operation was to be commanded by Model's Army Group B. The attack would be over a sixty-mile front between Monschau and Echternach and would be spearheaded by the recently formed Sixth SS Panzer Army, commanded by SS Oberstgruppenführer Josef 'Sepp' Dietrich, an old friend of Hitler's from their street-brawling days who had been a paymaster NCO in the first war and one of the first recruits to the SS. During this war he had successively commanded the Leibstandarte Adolf Hitler regiment, a Waffen SS division and then a corps.

Dietrich possessed no great intellect and most of the detailed planning and the operational direction of his various commands was carried out by the chiefs of staff, but he was tough, a natural leader popular with his men and, above all else in these troubled times, totally loyal. Dietrich would move through the Ardennes, cross the Meuse between Liège and Huy and press on to Antwerp. His left flank would be protected by Fifth Panzer Army commanded by General of Panzer Troops Hasso-Eccard Freiherr von Manteuffel, who would cross the Meuse at Dinant and advance towards Brussels and then Antwerp, while General of Panzer Troops Erich Brandenberger's Seventh Army would attack through Luxembourg and keep Patton's US Third Army from interfering with the main thrust. In support of the main operation would be around 2,000 English-speaking soldiers under the command of SS Obersturmbannführer Otto Skorzeny, the hero of the Mussolini rescue, who would be dressed in American uniforms and supplied with captured Allied vehicles and weapons and whose job it was to sow confusion and seize road junctions and bridges. Contrary to popular belief, such a *ruse de guerre* was not contrary to the laws of war provided those involved changed into the correct uniforms before taking any warlike action, but as Skorzeny's men had no intention of holding a changing parade, it rendered them liable to execution if captured. Additionally, parachute troops, properly dressed this time, would be used to take and hold the passes through the hills north of Malmedy.

For the first phase of the operation the Germans assembled 200,000 men, in thirteen infantry and motorized divisions and five panzer divisions, supported by 1,600 artillery pieces. One of the major problems, as Hitler freely admitted, was the absolute air superiority of the Allies but, in case the Germans were unable to rely on bad weather to negate that, they did manage to concentrate 1,770 ground attack fighters and light bombers on airfields in the West, almost two thirds of the total Luftwaffe strength, whose role was to keep the enemy air forces away from the heads of the armoured columns. Absolute secrecy was paramount: only the most senior commanders and those staff officers who had to know for planning purposes were told the objective for which they were being concentrated, until Hitler, who had moved his headquarters from Berlin to Bad Nauheim, personally briefed divisional commanders and above four days before *A-Tag*. Movement of the troops to the assembly areas could only be done at night and, as many of the formations to be employed had only recently been pulled out of the line elsewhere, they were battle-weary and had received only inexperienced recruits as reinforcements. Very few officers had any opportunity to reconnoitre the ground over which they would have to move, but the Germans believed that these disadvantages could be compensated for by their ability to react faster than the British or Americans and their superior planning and tactical skills. As movement to the assembly areas was much slower than had been anticipated, largely due to the state of the roads and the need to travel by night, the original jump-off date was postponed from 27 November to 10 December, and then, after the meteorologists predicted favourable (i.e. bad) weather later in the month, to 16 December.

That the Allies were caught by surprise was partly their own fault: they were convinced that the Germans were beaten and that they were incapable of mounting other than local spoiling and counter-attacks; they failed to understand the significance of intercepted requests for aerial photographic reconnaissance of the Meuse; they knew that aircraft were being moved but they did not know why; information from civilian refugees that the Germans were massing tanks and armoured vehicles in the Eifel were discounted, and reports that U-boats in the Atlantic and Baltic were sending far more weather reports than was normal were ignored. All these indications were considered by the Allied staffs at SHAPE and attributed to the Germans using the Ardennes as a rest area, or as a retraining area before moving to the Eastern Front, or possibly to block an Allied attack from the direction of Aachen. The Germans were far too short of fuel to mount an offensive; Rundstedt, Commander-in-Chief West, was known for his caution and would surely never risk an offensive at this stage of the war; and anyway, as nothing had been heard from Ultra, upon which Allied senior commanders had become obsessively reliant, then there could not be anything of significance happening. Montgomery had been given permission to spend Christmas on leave in England, and he had stopped his nightly situation conferences 'until the war becomes more exciting'.

However, *Wacht am Rhein* was not Rundstedt's idea but Hitler's, and the Allies had heard nothing from Ultra because the Germans had imposed radio silence, with all reports and instructions delivered by secure telephone, by

---

*After the war Rundstedt expressed anger that the operation was being described as 'The Rundstedt Offensive' as he claimed he had argued against it from the start and had never believed in it. That may be so, but he certainly agreed to it at the time and his final order of the day to the troops before they crossed the start line contained such phrases as 'Everything for Führer and Fatherland' and 'We are now entering a new phase of the war in the West.'

hand of courier or mouth of staff officer.* When at 0700 hours on the morning of 16 December, after an hour's artillery bombardment, Model's spearhead suddenly appeared out of the mist, the result was complete surprise, panic and shock. He faced 83,000 Americans in five divisions with 400 tanks and 504 artillery pieces spread all along the front and he outnumbered them in men, tanks, guns and motivation. At first it looked as if the Germans might achieve a shattering success: Sixth SS Panzer Army failed to break through in the north of their area of responsibility but penetrated as far as Malmedy in the south. Fifth Panzer Army did break through and forced the surrender of the US VIII Corps on 18 December, while to the south Brandenberger's horse-drawn army made modest gains. Fifth Army was now poised to seize the important crossroads at Bastogne, for if they could take that, then they had a clear run towards the Meuse. On 20 December, Eisenhower ordered that all troops north of the German breakthrough should come under the command of Montgomery's 21st Army Group, and all those south of it to be under Bradley. This made eminent sense as Bradley had refused to move his army group headquarters to the rear (he said he had never retreated and that anyway it would upset his soldiers) and his communications with the US First and Ninth Armies north of the Bulge had been severed, but it was to be the cause of yet another major inter-Allied row in due course. On 21 December the Germans took St Vith when Montgomery ordered a withdrawal to shorten the front, and Rundstedt ordered that this success should be reinforced by allocating the reserves to Manteuffel's Fifth Panzer Army and moving elements of Sixth SS Panzer Army south to him.

Despite their achieving complete surprise, not everything was going the Germans' way, however. The bad weather and the snow had helped but also hindered, as roads turned to mud and snow flurries forced tank crews to drive almost blind; the Luftwaffe was unable to find the dropping zones for the paratroops and dropped many in the wrong places, where most were captured; the fuel situation was critical as the Allied dumps that the Germans had hoped to capture had been moved west or destroyed, and Bastogne, which had to be taken speedily, was holding out under Brigadier-General Anthony McAuliffe, who refused repeated calls to surrender and, even when completely encircled, held on, being resupplied by air. Skorzeny's men generally failed in their mission to capture strategic junctions and many were captured and after hasty courts martial shot, but their very presence did sow distrust amongst the Allies, who could no longer assume that people dressed as them in vehicles with Allied markings were actually who they purported to be. At Malmedy 1 SS Panzer Division shot a number of American prisoners, presumably because they did not want to have to detail troops to guard them, and, as atrocity breeds atrocity, this in turn led to German prisoners being shot.

On 23 December, Manteuffel's leading elements had got to within four miles of Dinant on the Meuse, but that was as far as *Wacht am Rhein* was going to get, for on that same day the Allies shifted from running aimlessly about in circles to stabilizing the front, the Germans ran out of fuel, the weather cleared, allowing the Allied air forces to operate, and Patton – reluctantly, because he badly wanted to capture the Saar – was attacking from the south towards Bastogne. On 26 December, Patton's armour broke through to Bastogne, and now Eisenhower saw an opportunity to cut off the German salient and encircle and destroy the armies within it. Here was exposed a fundamental difference in the thinking of the two Western Allies. Montgomery concentrated on blocking the German advance, and only intended to counterattack much later, once men, stores, ammunition and guns were in place. Eisenhower and his American subordinates, however, wanted to attack straight away while the opportunity existed. On 28 December, Eisenhower ordered Bradley to form the southern pincer that would meet with Montgomery's thrust from the north and cut off three German armies. Montgomery, whom Eisenhower flew to brief that same day, would not agree. He stated that he could not be ready to attack before 1 January (later postponed to 3 January) and recommended that the American armies to the south withdraw to consolidate and prepare for the offensive when all was in place. Montgomery also renewed his request for a single Land Forces Commander, under Eisenhower, in a remarkably insensitive letter sent to Eisenhower on 30 December. This, along with the suggestion in the British press that Montgomery had saved the Americans' bacon and was the hero of the hour, an impression reinforced by a press conference he gave, infuriated the American generals and was the last straw as far as Eisenhower was concerned, particularly as Montgomery had only deployed three British divisions and they had not done very much. He drafted a signal giving the Joint Chiefs the choice of Montgomery or himself. Had the signal been sent, there can be no doubt that it would have been Montgomery who would have been sacked (and it was not only American officers who would have been happy to see the last of him) and only a last-minute intervention by his Chief of Staff, Lieutenant-General Sir Frances 'Freddie' de Guingand, on 31 December, persuaded Montgomery to write a cringing letter of apology and Eisenhower to tear up his signal.

As it was, Bradley's attack from the southern shoulder of the salient was launched on 1 January and coincided with *Fall Bodenplatte*, an attempt by the Luftwaffe to prevent the Allied air forces from interfering with Model's withdrawal. Nine hundred German aircraft attacked twenty airfields in Holland, Belgium and northern France, destroying or damaging 260 RAF and USAAF aeroplanes, but the Luftwaffe lost 300 of their own, and, while the Allies could replace theirs, the Germans could not. Since Montgomery did not launch the northern pincer until two days after Bradley, the opportunity to cut off the Germans was lost, and they were able to withdraw steadily and to avoid being encircled. On 8 January, Hitler authorized the abandonment of the Bulge pocket but it was not until 16 January that the two Allied pincers met, and not until the first week of February that all resistance in the salient was eliminated. The next objective for the Allies would be the Rhine, the largest water obstacle in Europe.

The so-called Battle of the Bulge cost the Germans 10,749 dead, 34,225 wounded and over 600 armoured vehicles destroyed or abandoned having run out of fuel.[92] It robbed them of their last reserves that could have been sent East and, combined with the wasteful despatch of troops to Hungary, left very little to defend the Homeland when Stalin launched his Vistula offensive in response to a plea from Churchill to take the pressure off the Ardennes.

* * *

Colonel-General Guderian predicted that the next Soviet offensive would come through Poland across the Vistula; he even predicted the date, but Hitler did not believe him, being convinced that the Red Army would need far longer to sort itself out and regroup after Operation Bagration. Sure enough, on 12 January five Soviet Fronts hurled themselves at the German lines and found a weakened opponent. They ripped a twenty-mile gap in Army Group Centre through which the Russian armour poured, with infantry riding on the tanks, and leaving any German units that still held their ground for the following waves to mop up. Warsaw fell on 17 January, relieved by the Polish Army under Russian command, but only after it had been held back long enough to allow the Germans to destroy Bór-Komorowski's, anti-communist Home Army. Cracow fell the next day and the Red Army caught the German counter-attack forces deploying, pinned them against the River Oder and destroyed them. In Hungary, Budapest fell on the 18th and two Fronts burst into East Prussia, pinning the Third Panzer Army around Königsberg, where they were joined by the garrison of Memel, evacuated by the German navy in the teeth of the Red Army. Now the German army could only retreat, with hastily formed ad hoc battle groups of a battalion or two, a few tanks and what guns could be scraped together desperately trying to buy time for the armies to withdraw and then scuttling back themselves. Two weeks after the launch of the Vistula offensive, the Red Army had advanced nearly 250 miles, and stood on the Oder, only fifty miles from Berlin.

The very last German offensive of the war took place in Hungary, when, on 6 March, Sixth SS Panzer Army, withdrawn from the Ardennes and still commanded by Dietrich, scraped together eleven panzer and motorized and twenty infantry divisions and attempted to retake Budapest from Lake Balaton, sixty miles away. It was a totally pointless exercise – the troops would have been far better employed along the Oder or on the Austro-Hungarian border – and some of the armoured divisions were down to twenty tanks each, while none of the infantry divisions was more than 50 per cent manned, but they did have a batch of the brand-new Tiger II tanks, sixty-ton monsters with an 88mm gun and totally impervious to any tank or anti-tank gun. Extraordinarily, some of the old tactical flair was still there and the Germans broke through the Soviet defences, but the early thaw meant that the Tigers sank in the mud once they ventured off roads, the attack soon ran out of steam in the marshes, the Soviets counter-attacked in overwhelming strength and Sixth Army could only retreat towards Vienna, leaving most of their brand-new tanks stuck in the swamps.

The thought of Russian troops on German soil struck panic into the civilian population. In Budapest the Red Army had shot out of hand any member of the SS that it captured, rounded up every Hungarian civilian with a German name and deported them to Siberia, raped everything in skirts regardless of age and helped themselves to anything moveable. If that was what they would do in Hungary, how much worse would it be in Germany?

* * *

In the Far East, General MacArthur was concentrating 200,000 troops to invade Luzon, the main island of the Philippines and the site of the nation's capital, Manila. In order to provide air bases from which the Fifth United

States Army Air Force could provide air cover for the Luzon operation, he needed to capture the island of Mindoro to the south of Luzon. It would be a tricky operation, as Mindoro was 260 miles from Leyte and thus out of range of land-based aircraft, but, despite the efforts of what was left of the Japanese navy, 24 Division landed there against negligible opposition on 15 December and work to develop airstrips began. While what few Japanese surface vessels were left might be unable to do very much damage to Halsey's fleet, kamikazes and the weather could. From 4 January 1945 swarms of suicide planes attacked American ships, and, while they never came near to scoring a victory, they damaged thirty warships, some of them badly. On 6 January a kamikaze attack on the battleship *New Mexico* killed Lieutenant-General Herbert Lumsden, who, having been sacked by Montgomery for not being sycophantic enough, hung around in Home Forces in England before being appointed as British Liaison Officer to MacArthur's staff. Anti-kamikaze measures included reducing the fleet from four medium-sized task forces to three large ones, increasing the number of anti-aircraft weapons on ships and stationing picket destroyers sixty miles away from the main fleet to give early warning. And as if kamikazes were not enough, the American fleet then ran into a typhoon, which sank three destroyers and damaged a number of other ships, as well as costing Halsey 146 aircraft and 800 men.

The Japanese garrison of Luzon was around 80,000 combat troops, with the same number again of administrative, navy and air force personnel. In accordance with the latest Japanese doctrine, they did not attempt to oppose the first American landing at Lingayen 100 miles north of Manila on 9 January, which was supported by a ferocious naval bombardment, but withdrew into the centre of the island. American progress thereafter was slow, despite MacArthur's urgings, as the Sixth Army's commander, Krueger, was concerned that to drive into the hinterland too early might allow the Japanese to emerge and cut him off from his supply base. On 29 January another landing took place, by IX Corps at San Antonio and Subic Bay, west of Bataan, and on the 31st 11 Airborne Division went ashore fifty miles south-west of Manila. MacArthur could now attempt to attack and recapture Manila, which was not only a politically important objective as the capital but also where large numbers of prisoners of war were being held who, if not rescued quickly, might be massacred by the Japanese as they withdrew. General Yamashita, who was responsible for the defence of the Philippines, had, in an unchar-acteristic act of humanity, ordered that Manila was to be an open city, that is, abandoned by the Japanese Army and not to be defended. Yamashita did not, however, have full powers of command over the naval infantry on Luzon, and Vice-Admiral Sanji Iwabuchi determined that he and 17,000 of his men would defend Manila, whatever Yamashita ordered. On 4 February the Americans got into the northern suburbs of the city and freed a large number of sick and malnourished prisoners, but it took another month to clear the entire capital. Fighting degenerated into a house-to-house slog, with all the bitterness and brutality that goes with such short-range battles, and, by 3 March, when the Japanese defenders, who refused to surrender and had to be killed, were no more, the city was a wreck. While the American death toll was only around 1,000, huge numbers of Filipino civilians lay dead, crushed by falling buildings, shot by the Japanese on suspicion of helping the Allies or caught in the middle of an exchange of fire.

In the centre of the island, the Americans pushed Yamashita's men slowly back into the mountains, while clearing the area surrounding Manila Bay. On 16 February the Bataan peninsula fell relatively easily, but that was not the case with the island of Corregidor, defended stoutly by the Americans and Filipinos in 1942 and defended as stoutly now that the roles were reversed. The 4,500-strong Japanese garrison retreated into the maze of caves and tunnels, made the Americans fight for every one of them and, when there was no hope left, exploded their ammunition dumps, taking attacker and defender alike to glory. It took ten days and a subsidiary airborne landing to subdue Corregidor, and another two days to mop up. Now the Philippines were secure, all that was left was for MacArthur to clear the remaining Japanese from the island of Mindanao, which fell in July, and from the north-east of Luzon. There Yamashita held out, impotent and unable to do more than defy the Allies, who were happy to allow him to stay in his jungle hideout to be mopped up when convenient, and there he remained until the end of the war.

* * *

Iwo Jima is a tiny island of less than twelve square miles in the Bonin Group, 700 miles from Japan and about halfway between Japan and the Marianas. Apart from Mount Suribachi, a 560-foot-high extinct volcano in the south, the island is relatively flat and thus an ideal site for air bases, of which there were two. To the Japanese, it was psychologically important, being part of the Japanese homeland as opposed to a colony or captured territory, and militarily important as a staging post between Japan and the South Pacific – an importance that was enhanced when the Japanese lost the Marianas in 1944. To the Allies, Iwo Jima was also vital ground because from it they could bomb Japan with land-based aircraft which could be escorted by fighters, and because it could also be used as a mounting base for an eventual invasion of Japan. The Japanese were well aware of the significance of Iwo Jima and in early 1944 Major-General Tadamichi Kuribayashi and 21,000 men of 109 Division were sent there with instructions to turn it into an impregnable fortress. Unusually, he was bade farewell by the emperor in person and it was clear that he was not expected to return. The construction of defences and a third airstrip began immediately and by the end of 1944 there were dug-in tanks, concrete emplacements, bunkers, trenches, tunnels, wire obstacles, mines offshore and on the beaches and concealed artillery pieces covering all the possible landing areas. Kuribayashi, of samurai descent, was a fluent English-speaker who quoted Shakespeare, had been an assistant military attaché in Washington (where he ridiculed the Western custom of standing up for ladies) and was opposed to the war from the beginning. He was well aware that he could not prevent a landing, nor an eventual capture of the island; what he could do, he thought, would be to kill so many Americans and delay them for so long that they would realize that an invasion of Japan proper would be too expensive to contemplate.

Admiral Nimitz delegated the capture of Iwo Jima to Vice-Admiral Spruance and his fleet, which was no longer needed by MacArthur now that he had the Philippines. Spruance had replaced Halsey in February – the latter was now enjoying well-earned shore leave, although he would return to the Pacific before the end of the war* – and in view of the immense strength of the defences he decided upon day and night bombing by Seventh Air Force from 31 January to 15 February, followed by three days of intensive naval bombardment before the US Marines would land on D-Day, 19 February. Diversionary air raids were also mounted against Tokyo by carrier-borne aircraft, and, although bad weather prevented them from doing very much damage, it was the first time a carrier force had come so close to Japanese

---

*The American system in the Pacific was to have two admirals and staff for each fleet and they rotated. While one was commanding the fleet, the other was planning the next operation. When Halsey was in command, the fleet was titled Fifth Fleet; with Spruance the same fleet became Third.

shores and the raids caused alarm at Imperial Headquarters as a sign of things to come. At Iwo Jima the bombing and the naval gunfire ripped off much of the camouflage over the defences, but the garrison was sheltered in concrete bunkers and trenches and survived relatively unscathed: many of the artillery positions were exposed, but as many were not. At 0900 hours on 19 February the three Marine divisions of the US V Amphibious Corps landed on the south-east side of the island. The Japanese defences made little reply until the first wave was ashore, and then opened up with artillery and mortar fire. At first the Marines were pinned down and unable to move, their problems compounded by worsening weather that made the landing of tanks and vehicles a difficult and dangerous undertaking. Massive naval gunfire and air support prevailed, however, and although casualties were heavy (about 2,500), by nightfall the Marines had established a beachhead a mile long and 1,000 yards deep. Then began some of the most vicious fighting of the Pacific war. Infantry with flame-throwers and engineers with explosives had to blast every Japanese defender out of his bunker or tunnel and it was not until 23 February that Mount Suribachi was scaled and the iconic photograph of the raising of the Stars and Stripes taken. That was by no means the end of the battle, for it took until 1 March before the two southern airstrips were taken, and still Kuribayashi and his men fought on. By 16 March they had been forced into two enclaves on the north and north-east of the island and only on the 26th did resistance cease, when all that was left of the garrison alive were 200 men wounded so badly that they could neither fight nor kill themselves. Kuribayashi's last letter apologized to the emperor for failing to defeat the landing, and said that he and his men would fight to the end. He had lived up to the expectations of his samurai tradition, and his body was never found.

Iwo Jima cost the US Marines 6,800 dead, over a third of the total of Marine dead in the whole war. The American fleet did not emerge unscathed either. Kamikaze attacks damaged the carrier USS *Saratoga* so badly that she had to be sent back to America for extensive repairs, and they sank the carrier USS *Bismarck Sea*. But the Americans wasted no time, and by 8 March the USAAF was operational on Iwo Jima. Now Japan could be attacked by B-29 bombers escorted by fighters from Iwo Jima, and Nimitz's next target would be Okinawa.

With a population of around 400,000 in 1945, Okinawa, sixty miles long and four to five miles wide, is the largest island of the 600-mile-long Ryukyu chain which runs from the northern tip of Formosa to Kyushu, the southernmost of the main Japanese home islands. At some 350 miles from Japan, it was an obvious target for the Allies and the Japanese had drawn up plans to defend it which hinged round holding the island long enough for the huge Allied fleet that must be assembled to be destroyed by air attack. In the event, and fortunately for the Allies, the Japanese had not reckoned on the Americans reacting as quickly as they did after the capture of Iwo Jima, and from 18 March American and British aircraft began attacking airfields in southern Japan and shipping in the Inland Sea. The Americans had assembled the largest military force yet seen in the Pacific: not far short of that mounted for Overlord in Normandy, it mustered 1,440 naval and merchant ships, including the British Pacific Fleet, the US Fast Carrier Force, the Joint Expeditionary Force and the Gunfire and Covering Force, which between them had nineteen battleships, fifteen fleet and six light carriers, thirty cruisers and 107 destroyers, there to support the fifty-nine-year-old Lieutenant-General Simon Bolivar Buckner Jr's US Fourteenth Army consisting of three Marine and five army divisions.

The defence of Okinawa was entrusted to Lieutenant-General Mitsuru Ushijima and his Thirty-Second Army. After garrisons on the outlying islands were deducted, Ushijima had around 60,000 combat troops and another 20,000 local militia who were used for labouring duties in the preparation of defences, and, knowing that he could not defend the whole island, he decided to concentrate in the south with defences in depth, positions concreted in and with the usual mix of tunnels and caves. In addition, he had a number of Sea Raiding battalions armed with a naval equivalent of the kamikaze, small patrol boats packed with explosives which were intended to be driven at speed into enemy warships and then detonated.

On 26 March the Americans seized the Kerama Retto islands, eleven miles west of Okinawa and with natural harbours where repair and refuelling facilities could be established. On the same day, air raids and naval bombardment of Okinawa began, with no great effect on the well-dug-in defenders. On 1 April the first waves of the US Fourteenth Army landed on the west of the island to little opposition, and by last light the two airfields were in their hands and operating aircraft the following day. By 6 April the whole of the centre of the island was in American hands, whereupon the first major Japanese retaliation began. This took the form of massed kamikaze attacks on the great concentration of shipping around Okinawa, and should have begun as soon as the fleet appeared, but disagreement between the

Japanese navy, which saw Okinawa as the vital battle of the war to which every consideration should be subordinated, and the army, which thought that Okinawa could not be held and wanted to keep the aircraft back for the defence of the homeland, caused a delay. Up until now, there had been kamikaze attacks but they had been sporadic, and by 5 April had sunk an escort carrier, a destroyer and three landing craft, and damaged other ships. On 6 April, however, came a mass wave of 660 kamikazes, supposedly coordinated with a foray by the 60,000-ton *Yamato*, the world's largest battleship, which headed for Okinawa with a light cruiser and eight destroyers. In their tanks were the last drops of fuel oil the Japanese could find and *Yamato* had enough to get there but not to return. It was a suicide mission, and all her crew knew it, and it achieved nothing: spotted by an American submarine on 7 April, she was attacked by aircraft of the Fast Carrier Force and she, the cruiser and four of the destroyers were sunk, her captain and nearly all her crew going down with her. It was the last hurrah of the once mighty Imperial Japanese Navy.

The kamikaze attacks mounted between 6 and 8 April hit twenty-five ships, sinking eight and damaging another ten so badly that they were out of action for the rest of the war. Then, on 11 April, a kamikaze attack was co-ordinated with a counter-attack launched by Ushijima. The counter-attack failed with heavy losses, but another two ships were sunk. Now Admiral Nimitz ordered USAAF bombers to switch from bombing Tokyo to eliminating the airfields in Kyushu from where the kamikaze were operating. Worrying though the suicide attacks were, increasing numbers of aircraft were being shot down, and the statistics – twenty attacks (and therefore twenty aircraft lost) for each ship damaged – were telling: this was simply not an effective use of scarce aircraft and scarcer pilots. That said, by 16 April the Allies had lost a total of one carrier, six destroyers, three landing craft and two ammunition ships sunk and thirty-one ships so badly damaged that they were out of action for long periods, including four carriers and a battleship. The British carriers were less vulnerable because their heavy deck armour plate prevented the diving aircraft from penetrating into the bowels of the ship, but they still suffered damage and the destruction of any aircraft exposed on the flight deck.

On land, the Japanese took to landing parties of engineers well equipped with explosives behind the American lines with instructions to cause as much damage as possible, while more massed kamikaze attacks built up to a peak from 23 to 25 May. Now another aerial weapon appeared: the Japanese sent five twin-engined bombers with a platoon of infantry packed into each one, ordered to crash-land on the Okinawa airfields and cause as much mayhem as possible. The Americans shot four of them down, but a fifth belly-flopped on to the strip and, before the occupants could be killed, they managed to inflict considerable damage on parked aircraft and installations, as well as setting on fire an aviation fuel storage depot.

At sea Admiral Spruance handed over to Admiral Halsey once again on 27 May, and on land torrential rain slowed up even further the infantry's already tortuous progress in reducing the Japanese defenders in their tunnels and caves. Now tanks could not operate in the mud and even amphibious vehicles had problems, but the weather hindered both sides and the Japanese were running short of ammunition and rations, their artillery was nearly all destroyed or had been abandoned through lack of shells, and even small arms were in short supply. Thousands of leaflets telling the Japanese that their situation was hopeless and urging them to give themselves up were dropped all over southern Okinawa, and Japanese-speaking Americans invited surrender over loudspeakers. Thirty-Second Army was reduced to around 10,000 combatants and for the first time in the war Japanese prisoners were being taken, as men surrendered an intolerable position – admittedly most of them were militia or wounded, but it was a sign that the belief in invincibility was wearing thin, and that the end of the battle might be in sight. General Buckner did not live to see the victory that his men won at terrible cost, for on 18 June a shell from one of the few remaining Japanese artillery pieces hit an observation post from where he was surveying progress and killed him. He was replaced by 'Vinegar Joe' Stilwell, now aged sixty-two and brought back from rustication to Washington, where he had been since the previous November. On 21 June, Ushijima realized that, having held out for three months, there was nothing more he could do. He ordered his remaining soldiers to break out individually to the north of the island and carry on the war as guerrillas, and he and his chief of staff committed ritual suicide by cutting open their stomachs with short swords and then being decapitated by their respective ADCs. Around 80 per cent of the Japanese army defenders were killed, around two thirds of the militia and countless civilians, many of whom committed suicide rather than be captured by the Americans. The Japanese had lost around 8,000 aircraft including 2,000 kamikazes. For the Allies, the death toll was 12,520 Americans killed, 763 aircraft lost, thirty-four ships sunk and another seventy that could not be repaired before the war's end. It was an expensive victory, but a very necessary one. Now the Americans had the bases and airfields they needed to prepare for the final invasion of the Japanese main islands.

* * *

In Burma, 'Uncle Bill' Slim had never been in favour of frontal attacks, and, given that reinforcements for the Far East were a low priority, he knew he could not afford costly battles of attrition. All the signs were that General Kimura, the Japanese commander of the Burma Area Armies, intended to fight on the other, east, side of the Irrawaddy and that a direct attack on him would bring on just the sort of battle Slim wanted to avoid and just the sort that the Japanese were good at. Yet Slim had turned the battered and defeated army of 1943 into a well-honed, confident and well-led team that after its victory at Imphal and Kohima knew that the Japanese soldier was not invincible and that he could be beaten. It was very much an imperial army, with just over 75 per cent of the troops being Indian, Gurkha and East or West African. Slim now decided to recast his plans for 1945 and embark on a strategy he could not possibly have contemplated a year before but which, if it succeeded, would win the war in Burma. The Japanese supply lines to the Fifteenth and Thirty-Third Armies in central Burma ran north through the town of Meiktila to Mandalay. Meiktila was seventy-five miles south of Mandalay and in and around the town were Japanese hospitals, ammunition and ration dumps, repair workshops and airstrips, while the main road and the railway from Rangoon to Mandalay ran through it. If Slim could capture Meiktila and hold it, then Kimura's position to the north would become untenable and he could be defeated in detail. The key was secrecy: if Kimura had an inkling of Slim's intention, then he would reinforce Meiktila and the plan would fail. Slim's orders were for XXXIII Corps, commanded by Lieutenant-General Sir Montague Stopford, to cross the Chindwin and make for the Irrawaddy and Mandalay, with the aim of drawing the maximum Japanese forces on to him, while Lieutenant-General Frank Messervy's IV Corps would go south, cross the Irrawaddy and take Meiktila. With the distances to be covered and the lack of roads, resupply would be a problem, but the army could rely on overwhelming Allied air supremacy and its engineers were capable of prodigious feats. The army was experienced in using mules as pack animals and could transport supplies by river craft on the Chindwin itself. Slim's staff calculated that, provided they captured airfields as they went along, the two corps could be maintained – just.

Then, when it appeared that all was set, Chiang Kai-shek threw a chopstick in the works when, without any warning, he demanded that all Chinese and American troops in Northern Area Combat Command be returned instantly to China – where the Japanese had launched an offensive to try to salvage something from their increasingly precarious position – and that they were to be flown out by the USAAF. This would mean losing three squadrons of transport aircraft, or seventy-five Dakotas, which would seriously compromise Slim's resupply plan and might even jeopardize the whole operation. Protests and appeals from Mountbatten to the Joint Chiefs secured a partial stay of execution: two squadrons would be returned to Slim and would remain in support of Fourteenth Army until the capture of Rangoon or until the end of June 1945, whichever was the earlier. Meanwhile, since it was critical that the move of IV Corps, heavily augmented with tanks, self-propelled artillery and troop-carrying vehicles, was not discovered by the Japanese, extensive deception measures were implemented, including the setting up of a dummy corps headquarters at Tamu in the north, and the routing of all communications through it, thus ensuring that Japanese intercepts could not pinpoint the real location of the corps. When the Japanese did detect some movement to their south, they were convinced that it was either a diversion to make them move troops south from Mandalay or a probe farther south towards the oil fields, an impression strengthened by Slim's dropping of dummy parachutists well south of IV Corps's line of advance.

When XXXIII Corps advanced from the Chindwin, the Japanese, in accordance with Kimura's plan, fell back towards the Irrawaddy, behind which they had concentrated eight divisions and the Indian National Army. This latter had now been exposed for the militarily unreliable organization that it was, but could still be used for labouring and carrying duties provided its members were given no opportunity to desert back to the British. XXXIII Corps established two bridgeheads across the Irrawaddy; they were furiously attacked by Japanese infantry but held their ground, using every possible stratagem to convince the Japanese that they were defending against two corps, not one, and steadily pushing the Japanese back until Slim could move Fourteenth Army headquarters to Monywa, on the lower Chindwin, while 200 miles to the south Messervy's corps crossed that river on 13 February. Now they were out of the mountains and the jungle and into the plains of central Burma where armour could be used in wide outflanking sweeps to which the Japanese had no answer. The attack towards Meiktila by Messervy's spearhead, Major-General 'Punch' Cowan's 17 Indian Division, on 21 February came as a severe shock to Kimura in his Burma Area Headquarters in Rangoon, but the 12,000-strong garrison fought grimly, and it was not until 3 March that the town fell, Cowan going on to take the main airfield complex ten miles to the east and the surrounding villages over the following two days.

Kimura was very well aware of the implications of losing Meiktila and now began to move troops south to retake it. For three weeks, IV Corps and 17 Division in particular were subject to constant counter-attacks as the Japanese tried desperately to reopen their supply and withdrawal route, and Twenty-Eighth Army, so far uninvolved and still west of the Irrawaddy, attempted to relieve its battered comrades, but without success. Cowan adopted a policy of aggressive defence, using groups of mobile infantry, self-propelled artillery and tanks supported by fighter-bombers to range up to twenty miles from the Meiktila perimeter to seek out the approaching Japanese columns and destroy them, but it was a close-run thing and on 17 March Slim flew the 5 Indian Division into Meiktila to bolster the defence. In the north, XXXIII Corps broke out of its bridgeheads forty miles north of Mandalay and on 20 March, after bitter fighting, Mandalay fell to the 29 Indian Division. The Japanese were now in serious disarray. With their retreat to the south cut off and with no possibility of reinforcement or resupply, Kimura could only order the remnants of Fifth and Thirty-Third Armies to fall back eastwards into the Shan Hills and retreat south.

Now the race was on to get to Rangoon before the monsoon broke; IV Corps headed south from Meiktila down the Sittang valley while XXXIII Corps followed the Irrawaddy. Kimura had left small delaying parties along the Irrawaddy, which were a nuisance and caused delay, but were no match for Grant tanks, but IV Corps met much more serious resistance as Kimura decided that theirs would be the main Allied axis towards the capital. Thirty miles south of Meiktila there was a stiff battle at Pyawbwe, and a farther 100 miles south of that the Japanese fought tenaciously to hold the airfield at Toungoo, from where a handful of their fighters attacked the approaching IV Corps column, destroying a number of soft-skinned vehicles but failing to stop the advance. Slim now adopted a policy of what he called 'Hammering on the back door while I burst in through the front', and on 1 May a Gurkha parachute battalion was dropped on Elephant Point, commanding the entrance to Rangoon harbour. In a desperate little battle, with no quarter given by either side, the Gurkhas killed all the defenders and at 0700 hours the next morning landing craft with the 29 Indian Division were able to enter the harbour and land on the docks, while the advance elements of IV Corps arrived overland the next day. In fact, the Japanese, realizing that holding on to Rangoon was utterly pointless, had abandoned the city. Within two weeks the port's facilities, destroyed by the Japanese before they left, had been put in working order again and the Allies were using them for much-needed resupply. All that was left now was to mop up the scattered Japanese, many of whom were already being ambushed and subjected to the most bestial atrocities by the delightful Burmans, and to prepare for the next great leap forward – the liberation of Malaya.

Now occurred a most extraordinary faux pas in the reorganization of the British higher command as Slim was sacked and then un-sacked. The details are still argued over and Slim was too much of a gentleman to make his true feelings known at the time, but Lieutenant-General Leese, Commander Land Forces under Mountbatten, told Slim that he was to be relieved as Commander Fourteenth Army and replaced by Leese's old chum from Staff College days, Lieutenant-General Sir Philip Christison, currently Commander XV Corps. Fourteenth Army was to reconquer Malaya, while a newly formed Twelfth Army (actually little more than a corps), which Slim would command, was to mop up in Burma. Slim was deeply disappointed – 'I didn't think I'd done anything wrong' – and his staff were horrified; the Indian Army, who had never had much time for Leese, was outraged; and back in London, the CIGS, Brooke, was affronted. The upshot of it all was that Leese himself was sacked and Slim stayed at Fourteenth Army.

What appears to have happened is that Leese carried the can for Mountbatten,* who was hyper-sensitive to any criticism or any negative publicity that might rebound on him, and was quite happy to hang Leese out to dry once he saw that nobody, from the most junior rifleman in Fourteenth Army to the CIGS, wanted rid of Slim.[93] Slim went on leave to the UK, met Churchill for the first time and informed him bluntly that the

---

*Mountbatten had apparently claimed that Slim was 'tired', but the real truth is probably that the Supreme Commander did not find Slim an easy or congenial subordinate. In personality and professional attitudes the two were poles apart.

British soldiers of Fourteenth Army would not vote for him in the coming general election, and then returned to the Far East in a new appointment as Commander Land Forces – the post that Leese once held. It was while he was making his way to his new headquarters at Kandy in Ceylon that he heard that the Japanese war was over.

19

CHECKMATE

JANUARY 1945–DECEMBER 1946

In North-West Europe, the mighty Rhine was the last great obstacle facing the Western Allies and preventing them from driving deep into Germany, and Eisenhower intended to clear the approaches to it and then cross on a broad front. Montgomery dissented: he still clung to the view that the full power of logistic and air support should be given to him to drive an armoured spearhead across the river which would stab through the German vitals to Berlin and end the war. In hindsight there are many who believe Montgomery was right, but Eisenhower was not convinced that the Germans were beaten yet – they had shown with their Ardennes offensive that they could still snarl if not roar – and that an advance on a narrow front would only risk being cut off and annihilated. Montgomery was instructed to clear to the Rhine between Antwerp and Düsseldorf starting on 8 February, but, owing to flooding and stiff resistance from German parachute troops, the Canadian First and US Ninth Armies, the latter still under Montgomery's command, could not close up to the river until 10 March. Farther south, Bradley closed up between Düsseldorf and Koblenz with Hodges's US First Army and Patton's Third, while the US 6th Army Group would advance north-east to the Rhine from south of Saarbrücken and trap elements of the German Seventh Army between Patch's US Seventh Army and Patton.

Once again, Hitler had placed impossible strictures on his generals by ordering them to fight west of the Rhine, instead of making full use of it and fighting behind it, with the result that, by the time the Allies had closed up all along the river, they had taken over 200,000 prisoners. First to get across were men of the US First Army's Twenty-Seventh Armoured Infantry Battalion who found a road and railway bridge at Remagen, between Cologne and Koblenz. The Germans had attempted to demolish it but the charges were incorrectly placed and while the bridge was damaged it still stood, and the Americans charged across and established a bridgehead on the far side. The wretched members of the demolition party were blamed with dereliction of duty and at least one, the officer commanding, was shot (and duly pardoned by the Federal Republic of West Germany years later). Next over was Patton, south of Mainz on 22 March, and then Montgomery, on a thirty-five-mile front between Rees and Emmerich on 23 and 24 March. Typically, Montgomery had orchestrated a set-piece battle: as Churchill, Brooke and Eisenhower looked on, 3,500 guns carried out a preliminary bombardment before two divisions, one British and one Canadian, crossed. By 26 March, 21st Army Group had twelve bridges in place and the troops were swarming over. The day before, Patton's armour broke out of the bridgehead south of the Ruhr and was heading north-east for Kassel. In the space of three weeks, the Allies were across the Rhine on a front of almost 200 miles and poised for the last leap into the heart of Germany.

In Berlin, Guderian, Chief of the General Staff of the army, was increasingly pessimistic about the course of the war and began to argue for the opening of negotiations with the Anglo-Americans for an armistice in the West, which would allow the full weight of what was left of the Wehrmacht to be directed against the Red Army in the East. Such a possibility would have been out of the question (although Stalin suspected otherwise) as the Western Allies had agreed upon a policy of no separate peace, but Guderian was sacked anyway and replaced by General of Infantry Hans Krebs, who had spent most of his career on the staff and had recently been brought in as Guderian's deputy, having previously been Chief of Staff at Army Group B on the Western Front. Rundstedt, too, was sacked yet again, and for the last time; blamed for the fiasco at Remagen and regarded as defeatist, he was replaced by Kesselring, who was recalled from Italy. At the same time Hitler ordered a scorched-earth policy to be implemented in Germany. As they were pushed back, army units were to leave nothing to the invaders. Crops, buildings, factories, roads, bridges, airports, docks and railways – all were to be comprehensively destroyed. In the event, ministers such as Albert Speer, who was responsible for armaments, local party officials and army commanders ensured that these orders were evaded: if Germany was to lose this war, then something had to be left for regeneration after it.

Once across the Rhine, 21st Army Group began to clear the Germans out of Holland. The priorities were to bring in food for a population which was on the brink of starvation and to deal with the remaining V2 launch sites, since these rockets were still being used not only against London but also against European cities in Allied hands. By now the German army was on the brink of dissolution: the *Volksturm* of old men, boys and even women fought bravely but they were no match for tanks and artillery, and it did not escape Stalin's notice that army units were surrendering much more readily in the West than to the Red Army in the East. An exception was in the Ruhr pocket, cut off when the US First and Third Armies met at Lippstadt on 2/3 April, when remnants of Field Marshal Model's surrounded Army Group B held out against repeated American attacks. Meanwhile, Montgomery was downcast to find that the US Ninth Army was now to be removed from his command (he was still insisting that with it he could take Berlin) and returned to Bradley, whose army group was to drive for Leipzig and Dresden, while 21st Army Group was to push north-east to Hamburg on the River Elbe, that being the agreed meeting line of the Anglo-American and Soviet armies.

Despite Patton's protests that he could take Prague, Eisenhower insisted that the Western Allies adhere to the agreement with the Soviets that they would advance no farther east than the Elbe. Churchill, egged on by Brooke and Montgomery, had now become alarmed at the prospect of the Russians getting to Berlin first and appealed to Roosevelt. Eisenhower, supported by Marshall, insisted that Berlin was but a geographical location and what mattered was the destruction of the German armies, not mere occupation of territory, and Roosevelt backed him. But for all Eisenhower's insistence on the military necessity taking priority over the political, he none the less impressed on Montgomery the importance of his reaching the Baltic before the Red Army: if Denmark and Norway had to be liberated, it had better be by the British or Americans, rather than by the Russians. On 11 April the US Ninth Army got to the Elbe at Magdeburg, and the next day Roosevelt died of a cerebral haemorrhage in Warm Springs, Georgia. Hitler was overjoyed, but of course it made no difference to the course of the war, except that Vice-President, now President, Harry S. Truman cancelled plans to bombard German industrial sites with pilotless bombers packed with explosives, for fear of retaliation in kind against London. German industry was still operating, albeit most of it far underground: the first jet fighters were taking to the skies and the latest in long-range submarines to the seas, but it was all far too late. Resistance in the West was now sporadic, albeit at times spirited. The situation in the East was very different.

* * *

For the Soviets, after they had thwarted the last German attempt to recapture Budapest and the Hungarian oil fields, the next objective was Vienna. They smashed the Hungarian Third Army, and forced back the furiously resisting Germans, whose Hungarian allies were now deserting them in droves. By 28 March the Red Army was on the Austrian border and heading for Vienna. In the north of the front, the priority for the German army now was to hold off the Russians and maintain the road and rail network until the civilian population could be evacuated overland or by the German navy. In the Baltic, Russian submarines were active, sinking anything they could find, even clearly marked hospital ships. When the 5,000-ton freighter *Goya* was sunk on the night of 16/17 April, 6,000 civilian refugees went down with her. The strategically irrelevant Army Group North, now renamed Army Group Kurland, withstood all comers in the Courland Pocket, and in Königsberg General of Infantry Otto Lasch, unable to be evacuated by sea because of constant air attacks, held out with his three badly under-strength divisions against thirty-six Russian ones, disputing every yard and counter-attacking with all the old skill and courage, until the Red Army finally penetrated to the centre of the city and Lasch surrendered on 9 April. A quarter of his soldiers lay dead in the ruins, along with about a quarter of the civilian population, but Hitler insisted that he was a traitor for surrendering at all and had him and his family condemned to death.*

On 13 April the Soviets took Vienna after suffering fearful casualties: the Germans had absolutely refused to give up the bridges over the Danube while the remotest possibility of holding on to the city remained. But now that the Russians were into Greater Germany proper, they reverted to barbarism. For years, German propaganda had warned what would happen if the Slavic hordes got into Europe, and it had not exaggerated. Red Army soldiers had behaved abominably in Budapest and Königsberg and now it became endemic. Russians butchered, tortured, shot and raped with impunity: military or civilian, adult or child, old or young, it mattered not, and often they were egged on by their commanders. Partly, of course, this was revenge for the German atrocities in Russia, but rape had not been a German sport, partly because military discipline had generally held, and partly because Russians and Jews were deemed inferior beings and so it would not have been fitting

---

*His family were arrested, but the war ended before they could be executed. Lasch was put in a Russian prison camp and not released until 1955.

to have sex with them. Nobody knows how many German women and girls were raped by Russian soldiers – and, for many who were, suicide was seen as the only way out – but it was so widespread that after the war the Catholic Church's bishops absolved German doctors from the sin of performing abortions. For years, Soviet commanders had kept their men going with appeals to patriotism reinforced by savage discipline while holding out promises of the pleasures of revenge once they had reached Germany, and now that time had come. Three days after the Russians took Vienna, their final offensive to take Berlin began, although Stalin had told the Western Allies that he could not attack Berlin until May, and that this offensive was aimed at Dresden. Naturally suspicious, and judging the Americans and the British by his own duplicitous standards, Stalin seems to have believed that the Germans were going to open the Western Front and do a deal with the Anglo-Americans to the detriment of the Soviet Union. In fact, although there were many who urged him to do so, Kesselring set his face firmly against any armistice that was not sanctioned by the political leadership, and Hitler himself was firmly set against any such agreement.

The Berlin offensive would be carried out by two Fronts: Marshal Zhukov's First Byelorussian with nine armies including two tank armies, which was directly east of Berlin along the River Oder, and Marshal Konev's First Ukrainian Front of eight armies, two of them tank armies, which was situated farther south, along the River Neisse. The Neisse is in fact the upper reaches of the Oder, so Konev had rather more ground to cover than Zhukov and would have to cross the River Spree before turning north for Berlin, although this would be compensated for by the fact that Zhukov would have to negotiate the formidable lines of obstacles the Germans had established before Berlin. Altogether, the Russians had assembled 2 million men, 6,000 tanks and self-propelled guns and 40,000 artillery pieces, mortars and Katyusha rocket-launchers. Facing them was Army Group Vistula, previously Oberhein, which had been commanded by Himmler until Guderian managed to persuade him to stand down 'for reasons of health' and was now in the hands of Colonel-General Gotthard Heinrici, who had previously commanded Fourth Army on the Eastern Front. Heinrici had General of Panzer Troops Hasso von Manteuffel's Third Panzer Army, Colonel-General Walter Weiss's Second Army, Colonel-General Theodor Busse's Ninth Army and General of Infantry Kurt von Tippelskirch's Twenty-First Army. All of these armies had taken a considerable battering, most were amalgamations of parts of previously shattered units and formations, all were seriously under-strength and Weiss's Second Army was cut off in Danzig, where it continued to resist stoutly but was unavailable to Heinrici for the defence of Berlin. Altogether, Heinrici could field around 300,000 men with 900 tanks and around 1,500 artillery pieces, and he was already losing faith in the competence of Berlin after being ordered to launch a counter-attack on the concentrating Russian troops at Küstrin (now Kostrzyn), one which had failed with heavy losses on 1 April.

The Russian tactics were those that they had used with considerable success so far: with one artillery piece per ten yards of front, they would unleash a devastating bombardment, after which the infantry would move forward and attack the German defences. Once the infantry had created a breach, the armour would pour through and the advance would continue. For the Germans, Hitler had at last sanctioned the methods that his generals had constantly been urging but had not been allowed to use. Two lines of defences would be prepared, and the troops would move back to the second line while the Russian artillery barrage came down, emerging and moving forward again when it lifted. This would protect the infantry from the preliminary bombardment and allow them to destroy the attacking infantry with artillery, mortars and machine-guns, and the armour which followed with anti-tank weapons including the primitive but highly effective hand-held *Panzerfaust*.

At 0500 hours on 16 April, Zhukov began his attack with the usual artillery bombardment and then launched his infantry against the German Ninth Army on the Seelow Heights. The Germans emerged more or less intact from their bunkers and took on the Soviet infantry, who could not break through. Infuriated, Zhukov sent in the armour of his First Guards Tank Army, but the tanks found themselves mixed up with the infantry and in a minefield with the Germans picking them off with 88mm guns and *Panzerfaust*s. Losing his temper completely, Zhukov sent in his second tank army, which only produced complete traffic gridlock and gave the Germans a host of juicy targets. Zhukov had mounted batteries of searchlights in his own forward positions and also on his tanks, the idea being that their beams would reflect off the clouds and illuminate the Germans, but now they worked in reverse, reflecting off the dust and smoke caused by the artillery and illuminating themselves, for which the Germans were no doubt suitably grateful. The following day, with more and more Russian troops thrown in and supported by constant attacks from the air, the town of Seelow eventually fell in the early afternoon, and Busse withdrew his units back to their next prepared defence position. It was not until 19 April that Zhukov finally broke through the defences on the Seelow Heights and was able to continue the advance towards Berlin. In the south, Konev had more success: attacking behind a smoke screen, he managed to force a crossing of the Neisse and establish a bridgehead big enough to get his tanks across on pontoon bridges, and the Soviet armour then penetrated Fifth Panzer Army's forward defences. The following day he reached and then crossed the River Spree and hooked north. Meanwhile, on 19 April, Stalin removed the Front boundaries and declared that whichever Front got there first would have the honour of capturing the German capital.

In Berlin itself, it was apparent that the city now risked encirclement and officials not essential to the defence and archives were being moved southwest into Bavaria – Hitler had already allowed Ribbentrop and his Foreign Office staff and those diplomats still accredited to Germany to go on 13 April, but announced that he himself would remain in Berlin to direct its defence along with Eva Braun, his long-term girlfriend, and his immediate entourage, including General Krebs and the OKH staff, while OKW moved to Zossen, thirty miles to the south. Hitler still seems to have clung to the notion that the alliance between East and West would break down, and he had ordered that Berlin should be stocked with sufficient stores, ammunition and rations for three divisions for three weeks, presumably calculating that, if the expected rupture did not come in that time, then the game would be up. On 20 April it was Hitler's fifty-sixth birthday. He had told his staff that he wanted no celebrations, but that afternoon he presented awards to members of the Hitler Youth and the *Volksturm* for bravery on the Oder Front. That day too, Göring, the titular head of the Luftwaffe, and Himmler, the head of the SS, left Berlin, supposedly to galvanize resistance against the Soviets.

Despite the heroic struggle of General Busse with Ninth Army and that of Third Panzer Army in support, the Russians were getting closer and closer, Zhukov from the east and Konev from the south, so much so that from 20 April onwards Hitler could not use the Reich Chancellery building but stayed in the extensive headquarters bunker dug deep into the ground beside it. On 21 April the Russians got to within artillery range and began to pour a rain of shells into the heart of the city. Observers reported the gun battery in question was only eight miles away. Hitler now ordered Heinrici to cut off the Russian salient created by Zhukov and Konev's advance by a pincer attack using SS Obergruppenführer Felix Steiner's Army Detachment Steiner attacking from the north and Busse's Ninth Army from the south. Theoretically this was all very well, but Army Detachment Steiner was in fact only a corps of three divisions, one police, one panzer grenadier and one light infantry, all well under-strength, and Busse's army was almost surrounded and pinned against the Oder. When Steiner pointed out that he himself was defending against the Second Byelorusian Front with his back to the Baltic and unless relieved had only three battalions available for anything else, Heinrici accepted that the attack could not happen. Hitler flew into a rage, fulminating against his generals. A summons to Heinrici to come and see him was evaded by the army group staff, who said that the commander was too busy planning the relief of Berlin to see anybody. That same day, Konev's Third Guards Tank Army stormed Zossen, arriving just after the staff of OKW had hurriedly evacuated their headquarters and dashed to Berlin before moving again to Neu-Roofen, forty miles north-west in Brandenburg, and Hitler was given the news that Field Marshal Model, whose Army Group B had held out in the Ruhr until all hope and ammunition was gone, had committed suicide, with 300,000 of his men being taken prisoner.

Further bad news arrived when it was reported that Nuremberg, the spiritual capital of National Socialism, had fallen to Patton's US Third Army after five days of bitter fighting. The next day, 22 April, largely to mollify Hitler and without much expectation that it would actually work, Keitel and Jodl of OKW presented a new plan involving an attack eastwards and north-eastwards by Busse and General of Panzer Troops Walter Wenck's Twelfth Army, which was currently on the Elbe fifty miles from Berlin and facing west against the American Ninth Army at Magdeburg. Wenck was to about turn and drive east, linking up with Busse south of Berlin, whereupon both armies would strike north-east and cut off the Russian forces attacking Berlin. At the same time Lieutenant-General Rudolf Holste's LXI Panzer Corps, part of Fourth Army on the Baltic coast, was to attack south.

Wenck did manage to turn his army round and initially made good progress towards Berlin, but he was stopped at Potsdam by strong Russian forces, and on 25 April the Red Army closed the ring around the city and Berlin was cut off, while in the west the British were into Hamburg. It is likely that Heinrici had now given up any idea of relieving Berlin and was concerned only with keeping the routes to the west open to the south of the capital to allow civilians to flee the Russians, and with trying to withdraw Busse's Ninth Army to the west. Now the Russians were in the suburbs of Berlin and only a few miles from the central government quarter. The garrison totalled around 150,000 under the command of General of Artillery Helmuth Weidling, but of those only 45,000 were regular soldiers or Waffen SS, the rest being made up of police, anti-aircraft gunners, Hitler Youth (schoolboys on bicycles armed with *Panzerfausts*) and *Volksturm*. The defence was fierce, for many of the defenders – including Dutch and French SS – had nothing to lose, and even at this last minute of the last hour Hitler's baleful presence stiffened resistance, as did 'flying' courts martial mainly composed of very young SS officers who were charged with the summary execution of anyone who appeared not to be doing their duty. These bodies tended to keep away from formed army units, whose commanders threatened to shoot them should they interfere, but they did inject a certain amount of terror into members of the *Volksturm* or the Hitler Youth whom the SS considered were displaying insufficient enthusiasm for the fight. Politically, too, the Reich was collapsing: Göring had signalled Hitler suggesting that, as the Führer was now cut off in Berlin and unable to discharge his duties as head of state, then perhaps he, Göring, should assume the leadership of Germany and try to arrange peace terms with the Western Allies. Hitler ordered him arrested and stripped of all his offices. The news that Himmler was trying to arrange an armistice through Swiss intermediaries brought an order for his dismissal too, and the fact that SS Obergruppenführer Hermann Fegelein, Hitler's Waffen SS liaison officer, was married to Margarethe Braun, Eva's sister, did not save him from being shot when he attempted to get out of Berlin in civilian clothes.

The last attempt to relieve Berlin failed when Wenck could make no progress beyond Potsdam, and Busse realized that his only possible choice was to try to break out west to join with Wenck, and on 24 April this he attempted to do, striking to the south of Berlin. Under heavy attack from Konev's troops in his flank and rear, Busse did manage to get some 25,000 of his men out to link up with Wenck, which at least meant that they could eventually surrender to the Americans rather than to the Russians.

With the Russians on the Elbe meeting the Americans at Torgau, Germany was now split in two, and on 25 April an RAF raid on Obersalzburg destroyed the Berghof, Hitler's erstwhile mountain retreat. As the Russians came closer and closer to the centre of Berlin and headed towards the *Reichstag*, from where they thought the defence was being directed, and Weidling's men began to run out of ammunition, it was none the less still possible, just, for aircraft to get in and out, and on 25 April a few naval infantry and SS did arrive. But with the only German formation still intact and capable of action – Army Group Centre, commanded by Ferdinand Schorner, a field marshal since 5 April – too far away in Czechoslovakia to help and with the loss of Gatow and Tempelhof airports over the next few days, there really was now no hope of salvation. On 27 April the Berlin underground system was flooded to prevent the Russians using it, in the process drowning many civilians who had taken shelter there. By 28 April the Chancellery was under direct shellfire and Keitel had discovered that Heinrici had no intention of coming to the relief of Berlin – such a move would anyway have been futile – but was instead pulling his troops back west as fast as they could go. Keitel dismissed Heinrici and his chief of staff, but in practice there was nothing he could do to enforce the sacking.

At last Hitler accepted the inevitable, and in the early hours of 29 April, with the bunker vibrating under the weight of high explosive raining down above, he issued cyanide capsules to his staff and dictated his political testament to his secretary, Frau Traudl Junge, widow of SS Obersturmführer Hans Junge, who had been killed in action in Normandy in 1944. In it, Hitler appointed three men as his successors: Grand Admiral Dönitz, Commander-in-Chief of the German navy and based in Flensburg in Schleswig-Holstein, as president of the Reich; Josef Goebbels as Reich chancellor; and Field Marshal Schorner as Commander-in-Chief of the army. Next, a registrar was summoned from Goebbels's ministry to preside over the marriage of Hitler and Eva Braun. There was a necessarily small wedding reception, during which Hitler spent most of his time discussing with Bormann and Goebbels the composition of the new cabinet, as if it could possibly matter now. That evening, General Weidling reported that there were no more *Panzerfausts*, tanks could not be repaired, his men were nearly out of small arms ammunition, there was heavy fighting less than a mile away from the Chancellery and that in his opinion they could hold out for no more than twenty-four hours. Hitler asked SS Brigadeführer Wilhelm Mohnke to become responsible for the immediate defence of the Chancellery if he agreed, and he did. The following day, at around 1530 hours in his study in the bunker, Eva Braun took poison and Hitler put a cyanide capsule in his mouth and, as he bit down on it, shot himself through the head. The bodies were taken out into the open, doused with petrol and burned in a shell crater.

The next day, 1 May, General Krebs, a Russian-speaker from his days as an assistant military attaché in Moscow, went out with a white flag to arrange a ceasefire. He was eventually taken to Colonel-General Vasili Chuikov, the commander of Zhukov's Eighth Guards Army that had spearheaded the final assault on Berlin. Krebs wanted to discuss terms but, after Chuikov had consulted Zhukov and he Stalin, Krebs was told that only unconditional surrender was acceptable. As Krebs did not have the authority from Goebbels to agree this, he returned to the bunker and the fighting continued. On 2 May, with his men out of ammunition and many surrendering on their own account, Weidling surrendered the Berlin garrison unconditionally. Krebs committed suicide, as did Goebbels and his wife, but only after first poisoning their children, while the party secretary, Bormann, and all those who could go with him attempted to break out west through the Russian lines in small groups. Many never made it.

Now the long nightmare of the civilians in Berlin began as Russian troops searched for alcohol, plunder and women, and began to exact vengeance for the 67,000 Red Army soldiers killed in the battle. The cost to the Germans of the fighting from the Oder–Neisse line to the fall of Berlin was around half a million killed or captured, with commensurate losses of equipment that could not be replaced. Elsewhere on the Eastern Front, the priority was to get as far away from the Russians as possible, and on 3 May the German navy began the evacuation of Army Group Kurland. Any Russian designs on Denmark were scuppered on the same day when the British Second Army reached Wismar on the Baltic, meeting the Russian Seventieth Army there; in Czechoslovakia, despite a partisan uprising in Prague and the re-defection back to the Red Army of General Vlasov's Russians (which did them no good at all, most subsequently being either executed or sent to the gulags), Schorner continued to hold out and edge westwards, and on the Elbe the American First and Ninth Armies met the Soviet First Byelorussian and First Ukrainian Fronts.

With Hitler dead, suggestions of negotiations for an armistice no longer risked court martial and a firing squad, and Admiral Dönitz, having consulted with Kesselring and all the senior officers who could be contacted, accepted that the war could not be continued. Emissaries were sent out under flags of truce and at 0500 hours on 4 May Generaladmiral Hans-Georg von Friedeburg and a delegation arrived at Montgomery's headquarters on Lüneburg Heath, twenty-five miles south-east of Hamburg. After being unnecessarily humiliated by the British field marshal by being kept waiting and then not allowed to smoke, von Friedeburg surrendered all German forces in Holland, Denmark and north-west Germany. The German party were then taken to Eisenhower's headquarters in Reims, where they were joined by Jodl from OKW. They again suggested a separate peace, which was turned down, and, when it became apparent that the Germans were playing for time to get as many of their troops and civilians into the West as they could, Eisenhower responded that, unless they signed, he would close his front and allow no more refugees through it. At 0241 hours on 7 May, Jodl signed the instrument of unconditional surrender of all German forces, wherever they were, the ceasefire to come into effect no later than midnight on 8 May. This was not acceptable to Stalin, who demanded a further surrender ceremony in Berlin, where at 2330 hours on 8 May Jodl signed again. Victory in Europe Day (VE Day) is therefore 8 May 1945 in Britain and America, and 9 May in Russia and the states of the former USSR. Although fighting officially ended on 8 May, many German units fought on and it was not until 15 May, in Yugoslavia, that the last German laid down his arms.

* * *

The victory parade in Burma took place in Rangoon on 15 June 1945, although mopping-up operations continued and the formal surrender did not take place until August. While the Americans had ordered that Japanese officers were permitted to retain their swords, Slim insisted that Japanese officers surrendering to or taken prisoner by the British were required to surrender their swords to a British officer of the same or higher rank, for only by doing so could they be made to understand that they had been defeated.* For now the next objective for the British was Malaya and Singapore – Operations Zipper and Mailfist – followed by Thailand and the Dutch East Indies, and it was intended to launch Zipper on 1 September 1945. There were 86,000 Japanese troops in Malaya, seasoned combatants, and, as the Malayan terrain was unsuitable for the employment of mass armoured sweeps, the British preponderance of

---

*Many Japanese officers' swords were prized family heirlooms with great cultural and almost religious significance. When Mountbatten accepted the surrender of Field Marshal Count Hisaichi Terauchi in Saigon in November 1945, he sent the field marshal's short sword, forged in the sixteenth century, to King George VI (it is now in Windsor Castle) and kept the long sword, forged three centuries earlier, for himself.

tanks and self-propelled guns would no longer be a major advantage. Slim, backed by Mountbatten and Auchinleck, thought that the minimum force for Zipper was seven divisions, but there were problems. In June the British government intimated that it was intending to reduce even further the length of a Far East tour to three years and four months for British soldiers – the Python scheme – after which they were to be repatriated to the UK. Theoretically, these men would be replaced, albeit by men with no experience of the East and who would require training on arrival, but the main problem was transport and the wherewithal to organize it. If all the British officers and men due to be sent home were to be withdrawn from their units, moved to and accommodated at ports of embarkation, and shipped to the UK, then the rail and transit facilities in India would not be able to cope, and nor would the available shipping. Not only that, but, as Auchinleck pointed out in a letter to the CIGS, there would be no shipping available for the Indian Army units in the Middle East and the Mediterranean, most of whom had been away from home for longer than the British and were long overdue for leave, to say nothing of the 23,000 West African troops in India waiting to be sent home to Africa. While Brooke understood the problem, there was little sympathy from British politicians – there was a general election due and Indians, Gurkhas and West Africans had no votes. The end result was an unhappy compromise: Zipper would be postponed until 9 September 1945, all British soldiers whose three years and four months was up before the end of the year would be withdrawn and repatriated when shipping became available, and Zipper would be mounted with six divisions rather than seven. In the meantime, with Iwo Jima and Okinawa secure, the Americans were planning for the invasion of Japan, with a view to landing on the southern island of Kyushu in November 1945 and then moving on to Honshu in March 1946.

In Japan huge merchant shipping losses and the effective destruction of the Imperial Navy threw the country back on its own resources. Reserve stocks of raw materials that could not be replaced were running out, there was only sufficient vehicle fuel to last until the end of June and just enough aviation fuel, if carefully used, to last until September. There was a shortage of rice, which was expected to be worse with a projected bad harvest in 1945, and salt was in very short supply. There was little industry still operating, but what there was suffered even more from the depredations of the army conscripting its workers and calling up those who were reservists. The introduction of price controls and rationing led to a thriving black market and competition between army, navy and civilian purchasing organizations for the limited stocks of oil, raw materials, and processed steel and rubber that were available. The Allied incendiary bombing had wreaked massive destruction on Japanese cities and rendered hundreds of thousands homeless, a situation exacerbated by the order to demolish yet more houses to create fire breaks through built-up areas. It was obvious that the next phase of the war would be an Allied invasion of the homeland, preceded by heavy aerial bombardment, and in Operation Ketsu-Go the Japanese now reorganized the balance of their forces to deal with it. In December 1944 seven divisions had been moved from Manchuria to Japan, leaving only twelve divisions, eight of which were newly raised and had no combat experience. These were barely enough to mount some sort of defence if the Russians attacked, something which the Japanese worked very hard diplomatically to avoid but suspected might happen anyway. Now every available man was called up and new divisions raised, anti-aircraft guns were brought in from outlying islands and every available aircraft brought to a state of readiness. By the summer of 1945 there were fifty-six infantry and two armoured divisions, in five area armies, ready to defend the homeland, along with 537 fighter and eighteen reconnaissance aircraft and 1,250 anti-aircraft guns. The fighter cover was totally inadequate to defend the whole country and it was intended that the main air effort would be by kamikaze attacks against Allied shipping, with the navy pilots going for warships and their army counterparts concentrating on troopships.

There had always been a peace party in Japan, politicians, civil servants and officers who knew that Japan could never win a war against the West, but they had perforce to be circumspect for fear of assassination. Now, while still unable openly to recommend making peace, they were able to attempt discreetly to influence the power brokers. In April the Cabinet resigned and the elder statesman Admiral Baron Kantarō Suzuki, untainted by warmongering, became prime minister, an appointment that it was hoped would send a mollifying signal to the Allies. As early as February, Prince Fumimaro Konoe, a former prime minister, had advised the emperor that there was a danger of a communist revolution unless the war ended very soon, and in June and again in July Hirohito instructed his Supreme War Council to take steps to restore peace. The difficulty was how to do it. Approaches were made to Russia, citing the Russo-Japanese neutrality agreement, and were rebuffed; the Swedes would not act as brokers without a formal request from the Japanese government; an attempt through the unlikely medium of Chiang Kai-shek failed; and unofficial soundings indicated that the British, who were thought to be more likely to compromise than the Americans, were not prepared to stray from the Allied policy of unconditional surrender. Unconditional surrender, though, was out of the question: the army would never accept the loss of face and the disgrace, nor any threat to the position of the emperor, and the population would probably follow the army. If some form of compromise could be arrived at, one that allowed the army to retain its honour, did not involve an occupation of the country and preserved the position of the emperor, then the army leaders might be prepared to accept an end to the war and the evacuation of the conquered territories and perhaps China and even Korea as well. Discussions were kept strictly secret from the younger army officers: history showed that they were quite liable to draw swords and slaughter anyone who suggested that the war was lost.

The Potsdam Declaration of 26 July 1945 effectively killed any chance of the Japanese government and army surrendering under terms that were acceptable to them. Given the imaginative name of Terminal, the conference was the last held by the wartime Allies, the United States being represented by her new president, Truman, and Churchill, defeated in the British general election, being replaced halfway though by Attlee, the new Labour prime minister. The Japanese ambassador in Moscow was instructed to inform his government that the Allies demanded the unconditional surrender of all Japanese forces everywhere; that those who had led Japan into war be removed, with the country occupied until this had been achieved; that all territories acquired by Japan since 1914 be given up, including Chinese territories; that Korea be granted independence; that Japanese sovereignty be restricted to the four main islands; that all servicemen be disarmed and returned to their homes; and that war criminals be brought to justice. The Japanese foreign and prime ministers pointed out to the Cabinet that with such terms attached the demand was not unconditional surrender as the term was usually understood: nothing was said about the position of the emperor and occupation was only to be until those responsible for the war were removed. The emperor thought the terms were acceptable, but the service chiefs were for rejection. It was decided to seek clarification and perhaps some amelioration through Stalin, who, although he had denounced the

Neutrality Pact in April, had not signed the Potsdam Declaration. As the declaration had been published all over the world, the Japanese government had to make some response, but it had to be one that would not reject the declaration outright, nor imply favourable consideration, since the latter was not yet acceptable to the army and the navy.

The Japanese, however, failed to brief their own press properly and, critically, the Japanese words 'take notice of' were mistranslated. As a result, the impression was given that the government in Tokyo had rejected the declaration. In his answer to a question at a press conference on 28 July, the prime minister, Suzuki, stated that the government would ignore the declaration and press resolutely on to bring the war to a victorious conclusion. It has been suggested that, had the Allies enquired more closely into the Japanese government's intentions, peace might have been achieved at this point, but that is to ignore the attitude of the army, and even more so of the senior naval officers, who, even though they now had no navy to speak of, would never accept a surrender that involved disarmament and occupation, and the fact that, as Stalin was intending to declare war on Japan in ten days' time, there was no chance of his interceding to get better terms.

Given that Japan intended to hold out come what may, the Allies had a number of options. They could invade, they could blockade or they could use new weapons to bring such destruction that Japan would have no choice but to give in. An invasion was already being planned and the command structure had been reorganized to put all land forces in the Pacific (including the British Fourteenth Army once it had regained Malaya) under MacArthur, and all naval forces under Nimitz, with Lieutenant-General Carl Spaatz, lately the USAAF commander in Europe, supporting with the Strategic and Far East Air Forces. For the first phase, fourteen divisions, including some released from the European theatre, were earmarked to take the southern half of Kyushu. The snag, though, about reducing Japan by invasion was that it might take a very long time, and, as the whole population would resist to the utmost, it could cause very many Allied casualties. Experience in Iwo Jima and Okinawa showed that, even with defeat staring him in the face, the only time a Japanese soldier was beaten was when he was dead, and, while figures still bandied about today of a million Allied casualties to subdue Japan by invasion are almost certainly a gross overestimate, the death toll could easily have been in the region of 100,000. An alternative would have been an air and sea blockade accompanied by air raids, as MacArthur recommended.

This would save Allied lives and would slowly strangle what was left of Japan's economy and starve her population, but this too might take a long time. Already the Japanese government had instructed its people to gather acorns to be made into foodstuffs, inshore fishing could still continue and, by eating everything that walked, crawled, swam, grew or flew, the population of the home islands could hold out for a very long time, whereas both the Americans and the British wanted a swift end to the war.

A third option was to use a weapon of such power that Japan could not possibly continue to fight on, for if she did she would face complete and utter destruction, and such a weapon did indeed exist. Since 1941 British scientists had been convinced that a bomb relying on atomic fission could be constructed, but given the need for an area large enough to test it, and the expense of developing it, it had been decided to share the knowledge acquired so far with the Americans and develop the bomb jointly, as the Manhattan Project. Developed and tested in great secrecy, two bombs would be ready by August 1945 and in July both Truman and Churchill, and then Attlee, agreed that they would be used if Japan could not be persuaded to surrender before the date fixed for an invasion of the main islands. And following the Japanese prime minister's July press conference, it was clear that his government was not about to surrender. So on the morning of 6 August three B-29 bombers approached the southern Honshu city of Hiroshima, one carrying an atomic bomb and two flying as observers. At 0815 hours the bomb was dropped by parachute and detonated as planned above the centre of the city, which had been selected because it housed both military and industrial targets. Of a population of 343,000, 78,000 were killed outright and 51,000 injured, mainly with burns. Many more would die of radiation sickness in the years to come and many women not sterilized by the radiation would give birth to deformed children. Of the 76,000 buildings, 48,000 were destroyed and most of the rest damaged to some extent.

When the news reached Tokyo later that morning, it was apparent that a weapon of unprecedented destructive power had been used but few details were known. When the Commander-in-Chief Second Area Army, whose headquarters was in Hiroshima, and his chief of staff flew into Tokyo on the morning of the following day, 7 August, they claimed that their headquarters was virtually untouched and that only a few soldiers had been injured: it appeared that the bomb had only damaged those with no protection – anything underground was safe – and that, whatever had been used this time, conventional Allied incendiary bombing had caused greater casualties and more damage. The officers exaggerated: much of their headquarters was above ground, including a military hospital, and that had been obliterated, but they were partly right about incendiary bombing, the effects of which were more widespread, even if they did not cause subsequent deaths from residual radiation, a particularly unpleasant after-effect which was not fully understood at the time. Then, on 8 August, the USSR declared war on Japan, effective from midnight, and 1.5 million Red Army soldiers stormed across the border against the Japanese Kwantung Army in the puppet state of Manchukuo.

The Japanese Supreme Council met on the morning of 9 August. All were agreed that peace must be made but there were serious differences as to the terms of acceptance. The foreign minister, Togo, urged that the Allied terms be accepted as they stood, while the army representatives insisted that there should be no occupation, the position of the emperor should be guaranteed, and the Japanese Army should disarm itself and be responsible for war crimes trials. They also pointed out that surrender was specifically forbidden under Japanese military law, which prescribed heavy penalties for anyone who did surrender, and it was doubtful whether any such orders from Tokyo would be obeyed. Despite what was undoubtedly a desperate situation, the army could still fight a battle, and a resurgence of patriotic nationalism would meet any attempt at invasion. Japan should hold out for acceptable terms.

While the council were arguing, a second atomic bomb was dropped, at 1130 hours on 9 August, on Nagasaki on the east coast of Kyushu. As it did not explode over the centre of the city, the damage was not as great as that at Hiroshima, but it was impressive nevertheless, killing 24,000 of the 270,000 inhabitants outright and injuring 43,000. The council met again on the evening of the 9th, before knowledge of the second atomic bomb had reached Tokyo, and again could not reach a conclusion, and neither could the Cabinet. Suzuki, the prime minister, briefed the emperor, who ordered an imperial conference for the next night, that of the 10/11th, by which time the news of Nagasaki had come in. Shortly before midnight, all the arguments were once again rehearsed at this conference. The positions of both the peace and the war parties had hardened, and Suzuki announced that there was now no alternative but to seek a decision from the emperor, who directed that the Potsdam Declaration should be accepted subject only to the imperial house not being deposed. The next morning, the message was sent through the Swiss and Swedish embassies:

> In obedience to the gracious command of His Majesty the Emperor, who, ever anxious to enhance the cause of world peace, desires earnestly to bring about a speedy termination of hostilities with a view to saving mankind from the calamities to be imposed on them by further continuation of the war... the Japanese government are ready to accept the terms enumerated in the joint declaration... with the understanding that the said declaration does not comprise any demand which prejudices the prerogatives of his Majesty as a Sovereign Ruler...

A masterpiece of weasel-wording, this initiated great debate in Washington, where some felt that the emperor should have no part to play in the future of Japan, while others felt that only the authority of the emperor could ensure obedience to a surrender order. The Allied reply stated that, from the moment of surrender, the authority of the emperor to rule the state would be subject to an Allied Supreme Commander and that he would be required to issue such orders as the Supreme Commander might require, and that the ultimate form of government in Japan would be established in accordance with the freely expressed wishes of the Japanese people.

The Allied reply was received in Japan on 12 August and again prompted vigorous debate. By now word had got out: posters denouncing the peace party as traitors were appearing on the streets and there were reports of unrest amongst junior army officers. Clearly a decision was urgently needed and this was reinforced by information from the Japanese embassy in Sweden which averred that the Allied reply constituted a narrow diplomatic victory for the Americans over the British, who had been against retaining the emperor. Any more delay and the Americans might change their stance. This was actually a complete and deliberate falsehood instigated by Allied intelligence – the British were in complete agreement with the Allied note – but it did concentrate minds in Tokyo. Meanwhile, Allied aircraft had been dropping leaflets over Tokyo setting out the peace terms and there was now a real danger that if the leaders of the army saw them – and how could they not? – they would institute a coup to isolate the emperor from his evil councillors who were advocating surrender. An imperial conference was called for the morning of 14 August and the emperor was asked once more to decide. He directed that it was time to 'accept the unacceptable' and to agree to the Allied terms. As was the protocol, the Cabinet and the Supreme Council now announced their unanimous acceptance of the emperor's decision. At 2330 hours Tokyo time (1430 hours GMT), the Japanese government sent a telegram to its ambassadors in Sweden and Switzerland accepting the terms of the Potsdam Declaration. Unlike her German ally, Japan had managed to end the war with head of state, government and civil service intact.

It was one thing for the emperor and his government to agree a surrender, quite another to enforce it. That night army officers who wanted to fight on attempted a coup. Army aircraft dropped leaflets claiming the announcement was a fake, the commander of the Imperial Guards Division stationed next to the Imperial Household ministry was assassinated when he refused to take part in the coup and the prime minister narrowly escaped the same fate by going into hiding, although his house was burned down. The coup narrowly failed and, on the morning of 15 August the army minister, General Korechika Anami, Admiral Onishi, the initiator of the kamikaze campaign, one field marshal, four full generals and a host of lieutenant-generals committed ritual suicide. That same day, Japanese radio announced at intervals during the morning that the emperor would speak to the nation at 1200 hours. This had never happened before and at 1200 all traffic stopped and most of the nation listened.

In his unprecedented address, Hirohito said that, despite the gallantry of the naval and military forces, the diligence of the civil service and the devoted service of the whole nation, the war had not developed to Japan's advantage and he had decided to accept the terms of the Potsdam Declaration. He asked his people to accept his decision loyally and to work to enhance the glory of the imperial state. There was no mention of unconditional surrender. An imperial rescript or proclamation was issued reinforcing the emperor's words. Despite some residual resistance, including the dropping by naval aircraft of leaflets denying that the rescript was genuine, most people in Japan obeyed, and, to ensure obedience by garrisons abroad, a message was sent to all overseas commands stating that Japanese soldiers and sailors taken into the hands of the Allies would not be considered as prisoners of war, thus there was no need for them to kill themselves. At the same time, the three imperial princes were sent by air to Saigon in French Indo-China, Nanking and Peking in China, Manchuria, Singapore and Korea to confirm the emperor's wishes. All over the Far East, the Japanese Army burned its regimental colours – they were not going to be exhibited in American and British museums as trophies of war.* Despite some mutterings from the Russians, who had launched a lightning invasion of Manchuria, cut off forty Japanese divisions, penetrated into the north of Korea and stood poised to take the Kuriles and the Sakhalin peninsula before fighting on this front came to an end on 23 August, General MacArthur was nominated as Supreme Commander in Japan, but the Japanese government asked for a delay in the arrival of occupation forces until it could ensure that there would be no 'unfortunate incidents' – by which it meant that it would lock up potential assassins and disable all serviceable aircraft, thereby foiling the threats of unreconstructed officers who insisted that they would carry out kamikaze attacks on the Allied fleet as it steamed into Tokyo Bay.

On 2 September 1945, on the deck of the battleship USS *Missouri* in Tokyo Bay, the representatives of the Japanese emperor, government and armed forces signed the instrument of surrender. Other ceremonies followed in Malaya, Singapore, Hong Kong, British Borneo, the Dutch East Indies and French Indo-China. The reoccupation of these territories was to take the Allies some considerable time, and in not all of them were they welcomed. In the Dutch East Indies a nationalist movement, some of whose members had cooperated with the Japanese, had no intention of reverting to Dutch rule, and, as the Dutch had no armed forces to retake the islands, the British, or more accurately the Indian, Army had to do it for them. As troops were in short supply, the surrendered Japanese garrisons were rearmed and used to restore law and order. It was commonplace for a young British officer, with a Gurkha orderly and a couple of signallers, to have under command an entire Japanese battalion, with beswords officers bowing and hissing, and obeying orders promptly and efficiently.

And so the Second World War ended, but now its consequences had to be dealt with, an eventuality for which the Allies had been planning since well before the end of the conflict and about which they had enunciated and agreed in principle at the Yalta Conference in February 1945. Germany was to be divided into occupation zones to be governed by Allied Military Government Control Commissions, the Russians in the east and the British

---

*They didn't manage to burn them all. This author's regiment has a number on the walls of its various messes, along with a goodly selection of samurai swords.

and Americans in the west, with the French granted an occupation zone at the last minute. There was no justification whatsoever for a French zone – they had done little or nothing to defeat the Germans, although the Free French had perhaps prevented France from going communist – but it was in the Western Powers' interest to restore France to Great Power status as a counterweight to the USSR and so the French got their zone, as they did in Berlin, which was the subject of a separate division, again into four occupied zones. Other matters settled were the borders of post-war Europe, and here Poland was the major stumbling block, a Russian solution being reluctantly agreed to when the USSR refused to recognize the London-based government-in-exile. Another – latterly contentious – stipulation, insisted upon by the Russians, was that Allied nationals in the German army should be returned to their home country (which meant Russians, Cossacks, Poles, Latvians, Ukrainians et al). In a form of déjà vu in reverse, it was the Jewish Brigade in northern Italy that supervised the herding of Uzbeks in German uniform across a bridge from the British into the Russian zone, where they were shot as they arrived.

As far back as the Moscow Conference of October 1943, the Allies had agreed that at the end of the war those whom they regarded as having been responsible for the war should be punished, and that this should be carried out as a result of proper legal proceedings. Not all agreed with this approach; some British jurists were concerned about *ex post facto* justice, and pointed out that it was a long-standing principle of British law that no offence could be made retrospective: that is, you could make it a capital offence to ride a bicycle without lights and that could be enforced from the date the king signed the act, but you could not then hang somebody for careless cycling before the act came into force. Even Churchill was at first of the view that the best solution would simply be to line up the leadership of Germany and Japan and shoot the lot out of hand, but more sober counsel prevailed and many legal brains had been occupied long into the night to devise a framework within which trials could be held, a framework that had to satisfy the legal systems of Britain, America and the USSR and which would be seen to be fair by the rest of the world. It was not finally agreed until August 1945.

There was an existing legal code – the Hague and Geneva Conventions – that dealt with some aspects of armed conflict, such as the treatment of prisoners of war and enemy civilians, but there was no charge that could be brought against those people who had been acting in accordance with the laws of their own country within that country, nor with behaviour that had not been thought of when the conventions had been drawn up. The Allies therefore devised a set of charges which they intended to bring against the civil and military leaders of the defeated nations before International Military Tribunals (IMT), one in Nuremberg in Germany and one in Tokyo. The one trying the Germans would have a judge from each of the UK, the USA, the USSR and France, and was to be presided over by Lord Justice Lawrence, who was a distinguished British law lord, the son of a Lord Chief Justice and the winner of the DSO as an artillery officer in the First World War, and who had incidentally been at school with Clement Attlee. There were four 'catch-all' charges that would be relied upon: Count One, making a common plan or conspiracy to commit any of the other counts; Count Two, crimes against peace; Count Three, war crimes; and Count Four, crimes against humanity. Of these, Count One, conspiracy, was well understood in English and American law, albeit not in others, while Count Three, war crimes, was straightforward and already covered by the conventions, but Counts Two and Four were more difficult to agree upon, and eventually it was decided that crimes against peace were defined as planning, preparing, initiating and waging a war of aggression and wars in violation of international treaties or agreements, while crimes against humanity covered murder, deportment, enslavement and persecution on racial, religious or political grounds, whether or not – and this was crucial – such actions were in violation of the domestic law of the country where they were perpetrated. This was intended to cover slave labour, the concentration camps, the extermination of Jews and others and the behaviour of the *Einsatzgruppen* on the Eastern Front.

There were, inevitably, objections. In regard to crimes against peace, Count Two, every general staff in the world plans aggressive war, whether they actually carry it out or not, and, if they did not, they would not be doing their job. In the bowels of the Ministry of Defence in London there are plans for attacking just about every country in the world. Admittedly the one against France has not been updated since the 1920s, and the one against the USA has gathered dust for almost 200 years, but they are there. If the tribunal was going to arraign Germans for the unprovoked invasion of Norway, for example, then it was to be hoped that the subject of the British plans to do exactly that in 1940 would not arise. This tricky little matter was resolved by the IMT declaring that the *Tu Quoque* defence ('You did it too, so how can you prosecute me?') could not be deployed. Even Count Three, war crimes, was not entirely straightforward, as it covered 'wanton destruction of cities, towns and villages not justified by military necessity' and this, it might be argued, could equally well be applied to the Allied bombing offensive against Germany. There was also another snag, particularly in regard to Count Four, where the practitioners of nastiness would doubtless claim obedience to superior orders. This, it was decided, would not be an acceptable defence, and only at the last minute was a serious embarrassment avoided when it was pointed out that in the Army Act, the law as far as British soldiers were concerned, a chapter explaining how they were affected by international law concluded by saying that orders from government or an individual soldier's superiors were an absolute defence to an accusation of breaching the various conventions. An amendment removing this protection was hurriedly issued.

Eventually, the Nuremberg Tribunal arraigned twenty-two Germans accused before it. It would have been twenty-four but Robert Ley, the leader of the Deutsche Arbeitsfront, the one trade union permitted, had committed suicide and the head of the Krupp industrial dynasty was found unfit to plead. Hitler, Himmler and Goebbels had all committed suicide, otherwise they would have been there too. The idea was to cover the widest spectrum of the NSDAP state, and the accused included politicians, industrialists, political theorists, government ministers and representatives of the military: from the army, there were Field Marshal Keitel and General Jodl; from the navy, Admirals Raeder and Dönitz; from the air force, there was Reichsmarschall Göring. It was perhaps ironic that the Russians, those masters of the art of mass murder and rigged trials, were represented, and that much hand-wringing reference was made to the principles of the League of Nations, which the United States had declined to join and from which the USSR had been expelled. The Molotov–Ribbentrop Pact was hurriedly skated over, even though Ribbentrop was one of the accused; the Russians insisted on including in the charge sheet the Katyn Forest massacre in Poland, which everyone knew had been carried out by them and not the Germans, and objected strongly when the wretched Rudolf Hess, who had been in British custody since long before most of the crimes complained of had been committed, and before the attack on the Soviet Union had even begun, was not sentenced to death.

The indictments took two days to read, and 218 days to try. In the end, three of the twenty-two were acquitted – the economist Hjalmar Schacht,

Franz von Papen, who had briefly been Hitler's deputy chancellor, and Hans Fritsche, head of the radio division of the Ministry of Propaganda – and, of the nineteen found guilty on one or more of the counts, eleven were sentenced to death. Göring managed to commit suicide before the sentence could be carried out but Keitel and Jodl were both hanged. These were dishonourable deaths for military men – and deliberately intended to be so – and a West German court many years later pardoned Jodl as a soldier who had simply been doing his duty and who confined his activity to operational matters. The two admirals were found guilty but sentenced to imprisonment. Once the IMT trials were over, each occupying power conducted further trials in their own zones of occupation, which continued until 1949. In both West and, much later, reunified Germany, the trials went on as post-war German politicians sought to distance themselves from their nation's past. It is difficult to see what is achieved now by putting a ninety-year-old former concentration camp guard on trial, when identification is doubtful and the witnesses' recollection must be impaired, but it still happens.

In Japan, the Allies took a rather different view. War crimes trials there must be, but the wartime alliance was fast unravelling and the West needed Japan as a bulwark against communism in the region. Most notable was the absence of the emperor in the dock, along with a number of leading military and naval figures, while many of the most wanted had already killed themselves. There were those both then and now who felt that Hirohito was as guilty as Hitler and should have been hanged, but expediency ruled and the Allies needed the authority of the emperor to keep order during the occupation. The International Military Tribunal Far East (IMTFE) was made up of eleven judges, reflecting the wide scope of Japanese aggression, and was presided over by Judge Sir William Webb of Australia. The Tribunal put twenty-eight Japanese on trial and found all of them guilty. Seven were hanged, all having been found guilty of atrocities against prisoners of war or civilians. Subsequent regional trials by the individual nations went on until 1951, and of the 5,700 defendants 920 were executed, nearly all found guilty of atrocities.

In hindsight, the conduct of both tribunals, and particularly that in Tokyo, leaves one uncomfortable. Hearsay evidence was permitted, as were diaries and written matter, even though the writers of these were not questioned, the defendants were accused of crimes that were not crimes when committed, the Russian judges were concerned only with doing what

Moscow wanted without regard to legal principles (the Russian judge in Tokyo could not understand English or Japanese, the two languages of the trial). There can be little doubt that most of the Germans and Japanese executed were thoroughly nasty people, and deserving of no sympathy, but it was of questionable legality all the same. That said, it is difficult to see what else the Allies could have done. The United Kingdom and the United States were democracies, and their populations would have insisted that those seen as being responsible for slaughter on such a scale were held accountable, regardless of legal niceties. To punish every single German or Japanese who had stepped out of line was not a practical proposition, and, for all the undoubted flaws in the procedure, the execution or imprisonment of a representative sample was probably the only realistic – and quite possibly the fairest – option.

EPILOGUE

The Second World War affected more people than any other in recorded history. Estimates of the total death toll vary widely and are of little assistance in assessing the results of the war, for it was not merely the relatives of those killed in battle that were most affected. When we add civilian deaths by bombing, famine, disease and deliberate genocide, the grand total may well be somewhere in the region of 50–60 million. Some authorities estimate a much higher figure but the truth is that, while the American and British records are accurate, and the German ones reasonably so, nobody really knows the figures for the USSR and China, even though there can be little doubt that they topped the league. The USA and the British Empire got away relatively lightly, with less than a million military and civilian dead between them, although this does not include those who died in the Bengal famine – a disaster which would not have happened but for the war preventing rice from being imported from Burma. In strictly demographic terms, populations, at least in the West, recovered relatively quickly, as they always do after a major conflict. Far more long-lasting, however, were the political and economic consequences of the war.

Militarily, the Red Army, with huge swathes cut out of it by Stalin's purges and with decision-making constipated by the presence of the commissars, probably made the steepest conversion. From being a force with obsolete equipment, a lack of mobility and ignorant commanders, it became one that was able to take on the Germans and beat them at their own game, admittedly only when greatly outnumbering them.

The United States started the war with an old-fashioned and tiny army and a large but pedestrian navy, but in an astonishingly short space of time her industries were galvanized into producing the materiel required to wage total war. American commanders knew that both officers and men were inexperienced and so they relied on machines, becoming by far the most mechanized of the combatants – the amount of firepower US forces could deliver, from ships, aircraft, artillery and tanks, was nothing short of awesome. As for the British, they feared the Germans' speed of reaction and ability to manoeuvre, and so they tried always to keep their forces balanced – with the right mix of armour, infantry and artillery – and to avoid taking risks, risks that they knew the Germans would exploit. The result was a plodding approach to war on land and cautious commanders who, despite protestations to the contrary, often fought battles of attrition reminiscent of the First World War. The thoroughly militarized society of Japan produced a superb fighting machine, with soldiers, sailors and airmen who were loyal, robust, capable of enduring great hardship and devoted to their cause. It was their misfortune that the machine was not backed up by an industrial base that could sustain it in a long war, and the appalling behaviour towards civilians and prisoners has left an indelible stain on Japanese honour.

In terms of pure military ability, however, the German army was by far the best. Time and again, even when the end was almost upon them, German soldiers showed a tactical flexibility and a professionalism which no other army came near to rivalling. While the British would require time for a formation newly arrived in theatre to train and marry up with others already there, the Germans could take a plethora of units of different arms, units which had never met each other before, give them a commander and send them out to do battle straight away. All German soldiers were trained in the same way and in the same battle drills, unlike the British, who relied on individual units having their own ways of doing things. After the war, the German generals mostly blamed Hitler for not allowing them to fight the sort of war that they were trained for and were good at. The question then arises: could the Germans have won the war without Hitler? Disregarding the fact that the Germans would not have gone to war without Hitler or someone very like him, the answer has to be 'No'. Once they had failed to win the war in 1940 by knocking Britain out of it, and then failed to take Moscow and topple the Soviet regime or at least force it to sue for peace in 1941, the Germans were always bound to lose: Russia was just far too big to conquer, and a country with Germany's population and industrial capacity simply could not take on the British and French empires, the USSR and the USA at the same time, however good her soldiers were – and they were very, very good. This was a lesson that Germany should have learned from the first war but chose not to.

As for the generals, many of the outstanding Russian commanders were rusticated immediately after the war for fear they might pose a threat to Stalin, and their talents only recognized, at least in their own country, many years later. Russian tactics were never particularly sophisticated, yet, given the size of the manpower pool from which the Red Army could draw, they did not have to be. It is difficult, therefore, to pass judgement on Zhukov, Konev and their ilk by Western standards, but there can be no doubt that it was they who directed the army which did most of the fighting on land and contributed in blood more to the defeat of Germany than any other.

In the United States, Eisenhower served two terms as president, following a long American tradition of successful military leaders turning (or being turned) to politics after a successful war. While there were those who dismissed Eisenhower's military capabilities, only he could have made the Alliance in the last phase of the war work – he was a past master at getting mutually antipathetic prima donnas to work together: nobody else, British or American, could have succeeded in the way that he did, and the free world owes him a huge debt. General Marshall, as Chief of Staff of the US Army, did a superb job in balancing the demands of the different theatres, coping with inter-service rivalry and ensuring that, even where British and American policies and interests differed widely, the Alliance never faltered. Douglas MacArthur became the viceroy of Japan, and nursed that nation back to health and brought it into the Western camp. Later, as American and United Nations Commander-in-Chief in Korea, he wanted to invade China and use atomic weapons against her. In hindsight, he may have been right, for as Napoleon so wisely said, 'Let China sleep, for when she awakes the world will tremble.' Bombing China back to the Stone Age might have nipped in the bud the economic threat now posed by that nation and the military threat that she may pose in the not too distant future, but it was not remotely acceptable politically. MacArthur himself was sacked and, in his own words, 'just faded away' after an emotional address to Congress.

Of the other American generals, Bradley, inoffensive and mild-looking, shunning publicity and getting on with the job without fuss, is perhaps the forgotten hero of the North-West European campaign, having commanded first an army and then an army group which did little wrong. In Italy, Lucian Truscott was a far better general than Mark Clark, while, if Patton, whose showmanship and shameless pursuit of personal glory rivalled that of Montgomery, had not been killed in a motor accident in December 1945, he would anyway have had to be removed.* While there may have been considerable merit in his public urgings that the Wehrmacht should be rearmed and, together with the American and British armies of occupation, marched on Moscow, there was not the slightest chance of any politician (or member of the public) agreeing to it, even though with the great benefit of hindsight it could have avoided fifty years of the Soviet boot on the neck of Eastern Europe.

Given the lack of defence funding between the wars, it is perhaps not surprising that most British generals were cautious, conservative and un-adventurous. Montgomery was made into a national treasure, largely because Alamein was a victory of sorts and the British badly needed a victory, but historians of the future will not, this author suspects, be kind to him. His personality traits, his desperate desire for success and recognition, his complete inability to understand the feelings of others and his determination to do everyone else down make him a deeply unattractive figure. He won victories, but many of them were flawed and, given the vastly improved state of British industry and the substantial benefits Lend-Lease had delivered by 1942, there were any number of generals who could have achieved as much, and in some cases a lot more. Montgomery went on to become Chief of the Imperial General Staff and was described by Field Marshal Templar as having been the worst one for fifty years, after which he became Deputy Supreme Commander of NATO, where he quarrelled with everybody. He did enormous harm to Anglo-American relations, insulted Eisenhower when the latter was president, and wrote love letters to a thirteen-year-old Swiss schoolboy – which might not have any bearing on the man's military ability, but it would certainly call his judgement into question.

Otherwise, there were plenty of solid, reasonably competent British generals but not many who really stand out. Alexander was perhaps the perfect coalition warrior. He got on with everybody, smoothed ruffled feathers and was respected by the Americans. He had a hugely difficult job in Italy, which remains almost a forgotten theatre, and he did as good a job as anyone

---

*Inevitably conspiracy theories as to Patton's death abound, one of the better ones suggesting that the accident was engineered by General 'Wild Bill' Donovan, head of the OSS, who arranged for an army truck to drive into Patton's staff car, while at the moment of impact an OSS operative shot him in the head. It is probably unnecessary (or perhaps it isn't) to say that there is no evidence whatsoever to suggest that the accident was anything more than just that – an accident.

could have done given the limitations that he had to work under. Brooke as CIGS did a reasonably competent job, trying to balance conflicting requirements with limited resources, but he was far too inclined to protect and advance his own favourites and he could have exercised far more control over Churchill than he did. The one British general that does stand out is Slim, who brought back a defeated and demoralized multi-racial army and turned it into a force that not only defeated the Japanese but also defeated them totally. He has had little recognition but future historians may well regard him as the best British general of the war.*

It was, however, the German generals who had the most difficult war to fight, that on the Eastern Front. They had hoped for and expected a short, sharp war but instead had to engage with a doggedly persistent enemy in a seemingly endless country and, even when everything went wrong after Stalingrad, managed to hold the Russians off for another three years, despite being outnumbered in tanks, aircraft and, of course, men. Elsewhere, too, there was not a theatre where German generals did not distinguish themselves: Manstein, Bock, Leeb, Model, Kesselring, Kluge, Guderian, even Rommel – the names trip off the tongue and the list goes on and on. These men were giants – flawed giants perhaps – and many of them were complicit in outrages and atrocities that they should never have allowed themselves to become involved in, but in purely military terms they stand head and shoulders, waist and ankles above anyone else on the Allied side. In a war that was biting off far, far more than Germany could ever chew, and despite their having to contend with constant political interference and distrust, they remained the epitome of professionalism. It is a great shame that in modern Germany, in the wish to disown the nation's past and throw perfectly respectable babies out with admittedly some very grubby bathwater, their achievements are hardly ever mentioned.

Japanese generalship was mixed: after the initial successes ambition frequently outreached the possible; they were too often let down, or allowed themselves to be let down, by logistic failures, and, while personally courageous and utterly loyal to an imperial ideal, many spent far too much time in political manoeuvring and plotting to the detriment of coherent campaign planning. Against incompetent or under-resourced or just plain worn-out enemies in Malaya, Singapore, Burma, the Dutch East Indies, the Philippines and Hong

---

*And, yes, he was in this author's regiment…

Kong, men like Mutaguchi, Yamashita and Homma did well, but, once the Allies had recovered and began to hit back, their weaknesses were exposed. For most, the best that could be said is that they were competent divisional commanders, but not much more. Senior Italian commanders suffered from a lack of modern equipment and a supreme commander in Mussolini who demanded far more than they could ever achieve. Messe did as well as anyone could in Russia, and was a competent enough commander during the last days of the North African campaign, but for most of his fellows, frequently snubbed by their German allies, their hearts simply were not in it.

At sea, the Royal Navy's Sir Andrew Cunningham, Commander-in-Chief Mediterranean and successor to Sir Dudley Pound as First Sea Lord, was outstanding, and men like Sir Bruce Fraser, well known as the commander of the Home Fleet from 1943 but whose development of naval aviation and ship construction as Third Sea Lord and Controller of the navy from 1939 to 1942 made a significant contribution to Britain's survival, and Sir Bertram Ramsay, architect of the Dunkirk evacuation and the naval aspects of the Normandy landings, were highly competent. Of American naval commanders, it is hard to fault Raymond Spruance, William Halsey and Chester Nimitz, while Ernest King, despite his extreme Anglophobia and personal disagreement with Roosevelt's 'Germany first' policy, was an able Commander-in-Chief of the US Navy. As for Germany's navy, even though it was instrumental in effecting the Norwegian landings in 1940 and the *Bismarck* shocked the British by sinking the *Hood* in 1941, these proved fleeting successes. Norway was to prove hugely wasteful to occupy, and the *Bismarck* was herself sunk a few days later. Indeed, the Kriegsmarine was never much more than an instrument for commerce raiding and coastal defence, and the most dangerous threat to Britain, and the one that might conceivably have forced her out of the war, Karl Dönitz and his submarines, was defeated by the convoy system and technology. By the time that Germany was able to deploy a new generation of super-submarines, it was far too late. As for Japan, her admirals were generally much more aware than their army colleagues of Western industrial potential, and many of them, including Isoruku Yamamoto, the architect of the Pearl Harbor attack, were not in favour of going to war but were too fearful of assassination to voice their opposition – either that, or they were simply unable or unwilling to be seen not to conform. Having been originally trained by the British, the commanders of the Imperial Navy held to many of the traditions of the Royal

Navy but lacked the technology and resources to go with them. Some of Japan's fighting ships – her heavy cruisers, for instance – were powerful units, but their communications and early-warning systems remained rudimentary by Western standards. Many Japanese naval operations – such as that for Midway – were brilliant in concept but just far too complicated to succeed in practice. And the climactic encounter between the Japanese and American battlefleets, one for which the Imperial Navy had so long and so assiduously planned, simply never happened.

In the air, the one arm of the British services that was reasonably ready for war was the Royal Air Force and men such as Hugh Dowding, for all his prickly personality and inability to get on with his seniors, Keith Park and Trafford Leigh-Mallory are justly acclaimed for the part they played in winning the pivotal Battle of Britain in the summer of 1940 – even if they were greatly assisted by poor German leadership, bad target selection and the Luftwaffe's lack of a true heavy bomber. As it was, both Dowding and Park were treated poorly in the aftermath of their victory, and similar treatment was meted out to Arthur 'Bomber' Harris, whose single-minded determination to hit the German homeland the only way Britain could – by bombing its cities – deserved more credit than he got from Churchill. In less vital theatres, too, the RAF produced some excellent commanders: Sir Arthur Coningham's Desert Air Force was a major contributor to North African success in spite of Montgomery's dismissive attitude towards him, and the conduct of the handful of pilots who defended Malta was nothing short of heroic. Meanwhile, the USAAF's Curtis Le May, who served with uncompromising distinction in both the Pacific and European theatres, and Carl Spaatz, who masterminded the American bombing campaign over Germany, warrant much praise, as does Claire Chennault for his efforts in the China–Burma theatre.

The Luftwaffe generals were successful when employing their forces in the role for which they were designed – tactical support for the army in a short war – but failed when they attempted to take on a strategic role. Political interference, Göring's idleness, dispersion of development effort with far too many new designs and the need to drastically reduce air crew training time as the war went on all conspired to make the Luftwaffe largely irrelevant by the latter stages of the war. As for Japan, her naval and army aircraft were initially first class, and more than a match for those the Allies had in the Far East and Pacific theatres, but this superiority was soon reversed and eventually Japanese aviation was reduced to the despairing last resort of suicide attacks.

* * *

The fighting did not, of course, end with the German and Japanese surrender; China's civil war continued and the precipitate Italian surrender left a vacuum in Greece, which had been under Italian occupation, precipitating a communist uprising in December 1944 that then developed into a civil war in which a communist takeover was only prevented by the intervention of British troops and a massive injection of American money, a commitment that lasted until 1949, long after the big war was over. The division of Korea, hitherto a Japanese colony, into an American client state in the south and a Russian, and then a Chinese, one in the north, led to the Korean War of 1950–53. Neither the communist uprising in Malaya in 1948, not finally put down by the British until 1960, nor its spin-off, the Brunei Revolt and Borneo campaign from 1962 to 1965, would have happened without Chinese communist support, while the collapse of the Dutch empire in the East and the eventual French defeats in Indo-China, which would almost certainly not have occurred had the Japanese not attacked those territories in 1941, led directly to the Vietnam War.

Indeed, in the Far East the most significant result of the war was the emergence of communist China. Had China not been involved in war with Japan, then Chiang Kai-shek's regime, looked upon kindly by the Americans, could almost certainly have contained the communists, and, while no Chinese dynasty has ever or will ever subordinate national interests to the greater good of the world, a Kuo Min Tang China would have caused a lot less trouble globally than Red China has and does. Britain's own empire in the East had been fatally weakened by the Japanese. The British had long conceded that India would one day be self-governing, but, had it not been for the war, home rule could have been delivered in stages, rather than in the rushed scuttle that did ensue, and both partition and the bloodshed then and Indo-Pakistani enmity now might well have been avoided. As for Japan, a regime founded on militarism and favouring expansion at the expense of others had been toppled, but Great Power politics meant that the country's national polity was retained and the Japanese were never forced to face up to what they had done – indeed, by some calculations they are now the second-richest country in the world.

It is quite likely that the state of Israel would not exist but for the war. Britain had promised a national home (but not a state) for the Jews in the

Balfour Declaration in 1917, promulgated to get Jewish opinion in the USA on the Allied side, despite the USA having already entered the war. Chamberlain's government had repudiated that declaration in 1939 as a result of Jewish terrorism and Arab protests, and in any case Britain had been traditionally Arabist: without the war she would never have agreed to the partition of Palestine, but the appalling treatment of the Jews during the war made it impossible after it for the British to be seen to be nasty to them, or to resist American pressure, and so the state of Israel, and decades of turbulence in the Middle East, was born.

In Europe, a thoroughly unpleasant regime had been destroyed, only for it to be replaced in Eastern Europe and the Balkans by an even more unpleasant one that stayed there for fifty years. Life for a Hungarian, Bulgarian, Romanian, Slovak, Lithuanian, Latvian or Estonian, provided he were not a Jew, would have been a lot more comfortable under Hitler's occupation than that of Stalin, and for a Czech and a Pole no worse. Stalin murdered far more people than the Nazis, although he admittedly had more time to do it in, and was just as anti-Semitic.

* * *

It is usually the case, or at least it is expected, that those on the winning side of a war are better off – or at least no worse off – than they were before the war. Britain, whose electorate decisively rejected Churchill, their wartime leader, in the 1945 general election, was certainly worse off after the conflict: she was financially gravely in hock; she was about to lose her Empire (which would have happened anyway, but not in such unseemly haste), and even two years after the cessation of hostilities she was unable to meet export orders through a shortage of steel, while rationing of food and petrol and restrictions on foreign exchange were more severe than at any time during the war. It has occasionally been suggested that, had Britain stayed out of the war or made peace with Germany in 1940, we would then have been in much better shape, much more quickly after a German victory in Europe and Russia. That suggestion can be instantly dismissed. Quite apart from the inevitability of war at some time between a German-ruled Europe with no threat to it from the East and a hitherto neutral Britain, a war that Britain could not have won, common decency and national pride and, yes, honour demanded that Britain did declare war when she did. In the first war, the American ambassador at one stage asked King George V why Britain had entered the war. His reply was 'What else could we do?' – an answer that stands equally well for the second great conflict of the twentieth century. British national interests demanded that she entered the war, but the vast majority of the population genuinely saw it as a moral issue: evil was abroad and it had to be stood up to.

After this war, Britain was no longer the leader of the free world, and D-Day for the Normandy landings, 6 June 1944, may well be said to begin the American Century. But at least it is the American and not the Russian or Chinese Century, and, however much the British and the Europeans are irritated by what they see as American naivety, and a belief that only the American Way is the right way, it was the Marshall Plan – American money and investment – that picked Europe up off the floor after the war (although it was a little unkind of Truman to stop Lend-Lease to the UK two days after VJ Day) and it was America that put the backbone into Europe and provided most of the muscle for the NATO alliance that deterred Soviet aggression for fifty years – aggression that would surely have come had NATO not existed – backed up by the nuclear deterrent, itself a product of the war. America opposed British policy during the Suez Crisis of 1956 and in 1970 the British government turned down a request by the Americans to provide troops for Vietnam. These disagreements have been laid to rest, and for the future America is the only country that matters to the United Kingdom, the only one that has the assets and conceivably the will to come to Britain's assistance if needed, and it is for that reason, if for no other, that if America goes to war – in Iraq, in Afghanistan or anywhere else – then British troops must be there too.

Perceptions of the war vary: in Britain it has become heroic myth, where plucky little Britain stood alone against the might of the dictators until the New World came to the aid of the Old; in America it is still seen as a moral crusade in which once again they rescued the Europeans from unseemly quarrels and spread freedom and apple pie around the world; in Germany the war is not mentioned except to embellish the legend of an anti-Nazi resistance that did not really exist; in Russia it is still celebrated – and understandably so, since the USSR lost a far greater proportion of its population than any other participant – as the Great Patriotic War, won by the USSR with minimal input from anyone else; in Italy, it is for the most part ignored, although many who should know better still hanker for the days of Mussolini's fascist regime; in France, the legend of a wider, general resistance to German occupation has become self-perpetuating, and there is still a reluctance to scrutinize the events of 1940 and after and the Vichy regime with any great rigour. In Japan, the war has quite literally been written out of the history books, and, even if it did happen, then allegations of Japanese misbehaviour are lies: the occupation of Manchuria and China was utterly benign and the Rape of Nanking never happened.

When lawyers are trying to establish a motive, they have a useful Latin tag: *Cui bono?* ('To whom the advantage?') So to whom was the advantage in this war? Certainly not to demilitarized, divided and occupied Germany, and not to Britain, bankrupt and with her Empire breaking up. While the Japanese did not do too badly out of it, despite being on the losing side, it was only Stalin, who gained half of Europe, and the American economy, which the war accelerated out of recession, that can actually be said to have gained from it – which does not imply that it was an unnecessary war, nor that German and Japanese ambitions should have been allowed free rein.

Much as one might regret it, conflict, and hence war, is an inescapable part of the human condition, and we should not discount the possibility of another war between major powers, which might or might not become nuclear, happening at some time in the future – but not within Western Europe. Whatever one may think of the European Union – a direct result of the war, beginning with the innocuous-sounding European Coal and Steel Community in 1952 and mutating over the following half-century into the organization that issues fiats that can override decisions of British ministers and which pronounces on the shape of fruit and vegetables – the interlocking and intermeshing of European economies, culminating in the adoption of a common currency, make it almost impossible – nay, inconceivable – for there ever to be another European war. Indeed, as Britain has stayed out of the Euro zone, she is the only country that could go to war against a European power, and that is not going to happen. While we cannot dismiss the possibility of minor squabbles in the Balkans along the line of Bosnia and Kosovo, or Greek and Turkish antagonism spilling over into frontier skirmishes, the Second World War is the Last European War.

Whatever shape a future war may take, however, it is a fair bet that it will be in a form that we have not anticipated, whether effects-based (a range of political, economic and military actions designed to induce the opponent, neutral or allied parties to pursue a course of action in keeping with the instigators' interests), concentric, hybrid, systemic, asymmetric, within peoples, between peoples, or whatever cry is yet to be coined. There is a danger in concentrating too much on current campaigns. The 2003 invasion of Iraq began as a conventional military operation; the war-fighting phase successfully completed, the campaign then became an insurgency which, owing to a failure to plan for the subsequent governance and reconstruction of the country along lines acceptable to the West, became a very violent one. Similarly, the Afghanistan operation began with the straightforward aim of removing the Taliban government and, when that was achieved, it staggered into guerrilla war between on the one hand tribesmen motivated partly by money (the Taliban pay better than the Afghan government), partly by religious fanaticism and partly by their traditional dislike of foreigners, and NATO (meaning mainly US, British, Canadian and French) troops on the other. In both cases, more damage has been caused by bombs planted and ambushes carried out by combatants who wear no uniform, are governed by no recognized military legal code and have at least the tacit support of the community within which they operate.

As far as the United Kingdom is concerned, the public demand that the troops involved should be given more of the equipment they are thought to need – helicopters, drones, bomb-detection and disposal equipment are only a few of the items in short supply – and, with the certainty of savage cuts in defence expenditure just round the corner, unseemly inter-service bickering has begun. It is tempting to argue that, as current operations follow a particular pattern, then future ones will too, and that we should structure our armed forces accordingly instead of trying to retain the capability to do everything. This would mean increasing the manpower and the equipment procurement budget of the army at the expense of the other two services and structuring the army to cope with anti-terrorist and counter-insurgency operations rather than in deploying main battle tanks and missiles. Such a policy may be attractive to politicians anxious to take money away from defence and spend it on bribing the electorate but it would be short-sighted in the extreme if Britain still wishes to remain a major power, or at least in the front rank of the medium powers. Every conflict is different, and true independence means the ability to defend the nation and the capability to project power abroad. That is why Britain should retain balanced forces including at least two fleet carriers, a replacement for the Trident nuclear deterrent and sufficient modern aircraft to ensure that the RAF can support and transport the army and provide a credible air defence of Great Britain.

It will be said that Britain cannot afford it. Of course she can afford it – by taking money away from other things. Whether she will afford it is a political decision, but, if British politicians and the British people want to retain a global influence, then that is the price that they must pay.

Regardless of what might come, it would be as well for us in the West to keep at least an adequate guard up, and not to allow our defences to languish to the state they were in 1939 and 1940. We are unlikely in any future war to have the luxury of being able to spend the first two or so years of the conflict girding our military loins, and that means a reasonable spending on defence now. Democracies must persuade their peoples that the way to safety and security is, in the words of Theodore Roosevelt, to speak softly and carry a big stick. That big stick means spending a larger proportion of national gross domestic product on defence than we do now. It will not happen, of course, for there are no votes in defence.

Second only to the Black Death of the fourteenth century, the Second World War killed more people than anything else in recorded history, and caused more destruction than earthquake, fire or flood ever did. Whether it was worth fighting depends on the standpoint of the observer: for the US and the USSR it obviously was, and for Britain the alternative of not fighting would have been much worse. The seemingly endless years of fighting certainly demonstrated mankind's ability for mass destruction, and most of the military lessons of the war have been forgotten or are no longer relevant. Not all is doom and gloom, however. Frightful though nuclear weapons were and are, their possession by East and West has forced a certain caution in international disagreements and the United Nations, child of the war and inefficient, corrupt and often incompetent though it may be, is a better by far forum for discussion and concerted action than anything that went before. While we should remember this war for the horrific impact that it had on nations and on people's lives, we should also respect and remember the stoicism, the bravery and the loyalty of millions of soldiers, sailors, airmen and civilians, Americans and Germans, British and Japanese, Italians and Russians, Chinese and Indians and all who believed in a cause, whether right or wrong, justified or not, deserving or not, and who were prepared to suffer and if necessary die for it.

NOTES

1 *The Times*, London, 17 March 2008.
2 Thomas and Gordon-Witts, *The Day the Bubble Burst*.
3 Ibid.
4 For the sources to support this statement see my *Mud, Blood and Poppycock*, Cassell, London, 2003.
5 Robin W. Winks and R. J. Q. Adams, *Europe Crisis and Conflict*, OUP, Oxford, 2003.
6 Paul-Marie de la Gorge (trans. Kenneth Douglas), *The French Army – A Military-Political History*, Weidenfeld & Nicolson, London, 1963.
7 Service, *A History of Modern Russia*.
8 Buruma, *Inventing Japan*.
9 Harvey, *American Shogun*.
10 Quoted in Neville, *Mussolini*.
11 Neville, *Mussolini*.
12 David Evans and Jane Jenkins, *Years of Weimar & The Third Reich*, Hodder Murray, London, 1999.
13 Tooze, *The Wages of Destruction*.
14 Election statistics from Evans and Jenkins, *Years of Weimar*.
15 Manchester, *The Glory and the Dream*.
16 Quoted in Parrish, *Anxious Decades*.
17 Research Institute for Military History, Freiberg, Germany (ed.), *Germany and the Second World War*, Vol. I. Pending the translation of the German Official History into English, this is the definitive history of the war from the German viewpoint.
18 Roy Jenkins, *Baldwin*, Collins, London, 1987.
19 J. Ramsden, *The Age of Balfour and Baldwin, 1902–1940*, Longmans, London, 1978.
20 Figures of Soviet, Italian and German assistance from P. H. Bell, *The Origins of the Second World War in Europe* (3rd edn), Pearson Education Ltd, Harlow, 2007.
21 Figures for the elimination of senior figures from Service, *A History of Modern Russia*, and total overall figures from J. Lee Ready, *World War Two Nation by Nation*, Arms and Armour, London, 1995. These latter are probably too high, but the order of magnitude would be about right.
22 Quoted in Citino, *The Path to Blitzkrieg*.
23 Research Institute for Military History, Freiberg, Germany (ed.), *Germany and the Second World War*, Vol. II.
24 Alanbrooke, *War Diaries 1939–1945* (Danchev and Todman (eds.)).

25 For a detailed account of the move through the Ardennes, see Rothbrust, *Guderian's XIX Panzer Corps.*

26 Figures from Thomson, *Dunkirk*

27 Colville, *The Fringes of Power.*

28 For a detailed account of German designs on Gibraltar and attempts to bring Spain into the war on the Axis side, see Burdick, *Germany's Military Strategy and Spain.*

29 Quoted in Manchester, *The Glory and the Dream.*

30 Paoletti, *A Military History of Italy.*

31 Burdick and Jacobsen (eds.), *The Halder War Diary.*

32 Unpublished memoir 2334728, Raymond Glassborrow, Royal Corps of Signals (transcribed Dominic Borrelli).

33 Alanbrooke, *War Diaries* (Danchev and Todman (eds.)).

34 Details of the Berghof conference of 31 July 1940 from Research Institute for Military History, Potsdam (ed.) (trans. Ewald Osers), *Germany and the Second World War*, Oxford University Press, Oxford, 1996.

35 Ibid.

36 Quoted in Braithwaite, *Moscow 1941.*

37 Viktor Suvorov (possibly a pseudonym), *The Chief Culprit*, US Naval Institute Press, New York, 2008.

38 Research Institute for Military History, Potsdam (ed.), *Germany and the Second World War.*

39 Ibid.

40 Ibid.

41 Ibid.

42 Ferrell (ed.), *The Eisenhower Diaries.*

43 Charmley, *Churchill.*

44 Memorandum on sea power, Churchill to the prime minister, Chamberlain, The National Archives (TNA) PREM 1/345.

45 TNA CAB 69/2.

46 Quoted in Toland, *Rising Sun.*

47 Quoted by Brian Bond, in *Dictionary of National Biography*, Oxford University Press.

48 Quoted in Barrie Pitt, *The Crucible of War.*

49 Burdick and Jacobsen (eds.), *The Halder War Diary.*

50 Jewish population figures taken from Goldhagen, *Hitler's Willing Executioners.*

51 Kleinfeld and Tambs, *Hitler's Spanish Legion.*

52 Research Institute for Military History, Potsdam (ed.), *Germany and the Second World War.*

53 Quoted in Toland, *Rising Sun.*

54 Quoted in Thorne, *Allies of a Kind.*

55 Kirby, *The War against Japan*, Vol. I.

56 Field Marshal Viscount Montgomery, *The Memoirs of Field-Marshal the Viscount Montgomery of Alamein*, Collins, London, 1958.

57 Alanbrooke, *War Diaries* (Danchev and Todman (eds.)).

58 Montgomery, *Memoirs.*

59 Author's interview 1964.

60 Joslen, *Orders of Battle*.
61 Research Institute for Military History, Potsdam (ed.), *Germany and the Second World War*.
62 Alanbrooke, *War Diaries* (Danchev and Todman (eds.)).
63 Details from William G. Dyess, *Bataan Death March – A Survivor's Account*, University of Nebraska Press, Lincoln, Nebr., 2002.
64 Slim, *Defeat into Victory*.
65 Mitsuo Fuchida and Okumiya Masatake, *Midway, the Battle That Doomed Japan*, Naval Institute Press, Annapolis, 1955.
66 Parshall and Tully, *Shattered Sword*.
67 Kirby, *The War against Japan*, Vol. II.
68 Manstein, *Lost Victories*.
69 Research Institute for Military History, Potsdam (ed.), *Germany and the Second World War*.
70 Airlift figures from ibid.
71 Alexander Stahlberg, *Bounden Duty*, Brassey's, London, 1990.
72 Research Institute for Military History, Potsdam (ed.), *Germany and the Second World War*.
73 Stahlberg, *Bounden Duty*.
74 Mellenthin, *Panzer Battles*.
75 Quoted in Harvey, *American Shogun*.
76 Heiber and Glantz (eds.), *Hitler and His Generals*.
77 Essay by von Gersdorff in Isby (ed.), *Fighting the Breakout*.
78 Bradley, *A Soldier's Story*.
79 Figures of tonnages sunk and submarine strengths and losses from Roskill, *The War at Sea*.
80 Ibid., Vol. II.
81 Figures from Neillands, *The Bomber War*. The British Official History gives an estimate of 40,000.
82 Richard Overy, *The Air War 1939–1945*, Europa, London, 1980.
83 Toland, *Rising Sun*.
84 Statistics from Samuel Eliot Morison, *History of the United States Naval Operations in World War II* (15 vols.), Little, Brown and Company, New York, 1956–60.
85 Foot, *SOE*.
86 Thomas, *An Underworld at War*.
87 Office of National Statistics, *Labour Market Trends*, HMSO, London, 1946.
88 Mark Connelly, *We Can Take It*.
89 Addison and Calder (eds.), *Time to Kill*.
90 Owen Chadwick, *Britain and the Vatican during the Second World War*, Cambridge University Press, Cambridge, 1988.
91 Morris Beckman, *The Jewish Brigade: An Army with Two Masters*, The History Press, London, 2008.
92 Research Institute for Military History, Potsdam (ed.), *Germany and the Second World War*, Vol. VII.
93 All the likely explanations for this extraordinary episode are given in Hickey, *The Unforgettable Army*.

BIBLIOGRAPHY

Addison, Paul and Angus Calder (eds.), *Time to Kill: The Soldier's Experience of War in the West*, Pimlico, London, 1997

Alanbrooke, Field Marshal Lord (Alex Danchev and Daniel Todman (eds.)), *War Diaries 1939–1945*, Weidenfeld & Nicolson, London, 2001

Argyle, Christopher J., *Japan at War 1937–1945*, Arthur Barker, London, 1976

Barnett, Corelli, *The Desert Generals* (2nd edn), Allen & Unwin, London, 1983

——, *The Audit of War*, Macmillan, London, 1986

Baverstock, Kevin, *Breaking the Panzers: The Bloody Battle for Rauray, Normandy, 1 July 1944*, Sutton, Stroud, 2002

Bayley, Christopher and Tim Harper, *Forgotten Armies: Britain's Asian Empire and the War with Japan*, Allen Lane, London, 2004

Beevor, Anthony, *Stalingrad*, Viking, London, 1998

——, *Berlin: The Downfall 1945*, Viking, London, 2002

Beneš, V. L. and N. J. G. Pounds, *Poland*, Ernest Benn, London, 1970

Bennett, Ralph, *Behind the Battle: Intelligence and the War with Germany 1939–45*, Sinclair-Stevenson, London, 1994

Best, Geoffrey, *Churchill: A Study in Greatness*, Hambledon & London, London, 2001

Betthell, Nicholas, *The War Hitler Won*, Allen Lane, London, 1972

Bialer, Seweryn (ed.), *Stalin and His Generals*, Pegasus, New York, 1969

Bidermann, Gottlob (trans. Derek S. Zumbro), *In Deadly Combat*, Kansas University Press, Lawrence, Kan., 2000

Bishop, Chris, *Hitler's Foreign Divisions*, Spellmount, Staplehurst, 2005

——, *Order of Battle: German Infantry in WWII*, Amber, London,

Blennemann, Dirk, et al., *Hitler's Army*, Da Capo, Cambridge, Mass., 2003

Blumentritt, Günther, et al. (ed. David C. Isby), *Fighting the Invasion*, Greenhill, London, 2000

Bond, Brian and Michael Taylor (eds.), *The Battle for France and Flanders: Sixty Years On*, Pen & Sword, London, 2001

Bradley, Omar N., *A Soldier's Story*, Henry Holt, New York, 1951

Braithwaite, Rodric, *Moscow 1941*, Profile, London, 2006

Brooks, Stephen (ed.), *Montgomery and the Eighth Army*, Army Records Society, London, 1991

——, (ed.), *Montgomery and the Battle of Normandy*, Army Records Society, London, 2008

Brown, David, *Carrier Operations in World War II: Volume I: The Pacific Navies*, Ian Allan, London, 1974

Bungay, Steven, *The Most Dangerous Enemy: A History of the Battle of Britain*, Aurum, London, 2000

Burdick, Charles and Hans-Adolf Jacobson (eds.), *The Halder War Diary 1939–1942*, Greenhill, London, 1988

Burdick, Charles B., *Germany's Military Strategy and Spain in World War II*, Syracuse University Press, New York, 1968

Buruma, Ian, *Inventing Japan: From Empire to Economic Miracle*, Weidenfeld & Nicolson, London, 2003

Calder, Angus, *The People's War*, Jonathan Cape, London, 1969

Carell, Paul (trans. David Johnson), *Invasion! They're Coming!*, Schiffer, Atglen, Penn., 1995

Carius, Otto (trans. Robert J. Edwards), *Tigers in the Mud: The Combat Career of German Panzer Commander Otto Carius*, Stackpole, Mechanicsburg, Penn., 2003

Carton de Wiart, Sir Adrian, *Happy Odyssey*, Jonathan Cape, London, 1950

Carver, Field Marshal Lord, *Out of Step*, Hutchison, London, 1989

Charmley, John, *Churchill, the End of Glory*, Hodder & Stoughton, London, 1993

Citino, Robert M., *The Path to Blitzkrieg*, Stackpole, Mechanicsburg, Penn., 1999

Clisby, Mark, *Guilty or Innocent? The Gordon Bennett Case*, Allen & Unwin, Sydney, 1992

Colville, John, *The Fringes of Power: Downing Street Diaries 1939–1955*, Hodder & Stoughton, London, 1985

Connelly, Mark, *We Can Take It: Britain and the Memory of the Second World War*, Pearson Longman, Harlow, 2004

Cooke, Alistair, *The American Home Front 1941–1942*, Grove, New York, 2006

Corrigan, Gordon, *Blood, Sweat and Arrogance and the Myths of Churchill's War*, Weidenfeld & Nicolson, London, 2006

Cross, Robin, *Citadel: The Battle of Kursk*, Michael O'Mara, London, 1993

Croucher, Richard, *Engineers at War 1939–1945*, Merlin, London, 1982

D'Este, Carlo, *Eisenhower*, Weidenfeld & Nicolson, London, 2002

Dank, Milton, *The French Against the French*, Cassell, London, 1974

David, Saul, *Mutiny at Salerno*, Brassey's, London, 1995

Deane-Drummond, A. J., *Arrows of Fortune*, Leo Cooper, London, 1992

Dear, Ian, *Sabotage and Subversion: The SOE and OSS at War*, Arms and Armour, London, 1996

Deighton, Len, *Blood, Tears and Folly*, Jonathan Cape, London, 1993

Delaforce, Patrick, *Monty's Ironsides*, Sutton, Stroud, 1995

——, *Monty's Highlanders: 51st Highland Division in World War Two*, Tom Donovan, Brighton, 1997

——, *Churchill's Desert Rats* (2 vols.), Sutton, Stroud, 2002

Demeter, Karl (trans Angus Malcolm), *The German Officer Corps in Society and State 1650–1945*, Weidenfeld & Nicolson, London, 1965

Dilks, David (ed.), *The Diaries of Sir Alexander Cadogan*, Cassell, London, 1971

Doherty, Richard, *A Noble Crusade: The History of the Eighth Army 1941–45*, Spellmount, Staplehurst, 1999

——, *Normandy 1944*, Spellmount, Staplehurst, 2004

Eich, Herman, *The Unloved Germans*, Macdonald, London, 1963

Ellis, John, *The Sharp End of War: The Fighting Man in World War II*, David & Charles, London, 1980

——, *Brute Force*, André Deutsch, London, 1990

——, *The World War II Databook*, Aurum, London, 1993

Evans, Richard J., *The Coming of the Third Reich*, Allen Lane, London, 2003

Farrell, Charles, *Reflections 1939–1945: A Scots Guards Officer in Training and War*, Pentland, Bishop Auckland, 2000

Felton, Mark, *The Coolie Generals*, Pen & Sword, Barnsley, 2008

Fenby, Jonathan, *Alliance: Roosevelt, Stalin and Churchill*, Simon & Schuster, London, 2006

Ferrell, Robert H. (ed.), *The Eisenhower Diaries*, Norton, New York, 1981

Fey, Will (trans. Henri Henschler), *Armor Battles of the Waffen SS*, Stackpole, Mechanicsburg, Penn., 2003

Flood, Charles Bracelen, *Hitler: The Path to Power*, Hamish Hamilton, London, 1989

Foot, M. R. D., *SOE in France*, HMSO, London, 1966

——, *SOE: The Special Operations Executive 1940–1946*, Mandarin, London, 1984

Forty, George, *The Reich's Last Gamble*, Cassell, London, 2000

Foss, Christopher P. (ed.), *The Encyclopedia of Tanks and Armoured Fighting Vehicles*, Spellmount, Staplehurst, 2003

Fournier, Gérard and André Heinz (trans. Heather Costil), *If I Must Die…*, OREP Editions. Cully, France, 2006

Fowler, Will, *The Commandos at Dieppe*, Collins, London, 2002

Fraser, David, *Alanbrooke*, Collins, London, 1982

——, *And We Shall Shock Them: The British Army and the Second World War*, Hodder & Stoughton, London, 1983

Fraser, George MacDonald, *Quartered Safe Out Here: A Recollection of the War in Burma*, Harvill, London, 1992

French, David, *Raising Churchill's Army*, OUP, Oxford, 2000

Fullbrook, Mary, *History of Germany 1918–2000*, Fontana, London, 1991

Gellately, Robert, *Lenin, Stalin and Hitler*, Jonathan Cape, London, 2007

Glantz, David M., *The Battle for Leningrad 1941–1944*, Kansas University Press, Lawrence, Kan., 2002

Goldhagen, Daniel Jonah, *Hitler's Willing Executioners*, Little, Brown & Co., London, 1996

Gorodetsky, Gabriel, *Grand Delusion*, Yale University Press, New Haven, 1999

Granatstein, J. L. and Desmond Morton, *A Nation Forged by Fire: Canadians and the Second World War*, Lester & Orpen Dennys, Toronto, 1989

Guderian, Colonel General Heinz (trans. Constance Fitzgibbon), *Panzer Leader*, Michael Joseph, London, 1952

——, (trans. Christopher Duffy), *Achtung – Panzer!*, Arms and Armour, London, 1992

——, et al. (trans. Alan Bance), *Blitzkrieg in Their Own Words*, Pen & Sword, Barnsley, 2005

Gunston, Bill (foreword), *Jane's Fighting Aircraft of World War II*, Random House, London, 2001

Hamilton, Nigel, *Monty: The Making of a General*, Hodder & Stoughton, London, 1985

——, *Monty: Master of the Battlefield*, Hodder & Stoughton, London, 1985

——, *Monty: The Field Marshal*, Hamish Hamilton, London, 1986

——, *The Full Monty*, Allen Lane, London, 2001

Harvey, Robert, *American Shogun*, John Murray, London, 2006

Hastings, Max, *Overlord*, Michael Joseph, London, 1984

Heathcote, T. A., *The British Field Marshals*, Leo Cooper, Barnsley, 1999

——, *The British Admirals of the Fleet*, Leo Cooper, Barnsley, 2002

Heiber, Helmut and David M. Glantz (eds.), *Hitler and His Generals: Military Conferences 1942–1945*, Enigma, New York, 2003

Hickey, Colonel Michael, *The Unforgettable Army: Slim's XIVth Army in Burma*, Spellmount, Staplehurst, 1992

Hiden, John, *Germany and Europe 1919–1939*, Longman, Harlow, 1993

Hoare, Oliver (intro.), *Camp 020 – MI5 and the Nazi Spies*, Public Record Office, Kew, 2000

Hogan, George, *Malta – The Triumphant Years 1940–43*, Robert Hale, London, 1978

Holmes, Richard, *Battlefields of the Second World War*, BBC, London, 2001

Holt, Thaddeus, *The Deceivers: Allied Military Deception in the Second World War*, Weidenfeld & Nicolson, London, 2004

Howlett, Peter, *Fighting With Figures: A Statistical Digest of the Second World War*, HMSO, London, 1995

Hylton, Stuart, *Their Darkest Hour: The Hidden History of the Home Front 1939–1945*, Sutton, Stroud, 2001

Irving, David, *The Rise and Fall of the Luftwaffe*, Weidenfeld & Nicolson, London, 1973

——, *Hitler's War*, Hodder & Stoughton, London, 1977

——, *The Trail of the Fox: The Life of Field Marshal Erwin Rommel*, Weidenfeld & Nicolson, London, 1977

——, *The War Path: Hitler's Germany 1933–9*, Michael Joseph, London, 1978

——, *The War Between the Generals*, Allen Lane, London, 1981

——, *Göring: A Biography*, Macmillan, London, 1989

Isby, David C. (ed.), *Fighting the Breakout*, Greenhill, London, 2004

Ismay, General Lord, *The Memoirs of Lord Ismay*, Heinemann, London, 1960

Jackson, Julian, *The Fall of France: The Nazi Invasion of 1940*, OUP, Oxford, 2004

Jackson, General Sir William and Field Marshal Lord Bramall, *The Chiefs: The Story of the United Kingdom Chiefs of Staff*, Brassey's, London, 1992

Jones, Michael K., *Stalingrad – How the Red Army Won*, Pen & Sword, London, 2007

——, *Leningrad – State of Siege*, John Murray, London, 2008

——, *Retreat – Hitler's First Defeat*, John Murray, London, 2009

Jones, R. V., *Most Secret War*, Hamish Hamilton, London, 1978

Joslen, Lieutenant Colonel H. F., *Orders of Battle Second World War*, HMSO, London, 1960

Keegan, John, *Six Armies in Normandy*, Jonathan Cape, London, 1982

——, *The Price of Admiralty*, Hutchison, London, 1988

——, *The Collins Atlas of World War II*, HarperCollins, London, 2006

——, (ed.), *Churchill's Generals*, Weidenfeld & Nicolson, London, 1991

Keitel, Field Marshal Wilhelm (trans. David Irving), *The Memoirs of Field Marshal Keitel*, Sten & Day, New York, 1966

Kennedy, Paul M., *The Rise and Fall of British Naval Mastery*, Allen Lane, London, 1976

Kershaw, Robert J., *It Never Snows in September*, Ian Allan, Hersham, 1994

Kesselring, Field Marshal Albrecht, *The Memoirs of Field Marshal Kesselring*, William Kimber, London, 1953

Kirby, Major General S. Woodburn, *The War Against Japan* (5 vols), HMSO, London, 1957–69

Kleinfeld, Gerald R. and Lewis A. Tambs, *Hitler's Spanish Legion: The Blue Division in Russia*, Hailer, St Petersburg, Fla, 2005

Knopp, Guido (trans. Angus McGeoch), *Hitler's Warriors*, Sutton, Stroud, 2005

Koch, H. W. (ed.), *Aspects of the Third Reich*, Macmillan, London, 1985

Kurowski, Franz (trans. David Johnston), *Panzer Aces: German Tank Commanders of World War II* (2 vols), Stackpole, Mechanicsburg, Penn., 2004

Lamb, Richard, *War in Italy 1943–1945*, John Murray, London, 1991

Leutze, James R., *Bargaining for Supremacy: Anglo-American Naval collaboration 1937–1941*, University of North Carolina Press, Chapel Hill, NC, 1977

Lewin, Ronald, *Slim the Standard Bearer*, Leo Cooper, London, 1976

Liddell Hart. B. H. (ed.), *The Rommel Papers*, Collins, London, 1953

Lindsay, Oliver, *The Battle for Hong Kong 1941–1945*, McGill-Queen's University Press, Montreal, 2005

Linklater, Eric, *The Campaign in Italy*, HMSO, London, 1951

Lord, Walter, *The Miracle of Dunkirk*, Allen Lane, London, 1983

Lowe, Keith, *Inferno: The Devastation of Hamburg 1943*, Viking, London, 2007

Lucas, James and James Barker, *The Killing Ground: The Battle of the Falaise Gap, August 1944*, Batsford, London, 1978

Lunt, James, *A Hell of a Licking: The Retreat from Burma 1941–2*, Collins, London, 1986

Lynam, Robert, *Slim, Master of War*, Constable, London, 2004

——, *The Generals*, Constable, London, 2008

Lys, Graham (ed.), *The Russian Version of the Second World War*, Facts on File, New York, 1976

MacKenzie, William, *The Secret History of SOE: Special Operations Executive 1940–1945*, St Ermin's, London, 2000

Mack Smith, Denis, *Mussolini*, Weidenfeld & Nicolson, London, 1981

Macleod, Roderick and Denis Kelly (eds.), *Time Unguarded: The Ironside Diaries 1937–1940*, Greenwood, Westport, Conn., 1962

Magenheimer, Heinz (trans. Helmut Bögler), *Hitler's War: German Military Strategy 1940–1945*, Arms and Armour, London, 1998

Mallman Showell, Jack P., *German Navy Handbook*, Sutton, Stroud, 1999

Manchester, William, *The Glory and the Dream*, Michael Joseph, London, 1975

Manstein, Field Marshal Erich von (trans. Anthony G. Powell), *Lost Victories*, Methuen & Co., London, 1958

Marston, Daniel (ed.), *The Pacific War Companion: From Pearl Harbor to Hiroshima*, Osprey, Oxford, 2005

Mawdsley, Evan, *The Russian Civil War*, Allen & Unwin, London, 1987

McKee, Alexander, *The Race for the Rhine Bridges*, Souvenir, London, 1971

Megargee, Geoffrey, *War of Annihilation: Combat and Genocide on the Eastern Front*, Rowman & Littlefield, Lanham, Md, 2006

Mellenthin, Major General F. W. von, *Panzer Battles*, Cassell, London, 1955

Merridale, Catherine, *Ivan's War: Inside the Red Army 1939–45*, Faber & Faber, London, 2005

Meyer, Obersturmbannführer Hubert, *The 12th SS* (2 vols), Stackpole, Mechanicsburg, Penn., 2005

Middlebrook, Martin, *Arnhem 1944: The Airborne Battle*, Viking, London, 1994

Middlebrook, Martin and Chris Everitt, *The Bomber Command War Diaries: An Operational Reference Book 1939–1945*, Viking, London, 1985

Milner, Marc, *The Battle of the Atlantic*, Tempus, Stroud, 2003

Milton, Richard, *Best of Enemies: Britain and Germany – 100 Years of Truth and Lies*, Icon, Cambridge, 2007

Mitcham, Samuel W., Jr, *Hitler's Field Marshals*, Guild Publishing, London, 1998

——, *Crumbling Empire: The German Defeat in the East*, Greenwood, Westport, Conn., 2001

Montefiore, Simon Sebag, *Stalin – The Court of the Red Tsar*, Weidenfeld & Nicolson, London, 2003

Montgomery, Field Marshal Viscount, *Normandy to the Baltic* (2 vols), Hutchison, London, 1947

Morison, Samuel Eliot, *The Two Ocean War: A Short History of the United States Navy in the Second World War*, Naval Institute Press, Annapolis, USA, 1963

Natkiel, Richard, *Atlas of World War II*, WH Smith, London, 1985

Neillands, Robin, *The Bomber War: Arthur Harris and the Allied Bombing Offensive 1939–1945*, John Murray, London, 2001

Neillands, Robin, *The Battle of Normandy 1944*, Cassell, London, 2002

Neitzel, Sönke (ed.), *Tapping Hitler's Generals: Transcripts of Secret Conversations 1942–45*, Frontline, Barnsley, 2007

Neville, Peter, *Mussolini*, Routledge, Abingdon, 2004

Nicolson, Nigel (ed.), *Harold Nicolson: The War Years* (3 vols), Atheneum, New York, 1967

Ousby, Ian, *Occupation: The Ordeal of France 1940–1944*, John Murray, London, 1997

Overy, Richard, *Why the Allies Won*, Jonathan Cape, London, 1995 (rev. edn 2006)

——, *Russia's War*, Allen Lane, London, 1998

——, *The Battle of Britain: The Myth and the Reality*, Penguin, London, 2004

——, *Countdown to War*, Allen Lane, London, 2009

Paget, R. G., *Manstein: His Campaigns and His Trial*, Collins, London, 1951

Paoletti, Ciro, *A Military History of Italy*, Praeger, Westport, Conn., 2008

Parish, Michael E., *Anxious Decades*, Norton & Co, New York, 1992

Parshall, Jonathan and Anthony Tully, *Shattered Sword: The Untold Story of the Battle of Midway*, Potomac, Washington DC, 2005

Paterson, Michael, *Code Breakers*, David & Charles, Cincinnati, Oh., 2007

Peattie, Mark R., *Sunburst: The Rise of Japanese Naval Air Power, 1909–1941*, Naval Institute Press, Annapolis, 2001

Picot, Geoffrey, *Accidental Warrior: In the Front Line from Normandy Till Victory*, Book Guild, 1993

Pitt, Barrie, *Churchill and the Generals*, Sidgwick & Jackson, London, 1981

——, *The Crucible of War* (3 vols), Jonathan Cape, London, 2001

Prasad, Bisheswar, *The Indian Armed Forces in World War II* (10 vols), Combined Inter-Services Historical Section (India and Pakistan), New Delhi, 1960

Probert, Air Commodore Henry, *Bomber Harris: His Life and Times*, Greenhill, London, 2003

Public Record Office London, *The Rise and Fall of the German Air Force 1933–1945*, Public Record Office, Kew, 2001

Research Institute for Military History Germany, *Germany and the Second World War* (9 vols), OUP, Oxford, 2000–2008

Reynolds, Michael, *Steel Inferno: I SS Panzer Corps in Normandy*, Spellmount, Staplehurst, 1997

Reynolds, Michael, *Men of Steel: SS Panzer Corps, the Ardennes and Eastern Front 1944–45*, Spellmount, Staplehurst, 1999

——, *The Devil's Adjutant: Jochen Peiper, Panzer Leader*, Spellmount, Staplehurst, 2002

——, *Eagles and Bulldogs in Normandy 1944*, Spellmount, Staplehurst, 2003

Rings, Werner (trans. J. Maxwell Brownjohn), *Life with the Enemy: Collaboration and Resistance in Hitler's Europe 1939–1945*, Weidenfeld & Nicolson, London, 1982

Robbins, Keith, *Munich 1938*, Cassell, London, 1968

Rogers, Anthony, *Churchill's Folly: Leros and the Aegean*, Cassell, London, 2003

Rohmer, Major General Richard, *Patton's Gap*, Arms and Armour, London, 1981

Roskill, Captain S. W., DSC, RN, *The Navy at War 1939–1945*, Collins, London, 1960

——, *A Merchant Fleet at War 1939–1945*, Collins, London, 1962

——, *The War at Sea* (4 vols), HMSO, London, 1976

——, *Churchill and the Admirals*, Collins, London, 1977

Rothbrust, Florian K., *Guderian's XIX Panzer Corps and the Battle of France*, Praeger, Westport, Conn., 1990

Scarfe, Norman, *Assault Division*, Spellmount, Staplehurst, 2004

Seaton, Albert, *The German Army 1933–45*, Weidenfeld & Nicolson, London, 1982

Service, Robert, *A Modern History of Russia: From Nicholas II to Putin*, Allen Lane, London, 1997

Shaw, Anthony, *World War II Day by Day*, Brown Partworks, London, 2000

Shepperd, G. A., *The Italian Campaign*, Arthur Barker, London, 1968

Shlaes, Amity, *The Forgotten Man*, Jonathan Cape, London, 2007

Slim, Field Marshal Viscount, *Defeat into Victory*, Cassell & Co., London, 1956

Smart, Nick, *British Generals of the Second World War*, Pen & Sword, Barnsley, 2005

Smith, Bradley E. and Elena Agrossi, *Operation Sunrise – The Secret Surrender*, André Deutsch, London, 1979

Smith, Colin, *Singapore Burning*, Viking, London, 2005

Smith, Major General Dale O., *Screaming Eagle: Memoirs of a B-17 Group Commander*, Algonquin of Chapel Hill, Chapel Hill, USA, 1990

Smith, E. D. *The Battles for Cassino*, Ian Allan, London, 1975

Stahlberg, Alexander (trans. Patricia Crampton), *Bounden Duty*, Brassey's, London, 1990

Stettinius, Edward R., Jr (ed. Walter Johnson), *Roosevelt and the Russians*, Doubleday, New York, 1949

Sweetinburgh, Sheila, *The Role of the Hospital in Medieval England*, Four Courts Press, Dublin, 2004

Taylor, Brian, *Barbarossa to Berlin* (2 vols), Spellmount, Staplehurst, 2003

Terraine, John, *The Right of the Line: The Royal Air Force in the European War 1939–1945*, Hodder & Stoughton, London, 1985

Thomas, Donald, *An Underworld at War*, John Murray, London, 2003

Thomas, Gordon and Max Morgan-Witts, *The Day the Bubble Burst*, Doubleday, New York, 1979

Thomas, Martin, *The French Empire Between the Wars*, Manchester University Press, Manchester, 2005

Thompson, Major General Julian, *Dunkirk: Retreat to Victory*, Sidgwick & Jackson, London, 2008

Thorne, Christopher, *Allies of a Kind: The United States, Britain, and the War against Japan, 1941–1945*, Hamish Hamilton, London, 1978

Toland, John, *Rising Sun*, Cassell, London, 1971

Tooze, Adam, *The Wages of Destruction*, Allen Lane, London, 2006

Tusa, Anne and John Tusa, *The Nuremberg Trial*, Macmillan, London, 1983

Vinen, Richard, *The Unfree French: Life under Occupation*, Allen Lane, London, 2006

Wacker, Albrecht, *Sniper on the Eastern Front*, Pen & Sword, Barnsley, 2005

War Office, *Combined Operations*, Macmillan, New York, 1943

Warner, Philip, *Auchinleck the Lonely Soldier*, Buchan & Enright, London, 1981

Weinberg, Gerhard L., *A World at Arms*, CUP, Cambridge, Mass., 1994

Wellum, Geoffrey, *First Light*, Viking, London, 2002

Wette, Wolfram (trans. Deborah Lucas Schneider), *The Wehrmacht: History, Myth, Reality*, Harvard University Press, Cambridge, Mass., 2006

Whiting, Charles, *The Battle of the Bulge: Britain's Untold Story*, Sutton, Stroud, 1999

——, *The Field Marshal's Revenge*, Spellmount, Staplehurst, 2004

Wilson, Theodore A., *The First Summit*, Macdonald, London, 1970

Winchester, Charles D., *Hitler's War on Russia*, Osprey, Botley, 2007

Wistrich, Robert S., *Who's Who in Nazi Germany*, Weidenfeld & Nicolson, London, 1982

Wood, Derek and Dempster Wood, *The Narrow Margin*, Hutchison, London, 1961

Wragg, David, *A History of Naval Aviation*, David & Charles, London, 1979

Zaloga, Steven J. and Leland S. Ness, *The Red Army Handbook 1939–1945*, Sutton, Stroud, 1998

Zeigler, Philip, *Mountbatten*, Collins, London, 1985

ACKNOWLEDGEMENTS

There are not all that many military historians about, and I owe a huge debt to those there are, most of them fellow members of the British Commission for Military History. Without exception, they have been unstinting in pointing me in all sorts of directions, many of them useful but all interesting. I have not experienced the oft-cited arrogance of academe, and have always found scholars of far greater eminence than myself to be unfailingly helpful, even those who have not necessarily agreed with my conclusions. They know who they are and I am grateful to them all.

There are, of course, some perks available to historians. One can be very fortunate and be invited to become an honorary research fellow of a university. The quid pro quo for a minuscule return (the occasional lecture) is, apart from a parking pass, access to libraries – and at a time when some books essential to the student of military history can cost up to £200 a volume,* this is an enormous help. Much thanks, therefore, to the Universities of Kent and Birmingham. Military history is but one aspect of history generally. It cannot, as I have also said above, be divorced from social, political and economic history – all are intertwined. Every so often, the question is raised as to whether schoolchildren and university students should be encouraged to study 'useful' subjects like engineering or chemistry, rather than 'academic' ones like literature or history. While in no way suggesting that engineering and chemistry are not vital to our economy (my own A Levels were in Physics and Pure and Applied Maths), history, it seems to me, is essential to our understanding of ourselves as a nation. It is rather like map-reading: how do you know where you are if you don't know where you've been? And how do you know where you're going if you don't know where you are?

We are incredibly fortunate in the availability and standard of proven records and information in Britain. The British Library, the National Archives at Kew, the National Army Museum, the Prince Consort's Library in Aldershot and the Imperial War Museum, to name but some, are veritable treasure troves of historical fact, as are the German Federal Archives in Koblenz, and their staffs have, as always, been enormously helpful and informative. I owe a particular debt to Alan Wakefield, curator of the Photographic Archive at the Imperial War Museum in London, to Professor Kearby Lyde of San Jacinto College, Houston, Texas, and to Michael Orr, late of the Royal Military

---

*The nearest equivalent that Germany so far has to an official history translated into English, *Germany and the Second World War*, costs up to £180 a volume. There are nine volumes – and more to come.

Academy Sandhurst. I am especially grateful to Angus MacKinnon, my editor at Atlantic Books, who has become not only a professional moderator of my occasional purple prose, but a friend in the very real sense, and Caroline Knight, Margaret Stead, Orlando Whitfield, Sachna Hanspal, Mark Handsley, Martin Lubikowski, and of course Toby Mundy, Chief Executive and Publisher, all of whom have not only cooperated hugely in the preparation of this book but without whom it simply could not have appeared. As always, my wife has been my intelligent reader and has done her best to prevent me from becoming too pompous. That she has failed is no reflection on her.

INDEX

Christie tank suspension, 42
and invasion of Soviet Union, 150, 167–8, 359, 361, 363
and North Africa campaign, 193–4, 196–201, 205–6, 210, 215, 217–18, 289–90
tanks, types of
Char B, 101
Churchill, 292
KV, 168, 242
M3 (Grant), 217, 290, 438, 549
M4 (Sherman), 214, 290, 306
Panzer Mk III, 101, 147
Panzer Mk IV, 101, 147, 168, 290
Panzer Mk V (Panther), 358, 360, 363, 473
Panzer Mk VI (Tiger), 6, 289, 301, 308, 358, 360
Scorpion, 292
Somua, 101
T-34, 42, 168, 243, 247, 344–5, 352, 358–9, 363, 473
Tiger II, 539
Valentine, 430
Taranto, 120, 254, 404–5, 439
Tarhuna-Homs, 303
Tauragé, 157
Tavoy, 319
Tebessa mountains, 306–7
Tedder, Air Marshal Sir Arthur, 207, 405, 426
Televaag, 494
Tempelhof airport, 561
Templar, Field Marshal Gerald, 581
Tenasserim, 318
Tengah, 19
Ten-Year Rule, 34, 97
Terauchi, Field Marshal Count Hisaichi, 463, 470
Terraine, John, 13, 15
Territorial Army, 75
Teschen, 86
Teutonic Knights, 139
Thailand, see Siam
Tharrawaddy, 326–7
Thoma, General Wilhelm Ritter von, 293
Thomas, Sir Shenton, 180, 277
Thrace, 133
Tiddim, 391
Tilsit, 157
Time magazine, 511
Times, The, 440
Timor, 178, 281
Timoshenko, Marshal Semyon, 143, 156, 163, 222, 239, 241
tin, 26, 176, 178
Tinian, 457–8, 460
Tippelskirch, General Kurt von, 556
Tito, Marshal (Josip Broz), 499, 529
Tobruk, 128, 135, 193, 196, 199–204, 206, 213–4, 302

Todt Organization, 488
Togo, Admiral Heihachiro, 188, 569
Tojo, General Hideki, 12, 185–6, 370, 444, 460, 463
Tokyo, 144, 171, 185, 370, 376–7, 380
air raids, 4, 337, 451, 518, 543–4, 545
'Tokyo Express', 374, 376, 466
Tokyo war crimes trials, 174, 574, 576
Tonga, 179
Tonkin, 183
Torgau, 560
Toulon, 299, 486
Toungoo, 549
Toyoda, Admiral Soemu, 464
trade unions, 33, 59, 61–2, 508, 510
Trafalgar, battle of, 443
Trans-Siberian railway, 37
Treaty of Brest-Litovsk, 36–7
Treaty of Tirana, 124
Treaty of Utrecht, 115
Treaty of Versailles, 3, 28–9, 37–8, 50, 53, 56–7, 60–1, 68–71, 84, 136
and German rearmament, 8, 81, 85–6
and US ratification, 7, 512
Treblinka, 477
Tresckow, Lieutenant-Colonel Henning von, 153
Treviso, 528
Trieste, 49, 50, 528
Trincomalee, 442
Tripartite Pact, 132, 140, 259
Triple Alliance, 49
Tripoli, 132, 134, 206, 211–2, 297, 303, 306–7, 407
Tripolitania, 196
Trotsky, Leon, 36, 38, 41
Truman, Harry S., 513, 554, 566, 568, 587
Truscott, General Lucian, 300, 411, 414, 522, 580
Tsunoda, Admiral Kanji, 458, 459
Tsushima, battle of, 188
Tukachevsky, Marshal Mikhail, 143
Tuker, General Francis 'Gertie', 310–1, 313, 413
Tula, 223
Tulagi Island, 338, 373
Tungale, 321
Tunis, 296–7, 301, 306, 312–3
Tunisia, 21, 285, 298–9, 299–301, 306–7, 350, 357, 396–7, 441
Turin, 529
Turkey, 49, 232, 306, 406
typhus, 221, 328
Tyrol, 50, 148, 517

Ukraine, 36, 40, 136, 139, 143, 160, 162, 167, 230, 231–2, 235, 347, 355, 361–7, 514
Ulster, 434
Uman, 165
Umberto, Crown Prince, of Savoy, 235
unconditional surrender, 304–5, 479, 562–3, 566, 571
Union Sacrée, 30
United Nations, 512, 590
United States of America, 63–8, 109, 510–14
death toll, 578
domestic conditions, 510–14
and economic recession, 23–8, 30
entry into war, 7, 120–4, 192–3, 259–60
and history, 14
and invasion of Soviet Union, 136–9
and Israel, 585–6
and Japanese internment, 512–13
Japanese invasion threat, 394
New Deal, 65–6
and the Philippines, 176–8
post-war, 587–8
relations with Britain, 260–3, 581, 587
unemployment, 26–7, 65–6, 68, 510
war economy, 510–11
United States Army, 7–8, 89, 121–2, 337, 370–1, 578–9, 513–14
United States Navy, 8, 121, 189–90, 193, 259–61, 371, 429–30, 434–5, 436, 443, 461, 465–6, 513–14, 578–9
United States Air Force, 584
and gliders, 399–400
and strategic bombing campaign, 453
Ural mountains, 167
US Federal Reserve, 27–8
Ushijima, General Mitsuru, 544–6
USSR, see Soviet Union

van der Lubbe, Marius, 61
Vasilevsky, Marshal Aleksandr, 472
Vatican, 52, 298, 403, 517–18
Vatutin, General Nikolai, 364, 367
VE Day, 563
Vella Navella, 395
Vemork heavy water plant, 501–3
Vengeance weapons, 486, 553–4
Venice, 408, 528
Verdun, 97, 104, 350, 487
Verona, 524, 528
Viareggio, 484
Vichy France, 7, 119, 130, 140, 183, 262, 490–93, 587–8